E. Lawrence
222 W. Adams, #997
236-0991

ARTHUR M. WEIMER, Ph.D., University of Chicago, M.A.I., is Special Assistant to the President at Indiana University and Professor of Real Estate and Land Economics. He was for many years Dean of the School of Business at that institution. Early in his career, Dr. Weimer taught at Alma College and Georgia Institute of Technology, and served as an economist with the Federal Housing Administration. He is recognized as one of the country's foremost economic consultants, and is a member of the Board of Directors of Mead Johnson and Company, National Homes Corporation, Railroadmen's Federal Savings and Loan Association, and Business and Real Estate Trends, Inc. Dr. Weimer serves as consulting economist for the U.S. Savings and Loan League, and is a past president of the American Finance Association and the American Association of Collegiate Schools of Business.

HOMER HOYT, Ph.D., University of Chicago, M.A.I., is President of Homer Hoyt Associates, Consulting Real Estate Economists. Dr. Hoyt previously taught economics at the University of North Carolina, the University of Missouri, and Columbia University and served as Principal Housing Economist for the Federal Housing Administration in Washington. Homer Hoyt Associates, founded by Dr. Hoyt, had the distinction of conducting economic, market, and appraisal surveys for such nationally known real estate projects as the Prudential Buildings in Chicago and Houston, Century City and Bunker Hill in Los Angeles, and regional shopping centers in Detroit, Kansas City, Chicago, Atlanta, Houston, Boston, and Dallas.

REAL ESTATE

ARTHUR M. WEIMER
Indiana University

HOMER HOYT
Homer Hoyt Associates

FIFTH EDITION

THE RONALD PRESS COMPANY · NEW YORK

Preface

The Fifth Edition of this book extends the emphasis given in the preceding edition to real estate decisions and decision-makers. The types of analysis that are helpful in the real estate decision-making process are given special attention. As in earlier editions, real estate operations are discussed with emphasis on principles and concepts rather than on current practices. Efforts are made to understand the nature not only of real estate decisions, but also the implementing of decisions through effective administrative processes.

Of special importance in making real estate decisions are factors related to income production at fixed sites. To a considerable degree these are the factors that set real estate decisions apart from other personal, business, and governmental decisions. Income production, of course, affects real estate values and valuations; hence valuations serve as basic decision guides.

Efforts have been made to show the relationships between the real estate business and other areas of business administration, between real estate resources and other types of resources, and between problems of the real estate sector of the American economy and those of our general social organization. A special feature of the Fifth Edition is the inclusion of a chapter dealing with "International Real Estate Trends."

The outline of this edition provides for a general introductory treatment of the subject in Part I. Real estate decisions and decision-makers are considered along with various physical, legal, and economic characteristics of real estate resources. Valuation principles are then introduced as decision guides.

Part II relates to the general subject of analysis for real estate decisions. Such types of analysis as appraising, the analysis of political and business trends, real estate market analysis, the analysis of city structure and land uses, and neighborhood and district analysis are discussed in an introductory manner.

In Part III the major decision areas of the real estate field are considered. These include production, covering subdividing, land development and building processes; marketing, including brokerage and promotion, and property management; and financing, with such topics as financing methods, instruments, institutions, and agencies being given special treatment.

Part IV pays particular attention to special types of properties and decision problems. Residential, business, and farm and other rural real estate are considered as well as international real estate trends and the relationship of real estate to future economic growth.

The Fifth Edition, like its predecessors, presents a variety of study projects, cases, and problems to aid the student in attaining a basic understanding of this subject.

ARTHUR M. WEIMER
HOMER HOYT

Bloomington, Indiana
Washington, D.C.
April, 1966

Acknowledgments

We are grateful to many friends and associates in a number of universities, business firms, and government agencies for their assistance. A number of those who used earlier editions for textbook purposes made highly valuable suggestions.

We are indebted especially to the following faculty members of the School of Business of Indiana University: W. George Pinnell, Edward E. Edwards, John F. Mee, George F. Bloom, Donald H. Sauer, John D. Long, E. W. Martin, Jr., John H. Porter, Edward J. Kuntz, L. L. Waters, Harold F. Lusk, Jean Halterman, Robert R. Milroy, Howard L. Timms, D. Lyle Diterle, Charles M. Hewitt, Robert C. Turner, John P. Lewis, J. W. Milliman, and S. F. Otteson. Mrs. D. Jeanne Patterson provided general editorial assistance, helped with the revision and development of the Study Projects and also revised the Glossary. Richard L. Mills, Gilbert D. Churchill, Rex D. Schrader, and Roger K. Harvey assisted with the development of study materials. The current classes in Indiana University's Graduate Program in Real Estate and Land Economics helped in reviewing various study projects and discussion questions.

We appreciate especially the suggestions provided by Fred E. Case and James E. Gillies of the University of California at Los Angeles and by Robert O. Harvey of the University of Connecticut.

Assistance with the current edition or with earlier editions was also provided by Lyle C. Bryant, Washington, D.C.; Norman Strunk, U.S. Savings and Loan League; Arthur E. Warner, University of Tennessee; Earl L. Butz, Purdue University; Maurice Seldin, American University; Gail E. Mullin, Kent State University; Troy J. Cauley, Indiana University; Ernest M. Fisher, formerly of Columbia University; Richard U. Ratcliff, University of Wisconsin; Paul M. Green, University of Illinois; David W. Thompson, Peat, Marwick, Mitchell and Company; and a number of others, including: Graham Aldis, L. Durward Badgley, Harry G. Atkinson, Frederick M. Babcock, Kenneth C. Beede, Morton Bodfish,

Gordon Chapman, Paul I. Cripe, Albert E. Dickens, Carl F. Distelhorst, Howard W. Greene, Robert W. Kautz, Max Lieurance, Lawrence V. Conway, Curt C. Mack, Helen Monchow, J. Bion Philipson, Ernest W. Walker, and Herman O. Walther.

Stenographic and editing assistance were provided by Mrs. Betty Herman and Mrs. Doris-Jean Burton. Mrs. Burton prepared the indexes and coordinated the many activities related to the preparation of the materials for publication.

A. M. W.
H. H.

Contents

Decisions. Decisions and Income at Fixed Sites. Implementing Decisions. Administrative Process. Management by Objectives. Social and Business Objectives. Planning Operations. Organizing Resources. Controls. Leadership. Registering Decisions. The Real Estate Environment.

Part II

ANALYSIS FOR REAL ESTATE DECISIONS

Part III

DECISION AREAS

Policies. The Federal Home Loan Bank System. VA Loans. Department of Housing and Urban Development. The Federal Housing Administration. The Federal National Mortgage Association. Other Housing Programs. Federal Farm Programs.

Importance of Mortgage Credit. Mortgage Lending Policies. Management Problems of Lenders. Lending Risks. Sources of Risks. Lines of Defense. Borrower Risks. Property Risks. Market Risks. Legal Risks. Administrative Risks. Portfolio Management.

Part IV

SPECIAL PROPERTIES AND PROBLEMS

Residential Real Estate Market. Supply of Residential Real Estate. The Demand for Housing. Personal Incomes. Trend Toward Home Ownership. Pattern of Home Ownership. Rental Housing. Condominiums and Cooperatives. The Suburban Trend. Financing and Housing Demand. Population and Housing Demand. Consumer Preferences and Expenditures. Second Homes. "Filtering Down." "Doubling Up." Technological Advances. Marketing Changes. Trade-in Problems.

Decisions on Business Real Estate. Administration of Real Estate. Retail Business Property. Space Demands in Central Locations. Lease Information. Determination of Prices and Rents for Retail Space. Changes in Shopping Center Pattern. Changing Character of Retail Sales. Types of Shopping Centers. Parking. Location of Outlying Retail Centers. The Department Store. The Discount House. Future Retailing Trends. The Retail Brokerage Field. The Modern Office Building. Supply of Office Space. Office Rentals. Types of Office Building Occupancy. Types of Office Building Locations. Advantages of Various Office Building Locations. The Demand for Office Space. The Owners of Office Buildings. Problems of Office Building Management. The Industrial Real Estate Market. Demand for Industrial Space. Selection of Industrial Locations. Manufacturing Districts. Trends in Industrial Construction. Wholesale and Storage Warehouses.

I

INTRODUCTION

1

The Study of Real Estate
Administration

Importance of Real Estate

You make use of real estate in some manner during every day of your
life. Real estate resources provide shelter, comfort, convenience, privacy,
a place of work, recreational facilities, and related services. Nearly all
business firms need a place of business—a store, office, plant, or other parcel of real estate—in order to carry on operations. Farms and ranches, of
course, rely heavily on real estate. Governmental, educational, religious,
and cultural institutions all make use of real estate. Our real estate resources—the homes, factories, office buildings, stores, shopping centers,
farms, rights of way, roads, streets, parks, recreational areas, and other
types—represent more than half of our national wealth.

Obviously, the manner in which resources of this magnitude are used
has an important effect on the well-being of our people, the success or
failure of business firms, and the general prosperity of the country. Effective utilization of real estate resources requires good administration on the
part of owners and users, whether they are home owners or the managers
of business firms, those engaged in the real estate business, or the officials
of government agencies and quasi-public institutions.

Objectives of Study

Decisions made by business executives, government officials, or private
citizens determine the amount and kind of real estate resources we have

and the effectiveness with which they are used. Thus, we may begin our discussion of objectives by suggesting that a major objective of studying this field is that of improving decisions relating to real estate resources.

For example, a business manager faced with a decision regarding the choice of a site for a new plant needs an understanding of real estate resources and the forces that affect them. As a minimum, he needs enough knowledge to make use of the assistance of specialists in the field. Similarly, a government official who must decide on an appropriate tax rate for real property needs at least a basic familiarity with this field. A private citizen trying to decide whether to buy or build a home or to continue to rent housing facilities will be aided greatly by a knowledge of this area of study. The owner or manager of a firm in the real estate business, of course, needs a command of this field of knowledge.

We are concerned, however, not only with the improvement of decisions relating to real estate but also with the *implementation* of such decisions. Thus, we are interested in the processes of putting decisions into effect, of "getting things done" that decisions indicate should be done —or, stated in another way, the administrative or management process. Hence, we might state the general objective of our study of this subject as the improvement of decision-making and implementation in the real estate field, both with respect to the utilization of real estate resources and the operation of real estate enterprises.

Your interest in this subject may arise from several sources. As a user, and owner, or potential owner of real estate, or as an investor in securities based on real estate, you need information about its uses and capacity to produce income. As an owner, manager, or employee of a business firm, or of a governmental or institutional agency, you will find a knowledge of this subject highly useful. If you are now connected with the real estate business or intend to engage in it, you have a particular interest in the study of this subject. As a voter, you are concerned with such problems as property taxation, land planning, zoning, slum clearance, housing programs, and the general efficiency with which we make use of our real estate resources.

Decisions and Economic Growth

As we have suggested above, a major objective of studying this field is that of improving decisions relating to real estate resources. Such decisions may have major significance for our future prosperity and well-being. Recent projections indicate that prospects for economic growth to the year 2000 are highly favorable. By that time, there probably will be more than 300 million people in this country (compared to 180 million in 1960); the labor force will increase somewhat more rapidly than total population because of age composition; the gross national product (the total output of goods and services) may advance from slightly over $500 billion in 1960 to approximately $1 trillion by 1980 to over $2 trillion by 2000 (in constant dollars). Disposable personal income for the average family may advance from somewhat over $6,000 to nearly $10,000 by 1980 to between $13,000 and $15,000 by 2000 (in constant dollars).[1]

Decisions affecting the utilization of real estate resources will play a major role in making such economic growth possible. Reaching sound decisions in the real estate area will not be a simple matter because of a number of important current trends, which, undoubtedly, will continue. Consider, for example, the following:

1. There will be more people, and they will require proportionally more resources for their support.
2. Housing will be one of our more difficult problems, in part because of the greater number of people, but also because rising prosperity will mean that people will demand better housing; for example, the two-house family will become more commonplace.
3. People will continue to move about a good deal, and the population is likely to be increasingly mobile.
4. The rate of technological and scientific change will continue to accelerate. The "knowledge explosion" will mean higher rates of obsolescence for many real properties.
5. The scientific and technological revolution may help us to find solutions to problems related to congestion and pollution, including sanitation and waste disposal, air purification, better and more reliable water supplies, and the like.
6. Although we have solved some of our longer-distance transportation problems, shorter-distance and local transportation continue to present some very difficult challenges. It may be that travel requirements can be reduced by improved communications facilities such as the wider use of closed-circuit television, interconnecting computer centers, and the like.
7. People will continue to move from farms to urban, suburban, and quasi-rural areas.
8. Some people will continue to refuse to live side by side with others. Some will want to live in exclusive neighborhoods. Probably none will want to live in slums; but many will continue to desire the excitement and stimulation that is often associated with some of the more highly concentrated and older parts of our cities.
9. Business firms will move about even more than in the past in search of desirable locations. At one time, factories and stores concentrated in or near city centers; recent years have seen the

[1] Hans H. Landsberg, Leonard L. Fischman, and Joseph L. Fisher, *Resources in America's Future* (Baltimore: Johns Hopkins Press, 1963), pp. 3–21.

decentralization of such installations to suburban and even rural areas. These trends are likely to continue, but many new developments may also emerge.

10. Increasing attention may be given to problems of the local area and region. We have been making better policy decisions on the national level as our information and data have improved. There is great need for improved data and information on the local level however, with much remaining to be done.

11. Problems of local government will become more complex; the overlapping and expansion of many local governing units is already posing major problems.

12. Competition between regions and localities probably will grow more intense.

13. Tax factors will continue to bulk large. The impact of local taxes on real estate resources is likely to be especially heavy.

14. There are likely to be increasing demands for land planning and zoning and related regulations, but the problems of imposing regulations and still making provision for enough flexibility so as not to inhibit growth are difficult ones indeed.

15. The already large blocks of leisure time available to many people mean improved recreation and better entertainment. A cultural renaissance may be possible. All this holds many implications for real estate decision-makers.

We could add to this recital of important factors likely to affect our lives and to complicate the problems of the real estate decision-maker. Interesting and dramatic as the events of recent years have been, the future promises to be even more challenging and demanding, particularly for those with interests in this dynamic field of real estate decision-making and implementing.

Method of Study

The study of the real estate field offers some excellent possibilities for an unusual form of "laboratory work." The house or apartment building in which you live, a store, a farm, a vacant lot or any other piece of real property with which you are familiar can serve as an excellent starting point for your study of this subject. You can use it as your own special laboratory or as a point of "reference" for the various materials you will be studying, especially those that pertain to real properties and to the forces that affect the decisions of people regarding them, thus bringing about changes in property incomes and values. You should recognize that the study of real estate involves primarily the study of people and their reactions to real properties or to business transactions relating to real properties.

Your home neighborhood and the town or city in which your reference property is located may also be considered as a part of your laboratory. Decisions in regard to every parcel of real estate are affected by its surroundings, since it is a *share* in the community of which it forms a part. By carefully training your powers of observation, you can learn a great deal about the effects of economic, political, and social forces on the uses to which people put different types of real estate, on the trends of real estate values, and on business and personal decisions.

Another interesting method of studying this subject is through discussions with people who are in one or another branch of the real estate business or who dabble in real estate investments. Find out what their experiences indicate as the most important things to learn about real estate. Discuss career opportunities in real estate or related fields. Ask about current conditions in the real estate market and about potential market changes. Inquire about trends of land uses and the development of new subdivisions, shopping centers, and industrial locations. Find out about real estate investment possibilities.

Market forces, both national and local, have important effects on real estate. Such forces, of course, are the results of billions of decisions made by millions of people. Local market factors are especially important in their influence on residential real estate. Even a small operator in the real estate field, whose interests are purely local in character, can often be of great help to you in gaining an understanding of market conditions and trends.

In addition, people who are actively engaged in business—especially those in real estate practice—will supply you with examples of the many forms and documents that are involved in real estate transactions. Sales agreements, listing agreements, deeds, leases, sales contracts, mortgages, and many other documents are in constant use. It is often easier to learn about these from actual cases and situations than from merely reading descriptions of them in books.

Therefore, select a "reference property" and if possible a "reference real estate operator," and refer to each of them again and again. You will find that the reference property and its environment will help you to gain an understanding of location and related factors. The reference real estate operator will help develop your understanding of market forces and your knowledge of the various practices involved in real estate transactions.

Study Techniques

Development of your ability to read, write, and speak properly, and to handle basic mathematics should be one of the important results of work

in this field. Clear and precise writing is an essential tool of every businessman regardless of the field or the level on which he operates. The
development of proficiency in writing and clarity of expression is a process that should go on throughout life. Of interest in this connection is
Benjamin Franklin's description of the process by which he taught himself
to write clearly:

About this time I met with an odd volume of the Spectator. I had never
before seen any of them. I bought it, read it over and was much delighted with
it. I thought the writing excellent, and wished if possible to imitate it. With
that view I took some of the papers, and making short hints of the sentiments
in each sentence, laid them by a few days, and then without looking at the
book tried to complete the papers again, by expressing each hinted sentiment
at length and as fully as it had been expressed before in any suitable words that
should occur to me. Then I compared my Spectator with an original, discovered
some of my faults, and corrected them. I also sometimes jumbled my collection
of hints and confusion, and after some weeks endeavored to reduce them into
the best order, before I began to form the full sentences and complete the
subject. This was to teach me method in the arrangement of the thoughts. By
comparing my work with the original, I discovered many faults and corrected
them; but I sometimes had the pleasure to fancy, that in particulars of small
consequence I had been fortunate enough to improve the method or the language, and this encouraged me to think, that I might in time come to be a
tolerable English writer, of which I was extremely ambitious.

In recent years considerable attention has been given to increasing the
speed of reading and the rate of comprehending written materials. By
constant practice, you can do a great deal to improve your capacity to
read.

The real estate field, like other business fields, deals to a considerable
extent with figures, financial statements, and accounting reports of various
types. Thus, your ability to use basic mathematics, accounting, and
statistics should be developed in the course of studying this subject. You
may find it desirable to become familiar with the work of the computer,
since its role is expanding rapidly in the business world.

Another ability that is valuable in the field of real estate, as it is in
many other areas, is that of *listening*. Many of us fail to learn because we
are not good listeners. Many business transactions are not successful because one or another of the parties involved failed to listen carefully
enough to make possible a real understanding or a meeting of minds.
Listening requires attention and concentration.

Creative Thinking

One of the important abilities you should acquire through your study
of this subject or others has been referred to by James Webb Young as

"a technique for producing ideas." [2] Sometimes it is called *creative thinking*. Professor John F. Mee has summarized the steps in this process as follows: first, selection and definition of the problem; second, exploration and preparation; third, the development of partial solutions or hypotheses; fourth, the stage of incubating ideas, mulling over the problem, or engaging in "unconscious cerebration"; fifth, illumination or the appearance of the idea; and last, verification and application of the idea.[3]

Since all business progress, including that in the real estate field, depends so much on new methods, techniques, products, and ideas, you will find it advantageous to develop your ability to think creatively and to develop your imagination and ingenuity. The creative thinking process is to a large extent an adaptation of the scientific method. Both inductive and deductive processes are involved, the former including the collection and analysis of pertinent information in order to arrive at a general summary or theory or principle, the latter including the process of reasoning from a general principle or theory to a specific situation or problem.

Creative thinking is especially important in the real estate field. For example, it often provides the basis for a plan for developing a new subdivision, a way of financing a challenging project, or a method of selling a property that has been on the market for a long time.

Current Publications

Students of real estate must also know how to find and use the major types of published information that are available. You should learn how to use the library and should familiarize yourself with the more important services that are published giving information about specific business firms and their operations. These services include Poor's, Moody's, Prentice-Hall Real Estate Service, and others. Increasingly, reference materials are organized in such a manner as to permit the use of the computer in speeding up the processes of identifying and retrieving significant information.[4]

Real estate transactions do not take place in a separate division of the business world but are a part of the total economic system. Consequently, you should cultivate the habit of reading current newspapers and magazines. The *Wall Street Journal*, the *New York Times* (especially the Sunday edition), and one or another of the weekly news magazines, such

[2] James Webb Young, *A Technique for Producing Ideas* (8th ed.; Chicago: Advertising Publication, Inc., 1953).

[3] John F. Mee, "The Creative Thinking Process," *Indiana Business Review* (February, 1956), pp. 4–9. See also, Arthur Koestler, *The Act of Creation* (New York: The Macmillan Co., 1964), chap. x.

[4] Joseph Becker and R. M. Hayes, *Information Storage and Retrieval: Tools, Elements, Theories* (New York: John Wiley & Sons, Inc., 1963).

as *U. S. News and World Report, Newsweek,* or *Time* will be helpful. *Business Week* provides a good weekly summary of business developments, and *Barrons, The Commercial and Financial Chronicle, Nation's Business,* and *Fortune* are also good current publications to follow. *The Survey of Current Business* published by the Department of Commerce, the Federal Reserve *Bulletin,* and *Economic Indicators* published by the President's Council of Economic Advisers present summaries of business conditions. For regional and local information, the publications of Federal Reserve District Banks and various university bureaus of business research are valuable.

Approaches to the Subject

The study of real estate may be approached from several directions. For example, we may emphasize principles and general concepts rather than practices. We may stress the administrative point of view or that of the land or urban economist. We may pay particular attention to those activities related directly to the real estate business or pursue a broader approach with emphasis on the relationships between real estate and business administration in general.

In our discussions we are concerned primarily with the administrative point of view. We stress concepts rather than practices and procedures. We emphasize the processes of decision-making and implementation, and their relationships to the efficient utilization of real estate resources in the achievement of desired results. Although we stress the administrative approach, we recognize that the processes of managing and administering real estate resources and activities take place in a broad economic, political, and social environment.

Other approaches to the study of this subject may also be followed, of course. An engineering and architectural approach would emphasize the physical factors involved in real estate resources, the character of the land, its size, shape, and other physical qualities, the character and quality of buildings and other improvements, the design, style, and functional arrangements relating to the property as a whole. A legal approach would stress the property rights involved in real estate ownership and use. An economic approach to the study of this subject would emphasize cost and benefit relationships, income-producing characteristics, and the interrelationships between real estate and other resources.

Each of these points of view is important to decision-making and to decision implementation in the real estate field. We refer to them often in our discussions.

Some students of this subject emphasize the investment approach. They contend that the essential factors involved in real estate decisions may best be understood in terms of their investment implications. Although this approach is attractive, it leaves something to be desired when real estate decisions are considered within the context of the over-all objectives of a business firm or the general social objectives that may be served by those responsible for public and quasi-public programs. We will, however, give special consideration to investment factors in real estate decisions.

There are also those who believe that value and valuation should form the central themes for the study of this subject. We pay special attention to these areas. We do so because we consider the factors affecting value to be of major importance in guiding real estate decisions and programs for their implementation.

Other approaches to the study of real estate administration might be followed as well. We believe, however, that decision-making and implementing provide both a stimulating and a highly useful approach to the study of this subject. We believe, also, that valuation concepts provide basic decision guides.

Why versus How

We emphasize the "why" rather than the "how" or "how to" aspects of the subject. This is not intended to minimize the importance of current practices in the business world or in the real estate field. Many current practices will be covered. It is well to recognize, however, that many business practices change in response to altered conditions, increased knowledge, legislative enactments, or for other reasons.

We are concerned with generalizations based on experience, that is, with hypotheses, theories, principles, and laws. Experience may be personal or it may involve the experience of others based on experiments or special studies. The degree of relative validity varies from hypotheses, which are very tentative generalizations, to laws, which are accepted universally. Principles are usually thought of as generalizations from experience that have sufficient validity to be everywhere acceptable but which do not have the status of laws. In the social sciences, and we consider the study of business as a part of this area, we seldom are sufficiently sure of our generalizations to classify them as laws.

Thus, we shall try to develop our abilities to understand the "why" rather than the "how" aspects of the real estate field. If you are able to acquire an understanding of the major forces that affect decisions in regard to real properties and the real estate business, and if you know the principles that explain changes in property incomes or in business practices, then you should be able to develop the necessary know-how to meet specific problem situations as they arise. In the short run, a how-to-do-things approach might be more valuable. In the longer run, however, a broader approach based on general concepts and principles undoubtedly will be the more practical, since it provides a basis for continuing growth and development.

Economics, Land Economics, and Urban Economics

The fields of economics, urban economics, and land economics provide many of the principles that help to explain operations and practices in the real estate field. What do we mean by economics? By land economics? By urban economics?

Suppose we begin by considering the meaning of the word *economy*. This term can have no real meaning unless it is considered in connection with a *stated objective*. Economy, like efficiency, is a relative term. Usually we think of economy in terms of savings, or in terms of return per dollar of investment. *Efficiency*, in the language of management or of economics, is usually considered as reflecting a relationship between input and output of energy, materials, or manpower. It is obvious that neither term can have any meaning unless there is a stated objective to measure against.

In the case of your "reference property," for example, you may be concerned with securing from it the greatest possible money return per year over as long a period of time as possible. Such an objective would require a careful program of management and use with a view to prolonging the economic life of the property. This is one type of objective. On the other hand, your concept of economy in the use of this property would have an entirely different meaning if you were trying to get the greatest money return from it for, say, a five-year period only.

Similarly, our concepts of economy in the use of our national resources change markedly after we enter a war and then change back again when war ends. The objectives of a wartime and of a peacetime economy contrast sharply.

Economy, then, in its most general sense, means getting as much as possible of what one wants (in terms of objectives) by the use of the means which are available.

Specifically, economics as a branch of organized study deals with the social organization for the utilization of resources in the attainment of the objectives which the society or community sets for itself. *Land economics*, which traditionally has been the branch of general economics most nearly related to our subject, deals with the social organization for the utilization of land resources in the attainment of the objectives that the community as a whole sets for itself.

Recently the area of urban economics has been given increasing attention. The area tends to be broader than land economics since it views the urban community as an integral part of the national economy but stresses the particular sets of problems related to specific local communities. On the other hand, it is narrower than land economics since it deals with urban communities only. Primarily urban economics deals with the effective use of urban resources in achieving community objectives. Students of business administration are becoming increasingly aware of the impact of urban economic problems on business policies and, in turn, of the effect of business policies on the urban economy.

The Administrative Approach

The basic problems of the economist and of the manager or administrator are very similar. Both are concerned with the effective utilization of resources in the attainment of desired objectives. The economist deals with society or the economic system as a whole, while the manager deals with his particular enterprise or program. Typically, also, the economist serves in an advisory capacity, while the manager is a man of action whose job is to get things done. Thus, the administrative approach differs from that of the land economist or urban economist primarily in that administration involves *action*. It includes analysis, investigation, and prediction; and the work of the economist will also include such activities. But administration or management is concerned ultimately with action, that is, with the use of ways and means to achieve desired results.

As Robert D. Calkins has said:

Administration is fundamentally the direction of affairs. It is purposive action, and to an increasing degree it is informed, rational, and deliberate action. It draws upon the knowledge of the physical sciences and the practical arts; it employs the knowledge and techniques of the social sciences; but it is overwhelmingly concerned with the choice of ends, ways, and means for the attainment of desired results. It is curbed by moral codes and ethical principles; and it is driven by springs of ambition and devotion that largely escape analysis. . . .

The three main elements of administration are the formulation of goals, the choice of ways and means, and the direction of people in some group purpose. These activities may be considered as consisting mainly of two processes: the process of decision-making and the process of execution, or action. The former determines what is to be done and how, while the latter puts decisions into action and oversees the process.[5]

Real Estate Administration

Real estate administration, then, like the processes of administration or management in other fields, includes decision-making and implementation in the use of resources to achieve desired objectives. In terms of *objec-*

[5] Speech given at the annual meeting of the American Association of Collegiate Schools of Business, Marquette University, Milwaukee, Wis., April, 1955.

tives, our interest centers in those of property owners and users (including individuals, families, business firms, or governmental or institutional agencies), the objectives of those engaged in the real estate business, and the ends or goals of our society as a whole as well as their relationship to private objectives.

We are interested in *resources*—primarily in these discussions with real estate resources—but also in the relationships between real estate and other types of resources. We emphasize the fact that real estate resources, like others, have no significance except in terms of people. We pay special attention to the distinguishing characteristics of real estate resources and to those factors which have a major impact on decisions regarding the use of real estate resources in the attainment of objectives. Of primary importance in this connection is the *capacity of real estate to produce income at fixed locations.* We are concerned not only with income production but income in excess of costs and in proper relationship to the risks that are assumed.

We consider in our discussions the general *environmental factors* that influence the decisions of property owners, users, developers, investors, and marketers. Thus, we are concerned with location factors, market forces, general business conditions, political trends, the legal framework, and governmental regulations and programs.

Real Estate Objectives

As we have indicated, administration is concerned with the use of resources to achieve objectives. In the real estate field we have two principal sets of objectives: those of property owners and users, and those of the people engaged in the real estate business. To a significant degree these two sets of objectives tend to coincide. Each of these two sets of objectives must also bear an appropriate relationship to the objectives of our society as a whole. While we have a system which largely allows each of us and each business firm to pursue individually determined objectives, the community or society as a whole will not long allow the pursuit of private objectives that are detrimental to the public interest. We have found that in our system of democracy and competition it is possible for us, within rather broad limits, to pursue individually determined objectives and still serve the best interests of the community as a whole.

Various types of business enterprises operate in the real estate field. These include not only real estate brokerage and property management firms, which popularly are referred to as "the real estate business," but land development and building companies and financial institutions as well. In addition, we include various specialists such as appraisers, engineers, architects, real property lawyers, market analysts, and others.

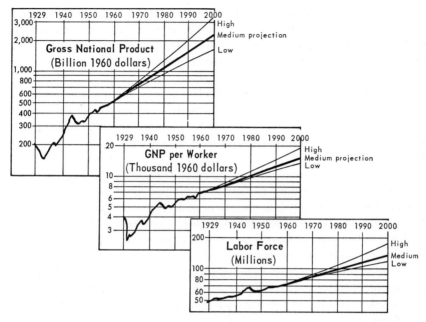

Fig. 1–1. Growth of gross national product, labor force, and output (GNP per worker), 1929–1960, and projections to the year 2000. (*Source: Resources in America's Future,* p. 20.)

The business firms in the real estate field will pursue objectives that are similar to those of business firms in other areas. Typically, business firms pursue such objectives as survival, growth, and the attainment of recognition or prestige. In order to do these things, they must make a profit. Some firms attempt to maximize profits, others to gain a "reasonable" or some other level of profit. Their specific objectives may vary widely; but, as we shall see, it is virtually impossible to manage a business firm in the real estate or in any other field without a clear understanding of the objectives that are being pursued.

Similarly, the owners or users of real estate resources may pursue a wide variety of objectives. Many will try to maximize profits. Some will hope to achieve maximum monetary returns over the long run, others in the short run. Some will try to maximize satisfactions from the direct use of real properties. In some cases objectives may be stated in terms of using real properties in connection with other resources to achieve a maximum total result, as in the case of a business firm using real estate and other resources in producing and marketing goods and services.

To an important degree in the field of real estate, as in many other fields, the interests of the community as a whole are closely related to the activities of private real estate owners, users, dealers, managers, and investors. Despite differences in the reasons behind their decisions and actions, both the community as a whole and practical men of affairs in their private capacities demand the development of each parcel of real estate to its *highest and best use.* This is a convenient concept, and the term is used often in the real estate business. One should recognize, however, that it involves some logical pitfalls and must be used with care. In general it means the utilization of a property to its greatest economic advantage. The term has been defined in terms of *greatest net income, highest land value,* and *largest return in money or amenities* over a period of time.

In addition to economic factors, social and political considerations have a bearing on the meaning of "highest and best use." The term would have different meanings in a society organized under a dictatorship than in one organized on democratic principles. Even in our own society, the highest and best use of a property may change with shifting consumer preferences, improved techniques and equipment, or for other reasons. The market reflects changes in buyer preferences and production methods. Changing attitudes and techniques are also reflected in zoning laws, building codes, and other regulations governing the development and use of real property.

Real Estate Resources

Real estate resources include land and buildings plus property rights in these physical objects. These property rights represent income or income potentials. These rights have value to the people who own, use, produce, finance, or market them.

As we shall see, real estate resources may be considered in terms of their physical, legal, or economic characteristics. From a physical standpoint, a piece of real property is made up of land and buildings or other improvements. From a legal point of view, a real property represents certain legal rights in land and buildings or other improvements. From an economic or business standpoint, the land and buildings and the property rights they represent have significance primarily because of their ability to serve the needs of people—that is, to produce income either in terms of monetary returns or in terms of direct use, thereby providing convenience, shelter, protection, privacy, or other property services.

Real estate resources include residential properties of many types: single-family houses, doubles, duplexes, three and four dwelling-unit structures, and apartments such as walk-ups, elevator or high-rise buildings, garden apartments, and others. The general classification of business properties covers both commercial and industrial properties. Commercial properties include stores, office buildings, shops, places of amusement, and the like. Industrial properties include both light and heavy manufacturing installations and various types of warehouses and related properties. In addition, we may distinguish farms and other rural real estate, government and institutional real estate, and special-purpose properties.

Values, Valuations, and Decisions

The market value of stocks, or the current price of stocks in American corporations listed on the New York Stock Exchange, on any given trading day, may be quickly ascertained by referring to the quotations on ticker tape. Many business decision-makers refer to such quotations frequently. As one of the authors of this book has pointed out in another connection:

Stocks are homogeneous, interchangeable shares in the equity of the companies and there are always holders willing to sell and persons willing to buy at prices established by the trading on the floor of the Exchange, in the case of all of the larger American corporations.

Unlike stocks, each real estate property is unique, and no two properties are exactly alike, since each parcel of land occupies a separate and distinct spot on the earth's surface and each building on the land may differ in some respect, either in type, size, age or utilities, from other buildings. There are usually no prospective buyers waiting to make bids on any specific real estate property on a given day, and on the other hand, the majority of real estate properties are not being offered for sale at any given moment. Sometimes there is a very wide difference between the asking price and the offer in the case of real estate properties that are available for purchase. Consequently, to establish the value of any real estate property, it is necessary to estimate at what price a hypothetical willing buyer and a hypothetical willing seller would consummate a sale, after sufficient time had elapsed for prospective buyers to have an opportunity to make bids. This estimate of value (or valuation) cannot be arrived at by looking at the last quotation on the stock market; it requires calculations by specialists known as real estate appraisers, who have studied all the factors in the local real estate market having a bearing on the selling price of a particular property.[6]

This statement emphasizes the importance of estimates of value in the real estate field and their usefulness as guides to decisions. It also indicates some of the difficulties of arriving at good value estimates. This is one of the major problems of the field and indicates why value factors are so important in our studies.

The Localization of Income

The study of real estate may be thought of as the study of the decisions of people relative to real estate resources and the programs of action

[6] Homer Hoyt, "Application of the Three Appraisal Approaches to Different Types of Real Estate," *The Appraisal Journal* (July, 1964).

that are based on such decisions. An understanding of such decisions and programs of action depends to a considerable extent on a knowledge of the interrelationships among the following:

1. Income production, and more specifically, income production at fixed and unique locations
2. Real estate values
3. Valuations and methods of analysis helpful in the making of valuations
4. Real estate decisions
5. The implementation of real estate decisions

We will be emphasizing these factors at many points. We need to understand the importance of income, and more specifically, *income production at fixed locations.* Income, of course, is the fundamental fact of economic life; it is the basic factor in almost all business and economic studies. Income is of major importance in nearly all business decision-making processes. The production of income is one of the chief motivating forces of workers, investors, business owners and managers, farmers, and professional people. Real estate, however, is fixed in location. If it is to have value, each parcel of real estate must be able to produce income *at the point of its location.*

Locations—Fixed But Dynamic

Although real estate income has to be produced at a fixed location, we should not tend to think of such a fixed location as having essentially a stable character. As a matter of fact, quite the opposite has been the case throughout most of our history. Each piece of real property may be a fixed point on the earth's surface, but this fixed point is a part of a highly dynamic framework. All manner of forces—economic, political, and social; international, national, and local—are operating constantly to add to or to detract from the property's capacity to produce income at a given site. If we tried, for example, to make certain that so far as location factors were concerned, a given piece of property representing a given investment would always produce the same income, we would have to move it about substantially. It is important, therefore, to pay particular attention to those factors. In our discussions we tend to emphasize particularly *market* factors and *location* factors which are likely to change either favorably or unfavorably the income-producing capacity of a real estate property.

Thus, in connection with real estate resources we shall try to stress *the forces that add to or detract from income-producing potentials at fixed locations.* Such forces will have an important bearing on decisions related to programs of land development, building, brokerage, property management, and real estate financing.

Each parcel of real estate, of course, is a share in our total national wealth. General economic trends will have a bearing on the predictions and decisions of people in regard to the ability of real estate to produce income. As we have said, each piece of real estate is a share in the community in which it is located. The income potential of a piece of real estate is dependent on the economic strength of the city and the character of its district or neighborhood. Similarly, the economic future of any piece of property is dependent to a large degree on market forces; typically, it is affected more by local market conditions than is almost any other type of goods or services. Analyses of such forces and predictions based on these analyses play a major role in programs for carrying out decisions related to property ownership and use.

Insofar as this book may have a central concept, the concept might be stated in this way: Real estate decisions and the manner of their implementation are closely related to the factors involved in income production at fixed but dynamic locations and in special types of markets; incomes are the basic factors in real estate values; valuations and other types of analysis are undertaken to provide the basis for income projections and value estimates which, in turn, provide guidelines for decisions and the development of programs to implement such decisions. There will be wide variation as between types of properties, markets, and locations, as well as variations in time. Summary statements, of course, are usually oversimplified and this statement is no exception. Even so, it may be helpful to you as you continue your exploration of this subject.

SUMMARY

As suggested above, we are concerned primarily with the improvement of decision-making and implementation in the real estate field. We stress the concepts that help us to understand the effective use of resources in achieving desired objectives. This is essentially the administrative process.

This process includes both decision-making and implementation. Decisions and programs of action are influenced by the objectives to be achieved, the resources available, and the general environment or climate within which the decisions are made and the programs are carried out. In our discussions, we pay special attention to the objectives of the owners and users of real estate resources (including individuals, families, business firms, or governmental and institutional agencies), the objectives of those engaged in the real estate business, and the interrelationships between these objectives and those of our society as a whole.

In order to give you a general introduction to the discussions in this book, the following outline may be helpful.

In Chapter 2 our attention centers on decision-makers and the real estate business; in Chapter 3 on real estate decisions and administrative processes. Chapters 4, 5, and 6 consider various physical, legal, and economic characteristics of real estate. In Chapter 7 we discuss valuation principles as decision guides. These seven chapters constitute the introductory section of the book.

Part II covers various analytical tools and decision guides related to the localization of income and real estate values, including valuations and appraisal methods, governmental and political trends, business conditions and industry trends, regional and local economic analyses, real estate market analysis, and location factors including city structure and land use patterns as well as neighborhoods and districts.

Part III centers on the major real estate decision areas: production, including subdividing; land development and building operations; marketing, which involves brokerage and promotion and property management; and finance, covering financing methods and instruments, financial institutions and agencies, and the processes of mortgage lending.

In Part IV we consider a variety of special properties and decision problems, including residential, commercial, industrial, and farm and other rural real estate. International real estate trends are reviewed and analyzed. In addition, various relationships of real estate resources to economic growth are considered along with some of the implications of current trends for the improvement of real estate administration.

QUESTIONS FOR STUDY

1. What are *your* objectives in studying real estate?
2. What is meant by the term "highest and best use"?
3. Identify some of the major problems faced by real estate decision-makers in a growing economy with a prosperous future.
4. What is the administrative approach to real estate and how does it differ from other approaches?
5. Compare the approaches to the study of urban economics and land economics to that of real estate administration.
6. How can you explain the recent trend toward increased attention to urban economics?
7. What are the major differences in the principles approach and the practices approach to the study of real estate?
8. What meaning do you attach to the statement that refers to a piece of real property as a share of the community of which it forms a part?
9. What are the major economic services provided by real estate resources?
10. Why is the study of income so important in the fields of economics and business administration? In what ways is the study of real estate a study of income production at fixed sites?

11. Why is the study of real estate administration concerned with the legal and physical characteristics of real properties?

12. *Study Project 1.* Select a reference property and prepare a report on it similar to the one outlined in the Study Project.

SUGGESTED READINGS

BARLOWE, RALEIGH. *Land Resource Economics.* Englewood Cliffs, N.J.: Prentice-Hall, Inc., 1958. Chap. i.

CASE, FREDERICK E. *Real Estate.* Englewood Cliffs, N.J.: Allyn & Bacon, 1962, Chap. i.

LANDSBERG, HANS H., LEONARD L. FISCHMAN, AND JOSEPH L. FISHER. *Resources in America's Future,* Baltimore: Johns Hopkins Press, 1963. Pp. 3–68.

WRIGHT, DAVID McCORD. *Growth and the American Economy.* New York: Charles Scribner's Sons, 1964. Chaps. i–iii.

NOTE: It is suggested that you become familiar with a number of general references and current publications, including the following: census reports, especially the *Census of Housing, House and Home, Land Economics, The Appraisal Journal, The Real Estate Appraiser, The Survey of Current Business, The Federal Reserve Bulletin, Economic Indicators, Business Horizons,* and *The Harvard Business Review.*

You might also write your local district Federal Reserve Bank and ask to be included on the mailing list for their monthly economic bulletin. These reports may be followed as a guide to regional and local economic trends.

2

Decision-Makers and the
Real Estate Business

Decision-Makers

Nearly everyone participates to some extent in real estate decisions, since each of us uses real estate in some way every day. The *primary* decision-makers in the real estate field, however, may be thought of as those who *own* real estate resources. In some cases owners also are *users* of properties; in others, ownership and use are separated. As we shall see in Chapter 5, ownership has a wide range of meanings; and sometimes the owner has relatively little power or control over his property. Typically, however, ownership provides the major basis for controlling decisions.

When ownership and use are combined, decisions are based both on the authority of the owner and his experience as a user of the property. When ownership and use are separated, the ultimate decision is made by the owner; but he is likely to be influenced considerably by the recommendations of the user of the property. In some cases, the user of the property may specify very definitely the conditions under which he will undertake to use it, and hence exercises significant influence on the owner's decisions. This is often the case when a long-term lease is being negotiated, or when the user plans to improve the property in some specific manner.

Another group of decision-makers consists of those engaged in one or another branch of the real estate business, including those who build, subdivide, market, and finance real estate resources and operations.

Those engaged in financing real estate play an important role in real estate decision-making. Typically, the *equity* or the owner's investment represents a small percentage of total property value, the remainder being provided by borrowed funds. Hence, the lender of these funds, whether an individual, a commercial banker, a savings banker, a savings and loan executive, an insurance company official, or a mortgage broker, may through his decisions to finance or not to finance a program of property purchase or development exercise a highly important influence on the owner's decisions.

Similarly, a land developer and subdivider, by his decisions as to the way a tract of land is laid out and subdivided, the types of streets, sewers, and other facilities that will be provided, and by related decisions, may exercise a controlling influence on future uses of the property. Future owners may thus be able to make decisions only within a fairly limited range of possibilities. The builder also plays an important role in real estate decisions in terms of both original construction and subsequent modernization and repair programs. A builder who does high quality work, for example, prevents the occurrence of many problems that may cause difficulties for the original owner or future owners.

Real estate brokers, by the provision of information for prospective sellers or buyers of real properties and by making available as wide a variety of choices as possible, also influence decisions in this field. They play an even more important role when they assist in arranging financing programs. Property managers may influence the decisions of the owners and users of properties by recommending programs of development, improvement, more effective use, and the like.

Various specialists in the real estate field such as appraisers, architects, engineers, property lawyers, and market analysts also influence the decisions of real property owners and users. By providing expert information and opinions, they make possible carefully considered decisions.

Still another group of decision-makers in this field includes government officials on federal, state, and local levels; officers and staff personnel of trade associations; leaders of labor unions; teachers, editors, and various molders of public opinion; and others who help to determine the general climate and the regulative framework within which real estate decisions are made and carried out. For example, zoning laws control property uses; taxes often are controlling factors in real estate decisions; and trade union practices may have a major effect on construction costs.

Real Estate Ownership

The ownership of real estate in this country is widely dispersed. Indeed, the opportunity to acquire ownership interests in real property was one of the main attractions for those who first settled in this country.

Around 60 per cent of our homes are owned by those who occupy them. Many others are owned by small investors. A high percentage of our farms are owned by those who operate them, and a substantial number are owned by retired farmers. Although no exact figures are available, a great many of our business firms own their places of business. Some firms lease their places of business for long periods of time. Thus, there is little concentration of ownership of real estate in this country. There are many owners of real property including home owners, farmers, small business-men, and individual investors.

Government agencies, of course, own a substantial amount of real prop-erty. Such ownership includes the areas devoted to roads, streets, parks, national and state forests, conservation areas, military reservations, gov-ernment office buildings, schools, and many others. The uses to which publicly owned real estate is put, of course, may have important effects on the ways in which privately owned property is developed or used.

We have not had a large concentration of real estate ownership in major companies or in private estates. In some cities, the land in the cen-tral business district has been held by a relatively few families, but even this condition is changing. Inheritance taxes have forced the breaking up of some holdings that might have resulted in relatively large concentra-tions of ownership. The competition of other types of investments has also had its effect.

The people in the real estate business may or may not be real property owners. Some of them are. Some of them speculate in real estate through ownership. On the other hand, some acquire few, if any, ownership in-terests. As we have suggested, the decisions of owners are highly impor-tant in determining the use and rate of development of real estate resources. But ownership of real estate is not complete as we shall see in Chapter 5, although it is more nearly so than is possible in most parts of the world. Owners exercise their rights to control property within certain broad limits, the principal restrictions arising from taxation, emi-nent domain, and the police power.

Users of Real Estate

Although we all use real estate, the decisions of some users tend to have a greater impact than those of others. We may distinguish between (1) owner-users and (2) nonowner-users or those who typically lease property. The latter group, in turn, may be divided between (a) those who have widespread decision-making power, such as those who use property under long-term leases or under leases which grant substantial rights to determine the way in which the property will be used, and (b) those who use property under short-term leases or other limited arrangements—for example, a student who rents a room, or a newly married couple renting a furnished apartment, or a business firm renting a storeroom on a temporary basis.

Those who lease property under arrangements which allow wide latitude for decisions stand in much the same relationship to real estate as owners. Either directly or indirectly, however, the users of property, even if they are not owners or those leasing it under broad grants of power, influence decisions greatly. In order to lease a property, the owner must provide it on terms that are attractive enough to make it marketable.

Buildings are constructed, modernization and repair programs are carried out, and conveniences and facilities are provided of a type that will attract users. In some cases, of course, the users spell out very definitely how property will be developed and improved. For example, under "sale and lease-back" arrangements, which we will consider at greater length later, an owner of property such as a chain store company sells it to an investor who improves it according to specifications laid down by the company which then leases it back for a period of years.

Scope of the Real Estate Business

The real estate business includes a wide variety of enterprises. Many of the real estate brokerage firms in this country are small concerns. The office with one man and a part-time secretary is not unusual. Relatively few brokerage and property management firms attain great size, being limited by the local nature of many markets and by the volume of business. Although large financial institutions play an important part in the field of real estate financing, there are also many medium-sized and smaller financial institutions—including small insurance companies, savings and loan associations, savings banks, and commercial banks—which service principally local markets. Even building enterprises often are small in size. Some construction companies, operative builders, and prefabricated house companies are large concerns, but many builders operate on a small scale.

In addition to those who engage in one or another branch of the real estate business on a full-time basis, many others dabble in real estate, owning and managing a few rental properties, lending money privately on the basis of mortgages on small homes, speculating in subdivision developments or other properties, or "taking a flyer" in the construction of a house or two for sale. A widow may be renting two or three dwelling units; a retired grocer may lend his savings to former customers who want to build houses; a dentist may be holding several acres of suburban land until it is ripe for development; a clerk's wife may be renting a few rooms to piece out the family income.

Of growing importance are the *real estate departments* of business firms. We have suggested that business firms are among the important users of real estate resources; their real estate departments are playing a growing part in the real estate business itself. Such departments specialize in the types of real estate transactions which are of major significance for the operation of their companies. The real estate departments of chain store organizations, for example, have developed rapidly in recent years. We shall have more to say about this aspect of the real estate business in Chapter 23. We should note here, however, that this is one of the areas of expanding opportunity for young people in the real estate field.

Functions of the Real Estate Business

Real estate enterprises exist because they perform useful functions for the community, functions for which people are willing to pay. Similarly, private real estate operators and speculators are allowed to pursue their activities because their functions are considered useful. In an economic sense, all of them are engaged in producing goods and services for which people are willing to pay varying amounts.

We may divide the principal functions of the real estate business into three divisions: developing, financing, and marketing. We use the term *developing* to describe the processes of preparing land for use, constructing buildings and other improvements, and making the completed properties available for use.

Financing provides for the channeling of a portion of the savings of the community into the production of real estate resources. It is also concerned with facilitating the consumption and use of these resources, which, because of their long life, require special types of financing arrangements.

Marketing includes the processes of putting real properties or their services into the hands of consumers. Brokerage and property management constitute the two main subdivisions of the marketing function. Promotion, including advertising and public relations, also forms an important aspect of marketing activity. It may serve the functions of real estate development and financing as well as marketing.

We should note that while certain business firms may specialize in the production, marketing, or financing of real estate resources, such firms have their own problems of production, marketing, or financing operations. While a firm engaged in house building, for example, is producing real estate resources, it must also market the houses it builds and provide adequate financing to carry on its operations. By contrast, a brokerage firm specializes in marketing activities, but it must "produce" listings and the necessary services essential to carry on its work and, of course, must finance its own operations. Thus, while the real estate business as a whole engages in the production, marketing, and financing of real estate resources for the community at large, each firm in one or another branch of the business also must perform these basic functions in support of its own programs.

Specialized activities such as appraising, legal work, engineering and architecture, land planning, and market analysis aid in the performance of the three basic functions of real estate development, financing, and marketing.

Similarly, the process of *managing real estate firms* involves decision-making and implementation, and the application of the basic managerial activities of planning, organizing, and controlling operations toward the achievement of established objectives. These activities may be thought of as methods for helping to accomplish the basic functions of the real estate business.

The activities of the federal, state, and local governments, and the trade associations and other quasi-public organizations in this field may also be viewed as aiding in the performance of the functions of developing, financing, and marketing real estate resources and the services provided by these resources for the community.

The Framework in Which the Real Estate Business Operates

The three functions of developing, financing, and marketing real estate must be performed regardless of how a society is organized. For example, in a dictatorship one huge government agency might perform all of them. Those in charge of such an agency would decide how much subdividing and building should take place, how the properties should be financed, who should be allowed to buy or rent them, and for how much. The government officials would be paid government salaries rather than commissions, fees, rents, interest, or profits.

In an enterprise system these functions are not organized formally. Through competitive bidding, each person, within the limits of his economic resources, by buying or not buying, or by buying more or less, or by selling or not selling, or selling more or less, helps to make the decisions which govern the development, financing, marketing, and use of real estate resources. Government, of course, has the responsibility for making competition work and for supplementing it when necessary.

A large portion of the real estate business is carried on by private enterprises such as brokerage firms, management organizations, subdividing and building companies, financial institutions, and individual operators on a full- or part-time basis. In addition, however, federal, state, and local governments participate in varying degrees in real estate administration.

Government agencies, for example, establish the rules of the game within which the private firms and individuals operate. Government defines and protects property, organizes and enforces a system of private contracts (in effect a system of "private law"), provides protection for private owners in the occupancy and use of their property, and regulates the uses to which property may be put. Government also taxes property, conducts research, collects and disseminates information, provides counsel, facilitates the financing of property ownership and use, lends money, insures and guarantees mortgages, and also develops, leases, owns, and operates certain real properties. In addition, government may regulate the practices of those engaged in the real estate business by licensing laws and similar devices.

The relationships between business and government appear to be growing more and more complex. This is particularly true in the real estate field. No commodity except narcotics is more definitely regulated and controlled than real estate. In part this is because the concept of real property ownership is itself a creation of the law. Also, the close relationship between public and private property in the real estate field helps to account for this situation. Accessibility alone virtually requires the use of public and private real estate in combination. In addition, the use of one property is likely to have significant effects on the use and hence the value of real estate located adjacent to it or nearby.

Obviously the effectiveness with which government agencies are administered has a special bearing on the utilization of real properties. This is important on the federal and state levels, but in the case of real estate, especially important on the local level. Local government agencies may on occasion be hampered by limitations of funds or personnel, but they are tending to respond to the increasingly demanding requirements of the modern business community.

Another set of agencies of major importance in the real estate field includes trade associations, nonprofit organizations, mutual benefit societies, and a number of similar quasi-public institutions. These agencies carry on a number of activities such as providing information, advice, and assistance to member firms, lobbying and other legislative activities, and serving as coordinators of government and private activities. In addition, labor unions play a significant role, especially in the construction industry.

It is not easy to present a diagram showing the relationship between these heterogeneous groups of private enterprises, government agenies, and quasi-public organizations; but the accompanying chart may be helpful (see Fig. 2–1). This chart stresses the fact that when we think of the real estate business or of real estate administration, we must think of all of these agencies, rather than only of one or another type.

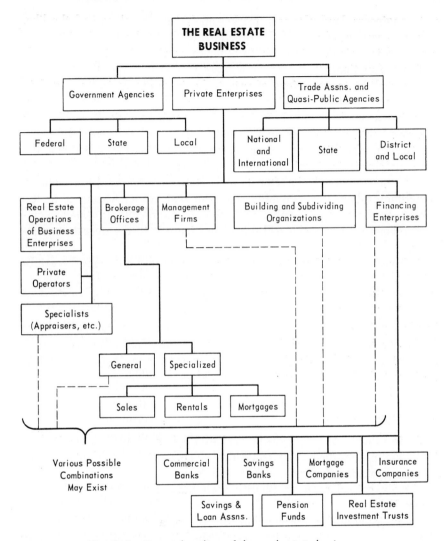

Fig. 2–1. General outline of the real estate business.

Private Enterprises

As is indicated by the chart, the typical enterprises which operate in the real estate field are brokerage offices, management firms, building and subdividing organizations, and financial institutions. Recognition must also be given to the real estate departments of business enterprises such as manufacturing or marketing companies. In addition, there are full- and part-time operators and various specialists, including appraisers, architects, engineers, land planners, market analysts, counselors, and the like. In some cases, nearly all of the functions of the real estate business are combined in a single enterprise. In other cases, there is extensive specialization of function.

The real estate operations of private business enterprises engaged in the production and marketing of various goods and services are often extensive, as we have noted. In larger firms such operations are likely to be carried on directly by company officials. In some cases, special departments, set up for this purpose, may occupy a position of importance in the company's organizational structure. In other cases, a company official such as the treasurer looks after its real estate resources and transactions. Sometimes subsidiary companies own the real estate, leasing it to the parent company. Or a member of the board of directors or a major company official may own the real estate and lease it to the operating company.

Although special departments and other arrangements may be established in larger companies to handle real estate matters, considerable reliance still is placed on specialized persons and organizations in the real estate business. The smaller firms in various fields of business seldom have special arrangements for real estate transactions. Usually the owner of the company or one of the partners or the principal officer of a small corporation will do this. He may rely on specialists in the real estate business to assist him or try to operate independently.

Organization of Firms

As in other fields of business, real estate firms may be organized as individual proprietorships, partnerships, or corporations, or they may take other organizational forms such as trusts or syndicates. You have undoubtedly gained some familiarity with these basic forms of business ownership.

In an individual proprietorship, of course, a single individual owns the business firm. He may have established it or purchased it. He may manage it himself or hire others to do this for him. No legal formalities are required to set up an individual proprietorship, although in the real estate field licenses are necessary in nearly all states for brokerage operations. This means that the owner of a brokerage firm needs a broker's license, and his salesmen also need licenses indicating that they are qualified to engage in this business. Financial institutions are required to obtain federal or state charters in order to engage in business. Usually no special licenses or other permissions are required to engage in land development or building activities. But, while the firm as such is not licensed, permissions usually must be secured to subdivide and improve land, especially when zoning laws are in operation; and building permits typically are required before construction can be undertaken.

Partnerships include two or more persons who jointly are owners of a business firm. Again, no special legal formalities are required for the establishment of a partnership, except for such license or other regulations as must be complied with. Partnerships often are formalized by written contracts between those making up the firm, although this is not essential from a legal standpoint. Both individual proprietorships and partnerships are widely used in real estate brokerage, property management, land development, and building activities. The corporate form is also used. Indeed, in the financial field almost all firms are set up as corporations.

A corporation is a legal entity created by state or federal charter for the purpose of carrying on specifically authorized activities. There are corporations for profit and also those not for profit, the latter usually being established for educational, research, religious, or similar purposes. There may also be government corporations of various types.

In corporations organized for profit, the owners are the stockholders. Bonds may be issued to creditors. Bondholders have no ownership interest, although they may become owners in case of reorganization. The owners of a corporation enjoy limited liability for the obligations of the firm—that is, the liability is limited to their stock interests. Individual proprietors are personally liable for the obligations of their firms. Partners are liable for all of the obligations of the firm unless special limitations are established, and this type of arrangement depends on the statutes of the states where the partnerships are set up. Since a corporation is a legal entity, it is taxed directly and its owners are also taxed on dividends received from the corporation (except in some small corporations whose owners may elect to be taxed as partners). This is not true of individual proprietorships and partnerships.

We should note that a specific piece of real property may form the basis for an enterprise established in any of the above forms. For example, the ownership of a store building might be set up as a corporation, and this property could be purchased by buying a majority of the shares of the corporation.

Some real estate ventures are undertaken as syndicates. Usually this is done for a specific operation such as carrying out a major contract or developing a large tract of land. Syndicates may be made up of individuals or of several firms. The organization of a syndicate depends on the arrangements made to govern the interests of the syndicate members at the time it is established.

Trusts are often established for various purposes in the real estate field. An owner of property may establish a trust for his heirs. Title to the property is transferred to a trustee who administers the property in accordance with the trust agreement. The trust form may be used in other cases as well. For example, the owners of land may pool their interests in a trustee who agrees to develop it for them. A shopping center may be set up as a trust. Real estate investment trusts are growing in popularity, in part because of tax considerations.

Production: Land Development and Building

The processes of developing raw land for use include land planning, subdividing, building, and related activities. Sometimes real estate firms specialize in land planning and subdividing activities. In a growing number of cases, these activities are combined with building and sometimes with marketing operations as well. Sometimes a company undertakes to develop an entire community.

There are two principal groups of builders in this country: (1) custom builders and contractors who serve individuals or firms on a contract basis; (2) operative builders who build for the general market.

Custom builders may be large or small firms. They enter into contracts for the construction of specific buildings or other improvements. They do not sell the buildings or other improvements but construct them under various contractual arrangements.

The operative builders, on the other hand, produce for an impersonal market. While the custom builder's product is sold before construction begins, operative builders may sell in advance or take their chances of disposing of their products in the general market.

Operative builders, or speculative builders as they are sometimes called, often are large contracting organizations, combining subdividing and building activities. They may build on a very large scale. The larger organizations may produce hundreds of homes and other buildings as a single project. Indeed, a community rather than a single building may be thought of as the unit of production in such cases. Large-scale builders bring factory methods of production to the building site. Often they have an ownership interest in the projects on which they work. The prefabricators, by contrast, build houses or other buildings in a factory and then transport them in sections to the building site for final assembly.

Architects serve as specialists who are retained by private individuals and business firms or by a building organization to design and plan buildings, to supervise construction, and to help solve building problems. Chapters 15 and 16 deal with land development and building operation in greater detail.

Brokerage

A broker is usually an agent who acts for the owner of a property and arranges for the sale, leasing, management, or financing of property on a commission basis. Some brokerage offices specialize in the selling of property and even in the sale of particular kinds of property. Some firms specialize in mortgage brokerage, others in lease brokerage. Frequently brokerage firms will handle the sale and leasing of residential, commercial, farm, or industrial properties and will also arrange for the financing of the transactions in which they participate. In some cases property insurance is combined with real estate brokerage. Brokers are paid on a commission basis, 5 to 6 per cent being a typical commission for the sale of a property, while lease and mortgage brokerages command varying commissions. The work of brokerage firms is discussed in Chapter 17.

Property Management

The growing complexity of the problems involved in planning, operating, maintaining, and marketing real property services (rather than the properties themselves) has resulted in the growth of specialized property management firms or in the combination of management and brokerage operations. Other factors contributing to the growth of property management are absentee ownership, more extensive governmental regulations, complicated taxes, the holding of properties by various types of financial institutions, technological changes, and the increased managerial skill required in this field.

A property manager is more than a lease broker, although many management firms start in this way. Typically, a property manager acts for the owner of real estate in all matters pertaining to the operation of the property or properties which are under his direction, including the leasing of space, the collection of rents, the selection of tenants, and the repair and renovation of buildings and grounds. For his services, the manager is paid a commission, usually 5 per cent of the rents collected, although other types of arrangements may be found.

Some management firms specialize in one type of real estate. For example, the management of farm property involves a set of problems quite different from those involved in commercial real estate. Similarly, specialized management problems characterize single-family residences, doubles and duplexes, apartment buildings, stores, shopping centers, office buildings, and industrial property.

The owners of some real estate firms prefer to combine brokerage and property management, since the latter types of activities are not affected so greatly by the upward and downward swings of general business conditions. Furthermore, a property management department often provides listings of property for sale by owners. In addition, the tenants in the buildings which are managed provide a prospective group of property buyers. Property management is considered at greater length in Chapter 18.

Financing Enterprises

The financing of the ownership and use of real estate is carried on by private investors and by a number of types of financial institutions, including commercial banks, savings and loan associations, mutual savings banks, insurance companies, mortgage companies and the like.

This type of financing is long range in character and is usually done by the use of mortgages or similar legal documents which provide for the pledge of greater or lesser degrees of interest in real property as security for the loans. Sometimes leases are used as a means of financing, as in the case of sale and leaseback agreements. Construction loans are made for short terms during the building period, but sometimes are merged with long-term financing. Many commercial banks carry on some real estate financing. Savings and loan associations and cooperative banks are engaged primarily in the financing of home ownership. Mutual savings banks, trust companies, and insurance companies have found the financing of both large and small real estate projects an outlet for substantial proportions of their investment funds. In recent years real estate investment trusts and pension funds have grown in importance in this field.

In financing transactions, interest is charged as a percentage of the funds loaned, and in addition origination, servicing, and brokerage fees may be charged. The federal government, especially through the new Department of Housing and Urban Development, the Federal Home Loan Bank System, Federal Housing Administration, and the Veterans' Administration, plays an important role in real estate financing. In Chapters 19, 20, and 21 we consider the subject of real estate finance at greater length.

Operators

Those who buy and sell or rent properties directly are referred to as real estate *operators* rather than as brokers, who act for others. The real estate operator may be a land speculator or an investor in income-producing properties. He may buy vacant land and hold it until it is ripe for development. Sometimes operators develop small or large apartment houses or own and manage blocks of single- or two-family rental houses. In many cases they specialize in business property. If we include with this group all those who dabble in real estate on a part-time basis, we have represented a highly important group of real estate decision-makers.

Appraising

Because the market for real estate is not highly organized, it is often necessary to estimate the value of properties for various business and other purposes. Appraisals or estimates of value serve as one of the major sources of information on which the business decisions related to real estate are based. Such estimates are usually made by appraisers, although others at times undertake to do this work. Because of the complexity of the appraisal process, numerous laws which require property appraisal, policies of large corporations, and similar developments, more and more valuation work is being done by specialists in this area. Such organizations as the American Institute of Real Estate Appraisers and the Society of Real Estate Appraisers have helped to develop training programs and standards of practice.

Appraisers may be employed on a full-time basis by a manufacturing or marketing company, a real estate firm, or financial institution; but the more typical arrangement is to employ them on a fee basis, paying a stated amount for each appraisal report. In some instances appraising is carried on in connection with brokerage or property management, while some appraisers specialize in this work exclusively.

Government Agencies

Federal, state, and local agencies of government carry on a wide variety of activities that have a bearing on real estate administration. To some extent the practices of the individuals and firms engaged in the real estate business are regulated—for example, by licensing laws. Some government agencies provide information and counsel. There are also some activities that are designed to stimulate or retard private activity.

The federal government does not regulate the real estate business specifically, other than to apply to it the regulations which are imposed on all business practices. Thus, antitrust laws and those regulating monopolistic practices apply in this area, as in others. Many of the informational activities of such federal agencies as the Department of Housing and Urban Development, Housing and Home Finance Agency, Bureau of the Census, Department of Commerce, Bureau of Labor Statistics, Department of Agriculture, and others are of importance to those engaged in the real estate business.

Probably the influence of the federal government on the real estate business is felt principally through real estate finance. The work of the Federal Housing Administration, the Federal Home Loan Bank System, the Veterans' Administration, and the Federal National Mortgage Association has been of major importance, as we shall see in Chapter 22.

License Laws

The principal activities of state governments which have a bearing on real estate administration and practice are license laws.[1] The first real

[1] See George F. Bloom's "Real Estate License Laws" in Appendix B of this book.

estate license law was enacted in California in 1917 but was declared unconstitutional. Another act was passed in 1919 which met constitutionality requirements, and Michigan enacted a similar law in the same year.

Nearly all of the states now have some type of license law. Many of these laws were patterned after a model law which was prepared in 1914 by N. W. MacChesney, who was then general counsel for the National Association of Real Estate Boards.

A license law makes provision for regulating the practices of real estate brokers and real estate salesmen in the interests of the public. Typically, such laws require that each person desiring to carry on brokerage or other marketing activities in the real estate field secure a license, and that only persons with stated qualifications may obtain licenses. Usually the people licensed are divided into two classes, brokers and salesmen, with supervision being exercised directly over the brokers, who are responsible for the salesmen working for them. Provisions are made for machinery to administer and enforce the licensing laws, and for the revocation of licenses and exaction of penalties if the laws are broken. Although penalties vary widely, Harold F. Lusk says, ". . . in no state can an untrained broker or salesman receive a judgment for the agreed commission in a court action, since the contract to pay the commission is an unlawful one." [2]

In order for a new applicant to secure a license he normally is called upon to (1) secure the endorsement of a certain number of responsible citizens (usually two) who vouch for his reputation, (2) meet certain minimum educational requirements, (3) pay a nominal fee, and (4) in some cases post a bond. Examinations are often required. These regulations are generally administered by a real estate commission.

There appears to be general agreement that license laws have helped to improve the personnel of the real estate brokerage business, that fraudulent practices have been reduced, and that the confidence of the public in real estate brokers and salesmen has been increased. It is probable that these license laws have helped to stimulate educational activity in the real estate field and that greater uniformity of practices among different regions has resulted.

License laws also regulate the entrance of architects and engineers into their respective fields and thus have an effect on the real estate business. In addition, some state governments require that contractors and workmen in the plumbing and electrical trades be licensed.

Of course, financial institutions are regulated as to establishment and practice. In some cases, the regulations are on a federal basis as is true of

---

[2] Harold F. Lusk, *Law of the Real Estate Business* (Homewood, Ill.: Richard D. Irwin, Inc., 1958), pp. 15–16.

national banks or federal savings and loan associations. In other cases such institutions operate under state authority.

When properly administered, laws licensing certain activities have advantages. It should be noted, however, that they may be used as a means of restricting competition if administered in a manner which is unfavorable to newcomers to the business or to people outside the state or locality. In their manner of enforcement, some of these laws may be open to criticism on this score. In a few cases, license laws have turned into little more than devices for raising revenue.

Local Regulations

Although there are many variations, local governments seldom regulate the real estate business directly but exercise profound influence on it by their tax policies, zoning and planning regulations, building codes, and related controls. Of special importance are building regulations, building permit requirements, regulations affecting the safety and health standards of buildings, changes in transportation systems and regulations, local public housing projects, and the like.

Trade Associations

A number of trade associations are of importance in the real estate field. The National Association of Real Estate Boards and its affiliates, a nationwide organization, has branches in each state and in many cities. It includes such institutes, societies, and councils as the following: American Institute of Real Estate Appraisers, Institute of Farm Brokers, Institute of Real Estate Management, National Institute of Real Estate Brokers, American Society of Real Estate Counselors, Secretaries Council, Society of Industrial Realtors, International Real Estate Federation, States' Council, and Women's Council.

The National Association of Home Builders, the National Association of Building Owners and Managers, and the Home Manufacturers' Institute are important organizations in this field. In finance, a number of organizations carry on work of importance to real estate, including the American Bankers Association, U.S. Savings and Loan League, Society of Real Estate Appraisers, National Association of Mutual Savings Banks, Life Insurance Association of America, and Mortgage Bankers Association. Others might also be mentioned.

Most of these organizations strive to serve their members by representing them before the public, collecting and disseminating information, carrying on educational activities, undertaking such lobbying and legislative activities as appear to be in the interests of their members, and conducting numerous related types of work. Of special importance are their attempts to raise the standards of business practice in their areas by educational programs, recognitions of various kinds, and restriction of membership to qualified personnel.

Educational and Operating Standards

Organizations that play a leading role in educational activities include the American Savings and Loan Institute, the American Institute of Banking, the American Institute of Real Estate Appraisers, the Society of Real Estate Appraisers, the American Real Estate and Urban Economics Association, and others.

The efforts of the National Association of Real Estate Boards to establish and maintain certain minimum standards of practice are deserving of special mention. In 1916 this organization adopted the term *Realtor* as "a distinctive name to be applied solely to persons who are members of a constituent board of, and as such having membership in, the National Association of Real Estate Boards." This name may be used only by those who are affiliated with the Association. To the extent that members follow high standards of practice, this term acquires value in distinguishing them from other persons engaged in the real estate business.

Code of Ethics

In order to guarantee high standards of practice, the National Association of Real Estate Boards adopted in 1924 an official code of ethics. Every local organization which becomes affiliated with the Association is required to adopt and enforce this code. Its principal objectives are to regulate relationships between those in the real estate business and the public and also to regulate relationships of brokers with other brokers, with owners, with operators, and with others in the real estate field. (See Study Project II.)

Is Real Estate a Profession?

Many people engaged in the real estate business believe that they are doing work of a professional type and that they should be accorded recognition as members of a profession or professions. Such recognition in a final sense depends on the general attitudes and standards of the public rather than on published rules, codes, or distinctive names. To date, those in the various divisions of real estate business have not been considered by the public at large to be members of a profession. This does not suggest that those in business activities in these areas occupy any lower position in the public mind than do those in medicine, law, or the ministry. It is a different position, to be sure, since the public in general appears to think of work related to real estate in terms of business rather than in professional terms. Whether this public estimate is correct or not may be determined by considering some of the basic criteria of a profession, concerning which J. M. Clark has made the following observations:

1. The professional man is an expert, selling services of guidance to persons who are in the nature of the case not experts. Moreover, their need is peculiarly vital to their well-being, whether it is the need of a man threatened with a lawsuit, the sick man's need for health, or the adolescent's need for wise and dependable counsel. Thus, the customers are in a peculiar relation of dependence on the one who is serving them, and the rule of *caveat emptor* is peculiarly out of place.

2. So much for the elements creating the need for codes of professional conduct. As for the facilitating causes, they consist largely of the common discipline through which all members of the professions have gone. Students are naturally group-conscious and keenly alive to all things making for the honor and prestige of the group, and this likemindedness continues if their lifework is a direct continuation of their training. Even the ceremonials help materially: a medical graduate taking the oath of Hippocrates can hardly be unaffected by the sense of obligations which he is assuming. On the whole, however, the schools appear to make relatively little attempt to focus this force on the development of professional ethics. The results achieved are largely natural by-products of the general character of professional training.

3. Another feature is the fact that professional services are rendered by the professional men in person. In this they differ vitally from the services of the typical man of business. This has two important results: it favors the development of sympathy, confidence, and honorable relations, and it is a fairly effectual obstacle to the growth of large-scale production, thus removing the chief incentive to commercialized methods of sales-promotion. This constitutes what is probably a permanent difference between the professions and business.

4. To sum up, the profession assumes responsibility for the quality and sincerity of its workmanship, for rendering service, to some extent, according to the rule of need rather than the rule of maximum profit, and for maintaining a level of competition which centers in service rather than salesmanship.[3]

If we accept this general description of the requirements of a profession, only a limited number of those in the various branches of real estate qualify on all counts. The appraisers come close to meeting many of these requirements and may develop at an early date into a truly professional group. Architecture is already recognized as a profession. Land planners and market analysts also are moving in the direction of professional status. Some of the other branches of the real estate business, however, may move in the direction of the professions more slowly. Brokerage, management, financing, developing, and related activities are likely to develop into areas of larger- rather than smaller-scale activity by virtue of the increasing needs for more economical production, marketing and

---

[3] By permission from *Social Control of Business*, by J. M. Clark, p. 206. Copyright, 1939, McGraw-Hill Book Co., Inc., New York.

financing of properties, and property services. Since professional services are always rendered on a personal basis, they cannot be adapted easily to large-scale production methods.

SUMMARY

The primary decision-makers in the real estate field are the owners of real estate resources. The influence of users of real estate on real estate decisions varies greatly depending upon whether they own or lease. If they lease real estate, they may have broad or limited decision-making power, depending upon the nature of the leasing agreement. Those who build, subdivide, market, or finance real estate also make or influence decisions about the use of real estate resources. Decisions by government officials, trade association executives, labor union leaders, and various molders of public opinion help to determine the general framework in which real estate decisions are made.

The ownership of real estate in the United States is widely dispersed, and private real estate enterprises exist in large numbers. There is no lack of large organizations in this field, but many are small. Real estate enterprises may be engaged in one or more of the basic functions of the business: production, including developing and building; financing; marketing; or other specialized activities. Within the framework of social, institutional, and governmental factors, these enterprises have broad discretion in the performance of their functions.

QUESTIONS FOR STUDY

1. List three ways in which the federal government influences real estate decisions.
2. Explain the functions of real estate license laws. Do you favor such laws? Why or why not?
3. How might license laws, building codes, and other restrictions on real estate adversely affect the allocation of real estate resources?
4. Who would be the principal decision-makers in the planning and construction of an apartment building? Who would be the principal decision-makers in the operation of this building?
5. How are financing groups and institutions able to exercise influence in decisions involving real estate resources?
6. List the principal local governmental regulations that influence the activities of subdividers. Which regulations apply most directly to brokers?
7. By what method could the various specialists in the real estate field strive toward the classification of "professional"? Which specialists are most likely to obtain that goal and why?
8. Who can use the title "realtor" and what is its advantage?
9. Which business firms are likely to have real estate departments? Which official would probably make the real estate decisions for: (a) A large

manufacturing firm? (b) A chain of supermarkets? (c) A local department store?

10. *Study Project 2.* Prepare an evaluation of the Code of Ethics of the National Association of Real Estate Boards. Include in your report a discussion of: (a) The purpose of the Code. (b) The extent to which your experience indicates that the Code is being followed. (c) Recommendations for improvements or additions to the Code. (d) The contribution made by the Code to real estate decision-making.

SUGGESTED READINGS

CASE, FREDERICK E. *Real Estate.* Englewood Cliffs, N.J.: Allyn & Bacon, 1962. Chap. i.

WEIMER, ARTHUR M. *Business Administration: An Introductory Management Approach* (3d ed.). Homewood, Ill.: Richard D. Irwin, Inc., 1966. Chap. i.

WRIGHT, DAVID McCORD. *Growth and the American Economy.* New York: Charles Scribner's Sons, 1964. Chaps. iv, v.

3

Real Estate Decisions and Administrative Processes

Decision-making

Decisions related to real estate resources or the real estate business are similar in most respects to those made in relation to other resources or other areas of business. Some of them are made on a logical and rational basis, others are the result of hunches, intuition, or snap judgments. Decisions in the real estate field, however, are likely to be influenced by several sets of factors that are unique: (1) income from real estate resources must be produced at fixed sites; (2) long-term commitments usually are required in real estate matters; (3) relatively large amounts of money usually are involved; and (4) public factors—streets, utilities, conveniences, and the like, plus laws and regulations—play an important part in determining private decisions.

Much has been said and written about decisions and decision-making. One may develop a logical, step-by-step procedure to illustrate the process, for example: (1) collecting and analyzing information, (2) developing predictions or postulates, and (3) arriving at a decision on the basis of value judgments and strategic consideration. When a decision is reached, it is translated into action or implemented. It is probably not advisable to separate decisions and operations; however, some insight may be gained by viewing levels of decisions in terms of their importance. It is desirable also to review and reconsider decisions in order that better decisions may be made in the future.

Dr. Robert D. Calkins believes that there are five general steps inherent in the process of rational decision-making, and he outlines them as follows: "(1) to identify the problem and understand it, (2) to define or clarify the goals sought, (3) to pose alternatives for the attainment of those goals, (4) to analyze the anticipated consequences of each major alternative, and (5) to appraise the alternatives and choose." [1]

Decisions involve choices among alternatives. In this respect a decision problem differs from an information problem or a prediction problem. An information problem is solved by securing the required information. (Getting the required information in some cases, of course, may be a major problem in itself.)

Suppose that you want to know the tax rate on a particular piece of property. You call the tax collector's office and secure the information. Your problem, which is an *information* problem, is solved. Now, suppose that you would like to determine the future taxes for this piece of property. This is a *prediction* problem. You study the trend of taxes for similar types of property and predict that taxes will advance at an increasing rate. Your problem, which requires prediction, is tentatively solved.

Now, suppose you have the alternative of buying this property (call it property A) or another one (property B). Here you are faced with a choice among alternatives. This is a *decision* problem. It may be that the tax factor will be the final basis of judgment. In any event, you compare the alternative properties with care, securing as much information as you can about each, analyze this information, consider the advantages and disadvantages of each property, estimate or postulate or predict the probable costs and results of buying each one, consider the values you hope to gain, and finally arrive at a selection—a decision.

Here we see that the decision problem is a combination of the information and prediction types of problems. But it is also something more. It finally involves a judgment as to the best of two or more alternatives. Such a judgment may be based on relative values such as personal preferences, objectives established, or other standards. In many business activities, considerations of strategy are also present, which require the anticipation, matching, or excelling of the moves of competitors who may also be considering the purchase of these properties.

As Calkins has pointed out:

For many years the prevailing view in management was that if we got the facts, the solution would be indicated. . . . But few problems are resolved so simply. In the first place, getting the facts is often a large investigation in itself. . . . When the facts are known, the causes of the difficulty are usually not apparent and must be discovered, often by testing hypotheses and experi-

[1] Robert D. Calkins, "The Decision-Making Process in Administration," *Business Horizons* (Fall, 1959).

mentation. And when the causes are found the question still remains: Are they the strategic factors through the control of which, or modification of which, a more favorable set of conditions can be created that will yield the results desired? [2]

Although we follow the point of view suggested by Robert D. Calkins in these discussions, a number of other interesting approaches might also be followed. Of special importance are the discussions of Herbert A. Simon. He considers decision-making and managing to be synonymous and identifies three principal phases of the process:

. . . finding occasions for making a decision; finding possible courses of action; and choosing among courses of action. . . . The first phase of the decision making process—searching the environment for conditions calling for decisions—I shall call *intelligence* activity (borrowing the military meaning of intelligence). The second phase—inventing, developing and analyzing possible courses of action—I shall call *design* activity. The third phase—selecting a particular course of action from those available—I shall call *choice* activity.[3]

We should note that decisions are always forward looking; they are oriented to the future since they deal with programs that are to be under-taken in the future. Further, decisions are almost always influenced by environmental factors, by general economic, political, or social conditions and potential changes in such conditions. Indeed management may be considered as largely a process of creating a favorable environment within the firm and relating this to the external environment.[4]

It is helpful to think in terms of the processes of problem identification; clarification of goals; the posing of alternatives, which requires the collection and analysis of pertinent information; predicting and postulating the consequences of the alternatives selected, which includes a consideration of strategic factors; and the making of value judgments and, finally, the choice of an alternative—that is, the decision itself. We will consider these processes in order briefly. Even a brief discussion may help us to gain insights into the decisions that are made in the real estate field, as well as their importance in determining how effectively real estate resources are utilized and real estate firms are managed.

Problem Identification

The identification of problems may be a very simple or a highly complicated matter. Often problems must be discovered. They are difficult to

[2] Robert D. Calkins, "The Art of Administration and The Art of Science," *Indiana Business Report No. 29* (Indiana University, Bureau of Business Research, 1959), pp. 15–16. See also *Business Horizons* (Fall, 1959), by permission.

[3] Herbert A. Simon, *The New Science of Management Decision* (New York: Harper & Row, Publishers, Inc., 1960), pp. 5–6, by permission.

[4] See Harold Koontz and Cyril O'Donnell, *Principles of Management* (3d ed.; New York: McGraw-Hill Book Co., Inc., 1964), p. 1.

identify. It is necessary to anticipate them or to know that they are developing. This is especially true in the real estate field because changes often occur so slowly that they are difficult to identify. The administrator is concerned not with an event but with its meaning and implications— that is, what it might lead to in the way of problems or risks. For example, the adoption of a new one-way street plan may be of special concern to the owner of a store building; he is not concerned so much with the fact that such a plan is adopted as he is with its possible implications for the income-producing ability of his property. He may be concerned also with its impact on competitive properties, or with longer-range changes that may grow out of the new traffic pattern.

Definition and Clarification of Goals

A primary responsibility of management in any situation is the definition of objectives. Without objectives it is impossible to manage any program. The goals set determine the relative value of supporting programs, the priorities that may be assigned to various resources and processes, and the various relationships between real estate, equipment, machines, manpower, and other resources.

There are various levels of goals ranging from broad ones for the whole organization to specific ones for particular operations. In making decisions, it is necessary to define and to clarify the specific goal that is being served. Often this is done on economic grounds, on the basis of cost, return, or risk relationships. But often it involves consideration of the broader purposes of the organization; and this may make it necessary to clarify relationships between immediate, intermediate, and general or long-term goals. We consider this subject somewhat further in the discussion of "Management by Objectives" later in this chapter.

Posing Alternatives

The alternatives open in a given decision are often far from clear. Only in relatively simple situations is there a choice between one alternative and another. More often there are many alternatives. For example, you are seldom faced with a choice of buying or not buying a property at a given price; you also have a number of "more or less" alternatives. The price may be less if there is a larger down payment, or the terms may be more favorable if additional security can be provided to assist in financing, or adjustments may be possible in assuming tax obligations or assuming an existing mortgage or other possibilities. In short, the choices in most business transactions and decisions are usually wide. Sometimes they must be sought out and their possibilities explored.

Often past experience provides guides to the posing of alternatives in various situations. Or the experience of others or typical practices in one or another field of business offer suggestions as to possible alternatives. Some alternatives will be ruled out on various bases. For example, they may not coincide with the objective sought or they may be considered unethical or not acceptable to the public or customers. Some alternatives are too costly or too risky to be considered. Some may conflict with other programs that are being pursued.

For example, a business firm may wish to purchase real property to provide room for expansion. One alternative may require the rezoning of several properties. This may be decided against because it might arouse the opposition of customers or union leaders or persons of political importance.

Collection and Analysis of Information

A wide variety of information is used as a background for decisions in the real estate field. Such information ranges from major reports of the Bureau of the Census dealing with population and housing to financial reports pertaining to a single piece of real estate. The volume of data has been growing, but there continues to be need for more complete and more accurate data to provide an adequate background for real estate decisions.

The analysis of data includes classification and the determination of points of similarity and difference. We may classify information for our purposes, for example, as (1) that pertaining to the environment of real estate—national, regional, and local data relating to real estate markets and location influences, including information about business conditions, population changes, money markets, prices, construction volume and costs, government programs such as taxes, and the like; (2) that pertaining to real estate resources—residential, commercial and industrial, farm and other rural real estate, and special purpose properties—including income and expense and related operating data, risk factors, construction and operating standards, and trends of development; and (3) that pertaining to the real estate business, including information about subdividing, building, brokerage, property management, and financial activities such as financial reports, operating data, and related information.

In the real estate field we make use of accounting and statistical techniques, historical studies, comparative studies, legal techniques, and others. In addition, we use valuation and appraisal techniques, location analyses, methods of market analysis, plus analyses of business, political, and government conditions. We discuss these topics in Part II.

Postulates and Predictions

We have indicated that decisions are, in effect, choices among alternatives, and that the alternatives are seldom given. Often they must be sought out. In most situations, however, the administrator does not explore all alternatives; rather, he explores those he selects as most important.[5]

Once the principal alternatives are identified, it is necessary to consider the consequences of each. This involves predictions, or perhaps more properly the establishment of *postulates.* Calkins says in this connection:

> As I have observed administrators they do not *predict* the future, they postulate it, and ask how a given course of action will work and what results it will have under these postulated conditions. . . . Prudent administrators seldom risk a major decision on the basis of results expected under only one set of postulates. They also ask: How will this course of action work if we have war, or a depression, or a boom? They postulate a number of contingencies and consider the consequences under each. They may, and sometimes do, fail to postulate the most likely future, or the one that is later realized, but their several efforts are intended to come fairly close to any set of conditions that may emerge.[6]

It should be noted that the administrator allows for some margin of error in making his estimates. He may allow a margin of safety in his commitments, keep a cash reserve for uncertainties, maintain reserves of personnel, space, raw material, and other things. Or he may set up alternative objectives, some more difficult to achieve than others.

Somehow the administrator must make commitments against an uncertain future. His predictions, postulates, or assumptions may be based on adequate or inadequate information, his selection of alternatives may be favorable or unfavorable, or the strategic factors he considers may or may not be pertinent. Still he must proceed.

Simon has aptly said in this connection:

> Administrative man recognizes that the world he perceives is a drastically simplified model of the buzzing, blooming confusion that constitutes the real world. He is content with this gross simplification because he believes that the real world is mostly empty—that most of the facts of the real world have no great relevance to any particular situation he is facing, and that most significant chains of causes and consequences are short and simple. Hence, he is content to leave out of account those aspects of reality—and that means *most* aspects—that are substantially irrelevant at a given time. He makes his choices using a

[5] Herbert A. Simon, *Administrative Behavior* (2d ed.; New York: The Macmillan Co., 1957), pp. 67, 81.
[6] Calkins, "The Decision-Making Process in Administration," *op. cit.,* p. 23.

simple picture of the situation that takes into account just a few of the factors that he regards as most relevant and crucial.[7]

Prediction Methods

The making of decisions may be facilitated by a knowledge of methods of prediction. A number of methods of prediction may be distinguished.[8] For example, we may make use of *persistence prediction*—that is, we may assume the continuation of conditions that currently exist. In predicting changes in the real estate market, we may assume that tomorrow will be like today—that is, that current conditions will persist unless there are good reasons for believing otherwise. If conditions have been generally stable, persistence prediction often works very well; when conditions are unstable, other types of prediction usually are preferable. If change has been occurring in a given direction—for example, if prices are generally advancing—we may make use of such a *trend* as the basis of prediction. Or if the market is moving upward and downward, predictions of the *cycle* type may be useful. Much has been said and written about the real estate cycle, which is presumed to be a long-term pattern of advances and declines in the volume of real estate activity and in prices and values. In recent years attention has centered more in short-term cyclical movements rather than in long cycles.

Associate prediction is another method that is often used. This is based on an assumed or established relationship between two sets of events—for example, an increase in real estate market activity may precede a rise in real estate prices, or a lowering of interest rates may be followed by an increase in the volume of building.

Predictions may also be made on the basis of *analogy*. A mathematical model of a real estate market may be considered as analogous to the market. An analogy may be drawn between the reactions of a sample of people in the housing market and the entire market.

Value Judgments

Ultimately decisions turn on value judgments. What is considered "best" by one decision-maker may be considered "worst" by another, since value scales will vary from person to person.

In most business situations, value judgments depend greatly on impersonal bases such as anticipated incomes and costs in relation to risks.

---

[7] Simon, *Administrative Behavior*, pp. xxv–xxvi, by permission of The Macmillan Co.

[8] See Irwin D. J. Bross, *Design for Decision* (New York: The Free Press of Glencoe, Inc., 1965), chap. iii.

Our competitive markets reflect the standards of buyers and sellers. Unless it has a monopoly, a business firm's selling prices are set by the market. Objective market standards usually dominate business decisions but personal values and prestige considerations sometimes modify market standards.

The specific objectives that a decision-maker is trying to achieve typically form the basis of his value judgments. For example, different decisions are likely to result if short-run rather than long-run objectives are given priority.

Strategic and Related Factors

Decisions are often weighted by strategic considerations, factors of timing, availability of opportunities and resources, and related factors. Often a decision is influenced by the anticipated actions or programs of competitors. For example, an investor may decide that the development of a shopping center of modest size is best at a given location; but in order to prevent the establishment of another center nearby, a somewhat larger project may be decided upon.

Timing may be a factor in decisions. A program of subdivision development may be started now rather than later because of the expected timing of a rival subdivision. Or it may be possible to borrow money to advantage now, and this may bring a decision to act sooner than had been planned. An advance in materials prices, on the other hand, may lead to the cutting back of a building program.

Continuity of Decisions

As one of the authors has pointed out in another discussion:

We have a tendency to think of a decision as final. This may be true in a literal sense, but we should recognize that we reappraise and review most decisions and frequently modify them, change them entirely, or supplant them by new decisions. . . . For example, a manager may decide to lease space for his store. Even before he occupies the location, however, he may have found another one that offers many additional advantages. He may then sublease the first location and occupy the new one. Business managers are constantly reviewing and reappraising the results of past decisions. Often decisions are modified or changed or canceled out. In some cases, of course, it may be impossible to change a previous decision even if the manager wished to do so. In the illustration above, for example, the manager might have found it impossible to take the new location if he had been unable to sublease the first one. Even in this case, however, he may occupy the first location for a time and later be able to make a shift.[9]

[9] Arthur M. Weimer, *Business Administration: An Introductory Management Approach* (3d ed.; Homewood, Ill.: Richard D. Irwin, Inc., 1966), pp. 280–81, by permission.

The idea of continuity in business decisions, the lack of finality in many decisions, and the interrelationships between decisions and actions are illustrated in Figure 3–1.

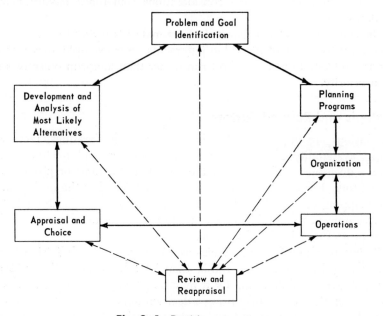

Fig. 3–1. Decision processes.

To continue the above quotation:

The business manager is engaged constantly in the making of current decisions, reviewing and reappraising past decisions, postponing some decisions, and undertaking new decisions. The decision-making process is not done in isolation; one decision seldom can be separated from others.[10]

Decisions and Income at Fixed Sites

Although we recognize that decisions may be made on various bases, those in the real estate field are likely to turn to a large extent on factors related to real estate values, and this means on factors affecting *income production at fixed sites*. As we suggested above, income is a basic factor in most business decisions and, more specifically, income or anticipated income in relation to the cost or anticipated cost of producing income. In the real estate field, however, the income from real properties must be produced at fixed sites, at specific locations; in this respect decisions in the real estate field are influenced by special factors somewhat different from those in other sectors of business life.

[10] *Ibid.*, p. 246, by permission.

We will have more to say about this important factor in real estate decisions throughout our discussions. It is important to note here, however, that if other factors are normal in a business sense, decisions in this field are more likely to be based on the capacity of a property to produce income, whether direct or indirect income, and income in excess of costs and in proper relation to risks, than on other factors.

Obviously the objectives of the owner or user of property may be such that income factors will be of secondary rather than primary importance. Because of tax factors, for example, an investor may prefer to limit income from a piece of property; or an owner of property may prefer to use it himself for purely personal reasons rather than to lease it to others who could use it to better advantage and enable it to yield a higher income. But such cases are likely to be exceptions.

We usually have tended to assume that property owners preferred to maximize net income or to maximize income over the long run. Indeed, this is the basis of the concept of highest and best use (see Chapter 1).

There are questions, however, as to whether this is actually the case. To quote again from Simon:

> In most psychological theories the motive to act stems from *drives,* and action terminates when the drive is satisfied. Moreover, the conditions for satisfying a drive are not necessarily fixed, but may be specified by an aspiration level that itself adjusts upward or downward on the basis of experience.
>
> If we seek to explain business behavior in the terms of this theory, we must expect the firm's goals to be not maximizing profit, but attaining a certain level or rate of profit, holding a certain share of the market or a certain level of sales. Firms would try to "satisfice" rather than to maximize.[11]

There may also be differences in the aspirations of those who own and those who manage or use properties. In this connection Simon says, "While economic man maximizes—selects the best alternative from among all those available to him; his cousin, whom we shall call administrative man, satisfices—looks for a course of action that is satisfactory or 'good enough.'" [12]

Thus we must recognize that some owners, managers, and users of real property may wish to maximize net income or maximize income over the long run, but that others may have different objectives and motives. These will clearly affect the decisions that are made relative to programs of property use and development.

Implementing Decisions

As we have suggested, decisions mean little unless they are implemented—that is, translated into action. In some cases a decision may indi-

[11] Herbert A. Simon, "Theories of Decision-Making in Economics and Behavioral Science," *American Economic Review,* Vol. XLIX, No. III (June, 1959), pp. 262-63.
[12] Simon, *Administrative Behavior,* p. xxv.

cate no action, or the failure to reach a decision may in itself be a decision to take no action. A decision may be a prelude to action, or it may be intertwined with the action. It may not be possible to distinguish between decisions and the implementing of decisions.

A decision may be a very broad one such as undertaking the development of a large shopping center, or it may be a special one involving, for example, a change in the copy for an advertisement of a house for sale. Broad decisions often are referred to as policy decisions or as major decisions. Usually they involve the establishment of basic objectives or programs. Supporting decisions are those which follow and which support the general objectives or policies or programs.

For example, a decision to develop a large shopping center may require numerous other decisions, some broad, some special in nature. Of the broader type will be decisions as to the general layout of the center, the relationships between land and buildings, relationships between store space and parking space, type of financing plan to be followed, leasing policies, and the like. Of a more special type will be decisions as to whether to work out a financing plan with one or another financial institution, or whether to lease a space to one or another store.

Thus, a decision may involve what is to be done, how it is to be done, by what means, at what time, by whom, and many other things. To translate a decision into action at least the following steps are usually required: (1) planning to achieve the objective or desired result; (2) organizing resources in order to carry the plan into effect; (3) controlling operations to assure conformance with the plan; and (4) leadership—the setting off or sparking of action—putting the organization and the available resources to work.

Administrative Process

These steps are often referred to as *the management or administrative process*. This process is applicable to large, comprehensive activities such as developing a multimillion dollar subdivision, or to a very specific activity such as selling or leasing a piece of property. *The management process provides an orderly method for getting things done.* It is a guide to action, to the implementation of decisions. It applies to all aspects of business administration and to all parts of the real estate business, to land development and subdividing, to building, to brokerage or property management, to financing, and to the effective utilization of real properties by business firms, institutions, or individuals.

The management process may be used by an individual operator who has a few real estate investments, by an executive responsible for the effective use of the real estate resources of a business firm, or by the head of a real estate firm or one of its divisions. Many who are responsible for carrying out decisions follow the management process without realizing the specific steps they are taking. An awareness of the steps of this process, however, tends to make for orderly and efficient operations. Recognition of the need for planning in advance of organizing resources makes for better operations; recognizing the importance of proper controls improves planning and organizing activities.

To use a simple illustration, suppose you are asked to arrange for the sale of a small residence. You would find it advisable to begin by developing a plan, determining exactly what is to be done, how, where, when, and by whom. In this case, for example, you would decide whether or not to advertise the property, and if so, the kinds of advertising you would use; whether you would sell the house yourself or arrange for someone else to do it. You would develop a tentative time schedule. You would decide whether to develop special sales aids and the like.

Once you had laid out a plan of action, you would organize the effort that you or someone else would make to carry out the action. For example, you might set up certain times when various things should be done; you would coordinate this particular assignment with others, and do various related things.

Throughout the process you would be aided by controls—by checking up on your activities to determine whether they were proceeding according to the plan that was established. If the plan were not being followed, you would need to determine why not, or whether some modification in the plan might be necessary.

This simple illustration of the processes involved in carrying out an action gives you a preliminary indication of the relationships between the basic steps of planning, organizing, and controlling operations. In most business situations, of course, the processes become much more complex. Typically, a number of people are involved, and the organizing step requires the establishment of appropriate working arrangements for them. Controls may require elaborate statistical and accounting reports, for example, and the development of elaborate standards for measuring performance. Also, when a number of people are involved, leadership activities increase in importance. Basically such activities include the direction of operations, the development of effective work teams, and the motivation of the people in the organization to put forth their best efforts.

Management by Objectives

Decisions in the real estate field or in any other field depend to a large extent on the objectives that are set up for accomplishment. The selection of an objective is a decision in itself, of course. Once an objective has been set up, it provides a guide to decisions. As we suggested above, an objective sets a general value scale which serves as a basis for reaching decisions.

The implementation of decisions also requires that objectives be set, that targets or goals be understood. Otherwise, there is no sound basis for developing plans, organizing resources, or applying controls. The leadership functions of management cannot be discharged unless the goals are understood.

Thus, the concept of *management by objectives* is basic to the effective management and administration of activities in the real estate field or in other areas of business. It may be helpful to state this proposition in re-verse—that it is impossible to manage without objectives, goals, or targets. An owner of an apartment building may have as his major objective the maximizing of net income or the development of the reputation of his building as a "good address," or he may wish to pursue other objectives. Sometimes two or more objectives may be pursued simultaneously, pro-vided they do not conflict. Usually, however, priorities must be indicated in such cases. The determination of the objectives to be achieved by means of a piece of real property usually is made by its owners. The owners may be influenced by those who use the property and by various environmental forces. Sometimes owners of property can determine ob-jectives only within limits. For example, a property may be zoned for a specific use or it may be under a long-term lease that allows little latitude for choice until the lease expires or can be bought in.

Similarly, the administration of a real estate firm depends on the deter-mination of objectives and on priorities between objectives in case several are being pursued. Such a firm may have survival as a basic goal, or growth, or the attainment of a prestige position. In any event, it will be necessary for it to make a profit if it is to continue in business and be able to pursue its objectives. In a final analysis, profits are the test of a real estate firm's performance, as they are of the performance of firms in other lines of activity. As Joel Dean has aptly pointed out, "Social criteria of business performance usually relate to quality of products, rate of prog-ress, and the behavior of prices. But these are tests of the desirability of the whole profit system. Within that system, profits are the acid test of the individual firm's performance." [13]

The general or specific objectives to be pursued by a real estate firm usually are determined by its owners. They may be influenced by com-petitors, employees, customers, market trends, general business condi-tions, government regulations, political trends, and many other factors. Hired managers may play an important part in determining objectives; but, in a final analysis, it is the owners who do this.

[13] Joel Dean, *Managerial Economics* (Englewood Cliffs, N.J.: Prentice-Hall, Inc., 1951), p. 3.

Social and Business Objectives

In our society, the owners of real property and those who own or manage various types of real estate firms are allowed to pursue their objectives within the general framework of our legal, governmental, and institutional arrangements. We allow this type of operation because we have found that in our competitive and democratic type of society the owners of real estate resources or real estate enterprises tend to serve the long-term interests of our society as a whole by pursuing their own best interests. This is not always the case, of course. For example, it is necessary to impose limits on the decisions of property owners through zoning laws to prevent the development of inharmonious land uses. Within certain limits, however, we rely on competition to regulate business activities for us and to assure buyers and users of good value per dollar of cost. Similarly, democratic political processes assure a fairly direct response to the programs of the owners and managers of properties or firms, either supporting them or not supporting them if they do not conform to the standards which the voting public expects of them.

A method of illustrating the relationships between the objectives of property owners, business owners, or managers on the one hand, and those of society on the other, is provided by an example from another field. We maintain a free press in this country and within very broad limits allow it freedom of expression. The objective of this arrangement is to disseminate the truth. This objective is achieved, not by requiring that all publications print nothing but the truth, but by allowing them (within the limits of the law of libel and other broad regulations) to print what they please. In this way we come very close to achieving our objective of disseminating the truth by means of freedom of expression and publication.

Much the same thing may be said about the real estate field. By allowing owners of property to pursue their own objectives, to maximize income or to develop properties to what they consider to be the highest and best use of such properties, general community as well as purely private objectives are served. In most cases such objectives are served better than if more direct and specific controls are set on the ownership, use, development, financing, or marketing of private real properties.

Similarly, by allowing the owners of real estate enterprises to pursue their own objectives—maximizing profits, surviving in the face of competition, achieving growth, or attaining prestige positions—they serve also to help further general social objectives. For example, if a savings bank, in order to increase earnings, charges interest rates on its mortgages that are higher than those of its competitors, it will lose business and hence income. Competition will force it to lower its rates. Thus, competition is a highly effective control process. It brings about a blending of private and general objectives.

Planning Operations

Basically, management planning sets up a program of action to achieve the objectives that have been established. This is why planning is carried on. A plan may be thought of as a blueprint or guide to action. Plans may be established to guide the operations of a real estate firm or a program for utilizing, developing, financing, or marketing a piece of real property. Thus, plans may be general or relate to specific actions; they may be for short or long periods of time; they may involve many people or a few; they may be simple or complex; and they may be independent or related to other plans.

Although planning may involve a wide variety of methods and processes, most plans may be thought of as providing answers to such basic questions as the following: (1) What is to be done in order to attain the established objectives? (2) Where is the action to take place? (3) When is the necessary action to be carried out? (4) Who will put the plan into action? (5) How will the plan be carried out?

In addition, most plans in the real estate field must consider matters of *costs* and, more specifically, relationships between estimated costs and anticipated *returns*. Cost and return factors also must be considered in relation to the *risks* that may be involved. For example, a mortgage lender may be paying 4 per cent for funds deposited with him for investment and may be able to place a mortgage for 7 per cent. The risk that the mortgage will result in losses may be so great, however, that the cost-return relationship will not be considered adequate.

Plans usually necessitate the consideration of *strategic factors*. For example, the development of a plan for marketing a new subdivision may require careful consideration of the probable programs of competitive subdivisions. Or the operator of a real estate brokerage firm may be developing plans for an intensive sales campaign but hesitate to put it into effect, fearing that it will be matched immediately by important competitors.

The *resources* that are available or can be made available often exercise a controlling influence in the development of plans. For example, a plan for expanding a store may be complicated by the inability to gain control of an adjoining property. A plan for developing a neighborhood shopping center may be limited by zoning regulations and inability to secure exceptions to such regulations.

Plans will be influenced also by general environmental factors—by such things as general business conditions, government programs or anticipated changes in programs, market trends, population movements, and many related influences. And as we have indicated, plans in the real estate field often must cover long periods of time. Hence, planning in this field tends to be somewhat more complicated than in other business areas.

Organizing Resources

In order for resources to be used effectively, whether these include the abilities of people or the productive power of real properties or capital goods, it is necessary to organize them in a manner which provides for a maximizing of total effort relative to cost. For example, the owner of an apartment building must determine how much effort will be put into advertising; into maintenance, modernization, and repair programs; into apartment house services such as janitors, elevator operators, and maintenance personnel. Similarly, the manager of a real estate brokerage firm will need to determine appropriate working relationships between the manager, salesmen, and other workers in the firm, assigning authority and responsibility in such a way that the people involved will work as an effective team in carrying out the plans that have been established to achieve the firm's objectives.

From a management standpoint, organization usually refers to the relationships between the various people who make up the firm's personnel. Good organization also includes, however, the determination of the relationships between people and the various things such as real properties, machines, and equipment which will help them do their work.

In the case of real estate, special organization problems exist with respect to such diversified activities as subdividing and land development, building, brokerage, and financing. Real estate poses some special problems from an organizational standpoint because real properties typically are available only in fairly large economic units; and it is not always easy to develop the best working relationships between real properties, the people who make use of them, and the various types of equipment, tools, and other resources that are necessary to give them their greatest productivity.

Controls

Basically, controlling is the process of making certain that operations are being carried out in accordance with established plans. Various standards may be set up such as sales quotas in the case of a real estate brokerage firm, return on investment in the case of a real property, or the maintenance of a certain occupancy ratio in the case of a shopping center.

Frequently, budgets are used both as a planning technique and as a means for exercising controls. In some cases the analysis of operations resulting from control processes indicates that plans are not feasible and must be modified. In other cases, of course, controls indicate poor performance and the need for improvement.

The principal steps of the control process may be stated as follows: (1) the development and establishment of standards, (2) the appraisal and analysis of performance, (3) the correcting of deviations from standards.[14] Adequate accounting records are of basic importance in control programs. Often statistical studies which make it possible to compare performance of one property with another or of one real estate firm with another provide substantial help in the development of adequate controls.

Leadership

The various steps that form parts of the management or administrative process are made effective through leadership. Leadership expresses itself in setting objectives, in developing plans, in establishing organizational arrangements, and in the selection of control methods. All of these things, however, might be done by staff specialists of one kind or another.

Leadership is the essential factor in setting off the action that is required to put these various steps into operation. Even in very small operations such leadership qualities as imagination, drive, and resourcefulness in meeting new problems or situations are highly important. Leadership is related to action. It involves the creation of power through proper channeling of the use of resources, and the fixing of authority and responsibility. It includes the direction of activities and the motivation of the people who carry out operations. Typically, an effective leader is also a good strategist who has the ability to anticipate the reactions of competitors to changed conditions and programs. The significance of leadership factors in management is being recognized more and more.[15]

Registering Decisions

In a general way, the basic decisions in this field, as in others, are registered in markets or through political elections. By buying or not buying, or buying more or less; leasing or not leasing, or leasing more or less; selling or not selling, or selling more or less; lending or not lending, or lending more or less; or developing land, building, and modernizing, or not doing these things—in this way market preferences are expressed. The relative importance of real estate resources in comparison to other goods and services, and also the relative importance of different types of real

[14] See Harold Koontz and Cyril O'Donnell, *Principles of Management* (3d ed.; New York: McGraw-Hill Book Co., Inc., 1964), chap. 28.

[15] See, for example, Rensis Likert, *New Patterns of Management* (New York: McGraw-Hill Book Co., Inc., 1961), chap. 2.

estate resources, are registered in markets and reflected through the prices and rents that are established there.

Similarly, in a very general way elections and actions by political agencies provide a means for registering decisions and preferences regarding the ownership, use, financing, development, purchase, or sale of real estate. Every voter may in local, state, or national elections indicate his preferences in regard to such things as the taxation of property, or the regulations that will govern the ownership, use, financing, and development of real estate. Through such elections the general political and governmental climate is determined within which real estate transactions are carried on and real properties are owned and used.

The Real Estate Environment

Real estate resources are utilized and real estate firms are operated in a highly dynamic economic, political, social, and cultural environment. Our general system of enterprise and democracy is usually referred to as "the enterprise system." This system provides for widespread decision-making among all members of our society, and social controls are exercised in large part through market competition. In this system, however, it is the responsibility of government to make competition work and to provide a general framework of laws and regulations that will help the system to work and to achieve its objectives. A primary principle in this system is freedom for individuals or private enterprises to act so long as the rights of others are not infringed upon. This system rests on freedom of thought, inquiry, and expression; freedom of enterprise, including the selection of careers and the ways in which one will spend or invest his money; political freedoms which assure the right of ballot, free elections, trial by jury, and general protections of the individual against the central authority of the state; religious freedoms; and related freedoms.

We should recognize, of course, that there are some things we seldom make conscious decisions about. These are institutional factors and arrangements—accepted ways of doing things, customs, and traditions that are so strong we almost never question them or make decisions about them.[16] Language is a good illustration of such an institutional arrangement. No one decided that a certain word, "book," should designate what you are now studying. In other countries other words are used. But we are not likely to change the word "book" or many other words. They are a part of our cultural and institutional arrangements. Attitudes toward land ownership, rights of individuals, family ties, loyalties, and the like are other examples that might be cited in this connection.

[16] See, for example, Clyde Kluckhohn, *Mirror for Man* (Greenwich, Conn.: Fawcett Publications, Inc., 1960).

To make a system such as ours work requires a careful balancing of the rights and obligations of the individuals, business firms, government agencies, and other organizations that go to make it up. Our society stresses such objectives as growth and progress in all desirable aspects of life. By stressing the freedom of individuals to make their own decisions and to accept the responsibility for them, the means constitute in large measure also the ends of our society.

Our system is both dynamic and progressive. Progress is characterized not only by higher incomes and better living conditions but by increasing equality of economic opportunity and by the improvement of the social and cultural standards of people generally. Professor David McCord Wright has said in this connection, "Not the ending of competitive acquisition should be our goal, but the competitive acquisition of nobler things in a nobler way." [17]

Our system reflects the attitudes, ideals, objectives, and general characteristics of the people who live and work in it. These characteristics give our system its capacity for growth and progress. For our system to grow and to progress, certain conditions must be present. Human and material resources must be available as well as knowledge and ideas, but in addition there must be a climate that is conducive to growth. Our system of widespread decision-making has tended to foster growth, but such a wide latitude for choices inevitably leads to change.

Although dynamic and changing conditions are conducive to economic growth and progress, since they allow for experimentation and the development of new ideas, it must be recognized that a dynamic system is also to some extent an unstable system. Thus, one of the problems of our type of society is to avoid wide fluctuations of economic activity and at the same time to maintain the conditions essential to growth and progress. Those interested in real estate have a particular stake in stable and orderly economic growth, since real estate resources have in the past often been affected adversely by rapid upward or downward movements in economic activity.

SUMMARY

Real estate decisions are influenced by several factors rather unique to the real estate field. Income from real estate must be produced at fixed sites; long-term commitments involving relatively large amounts of money usually are involved; and public facilities and regulations are important determinants of private decisions.

The successful administration of real estate resources involves the determination of objectives and the effective use of resources in attaining

[17] David McCord Wright, *Democracy and Progress* (New York: The Macmillan Co., 1948), pp. 24–25.

selected goals. Making and implementing decisions are the important aspects of administration. An important function of the market is to determine objective values which can be substituted for differing personal values, thus facilitating transactions. Real estate decisions turn largely on the capacity of property to produce income in excess of costs at its fixed location. The concept of highest and best use, referring to maximization of net income, serves as a guide to decisions in the real estate field. These decisions are made within a climate determined in part by governmental and institutional factors.

QUESTIONS FOR STUDY

1. Explain the difference between administration and decision-making.
2. Which of the factors influencing real estate decisions are largely unique to the real estate field?
3. If you were asked to sell your property to a proposed throughway project, would this involve a decision problem? Explain.
4. Why are not *all* alternatives considered in making a real estate decision?
5. How may value judgments affect real estate decisions? Explain.
6. How can "strategy" considerations alter a decision? Give an example.
7. Which types of decisions should be made by the top level of management?
8. What is the responsibility of a decision-maker after a "final" decision has been made?
9. In what respects might the objectives of a real estate firm differ from the objectives of society as a whole?
10. Give several reasons why a prospective property owner might choose a property *other than* that which maximizes his income from the property over the long run.
11. If, in light of several alternatives, a decision-maker fails to take action, what decision has he reached?
12. Outline at least two ways in which the dynamic character of our economic system affects real estate decisions.
13. *Study Project 3.* What do you think of the concept of "causative thinking"? How might causative thinking be used in the development of a new subdivision?

SUGGESTED READINGS

Koontz, Harold, and Cyril O'Donnell. *Principles of Management* (3d ed.). New York: McGraw-Hill Book Co., Inc., 1964. Part I.
Likert, Rensis. *New Patterns of Management.* New York: McGraw-Hill Book Co., Inc., 1961. Chap. ii.
Mee, John F. *Management Thought in a Dynamic Economy.* New York: New York University Press, 1963. Chap. ii.
Ratcliff, Richard U. *Modern Real Estate Valuation.* Madison, Wis.: The Democrat Press, 1965.
Simon, Herbert A. *The New Science of Management Decision.* New York: Harper & Row, Publishers, Inc., 1960. Pp. 1–13.
Weimer, Arthur M. *Business Administration: An Introductory Management Approach* (3d ed.). Homewood, Ill.: Richard D. Irwin, Inc., 1966. Chap. xii.

4

Physical Characteristics of
Real Estate Resources

Points of View

One of the first things a real estate salesman learns is the importance of selecting the proper route to a property when showing it to a prospective buyer. He knows that the same property approached from different routes often produces very different impressions. The decisions that people make in regard to real properties are influenced greatly by the way they think about them.

In Chapter 1 we suggested that you select a "reference property" as an aid to studying this subject. If we were to approach your reference property by one of the avenues leading to it, we would probably view it first as a physical entity, as land and buildings. This is the point of view of most people when they first think about real property. It forms the basis of our discussions in this chapter. The land may be studied in terms of its size, type, topography and relief characteristics, the condition of the soil and subsoil, and accessibility to streets, roads, utilities, and various conveniences. The building may be studied in terms of its size, type, design, condition, structural soundness, the floor plan, the mechanical conveniences available, the relationship of the building to the lot, orientation, and similar matters.

If our approach to the property were by another "street," however, we would look at it as a lawyer does and see it chiefly in terms of legal rights and obligations. To a lawyer the physical land and buildings have significance only to the extent that they represent *property rights*. These rights are evidenced by a great many types of legal documents and records. Many of these documents are recorded at the courthouse in the office of the local registrar of deeds or in the offices of other officials. The property may be identified in a plat book. The owner or his attorney will have an *abstract of title*, which contains a detailed history of the transactions which have had a bearing on the title to the property. Thus, property rights, although intangible, have a certain appearance of reality to many people because they are represented by many types of written documents and official-looking pieces of paper. The legal characteristics of real estate are considered at greater length in the next chapter.

If we approached your reference property from still another "street," we would look at it through the eyes of the business manager, investor, property user or owner, appraiser, or real estate broker. In this case, we would consider the physical land and buildings, of course, and we would also consider the property rights which the land and buildings represented. But we would view the property first and foremost as an economic resource, as a *vehicle of productivity*, as a means of providing protection, shelter, conveniences, privacy, and other services. In short, we would think of the property in terms of its *income-producing ability*, in terms of the dollars and cents which it may yield an owner over the period of its productive life, in terms of its contribution to the production and marketing activities of a business firm, or in terms of the direct satisfactions which an owner might derive from occupying it. This is the point of view with which we shall be chiefly concerned in our study of real estate decisions, resources, and operations. Our reason for stressing this point of view is the belief that factors relating to the income-producing ability of real properties are of primary importance in influencing the decisions of property owners and users. In Chapter 6 we discuss this subject at greater length.

For our purposes, the land and buildings on the one hand and the property rights they represent on the other have significance chiefly because they influence the decisions of people in regard to the direct satisfactions or income that may be derived from them. For example, good construction is important mainly because it is related to the ability of a property to produce money or real income. Similarly, property rights have significance for our purposes chiefly as they facilitate or interfere with sound programs of property use.

Nevertheless, it will be necessary to study the physical characteristics of real property. Our main purpose in this connection will be to study the *income characteristics* of the physical land and buildings and to learn that portion of the language of the architect, engineer, or builder which is essential to an understanding of the subject.

Similarly, we shall be concerned to some extent with the legal aspects of real estate, especially with the effect of specific property rights on the income-producing ability of real properties and hence on decisions related to them. We should learn to identify the more important property rights that may exist and to acquire an understanding of the principal documents which are used in real estate transactions. We must learn that portion of the lawyer's language which is pertinent to the subject. However, those who wish to pursue this phase of the subject very far should take a course in real estate law or real property law.

One of our primary purposes in considering the work of the architect and engineer on the one hand and the work of the lawyer on the other is to learn to recognize those situations in which it is essential to call upon these specialists for advice. To paraphase an old axiom, "He who is his own lawyer, architect, or engineer has a fool for a client."

Land Resources

In the early literature of economics, land was considered one of the ultimate factors of production: land, labor, and capital. Land included everything furnished by nature, labor all human services, and capital all artificial or produced goods used in the production process.

There are serious questions about differentiating between land and capital in the sense outlined above. As Professor Knight has said:

> What we call natural agencies, as they are used in production, are very different from "raw" nature, untouched and unexamined. Many things have been done to them, many costs incurred in bringing them into use; in fact, averaging out for any large group of natural agencies would probably show that they have cost as much as at any given time they were worth, or in short that their productive value is entirely accounted for by previous expenditure of productive power or "investment," undertaken for much the same motives as any other production of valuable things.[1]

For our purposes, land may be considered in a physical sense as including the earth's surface; under certain conditions we may also include the minerals below the surface, and the air above the surface. Mineral and air rights relate to surface land largely through ownership. In terms of land uses, the following classification may be helpful:

    I. Surface Land
        A. Agricultural land
        B. Forests
        C. Transportation and communication
        D. Recreational uses

[1] Frank H. Knight, *The Economic Organization* (New York: Augustus M. Kelley, 1951).

E. Building sites
  1. Urban
    (a) industrial
    (b) commercial
    (c) residential
    (d) governmental
    (e) institutional
  2. Rural nonfarm
II. Water Resources
III. Subsurface Mineral Rights
IV. Supersurface Air Rights [2]

Other classifications could be worked out, of course. This one will aid us in understanding the major types of land uses.

Table 4–1.

	1950	1960	Medium Projections 1980	2000
			(million acres)	
Cropland, including pasture [1]	478	447	443	476
Grazing land [1]	700	700	700	700
Farmland, non-producing	45	45	45	45
Commercial forest land [2]	484	484	484	484
Recreation (excluding reservoir areas and city parks)	42	44	76	134
Urban (including city parks)	17	21	32	45
Transportation	25	26	28	30
Wildlife refuge	14	15	18	20
Reservoirs	10	12	15	20
Total specified [2]	1,815	1,794	1,841	1,954
Other land (residential)	89	110	63	−50
Total land area	1,904	1,904	1,904	1,904

SOURCE: Hans H. Landsberg, Leonard L. Fischman, and Joseph L. Fisher, *Resources in America's Future* (Baltimore: The Johns Hopkins Press, 1963), p. 24.

[1] All adjustments for feeding requirements are made in cropland, with grazing land held constant.

[2] Does not provide for increased acreage to meet projected commercial forest demand. Requirements to close the projected gap in 2000 might run as high as 300 million acres to be put into forest use at this time.

Some idea of the way in which the land area of the United States is allocated among various types of land uses is presented in Table 4–1.

[2] See, for example, Raleigh Barlowe, *Land Resource Economics* (Englewood Cliffs, N.J.: Prentice-Hall, Inc., 1958), p. 10. Barlowe suggests a tenfold classification of land uses: cropland, pasture and grazing land, forest land, mineral land, recreational land, residential lands, commercial and industrial sites, transportation lands, service areas, and barren and waste land.

Building Classification

One basis for classifying buildings is provided by the land uses outlined above. Of major importance are farm buildings (including houses either with other farm buildings or with residential real estate); residential structures, ranging from single-family homes to large apartment houses; and industrial, commercial, governmental, and institutional buildings.

Various subclassifications are frequently used as well. Residential buildings may be divided as to number of dwelling units or by location. Single-family homes, two- to four-family dwellings, and dwellings with five or more units usually constitute the main classification groups by number of units; the division is usually by urban, rural nonfarm, and farm residences when the classification is made in terms of location. Industrial structures typically are classified as heavy manufacturing, light manufacturing, and warehouses. In addition, industrial structures may be classified by location, such as central, suburban, or outlying. They may also be classified by type of product.

Commercial structures include all types of stores, office buildings, hotels, and service establishments. Sometimes the commercial classification is limited to structures used for retail and wholesale purposes, with office buildings and hotels set apart as separate classes, and with theaters, service establishments, and others placed in a category of "special purpose properties." For our purposes the commercial properties will include all of these types, and the classification "special purpose properties" will be reserved for properties that involve specialized types of uses and therefore pose management, marketing, financing, and valuation problems.

Governmental structures include all types of buildings owned or operated by national, state, or local governments, whether used for residential, industrial, commercial, farm, or other purposes. Institutional buildings include those owned or operated by educational, research, or religious organizations, foundations, or others.

In some cases public utility buildings are separated from others. The Department of Commerce, for example, divides construction activities into private and public groups, with the former divided into residential (nonfarm) and nonresidential, including industrial and commercial, plus farm and public utility construction.

Factors Affecting Income

A listing of all physical factors that affect the income-producing ability of land and its buildings and other improvements would be an almost impossible task. The most important points that we shall consider include the following:

1. Land
   (a) Location
   (b) Size and shape of lot
   (c) Topography
   (d) Condition of soil and subsoil
   (e) Accessibility and availability of utilities and conveniences
2. Buildings
   (a) Type of building in relation to land
   (b) Quality and durability
   (c) Design or layout in terms of function
   (d) Style and attractiveness
   (e) Conformity
3. Other Improvements
   (a) Type
   (b) Quantity
   (c) Quality

You will find it helpful to study your reference property in terms of the items listed above, remembering to consider each of them from the standpoint of relationship to income-producing ability.

Location

Although fertility is the principal factor in determining the income produced by agricultural land, the location or *situs* of urban land is of primary importance in determining its income potential.

Since no two points on the earth's surface are exactly alike, every piece of urban real estate is unique. It differs in some respect from every other parcel of real property. In some cases the degree of difference is relatively slight, while in other cases it is of greater importance than any other single value characteristic. Each parcel of urban real estate is an immovable part of a neighborhood or district as well as of an entire town or city. To understand even a few of the important features of the relationships between location and income we shall need to study the factors related to national and international economic trends, industry potentials, regional and urban economic development, the dynamics of city growth and structure, and the character of specific residential neighborhoods and business and industrial districts. For the present it will be necessary for us only to note the importance of location as an element affecting property income and to proceed with a consideration of other income characteristics of land and buildings.

As we shall see in Chapter 24, there are important differences between the factors which affect the income-producing ability of farms and other rural real estate and those affecting urban properties. Natural resources such as soil fertility, climate, topography, and scenery play relatively greater parts in determining the income-producing ability of rural real estate than they do in urban properties. The factor of location, which is of primary importance in understanding urban real estate, also plays a vital role.

Size and Shape of the Land

Urban lot sizes are usually measured in square feet or the number of feet of frontage on the street and depth in feet. Farms and other rural real estate are measured in terms of acres (43,560 square feet) or sections (square miles—640 acres). Obviously, a lot with only 30 feet of frontage cannot be used as the site for a tall office building or a large department store. Size is an important factor in determining use, and use in turn has a very direct bearing on income-producing ability. Size also determines effectiveness of use; the trend toward larger farms as agriculture has become more highly mechanized is a case in point. Value, of course, is not directly proportional to size. Up to a point, additions to the size of a parcel of land tend to increase its income-producing ability and hence its value; thereafter, such additions tend to be of diminishing importance. *Plottage* is the term used to describe the extent to which value is increased when two or more plots are combined.

Babcock has this to say about plottage:

> Plottage value is not a characteristic of any single tract of land. As a concept it can apply only to the comparison between a given larger tract and the specific smaller units of which it is composed. All combinations of land parcels do not result in a plottage increment. Plottage value can be determined only by means of an actual comparison of valuations based upon the different sets of uses.[3]

The relationship between frontage and depth is important for many types of urban real estate. In the case of residential land, for example, there has been an increasing demand for lots with wider frontage and of somewhat shallower depth. Few lots of less than 50 or 60 feet in width are considered adequate for residential development, and those of wider frontage, around 100 feet, tend to be more salable. In an earlier period when many people owned horses, the long, narrow lots often found in older parts of our cities were more desirable, since they allowed for separation of the house and the barn. Under current conditions, however, there is less need for a lot of great depth. Lots used for business and

---

[3] By permission from *The Valuation of Real Estate,* by Frederick M. Babcock, p. 107. Copyright, 1932, McGraw-Hill Book Co., Inc., New York.

industrial purposes vary greatly in width and depth, depending on the specific uses to which they are put.[4]

The "new town" concept, in which a golf course, private parks, sites for industries, schools, churches, and shopping centers are provided, gives added plottage value to a 40- or 50-acre tract when part of another tract of 500 to 750 acres.

The shape of the land parcel may determine the possible uses to which it may be put and hence affect its income-producing ability. While lots of irregular shape may often be used to advantage for residential purposes, regularity is usually desirable for business, industrial, or agricultural uses. Many developers of new residential areas now plan lots of irregular shape, adapting them to curvilinear streets, cul-de-sacs, and park areas. This practice contrasts sharply with the gridiron pattern formerly followed almost exclusively in subdivision planning. The gridiron pattern often resulted in lots of odd shape when diagonal streets were involved.

Topography

A study of topography includes a consideration of contour and slope, the direction and steepness of slope, and such things as gullies, streams, knolls, and ravines. These factors may have a determining influence on the uses which may be made of the land. Lots with steep slopes, for example, are not easily adapted to business, industrial, or agricultural uses. They may allow for attractive residential developments, although the cost of a house built on a sloping lot is usually greater than that of one constructed on a level lot. Note Figure 4–1 in this connection. Topography has an important bearing on drainage, on erosion, on the ease or difficulty of constructing streets or roads, and on landscaping problems.

In addition to the topography of a specific land parcel, it is usually necessary to consider the topography of adjoining land, since drainage and related problems may be involved. Gently rolling land is usually considered desirable in residential neighborhoods and for farming operations, while level or nearly level land is more desirable in business and industrial areas.

It is well to give special attention to streams or bodies of water on or near a piece of land. The possibility of flooding is always an important consideration, and stagnant water may invite hordes of mosquitoes.

As a general guide to the study of the contour of a tract of land, consider on the one hand those factors which will be advantageous to its income-producing ability and on the other those things which will be

---

[4] "Depth rules" and tables have been developed as guides in determining the values of fractional parts of a lot. See Paul F. Wendt, *Real Estate Appraisal* (New York: Henry Holt & Co., Inc., 1956), pp. 276–77.

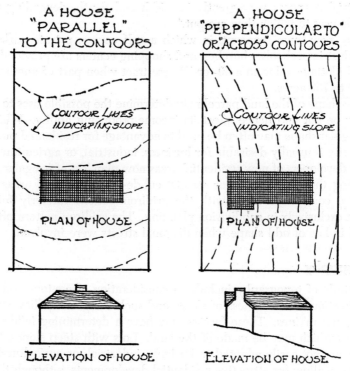

Fig. 4–1. Construction parallel and perpendicular to contours.

detrimental and which will increase costs. For example, drainage problems often require expensive tiling operations, while steep lots may require the construction of retaining walls.

Condition of the Soil and Subsoil

The condition of the soil and subsoil is of basic importance in determining the income-producing ability of farms. It also has a bearing on city lots. In some cities expensive piles must be driven to provide a bearing surface for any buildings of major size because of the unstable nature of the soil. If rock formations are encountered at a point only a few feet from the surface, it becomes expensive to excavate and to install water mains and sewer lines. In such cases special provision must usually be made for drainage as well. For buildings of moderate size, subsoils of clay, gravel, and coarse sand are usually the most desirable.

In rural nonfarm areas near cities but beyond sewer mains, percolation tests are important in determining whether the soils will absorb sewage.

The condition of the topsoil is of lesser importance in the case of lots used for business and industrial purposes, since they are usually covered over with concrete or asphalt. For residential and agricultural uses, however, the condition of the topsoil is of major importance. Surface rock, some types of clay, muck land, and quicksand often create special problems.

Accessibility and Availability of Utilities and Conveniences

Even the pioneer farmer had to have a road or a right of way over which he could carry his produce to market and bring back necessary provisions. The importance of accessibility tends to increase as our communities become more complex. As Babcock has said:

> The importance of access to land is apparent. Communication and transportation determine, in part, where cities will be located and how stores and apartments will be distributed within cities. While we define land as including climate and its natural features, it is also well to visualize, in the same category, the surrounding neighborhood, together with the kinds of accessibility enjoyed. The difference in value between two farms, one on a wide, hard road and one on an unimproved dirt road, is a difference in land value.[5]

A farm may be diminished in value if it is split in two by an express highway to which it has no access. Land at express highway intersections has a high value for motels, shopping centers, and industries.

The value of a parcel of land is related directly to the ease or difficulty of access to roads and streets, transportation facilities, water and gas mains, sewers, and electrical and telephone lines. Similarly, such services as mail delivery, police and fire protection, and garbage, trash, and snow removal are significant.

Distances to schools, shopping centers, places of employment, churches, community centers, parks, and playgrounds are of special importance in considering the value characteristics of land used for residential purposes. Nearness to main arteries of pedestrian traffic and to parking areas are of major importance in the case of business sites. Nearness to transportation lines often is important to industrial sites. Increasingly, accessibility has meant ease of access by automobile or truck transportation. Both shopping centers and industrial parks illustrate this trend.

Surveys

In connection with most development activities, or in cases of mortgage financing, surveys by licensed surveyors or engineers are often required. Such surveys usually show (1) exact dimensions and (2) boundaries in relation to streets or roads; they may show (3) levels of land by contour lines, (4) position of trees, rock formations, and so on, and (5) location

[5] Babcock, *op. cit.*, p. 27.

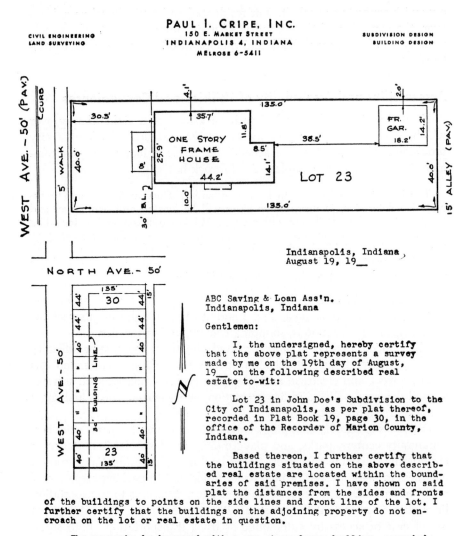

Indianapolis, Indiana,
August 19, 19__

ABC Saving & Loan Ass'n.
Indianapolis, Indiana

Gentlemen:

I, the undersigned, hereby certify that the above plat represents a survey made by me on the 19th day of August, 19__ on the following described real estate to-wit:

Lot 23 in John Doe's Subdivision to the City of Indianapolis, as per plat thereof, recorded in Plat Book 19, page 30, in the office of the Recorder of Marion County, Indiana.

Based thereon, I further certify that the buildings situated on the above described real estate are located within the boundaries of said premises. I have shown on said plat the distances from the sides and fronts of the buildings to points on the side lines and front line of the lot. I further certify that the buildings on the adjoining property do not encroach on the lot or real estate in question.

The property is improved with a one story frame dwelling, occupied by John Jones, and located at 2735 North West Avenue, Indianapolis, Indiana.

This survey is for Mortgage purposes and does not purport to be sufficient for the location of corner stakes and the establishment of lot lines.

Fig. 4–2. Surveyor's plat of a city lot for mortgage purposes. (Courtesy Paul I. Cripe, Inc.)

of sewer, water, gas, and electric lines. The purpose of the survey usually determines the items which are covered. See Figure 4–2 for example.

Buildings

Except for parking lots and a few other uses, it is necessary to construct a building in order to earn income from urban land. Thus buildings should be thought of as the means by which the earning power of urban land is released. Considered in another way, the services of buildings and other improvements on urban land may be thought of as similar in some degree to the crops which are produced on farm land. Buildings are also important to farming operations but play a lesser role than they do in urban land uses.

In this section we shall consider some of the characteristics which increase or diminish the income-producing ability of buildings and consequently have a bearing on value. Land value arises from residual income remaining after expenses of operating the building, real estate taxes, and interest and depreciation on the cost of the building are deducted from gross income. If the wrong type of building is constructed, the value of the land may be destroyed.

We should note that while a lot and a building together form a single income-producing unit, the building can be replaced while the land cannot. Every lot differs in some degree from every other one. In the case of especially well-located lots, the land is one of the paramount supports of the value of the entire property. In other cases it is of lesser importance. In some cases land can be "made," as in Miami or Chicago, where water-covered areas have been filled in or where bluffs have been graded down.

Type of Building in Relation to Land

As we pointed out in Chapter 1, it is desirable from both private and public standpoints for each piece of real estate to be put to its highest and best use. One of the important considerations in developing a property to its highest and best use is a balanced relationship between land, buildings, and other improvements. The income-producing ability of a property may be greater or less than required to pay a return on the investment. This difference is often referred to by appraisers as *improved value*.

For example, a building costing $50,000 to construct may be placed on a lot that cost $10,000. Faulty planning and improper improvement may result in a value based on anticipated returns of only $40,000. On the other hand, a proper combination of land and buildings based on careful planning by the architect, plus cleverness, imagination, and risk-taking by the promoter, may produce an income that will support a value of $80,-

000. Careful consideration of alternative plans for improvement, study of market potentials and present and prospective competition, guarding against hazards, development of cost controls, and the like are all involved.

Some buildings represent an *overimprovement*—that is, a larger expenditure than can be supported by the site. Others represent an *underimprovement*, an investment that is not great enough to bring out the full income-producing potential of the site. In some instances general-purpose buildings provide the best improvement, in others special-purpose buildings are preferable. In the case of residences, underimprovements or overimprovements are usually apparent by comparison with other houses in the area.

Orientation

The position of the structure on the land and its general relationship to its surroundings are usually referred to as its *orientation*. In solidly built business streets, of course, there is little latitude for special arrangements. Even in such cases, however, position on the street, easy access for customers, accessibility to delivery trucks, relationship to adjacent buildings, and the like are important factors in a property's income-producing ability. In the North, locations on the street facing the sun may command a premium; in the South the opposite is often true. An industrial building must be placed advantageously with respect to the movement of materials and workers into and out of the plant.

Orientation is a major problem in the case of residential buildings, particularly single-family homes. A house placed on the lot in such a way as to bring out the greatest potentialities of the entire property will be more valuable than an identical house located to lesser advantage. In addition, proper orientation to the sun, prevailing winds, and attractive and unattractive views are major considerations. Attention is often given to solar orientation in order to take greatest advantage of the sun's heat in the winter and protection from it in the summer. Also, houses should be located to advantage with respect to lot lines, setback lines, and other houses in the area.

Quality and Durability

The quality of workmanship and materials in a building have an important effect on its durability. If properly constructed a building will resist both the elements and usage over a long period of time and without incurring excessive maintenance costs. The durability of a building has a direct relationship to its life cycle—that is, to the period during which it can produce an income adequate to justify the investment involved. While the physical life of a building is usually longer than its economic life, there tends to be some relationship between physical life and the period during which satisfactory returns can be earned. These returns, of course, may be either in the form of monetary income or, in the case of an owner-occupied home, in direct usage.

It may be said in general that physical decay has been one of the less important factors in bringing the useful or economic lives of buildings to an end.[6] Generally, buildings are demolished in order to make room for a higher land use. Indeed, the rate of obsolescence of buildings appears to be higher than it was several decades ago. Rapid changes in the structure of cities, especially under the impact of heavy automobile traffic, have brought swift changes in land values and in the economic usefulness of many buildings. Competition of new outlying areas is affecting land uses in central business districts. Industrial suburbs often reflect unfavorably on "near in" industrial locations.

Depreciation

As we have indicated, the income-producing ability of a building tends to decline and its value to diminish with the passage of time if other things remain equal. This process is called *depreciation*.

The American Institute of Real Estate Appraisers has pointed out that depreciation may be due to deterioration resulting from wear and tear and the action of the elements or to obsolescence which may be functional or economic. Functional obsolescence results from poor planning, design, or equipment and related factors "evidenced by conditions within the property"; economic obsolescence results from changes "external to the property," such as neighborhood changes, shifts in market preference, technological advance, and the like.[7]

In this country obsolescence appears to be the major cause of loss of value, particularly the development of competition from more efficient structures and more desirable neighborhoods and districts. Over the long sweep of history there has been a general tendency for property values to rise, and this trend has sometimes obscured the importance of depreciation, especially that resulting from inadequacy, supersession, and obsolescence. The rapid economic changes of recent years focused attention on these factors. Many buildings with years of physical life remaining were torn down to make way for more productive uses.

[6] *Ibid.*, p. 110.
[7] See *The Appraisal of Real Estate*, Chicago, The American Institute of Real Estate Appraisers, 1964, pp. 199–204; also the Institute's *Appraisal Terminology and Handbook*, 1962, p. 52. See also James C. Bonbright, *Valuation of Property*, Vol. I, New York, McGraw-Hill Book Co., Inc., 1937; Babcock, *op. cit.*, Ch. xxvii, and Wendt, *op. cit.*, pp. 244–46. For other views see Richard A. Cherney, "The Problem of Depreciation," *The Appraisal Journal* (January, 1964); Richard U. Ratcliff, *Modern Real Estate Valuation* (Madison, Wis.: The Democrat Press, 1965), pp. 58–64.

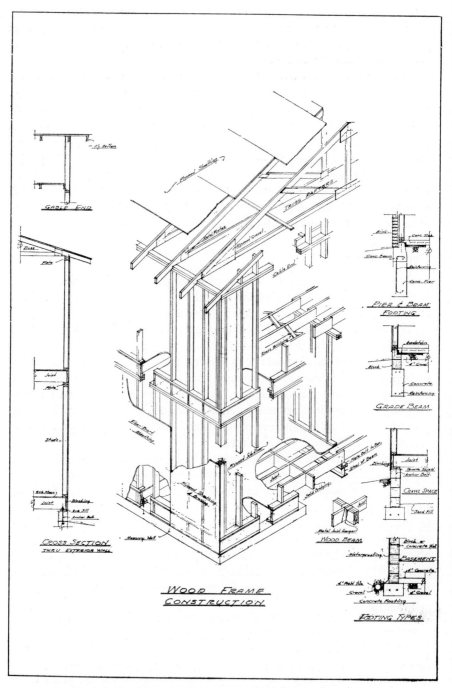

Fig. 4–3. Wood frame construction. (Courtesy Paul I. Cripe, Inc.)

Types of Construction

The four main types of construction used in this country are wood frame, wall-bearing masonry, reinforced concrete frame, and steel frame. Wooden frame construction, whether covered by weatherboarding or veneered with brick or stone, is the type most frequently used in building medium-priced houses (see Fig. 4–3). It is cheaper than other types, it can be built rapidly, and it is easy to insulate against heat or cold. Its chief disadvantage is susceptibility to fire. However, firestops, fireproof materials for insulation, aluminum coating, and flameproofed lumber help to reduce this hazard.

In masonry construction the exterior walls are of brick, stone, or concrete block. A brick wall may be of solid construction, or it may be built somewhat thicker than a solid wall to allow for an air space between the outer and inner courses of brick. Often brick or stone is backed up with hollow terra-cotta tile or cement blocks. Stucco on hollow terra-cotta tile is a better construction than stucco on wood, which is liable to shrink and crack the stucco. Masonry houses in the lower-price ranges usually have interior partitions and floor joists of wood. Steel joists may be used in more expensive types. Masonry structures tend to be more fire-resistant than frame types, and maintenance costs are typically lower. On the other hand, such structures are more expensive to build.

Concrete structures may have walls and floors of monolithic construction which are poured into place at the site, may be assembled from concrete block and precast joists and slabs, or may be constructed by a combination of these methods. The chief advantages of concrete buildings are their permanency, fireproof construction, and low maintenance costs.

Steel-frame structures are similar in principle to wooden-frame buildings. Studs, joists, and rafters made of steel are used, eliminating shrinkage; when noncombustible insulating material and exterior covering are used, the structure is relatively fireproof. Coverings may be of any of the usual building materials desired.

Another classification provides for two basic types of construction: skeleton frame and wall bearing. The former makes use of columns to transmit loads to the foundation; the latter uses the walls for this purpose.[8]

Functional Plan

Buildings are designed for many purposes, ranging from the functions of specialized industrial structures to those of small single-family residences. All of them provide protection against the elements, such as tem-

[8] See P. G. Falkner, "Understanding Basic Principles and Terms of Building Construction," *The Appraisal Journal* (January, 1964).

perature extremes, rain, and snow. Nearly all provide some degree of comfort and convenience.

The development of an adequate functional plan for a building is largely the work of the architect and engineer. Careful design of spans, proper distribution of weight, adequate openings for doors and windows, correct width of corridors, suitable combinations of materials, and related factors are all involved. In recent years even low- and medium-priced single-family homes have been studied in terms of functions to be performed and the most effective arrangements of the exterior and interior of the structures for the performance of these functions. The functional plan of special-purpose buildings must reflect the specific use for which the structure is intended. General-purpose buildings aim at simple arrangements with a maximum of flexibility of the use of interior space.

Constant improvement in design is one of the important causes of obsolescence in existing buildings. The efficiency of one-story manufacturing plants with continuous assembly lines, for example, has rendered many multistory industrial plants obsolete.

Of special importance to the functional adequacy of modern buildings is the mechanical equipment that is used. The cost of such equipment is now a major item, even in the construction of a small house. The adequacy, condition, durability, and operating economy of such equipment has an important bearing on operating costs and hence on the income-producing capacity of a building. For residences the most important types of equipment are plumbing and sewage disposal, heating and air conditioning, and electric light and power. Elevators are of major importance in many office, apartment, and store buildings. Indeed, the elevator was essential to the development of modern skyscrapers. Escalators are being used to an increasing extent. Industrial plants contain a wide variety of specialized equipment of many types.

Sometimes convertibility is a factor in building value. In the case of old buildings with limited economic lives in present uses, the possibility of conversion to alternative uses becomes a primary consideration in determining their value.

Usually a building is designed originally to serve its immediate contemplated use. In some instances, adaptation to other uses is a simple process. If there is a high degree of specialization, conversion to alternative uses may be so costly as to be inexpedient. As Babcock has pointed out:

An office building constructed with high ceilings because it is in a department store neighborhood may prove to be an office building 20 years later and to have suffered from both the presence of the high ceilings and the excess cost per square foot over the entire period. . . . Furthermore, if architectural advances are many (as they have been in the past), the very features built in to enable conversion may not prove adequate to the requirements of the second kind of use when the time comes.[9]

Provision for future additions and design which allows inclusion of additional equipment such as air conditioning and the like are desirable features, even in new buildings. Except for such factors convertibility is not usually considered in judging the adequacy of the functional plan of a new structure, but may be important in a building that is in the late stages of its economic life in its present use.

Style and Attractiveness

The appeal of a building to prospective users and investors is an important element in its ability to produce future income. The factors that make up appeal are difficult to identify. We know that architects and engineers often are able to impart to a building an appeal that is over and above that arising from utilitarian and economic considerations alone. Often this appeal continues over many years. Style in a building is usually considered to be one of the factors that provide long-range appeal to users and investors. In this connection Condit has this to say:

. . . the word "style" is much abused. Yet its connotation is such that the critic and the historian of art can hardly avoid it. In architecture it represents or stands for those essential characteristics of construction, form, ornament, and detail which are common to all the important structures of any particular period in history. But it also stands for those technical and aesthetic qualities of the artistic product which grow directly, logically, and organically out of the conditions of human existence and out of the aspirations and powers of human beings. We rightly feel that the buildings of a certain style—if it is a genuine style—reflect in their form the realities of man's experience and the attempt to master and give emotional expression to those realities. These buildings are constituent facts of man's history, and their revelation is a part of truth itself.[10]

There may, of course, be wide variations in the tastes and cultural standards of prospective users and investors. These tastes will vary from time to time and from region to region. In general, however, experience indicates that buildings which are constructed according to the dictates of good taste are more stable in value over long periods of time than others. For example, houses constructed in accordance with sound architectural standards are not subject to the wide fluctuations in price which arise from the unsettling influences of fads and the temporary popularity of a particular style. The mark of good taste is simplicity. This is manifest in simple masses, simple roof lines, and restrained and well-chosen detail. Good taste and good architecture depend on simplicity. Beauty

---

[9] Babcock, *op. cit.*, p. 99.
[10] Reprinted from *The Rise of the Skyscraper* by Carl W. Condit by permission of the University of Chicago Press, p. 1. Copyright 1952 by the University of Chicago.

is not created by gingerbread and other incongruous and superfluous features and ornaments, but by good proportions and the proper use of materials.

Architectural styles vary widely. Most architects try to select the style which will express most adequately the use of the building. Recent trends appear to be away from the limiting influences of some of the traditional styles, with greater emphasis on functional design. In the case of houses, for example, it is possible to list a number of styles which may be seen in our towns and cities every day, but in general many liberties have been taken with the prototypes of these styles so that no hard-and-fast classifications can be made.

We often refer to "English," "Spanish," "French," "colonial," or "modern" houses, and to such special types as "Cape Cod," "ranch house," "Dutch colonial," "Southern colonial," and the like. All of these architectural styles are found with many modifications and variations, but many houses of real distinction cannot be classified by style. Indeed, the trend has been away from the so-called traditional style and toward the modern or contemporary style. This trend is even more pronounced for business and industrial buildings.

Consider the following statement:

Today, a mere generation later, this thing we call "modern architecture" is firmly established; it is also well on the way toward becoming the hallmark of a new American civilization. Throughout the world, in places where America's culture is not always valued very highly, our architecture is invariably acclaimed. . . .

For architecture is not just a way of packaging a rather large product to attract potential impulse-buyers. Architecture is a system of organization, a way of putting things together. The same client's program, in the hands of architect A (who uses system A), will produce one sort of plan, one sort of space, one sort of exterior expression. In the hands of architect B (who subscribes to system B), the very same program may be solved in an entirely different manner, all the way through. . . .

And architecture—unlike "styling" or "packaging"—possesses another quality that is of the greatest importance to any client or consumer: it only starts to live after the job is done. A box of Kleenex tissue is through once it has been designed, manufactured, sold and used up. The cycle is short, simple, direct. But a good building is a living organism—it starts to do things of its own accord once it has been born. "We shape our buildings," Winston Churchill has said, "and, afterwards, our buildings shape us." [11]

Simplicity, balance, proper proportions, and quality of materials and workmanship, all considered in relation to the functions of the building, are the primary considerations in judging its attractiveness. It should be

[11] Peter Blake, "Modern Architecture: Its Many Faces," *The Architectural Forum* (March, 1958), pp. 77–78.

noted, however, that there are no absolute standards and that real estate value rests on what potential buyers, users, or investors *think* is attractive as well as on what may be considered attractive by experts.

Conformity

The degree to which buildings are compatible with their surroundings has a bearing on their value. A $25,000 house in a neighborhood of $15,000 houses is likely to be less marketable than it would be if it conformed to its surroundings. Similarly, a building which differs widely in architectural style from neighboring structures will tend to be less productive of direct or indirect returns than if it conformed more closely.

It should be noted that factors of this type must be judged in terms of the environment in which the building is found. A duplex in a neighborhood composed entirely of single-family houses does not conform. If there are a number of duplexes as well as three- or four-family houses in the same neighborhood, however, such heterogeneous uses would justify any of these types of buildings.

This matter is well stated in the FHA *Underwriting Handbook:*

A residential property of good physical characteristics necessarily may not be good security for a mortgage loan, even though situated in a good location. It may exhibit greatly diminished marketability if it is not in conformity with the desires and needs of persons who occupy or might wish to purchase properties in the neighborhood. It may be that the property would be entirely appropriate at another location, but decidedly out of favor in its actual location. It may be displeasing when viewed in relation to its surroundings. It may be too costly for the typical purchaser to own. It may not conform in other respects to the use which would be most marketable in the particular neighborhood. Several kinds of nonconformity may, therefore, adversely affect the marketability of properties.[12]

Other Improvements

In addition to the main buildings, any other improvements which form a part of a property have a relationship to its value. These other improvements may include (1) accessory buildings, such as garages; (2) walks, driveways, and parking areas; (3) protective barriers; (4) terraces; (5) service areas; (6) retaining walls; (7) landscaping, including lawns, trees, shrubbery, and gardens; (8) fences; and (9) other types.

We shall not attempt to undertake a detailed discussion of these items. Their type, extent, and quality are points to consider when studying the relationship of "other improvements" to the earning power of a property and their impact on real estate decisions.

[12] Federal Housing Administration, *Underwriting Handbook* (rev. ed.; Washington, D.C.: Government Printing Office, 1959), sec. 71416.1.

SUMMARY

We usually think of real properties as distinct physical units composed of land and buildings. As such, they possess many physical characteristics which may influence real estate decision-makers. This is because physical characteristics affect income-producing ability, either directly or indirectly.

As no two parts of the earth's surface are exactly alike, location is an important factor in determining income-producing ability. For agricultural land, fertility varies from one location to another. In the case of urban real estate, some locations are more accessible than others, or have more favorable surroundings.

Although the value of a parcel of real estate is not directly proportional to its size, the size and shape of real properties are among the factors which help to determine value. Additions to the size of a piece of real property tend to increase its income-producing ability and hence its value, up to a point. A large parcel of land may have, for some purposes, greater value than the sum of the values of the smaller land parcels of which it is composed. This is known as plottage value. The shape of land parcels, as well as their size, often determines the possible uses for the properties, and thus influences their income-producing ability.

Other physical characteristics such as topography, soil and subsoil conditions, and accessibility to transportation and utilities may limit or determine land uses, and hence land values. The income-producing ability of a parcel of real estate also is influenced by the buildings upon it and their quality of construction, their style and attractiveness, size, orientation, and conformity with the surrounding area.

QUESTIONS FOR STUDY

1. Develop a classification of existing land uses in the community in which your reference property is located.
2. Make a list of the physical factors affecting income-producing ability of real estate that would be most important if you were in charge of selecting a site for: (a) A new drive-in restaurant. (b) A television repair shop. (c) A new post office for your community.
3. Why is the economic life of a building likely to be less than its physical life?
4. What are the distinguishing characteristics of the principal types of construction?
5. If you were planning to build your own home, which factors would you consider most important in determining its orientation?
6. Give some specific examples of overimprovement and underimprovement of real properties.

7. Mr. Carey owns a vacant lot adjacent to his grocery store. This vacant lot has a frontage of 25 feet. Adjoining it is another vacant lot owned by Mr. Gibson, whose dry cleaning establishment is located on the next lot. Mr. Anderson offers Carey $5,000 for his lot, but says that if Carey also can secure Gibson's vacant lot, he will pay $13,500 for the two lots. Can you explain why Anderson would offer more than twice as much for the two lots as he would give for one of them alone?

8. What is meant by "depreciation"? What is its effect on the income-producing ability of a building?

9. In planning to build your own home, would you prefer to buy and build on a level lot or a sloping lot? How might the value of the house be a factor in the choice of lots?

10. Would you want to build a ranch-style house in a neighborhood where all existing houses were colonial style? If such a situation existed, would you want to buy the ranch-style house? Why?

11. What are the desirable and undesirable features in the elevation and floor plan presented in the figure below? Defend your answer.

ELEVATION

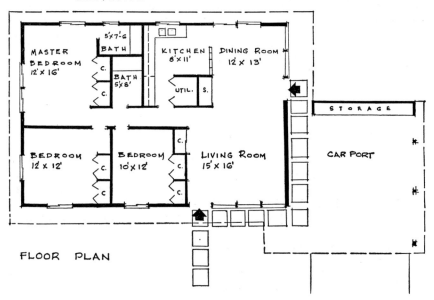

FLOOR PLAN

A house plan for study and criticism. (Courtesy Paul I. Cripe, Inc.)

12. *Study Project 4.* What additions can you suggest for this "complete" guide? How does the guide take into consideration conformity? Depreciation? Orientation?

13. *Study Project 5.* What is your general reaction to the statement? Do you believe that the role of the artist can be a significant one in the real estate field? Explain.

SUGGESTED READINGS

American Institute of Real Estate Appraisers. *The Appraisal of Real Estate* (4th ed.). Chicago: The Institute, 1964. Chaps. ix–xi.

Cherney, Richard A. "The Problem of Depreciation," *The Appraisal Journal* (January, 1964).

Falkner, P. G. "Understanding Basic Principles and Terms of Building Construction," *The Appraisal Journal* (January, 1964).

5

Legal and Governmental Characteristics of Real Estate

Regulations and Real Estate Decisions

The variety of regulations, laws, and governmental policies having an impact on real estate is so great as almost to defy comprehensive classification and analysis. You might try, for example, to prepare a list of all the regulations affecting your "reference property."

Real estate is more closely regulated as to ownership and use than any other commodity, with the possible exception of narcotics. (See Study Project 8.) In part, this is due to the face that private property rights in real estate are created, guaranteed, and enforced by government. In part, this situation arises from the great effects which the utilization of one piece of real property may have on another.

The ownership of real property is regulated by the laws governing titles and title transfers. Such regulation of ownership is in part the result of the gradual evolution of the common law and in part the product of legislative and administrative processes. Ownership is never "complete," since the exercise by government of the rights of taxation, eminent domain, or the police power may modify various private ownership interests substantially.

The influence of government on the income-producing ability of real property is profound. It ranges all the way from the definition and protection of ownership rights and the enforcement of contracts to the maintenance of full or nearly full employment conditions in our economy. Real estate is affected by all levels of government from the federal government to local townships, municipalities, and school districts. We should recognize that a major portion of the income from real estate each year is used for the payment of property and income taxes. Even so, we must also recognize that real property rights could not exist without government and that real properties would have much lower values without the opportunity to enjoy the protections and services of modern governmental organizations.

Not only governmental regulations and policies, but private agreements and regulations may also have important influences on real estate decisions and on the income-producing potential of real properties. We may think of all of the private agreements and contracts that involve real estate as constituting a system of private laws. In addition, such specific arrangements as deed restrictions or agreements of property owners' associations may have important influences on real estate decisions.

Decisions relating to the uses of various real properties, the contracts and agreements of owners, users, investors, and others, the rate of development of properties, and the rationing of available space are all influenced by market competition. Indeed, competition is the principal method of regulating real estate resources in this country. Through competitively determined prices and rents, decisions are made regarding what will be produced, how much, and for whom. Competition, of course, is governed by numerous laws, regulations, and informal controls that make it possible for the market to function. Competition does not work automatically; indeed, there never was such a thing as completely unregulated competition, and there never could be, especially in our complex kind of economic system.

In addition, the real estate market is limited by special types of regulations, including laws affecting the transfer and financing of properties, zoning and land planning laws, building codes, subsidies, taxes, price and rent regulations in some cases, government ownership, and other types of regulative methods.

Relation of Real Estate Law to Real Estate Decisions

The value of a parcel of real estate may be divided among many interests, depending on the property rights represented by the land, buildings, and other improvements. A property may represent a wide variety of interests or *estates*. It may be owned by Mr. and Mrs. X, leased to Mr.

Y, who in turn has subleased it to Mr. Z, who occupies it. Mr. A may hold a mortgage secured by the property, Mr. B may have the right to a path across it, and Mr. C the right to install utility lines on it. The degree, quantity, nature, and extent of interest which a person has in real property is that person's estate in the real property. Basically, the value of such rights depends on economic forces. In some cases the legal arrangements may limit decisions and programs regarding the utilization of the property and thus affect its value adversely. In other cases, legal arrangements may implement a sound program of property use.

The legal arrangements connected with property ownership, use, or transfer involve almost countless legal documents. The title, possession, or use of real property is usually evidenced by some written instrument. However, occupancy is notice to everyone of rights claimed in real property, and the rights of the occupant must always be ascertained.

Our interest in the legal aspects of real estate—in the papers and documents—arises from their effect on decisions of individuals or business or public officials. These decisions often turn on the economic implications of the legal arrangements which may be involved.

Those in the real estate business need to be familiar with the legal concepts and practices involved in real property ownership, use, investment, transfer, and financing. However, it is *not* their function to serve as substitutes for lawyers. Real estate operators, brokers, and specialists have a place in the business community primarily because of their knowledge of *economic* forces and the application of such forces to specific business practices. They should know enough about real estate law to determine when situations require that competent lawyers be consulted. Such legal counsel is readily available.

There are relatively few people outside the real estate business who may be consulted in regard to the economic and business aspects of this field. It is in this area, therefore, that the real estate broker, manager, developer, appraiser, or mortgage lender tends to become a "professional" or expert in his own right. Hence, it is on the administrative and economic rather than on the legal and engineering phases of the subject of real estate that we concentrate our attention.

The Meaning of Property

Property may be defined in a nontechnical manner as the exclusive right to exercise control over economic goods. This right may be exercised by one or more persons, corporations, associations, or by the community at large.

Between public property on the one hand and private property on the other, certain additional classes of property may be distinguished. One class is *common property*, which provides for the ownership of an un-divided unit of land by a number of people who hold their interests by virtue of their ownership of adjoining private tracts. The New England common of an earlier period is an illustration of such an arrangement.

The essential requirements for private property are (1) an owner, (2) a property object, which must be a thing of economic value, and (3) an organized government to protect and enforce property rights. Private property is essentially a matter of human relationships, a combination of rights and responsibilities which are recognized and sanctioned by the community.

The exercise of the *exclusive right* of private property is subject to at least three reservations by the state. These reservations arise from tax-ation, eminent domain, and the police power. We should note also that private property for which there is no owner reverts to the state in accord-ance with the doctrine of *escheat*.

Property Taxation

Taxation means the right to payments from citizens for the main-tenance of the state. Property taxation means that the state may collect payments from a property owner based on some relationship to the prop-erty, usually its value. If such payments are not made, the property may be sold by the state to satisfy the claim for taxes. Taxes may be thought of as interest payments on a mortgage that never matures and never can be paid off. The extent of the tax burden varies between properties but in some cases represents as much as a third or more of annual gross rent. Because land ownership was a fair indication of ability to pay taxes during the early years of our country's history, property taxation came to be used widely by state and local governments. The federal government cannot impose direct taxes on real property. However, the federal income tax has an important bearing on many real estate transactions and in some cases may exercise a determining influence on decisions regarding the purchase, sale, leasing, or financing of real property. Although state and local governments now make use of other forms of taxation in addition to the property tax, a heavy share of the tax burden which such govern-ments, notably local governments, impose is borne by real estate.

Taxes on real estate are of two principal types: (1) general property taxes imposed by states or municipalities and (2) those imposed by such special taxing authorities as sanitary districts or school districts. In addi-tion, special assessments may be levied against a property owner to cover all or part of the cost incurred for paving streets, building sidewalks, or making other improvements directly affecting his property.

Taxes and assessments are liens on property, ranking above all others;

and in some cases they become personal claims against the owner as well. As we have indicated, the state is a persistent tax collector. If taxes are not paid when due, interest and penalties may be added. If payment is still not made, the taxing authority may either (1) sell the property and collect the tax out of the proceeds, returning the balance to the owner, or (2) sell the tax lien. Redemption periods are provided in many states. Thus, if a sale is made, the purchaser receives a "tax title," which ripens into full ownership if the property is not redeemed.

If tax liens are sold, the taxing authority is, in effect, selling its claim to another. In such cases, the purchaser pays the tax and looks to the owner of the property for reimbursement. In effect, the purchaser of a tax lien becomes the holder of a mortgage which is superior to all other claims against the property. If payment is not made within a stated period, varying greatly from place to place, the certificate matures and proceedings are carried out similar to those of foreclosure.

The relationships between governments and individual property owners arising from taxes have created numerous problems. Taxes are important to the politician as well as to the owner or user of the property or the investor in the property. As a result, our tax structure is complex, often illogical, and in many instances unfair to real property owners, users, or investors.

Tax Capitalization

One of the serious difficulties with our taxation policies affecting real estate is that they have tended to ignore the effects of taxes on different members of the community and on the uses to which properties are put. For example, when a tax of any sort is imposed on a piece of real estate, unless it receives benefits from government activity financed by the tax corresponding in value to the amount of such payments, the tax (or that portion of it which exceeds the accompanying benefits) will be *capitalized,* which means that the owner of a property at the time a tax is imposed pays it for all time, under the conditions outlined above. In other words, if taxes on a piece of real estate are increased, its sale value is decreased by an amount equal to the *capitalized value of all future tax payments.* This is true because the buyer will consider the amount of the tax in determining how much he will pay—deducting a sufficient amount to allow for taxes. Thus, the present owner of the real estate pays the increased tax once and for all.

It is obvious that increases in real estate taxes which are not accompanied by corresponding benefits result in gross injustices to present property owners. It is equally obvious that removal of property taxes that have once been capitalized after a parcel of real estate has changed hands many times results in wholly undeserved windfalls to those who purchased properties after such taxes were imposed.

Eminent Domain

Eminent domain is the right of the sovereign government to take private property for public use. In effect it is the right to compel a sale by the owner, since compensation is always paid. The private owner has no choice in deciding whether to sell or not to sell. He must sell if his property is *condemned* for public use. Eminent domain may be exercised by the federal government, by the various states, and by municipalities, or by semipublic corporations whose existence is regarded as essential to the welfare of the public.

Before this right is exercised, attempts are made, in practice, to purchase directly from the owners such properties as are required. This avoids the formal processes of condemnation, which often are costly. However, if the owner of any parcel demands a "holdup" price, condemnation proceedings are instituted. The price is then fixed by the court, usually after hearing the testimony of expert appraisers. In the exercise of the power of eminent domain the government is not restricted to the property which is to be used directly for the public project involved. *Excess condemnation* is sometimes permitted by courts if this appears to be in the best interests of the public.

Governmental Ownership

Historically, we have been committed to the policy of encouraging private ownership of both urban and rural land. However, when public parks, schools, office buildings, army, navy, and air force installations, forest preserves, and the like are considered, our governments control a considerable amount of real property. In recent years special attention has centered on public ownership, often through the exercise of eminent domain, to cope with such problems as slum clearance and urban renewal and soil erosion and conservation.

When real estate is owned by government, several purposes may be served. For example, such properties may provide the basis for research and experimentation, or they may serve such purposes as income redistribution as in the case of providing improved housing for lower-income groups. Conservation of natural resources is often cited as a justification for public ownership. Even so, we continue in general to encourage the private ownership of real property. A large majority of our families are home owners; most of our farms are owned by those who operate them; and a large percentage of our business firms own the land used for their installations.

Police Power

The *police power* involves all regulations necessary to safeguard the public health, morals, and safety and to promote the general welfare.

The police power, in its broadest sense, includes all legislation and almost every function of civil government. . . . It is not subject to definite limitations, but is coextensive with the necessities of the case and the safeguards of public interest. . . . It embraces regulations designed to promote public convenience or the general prosperity or welfare, as well as those specifically intended to promote the public safety or the public health. . . .[1]

In exercising the police power the state does not become the owner of property and it is not obliged to compensate private owners. From the standpoint of real property the most important use of the police power is found in zoning laws. These laws have far-reaching effects on the uses of real estate, as do building codes and related regulations.

Land Planning and Zoning

Land planning and zoning, among the important examples of the exercise of the police power, are largely products of the present century, although some regulations of this type go back to ancient times. In this country several cities were planned at the time they were established, the most notable being Washington, D.C., under the L'Enfant Plan. In recent years the rapid spread of blighting influences in many of our cities has resulted in the further development of land planning and zoning activities.

Land planning involves over-all programs for development concerned chiefly with public or semipublic land uses such as roads, streets, parks, and related matters; it invades private property rights only in incidental ways. Zoning is a device for carrying out the plan with respect to land use and specifically limits the rights of private individuals, since it involves the regulation by districts under the police power of such matters as the height, the bulk, and the use of buildings as well as the use of land. Density of land use and hence of population may also be regulated. City, county, metropolitan area, state, and regional planning may all be involved.

Building Codes

Another illustration of the exercise of the police power is provided by building codes. Such codes are in force in most American cities. Such

---

[1] Sligh *v.* Kirkwood, 237 U.S. 52 (1914).

regulations are based on the grounds of safety and health. Hence, the quality and strength of materials are usually regulated and controls leading toward fire prevention and sanitation are imposed. Regulations may determine the ratio between the height and thickness of walls, the spacing of girders, and allowable stresses. Sanitary and health regulations necessitate control over plumbing, vents, ventilation, room height, and similar matters.

Although building codes provide many protections for citizens, they have been subject to numerous criticisms. In some cases they are unduly complicated; sometimes they afford certain types of protection for local firms or unions; often they "make work" for certain trades; frequently they fail to recognize new materials or practices and thus retard progress in the building industry. Despite problems, however, progress is being made in these areas.

Feudal and Alloidal Tenure

Except for the reservations arising from taxation, eminent domain, and the use of the police power, the ownership of real estate in the United States today may be thought of as being as complete as the ownership of a watch. The system of landholding that gives the owner such complete rights is referred to as *alloidal,* as contrasted with *feudal,* tenure. One of the issues of the American Revolution concerned some of the remnants of the feudal system which had been established in the New World.

In the feudal system no one except the king really owned land in the sense that an average citizen may hold it today. The feudal system of landholding originally grew out of military necessity. In return for grants of land, a king was able to assure himself of certain stipulated military services from his subjects. He granted lands to his lords, who granted them in turn to their followers. The feudal system has been aptly described as a pyramid with the king (the only real owner of the land) at the head and with the serfs or those who actually tilled the soil at the base.

After a period of time the *feuds* (grants of land) became permanent and could be inherited. If for some reason the lands were declared forfeit, the king reassigned them to a more favored subject.

William the Conqueror introduced the feudal system in England. Private ownership of land had previously been recognized there to a considerable degree, and the feudal system was introduced with difficulty. In succeeding centuries, as the country developed economically, the Crown found new ways to support its armies and other activities and the feudal system was gradually supplanted until private ownership in the modern sense became possible under the law.

Real versus Personal Property

Property objects may be tangible or intangible. Even though they are intangible, they generally are described as *things*. Things may be divided into "things real" and "things personal." The land and all things permanently attached to it are considered to be realty, and all other things are personalty. The line of demarcation between the two is sometimes very hard to determine in practical situations, however.

Land is considered by the common law to have an indefinite extent upward as well as downward, so that the word *land* includes not only the face of the earth but everything under it or over it. A strict interpretation of the concept of property as including the surface of the land plus an indefinite extent upward would make air traffic impossible. Consequently the right to space above 1,000 feet in congested areas and 500 feet elsewhere is considered as similar to rights on a navigable stream. *Air rights* have been purchased above railroad tracks to provide space for buildings, as in the case of the Daily News Building, the Merchandise Mart, and the Prudential Office Building in Chicago and the Pan Am Building in New York.

Types of Estates

Since it is possible to hold varying degrees of interest in land, lawyers have seen fit to divide these interests or estates into classes. The classification schemes commonly employed view these interests from one or another of the following standpoints: (1) duration or *quantity* of interest, (2) *time* of enjoyment, and (3) *number* and *connection* of the interested parties.

From the standpoint of quantity of interest, estates have been divided into those of *freehold* and those *not of freehold*. The concept of freehold has had a long historical development. It originally was synonymous with *possession,* but later came to be a more inclusive right than possession and was distinguished from it. Originally nonfreehold estates were considered as little more than contracts, although this concept was broadened with the passage of time. Since feudal society required that someone always hold a freehold interest, the legal doctrine developed that "the seisin [possession by virtue of feudal investiture] of land can never be in abeyance." Hence, with minor exceptions, there is always a freehold interest underlying an estate less than freehold. While this distinction between estates of freehold and those not of freehold is historical rather than logical, it helps to clarify the various types of interest which may exist.[2] Freehold estates

[2] Harold F. Lusk, *Law of the Real Estate Business* (rev. ed.; Homewood, Ill.: Richard D. Irwin, Inc., 1965), chap. vi.

include the *fee simple, fee tail,* other qualified estates, and the *estate for life.* Nonfreehold estates include estates for years, from year to year, and at will and at sufferance, or those commonly called *leasehold* estates. In this country a leasehold is now generally held to be personal property.[3]

From the standpoint of time of enjoyment, estates have been subdivided into those of *possession* and those which involve *possession at some future time.* Legally they are referred to as *estates in possession* and *estates in expectancy.*

The *number of owners* may be one or many. Legally this provides for the subdivision of estates into two groups: one owner, or *estates in severalty,* and more than one owner, or *joint estates.*

Fee Simple Estate

Lusk defines an estate in fee simple as ". . . the highest type of ownership in real estate known to law . . . the owner is entitled to all the rights incident to the property. . . . The terms *fee, fee simple,* and *fee simple absolute* are equivalent."[4]

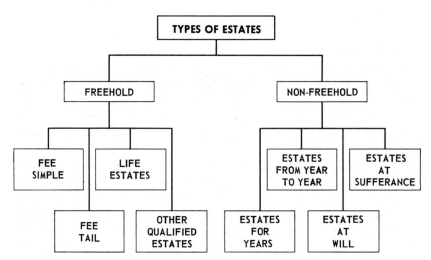

Fig. 5–1. Types of estates.

A fee simple estate carries with it the right to dispose of the property in any way the owner wishes. He may sell it, give it away, will it to his heirs or others, or trade it for other property. Furthermore, he may use his property in any way which will not interfere with the rights of other

[3] *Ibid.,* p. 64.
[4] *Ibid.,* p. 65. See also, Robert Kratovil, *Real Estate Law* (4th ed.; Englewood Cliffs, N.J.: Prentice-Hall, Inc., 1964), pp. 47–49.

property owners within the limits established by the state, which were discussed above.

Fee Tail Estate

A fee tail or limited estate restricts the alienation of the property in that it must pass to descendants of the owner. Originally this device was used to insure the passing of land in a direct ancestral line. When liberalizing tendencies caused modifications of this condition, statutes were enacted which restored the limitation. Later changes provided that fee tail estates could be created which could be transformed into fee simple interests by appropriate court action. The fee tail estate has been abolished by legislative enactment in a number of our states.

Estates for Life

Lusk explains estates for life as follows: "A life estate is a freehold estate in land and is limited in duration to the life of the owner, or to the life or lives of some other person or persons. It is not an estate of inheritance. A life estate may be terminated on the happening of a future, uncertain event." [5]

Thus, an estate so long as a specified person lives or during widowhood may be classified as a life estate. The life tenant may occupy the property or rent it to another and thus enjoy the income from it.

Estates for life are limited in time and involve a less complete form of ownership than the fee simple or (ordinarily) the fee tail. Estates for life may be created either by act of the parties (conventional) or by operation of the law (legal). Of the former, there are estates granted by one party for his life, or estates granted for the duration of the life of another. In the first case the estate ends at the death of the grantee, and in the second, at the death of the party named. [6] Life estates created by operation of the law include *curtesy* and *dower*. Curtesy is the life estate of the husband in the real estate owned by his wife, while dower is the life estate of the wife in the real property owned by her husband. These estates are no longer recognized in some states. A number of western states recognize the arrangement of *community property*. This provides that in the absence of a will the surviving husband or wife will receive half the estate and the heirs of the deceased the other half.

The right of *homestead* entitles the head of a family to an interest in his owned residence which is exempt from the claims of creditors. It is often referred to as *homestead exemption*. Statutes set limits to the amount of the exemption and usually require the filing of a written dec-

---

[5] Lusk, *op. cit.*, p. 69.
[6] This estate is technically called *estate d'autre vie*.

laration cf homestead. This type of interest has been created by statute, not through the common law.

Nonfreehold Estates—Leasehold Estates

The estates which are "less than freehold" include *estates from year to year, estates at will,* and *estates by sufferance.* These interests are commonly called *leasehold estates,* or rights of tenants as distinguished from those of a freeholder. An estate from year to year is a contract for a definite period of time—the period may be short or long. Estates at will are similar, but the duration of the lease depends on the will of both, as either party may terminate it. In the case of an estate by sufferance, the term of a lease for a definite period has expired and the tenant continues to hold over without special permission. However, *periodic tenancy* is sometimes involved in similar situations; for example, leases which run from year to year and month to month are assumed to be renewed if the owner accepts payment after the expiration of the lease and if appropriate notice of its expiration has not been given. It is necessary to differentiate between these types of tenancy and a tenancy for one year or for one month.

Estates Classified as to Time of Enjoyment

Estates may also be classified as to time of enjoyment. As we have pointed out above, one may either be in immediate possession of an estate or expect to secure possession at some future date. The latter type of estates include *reversions* and *remainders.* A reversion is the residue of an estate left with the grantor which entitles him to possession after the end of another estate. For example, if Mr. X leases his property to Mr. Y for ten years, Mr. X has the reversion.

A remainder is the right of a person to interests which mature at the end of another estate. For example, if Mr. G. I. Jones grants a life estate to Mr. I. G. Brown and thereafter to Mr. I. M. Smythe in fee, Mr. Smythe holds a remainder. If such an estate passed to Mr. Smythe only if he paid some obligation or fulfilled some other requirement, he would hold a *contingent remainder.* It should be noted, however, that a remainder must not be postponed for too great a period of time or it will be void because of the "rule against perpetuities." Usually this limits the postponement of estates to the lives of people who are living at the time the conditions are established.

Estates Classified by Number of Owners

Classification of ownership by number and connection of interested parties results in two main groups of estates: *joint estates* and *estates in severalty.* The latter are estates held by single owners, the former by more than one. In cases where more than one owner is involved, a number of possible arrangements may exist, the chief of which are *tenancies in common* and *joint tenancies.* If two or more persons own separate estates in the same property, each holding a distinct interest which may be sold or transmitted in any way, a tenancy in common exists. However, if two or more persons hold ownership in the same degree, acquired by purchase or grant, but not as separate shares, a joint tenancy exists. Joint tenancy is also distinguished by the doctrine of survivorship; that is, if one of the joint tenants dies, his interest passes to the survivor or survivors. While a joint tenant cannot will his share of such an estate, he may convey it while living. In such cases, however, a tenancy in common exists after such a grant. Any of the joint tenants may occupy the property without paying rent to the others, but if the property is leased to strangers, the rents are divided between the joint tenants. While the common law tended to favor joint tenancies, the present tendency is to favor the tenancy in common. In Oregon, for example, joint tenancies have been abolished by statute.

Another type of estate is *tenancy by entirety.* Since husband and wife are considered one person under the common law, each becomes the owner of the entire property when they take title to it together, and upon the death of either spouse the survivor is sole owner. Special statutes in the various states now fix interests of this type.

In case real estate is transferred to a partnership, the individual persons composing the partnership become the owners of the property. Hence, when a business operates as a partnership, it is usually found expedient to acquire real estate under a business name or in the name of one or more of the individual partners. Under such an arrangement the partners are the equitable owners. Since a corporation is a separate legal entity, it may own real estate in much the same manner as an individual if given this power directly or by implication in its charter or certificate of incorporation.

Corporeal and Incorporeal Rights

In addition to the types of estates which may be held by the occupant of a property or *corporeal rights,* there may be certain nonpossessory interests in real estate, or rights held by those who are not entitled to actual occupation. The latter interests are called *incorporeal rights* [7] and include (1) those rights which may ultimately develop into complete possessory or corporeal interests and (2) those which may not. Reversions and remainders, which have already been described, may be classified in the first group. In the second group of incorporeal rights in property the most important are *easements* and *rents.* Easements include the right

[7] Lusk, *op. cit.,* pp. 74–89.

to make a limited use of land without taking anything from it or having possession, such as the right to pass over another's property. Rent is the right of the grantor or lessor to receive a return or payment from the tenant. Sometimes these interests are classified as rights in another's property and include (in addition to easements and rents) profits and covenants running with the land, such rights as mortgages, statutory liens, and equitable charges or liens.

A *lien* is the legal right of a creditor to have a debt or charge paid or satisfied out of the property belonging to the debtor. Liens may be divided into specific and general classes, the former including mortgages, local taxes and assessments, and mechanics' liens, while the latter includes judgments, estate taxes, and the like.

Taxes, of course, are liens on real property when levied against it, and the property may be sold to satisfy the claim. Special assessments, which generally arise when all or a part of the cost of public improvements is charged against the property which is benefited, may be collected in the same way. In addition, there are ways for federal or state governments to obtain a lien on a delinquent taxpayer's property even though the tax was not levied on the property. For example, the federal government may have unpaid income taxes made a lien.

While at common law a *mortgage* amounted to a conveyance of an estate to the mortgagee or lender, the conveyance to become void when the terms of the mortgage agreement were fulfilled, today the mortgage is considered more in the nature of a lien upon a property to insure the repayment of a loan or the performance of an act. In many states a mortgage is restricted, by statute, to a lien. If the loan is not repaid, the mortgagee may take the necessary legal steps involved in foreclosure in order to recover his claim.

Mechanics' liens protect those who furnish materials and labor for the improvement of a property by giving them a claim against it. Such liens are governed by statute and vary widely among the states. Typically such a lien affects only the property that is benefited by the materials and labor involved. Usually such liens are enforcible by foreclosure.

When *judgments* involve money awards, they become liens on the property of the debtor, and his property may be sold to satisfy the claim. Estate taxes or inheritance taxes are a lien on the property of an estate, and such property may be sold to satisfy the tax if it is not paid.

Title to Real Estate

While one may hold a wide variety of interests in real property, he must be able to prove ownership. Such proof or evidence of ownership is called *title*.

At one time the fact of possession was considered evidence of title, just as the possession of most personal property is considered evidence of ownership today. Because of the complexity of the interests which may exist in real property, written evidence of ownership became essential. False statements or errors of memory created so many problems that the Statute of Frauds was enacted in England in 1677. It provided that all agreements affecting the title to real estate must be in writing to be enforcible. The party refusing to perform the contract can be held if he signed the written memorandum, whether or not the other party signed. Similar requirements were established in each of our states.

Public Records

Not only was written evidence of ownership needed, but permanent public records were found to be essential to systematic recording of real property ownership and of the transactions involving such ownership. The "recording acts" have met this requirement. In each of our states there is provision for the recording of transactions affecting real property.

Such records have been set up for two purposes: (1) to preserve evidence of all instruments affecting title, and (2) to provide any person with notice of their existence and content. If the records are complete, it is possible to determine all claims against a property and all transactions affecting it. If any questions exist regarding outstanding claims, the title is termed "cloudy" or "defective" and is not "clear." In such cases the property is not readily marketable, since "a good and merchantable title" cannot be given.

The registry laws do not make recording compulsory. They merely provide that recording of an instrument informs all who deal in real property of the transaction and that, unless an instrument is recorded, a prospective purchaser without actual notice of its existence is protected against it.

Various records must be kept in order to preserve adequate information about the status of title. These include deed books, mortgage books, plat books, and other records which preserve information about judgments, tax liens, attachments, mechanics' liens, wills, estate administration, divorce, marriage, bankruptcy, special assessments, and similar matters. In addition, restrictions on the use of real estate established by zoning laws or deed restrictions also affect the status of titles to real property.

Recording must be made in the county in which the land is located. If a property lies in two or more counties, the instruments pertaining to it must be recorded in each. A land records office is usually located in each county or similar subdivision in the state, and the officer in whose charge such records are placed ordinarily is called the *recorder* or *registrar of deeds*, although in some states the clerk of the county court or the county clerk keeps such records, and in others the auditor does this work.

Abstract of Title

The history of the title to a property may be traced by a study of those instruments in the public records which have affected it. Such a study is referred to as a *search of title*. It is usually made by abstracters who prepare an *abstract of title* or an *abstract,* which contains a summary of the documents having a bearing on the history of the title to a property. From this information it is possible for a competent lawyer to tell whether the title is *clear* or *defective*. He renders an *opinion of title*. This opinion may indicate that the title is clear or that certain matters must be cleared up before a purchaser can afford to take title to the property. The mere fact that an abstract is available is no assurance of good quality of title.

Title Insurance

Because of the many factors which may affect the title to a piece of real property and the countless risks which a purchaser may assume, title insurance companies have been established. In return for a premium such companies will guarantee that the title to property is clear, or that it is clear except for defects which are noted. Title insurance has been found to facilitate real estate transactions, since title insurance companies usually can act with greater speed in checking titles than individual lawyers and abstracters. Furthermore, such companies employ highly skilled personnel. Because of the care with which the work is done, and the fact that risks are spread over many properties, it is possible to carry out transactions which might otherwise be blocked because of minor defects in title. Title insurance does not guarantee title but will pay for damages resulting from defects in title.

The Torrens System

A system of land title registration by which the state guarantees title has developed from the work by Sir Robert Torrens in Australia during the middle of the last century. This system is in use in a number of our states. In a sense it does publicly what title insurance companies do on a private basis.

This system of land title registration provides for the establishment of title in an owner once and for all when he makes application to a duly elected or appointed *registrar*. The registrar institutes court proceedings in order that any claims against the property may be made. If none is made or such as are made are settled, the title is decreed to rest with the applicant, a decree is entered in a book of registry, and a certificate of ownership is issued to the owner or owners.

The owner pays a fee which becomes part of a revolving fund and which may be used to repay those who may have been cut off from their interests by the proceedings.

Acquiring Title to Real Estate

Property in real estate may be acquired in various ways, the most important of which are (1) by public grant, (2) by devise or descent, (3) by adverse possession, and (4) by private grant.

Title by public grant means that the federal government or a state issues a patent or grant to a private party. Much of the land originally held by the United States government was transferred to private ownership in this way.

Since one of the more important rights of property is the right to will it to survivors, a property owner may make a will. If the will is valid, he may dispose of his property as he wishes. Title secured in this way is called *title by devise.* After the death of the devisor the will is *probated*—that is, presented to a court for action. The property then passes automatically to those designated by the will if no one contests its validity. The right to convey property by will is subject to statutory limits which vary from state to state.

If a property owner dies *intestate*—that is, without making a valid will—the distribution of his property is governed by the statutes of the state in which the real property is located. Title acquired in this manner is said to be *title by descent.* The statutes governing the distribution of property in cases where the owner did not make a valid will vary widely from one state to another.

Deeds

The sale of property by one person to another is usually referred to as a *private grant,* and in such cases title is passed by the use of a *deed.*[8]

The principal requirements essential to the validity of a deed have been outlined by Kratovil as follows:

The validity and legal effect of a deed are matters governed by the law of the state where the land is located, and the requirements vary somewhat from state to state. Generally, however, and subject to the exceptions hereinafter mentioned, the essential elements of a deed are a competent grantor, a grantee, recital of consideration, words of conveyance, adequate description of the land, signature and seal of grantor, and a delivery of the completed instrument to the grantee. In addition, a deed may contain warranties of title, recitals show-

[8] *Ibid.,* p. 115.

CONSULT YOUR LAWYER BEFORE SIGNING THIS INSTRUMENT—THIS INSTRUMENT SHOULD BE USED BY LAWYERS ONLY.

THIS INDENTURE, made the   1st   day of   May   , nineteen hundred and
BETWEEN   WILLIAM J. JONES, residing at 115 Lenox Hill Avenue, in the City, County, and State of New York

party of the first part, and   JOHNATHAN WHITE, residing at 711 Front Street, in the City, County, and State of New York

party of the second part,

WITNESSETH, that the party of the first part, in consideration of ten dollars and other valuable consideration paid by the party of the second part, does hereby grant and release unto the party of the second part, the heirs or successors and assigns of the party of the second part forever,

ALL that certain plot, piece or parcel of land, with the buildings and improvements thereon erected, situate, lying and being in the Village of Lyons, in the County of Wayne, State of New York, and bounded and described as follows:

BEGINNING at a point on the southerly side of One hundred and seventh Avenue (Wayne Avenue) distant forty feet westerly from the corner formed by the intersection of said southerly side of One hundred and seventh Avenue with the westerly side of One hundred and thirty-fifth Street (Clinton Avenue) running thence southerly parallel with One hundred and thirty-fifth Street one hundred feet; thence westerly parallel with One hundred and seventh Avenue forty feet; thence northerly parallel with One hundred and thirty-fifth Street one hundred feet to said southerly side of One hundred and seventh Avenue and thence easterly along said southerly side of One hundred and seventh Avenue, forty feet to the point or place of beginning.

SUBJECT to covenants, restrictions and reservations contained in former instruments of record and to encumbrances of record.

TOGETHER with all right, title and interest, if any, of the party of the first part in and to any streets and roads abutting the above described premises to the center lines thereof; TOGETHER with the appurtenances and all the estate and rights of the party of the first part in and to said premises; TO HAVE AND TO HOLD the premises herein granted unto the party of the second part, the heirs or successors and assigns of the party of the second part forever.

AND the party of the first part, in compliance with Section 13 of the Lien Law, covenants that the party of the first part will receive the consideration for this conveyance and will hold the right to receive such consideration as a trust fund to be applied first for the purpose of paying the cost of the improvement and will apply the same first to the payment of the cost of the improvement before using any part of the total of the same for any other purpose.

AND the party of the first part covenants as follows: that said party of the first part is seized of the said premises in fee simple, and has good right to convey the same; that the party of the second part shall quietly enjoy the said premises; that the said premises are free from incumbrances, except as aforesaid; that the party of the first part will execute or procure any further necessary assurance of the title to said premises; and that said party of the first part will forever warrant the title to said premises.

The word "party" shall be construed as if it read "parties" whenever the sense of this indenture so requires.

IN WITNESS WHEREOF, the party of the first part has duly executed this deed the day and year first above written.

IN PRESENCE OF:

Wm. K. Murray   _William J. Jones_ ____(Seal)

Fig. 5–2. Warranty deed. (Courtesy The Title Guarantee Company, New York.)

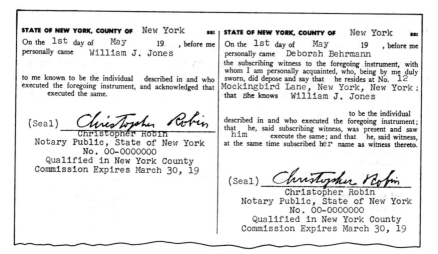

Fig. 5–2. Warranty deed (reverse).

ing mortgages and other encumbrances, a date, witnesses, an acknowledgment, and revenue stamps. Delivery is usually followed by filing or recording of the deed in the proper public office.[9]

The types of deeds which are used most frequently are the *warranty deed,* in which the seller warrants that the title to the property is "good and merchantable," and the *quitclaim deed,* in which the seller transfers only such title as he may possess. The *grant deed* is often used and may be classed between the warranty and quitclaim types. Also, there are various types of officers' deeds, such as the deeds given by sheriffs or other officials. In addition, there are trustees' deeds, executors' or administrators' deeds, conservators' or guardians' deeds, and related types. Since the most important is the warranty deed, the student is urged to study Figure 5–2 with some care.

Description of Property

In order for real estate to be described in a sufficiently clear manner so that it can be located without question, several methods have been developed. Except for the thirteen original colonies, much of the land in this country was surveyed before it was opened for sale to the public. The township six miles square formed the basic unit of measurement. Townships are identified by surveying lines running east and west, called *parallels,* and north and south, called *meridians.* North and south rows of

[9] Kratovil, *op. cit.,* p. 51.

townships are called *ranges,* and east and west rows are referred to as *tiers.* Within each township, sections are identified by numbers in accordance with the method illustrated in the accompanying diagram. Farms are ordinarily identified with respect to their location in sections and townships. However, when land is platted by a subdivider and a copy of the plat is made a matter of public record, the lots involved may be identified by block and number.

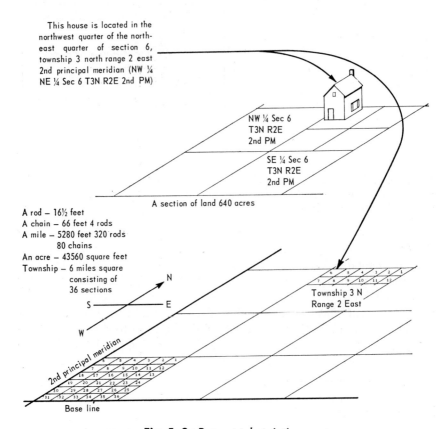

This house is located in the northwest quarter of the northeast quarter of section 6, township 3 north range 2 east 2nd principal meridian (NW ¼ NE ¼ Sec 6 T3N R2E 2nd PM)

NW ¼ Sec 6
T3N R2E
2nd PM

SE ¼ Sec 6
T3N R2E
2nd PM

A section of land 640 acres

A rod — 16½ feet
A chain — 66 feet 4 rods
A mile — 5280 feet 320 rods
80 chains
An acre — 43560 square feet
Township — 6 miles square
consisting of
36 sections

N
S —— E
W

2nd principal meridian

Township 3 N
Range 2 East

Base line

Fig. 5–3. Property description.

While the description of a property by the street and number of a house may be adequate for general purposes, a more detailed description is necessary when property actually changes hands. Indeed, it is usually considered advisable to have a careful survey made prior to undertaking purchase, mortgage lending, leasing, or improvement.

In those parts of the country which were not surveyed prior to being opened to sale to private individuals, the system of "metes and bounds" is used. The term *metes* refers to measures, and *bounds* to direction. For example, at a designated starting point, it is possible to indicate certain distances in various directions and return to the original starting point, thereby describing adequately a tract of land. The key to the success of such description is the adequacy of the description of the original starting point. Some difficulty is encountered, for example, if bodies of water. trees, and other natural formations are chosen as starting points. In such cases the destruction of a tree or a *monument* will invalidate the property description. For the purposes of land description, such things as bodies of water or trees are referred to as *natural monuments,* and fences, houses, or walls as *artificial monuments.* In case of conflict, monuments control over metes and bounds.

Since there are possibilities for error, descriptions by metes and bounds usually contain the words "more or less," which give some protection in case a new survey does not coincide exactly with the original. These terms are usually interpreted by the courts within the limits of a reasonable standard.

The Condominium

A recent innovation in real estate ownership, the condominium, presents another problem in property description. The condominium has been described as follows:

. . . the legal term for real property ownership providing fee simple ownership of an individual apartment or other enclosed space in a building; at the same time, it provides for common ownership by the individual unit owners of such areas as halls, elevators, and recreational facilities related to the building. . . . Traditionally, under Anglo-American law a fee simple title to land has meant the ownership of a certain area of the earth's surface that could be appropriately described. Generally, ownership of the airspace above this area, as well as the right to exploit whatever lay beneath, has attached to the ownership of the surface. However, separate conveyance of subsurface mineral rights has been well recognized. Not so commonly recognized has been the right of the owner to convey title to the airspace above the surface he owns in fee simple. The condominium makes possible the individual ownership, alienation, and mortgaging of a portion of the airspace occupied by an apartment—for example, one situated fifteen stories above the ground.[10]

Real Estate Contracts

Almost all transactions involving the sale, purchase, or exchange of real estate result in the drawing of a contract. Such contracts in the real estate business may be of a number of types, including purchase and sale contracts, listing contracts, land contracts, and others.

[10] Robert R. Milroy, "The Condominium," *Business Horizons* (Spring, 1964), p. 51.

The regulations governing contracts pertaining to real estate are similar to those governing contracts in general. The contract must be made by persons who are legally competent. There must be an offer and an acceptance. There must be a valid consideration. Each party must be obliged to do something. The object for which the contract is drawn must be legal.

In addition, however, contracts which involve real estate transactions must be in writing and must be signed by the parties who are to be bound by them. Real estate contracts differ in this regard from other types of contracts. This difference grows out of the provisions of the Statute of Frauds referred to above.

Contracts for the sale of real estate are usually drawn in accordance with forms which are approved by a local real estate board or similar group. Typically, such contracts provide for a property description, a financial statement, a closing date and place, and signatures. In addition, such contracts should contain an exact statement of the kind of deed involved and an agreement regarding the evidence of title which the seller will furnish. It should be noted that real estate contracts are "specifically enforcible." The courts may force either party to a real estate contract to carry out an agreement exactly. However, this decision is discretionary with the court. If specific performance is not requested, the contract may be rescinded with adjustments in the monetary arrangements. Also, one party may sue the other for breach of contract and damages.

Land contract, or *contract for deed,* is the term used to identify a purchase and sale contract which provides for the payment of the purchase price in installments over a period of time. Sometimes similar arrangements are made under a *lease with option to purchase.* Such leases allow the tenants to purchase the property at a specified price within a stated period with the understanding that all or part of the rent paid will apply toward this purchase price.

Listing contracts will be described more completely in Chapter 17. There are four general types of listing arrangements: (1) *open listing,* in which the seller may list his property for sale with a number of brokers; (2) the *exclusive agency,* in which the seller gives one broker an exclusive agency, but reserves the right to sell the property himself; (3) the *exclusive right-to-sell contract,* which gives the broker the sole right to dispose of the property for a given period and if the owner sells the property himself he still must pay the broker his commission, and (4) *multiple listing,* a system in which a number of brokers have an agreement by which any one of them may sell property for which another member of the group has an exclusive right-to-sell contract. Under such an arrangement, there is provision for dividing the commissions involved.

Leases

Leases are agreements entered into by an owner or lessor with a tenant or lessee in which the possession of the property is granted to the tenant, usually for a specified period of time, in return for a stated rental.

Leases may be oral or written. In some states, leases for periods of more than one year must be in writing to be valid, while in some states oral leases are valid for as long as three years. Property may be leased for a long period of time. There are leases that run for as long as 999 years. *Ground leases* are sometimes drawn up to run for long periods and allow the tenant to construct buildings or other improvements on the property. Because of the importance of the provisions of a lease, many real estate boards have drawn up standard lease forms, as have many business firms when the rental of property is an important part of their activities. In a transaction of considerable financial importance or involving any unusual rights of either lessor or lessee, it is advisable to have a competent real estate lawyer prepare the lease.

Rents may be fixed for a flat rate, or related in some way such as gross or net sales to the amount of business handled by the tenant. Sometimes there is provision for a *graded* or *step-up lease.* In such cases, the rent is established at one level for a given period and then advances for another period. A reappraisal is sometimes required in such cases. As has been pointed out above, some leases contain an option to purchase.

Leases are terminated either by expiration, by mutual agreement, by a breach of the provisions of the lease, or in other ways. Some leases are for an indefinite period and operate from month to month. Leases are important to the business of property management, and the details of lease agreements will be described in Chapter 18.

Uniform Commercial Code

The Uniform Commercial Code has now been adopted in more than half our states. Although not closely related to real estate law, there are a number of situations where it may be applicable. For example, such things would be included as a security interest in annual crops, fixtures, or goods before they become fixtures. There are many difficult problems involved as to the applicability of the code or traditional real estate law and they are too specialized for our consideration here. We should recognize the growing importance of the Uniform Commercial Code, however, and its current and potential significance for various real estate decisions.[11]

[11] Peter F. Coogan and Albert L. Clovis, "The Uniform Commercial Code and Real Estate Law: Problems for Both the Real Estate Lawyer and the Chattel Security Lawyer," *Indiana Law Journal,* Vol. 38, No. 4. (Summer, 1963)

SUMMARY

Real estate is one of the most heavily regulated sectors of our economy, being subject to the direct or indirect regulations of federal, state, and local units of government. Private ownership of real estate resources is never complete, as this ownership may be modified by the governmental powers of taxation, eminent domain, or the police power. The exercise of these powers may therefore be a key factor in private decision-making.

Real estate administration is conducted in an atmosphere of institutional arrangements and procedures which have developed within the legal system. Many legal details and legal documents are involved in the establishment of ownership or the transfer of ownership of real estate. Legal arrangements in some cases limit the utilization of property and thus reduce its income-producing ability; in other instances legal arrangements may promote sound property uses and enhance the value of real estate.

Property involves the right to exercise control over economic goods, including real estate resources. Various interests, or estates, in real property may exist and may be classified according to the quantity of interest, the time of enjoyment, or the number of interested parties. Also of importance are nonpossessory interests such as easements and rents.

The prudent individual or business manager will seek competent legal assistance in handling the detailed legal procedures involved in real estate transactions.

QUESTIONS FOR STUDY

1. Prepare a list of the various laws and regulations that have an effect on the income-producing ability of your reference property, and indicate whether the effect of each is to improve or reduce this income potential.
2. How could you establish proof of the ownership of your reference property?
3. Explain why organized government is necessary to the existence of private property.
4. Could an interest in real property exist that did not include either ownership or possession of the property? Discuss.
5. In what way is private property a matter of human relationships?
6. How did taxation on real estate develop? How significant are real estate taxes in the total tax receipts of state and local governments?
7. What is the purpose of title insurance?
8. Distinguish between "title" and "deed."
9. Explain the use of a tax lien.
10. Can a real estate tax be imposed upon all future holders of a specific property? Explain your answer.

11. Mr. Adams owns a building in which you intend to open a hardware store. He offers to negotiate with you either a flat-rate lease or a percentage lease. Indicate reasons why you might prefer one type of lease over the other.

12. *Study Project 6.* How would joint tenancy have changed this dispute? Discuss the significance of joint tenancy and tenancy in common and the differences between these concepts.

13. *Study Project 7.* Do you agree with the author's conclusion that police power and eminent domain should be considered separately in condemnation appraisal? By what methods could legal precedent be circumvented so that compensation could be awarded for both types of damages? Would you recommend this?

SUGGESTED READINGS

KRATOVIL, ROBERT. *Real Estate Law* (4th ed.). Englewood Cliffs, N.J.: Prentice-Hall, Inc., 1964. Chaps. vi–ix.

LUSK, HAROLD F. *Law of the Real Estate Business* (rev. ed.). Homewood, Ill.: Richard D. Irwin, Inc., 1965. Chaps. vi–xi.

6

Economic Characteristics of Real Estate

Decisions and Incomes at Fixed Locations

As we have pointed out, decisions relating to real estate turn largely on the analysis of income and estimates of income-producing potentials at fixed locations. Such incomes may be in the form of monetary returns or result from the direct use of a property. But the services produced by a property can be provided only at a given site, for all real estate is *fixed in location*. The land is immovable, and the cost of moving buildings and other improvements is so great that such projects are seldom undertaken.

All types of economic activity and decisions related to them are concerned with income—that is, the production of returns in excess of costs. Indeed, *income* has often been referred to as *the fundamental fact of economic life*. In real estate we are concerned with income and more particularly with the *localization* of income. In nearly all other types of business it is possible for the commodity or service involved to follow the market, to move to the point where the greatest income-producing potential exists. In the real estate field this is not true. The market must be induced to come to the property. Once a property has been developed, its future is dependent entirely upon its ability to command a market for its services at its specific location.

Fixity of Location

The fact of fixity of location is of major importance in decisions and programs of action related to real estate for these reasons:

1. Because of fixity of location, every parcel of real estate differs from every other one. It is a unique point in a changing economic framework. Not even a vacant lot is identical in every respect with an adjoining vacant lot. Physical structures differ with respect to condition, style of architecture, materials of construction, and in many other ways. Real properties also differ from each other with respect to distances from transportation lines, from places of employment, from civic and social centers, from other sections of the area, and from other parts of the country or the world. Decisions related to city properties are affected greatly by the "urban plant" which serves them, the system of streets, sewers, water mains, utilities, parks, playgrounds, schools, and the like. Similarly, decisions related to rural properties are influenced by the availability and cost of public or quasi-public facilities and services.

2. Because of fixity of location, real estate resources can never escape from developments of an economic, social, political, or physical character which may affect them favorably or adversely. If the street on which your home is located develops into a high-speed traffic artery, you cannot as a practical matter move even the house to a quieter or safer street. Nor can you move a house or any other piece of real estate out of the path of blighting influences. Conversely, you cannot help but reap the benefits of any developments which reflect favorably on the city or the district or neighborhood in which your property is located. The influence of factors of this type on real estate expectations and decisions is considered at greater length in Chapters 13 and 14.

Although fertility, annual precipitation, length of the growing season, and slope form the principal basis of the income-producing capacity of farm land, location or *situs* is of basic importance in the case of urban land. Babcock stresses this point:

> A land parcel, insofar as it is a described area on the face of the earth, cannot be destroyed. The value of land, on the other hand, is only relatively durable, and in some cases can be completely destroyed. The importance of certain locations may disappear. Fertility declines with continued use. But the land itself remains.[1]

3. Because of the fixity of location of real estate, the real estate market tends to be more limited in extent than are the markets for most other commodities. The market for owner-occupied homes typically is limited in geographic extent to a single city and often to a certain section of that city. The market for commercial and industrial real estate, however, is

[1] By permission from *The Valuation of Real Estate*, by Frederick M. Babcock, pp. 26–27. Copyright, 1932, McGraw-Hill Book Co., Inc., New York. See also Raleigh Barlowe, *Land Resource Economics* (Englewood Cliffs, N.J.: Prentice-Hall, Inc., 1958), pp. 18–19, and Sanders A. Kahn, Frederick E. Case, and Alfred Schimmel, *Real Estate Appraisal and Investment* (New York: The Ronald Press Co., 1963), pp. 43–47.

somewhat broader and may be thought of as at least regional in extent. Farm lands typically are bought and sold throughout a county or other relatively limited area. The market for a property varies somewhat with the point of view from which it is considered. Thus, a New York investor might buy an apartment house in Chicago. The people who rented the apartments, however, would in almost all instances be Chicagoans.

4. Fixity of location is the principal basis for the legal distinction between real and personal property as we saw in our discussions in the preceding chapter. Also, fixity of location makes it possible to establish definite boundaries and to describe the property for legal and business purposes.

Long Life of Real Properties

Decisions relating to real properties are influenced greatly by the long life of these resources. Income expected ten years hence is worth less today than current income. This is because we discount the future due to the many uncertainties and risks that lie ahead and because of the waiting involved. As a site for buildings and other improvements, land is relatively permanent. Buildings and other improvements on the land have a longer life than that of most other commodities. Hence, investments in real estate tend to be fixed for long periods of time. It is not easy to change urban land from one use to another. If an apartment house is built on a lot, it usually remains there for many years, even if the market at times is depressed to the point where the owner cannot earn a satisfactory return on his investment.

Although agricultural land can be shifted from the production of one crop to another from year to year, the farmer may be concerned with crop rotation which tends to place limitations on land use.

Long-Term Implications of Decisions

Some decisions in regard to the purchase, sale, or leasing of real estate are made for short-run purposes. They may be made for purposes of speculation, to provide space for temporary periods, or to protect a position previously taken. Most such decisions, however, are made for longer-term periods. Even the leasing of a dwelling unit usually covers a period of a year, often longer; most commercial leases are for a term of years. Purchases are usually made with a long-term program of property use or development in mind. Some speculative purchases, of course, are long term in character. Thus, the long-term nature of most real estate decisions is an important factor in understanding programs of property use and the operation of real estate markets.

Real Properties as Large Economic Units

The fact that real properties are relatively large economic units is one of the reasons for the existence of the real estate business. Brokers are needed to bring together buyers and sellers—investors in and users of various properties or property services. Property managers are essential to the operation of large buildings or blocks of properties. Since special financial arrangements usually are necessary in real estate transactions because of the large amounts of money involved, an elaborate system of financing has developed.

Interdependence of Private and Public Property

Rarely can a piece of real estate be used except in conjunction with some public land, and the interdependence of private and public land tends to increase as the community becomes more complex in structure and organization. In order to have access to private land, there usually must be either a public road or street or an easement providing a right-of-way over another private property. Since private arrangements of the latter type are usually difficult to make, we normally depend on public streets and roads for access to our properties. The proportion of the land area given over to public streets, alleys, parks, and similar uses increases as cities grow in size and complexity.

In addition to the problems of access to real properties, provision must be made for water, drainage, and disposal of sewage; for electricity, gas, telephones, and other utilities and conveniences; and for police and fire protection. Indeed, one of our problems in the future may center on channeling enough capital into public projects and properties to support private real estate resources.

Supply of Real Estate

The supply of real estate available at any given time may be considered from two standpoints: (1) the *properties* themselves, and (2) the *property services* provided by these real estate resources. The properties include all types of real estate: residential, commercial, industrial, agricultural, mineral, public, and special-purpose properties. They include the land, buildings, and other improvements as well as the legal rights represented by these physical resources.

In a sense real properties may be thought of as factories producing services—shelter, protection, privacy, comforts, conveniences, and other services. For example, a hotel may be thought of as a producer of the various services it provides its guests. Once a property is improved, property services must be utilized or they will be wasted through depreciation and obsolescence. In this respect, property services may be compared to labor: the loss of a day of a worker's time is an irrevocable loss, just as is the case with the loss of a day of property utilization.

Various arrangements may be made for the utilization of the available supply of real properties. An entire property may be purchased for a lump sum. This sum will represent the present value of the services the property is expected to render over the period of its productive life. Usually some borrowing is involved in such purchases because of the relatively large sums typically required. Or a property may be leased, with rental payments being made for the property services as used on the basis of fixed amounts per month or per year, or on percentages of gross or net earnings, or on some other basis.

Supply of Real Estate Inflexible

Because of the long life of real properties, the supply of real estate resources at any given time is relatively fixed.[2] These resources may be used more or less intensively, of course, and consequently the supply of *property services* is somewhat more flexible than the supply of *properties*. Even in terms of property services, supply is relatively fixed, however, since there are fairly narrow limits within which the property services from a given property can be expanded through more intensive use. Also, even though a property is not used, it tends to affect current market conditions by virtue of its being a part of the available supply.

The present supply of real properties has been accumulating over many years. The amount added in any one year represents a very small percentage of the total. In recent years, for example, we started around 1,500,000 nonfarm housing units annually. Yet this represented in any one year only about 3 per cent of the total nonfarm housing supply.

The supply of commercial and industrial properties also is not expanded rapidly year by year. We have actually reduced the acreage under cultivation for agricultural purposes in recent years, although we have increased, of course, the intensity of use and expanded productivity through improved methods and machines.

When new construction declines to low points because of sluggish market conditions, the supply of real estate is not reduced to any marked extent. The additions may be small but seldom are less than demolitions or losses from fire and other hazards.

[2] See Edward E. Edwards, "Real Estate Economics: A Return to Fundamentals," *The Appraisal Journal* (April, 1949); reproduced in Study Project 8. Also, Paul A. Samuelson, *Economics: An Introductory Analysis* (6th ed.; New York: McGraw-Hill Book Co., Inc., 1964), pp. 537–39.

Structures deteriorate with use and the passage of time. By 1975, for example, the remainder of the 20,264,000 dwellings built before 1920 will be at least 55 years old. Some of these will remain in good condition, but many will tend to deteriorate rapidly. On the basis of census reports and other estimates, it is estimated that between four and five million dwellings may now be in need of substantial improvement. Many of our present dwelling units have to be replaced every year.

Since the supply of properties and even of property services is relatively fixed, *demand* is the most important factor in determining market prices and rents during short-run periods of a year or two. When demand exceeds supply at current prices and rents, there is a tendency for prices and rents to move upward and to continue to advance for a prolonged period, since it takes a long time to add substantially to the supply available. When demand falls below supply at prevailing prices and rents, the market slows up and prices and rents fall and continue to decline for a long time.

Because of the relative inflexibility of supply and the informal nature of real estate markets, there probably never was a time when the markets were in balance. Tendencies toward balanced relationships between supply, demand, and price, however, do exist, and it is the identification of these tendencies that is of greatest importance in analyzing real estate markets, as we shall see in Chapter 12.

Demand for Real Estate

The demand for real estate is based on a wide variety of considerations. It reflects the standards, attitudes, and objectives of individuals, families, business firms, government officials, and others. It indicates preference for real estate relative to other goods and services. In the case of commercial and industrial real estate, demand is a reflection of company policies based on estimates of the potential income-producing capacity of real property in relation to cost, including construction costs and operating expenses, and in relation to potential return from other resources. Industrial firms demand more real estate when the market for their products is brisk and market potentials are good. Commercial properties are in heavy demand when profit prospects are favorable. As a result of the adoption of long-range planning programs by many business firms, there is more of a tendency to buy real estate well in advance of current or short-term needs.

The demand for residential real estate is largely a reflection of consumer incomes. To a large degree the demand for residential real estate is similar to the demand for luxury goods. Minimum requirements for shelter could be met with very small expenditures. The demand for hous-

PLOTTING DATA

Year	1960 Dollars	Year	1960 Dollars
1929	1,157	1947	1,494
1930	1,076	1948	1,496
1931	1,034	1949	1,508
1932	934	1950	1,574
1933	906	1951	1,559
1934	948	1952	1,574
1935	1,001	1953	1,622
1936	1,097	1954	1,615
1937	1,127	1955	1,706
1938	1,100	1956	1,730
1939	1,154	1957	1,743
1940	1,205	1958	1,728
1941	1,274	1959	1,796
1942	1,231	1960	1,817
1943	1,246	1961	1,819
1944	1,275	1962	1,874
1945	1,349	1963	1,905
1946	1,497	1964*	1,983

* Estimated.

Fig. 6–1. Personal consumption expenditures per capita, 1929–1960, and projection to the year 2000. (Source: *Resources in America's Future*, p. 81.)

ing, however, is much more than a demand for shelter. It includes the desire to have a "good address," to live in a neighborhood of congenial people, or to attain the comforts and conveniences that are provided by modern living accommodations. The demand for residential real estate increases as personal incomes rise. This increase may be both for more space and for space of higher quality. Conversely, demand drops sharply when incomes go down.

Figure 6–1 gives some indication of past and future personal consumption expenditures per capita. These, of course, include expenditures for housing. The average yearly income per household after taxes was running at about $6,500 in 1963. It could rise to about $10,000 in 1980 (in 1960 dollars) and be somewhere between $13,000 and $15,000 at the end of the century.[3] Thus, the long-term demand for residential real estate is likely to be strong, at least as suggested by these anticipated income levels. These figures are inflated somewhat by the inclusion of high-income families in the averages. If the median income is used—that is, the midpoint, with as many incomes above as below—the figures would show a rise from around $5,000 in the early 1960's to $7,500 by 1980 to $10,000 to $12,000 in 2000.

To the extent that residential real estate partakes of the nature of a luxury, and for a large majority of dwellings this is the case, it is in competition with other luxury goods for the consumer's income. But more than the consumer's income is involved. His *credit* plays an important part as well. Similarly, the credit of business firms plays a major role in the demand for commercial and industrial real estate. The demand for farm real estate is largely a reflection of both farm incomes and the credit position of farmers and investors in farm real estate.

Demand and Credit

Since real properties typically represent relatively large economic units, few buyers are able to pay for their properties as they are purchased. Credit usually plays a major part in such transactions. The amount that a prospective buyer is prepared to bid for a piece of real estate depends to a marked degree on the amount he can borrow. This is true of most home buyers and to a considerable degree of the buyers of commercial, industrial, and farm real estate as well. Except for loans arranged through friends, associates, or relatives, how much can be borrowed on a specific property depends on the attitudes and policies of the managers of lending institutions. Typically, financial institutions consider such factors as the following in deciding how much of a loan can be made to finance a specific transaction: (1) the borrower's income and income prospects, (2)

[3] Hans H. Landsberg, Leonard L. Fischman, and Joseph L. Fisher, *Resources in America's Future* (Baltimore: The Johns Hopkins Press, 1963), Chap. i. See also, "The Next Decade and Its Opportunities for the Savings and Loan Business" (Chicago: U.S. Savings and Loan League, 1959) and "A Second Look at the Decade of the 1960's" by Edward E. Edwards and Arthur M. Weimer, also published by the U.S. Savings and Loan League, 1963.

the present and potential value of the property, (3) the relative attractiveness of other forms of investment, and (4) the legal restrictions surrounding financing arrangements.

The policies of lending institutions are affected by market conditions. For example, their lending policies may tend to exaggerate the effect of incomes and income prospects on the demand for real estate. When incomes are high and income prospects are favorable, lending institutions tend to be optimistic about both the borrower's income and the value of the property. When incomes are declining and markets are sluggish, the policies of lending institutions tend to be very conservative.

The relative attractiveness of other forms of investment is an important factor in determining the availability of credit for real estate transactions. The availability of funds and the interest rate that must be paid are determined in part by conditions and events entirely outside the real estate market, such as the yield on government and corporate bonds and other investments. Relative attractiveness involves more than yield. There may be a preference for liquidity of investments, as is usually true during depression periods. At such times the funds available for real estate financing may dry up, even though high yields are offered, because investors place a heavy premium on liquidity.

The lending policies of real estate financing institutions are closely regulated by state governments and the federal government. The importance of the federal government in this field has grown with the insurance of deposits and savings accounts, the insurance and guarantee of mortgages, and the increasing role of the Treasury and Federal Reserve in the money markets. In periods of emergency the federal government may impose controls on real estate financing with regulation of down payments and terms of loans.

Thus at any given time the demand for real estate depends to a considerable extent on the willingness of financial institutions to finance property purchases. This is particularly true of residential real estate, but has considerable validity in the case of commercial, industrial, and farm property as well.

Population and Real Estate Demand

If a rising population is accompanied by favorable income prospects, the demand for real properties and property services tends to be high. But an increase in population will not bring a rise in the demand for real estate if incomes are falling, unless there should be a sudden shift in the preference of buyers for real estate relative to other goods and services. Thus, the primary factors in real estate demand are considered to be incomes and the terms and availability of financing. However, population trends and movements may be clues to real estate demand when considered in relation to income trends.

The age distribution of the population is an important factor to consider as well as the trend of total population growth. If there are a large number of people of marriageable age, as will be the case for some years, demand for residential real estate will tend to be strong—assuming that income conditions are favorable. As children reach school age, interest in single-family homes tends to rise. The trend toward more children per family in recent years undoubtedly stimulated the demand for somewhat larger houses than was the case earlier. (This trend may now be in process of modification.) With a larger number of people in higher age groups and with the expansion of pension funds, both public and private, there is a growing market for small, efficiently designed town houses and apartments for retired persons and couples. There is also increased interest in locations in warmer climates.

Cities with growing populations usually have more active real estate markets than those with stable or declining populations. But there must be income-producing opportunities in a city to induce people to move there. Except for resort areas or "dormitory towns," people are attracted to cities by good income prospects. Thus, income is again the primary factor in explaining real estate demand.

Population Trends

Thirty years ago, on the basis of the birth and death rates then prevailing, it was predicted that the population of continental United States would increase to 155 million and thereafter remain stable or decline. Such estimates were far from reality. The rapid rise of the birth rate after World War II and the continuation of relatively high birth rates, plus some increase in average longevity, resulted in a total population of 193 million persons in mid-1964 with prospects for an advance to 245 million by 1980 and 330 million by the end of the century.

As we have suggested, this expansion in numbers of people will not by itself bring an increase in housing demand or in the demand for other real estate. If accompanied by at least stable and preferably rising per capita incomes, plus favorable conditions in terms of availability and cost of financing, such a population growth may be translated into significant demands for real estate resources and their services. Rising incomes, even with a stable population and favorable financing conditions, would bring an expansion in real estate demand, provided that real estate remained in a reasonably competitive position relative to other goods and services. For example, people may wish to improve the quality of their housing, or more families might own two houses, perhaps a summer and a winter

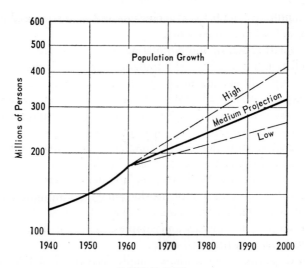

PLOTTING DATA

Year *	Population (in thousands)	Year *	Population (in thousands)
1940	132,122	1953	159,559
1941	133,402	1954	162,388
1942	134,860	1955	165,276
1943	136,739	1956	168,225
1944	138,397	1957	171,278
1945	139,928	1958	174,154
1946	141,389	1959	177,080
1947	144,126	1960	180,676
1948	146,631	1961	183,742
1949	149,188	1962	186,591
1950	151,689	1963	189,278
1951	154,283	1964	192,120
1952	156,947	1965	195,000

Projections	Population (in millions)	
	1980	2000
High	280	430
Medium	245	330
Low	225	270

* At July 1.

Fig. 6–2. Population growth, projected to the year 2000. (Source: *Resources in America's Future*, p. 73.)

place, or a downtown and a suburban home, just as increasing numbers of families are owning two or more cars. Also, high incomes enable single persons to have their own dwellings and enable older couples to live apart from their children. With rising populations and incomes (assuming that financing will be available) real estate demand may be stimulated particularly.

Our population pyramid now has a peculiar shape. The low birth rates of the 1930's created a situation which currently gives us a smaller number of people in the 30–40 age group than in others, except for those in advanced age groups. But filling in back of this age group are larger numbers in the 20–30 and in the 10–20 age groups, with consequent rises in the number of marriages coming along currently.

The population has been moving toward the suburbs and toward the south and west. These trends are likely to continue. For example, the Pacific Coast and Mountain areas are expected to grow faster than the rest of the nation in the years ahead because of the anticipated expansion of economic activities in these regions.

Growth of our cities is likely to occur primarily in the suburban areas in the years ahead, with another 80 per cent of the growth of our metropolitan areas and other urban places taking place in the suburbs. Whether the principal growth will occur in cities of more than 100,000 people or in other places is difficult to predict, although the larger urban areas are likely to continue to attract the lion's share of growth.

Our population will tend to be somewhat older on the average in the years ahead. It will hence contain a growing proportion of retired people and those in advanced years. As is true of other age groups, their demand for real estate resources and services will depend on their economic condition rather than their numbers. With the expansion of social security and retirement programs, the outlook for strong demands by these age groups for real estate appears to be good. Some of this demand will be centered in regions with warmer climates.

Market Competition

The basic force in markets is competition, and this is the key to understanding how markets work. Through competition, prices (and rents) are set and the market performs its functions of allocating space, determining rates of development of properties, and determining land uses.

If the owner of a parcel of real estate wishes to sell it, he offers it in the real estate market. If a prospective buyer wishes to purchase or lease real property, he "enters the market" and attempts to secure the property or property services that will meet his requirements. This market has no single geographical focus, but operates through scattered transactions of owners, brokers, and users of real estate resources or services. There is no organized exchange where real estate transactions take place, as in the case of the large security or commodity markets. "The market" is a highly informal series of negotiations ranging all the way from direct sales of properties by owners to complicated transactions in which numerous brokers and their principals participate.

The market process arises from the *mutually beneficial nature of exchange.* If the owner of a house sells it for $20,000, he must want the money more than the house. On the other hand, the buyer must want the house more than the $20,000. Unless these conditions were present no sale or purchase would be made. Both buyer and seller expect to benefit from the transaction at the time it is made. Later on, of course, changing conditions may prove that one of the parties to the transaction was benefited to a greater extent than the other. At the time of the agreement, however, both expected to benefit.

Competition for various kinds of space is a major factor in the setting of prices (and rents) and in establishing price relationships. This process largely determines how real estate resources are allocated among those who demand them, and it influences the rate of adding to and subtracting from the available supply.

We should recognize that markets are made up of people, and more specifically, of people with economic capacity, that is, available funds or the ability to command credit. The decisions of people are behind whatever happens in markets. Thus, when we refer to "market forces" we are really thinking of various actions that are being taken as a result of decisions made by people in connection with their personal, business, or governmental activities.

Scope of the Market

Because of the fixed location of real properties we usually tend to think of the real estate market as being local in character, typically including only one city or community. While stores, factory buildings, homes, and farms cannot be moved from one locality to another, there are wide variations in the scope of the market for different kinds of properties or property services. Typically the market for owner-occupied homes is a local one. It is confined to the people living in the community or moving to that specific area. The market for resort property, however, may be widespread, since such dwellings are usually occupied for only a portion of the year and purchasers or tenants may come from any part of the country or the world. Income property can be compared on a national and often on an international basis. Also, the market for investment properties of nearly all types tends to be regional and in some instances national in scope. An investor in Chicago might buy a farm in Kansas. A New York investor might purchase an apartment house in Los Angeles.

The market for commercial and industrial property tends to be regional or national rather than local in scope. Large industries like General Electric, Ford, and U.S. Steel buy, sell, and lease real estate on a national and international basis. Chain store organizations analyze the population and purchasing power of numerous trade areas throughout the country, determine new store locations, the volume needed to support stores of various sizes, and the population and income required to achieve such volume. Sales volumes of existing stores, of course, provide a valuable guide in making such estimates.

Many local department stores have been acquired in recent years by such national chains as Allied Stores, Federated Department Stores, and others. National organizations are prominent in apparel lines, drugs, variety stores, and supermarkets; Kresge, Woolworth, Krogers, and A & P are examples. However, many large independent department stores still operate chiefly in one city. For example, the J. L. Hudson Company confines its operations to Detroit, and Marshall Field and Company to Chicago.

In general, organizations which operate stores on a nationwide chain basis are gaining in importance. Nevertheless, local factors always play an important role in decisions regarding specific retail outlets, whether the decisions are being made by chains or local firms. The same thing is true in other real estate fields. An apartment house in Detroit may be purchased by a New York investor, but his decision will be based on his estimate of conditions in the Detroit real estate market. An industrial plant in Atlanta may be leased by a Chicago firm, but local factors in the Atlanta market will have an important bearing on the final decision.

Unimproved urban sites or vacant surburban tracts are sold in a series of local markets. Since their value depends on estimates of their future use and income, prices often advance quickly on favorable news. The market tends to be a "thin" one and a few sales may send prices up rapidly.

Basic Market Principles

A market is a set of arrangements for bringing together buyers and sellers. The market process is commonly symbolized by specialized trading rooms where major dealers assemble daily for making transactions and where the transactions are all promptly reported to the public. However, it is only in connection with a few highly standardized and heavily traded items like wheat, cotton, copper, and the securities of large corporations that highly organized exchanges are found. Such highly organized exchanges are often used as illustrations of the general economic theory of markets. This is partly because they are dramatic, but mainly because the geographic concentration of transactions and the comparative freedom from other complications make it fairly easy, in connection with them, to visualize the basic principles that operate in all kinds of competitive markets. In other words, in the great exchanges, actual operations resemble very closely the competitive model of economic theory. It should be understood, however, that other markets, including the real estate market, follow the same model, though not so closely.

The most fundamental of the general principles of market operation relates to the tendency, in a given market as of a given time, toward uniformity of prices for like commodities. Other basic principles of general market operations are these:

1. When demand exceeds supply at the current price, price tends to advance. When supply exceeds demand at the current price, price tends to decline.
2. An advance in price tends to reduce demand and to increase supply. A decline in price tends to stimulate demand and to decrease supply.
3. Price tends to move to the level at which demand and supply are in balance.
4. An increase in demand, or a decrease in supply, will tend to raise price at least temporarily; a decrease in demand, or an increase in supply, will tend to lower price at least temporarily.

In markets where specialized trading rooms are characteristic, these tendencies are easier to observe, but their operation can be detected no less certainly in markets like that for real estate which are characterized by other means for getting buyers and sellers together. This is the case, for example, in the over-the-counter securities market, where major dealers, despite their separation, get together by telephone and wire services.

The departures from the model outlined above are considerably greater in the real estate market, where the complications include lack of standardization as well as separation of buyers and sellers. However, even in the real estate market the basic principles of market operation outlined above are in evidence.

By and large, pieces of property approximately comparable in size, quality, and desirability tend to rent or sell for about the same prices at a given time in a given locality. Also, the rents and sales prices of properties of different sizes, qualities, or degrees of desirability tend to reflect more or less accurately these differences. While the processes by which adjustments take place do not operate as smoothly or as quickly as in the organized exchanges, they do regulate changes affecting real estate; and in a very fundamental sense they help to govern the uses of these resources.

Criteria of an Effective Market

In our preceding discussion we stressed the point that the real estate market corresponds in a general way to the theoretical model of market competition. It is equally important to understand how the real estate market departs from this model. In this connection we need to ask what are the criteria of a good or effective market. Competition can operate more easily if the goods involved are durable and capable of bearing long carriage, if they can be standardized, graded, and bought and sold from samples. Furthermore, a market requires good organization, preferably as a central exchange which is easily accessible to all and where offers to buy and sell can be cleared with a minimum of difficulty.

The more complete the knowledge which buyers and sellers possess of all forces bearing on the market, the more effective market competition becomes. Finally, buyers and sellers must be free from compulsion (as, for example, where some single group dominates the market) if competition is to be effective.

In the model of a competitive market, sellers and buyers are numerous and they are seen as bidding against each other until a price is set at which the market is cleared. The action of any single buyer or seller in this model has only an infinitesimal effect on the market as a whole; but the interactions of all operators taken together create changes in supply, demand, and price. All that any individual buyer can do is to buy or not buy, or buy greater or smaller quantities, as prices change. All that an individual seller can do is to sell or not sell, or sell more or less. If he is a producer, he can produce or not produce, or vary the amount of his production. The quantities supplied will thus be changed and this will affect price.

In the case of some real estate markets, for example, the market for vacant and unimproved land, a single buyer may exercise a significant effect. This is due to the relative "thinness" of the market. A comparable situation is that of stocks traded in limited volume on the over-the-counter securities market.

The real estate market ranks comparatively low in effectiveness among various types of modern markets and contrasts in several ways with the model of a competitive market we outlined above. In the market for agricultural staples like wheat, for example, the conditions mentioned above as essential for a good market are approached rather closely; but they are found only to a limited extent in the real estate market. In general, real properties cannot be graded or bought and sold from samples. Also, dealings in the real estate market take place in terms of an assortment of legal rights which vary in details from case to case. In addition, every transfer of real property involves many papers, documents, and legal formalities.

Functions Performed by the Market

Real estate market operations contribute to the performance of at least three important functions which are essential to satisfactory business and community life. Consideration of these functions is helpful in gaining an understanding of market operations.

First, adjustments must be made to sudden changes in the requirements for space. Thus, rapid changes in the needs for space may result from such things as the establishment (or disestablishment) within a community of a private business or of a governmental agency. When changes in space requirements occur on short notice, as they usually do, it is obviously impossible to expand or contract the supply of buildings simultaneously. When such changes occur only on a temporary basis, expansion or contraction would not be desirable even if it were possible. Hence, the situation calls for apportioning existing quarters in as satisfactory a manner as is possible among all of those who need to use them.

Second, unless changes in land or building requirements are only temporary, the situation calls for expanding or contracting the space available in order to meet the changed conditions. Otherwise the people in the community would be subjected to prolonged inconvenience and economic loss.

A third function which has to be performed relates to land use determination and has as its objective the creation of a proper balance in the development of a community by arranging to have each parcel of land devoted to its most important use in relation to other parcels in the area. The efficiency of a city as an economic and social unit depends largely on the adequacy with which this function is performed in the light of the needs of the community as a whole.

In periods of national emergency, of course, the market allocation of real estate resources is often superseded by laws and regulations. For example, the establishment of rent controls and the rationing of building materials during World War II drastically affected the supply side of the market. As a result, the competitive market forces became largely inoperative and the allocation of real estate resources was undertaken by government authorities.

Market principles assist us in understanding the types of controls that may be used with reasonable chances of success under such conditions, as we shall see in the following discussion.

Ordinarily we are not conscious of the fact that the market has anything to do with the performance of any of the functions outlined above, and because of this we frequently overlook the significance of market forces for business and government policies.

We should recognize that noneconomic factors often play an important role. Some owners, because of sentimental attachment to properties, or for similar reasons, would refuse to sell their properties for almost any price. Also, some real properties are kept off the market because they are tied up in estates or because of title difficulties. Despite factors such as these, the market still manages to perform reasonably well the functions we have outlined.

Short-Run Market Changes

Suppose City A, U.S.A., with a population of around 30,000 families, or about 100,000 people, is selected as the location for a new industry. As a result, suppose that approximately 1,000 families move to City A within a few months. Requirements for both office space and living quarters would expand suddenly. The situation would be complicated by the fact that the success of this industry may not be assured and investors may be unwilling to take the risk of adding new permanent housing facilities. Adjustments would be worked out, however, through market competition.

If a similar situation occurred in City B, located in a controlled society that did not rely on market competition, the processes of adjustment would be quite different. In both cases, it is apparent that the situation would call for a considerable amount of doubling up or crowding together of the prior residents to make room for the newcomers. In City B, this process would be attacked directly by administrative methods. The space would be catalogued and rationed out on some predetermined basis to those who had demands for it. In City A, similar results would be achieved through market competition. Rental levels would move upward to the point where the required adjustments would be made. Many families would be compelled to move to smaller quarters or to double up as rents advanced, thus making space available.

In City A, quarters would be provided for the newly arriving employees of the new industry, in the main, by price-induced crowding together on the part of the prior residents of the city. Some additional office and residential space would be made available by converting storerooms and other space to meet the new requirements, but such increases probably would not be of great importance quantitatively.

Illustration of Short-Run Changes

The various sets of conditions and the adjustments which would take place is illustrated diagrammatically in Figure 6–3.

Curve D_1 represents the character of the requirements (or demand) for residential space as of some moment of time prior to the coming of the new industry. It simply shows the amount of space and other house services that would have been required by the citizenry at all possible levels of rent per unit [4] within the range of rents shown. The dotted curve

---

[4] In drawing a diagram of the sort presented here, which seeks to describe certain features of the market situation for an entire city, one is obliged to reduce all existing and potential building space to comparable units. Definition of such a unit in physical terms is almost impossible, but some such concept must be used in this connection. This diagram and the one immediately following are based on *a priori* considerations and not on direct statistical data. For illustrative purposes, however, they should be helpful.

D_2 shows the new character of requirements for residential space as of some moment of time after the coming of the new industry.[5] Both curves imply that any given group of people under specified conditions would use less space as a result of rent increases.

Curve S reflects the amount of space that would be made available for various purposes within a fairly short period of time (a month or so) at different levels of rent. It will be noted that the curve has practically no elasticity; in other words, under the conditions shown, very little increase in the amount of space and property services available could be expected as a result of an increase in the level of rents.

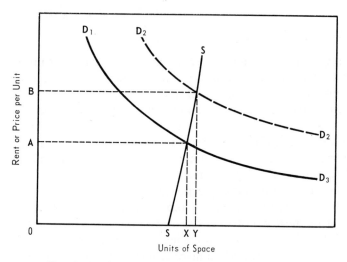

Fig. 6–3. Short-run supply-demand relationships.

If this diagram were drawn to reflect accurately the actual demand and supply conditions in City A at the time, it would indicate the direction toward which average rents would tend to move under each of the two sets of demand conditions stated. Under the conditions existing prior to the advent of the new industry, the rent per unit would tend toward the OA figure; under the conditions reflected by the D_2 curve, rents would tend toward the OB level.[6] At any time, of course, average rents might

---

[5] It is important to note that curves D_1 and D_2 both represent sets of demand conditions *as of a moment of time.* As new families moved to the city and as incomes of families already there increased, a steady day-to-day movement to the right of the actual demand curve undoubtedly took place.

[6] In the conventional language of economics, OA and OB, under the supply conditions represented by curve S, represent the equilibrium prices for the demand conditions represented by curves D_1 and D_2, respectively. They are the prices which, under the conditions specified, will just clear the market.

actually be higher or lower than those points—but, should rents be higher, there would tend to be a higher percentage of vacancies; likewise, if rents were ever to fall lower, demands for space would increase and rents would be raised.[7]

From the illustration it is apparent that when we are interested in knowing what will happen during some short period of time, such as a few months, as a result of a given change in the real estate market, demand forces are the determining factors, since supplies are relatively fixed. Consequently, any short-run analysis of the real estate market requires that demand considerations be given greatest attention. Over longer-run periods this is not the case, as the following discussion will show.

Longer-Run Changes

The second function which the real estate market performs is that of adjusting the available supplies of space to changes in requirements which are expected to be permanent. If a new industry moved into a city, there would be a tendency for rents to move upward, as we noted above. Now, if it became apparent after a year or two that this industry would succeed and remain prosperous for some time, this would provide grounds for expecting the level of rents to continue at a high plane and would give some assurance of higher than average profits to anyone who wished to construct new residential or office buildings in the city.

It is reasonable to expect that considerable building activity would result in areas near the new industry. The rapidity of the response would depend largely on how much the rent per unit in that city exceeded that in other cities. If the rent differential were large, adjustment would presumably be made in a shorter time than if the differential were smaller. (If diagrams are helpful, the supply curve in Fig. 6–3 would be drawn with a less sharply upward slope.)

Variations in the rate at which additional space is made available in a given real estate market depend not only upon variations in the rate of return on capital invested in real properties but also upon variations in the length of time allowed for adjustments to work themselves out. Differences in the rate at which supply may be increased in adjustment periods of different length reflect the fact that as soon as the rate of building in a given market exceeds the normal capacity of local builders and suppliers of materials, increases in that rate are possible only if greater remuneration is offered for those necessary services. Overtime must be compen-

[7] For a more complete discussion of demand, supply, and price relationships, see George W. Zinke, *The American Economy: An Introductory Analysis* (New York: The Ronald Press Co., 1959), chaps. xiv–xvii. See also Paul A. Samuelson, *op. cit.*, chaps. xx, xxi, and xxii.

sated, allowances must be made for lower efficiency of operations, and laborers and tradesmen must be attracted from other cities.

Periods of active building often result in excessive supplies of space. Builders may continue to develop new properties even after demand has started to decline. The vacancy rate then increases and a considerable time may be required for readjustments to be made due to the long life of real properties.[8]

Land Use Determination

In considering the ways in which market forces performed their first two functions, we must not overlook the fact that market competition is one form of social control. Frequently, some government action is necessary to harness the forces of competition, especially in the form of contract enforcement, the maintenance of order, and the counteraction of forces tending toward monopoly. In the performance of its third main function, that of land use determination, the community must rely to a much greater extent on governmental action to direct and regulate the operation of competitive forces than in the case of the rental market.

If we take for granted a particular pattern covering the layout of streets, public transportation routes, boarding points, and the like, it can be said that rents and market prices obtainable for various tracts of land provide the most serviceable indexes of their relative importance to the community as a whole. Within this sphere, market competition, which tends to force land into the uses from which the greatest returns can be secured, affords the most workable device for deciding the alternative uses to which these land resources may be put. We should note that returns cannot necessarily be computed in dollars. In some cases esthetic considerations or sentimental attachments may be major factors in decisions related to land use. Such decisions, however, will also tend to be reflected in the market. While some other qualifications are necessary, such as those arising from a given type of income distribution, it may be said that the use which can pay the most for a given site is the use which will be most advantageous for the community as a whole.

This, of course, is not the whole story. We have assumed a *given pattern* for the street and transportation system. Had the street plan been laid out on another basis or had the main transportation lines and breaking points been located elsewhere, altogether different parcels of land would have commanded the highest prices and rents.

[8] For example, the vacancy rate in Chicago rose from around 2 per cent to 10 per cent between 1928 and 1932. Some 8.5 million square feet of office space was added to Chicago's office building supply between 1923 and 1930 and as a result the market was depressed for twenty years before growth reduced vacancies and moved prices upward.

Modifying Factors

There are certain other factors which interfere with land use determination through competition. In the first place, it may not pay to demolish an existing structure and build another until the present building is in a late period of its economic life. Tax depreciation factors may play a major part in a decision to demolish or not to demolish a structure. Second, and more important, some land uses are very detrimental to adjoining properties. For example, a warehouse located in a residential area might bring great returns on the tract upon which it was built, but it might reduce the value of many near-by properties. The net result might represent a loss in the total property values of the area.

The net loss in a property value from the development of a particular parcel of land in a manner that is out of harmony with the character of the area in which it is located is likely to reflect a diminution in the economic welfare of the entire community. The effects are felt even beyond adjacent tracts of land, since the people who previously were the land users (and any potential users under the prior conditions) are now forced to seek new areas, which in all probability are less desirable than was the original district before the adverse development occurred. Furthermore, the very existence within an area of uncertainties as to whether such adverse developments may occur tends to exert a restraining influence on new investment and to make necessary a higher prospect of return before developments can be expected. For business risks of this type there can be no economic justification, either for private enterprise or for the community at large.

These observations suggest the conclusion that the potentialities of individualistic competition in connection with land use determination can be realized to the fullest extent only if government or private groups act to minimize the dangers and risks arising from the manner in which particular owners may use their properties. This provides the economic justification for zoning, land planning, and private restrictions on land use. Zoning can be economically beneficial or detrimental to a community depending on the extent to which it substitutes certainty for economically unnecessary and unproductive uncertainty. Zoning schemes obviously tend to lose their economic justification if they fail to lay down definite policies expressed in rules simple enough so that they can be generally understood. In other words, uncertainties of all sorts should be minimized —political and governmental as well as other types—and the area left for administrative discretion narrowed as much as possible.

Zoning may result in an uneconomic arrangement of land uses if more land is zoned for industrial or commercial uses than is required. If zoning authorities make use of market surveys, they may be able to adapt the regulations to the needs of the market. It would be desirable to do this without opening the door to unlimited "spot" zoning.[9]

SUMMARY

Real estate prices and rents are the regulators of real estate markets and they interact with supply and demand forces. Both supply and demand forces are influenced by the fact that all real estate is fixed in location. After a property has been developed, its future depends upon its ability to command a market for its services at its given site.

Because of fixity of location, (a) no two parcels of real estate are exactly alike; (b) the income-producing ability of real properties is affected by economic, social, political, and physical changes in the surrounding area; and (c) real estate markets tend to be more localized than markets for other commodities.

The supply of real properties available at any given time is relatively fixed. However, because of possible changes in intensity of use of real properties, the supply of property services tends to be more elastic than the supply of properties themselves.

With supply relatively inelastic, demand factors are the most important determinants of prices and rents in any short-run period. The expected profitability of investment in real estate as compared with investments in other resources is a key determinant of demand for commercial and industrial real estate. For residential real estate, consumer incomes are the most important demand factor. Because of the high unit values of real properties, the terms and availability of credit also play a crucial part in determining the demand for real estate. Population trends and movements do not constitute a demand for real estate unless income prospects are favorable, but population factors may provide clues to future real estate demand when considered in relation to incomes.

Real estate markets perform the major functions of rationing space in the short run, adjusting supplies over the longer run, and land use determination.

---

[9] Although it is not appropriate to discuss in detail here the relation of competitive forces to the problem of the social control of real estate, we should note that an important relationship exists between them. For example, in the case of the third market function which is discussed above, it should be noted that most programs for planning set the balanced and economical development of cities as their major goal. Of course, this goal can be achieved only by getting individual parcels of land assigned to their proper places in a comprehensive and generally satisfactory pattern. From what has been said, it should be apparent that the real estate market contains powerful forces which can be made to do a major part of this work if they are understood and skillfully harnessed.

QUESTIONS FOR STUDY

1. In which respects can it be said that the supply of property services is more flexible than the supply of properties?
2. Indicate the ways in which fixity of location affects the income-producing capacity of real properties.
3. Give illustrations of changing social or political conditions that may affect the value of real properties?
4. Which types of real estate (residential, commercial, industrial, agricultural, etc.) have the broadest market? Which have the most localized market?
5. If personal incomes of consumers were to double, would you expect expenditures on residential real estate to double? Defend your answer.
6. Why is credit an important factor in the demand for real estate? What factors determine the availability of credit for potential purchasers of real properties?
7. In which ways does the value of private properties depend upon the existence of public properties?
8. Why are demand factors more important than supply factors in determining real estate prices and rents in any short-run period?
9. Describe the effect of a growing population on the demand for real estate. How may age distribution be an influence?
10. Why is the market for owner-occupied homes more highly localized than the market for commercial or industrial property?
11. Explain the market process and its value to society. How does the real estate market differ from other types of markets?
12. List and explain the functions performed by real estate markets.
13. Explain this statement: "Competition represents a type of social control, not the absence of control."
14. How does the market serve as a rationer of space?
15. Compare and contrast the allocation of space under competitive market conditions and under administrative regulation.
16. In which ways does the market determine when additions will be made to the supply of real properties or of property services? How does the market determine the amount of such additions?
17. Explain some of the special regulations that are considered necessary to assist the market process in determining land uses.
18. *Study Project 8.* (a) What are the most important economic characteristics of real estate identified in this article? What other economic characteristics of real estate can you identify? (b) Do you agree with this statement by Professor Edwards: "Real estate, as it is known in this country, is not a necessity of life, but a luxury"?
19. *Study Project 9.* (a) How is the scope of the market for a particular type of real estate determined? (b) Is the role of Previews, Inc., as a broker any different from that of the typical broker in your city? Explain. (c) What are the characteristics of the market for the particular type of real estate in which Previews, Inc., specializes?

SUGGESTED READINGS

EDWARDS, EDWARD E. "Real Estate Economics: A Return to Fundamentals," *The Appraisal Journal* (April, 1949). See Study Project 8 in this book.

GRIGSBY, WILLIAM G. *Housing Markets and Public Policy.* Philadelphia: University of Pennsylvania Press, 1963. Chap. ii.

HOYT, HOMER. "Dynamic Factors in Land Values," *Technical Bulletin No. 37.* Washington, D.C.: Urban Land Institute, March, 1965.

REYNOLDS, LLOYD G. *Economics: A General Introduction.* Homewood, Ill.: Richard D. Irwin, Inc., 1963. Chaps. iv–v.

SAMUELSON, PAUL A. *Economics: An Introductory Analysis* (6th ed.). New York: McGraw-Hill Book Co., Inc., 1964. Chap. xix.

WENDT, PAUL F. *Real Estate Appraisal.* New York: Holt, Rinehart & Winston, Inc., 1956. Chap. i.

7

Valuation Principles as Decision Guides

Central Concepts

By this stage in our discussions, we can see the broad outlines at least of our central concepts. It may be helpful to summarize them, recognizing that they are stated here in somewhat oversimplified terms.

1. Income is the fundamental fact of economic life.
2. Like other areas of business administration, the real estate field emphasizes income, but more specifically in this field, the localization of income.
3. Real estate decisions turn largely on factors related to income and income production potentials at fixed locations.
4. Income production potentials can be translated into present values by the discounting process. Real estate values may be thought of as the present worth of future incomes.
5. Estimates of the future income stream that may be produced by a property are based on analyses of:
   a. national and international economic trends
   b. the outlook for specific industries
   c. regional and local economic conditions
   d. markets for various types of real properties and their services as well as the costs of producing such properties and services
   e. the outlook for the neighborhoods and districts of which a property forms a part
   f. the value characteristics of the property itself

135

Study Plans

In this chapter, it is our plan to outline various valuation concepts that may be useful as decision guides. To do this, we review and restate some of the materials that have been presented in the first six chapters as well as adding to these earlier discussions.

In the following chapter, we begin a series of discussions of various types of analyses that may be undertaken to aid the real estate decision-maker. We begin by considering the general subject of value analysis and appraisal methods. This is then followed by a series of discussions of analytical methods related to the topics outlined in point 5 above.

Valuations and Decisions

Real estate decisions often turn on the values of specific properties. Since it is difficult in the real estate field to secure evidences of value such as market prices, it is frequently necessary to make estimates of value. Such estimates of value or valuations or appraisals then become important guides to business and personal as well as to various governmental or institutional decisions in regard to real estate.

The estimate of the value of a property may be the critical factor in deciding whether to proceed with plans to buy, sell, finance, develop, or lease it. Valuations are also helpful in developing programs for implementing real estate decisions.

As we shall see, valuations may be undertaken for a variety of purposes. It may be necessary to determine how much may be realized from a property in terms of a quick sale, what it is worth for lending purposes, or its insurance coverage; or its value in terms of the settlement of an estate; or the development of a program of property improvement; or whether one or another property should be purchased for an expansion program, the relative importance of a property to a business firm's progress, and many other problems may be involved. Thus, valuations form the basis for decisions and programs of action of many types.

Value and Income

In our earlier discussions we emphasized the importance of thinking in terms of the income-producing ability of real properties and the factors that favored or militated against income production at fixed locations. We referred to real properties as "vehicles of productivity." In some cases incomes may be received through the direct consumption of property services, as in the case of an owner-occupied home or a merchant utilizing a store building that he owns. In other cases incomes are in the form of indirect or monetary returns—a landlord collecting rents or an investor receiving dividends or a mortgage lender earning interest on a mortgage.

As we have pointed out, income from real estate is peculiar in that it is produced in fixed locations, and specific properties typically produce income over relatively long periods of time. The present value of anticipated future incomes produced at specific sites is the most logical definition of *real estate value*. The process of reflecting future income in present value is called *capitalization*.

From this standpoint, *income* is of primary importance and *value* is a secondary consideration. Babcock has stated this proposition very effectively:

> The future income stream has been declared to be the most fundamental fact of economic life. It is certainly the very basis of transactions which concern real estate values, and it would appear that future income could hold no other than the basic and fundamental position ascribed to it. If it is true that future income is primary and fundamental, then the value of real estate will have to be granted a secondary position. In this sense *the property actually is the earning expectancy*, and the capitalized figure—the total value—is a derived fact depending upon the future income stream in some manner.[1]

The concept outlined in the above quotation represents the *basic principle* of real estate valuation. It also is the key to understanding real estate analysis, as well as decisions relating to real estate development, marketing, investment, use, management, and financing. The importance of income, and more specifically of income produced at a fixed site and over relatively long periods of time, has been stressed throughout our previous discussions and will be referred to frequently in the chapters that follow.

Babcock goes on to say, ". . . one of the characteristics of earning expectancy is that it can be purchased for a present lump sum, and that the price required to so purchase a future income is proportional to the amount, character, and certainty of the earning expectancy."[2]

Application of the Income Concept

The practical difficulties in applying this principle to actual real estate valuations and related decision problems in the business world are numerous. For example, it has been said by those who are critical of the income approach to valuation problems that the application of the present value concept involves dividing one unknown (the estimated future annual income) by another unknown (the capitalization rate) to arrive at a third unknown (value).

[1] By permission from *The Valuation of Real Estate* by Frederick M. Babcock, p. 129. Copyright, 1932, McGraw-Hill Book Co., Inc., New York. (Italics added.)
[2] *Ibid.*

Thus, if we assume that the annual net income of a particular piece of real property is $1,000 and that the rate necessary to attract investment into properties of this type is 10 per cent, then by dividing $\dfrac{\$1,000}{.10}$, we find that the estimated value of this property on the basis of capitalizing its anticipated income at a 10 per cent rate is $10,000. (In this case income is capitalized in perpetuity; that is, $10,000 now is equal to $1,000 per year forever in terms of a 10 per cent capitalization rate.)

Although it is true that anticipated future incomes can never be known exactly, buyers, sellers, investors, developers, mortgage lenders, appraisers, and others concerned with valuation problems must make the best estimates possible of the future income that a property can produce. Similarly, while the capitalization rate that will exactly reflect future earnings in present value is unknown, an estimated rate can and must be applied. This process is little different from those which are followed in arriving at many other types of business decisions. For example, a new product is available to a manufacturer. He estimates its income-producing ability, estimates the risks involved, and discounts them to the extent that he believes appropriate. On the basis of these estimates he decides to produce and market the new product or to pass it by.

Many business decisions involve similar types of postulates and analyses, notably capital investment decisions. As has been pointed out:

> The situation in which a manager is working will tend to indicate the factors to which he gives greatest weight in arriving at capital investment decisions. For example, he may stress the period of pay-back. It may be important to recapture the investment at an early period. Or he may stress returns per dollar of outlay, without respect to the timing of the return. He may emphasize average annual proceeds per dollar of outlay (that is giving consideration to the number of years and averaging the return per year). The manager may estimate average income on book value of the investment; that is, after depreciation has been charged against the investment. The method considered highly desirable by many managers is the discounted cash flow method; that is, computing the present value of the earnings that will be secured over a period of time.[3]

Factors Affecting Income

In Chapters 4, 5, and 6 we considered some of the factors that affect the income-producing ability of real properties. These included the prop-

---

[3] Arthur M. Weimer, *Business Administration: An Introductory Management Approach* (3d ed.; Homewood, Ill.: Richard D. Irwin, Inc., 1966), pp. 481–82. See also Harold Bierman, Jr., and Seymour Schmidt, *The Capital Budgeting Decision* (New York: The Macmillan Co., 1960), chap. ii; Donald F. Istvan, "The Economic Evaluation of Capital Expenditures," *Journal of Business*, Vol. XXXIV, No. 1, (January, 1961) pp. 45–51; Richard U. Ratcliff, *Modern Real Estate Valuation* (Madison, Wis.: The Democrat Press, 1965), pp. 56–57.

erty itself in terms of its physical characteristics and the legal rights involved. We emphasized the fact that sometimes legal arrangements are such as to interfere seriously with the income-producing capacity of a parcel of real estate. In other cases the legal arrangements may assist the income-production process in a manner that is out of proportion to the physical property. A case in point is a lease negotiated for a high rental for a long period prior to the time that the neighborhood surrounding the property deteriorated sharply.

Similarly, we considered various characteristics of land, buildings, and other improvements in terms of their effect on income-producing ability. We considered the concept of highest and best use, contrasted overimprovements and underimprovements, discussed the effect on income production of the quality and type of building in relation to the land, function, style and attractiveness, and other related factors. Depreciation factors were also discussed.

In addition, we pointed out the importance of governmental and political trends and general economic trends, as well as factors relating to the localization of income including industry analysis, regional and local economic conditions, market factors, and location influences. All of these will affect the income-producing ability of specific real properties. These topics are discussed briefly in the following paragraphs and will be considered in greater detail, along with methods of analyzing such forces, in succeeding chapters.

Governmental and Political Trends

The income earned by specific parcels of real estate is influenced by governmental and political trends and by various regulations and government services. For example, zoning laws regulate the uses to which real estate may be put and the height, bulk, and form of buildings which may be erected. Building codes regulate the quality of workmanship and materials which may be used in constructing improvements. The approval and protection of private property in land, the enforcement of contracts, police and fire protection, provision of water, sewage disposal, health services, provision for transportation facilities, parks, playgrounds, and similar conveniences are all closely related to the income produced by real properties. Rent regulations, financing services, public housing programs, renewal programs, and the like are also important in this connection.

Taxes, special assessments, and other charges and their relationship to services provided should be considered in determining the capacity of real properties to produce incomes. Any probable advance or decline in charges of this type relative to serviecs provided will affect property values. Similarly, private regulations, such as deed restrictions, set certain limits on property uses and hence affect incomes. The activities of property owners' associations, real estate boards, citizens' associations in local neighborhoods, trade-unions in the building field, and other organizations may exert a direct influence on property use and on income-producing ability.

Economic Trends

As we have suggested, levels of business activity have an important effect on the income-producing ability of real properties. Business trends nationally, regionally, and locally, as well as anticipated changes in the level of activity in specific industries, play vital roles in decisions governing the purchase, sale, leasing, financing, use, and development of real estate. When business prospects are generally favorable, decisions are made in an optimistic environment. If business prospects are unfavorable or highly uncertain, the opposite is the case. The analysis of general business conditions is far from a simple process. It is essential, however, that those who are concerned with the income-producing potential of real properties follow closely the major indexes of business activity. These are published in such financial newspapers as the *Wall Street Journal* and such news magazines as *Business Week*. Helpful references include the *Survey of Current Business*, published by the Department of Commerce, the *Federal Reserve Bulletin*, and *Economic Indicators*, published by the Council of Economic Advisers. Analysis of prospects for specific industries, regions, and localities present special problems. Such problems relate to the *localization of income* and the factors in the general economic system, various sectors of the economy, and in local economies that are likely to influence the income production potential of specific properties.

The entire structure of real estate values in a city or local economy depends on the sources of employment and income now available plus others that may become available in the future, as well as on the future prospects of these income sources. The income-producing ability and hence the value of every parcel of real estate in a city depends on the economic opportunities presently available there or new ones that may be added; the flow of income into the locality—the localization of income —is a basic ingredient in real estate values.

Market Forces

Conditions in the real estate market have a major bearing on the incomes of real properties. If the market is active, with rents and selling prices at high levels, it is necessary to determine whether such conditions are likely to continue, the kinds of variations which may be anticipated, and the probable effects of such changes on property incomes. Because the real estate market is not highly organized and because of the nature of real properties, market activity tends to fluctuate between fairly wide levels. These cyclical variations of the real estate market may have different effects on various types of properties. Hence, the process of determining the effect of market variations on the income-producing ability of a specific property is far from simple. For example, if high incomes are anticipated in the near future the effects on value are greater than if the same high levels of income cannot be expected until five years in the future, with relatively low incomes in the intervening period. This results from the fact that the present (capitalized) value of the high incomes received in the near future will be much greater than the present value of similar incomes postponed for a period of time.

Location Factors

The structure of the city and the character of the residential neighborhood or business district surrounding a property have a direct relationship to its income-producing ability.

If a property is located in a part of a city which is not in the main direction of city expansion, its income-producing ability and value may be affected adversely. Similarly, a property located in the path of expanding forces of blight may tend to lose income-producing capacity.

The character of the business district or residential neighborhood in which a property is located exerts an important effect on its capacity for producing income. For example, a sudden change in the character of a neighborhood as a result of the introduction of inharmonious land uses will cause value losses through lowered incomes. Similarly, the character of a business or industrial district will have a direct bearing on the incomes of the properties located there.

Operating Expenses

Operating expenses may rise or fall and thus affect property incomes. Since many operating expenses are relatively fixed, net incomes rise faster than gross incomes when rents advance, and conversely they fall faster when rents go down. This is especially true of planned shopping centers nearby, all of which make use of percentage leases. In general, it may be said that anything which affects the cost of marketing a property or its services will affect income-producing ability. For example, such charges as repairs, decorations, janitor services, insurance, supplies, management fees, taxes, and the like require individual consideration whenever the anticipated income of a property is being estimated.

The Capitalization Rate

As we have pointed out, the value of a property may be considered as equivalent to the present worth of anticipated future incomes. We have considered briefly some of the items which have a bearing on the income-producing capacity of real properties and on the expenses of producing income.

Such future incomes, however, must be capitalized at some rate in order that future earning power may be reflected in present value. The rate which is applied in the case of a specific property will depend on a wide variety of factors, the most important being (1) the current rate of interest, and (2) the amount of risk.

The rate of interest is not the capitalization rate. Theoretically, the term *interest* is used to designate a return on capital which does not include compensation for risk, management, or other costs. That is to say, pure interest is riskless interest. The return on government bonds is the closest approximation to riskless interest which can be cited. Such rates vary from time to time. To this basic interest rate we must add an allowance for various risks in arriving at a capitalization rate. Such risks will vary from property to property. Incomes from properties with prospects for stable, continued returns are capitalized at low rates; those with great risks, at higher rates. Such factors as marketability of property, changes in business conditions, investment preferences, and the like are important risk elements. Also, in some cases allowances are made in the capitalization rate for the management of the investment.[4]

Utility and Scarcity

Economists tell us that real estate, like other commodities, is valuable in proportion to its utility and scarcity. As an interesting case in point, consider the houses in one of the old western ghost towns. Many of these towns were established originally at points where new mineral deposits were discovered. People flocked there in the hope of amassing wealth. Real estate values of course rose rapidly. When the mineral deposits were exhausted, people moved on, leaving ghost towns to mark their earlier hopes. As a consequence, the real estate there became worthless because it no longer served a useful purpose and it was available in greater quantities than the demands for it.

As a general rule, people will demand things which are important to them. However, what is important tends to change over the years. The

[4] For more detailed discussions of capitalization see Sanders A. Kahn, Fred E. Case, and Alfred Schimmel, *Real Estate Appraisal and Investment* (New York: The Ronald Press Co., 1963), Chap. x.

modern supermarket might have faced early bankruptcy a generation ago. A few decades ago people demanded kinds of housing facilities which are not wanted today. Some of our modern homes with their low ceilings and compact arrangements might have been drugs on the real estate market two generations ago when houses with large rooms and high ceilings were preferred.

Even at the same time, housing means different things to different people. To some it is simply a matter of shelter and protection. Others consider housing in terms of social status, as a form of investment, or as a sentimental association with family history. In other words, what people demand in housing or other real estate, as well as in other things, depends on their standards and objectives. Similarly, their standards and objectives will determine the amounts of time, effort, and materials which they are willing to spend in order to satisfy their demands.

These standards are determined in part by custom, institutions, attitudes, technical knowledge, and social organization. The fertile prairies of Illinois, for example, had relatively less value to the Winnebago Indians than to the farmers of today. Even to the early pioneers these prairies had little value because of their crude plows. Improved plows later helped to make this land very valuable, thus reflecting the influence of technology.

Similarly, individual standards and objectives will have a bearing on the decision of a business firm, an individual, or a family regarding expenditures for properties or property services in relation to other needs. For example, the value of a home cannot be measured altogether in terms of what it will bring in the market. It may have a high subjective value to the family living in it, even though it might command a relatively low price on the market in case of sale. By contrast, the value of an office building is likely to depend almost entirely on the rents which it will command in the market.

Thus the value of real estate, like the value of other things, depends on its relative utility and scarcity. But the measure of utility and scarcity must be established in terms of the standards or objectives of the individuals, business firms, and communities involved. The term *value*, like the term *economy*, has little meaning unless considered in relation to community and individual standards and objectives.

Value and Price

To the nation as a whole, value is a matter of the comparative importance to its citizens of the different things, including real estate, that are essential to its welfare according to its standards, but that do not exist in sufficient quantities to meet the demands for them. To the individual citizen, concerned primarily with his own stake in the community, the value of a parcel of real estate depends fundamentally on how much of other things or the services of other things or persons he can get in exchange for a piece of real estate or the services which it renders. In practice, the relative importance of real estate is reflected in prices, which are values translated into monetary terms, such as dollars, pounds, or whatever monetary unit is commonly used. Frank H. Knight writes: "Since price is always the price of something and is a quantity or number, it is natural to think of it as the measure of some quality or attribute in the thing which bears a price. This quality or attribute measured by price is the simplest conception of value." [5]

Because the market for real estate is not highly organized, the prices paid for real properties may not coincide with their values at any specific time. Price and value will tend to be identical under conditions of perfect or near-perfect market competition. In such cases the full play of all forces having a bearing on the market results in prices which reflect with reasonable accuracy the values of the commodities involved.

Value and Cost

It is usually because costs must be borne in order to bring goods and services into the market that such goods and services are scarce relative to the demands made on them. In the case of real estate, the costs of new developments are usually substantial. Costs must be borne in order to acquire a lot and hold it until it is ripe for development. The cost of constructing a building and other improvements typically involves a relatively large sum. Costs of development and building are not undertaken unless the owner or developer believes that the returns will be sufficient to warrant the costs including those of bearing the risks incurred. Thus, when property prices or rents are high relative to costs of construction and land costs, there will be a tendency for people to build. When costs are high relative to prices or rents, very little or no construction will take place. Hence, we may say that costs affect values and prices only as they affect supply. Over long-run periods there is a tendency for costs and values to coincide, but at any given time costs may be far above or far below values as reflected in selling prices or rents.

The mere fact that a total of $25,000 was spent to buy land and build a house does not necessarily have a connection with the value of the property. It *may* have a bearing on value, and it will be one of the facts which will concern an appraiser. However, such costs are important only

[5] Frank H. Knight, "Value and Price," *Encyclopedia of the Social Sciences* (New York: The Macmillan Co., 1930), Vol. XV, p. 218. By permission of The Macmillan Co.

at the time that actual construction takes place. They are then price *determining* costs. Once completed, the building remains for a relatively long period of time and limits the possible uses which can be made of the land. Hence after the completion of the building production costs are passive factors. The investment originally made in the property is a "sunk" cost.

Babcock makes an interesting observation in this connection:

A standard illustration . . . is the one which assumes a 30-story hotel to have been built in a remote and inaccessible spot in a desert. It is self-evident that the building is not worth an amount represented by the investment which would be required to replace it. There is rarely, in fact, any connection between the cost of replacement of a building and its value. The notable exception and the only exception is the case of the building just completed which represents the highest and best use of its site. In the latter case a building is worth precisely its cost of replacement. However, its value at any future time may not bear any relation to either its replacement or original cost of construction.[6]

Depreciation and Obsolescence

Buildings and the equipment in them wear out over time. This usually takes place gradually. This process is referred to as *depreciation,* as we noted in Chapter 4. The term *depletion* is used to describe the using up of a natural asset and is most commonly used in the case of oil wells.

Loss of value not only results from wear and tear but from the development of more and better buildings and equipment and from general economic changes. We typically use the term *obsolescence* to describe this process. Obsolescence, as we have seen, may be functional or economic, the former relating to conditions within a property, the latter to external changes. Physically a building may be in excellent condition but will lose value if another building (usually a newer one, but the time difference may not be great) performs the same function more efficiently or more attractively.

In recent years as rates of change have accelerated, value losses from obsolescence have grown increasingly important. Higher discount rates are required in connection with many real estate decisions in order to reflect higher risks of obsolescence.

"Value Is a Word of Many Meanings"

The foregoing discussion emphasizes the validity of Justice Brandeis' remark, "Value is a word of many meanings." There is much confusion about the meaning of value because the term has been interpreted in so many ways. By thinking in terms of income, and the present worth of

[6] Babcock, *op. cit.,* p. 36.

future income, you may minimize some of these difficulties. Nevertheless, you will be drawn into arguments frequently because of the wide differences of meaning ascribed to the term *value*.

Economists tend to identify value with *market price*, provided that the price is set in a free market in which really competitive conditions exist. Appraisers tend to identify value with *warranted selling price*, or the price that a willing buyer would offer and a willing seller would accept, neither acting under compulsion. This concept is not far removed from that of the economist. Ratcliff stresses the "most probable selling price" of a property.[7] However, the courts have interpreted value in such a wide variety of ways that no single definition can be made to fit the many cases involved.

Appraisers sometimes make estimates of upper and lower limits of value. This enables them to deal with situations in which the purpose of the valuation is not stated or is not clear.

Appraisers have resolved this difficulty in part at least by raising the question, "Value for what purpose?" As we pointed out earlier, the term *economy* can have little meaning without reference to an objective. The same thing is true of the term *value*. For example, the value of the same property at the same time for one purpose may be quite different from its value for another purpose, as we shall see in the following discussion.

Is There "One True Value"?

The idea that a property should have "One true value" probably is a direct descendant of the medieval concept of "just price." The medieval church fathers argued that there was a "just price" for every commodity and that sellers should not ask more than this amount. Like many other concepts, this idea has come down to us in modified form, and today we hear about "fair price" or "reasonable price," terms which contain some of the connotations of the idea of "one true value." If one attempts to define what is "fair" or "reasonable," he soon finds it necessary to establish criteria or objectives against which he can measure. Similarly, value or "true value" cannot be defined except in relation to some standard. In part this is a reflection of the general standards of the community, but more specifically value is likely to be considered with respect to purpose or objective. Hence, an appraiser can only with considerable difficulty answer such a question as, "What is the value of the X property?" He answers most directly if he finds the answer to the question, "Value—for what purpose?" Difficult practical problems often arise if a client declines to reveal the purpose of a valuation to an appraiser.

[7] Ratcliff, *op. cit.*, chap. iii.

Appraisers sometimes make estimates of upper and lower limits of value. This enables them to deal with situations in which the purpose of the valuation is not stated or clear.

If the future income of a property could be predicted accurately, and if a sufficiently broad market for real estate existed, there would be less difficulty in solving value problems and less controversy about the question of "one true value." Valuations are affected by differences of opinion regarding future trends, the relative inefficiency of real estate markets, and variations in the availability of money for investment in real estate. If the property must be sold quickly for cash, a buyer must be found who can raise the required cash in a short time; and the price will be lower than if more time is available to find more buyers or to arrange favorable financing terms. If the property is being purchased for a long-term investment, the future income stream becomes the most important consideration.

If the property is being valued for taxation purposes, where uniformity is the main consideration, its comparability in value with other similar properties rather than the total value is the chief concern. In tax assessments it does not matter particularly whether all properties are assessed at 40 or 80 per cent of market price or cost, provided all are valued on the same basis. Here market price or cost is used, however, as a means of insuring uniformity rather than as a measure of value.

Valuation for mortgage loan purposes emphasizes safety of the loan, and may often result in values that are below market or sales price. In rate-making cases, such as for public utility regulation, where a return is allowed on the original investment, cost less depreciation may become the most important factor in valuation. Terms of the sale often are important. Properties sold with low down payments usually command a higher selling price than those sold for heavy cash payments, because the market is broader in the former case.

Plottage Value

If a city zoning ordinance requires that detached homes have a frontage of 60 feet, a single 30-foot lot would have little or no value, but if two 30-foot lots were joined together they would have a greater value than the sum of the two lots as separate units. This increase of value obtained by combining a number of lots into a larger tract is known as *plottage* value as we have seen. Value increases in such cases until the assembled tract is large enough for the maximum utilization of the site.

Recent changes in land uses have increased the size of plots necessary for the highest and best use of land. Thus tenements in New York City were once built on 20-foot lots. Later a frontage of 100 feet was considered necessary for an apartment building. Now it is considered desirable to acquire a number of blocks for one project so that streets can be closed, and the buildings placed on the basis of 25 per cent land coverage, oriented so that they will have the best view, and provided with the maximum light and air.

Department stores have found that plottage value can be obtained by acquiring an entire block so that the values of the main street are carried over to the side street. Rockefeller Center in New York City obtained a plottage value by erecting a series of buildings on a tract of several blocks, which permitted open plazas and yielded higher rents for the office space than buildings with 100 per cent land coverage.

Factories gain plottage value from combining several blocks, which permits more efficient layout of the plant and which avoids congestion of city traffic and policing of factory buildings on every side. Retail stores achieve plottage value by combining several tracts of land, which permits automobile parking near the store. The planning of complete communities of many acres and even many square miles is another case in point.

Plottage value can be secured by acquiring all of the lots in an old subdivision that had been planned with narrow lots and an obsolete street layout. Single ownership allows for the replatting of the subdivision according to the best planning standards. Similarly, plottage value is provided through the public acquisition of land for redevelopment purposes.

The power of condemnation is often necessary in order to assemble a large number of parcels at reasonable cost, because the owners of the last remaining parcels will usually demand a price so high as to defeat the entire project. Sometimes private firms assembling a tract will pay a nuisance value for one single parcel if it is in the middle of the proposed development, but if it is on the edge, development can often proceed without it.

Valuation Methods

The principal methods of evaluating or appraising real estate are: (1) capitalizing estimated future income, known as the income method; (2) determining cost of replacement, known as the cost method; and (3) comparing properties as to prices, rents, or other market data available, known as the market method. These methods are discussed in greater detail in the next chapter.

The capitalization of expected future annual income is the most conclusive method of real estate valuation. It is particularly applicable in the case of apartment buildings, retail store property, office buildings, and other income-bearing property. Such properties are often bought for investment purposes. Mining properties are also valued on the basis of a capitalization of their net income, allowing for depletion.

Single-family houses are not ordinarily purchased for an investment; and new homes, if rented, do not ordinarily yield a return on the purchase price comparable to commercial properties. Families buy houses partly as consumption goods. The value of a house can be established mainly by comparable sales, that is, by a comparison with the selling prices of other houses similar in size, quality of construction, and neighborhood. In the case of new houses market price is reflected by the current cost of construction (plus profit if any) and the price of the improved lot.

Vacant land in metropolitan areas on the edges of cities is valued by estimating the net income on the land that will be returned by the type of buildings for which it is suited, discounted for the waiting period that must elapse before it comes into use.

Factory buildings and such specialty buildings as hotels and theatres derive their value by their utility as part of a business enterprise. They are seldom sold in the market and are usually valued on the basis of reproduction cost less depreciation. Specialized buildings may become obsolete or suffer a great decline in value if the industry originally constructing them finds it no longer profitable to operate them.

The range in valuation estimates made by different appraisers for the same property varies according to the type of property. In the valuation of new single-family homes, when numerous houses of the same type are being offered for sale in similar neighborhoods, valuations made by various appraisers will be in substantial agreement. Also, in the case of income properties, particularly those on long-term leaseholds, when the tenant has triple-A credit, there will not be a great variation in different valuation estimates.

On the other hand, there can be a wide divergence in the valuation of vacant land on the edge of a growing city, because of differences of opinion as to the type of future land use and the length of time before the land will become income-bearing property. As soon as the use is determined by zoning and the land is ready for the building of houses of a given value, or for the erection of stores or factories, its value can be more accurately estimated. There can also be a wide range of estimates on the value of highly specialized buildings that are no longer suitable for the purpose for which they were originally constructed.

There appears to have been more concern about appraisal methods in recent years than with the theoretical basis on which sound appraisals may be made.[8]

[8] Paul F. Wendt, *Real Estate Appraisal* (New York: Holt, Rinehart & Winston, Inc., 1956), p. 40. See also Richard U. Ratcliff, "A Restatement of Appraisal Theory," *The Appraisal Journal* (January, 1964), pp. 51–57, and his *Modern Real Estate Valuation.*

Although theoretical concepts have not changed a great deal, except for some refinements, more elaborate sets of relationships can now be developed in a practical manner through the use of the computer. It should be recognized also that major changes have occurred that complicate the application of various value theories and principles. For example, the old depth and corner influence concepts have little or no applicability for the modern regional shopping center. Recognition must be given to the increasing importance of governmental influences, ranging all the way from farm price supports, transportation developments, and zoning laws to general federal programs for the maintenance of long-term prosperity.

We should recognize that appraisal methods are tools only. Unless they fit into a theoretically sound framework, they may lead to questionable results even if applied with care. Although the concept stressed by Babcock that the *property is the earning expectancy* often has been criticized by practicing appraisers, no other satisfactory basis for valuation has been advanced. Indeed, this concept is being applied more extensively over a wide range of situations as, for example, in connection with other forms of capital investment as mentioned earlier in this chapter.

Factors Modifying Value Estimates

Acceptance of the concept that value is directly related to the present worth of future income does not mean, as some seem to infer, that all appraisals must be made by the income method. Because of specific purposes as defined in the appraisal assignment, the nature of the income, or the absence or inadequacy of data, it may be impossible in many practical situations to use the income method. This does not alter the basic nature of the appraiser's task. Regardless of method used, he is attempting to determine the value of the earning expectancy. Most real estate decisions will be related to earnings but important modifying factors may be present.

It is often necessary to use sales prices of comparable properties as the basis of valuations and decisions since data may not be available on which estimates of the size or duration of a future income stream can be made. Sales prices of comparable properties, however, indicate what buyers and sellers in the current market believe the present value of that income stream to be.

For example, in the case of vacant land that appears to have potential use for urban sites, it is difficult to know how much time must elapse before the land is ripe for development and, when it is, what type of use may be indicated by market demand or permitted by the zoning regulations that will then be in force. Sales prices often are helpful guides even when data regarding future income are available. Two properties may be yielding the same net income currently, but one of them may be located in a declining area or be facing stiffer competition in the future than the other. Sales prices will indicate the current estimates of buyers and sellers of the differential between such properties.

Construction and development costs are important elements in the valuation of real properties and in decisions regarding them. They enter directly into the valuations of new properties and indirectly into value estimates of older properties. The owner of a vacant urban site can only secure a stream of income from the land, except in the case of parking lots or similar uses, by constructing a building and other improvements on it. If the building is constructed in an area where there is no demand for its services, or the demand is very limited or operating costs are too high for the income produced, the land may have a zero or even a negative income.

Properties located in declining areas present special problems because of the difficulty of estimating rate of decline, possibility of renewal efforts, and other uncertainties. Market prices of comparable properties often are helpful in the valuations of such properties since they reflect the opinions of buyers and sellers in regard to such uncertainties.

The type of property may pose special valuation and decision problems. For example, the value of a public building such as a library can seldom be estimated either on the basis of income or market prices. The only data available in such cases usually are those related to costs. Hence, valuations, of necessity, are based on such data.

Cash flow may be an important element in real estate decisions and may influence significantly what potential buyers and sellers are willing to offer or accept for a property. Cash flow is the amount of money available after deducting (1) operating expenses, including real estate taxes, and (2) payments on the principal and interest of the mortgage. Thus, cash flow is not equivalent to the net income of the property because the cash flow can be increased by securing long-term mortgage financing with low payments on the principal. Those properties that yield an immediate cash flow that is larger than normal often are attractive to investors.

Also, some real properties may be attractive to investors because depreciation allowances are favorable and depreciation is deductible from federal and state income taxes. After a property is fully depreciated (as rapidly as tax regulations will allow, usually ten years or more), it may become desirable to sell it to a new owner, who can start the depreciation charges all over again (and at as high a rate as allowable).

Elements of Valuation

Although it is impossible to reduce to a few simple statements the elements of valuation, the following points may help in summarizing some of the ideas and concepts that have been presented in our discussion.

1. Valuations and the analyses necessary to reach them are of major importance in real estate decisions and in developing programs of action to implement decisions.
2. The study of valuation, as is true of nearly all real estate topics, is essentially a study of income and, more specifically, income produced at a fixed site and over long periods of time.
3. "The property is the *earning expectancy*."
4. The legal property is important from the standpoint of the influence of ownership and other rights on the income-producing capacity of the real estate.
5. The physical property is the vehicle of productivity. It is important only in terms of its income-producing potential. It may be thought of as a machine producing property services over the remainder of its economic life.
6. Economic life is typically shorter than physical life.
7. Depreciation may be thought of as loss of value from (a) deterioration, that is, wear and tear over time, and (b) obsolescence, including functional and economic factors.
8. Value depends on purpose or objective. "Value is a word of many meanings." Like the term *economy*, it has greatest significance when related to purpose. Otherwise, appraisers may find it necessary to report upper and lower limits of value.
9. Future income can be bought for a present lump sum. The present sum represents the discounted value of future earnings. This amount may ordinarily be thought of as the value of the property. It is secondary to income.
10. Future income is less valuable than present income; the longer income is postponed, the smaller is its value at present.
11. The process of reflecting future income in present value is called *capitalization*.
12. Property values reflect the standards and attitudes of the buyers, sellers, owners, users, and investors in properties. These standards and attitudes change gradually over a period of time, and vary somewhat from region to region and country to country.
13. Gross incomes and costs and, hence, net incomes are affected by business conditions, by governmental and regulatory factors, by market conditions and changes, and by location factors.
14. Value will be identical with price under conditions of effective market competition, but may be greater or lower than price, depending on current market conditions.

15. Value may be identical with, or greater or less than, cost. Over long-run periods, costs and values will tend to coincide. In short-run periods, there may be wide variations between them.
16. The principal approaches to valuation problems are the income method, the cost approach, and the market method (see Chapter 8).

SUMMARY

This chapter outlines various valuation principles that may be used as real estate decision guides. The view is presented that there is no one true value. The value of a parcel of real estate varies with the purpose of the valuation. The sixteen points listed above provide a useful summary of the important elements of valuation.

The valuation of real property facilitates real estate decision-making since it involves the analysis of factors bearing on income-producing ability. Value, for most purposes, essentially is a derivative of income-producing ability.

As it is future income that is relevant for valuation purposes, valuation methods have been developed in an attempt to aid in the determination of the best estimate of the present value of future incomes. Specific methods of valuation are discussed in the next chapter.

QUESTIONS FOR STUDY

1. What is meant by the expression "The property is the earning expectancy"?
2. Assume that a property earns $20,000 per year. What will be its value at a capitalization rate of 7 per cent? How will its value be changed if the capitalization rate is increased from 7 to 8 per cent? How will the value be changed if the capitalization rate is dropped from 7 to 6 per cent?
3. Explain why capitalized value of income in the near future will be greater than capitalized value of similar incomes postponed for a period of time. Using the Capitalization Tables in Appendix C, provide an example for your explanation.
4. Explain the term "plottage value," and give an example.
5. Why should obsolescence affect the discount rate used in connection with a real estate decision?
6. Is a property always worth its cost of production? Why or why not?
7. What is meant by the statement "Over long periods, costs and values will tend to coincide"? How does this occur?
8. Why might a broader market for real estate and real estate services make it easier to estimate property values?
9. Do the operating expenses for a property have an effect on the value of that property? Explain your answer.
10. Assume that you are considering the purchase of an office building tenanted exclusively by physicians and dentists. The building has been

yielding a net annual return of $55,000. How would you determine the appropriate capitalization rate to use in the valuation of this property?

11. Evaluate this statement: "Any factor that affects the income-producing ability of a property likewise affects its value in the same direction."

12. Should cash flow be an influence in valuing property?

13. What is meant by "capitalizing in perpetuity"?

14. Mr. Beckworth was the owner of a first-class hotel in a small town. The hotel was constructed in 1952 at a cost of more than $700,000. The hotel never has earned more than 2 per cent on this investment; and average earnings have been approximately 1.5 per cent since the hotel was built. Mr. Beckworth recently died and left the hotel to his heirs. In order to settle the estate, a valuation of the hotel is needed, and you have been asked to testify as an expert appraiser regarding the value of the hotel. One of the heirs contends that it must be worth about $700,000 considering the original cost and rising property values since that time. What reasons can you give for agreeing or disagreeing with his contention? What method would you use to value the hotel?

15. (a) You are offered a piece of property for $5,000 cash and $1,000 at the end of each year for five years. What is the equivalent cash price if you use a 5 per cent discount rate? (b) You are offered a piece of property for $10,600, or for $7,000 cash and payments of $2,000 at the end of each year for two years. If you could invest your $4,000 at 4 per cent or pay cash for the property, which would you choose? (c) You are offered a piece of property for $4,000 cash and $1,000 at the end of each year for five years. What is the equivalent cash price if you use a discount rate of 6 per cent? 10 per cent?

SUGGESTED READINGS

BABCOCK, FREDERICK M. *The Valuation of Real Estate.* New York: McGraw-Hill Book Co., Inc., 1932. Chaps. xii–xiv.

BIERMAN, HAROLD, JR. and SEYMOUR SCHMIDT. *The Capital Budgeting Decision.* New York: The Macmillan Co., 1960. Chap. ii.

HOYT, HOMER. "Application of the Three Appraisal Approaches to Different Types of Real Estate," *The Appraisal Journal* (July, 1964).

KAHN, SANDERS A., FRED E. CASE, and ALFRED SCHIMMEL. *Real Estate Appraisal and Investment.* New York: The Ronald Press Co., 1963. Chap. x.

RATCLIFF, RICHARD U. *Modern Real Estate Valuation.* Madison, Wis.: The Democrat Press, 1965. Chaps. i–iii.

WENDT, PAUL F. *Real Estate Appraisal.* New York: Holt, Rinehart & Winston, Inc., 1956. Chaps. i–ii.

II

ANALYSIS FOR REAL ESTATE DECISIONS

8

Value Analysis and
Appraising Methods

Valuations as Aids to Decisions

In this chapter, we emphasize appraisal methods. We may think of them as methods of value analysis, as ways of arriving at value estimates that may serve as decision guides. As we have suggested, valuations or appraisals are important aids to real estate decisions. They provide one of the bases, and often the determining one, for reaching real estate decisions and for developing programs of action for implementing such decisions.

Thus, valuations are not usually ends in themselves. Appraisers do not make decisions. They provide information and forecasts which may aid business executives, government officials, or individuals in arriving at better conclusions and decisions than might otherwise be possible. If a mortgage lender asks an appraiser to estimate the value of a property for mortgage lending purposes, it is not the function of the appraiser to decide on the merit of the specific mortgage arrangement that the lender has under consideration. An appraiser may help a seller to decide how much to ask for a piece of property or a buyer to decide how much to offer, but the appraiser does not make the final decision.

Because of this, it is sometimes argued that the appraiser need not know the purpose of the valuation he is asked to make. If we could find some uniform basis for all appraisals, this might be the case. In view of the many different interpretations of value, however, it is almost impossible for an appraiser to proceed without such knowledge.

Defining Valuation Problems

Thus, the *purpose* for which a valuation is made is of basic importance, not only in defining value, but also in defining valuation problems. Other conditions that are of importance in defining valuation problems include *time* and the identification of the specific *property rights* involved.

In a general sense the function of the appraiser may be thought of as that of estimating the present value of the income potential of a given site. Specific situations, however, may require that he estimate the current market value of the property; the price that may be obtained in a quick sale; the price that a prospective buyer should offer for the property or a partial interest in a property; and the value of the property for insurance purposes, for mortgage lending purposes, for damages suffered under condemnation proceedings, or for the solution of many other business or personal problems. Thus, definition of the specific valuation problem to be solved is an essential first step in the process of making an appraisal of a piece of real property.

For example, Ratcliff has suggested that real estate transactions may be classified in the following ways and that this classification indicates the nature of the appraisal problem that is involved:

1. Transfer of ownership
   a. Sale
   b. Purchase
   c. Trade
2. Extension of credit secured by real estate
3. Compensation for damage or loss
   a. Through condemnation
   b. For damage compensable under property insurance contract
4. Taxation
   a. Assessment for property tax
   b. Basis for depreciation allowance
   c. Basis for inheritance tax
5. Selection of a program of utilization.[1]

The definition of the problem includes an identification of the *specific property rights* involved. As we indicated in Chapter 5, a wide variety of interests may exist in the same piece of real estate. Usually the appraiser estimates the value of *specified property rights* rather than the value of the physical land and buildings. He may be called upon to determine the reversionary right in a leasehold, the value to a tenant of a lease, the air rights over a piece of land, the value of an easement, and

[1] Richard U. Ratcliff, "A Restatement of Appraisal Theory," Chapter II, "The Economic Function of Appraisal," *The Appraisal Journal* (January, 1964), p. 59.

many other types of interests. The American Institute of Real Estate Appraisers points out:

> Since the value of real property does not solely reside in the physical land and the improvements, the appraiser cannot define his problem precisely until he knows exactly what property rights are involved.[2]

Time is another important element in defining appraisal problems. In some cases the appraisal requires that a value estimate be made as of some specified date in the past, rather than in terms of the current date. Such situations often arise in the case of tax problems or valuation for the purpose of settling estates. It may be necessary to estimate value as of some future date as well.

Appraising Methods

Professional appraisers have developed three principal (or "classic") [3] approaches to valuation problems:

1. Capitalizing estimated income
2. Determining cost of replacement
3. Comparing properties on the basis of the market data available

As we have suggested, the first of these approaches fits best the logic of valuation theory, since all property value is derived from future income, whether such income is in the form of monetary returns or results from the direct use of the property. (The latter are sometimes called *amenity returns* in connection with residential property.) In many cases, however, there are practical difficulties in using the capitalized income method. For example, if you have occupied your own home for a number of years, it may be easier to make an appraisal by the *market data* or *comparative method* than by capitalizing an estimated future income. Again, the appraisal of a public building requires almost inevitably the use of the *replacement cost method*, since neither income estimates nor comparable sales prices are likely to be available. In some cases (except for single-family owner-occupied homes) all three approaches are used in order that one result may be compared with another.

Regardless of the method used, however, the appraiser must always consider the purpose of the valuation, the property interest represented, and the time at which the appraisal is to apply. In almost all cases he will

---

[2] *The Appraisal of Real Estate* (4th ed.; Chicago: American Institute of Real Estate Appraisers, 1964), pp. 53–54.

[3] See Sanders A. Kahn, Fred E. Case, and Alfred Schimmel, *Real Estate Appraisal and Investment* (New York: The Ronald Press Co., 1963), chap. vii. For an interesting view see Richard U. Ratcliff, "A Neoteric View of the Appraisal Function," *The Appraisal Journal* (April, 1965); and his *Modern Real Estate Valuation* (Madison: Wis.: The Democrat Press, 1965).

Types of Incomes from Real Properties and Valuation Methods

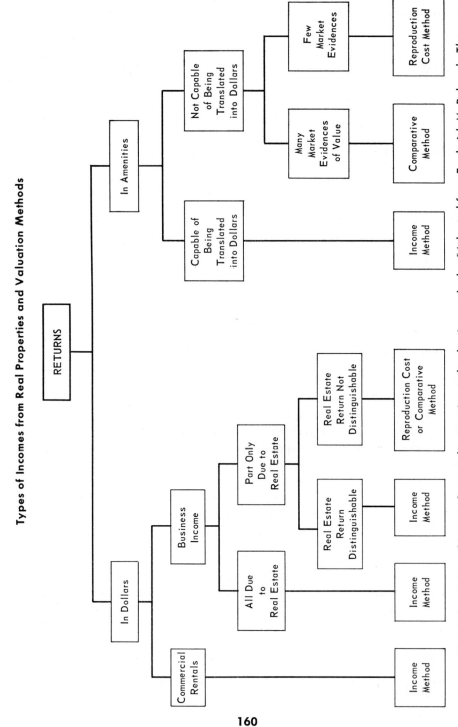

Fig. 8-1. Types of income from real properties and valuation methods. [Adapted from Frederick M. Babcock, *The Valuation of Real Estate* (New York: McGraw-Hill Book Co., Inc., 1932), p. 184.]

find it essential to think in terms of the income-producing ability of a property even though he is employing the market data or cost method in his work. Obviously, the costs of developing a site and constructing a building would not ordinarily be undertaken unless anticipated monetary or direct returns were expected to exceed such costs. Similarly, prices, rents, and other pertinent market data reflect more or less accurately the market's estimate of future income-producing capacity of properties.

Selection of Method

Three principal factors will guide an appraiser in his selection of the appraising method to be used for a specific case. Whether he selects the capitalized income, the market data, or the replacement cost method will depend on (1) the purpose of the valuation, (2) the type of income produced by the property or assumed to be produced under the use program that is projected, and (3) the kinds of data available for use.

In some cases the appraisal problem is stated in terms which specify the method to be followed. For example, an appraiser may be asked to determine the present value of a lease, which clearly indicates the use of the income method, or he may be asked to report the price which could be obtained for a property in a quick sale, which would require the use of the market data method.

If the purpose does not define method, consideration is given to the type of income produced or assumed to be produced by the property. As has been suggested, two principal kinds of returns may be considered: (1) dollars, and (2) direct returns resulting from the use of the property by the owner.[4] Babcock has pointed out that type of income may aid in selection of the appropriate appraisal method. If income is in dollars, it may be derived from several sources, the two main types being commercial rents and business profits. If the property earns commercial rents, the method of capitalizing income is indicated. If business profits are involved, they may be due entirely to the real estate or partly to the real estate and partly to the business enterprise. If profits are all due to real estate, the capitalized income method is preferred. To the extent that returns to the real estate and the business enterprise can be distinguished, the income method is considered preferable. However, if the returns on real estate cannot be distinguished from other returns, as in the case of a foundry or a railroad terminal, the replacement cost method is used.

If returns are in the form of direct use of the property, the income method may be used if such returns can be translated rather accurately into dollars. If, on the other hand, returns from direct use cannot be

[4] Frederick M. Babcock, *The Valuation of Real Estate* (New York: McGraw-Hill Book Co., Inc., 1932), p. 184.

translated into dollars, the selection of methods hinges on the extent to which market data are available. If there are sufficient market evidences of value, as in the case of comparable properties, the market data or comparative method should be selected. This is often the case in appraising a single-family owner-occupied residence. However, if there are few or no data available indicating market prices or rents for comparable properties, the replacement cost method is followed of necessity. Typical illustrations of this situation are provided by the problems of appraising a library or a government building. (See Fig. 8–1 illustrating the relationship of type of income to method.)

As we have already indicated above, the availability of data sometimes dictates the choice of appraisal method. While decisions based on the availability of information may not always be logical, there are times when the appraiser has no alternative. Cases such as a public library, a government building, hospital, a school, a grain elevator, an unused factory building, or a museum are likely to present data problems.

As we have pointed out, the appraisal method must be adapted to the type of property and the purpose of the appraisal. For example, in the case of a large department store on a principal corner of an eastern city, the lot was owned by the store, and the property and the business were parts of a total unit. The building was suited for only one purpose, that of a department store. The valuation was derived by capitalizing the percentage of sales the department store could afford to pay as rent. On the other hand, in valuing the property on the opposite corner, occupied by an obsolete bank building, the valuation was determined by ascertaining the net rentals that could be obtained from stores on that corner and capitalizing these rentals. That is, an assumed use program was set up. The building in this case was regarded as of no value in appraising a site on the best retail corner in the city, because it had to be wrecked to make way for the new stores from which the highest rent could be obtained.

Steps in the Income Method

The capitalization of anticipated incomes requires that estimates of revenues and expenses be made and that the estimated net income before depreciation be capitalized at an appropriate rate. While the procedures of appraisers vary somewhat, the three main steps usually involved in the process are these:

First, gross income is estimated by computing the total possible income at 100 per cent occupancy of the building and deducting for vacancies and collection losses.

In the second step in the capitalization of anticipated incomes, operating expenses are estimated, including allowances for replacement of certain items of equipment and the like.

The third step in the use of the income method is capitalizing the net income resulting from the deduction of estimated operating expenses from gross effective earnings by applying the appropriate capitalization rate or rates. This phase of the process is not simple, even when net income is capitalized in perpetuity. The selection of an appropriate capitalization rate usually means the difference between a sound and an unsound appraisal in such cases. Even more complicated problems arise if a split rate is used, with the application of one rate to the income attributed to the land and another to the income assigned to the building.

Estimating Income

Income estimates are based on the earning record of the property as well as that of comparable properties, with proper allowances being made for probable future developments. That is, past earnings may be used as an indication of future earnings only if there is reason to believe that the future will be like the past with respect to the subject property. Past income is only a part of the data to be considered by the appraiser. That is why it is important for him to consider general economic trends, governmental and location factors, and local market trends, as well as the specific property being appraised.

The difficulties of estimating the future income production of a property are emphasized by Leo Grebler's study of urban real estate investment experience based on the records of 312 cases with 518 properties in New York City. He says:

> The wide swings in gross and particularly in net income highlight the difficulties in using current earnings for projections of expected earnings. A projection of the 1930 net income for ten years, discounted at 6 per cent would have produced a present value of anticipated net almost 71 per cent higher than the present value of the net actually earned and discounted at the same time. A similar ten-year projection based on the 1926 net would have been 19 per cent higher than the actual net. Projection of the 1936 net income for ten years would have been almost perfect, although most market observers at that time probably would have hesitated to accept the 1936 figure for a period as long as ten years. If the 1940 net had been used for a ten-year projection, the result would have fallen 10 per cent short of actual earnings in spite of the ensuing control of rents. The process of arriving at expected income requires, of course, consideration of a whole range of probabilities. Among these, the straightforward projection of current earnings does not necessarily hold the promise of greatest realism.[5]

Since the anticipated future income is the most vital element in a valuation, the appraiser should make a careful survey to determine probable future incomes. If an apartment property is being appraised, he

[5] Leo Grebler, *Experience in Urban Real Estate Investment* (New York: Columbia Univ. Press, 1955), p. 51.

should obtain prevailing rents in a number of comparable properties, as-certain the number of vacancies, and study neighborhood and market trends for the purpose of determining whether the prevailing rents are likely to continue. The appraiser must determine also what would be a reasonable estimate of vacancy rate and collection loss.

In the appraisal of commercial properties, the appraiser must secure information about rentals on recent leases of comparable properties. Where properties are leased for long terms on net leases to responsible firms, the problem of estimating future income is somewhat less difficult.

The appraiser must be particularly careful in estimating future income in a period of business prosperity or after a sustained period of building. Some of the greatest errors in valuation have been made in projecting the income of boom periods into the future. Appraisers must also consider the competitive effect upon the market of new office buildings, new regional shopping centers, new apartment buildings, or houses that are under construction. Usually appraisals are made on the basis of price levels as of the time the appraisal report is prepared. In some cases the appraisal problem may require that potential price level change be re-flected.

Operating Expenses

In valuation, expenses are defined as all actual cash outlays involved in the ownership and operation of a property during the remaining eco-nomic life of the building except those arising from mortgage indebted-ness. They do not include vacancy allowances, rent concessions, collection losses, and allowances for deterioration or obsolescence. Operating expenses usually include heating, electricity, gas, wages and salaries, re-decorating, painting, insurance, property taxes, water, supplies, manage-ment fees, and periodic replacement of such equipment as furnaces, roofing, and similar items amortized over their useful life. The FHA lists four principal classes of expenses in the management and operation of a rental income property: renting and administrative; regular operating; repairs, maintenance, and replacements; and taxes, special assessments, and hazard insurance.[6] Note that the personal income taxes of the owner are not chargeable to the building and that interest payments on the mortgage are not operating expenses. If interest were included, it is obvious that a comparable property without a mortgage would have a higher value than one with a mortgage, yet both might bring the same amount in the market.

In estimating operating expenses, the appraiser must be careful to determine the accuracy of the records placed at his disposal. It is usually

[6] Federal Housing Administration, *Underwriting Handbook* (rev. ed.; Washington, D.C.: Government Printing Office, 1959), Sec. 71523.3.

advisable to compare figures for several similar properties or to consult the officials of real estate management firms, who are usually intimately acquainted with operating expenses. In addition care must be taken to include only annual charges; insurance, for example, is often paid for three-year periods and a division is necessary to reflect annual expenses. Such charges as special assessments may have only a definite number of years to run, and this must be reflected in future expense estimates.

As is the case with income records, the past experiences reported by records of operating expenses are *supporting data only*. They help to make possible estimates of future expenses, but past experience can be projected only when it appears that the future will resemble the past sufficiently to justify such a procedure. In estimating future operating expenses, allowances must be made for increased wages of building-maintenance workers, higher real estate taxes, higher insurance costs, and higher materials costs for repairs whenever such increases appear probable. Conversely, probable declines in such items may also be reflected in the estimates. Also, the condition of the structure should be considered since this may affect operating costs.

Capitalization Problems

It is obvious that a difference of 1 per cent in the capitalization rate will have a major effect on the value estimate. For example, if a property is expected to earn a net return of $5,000 per year and is capitalized in perpetuity at 10 per cent, the resulting value estimate is $50,000. However, if it is capitalized at 9 per cent the result leads to the higher estimate of $55,555.

How is an appraiser to know which capitalization rate to select? In most cases he selects a rate which will reflect the opinions of investors at the time. This rate should indicate how much investors expect to receive as a return if capital is advanced on one or another type of property or how much more or less they expect if capital is invested in real estate as against alternative types of investment. In a sense the selection of a capitalization rate is based on an estimate of the opinions of real estate investors. Financial institutions as well as investors themselves provide data of this type which the appraiser may find useful. The final selection of a rate will be an estimate, of course. However, it should be an estimate based on the most reliable information available to the appraiser.

Sometimes appraisers use a *summation method* in determining capitalization rates. For example, they may begin with the safe rate or as near a riskless rate as possible such as the return on government bonds. To this may be added an allowance for risk, an allowance for lack of liquidity of real estate investments, and an allowance for the costs of managing the investment. Thus, to a return of 3.5 per cent on government bonds might be added 2 per cent for risk, 1.5 per cent for nonliquidity, and 1 per cent for management—or a capitalization rate of 8 per cent. The Federal Housing Administration includes the following factors in building up a capitalization rate: safety of principal, certainty of return, regularity of return, liquidity, and burden of management.

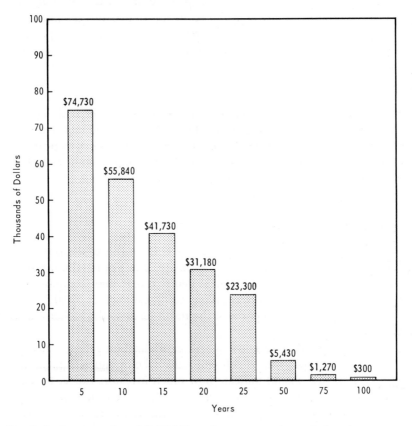

Fig. 8–2. Present value of $100,000 at 6 per cent at the end of various years.

The *band of investment method* is also used. This involves computing the returns on the property attributable to the various investments in
it, for example, the interest return on the first mortgage, the interest return on the second or other junior mortgages, and the return the owner
expects on his equity investment. This total is then related to the entire
investment. Thus, a first motgage of $5,000 at 5 per cent would yield $250
per year, a second mortgage of $2,000 at 6 per cent would yield $120—or
a total of $270. To this would be added the amount the owner believed
necessary on his equity investment, say 10 per cent on $3,000 or $300

for a total of $670 on a total investment of $10,000, indicating a capitalization rate of 6.7 per cent.[7]

Most appraisers attempt to base the capitalization rate on market experience, as suggested above. In some cases they work out *quality ratings* and use various grid rating systems to aid them in the selection of a rate. Ultimately, the capitalization rate selected is a matter of judgment. It reflects the appraiser's estimate of the degree of risk involved, the problems of managing the investment, and general market and investor attitudes.

Split Rates

Difficult problems are encountered if different capitalization rates (split rates) are to be applied to the return on land and on buildings. A property is a single income-producing unit, of course, but it is possible to make estimates of the proportion of the income which may be ascribed to land on the one hand and to buildings on the other.

For example, suppose that a small apartment house on a 100-foot lot is expected to earn a net return of $5,000 per year; if land in this area has been selling for $100 per front foot, one may estimate (by the market data method) that the lot is worth around $10,000. If investors are expecting a return of 5 per cent on improved land, then $500 of the earnings may be attributed to the land and the remainder to the building. The remaining $4,500 may be capitalized at a rate which will reflect the remaining economic life of the building and investors' expectations of earnings from such properties. In this case the *residual return* is assigned to the building, to use appraisal terminology.

If it is estimated that the building has a remaining economic life of 25 years and that a 7 per cent return would be expected by investors, the factor 9.46 may be selected from capitalization tables and multiplied by $4,500, the income attributed to the building. (See Appendix C.) The resulting $42,570 may be used as an estimate of the value of the building. To this the value of the land—$10,000—must be added to secure an estimate of the value of the entire property—say, $52,500. Appraisers follow the practice of rounding off totals, since there is no reason to make a final result appear to be more than a reasonable estimate.

The example above applies more definitely to properties in mid-life or late life than to properties improved with new buildings. When new buildings are involved, information is usually available regarding costs of construction. In such cases land is assigned the residual return. For example, suppose we assume that a new apartment property is expected

[7] Paul F. Wendt, *Real Estate Appraisal* (New York: Holt, Rinehart & Winston, Inc., 1956), pp. 154–62.

to earn $50,000 per year, that the building cost $500,000, that it has an estimated useful life of 40 years, and that it is expected to earn a 7 per cent rate of return. In this case we may assign $41,000, which is derived by selecting from Table II in Appendix C the factor 12.11 (7 per cent for 40 years) and dividing this into $500,000 or $41,200 or rounded to $41,000. This is assigned to the building. The residual amount, $9,000 is assigned to the land. This may then be capitalized in perpetuity at the selected rate, say 5 per cent, and the resulting amount, $180,000 (derived by dividing .05 into $9,000), may be considered an estimated value for the land. The total value of the property will then be around $680,000.

Note that if the capitalization rates were increased by 1 per cent, the earnings assigned to the building would be increased to approximately $45,500, leaving only $4,500 as the residual amount to be assigned to the land. Capitalizing this amount at 6 per cent results in an estimated land value of $75,000 or a total property value of only $575,000.

Because of the fact that several mathematical steps must be taken in the use of this type of appraisal method and because of the difficulty of selecting appropriate capitalization rates, many appraisers prefer to capitalize total net returns in perpetuity rather than to use split rates. One of the arguments favoring the use of different rates for land and building incomes is that it forces the appraiser to consider carefully the factors affecting both land and buildings and to study in detail the character of the income, its probable trend, and the capitalization rates applied.

Mathematical Models

Another problem involves the selection of a capitalization rate which will reflect the trend of income. Several mathematical models or assumptions may be set up, such as level annual returns to the end of the building's life or declining returns at different rates. Babcock, for example, has established four income premises and has set forth tables reflecting the different types of return under appropriate capitalization rates.[8] Various other tables have been prepared, based on different mathematical models or assumptions, including the Hoskold sinking fund and the Inwood tables. Almost any type may be used, if the appraiser understands the assumptions back of the tables and their meaning in the capitalization process.

[8] See Appendix C. See also Babcock, *op. cit.*, pp. 534 and 561. Babcock outlines four major income premises. The first assumes that income will be the same for each year of the property's economic life. The second assumes a decline to zero over a period of years, the annual amounts corresponding to a level annual annuity at 10 per cent. Premise three is similar to the second, the difference being that the annual annuity rate is 3½ per cent. The fourth premise assumes a regular decline to zero by equal amounts each year corresponding to a straight line.

In the Inwood method the principal is reduced each year by an amount equal to the periodic payment less the interest on the prior unpaid balance. The Hoskold method assumes that the portion of the investment returned each year is reinvested in a sinking fund at a lower rate of return; hence, the outstanding investment is not reduced.[9]

Gross Income Multipliers

In some cases, appraisers base value estimates on gross incomes, applying a multiplier based on experience and rules of thumb. One such rule of thumb is that value will be equal to 100 times gross monthly rent in the case of residential rental property.

The use of gross income multipliers has tended to increase somewhat in recent years. The Federal Housing Administration has made fairly widespread use of this procedure. Investors often base their decisions on some multiple of gross income, both in the real estate field and in other fields.

In some cases appraisers use current gross incomes in this process and in others a stabilized or adjusted annual income is established. The multiplier used varies with the type of property, economic life of the property, current investment preferences, and other factors.

The principal problem involved in the use of gross income multipliers arises from the fact that for many types of properties expenses do not change in the same proportion as gross incomes. That is, if gross rents advance, net incomes are likely to advance even more rapidly if many expense items, such as taxes and insurance, do not move up in the same degree or at the same rate as gross rents. The opposite is also true: When gross rents decline, net incomes may decline even more rapidly.

There is some justification for the use of gross incomes in the case of single-family residences, because expense ratios do not appear to vary in the same degree as in the case of larger residential or commercial properties. The FHA, for example, follows the method of using a gross monthly rental and an appropriate rent multiplier in the case of owner-occupied one- and two-family buildings.

When gross income is capitalized by using a rent multiplier, the selection of this multiplier must be made with as much care as the selection of any other capitalization rate. Rent multipliers will vary between rental ranges; they will differ for properties in the same rental or value range, depending on the appeal and competitive position of such properties; and

---

[9] For further discussion of the mathematics of appraising, see Fred E. Case, *Real Estate* (Englewood Cliffs, N.J.: Allyn & Bacon, Inc., 1962), pp. 178–92, and Sanders A. Kahn, Fred E. Case, and Alfred Schimmel, *op. cit.*, chap. xi.

there will be variation depending on the remaining economic life of the property. Rough approximations may be secured by relating prices for which properties have sold to their rental values. Such approximations, however, should be modified to allow for other variables.

This process of valuation by the use of gross income multipliers may be considered a variation of the capitalized income method. It also has a relationship to the market comparison method, since the multipliers employed may be developed by using data on the market prices of comparable properties and the relation of such prices to gross incomes.

Steps in the Market Data or Comparative Method

The process of estimating value by the use of this method includes the following four principal steps:

1. Analysis of the property under consideration in terms of its use and potential uses, characteristics of the land, characteristics of the structure or potential new structures, location factors, market trends, and the regulations and restrictions affecting the property. The detail with which this analysis is carried out will vary with the type of property and purpose of the appraisal. In many cases, established forms are used; for example, savings and loan associations, insurance companies, banks, and other mortgage lenders often indicate rather specifically the factors to be included in a property analysis.

2. Other properties having the same or nearly the same characteristics are selected. The appraiser has available or secures information about these properties to use for comparison with the subject property. Generally properties are selected for comparative purposes which have been bought in the open market (without such compulsion as forced sales) and for which price information can be obtained. Other information which is used in the absence of price data includes listings or offers to sell, offers to purchase, and rentals. Only "arms length" transactions should be used. Recent sales data are much more reliable than those going back a year or more.

3. The information about the comparable properties is analyzed carefully. For example, sales data are considered with respect to the number of sales involved, the period of time covered, the terms of the sales (including down payments, financing arrangements, and the like), the motivating forces back of the sales, if discoverable, and the degree of market activity, including the rate of turnover of properties.

4. Comparisons between the subject property and comparable properties are made, either on an over-all or "chunk" basis or by the use of cubic foot and square foot units for comparative properties.

Appraisers follow various techniques in carrying out the process of making comparisons between properties. In some cases, detailed rating forms are used to assist in the process. Typically, comparisons are made at least with respect to physical factors, location, market and related economic factors, and governmental and regulatory influences.

Physical factors include: (1) site and accessibility; (2) size and shape of the lot; (3) size, style, and functional plan of the building; (4) condition of the building; (5) materials of construction; (6) number of apartments, rooms, offices, or other space units; (7) equipment in the building and its condition; and (8) life expectancy of the building and other improvements.

Location factors include: (1) the general reputation of the neighborhood or district in which the property is located; (2) the desirability of the area as a place to live or do business; (3) the presence or absence of such blighting influences as inharmonious land uses; and (4) the economic future of the city or area (see Chapters 11, 13, and 14).

Market factors include present and anticipated sales prices, rentals, ease or difficulty of financing, volume of transfers, preferences for various types of properties, construction costs, and anticipated changes in market trends (see Chapter 12). Degree of marketability, currently and in the future, is one of the major considerations in determining comparability of properties for appraisal purposes. Related economic factors include: (1) earnings, (2) operating expenses, (3) competitive position of the property, and (4) special features.

Governmental and regulatory factors include: (1) tax rates and assessments, (2) zoning and building regulations, (3) deed restrictions, (4) traffic regulations, and (5) public improvements, such as streets, utilities, schools, and related facilities.

Use of Tables and Formulas

A number of tables, such as *depth tables* and *corner influence tables,* have been prepared for use by appraisers.[10] Depth tables are based on the theory that added depth will increase the value of a lot, but at a diminishing rate. Although this idea may have validity for some types of lots, particularly those used for commercial purposes in older parts of cities, its application to residential lots is questionable since some variations in depth have little effect on the value of homesites. These concepts have little applicability in shopping centers that provide free parking or in industrial areas.

Corner influence tables are of great value as an aid to the valuation of downtown office buildings and for smaller retail stores located on corners with frontage on two important streets. Such tables have practically no utility in the valuation of regional shopping centers.

[10] *Real Estate Appraisal Principles and Terminology* (Chicago: Society of Real Estate Appraisers, 1960), p. 75.

Sources of Market Information

Standard sources of information are insurance atlases, showing the dimensions of the land and buildings; the assessor's record cards, which usually show dimensions of the land and buildings, the assessed valuation, and data on sales; city zoning maps; real estate atlases, showing the occupancy of each store in the principal shopping districts; airplane maps of cities; the county recorder's records of leases and deeds; published accounts of transactions in newspapers and real estate magazines; files of other brokers and financial institutions; records of title companies; and interviews with brokers and clients.

Most appraisers follow the practice of building voluminous files of information. These are sometimes referred to as an appraiser's "data plant." [11] The classification and filing of pertinent information are prerequisites to successful appraising by any method. Successful use of the comparative or market data method, however, requires ready access to information about a variety of properties. In addition to information about specific properties, data are usually compiled on the volume of construction, the number of real estate transfers, vacancy ratios, and other facts which reflect market conditions. A complete "plant" of appraisal information will also contain data on construction costs, availability and cost of mortgage money, zoning and building regulations, tax information, insurance rates, and numerous related types of materials.

The computer makes possible the storage and retrieval of a large volume of data. It may play a big role in future appraisal data plants.

What Is Meant by Cost?

The use of the *cost* or *replacement cost* method of valuation requires that consideration be given to the meaning of these terms. Many terms are used with reference to costs, including actual cost, historical cost, original cost, and replacement cost, to mention but a few.

Actual cost usually refers to the amount actually paid for the development or acquisition of a property. Hence, the same property might have different actual costs under different conditions; it may have cost $4,000 to acquire a lot and $20,000 to build a house, an actual cost of $24,000; however, the property may have been sold for $27,500 and this amount would then represent actual cost to the new owner.

Original cost often is intended to refer to cost of construction rather than to subsequent sale price. Here again, however, problems arise.

[11] See George F. Bloom, "Practice of MAI's Regarding the Appraisal Plant," *The Appraisal Journal* (July, 1953). See also Bloom's doctoral dissertation of the same title, Indiana University. The Security First National Bank of Los Angeles has developed an excellent appraisal data plant.

What is to be included in cost of construction? Will contractor's profits be included? Financing costs? Other charges? Also, there is the problem of accounting practice, which tends to identify original cost with the acquisition cost to the present owner.

Historical cost has also been used to designate original construction cost, but almost any cost which has been previously incurred is a matter of history and might properly be included in this term.

Because of the many terms and meanings in common use, we need to define what we mean by cost in real estate appraisal practice. A number of terms have been used such as "estimated cost of replacement of building" and "required investment exclusive of land," the former referring to the costs involved in replacing a similar structure itself, whereas the latter includes all costs incurred in improving a site.[12] In the latter group are included (1) building costs, (2) carrying charges, (3) financial costs and interest, and (4) equipment and fixtures. Typically appraisers use current costs less depreciation.

Difficult problems are involved also in deciding what to include in replacement or reproduction costs when buildings are in mid-life or late life. Most appraisers tend to use the terms *cost of replacement* and *cost of reproduction new* synonymously, taking both terms to mean the *present cost of a property of equivalent utility.* The investor is concerned with an acceptable substitute. He is not interested in a replica.[13]

Bases of the Cost Method

A cost estimate with land value added is usually considered as establishing the upper limit of the value of a property. The *principle of substitution* serves as the basis for this position. Bonbright's statement of some years ago is still significant: "When property is replaceable, its owner has the option of replacing it with an effective substitute in case he is deprived of its use. This option limits the value of the property to the owner, since it permits him to mitigate the damages that he would otherwise sustain as a result of its loss." [14]

When a new building is constructed, the owner would not ordinarily undertake the project unless he believed that the return which the new property is expected to earn would more than justify the costs incurred. Hence, it is quite appropriate in the case of a new structure (assuming highest and best use of the site) to compute a return on the investment required to improve the land and to impute the remainder of the antici-

[12] Babcock, *op. cit.*, p. 447. See also *Appraisal Terminology and Handbook* (4th ed.; Chicago: American Institute of Real Estate Appraisers, 1962).

[13] Wendt, *op. cit.*, p. 224.

[14] By permission from *Valuation of Property*, by James C. Bonbright, p. 156. Copyright, 1937, McGraw-Hill Book Co., Inc., New York. See also chaps. viii–ix.

pated income to the land, as we explained above in our discussion of the income method.

Appraisal of an older building raises the depreciation problem. *Current cost less depreciation* is the principle applied to such properties in valuation by the replacement cost approach. While investors are concerned with estimates of this type, there are many problems involved in the use of the replacement cost approach in the case of older buildings. Market prices of comparable properties often provide more reliable guides in such cases.

When valuations are based on costs less depreciation, current construction costs should be used. As a general rule, when there are available data on a number of buildings of the same type as an older building being appraised, the market approach is preferable. It reflects obsolescence but does not exaggerate physical depreciation.

Despite these difficulties, there are cases in which the appraiser has no alternative but to use the replacement cost method in the case of older properties. The purpose of the appraisal may necessitate the use of this method, or it may be found impracticable to proceed in any other manner because of the lack of pertinent data. If proper considerations are given to the problems and difficulties involved, reasonable value estimates may be made. This is likely to be true if it is possible to relate such data to market prices or to the income production of comparable buildings. Often, an older structure would not be replaced. In some cases, it might even have a negative value.

The fundamental difficulty with the cost method, except in the case of new structures, is that the appraiser's view must of necessity be directed backward rather than forward. The income method stresses future probable returns; the cost method considers past outlays. These outlays may have been made at a time when they were justified by expectations; however, subsequent events may have provided the information whereby the original expectations were justified or proved to be in error. The key to the solution of the problem is the treatment of depreciation in terms of the ability of the property to perform its functions in the future rather than only in terms of past events.

Steps in the Cost Method

In the appraisal of new properties, cost estimates may be based on a quantity survey of the actual expenditures involved, or unit cost methods may be used. Special factors may arise in specific cases which cause costs to be well above or below the average for properties of the type under consideration. Unit costs are based on averages which are reduced to square feet, cubic feet, or some similar unit.

The various items which go into the building of a standard structure may be computed on an "in-place" basis. Cubic and square foot unit costs are derived from information of this type. A number of services supply information on a unit cost basis.[15] Appraisers often make use of bench mark houses to help in the appraisal of existing houses by the cost method. A bench mark house is representative of a size and style of property.

In computing the cubic feet of content of a structure, allowances are made for pitched roofs, open porches, bay windows, and the like. Square feet of floor area are computed on the basis of the exterior dimensions of the structure and the floor space in use. Adjustments are made for basement and attic floors which are finished for use. The square foot method is being used to an increasing extent.

Factors causing variations in square foot costs for different types of buildings include the following:

1. The floor-wall ratio. A one-story building 100 by 100 feet costs less per square foot of floor area than a building 20 by 100 feet. This is because the cost of the side walls is relatively more for the smaller building. Similarly, triangular buildings cost more per square foot than rectangular buildings.

2. Two-story houses cost less per square foot of floor area than one-story buildings because the roof area and basement area are half as great and it costs less to carry construction upward to the second story than to expand laterally.

3. Since kitchen and bathroom plumbing fixtures are the most expensive elements of cost in a residential structure, a six-room house or apartment costs less per square foot of area than a four-room house or apartment with the same kitchen and bathroom facilities because these plumbing costs are spread over a greater floor area in the former case.

4. The cost varies with the material of exterior construction. Houses constructed of solid masonry cost more per square foot than those with weatherboard over frame.

5. The cost varies with the quality of interior trim and fixtures. Houses that have expensive hardwoods for interior trim, copper pipes, and the highest-quality plumbing fixtures cost more than those built of cheaper materials.

6. The cost of commercial buildings varies according to the extras included, such as escalators, elevators, air conditioning, ceramic tile floors, and expensive store fronts.

Notwithstanding all of these variations, it is possible to set up unit costs for buildings of different standard types and to allow for variations from the standard type.

[15] For example, E. H. Boeckh and Associates.

Building costs include all of the expenditures required to construct a building—costs of materials, wages, contractors' fees or profits, architects' and engineers' fees, and allowances for extras and contingencies. Sidewalks, driveways, landscaping, and the like are also included, as well as costs of accessory buildings. To these are added carrying charges, financial costs, and equipment costs.

Carrying charges include costs incurred during the period of construction and the time that elapses before the building is put into operation, such as taxes and insurance during construction, costs of working capital, and expenses involved in rental campaigns. Financing costs include interest on invested capital or borrowed funds during the construction period, as well as discounts, commissions, consulting fees, related legal expenses, and the like. Costs of such equipment as becomes a part of the real estate are included, although furniture and removable equipment may or may not be included, depending on the valuation problem involved.

Land value is added and is usually estimated by the comparative method, although the actual amount paid for the land may be used if it is comparable to current prices of similar sites.

In some cases blueprints are used as the basis for making cost estimates for buildings that are to be constructed. Appraisers usually do this by the application of a unit cost factor, with allowances for extras or deficiencies.

As we have pointed out above, replacement cost new does not provide a usable result for the valuation of older structures unless allowances are made for depreciation.

Land Value

If the site is unimproved, or improved with old structures of little value, land may be appraised by the comparative method. Another method of determining land value is to set up a model of a hypothetical building that represents the best use of the site. The rents for this building are estimated on the basis of comparable rents in the vicinity, or sometimes by actual offers of responsible prospective tenants. Operating costs are estimated on the basis of comparable buildings. The process outlined above in the discussion of the income method is then followed.

Depreciation Problems

There are a number of methods in use for estimating depreciation, such as the straight line, weighted rate, reducing balances, and sinking fund approaches to the problem. However, their application without modification is likely to result in wide margins of error because of the differences in the definition of depreciation and the variations in the care and maintenance of different properties.

The term *depreciation* may be taken to mean loss in value from any cause, including physical wear and tear and obsolescence, both of the functional and economic types. However, many of the tables which are in common use limit depreciation to the physical wear and tear on structures.

The care and maintenance given to different properties are not reflected in many of the depreciation tables which are used. Two methods are often adopted to deal with this problem: (1) the quantity survey of observable depreciation with allowances for curable and noncurable defects, and (2) the effective age device. In the former method, a survey is made of the building and points of depreciation are divided into curable and noncurable classes; the cost of making the repairs and alterations necessary to remedy the curable defects is then computed and added to the estimated loss in value due to noncurable defects. Physical depreciation, obsolescence, and other causes of loss in value may be treated in this manner.

The *effective age* of a property may or may not coincide with the numbers of years since construction. A building may be 25 years old and the average life for structures of the type under consideration may be 50 years, but the estimated remaining economic life of the building may be 40 years. Hence, its effective age is only 10 years rather than 25. An appropriate depreciation percentage may then be applied on the 10-year basis and provide an estimate of value loss. This method has the advantage of forcing the appraiser to consider the future economic life of the building rather than to deal only with past events.

The application of depreciation tables often exaggerates the loss of value of well-maintained properties. There are examples of residential structures 50 years old that sell in the market for half of their present reproduction cost new, and yet, on the basis of the types of depreciation tables often used, would be almost valueless. Tests of all depreciation tables should be made by comparing market prices of old buildings with valuations based on current costs less depreciation. Rapidly rising construction costs, of course, offset many depreciation allowances, and structures over 20 years old have frequently sold for more than their original cost. When used, depreciation and obsolescence allowances should be deducted from the most recently available cost of construction estimates.

Depreciation has become a very important factor in income tax returns. By using the declining balance method, or double the straight line method, in the early years, owners of shopping centers and apartment buildings can minimize income tax payments during that period and obtain a large cash flow. At the end of this period, often ten years, when depreciation

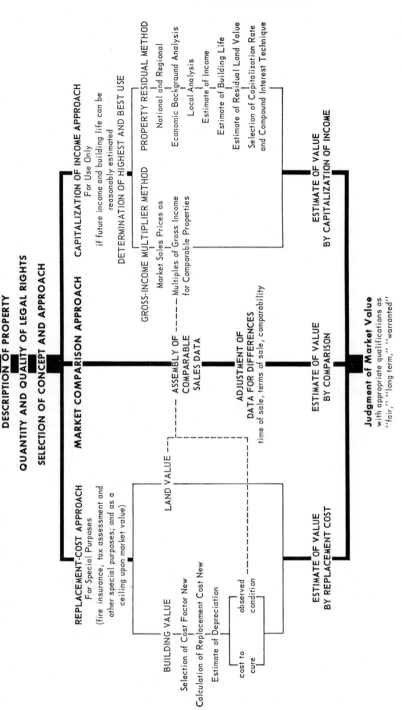

Fig. 8–3. The appraisal process. (By permission from *Real Estate Appraisal*, by Paul F. Wendt, p. 309. Copyright, 1956, Holt, Rinehart & Winston, Inc., New York.)

allowances are exhausted the property is sold to a new buyer who starts the process over again with a high rate of depreciation.

Methods of Valuation for Tax Assessment Purposes

In appraising real estate for tax assessment purposes, land and buildings are valued separately. A land value map is prepared by estimating current front foot values for every block in a city, with square foot values being prepared for industrial properties and acreage values for certain vacant land. These values do not necessarily represent full market price, but they should reflect the relative desirability of the different residential neighborhoods in the city and the relative value of business and industrial properties. Usually the assessor consults with local real estate brokers to secure a proper relativity of land values.

The building values generally are estimated on a reproduction cost basis. All the buildings in the community are classified according to types, which are determined by materials of construction, quality, height, area, plumbing facilities, and related items. Then unit square foot or cubic foot costs are established for each type. This cost may be a percentage of the current cost, which is to be preferred, since that is the cost which may be most easily ascertained, or it may be the costs in what is considered a normal year.

After all the buildings in the city are classified by types, field staffs visit every property, classify it as to type, take its external measurements, note the material of construction, type and quality of equipment, and related items. These facts are entered on field cards. The age of the building is determined for depreciation purposes, either from building permit records or from the architectural type and appearance of the building.

The field records are transferred to permanent property record cards. These show the land area, and the front foot or square foot value established for the block. The land value of a given parcel is calculated either by multiplying the number of front feet by the established front foot value and adjusting for differences in standard depth by depth tables or by using the square foot method.

The building value is determined by multiplying the dimensions to obtain the square foot or cubic content. The original cost new is determined by multiplying the total by the unit price for that class of building. Deductions are then made for depreciation according to the age of the building, with adjustments for such factors as physical obsolescence or neighborhood depreciation. The total value of the property is the summation of the land and building value.

Assessments derived by the method of construction costs for buildings should be checked against recent sales. Properties that sell for less than their reproduction cost less depreciation plus land value are probably suffering from obsolescence or neighborhood depreciation, for which allowances should be made.

The foregoing methods are generally used in wholesale assessments for taxation purposes. It is not possible to secure sufficient current sales data for all types of properties, particularly factories, office buildings, and large stores, to base assessments upon sales. In the case of commercial properties, rentals paid on current leases should be analyzed in making assessments. Valuations based largely on cost less depreciation can be related to values based on income by adjusting land values or the amounts allowed for obsolescence.

Factors Influencing the Judgment of Appraisers

Although the making of value estimates should be an objective process, there is little doubt that appraisers frequently are influenced by the state of the real estate market at the time an appraisal is made and by popular opinions. During periods of prosperity, when the real estate market is very active and the income from real estate is high, appraisers may tend to project this favorable income situation far into the future. On the other hand, during periods of extreme depression, when the volume of sales is limited and the return on real estate is low, appraisers may forecast a continuation of this low-income condition for a long period of time.

Similarly, prevailing opinions regarding the character of certain neighborhoods or sections of the city or the popularity of one or another type of property may influence the judgment of appraisers. For example, appraisers may continue to predict an optimistic future for fashionable residential neighborhoods for some time after such areas have started to decline. Similarly, certain types of commercial property (for example, some downtown stores) which have had a long record of past success often are expected to continue to maintain such a record even though forces are in operation which will tend to limit their future earning power.

Competent appraisers try to avoid pitfalls of this type. They try to study objectively all of the forces which will affect the future income-producing power of the properties which they appraise. Other appraisers, however, do little more than rationalize the popular beliefs prevailing in the real estate market.

The Use of Data

The best protection for an appraiser against current market psychology is the use of factual information. As we have indicated above, many appraisers follow the practice of collecting voluminous files of data for use as an appraisal tool. However, appraisals are not the product of such data; they are the result of the appraiser's judgment. The data available to him are of importance because they help him to formulate sound judgments. They supplement rather than supplant the judgment of the appraiser.

In order to use data, an appraiser or other analyst must understand the basic processes of collecting, classifying, and analyzing them. A considerable portion of appraisal data is statistical in nature, and its use is governed by sound statistical practice. Such general rules as the following apply:

1. *Isolated facts* are relatively useless. The facts used should have a direct bearing on the appraisal.
2. Observations must be sufficiently *numerous* to be representative.
3. The items of information collected must conform to *accuracy standards;* for example, *errors* should tend to cancel out rather than to be cumulative.
4. The sample collected must be *characteristic* of the area or problem or of the "universe," to use statistical terminology.
5. The data must be *classified* or *arranged* systematically, the basis of the classification varying with the purpose involved.
6. Analysis is carried on for the purpose of determining points of *similarity and difference* between items and classes or groups.

Too frequently, appraisers overemphasize one item of information and fail to put it into a proper relationship with other data. In many cases too few data are collected; conclusions may then be based on information which is not typical. During a boom period nearly all information may be weighted in the same direction and reflect the immediate market situation and immediate future expectations only, rather than long-range trends.

Basically, the use of data means borrowing from the experience of others. The complexities of real estate value problems are so great that few people can carry enough information around in their heads to solve them. Programs of data collection, assembly, and analysis are growing in importance in the field of real estate valuation, aided by the expanding use of the computer.

The Appraisal Report*

Appraisal reports may be relatively simple statements or involved and detailed reports, depending on the purpose of the appraisal and the complexity of the problem. Many firms use standard forms for appraisal reports. In such cases the appraiser has a definite guide as to the requirements of his client. In some cases a brief statement in the form of a letter or memorandum serves as an appraisal report.

With the growing importance of appraisals and with the development of standards of practice by such groups as the American Institute of Real Estate Appraisers [16] and the Society of Real Estate Appraisers, appraisal reports have tended to become more standardized than was formerly the case.

Usually a formal report contains three main parts: (1) an introduction, (2) the analysis and conclusions, and (3) the supplementary data in the form of appendixes or annexes. The introduction may include a letter of transmittal, which usually states the result of the value estimate; a statement of limiting conditions, such as a presumption that the legal description furnished is accurate; a photograph or photographs of the property; and in addition (if the report is of some length) a table of contents and title page as well as a statement of the appraiser's qualifications.

The second part, which is really the body of the report, usually includes the following: (1) purpose of appraisal, (2) legal description of the property, (3) property data (building and site), (4) location data, (5) market information, (6) a detailed outline of the value estimate, including reasons for selection of the method used and the main steps required in its application to the problem, (7) interpretation of the estimate, and (8) certification of the estimate.

The third part of the report includes maps, supplementary photographs, blueprints, floor plans, and other information. Materials of this type are ready for use if necessary but are supplementary to the first two parts of the report.

The main objective to be achieved by a carefully organized and prepared appraisal report is to provide the basis for following the steps taken by the appraiser in arriving at a value estimate. A more or less standardized form assures that all pertinent data will be presented and analyzed in a systematic fashion.

SUMMARY

Valuations or appraisals serve as aids to real estate decisions. Thus, appraising may be thought of as a technique to aid the decision-maker. As value differs depending upon the purpose of the valuation, property rights involved, and time, the appraiser needs to know the purpose for which the appraisal is to be made, as well as the specific property rights in question, and the time of their enjoyment or use.

The three principal approaches to valuation are the income method, the cost method, and the market data or comparative method. The first of these, capitalization of expected future income, is logically best; but the purpose of the valuation, the type of income produced, and the available

[16] See *The Appraisal of Real Estate.*

data determine which method may be most effective in any given situation. Regardless of which method is used, the appraiser is trying to determine the earning expectancy of the property.

In capitalizing expected future income, the choice of an appropriate capitalization rate is ultimately a matter of judgment, based on the knowledge and experience of the appraiser. Sometimes appraisers use the summation or band of investment methods of determining capitalization rates. Capitalization requires that assumptions be made as to the trend of future incomes and expenses. In recent years increasing use has been made of gross income multipliers, although this technique does not allow for the relatively inflexible nature of operating expenses.

A property often is divided into land and buildings for valuation purposes. The appraiser may use either the building-residual or land-residual methods of valuation, depending upon the age of the building and the availability of cost data.

The market data or comparative method is used widely especially when markets are active and information on sales is available. The cost method poses special problems but is useful when other methods cannot be applied.

The results of a valuation are presented in an appraisal report. These reports, which are becoming more standardized, usually consist of an introduction, analysis and conclusions, and appendixes of supplementary data.

QUESTIONS FOR STUDY

1. Why is it important to know the purpose of a real estate transaction before making an appraisal?
2. How might appraisals for the purposes of quick sale or estate settlement vary from each other in terms of the value estimates made?
3. Assume that your home is assessed for tax purposes at $8,500 and that you have been offered $20,000 for the property; you also know that you can get a bank loan of $12,500 on the property. Which of these amounts is indicative of the property's value? Explain.
4. Which appraisal method would you use in the valuation of the house in which you live? Why is this method better than others?
5. If capitalization of future income is the appraisal method most consistent with the theory of value, why are other methods sometimes used? For what purposes are these other methods applied?
6. What difference does it make whether the return on property is through dollar payments or amenities?
7. List the steps involved in the income method of valuation and discuss the primary difficulties involved in each step.
8. What difficulties do you see in attempting to apply the summation method to determine capitalization rates?

9. What does the gross income multiplier method have in common with the capitalized income method? How is it related to the market comparison method?

10. Which of the three valuation methods would you recommend for use in the valuation of: (a) The administration building of your college or university? (b) Your own home? (c) A newly constructed home that you might be interested in buying? (d) Your local post office building? (e) Your city's highest-class commercial property?

11. In which ways does the age of buildings influence the choice of valuation methods?

12. Why is the cost method easier to apply to new than to older structures? Discuss some of the difficulties involved in using this method for old structures.

13. Under what circumstances is full-market-price valuation unnecessary for tax assessment?

14. Explain how "the use of data means borrowing from the experience of others."

15. *Study Project 10.* (a) What is the purpose of the appraisal? What is meant by "market value"? For what other purposes might the appraisal have been made? Explain. (b) Would you include the value of the carpets and draperies in the value of the real estate? Why or why not? (c) Is the income approach to the estimate of value as reliable as the other approaches? Explain. (d) Of what significance, if any, is the quantity of data in applying each of the three valuation approaches? (e) Why did the appraiser stress the market data approach in arriving at the final estimate of value? Explain.

16. *Study Project 11.* How can the appraiser affect the growth of local and regional communities? Is it the social responsibility of an appraiser to be consistent in making valuations? Why or why not?

SUGGESTED READINGS

AMERICAN INSTITUTE OF REAL ESTATE APPRAISERS. *The Appraisal of Real Estate* (4th ed.). Chicago: The Institute, 1964.

BABCOCK, FREDERICK M. *The Valuation of Real Estate.* New York: McGraw-Hill Book Co., Inc., 1932. Chaps. xv–xviii.

ELWOOD, L. W. *Elwood Tables for Real Estate Appraising and Financing.* Ridgewood, N.J.: Published by author, 1959.

FRIEDMAN, EDITH J. (ed.). *Encyclopedia of Real Estate Appraising.* Englewood Cliffs, N.J.: Prentice-Hall, Inc., 1959.

HOYT, HOMER. *Dynamic Factors in Land Values.* Washington, D.C.: Urban Land Institute, Technical Bulletin No. 37, 1960.

HOYT, HOMER. "The Appraisal of Different Types of Property," *The Appraisal Journal,* July, 1964.

KAHN, SANDERS A., FRED E. CASE, and ALFRED SCHIMMEL. *Real Estate Appraisal and Investment.* New York: The Ronald Press Co., 1963. Chaps. vii, xi.

RATCLIFF, RICHARD U. *Modern Real Estate Valuation.* Madison, Wis.: The Democrat Press, 1965.

WENDT, PAUL F. *Real Estate Appraisal.* New York: Holt, Rinehart & Winston, Inc., 1956. Chaps. iii, vi–ix.

9

Analysis of Governmental and Political Trends

Analytical Problems

It is far from easy to analyze governmental and political trends and to determine their potential impact on real estate incomes, values, and decisions. Nevertheless, such analyses must be undertaken by real estate decision-makers. Every governmental and political development has a potential effect on real property. Those who make decisions regarding the purchase, sale, development, use, management, or financing of real estate find it necessary to try to anticipate political and governmental trends, to estimate their potential impact on real property in general and especially on particular properties, and to arrive at decisions on the basis of such anticipations and estimates. The generation and localization of income are influenced greatly by potential developments in the governmental and political sector.

Although information about governmental and political affairs is available in every newspaper, magazine, and radio or television broadcast, it is hard to select the key information, weigh its implications and determine its significance. Some assistance is available to the decision-maker. For example, there are a number of trade associations operating in the real estate field and in related fields as we noted in Chapter 2. Often they can provide pertinent information since they follow developments in Washington and in state capitols with considerable care. On the local level, real estate boards, chambers of commerce, and other business and citizens organizations may be helpful. Sometimes lawyers can provide assistance in analyzing proposed legislative changes and in assessing their chances for enactment. It is often possible to secure help from one's congressman, senators, or legislative representatives in state or local government.[1]

In some cases, various types of "public opinion polls" give indications of public attitudes and points of view although there are variations in their reliability. In addition, the real estate decision-maker usually follows opinion closely in his own circle of acquaintances.

Each of us can learn something from the evaluation of reports, headlines, news stories, and editorials. This is not always easy to do. As has been pointed out:

Often government officials or politicians issue statements that are designed to "smoke out the opposition" or to "send up a trial balloon" to test public reaction or to lay out a claim to an area in which there is likely to be new legislation. The business manager soon develops a healthy skepticism in regard to current news reports. He tries to understand what is back of them, what the motives of government officials or politicians may be, and what kinds of results may be anticipated. He attempts to think in terms of who exercises the real power in political and legislative campaigns. Often the actions of elected representatives or public officials are taken with one eye on those who control important blocks of votes or who provide substantial financial support for political campaigns. In short, *things are not always as they seem* to be in this interesting sector of our business environment.[2]

Special Interests

We should note also that while the bulk of regulations and controls are proposed or set up to serve the public interest, there are numerous cases where special interest groups are trying to secure an advantage. An example may be found in some of the building regulations which favor local builders and workers as against competition from other cities or localities.

As has been suggested above, things are not always what they seem to be in the governmental or political field. Governmental machinery often offers opportunities for closely knit groups to exert their influence and secure competitive advantages over other groups that are not situated in as fortunate a position. Such advantages usually last until the other groups become sufficiently organized to exert pressures for their own purposes. In most federal, state, and local governments these processes are going on more or less constantly. Their extent and nature is often difficult to determine without access to the kind of information that usually is *not* found in the official pronouncements.

---

[1] Arthur M. Weimer, *Business Administration: An Introductory Management Approach* (Homewood, Ill.: Richard D. Irwin, Inc., 1966), chap. vii.

[2] *Ibid.*, p. 159.

Points of View

The analysis of governmental and political (or other) trends varies somewhat with the point of view of the analyst and decision-maker. For example, the viewpoint of the private investor differs from that of the public official. The federal government official's outlook will differ from that of the local official. The point of view of a company executive differs from that of the home owner. As we indicated in Chapter 2, the viewpoints of buyers and sellers, borrowers and lenders, and owner-users and nonowner-users may differ widely.

We need to remind ourselves from time to time of the variety of points of view from which real estate decision-makers may consider their problems and their decisions. Similarly, we should recognize the variations that may arise between a short-term and longer-term outlook. Although we tend to follow the latter, we dare not ignore the former. The real estate decision-maker may be able to identify long-term governmental and political trends. We will consider several of these in the following discussion. He usually will find it helpful to follow our periodic elections on local, state, and national levels with care. In addition, he needs to be alert to the possibilities of sudden shifts in governmental or political conditions such as may result from a war "scare" or other emergency. Usually, opinions and attitudes change slowly but now and then sudden shifts occur. If they can be anticipated, of course, chances for sound decisions are greatly improved.

Types of Regulations

It is often helpful to think in terms of the various types of regulations that may have a bearing on real estate. Although we tend to emphasize public regulations and controls, we should recognize also that various private regulations may be important. For example, deed restrictions are very important as are policies, programs, and regulations imposed by groups such as labor unions, property owners' associations, business associations, and others.

The various types of regulations and programs that affect real estate may also be divided according to whether they are of the *coercive* or *inducive* types. Coercive regulations typically are of the "thou shalt" or "thou shalt not" types, with penalties imposed for failure to comply. Inducive regulations accomplish their objectives by offering rewards for compliance or by providing information on the basis of which individuals will tend to make decisions that are in line with the public interest. Subsidies are generally of this type, as are the information-giving services of federal, state, and local governments, trade associations, universities, business firms, and private individuals.

Regulations may also be classified as to whether they are imposed on properties or on the real estate business. For example, many informal controls such as custom, accepted procedures, status, personal relationships, and the like affect businessmen and business practices.

Regulations may also be classified as to whether they *supplement* or *supplant* competition. Usually, the former are favorable developments for real estate, while the latter are unfavorable, although special circumstances may at times require re-evaluation of this statement.

We should note that the rights and responsibilities that go with the ownership of real estate vary somewhat from generation to generation, even when no formal changes are made in our laws. General attitudes toward such rights and responsibilities reflect the economic, political, and social standards of the community. Thus, real estate is a part of the general *institutional* framework of our society. It is affected by customs, standards, mores, folklore, traditions, and generally accepted ways of doing things. It is often difficult to explain how various institutions or accepted ways of doing things came about or when or how they will change. But it is important to recognize their existence.

Position of Private Property

While trends in many parts of the world have been in the direction of limiting or reducing the private ownership of real property, this has not been the case in the United States. Property rights have generally been protected and encouraged, although public opinion appears to be moving more in the direction of justifying private property in terms of efficiency of use and opportunity of widespread participation in the economic system rather than in terms of guaranteeing the exclusive right of ownership as a special privilege.

However, a growing percentage of the income derived from real estate has been drained off in recent years for general community purposes through property and income taxes. The important consideration from the standpoint of analyzing income is to determine whether investments in real estate are being penalized or are likely to be penalized in the future relative to other types of investments as a result of taxes. With the expanding activities of governmental agencies on federal, state, and local levels, larger portions of the incomes from all types of investment have been taken for general public purposes than formerly. Because of the "double taxation" of real estate income with the payment of taxes on the property itself plus income taxes by the owner on returns from the property, it may be that other types of investment enjoy a greater competitive advantage over real estate than was the case a generation or two ago. In some cities the heavy tax burdens of downtown properties explain in part the slow progress of private urban renewal programs.

Maintenance of Competition

Traditionally this country has undertaken to maintain competition as a major method of social control and to use markets as devices for regulating the production, use, and consumption of goods and services. Monopolies have been attacked through the antitrust laws. Various products have been tested to guard the public against fraudulent goods. Competition has always been regulated in some degree. It has always been necessary to establish the rules of the business game and to enforce them.

As J. M. Clark has pointed out: ". . . when we speak of the 'social control of business,' we must take pains to avoid the implication that business exists first and is then controlled. Control is rather an integral part of business, without which it could not be business at all. The one implies the other and the two have grown together." [3]

The regulations imposed during periods of war often have set important limits to competition in real estate markets. Of major importance were rent controls, which have largely been eliminated except in special areas or for certain state and local controls. Such controls supplanted competition in important segments of our housing markets and shifted the use and development of many real properties.

In addition, government assists some portions of the real estate field to compete more effectively; for example, the insurance of mortgages by the Federal Housing Administration and the guaranteeing of mortgages by the Veterans' Administration have helped many people to become home owners. Activities of this type probably have stimulated and widened competition rather than restricted it. However, such programs hold the possibility of restraining as well as aiding competition in the future.

Competition is affected by subsidy programs, notably in the case of municipalities offering tax-free land for varying periods to induce industries to move to their localities. Such programs transfer tax burdens to other real estate within the jurisdiction of the local taxing authorities.

Public-housing programs, of course, bring the government into competition with private owners of rental properties. To the extent that such programs serve racial or national groups which are unable to compete effectively in housing markets, they do not change greatly the competitive situation. To the extent that they serve others, they may create com-

[3] By permission from *Social Control of Business*, 2d ed., by John M. Clark, p. 12. Copyright, 1939, McGraw-Hill Book Co., Inc., New York.

petitive problems. Renewal and redevelopment programs hold possibilities both for facilitating and restraining competition.

Inflation and Deflation

The historical trend in this country has been in the direction of gradual inflation. Downward adjustments in prices, of course, have occurred from time to time especially prior to World War II. But after each downward swing, prices typically have advanced to levels higher than previously.

This long-run tendency has been of great importance to real estate ownership and investments. Except for poorly located or improperly designed properties or those which were the victims of changes in the internal structure of land uses in our cities, the dollar investments in real estate over the years have tended to be maintained. The major problem has been the ability of owners and investors to hold on during depression periods.

An interesting case in point is the experience of the Home Owners Loan Corporation. Although over a million mortgages were financed during the depression of the early 1930's, by the time the Corporation was liquidated in 1952 it had been able to operate without loss and turned over nearly 14 million dollars to the Treasury.

On the basis of past trends it appears that gradual inflation will continue over future years, interrupted from time to time by recession periods. Gradual inflation tends to benefit equity investors in real property and is to the disadvantage of those who invest in mortgage loans or bonds. It would be a mistake, however, to assume that long-term inflation is inevitable. Technological progress, new products, better management, and improved production and marketing methods may prevent significant price increases. Or prices may advance but "dollar's worths," that is, the quality as well as the amount of goods and services may advance even faster.

War and Peace

International relations and defense programs are likely to have important effects on real estate decisions and on the income-producing ability of real properties in the foreseeable future. The unsettled condition of world affairs, the varying temperatures of cold to hot wars, and the many related uncertainties undoubtedly mean that the defense and related industries will continue to have an important place in the American economy. Factors of this type will complicate the making of decisions related to long-term commitments of the type involved in real estate ownership, management, and investment.

Fighting Depressions

The general concept that it is the responsibility of the federal government to fight depressions is rather generally accepted by the American people. The policy of maintaining full employment was enunciated in the Employment Act of 1946. Although it may be altered or modified in the future, for example, giving greater emphasis to stabilizing the value of the dollar, full employment appears likely to continue as a major policy objective. Maintenance of employment and incomes helps to strengthen the market for all types of properties.

In addition, the insurance of bank deposits and accounts in savings and loan associations helps to avert serious financial stringencies. Insured and guaranteed mortgages provide financial institutions with some assurance of liquidity. Improvements in the credit and banking systems, farm price support programs, unemployment insurance, and other related programs should go a long way toward mitigating the effects of future recessions.

Prior to World War II the declines in real estate prices, rents, and volume of activity were much greater than the average declines for other commodities. Modification of the swings of the business cycle, such as occurred in the postwar recessions, probably benefited real estate more than most other goods or services.

Progress and Economic Opportunity

In contrast to the general opinion that we had become a mature economy, which was prevalent during the 1930's, there now appears to be a widespread belief in an expanding and dynamic economy. Programs for expanding output are more popular than those for restricting output. Competing groups are concerned with increasing their respective shares of the total output at any given time, it is true, but they are also concerned about expanding total output.

Government programs for subsidizing research, for allowing rapid depreciation for tax purposes, for disseminating information, and for related activities appear to be generally accepted and supported. Programs undertaken in the interest of small business firms and farms are popular and help to guarantee a widespread distribution of economic opportunity. Continued support of our public school system, extending through universities, is one of the best guarantees that young people of ability will have a chance to rise on independent terms.

On the other side there is growing concern with provisions for security. Welfare legislation of many types has increased in popularity. The danger in such programs is not in their objectives but that they will tend to impose limits on expansion and progress. However, with the rapid expansion of the American economy in recent years, there appears to be no reason to fear that programs which have for their main objective the provision of security and stability are likely to be developed at the expense of economic growth and progress.

Public attitudes, of course, can change and often do. Proposals for limiting or licensing investment, building, or development have been made in the past and may be made again in the future. Trends of this type are significant from the standpoint of all real estate decision-makers, including investors, managers, users, buyers, and sellers.

Equality versus Excellence

John W. Gardner, former president of the Carnegie Corporation, now Secretary of Health, Education and Welfare, has aptly pointed out that our society has the difficult task of pursuing both equality and excellence, even though these are in some degree incompatible objectives.[4] Even in the pioneer community on the American frontier we believed that "all men are created equal," but still insisted, "let the best man win!"

Today we expect outstanding performance of scientists, managers, and government officials at the same time that we put restraints on them in the interests of equality. Requirements for employment continue to move upward and there is greater intensity of competition both at home and abroad. We take pride in fine residential developments but at the same time feel uncomfortable about wide distinctions between the homes of those in different income groups. We need the incentives that come from some exclusiveness, but cannot afford to allow this to emphasize inequality to a marked degree. This is particularly true if exclusiveness can lead to a stratified society. Gardner says:

No democracy can function effectively until it has gone a long way toward dissolving systems of hereditary stratification. This is presumably true of any democracy, but overwhelmingly true of the urbanized, industrial democracy with which we are familiar. On the other hand, no democracy can give itself over to extreme emphasis on individual performance and still remain a democracy—or to extreme equalitarianism and still retain its vitality.[5]

At the present time tendencies toward increased equality may be noted in the real estate field as efforts are being made to provide broader access to markets and to eliminate discrimination between color or religion with respect to living arrangements. This will create some uncertainties for real estate investors but should lead to a more democratic society.

[4] John W. Gardner, *Excellence* (New York: Harper & Row, Publishers, 1961), p. 27.

[5] *Ibid.*, pp. 28–29.

Public Ownership of Property

Despite generally favorable attitudes toward private property in real estate both historically and currently, we have always had a great deal of public ownership of such resources. The public domain, of course, was very large during the pioneer period of American history. Much of this domain was transferred to private ownership through a variety of land acts culminating with the Homestead Act at the time of the Civil War. Various changes were made subsequently to meet the needs of the Far West.

Even though much land was transferred to private ownership, much continued or was placed under public control, including our great national parks, forest preserves, highway rights-of-way, conservation areas, and many other types of land uses. Also, it has often been necessary to take land back from private ownership either through direct purchase or condemnation proceedings to provide for the new system of superhighways, wider streets, sites for schools or school expansion, flood control, urban renewal programs, recreational programs, and other types of requirements.

There is little doubt that programs of this type will continue and may expand. In some cases this will mean an expansion of public ownership, although in some programs such as urban renewal, provision is made for resale of various properties to private owners.

Government and Real Estate Finance

On the federal level, government probably has influenced real estate decisions through its financial programs to a greater extent than in any other way. In addition to the general governmental functions related to the regulation of currency, credit, and financial institutions through the work of the Department of the Treasury, Comptroller of the Currency, the Federal Reserve, the Federal Deposit Insurance Corporation, and related agencies, special developments have occurred through the establishment of a variety of programs and agencies. These include the Federal Home Loan Bank System and the Housing and Home Finance Agency, which coordinates the programs of the Federal Housing Administration, the Public Housing Administration, the Federal National Mortgage Association, and the Urban Renewal Administration. In addition, the mortgage guarantee programs of the Veterans' Administration have played an important role in real estate finance.

We will have more to say about a number of these agencies and programs in Chapter 20. We should note here, however, that governmental and political trends are very likely to involve the general area of real estate finance.

At the present time the areas that are most important are mortgage insurance and guarantees, secondary mortgage market operations, direct lending in some situations, the financing of cooperative programs with local governments, the insurance of savings accounts, and the regulation of financial institutions with strong interests in the real estate field.

In the area of mortgage insurance and guarantees governmental programs appear to have been relatively less important in recent years than previously. Conventional mortgage loans have tended to gain on the insured and guaranteed types. Private systems of mortgage insurance have been started. Demands of veterans have declined and provisions have not been made for extending the benefits of mortgage guarantees to those who served in the military forces following the Korean War. Direct lending has not been extensive. Financial arrangements related to federal and local urban renewal programs have tended to expand and probably will continue to do so. There have been plans for increasing the insurance of savings accounts in banks and savings and loan associations beyond the $10,000 level.

Subsidies

As our society grows more complex, the number and types of subsidies appear to increase. Subsidies may take a number of forms. The most important type used by local governments is the device of tax exemption. In many instances smaller cities and towns offer tax exemptions to industrial establishments in order to induce them to locate in such places. Churches, schools, government properties, and various others ordinarily are exempted from taxation. In some cases exemptions are allowed in varying amounts to home owners whose properties are mortgaged. However, if subsidization is to be employed at all, outright grants are preferable to tax exemptions. Subsidies which are open and aboveboard may be desirable or undesirable, depending on the objectives of the specific grant. In either case, it is relatively easy to count the cost involved.

Subsidies in the real estate field are of many types, the most important being those resulting from the activities of the federal government. To some extent, the activities of the Federal Housing Administration, the Mortgage Guarantee division of the Veterans Administration, and the Federal National Mortgage Association may subsidize various real estate activities. However, losses to date have been negligible in connection with these activities; and in addition, improved methods and practices resulting from the work of those agencies may well justify any subsidies involved.

There are cases of one government subsidizing another. The payments of the federal government toward urban renewal projects developed by local governments illustrate these practices. In these cases, subsidies, government ownership, and tax exemption may all be involved. It is probable that the number and type of subsidies wil continue to expand and to create special problems and uncertainties for real estate decision-makers.

Some subsidies operate in an indirect manner. For example, a tariff that protects the products of a locally produced industry may be an indirect subsidy to the property owners in that area. Similarly, federal payments under a crop control program may be of special benefit to the real estate in a particular locality.

As Thompson points out:

The purpose of evaluating the impact of national economic policies on the local economy is not only to prepare the urban area to correctly perceive its own interests so that it may pursue them intelligently—lobby rationally—but also to smooth local adjustments to national policy changes not of the community's own making or liking. Specifically, a clear conception of the vulnerability of the local economy to foreign imports may not enable the community to halt a reduction in the protective tariff, but this knowledge may well alert the community to the coming change and suggest alternative avenues of adjustment.[6]

Government Contracts

One of the important ways that federal or state programs may affect a particular locality and the real estate of the area is through the letting of contracts for the construction of important government installations or the purchase of products. The installations of the National Aeronautics and Space Administration in the southern part of this country are an interesting illustration of the impact of government building programs on local areas. The establishment on the one hand and the closing on the other of various military installations is another case in point.

Similarly, the letting of contracts for the production of major items of military or space hardware has had an important effect on economic activity in various localities. The cancellation of contracts tends to have depressing effects on the locality involved. The awarding of a contract to one firm as against others may benefit the property owners of one locality relative to those in the other areas that did not get the contract.

Taxation of Real Property

Of all of the ways in which government programs and political trends affect real estate decisions none is more important than taxation. It has aptly been said that the power to tax is the power to destroy. Real prop-

[6] By permission from *A Preface to Urban Economics*, by Wilbur R. Thompson, p. 83. Copyright, 1965, Johns Hopkins Press, Baltimore, Md.

erty cannot be concealed. Hence, it seldom can escape from taxation. As we have suggested, taxes tend to be capitalized. As a result, any change in the tax burden of a real property has a direct effect on its value.

Historically, we relied heavily on the property tax as a source of revenue for state and local governments. It continues as a prime support of local governments and to some extent of state governments. As demands for government programs and services have expanded, however, the property tax has been supplemented by other types, notably income and sales taxes. It may be that we are reaching the limits of taxes on real property for several reasons. First, the tax burdens themselves are already high; second, a substantial majority of homes are now owned by their occupants, a situation that contrasts with that of two or three decades ago; and third, other sources of revenue are proving to be productive.

It is doubtful, however, that property tax reductions are likely to occur. In part this is due to the tax capitalization process which would mean that owners at the time of the reduction would reap a major windfall. In addition, it would be politically unpopular in some quarters to reduce such taxes. (As property ownership becomes more widespread, this situation may change.) About all owners and prospective owners of real property may hope for in the near term is the approximate freezing of tax burdens at or near present levels.

Uniformity in Taxation

Problems related to uniformity in taxation point up some of the difficulties faced by real estate decision-makers. The real estate tax burden is considered to be equitably apportioned between real property owners if all property is valued uniformly at the same proportion of value. If a property which sold for $15,000 is assessed for $6,000, and another that sold for $10,000 is assessed for $4,000, both owners pay their fair share of the tax burden, because each property is assessed at 40 per cent of its value and the owner of the $15,000 house pays 50 per cent more than the owner of the $10,000 house. It would be unfair, however, if both houses were assessed at $4,000, because the owner of the more expensive house would be paying less than his fair share in taxes.

The tax levy is determined by making a budget of all expected local government expenses. All of the real and personal property is then valued for tax purposes. If the total budget of local government costs for the ensuing year is estimated at $4,500,000, and it is estimated that only 90 per cent will be collected, the amount of the levy will be $5,000,000. If the total assessed value of all the real and personal property in the local government jurisdiction is $200,000,000, then the tax rate will be $2.50 per $100 of assessed value. A house and lot assessed for $10,000 would then pay $250 in taxes. This assessment of $200,000,000 may be less than half of the actual market value of the property in the jurisdiction based on recent sales. However, if all the assessed values in the jurisdiction are doubled or raised from $20,000,000 to $400,000,000, the actual taxes paid by any specific property would not be affected if the increase were uniform. The budget of $5,000,000 should remain the same. The tax rate to raise this amount from a $400,000,000 tax roll would be only $1.25, or half the former tax rate. The taxes on a house on which the assessment was raised from $10,000 to $20,000 at a tax rate now reduced to $1.25 per $100 of assessed value would be $250, the same as before.

Whether assessments are relatively high or low does not automatically affect their uniformity or their equity in distributing the tax burden. However, it is believed that an extremely low level of assessment encourages lack of uniformity. An owner whose property is worth $10,000 and is assessed for $6,000, has a just cause for complaint if the average level of assessment is only 20 per cent of value; but if he complains, he is often asked whether he would sell his property for the assessed value and his complaint is dismissed. An extremely low assessment also limits the bonding power of the municipality. Sometimes, as in New York, there is a constitutional limit on the tax rate. This tends to cause high assessments which are above market value in depressions.

Where the state levies taxes on local real estate, it is to the self-interest of counties and cities to assess their properties at low valuations so that they will pay a lower share of state taxes. To overcome this, the state tax commission of some states (e.g., Illinois) may make its own appraisals and may order the local assessments raised by a factor that is supposed to equalize assessments throughout the state. Uniformity of assessment between all types of property in cities is difficult to achieve because of political considerations. Single-family homes, since they contain the most voters, are usually undervalued in comparison with apartments and commercial or industrial properties.

There are frequently many different local taxing districts which overlap. There are school districts, sewer districts, local city governments, park districts, mosquito abatement districts, and others. Each district imposes taxes upon real and personal property to cover its costs. The tax on any specific property is a component of local city taxes, county taxes, school district taxes, park district taxes, and others. All the taxes may be collected by one government authority and distributed to the others; or sometimes taxes must be paid separately to different authorities, such as the city and the board of education.

The need for reassessment of all the real estate in a given jurisdiction does not arise from the fact that real estate values change, but that they do not change uniformly. Some districts decline in desirability but they may still retain old levels of assessed values. Other new districts may have increased rapidly in value and are underassessed. Because of the rapid growth and change of many of our urban areas, we are likely to see a substantial increase in reassessments and related programs. This will add to the problems of decision-makers in the real estate field.

Relative Tax Burden

As we have pointed out, differences in tax burdens and in relative tax burdens often have a major impact on real estate decisions. There is a great difference in local tax burdens, not only between cities in different regions of the country, but even between local communities in the same metropolitan area. Such differences may be accentuated in the future since they are due to the following factors:

1. The number of surplus-producing properties such as stores, factories, vacant land, and high-priced homes compared with the number of low-valued single-family homes which typically do not pay enough in real estate taxes to cover their share of local government costs.[7] One community in a metropolitan area may have the regional shopping center and most of the high-priced homes. Its taxes will be relatively low compared with surrounding communities.

2. The quality and quantity of local government services. In some suburban communities taxes are low because no sewer or water systems are provided and there is inadequate police and fire protection. Highways are provided by the state without local government cost. Taxes are high in some central cities not only because of the cost of sewers, water mains, and streets, but also because of heavy payments for social services.

3. The amount of tax-exempt property. A large amount of tax-exempt property throws heavier burdens on other property.

4. Homestead exemption. In Florida, homestead exemption gives extremely low taxes to low-value homes.

5. The amount of subsidies, or grants-in-aid, or allocations of state revenues received from state income taxes, liquor license taxes, or gasoline taxes, or federal government aid for education, highways, or other purposes.

6. The amount of taxes collected locally from sources other than real estate, such as license fees, fines, local sales taxes, and so forth.

7. The amount of surplus received from local government-owned utilities, such as water and in some cases electricity. When a city-

---

[7] See Homer Hoyt Associates, "Economic Survey of the Land Uses of Fairfax County, Virginia" (1954) and "Economic Survey of Montgomery and Prince George Counties, Maryland" (1955).

owned utility incurs a deficit, such as the New York City subway, it adds to the taxes paid by real estate.

8. Differences in wage and salary scales paid teachers, policemen, and other municipal employees.
9. The efficiency of local governments. The number of municipal employees required to perform equal services varies in different cities.
10. The amount of the local government debt and the interest and principal payments.
11. The compactness of the city. Compact cities require less cost for sewers, water mains, highways, and police and fire protection than diffuse cities in which vacant blocks intervene between settled areas.
12. The amount of taxes levied and collected on such personal property as furniture, livestock, automobiles, stocks, bonds, bank deposits, and so on.
13. The number of overlapping jurisdictions.

For the reasons mentioned above, the local tax burden in some communities is now four to ten times as great as in others. Relative real estate tax burdens are not necessarily a decisive factor in the location of industries because they are comparatively small items in total production costs, and can easily be offset by other advantages. Lower taxes, however, may be the deciding element if other factors are equal or nearly so.

Conservation and Renewal

As a nation, we have placed relatively less emphasis on private and public programs for conservation, reclamation, and renewal of real estate resources than have many older countries. We have generally been more interested in the development of new properties than in conserving or renewing old ones. Cutover timberland, eroded agricultural land, and the deteriorated condition of some of the "near-in" areas of our cities all reflect the pioneer tendency to abandon worn-out land or structures and to develop new resources.

In recent years, however, relatively more attention has been given to programs of flood control, soil conservation, reforestation, urban renewal, and related activities than previously. Programs in these areas are gaining more recognition by government agencies at all levels as well as by private investors and developers.

We should recognize, of course, that there are some *nonrenewable* resources. For example, a natural recreational area may not be subject to renewal. The same thing is true of such resources as coal, petroleum, and natural gas. *Renewable* resources are subject to replacement either through natural processes or through human decisions and programs. Basic soil fertility may be destroyed but is also subject to renewal. The productivity of renewable resources can be increased, maintained, or diminished as a result of individual, business, or governmental decisions.[8]

Of special importance in recent years have been the urban renewal programs which reflect growing interest in some of the increasingly complex problems of our cities. In addition to various privately established and financed programs there have been a number of firms that have undertaken the redevelopment of land after it has been assembled and cleared by governmental or quasi-governmental authorities. Such names as Zeckendorf, Greenwald, and Kitchen come to mind in this connection. A number of larger business firms have taken varying degrees of interest in renewal programs including Mellon and Alcoa in Pittsburgh, the Rockefellers in New York, and the Downtown Business Group in Philadelphia. Various universities, hospitals, and other institutions have taken increasing interest in urban renewal as have voluntary civic groups. Of growing, and in many respects major, importance in recent years in the urban renewal field, however, have been government programs, notably on the federal level, but including various state and local efforts as well.

Approaches to Urban Problems

We have undertaken a wide variety of programs to try to cope with the growing complexity of our urban problems. The Chicago World's Fair of 1893 gave an early impetus to city planning and related problems, as did the reinstitution of the L'Enfant plan for Washington in 1900. Concern over some of the slum problems of New York had brought a tenement house law as early as 1867. A substantial revision was made in 1901. The first comprehensive zoning law, covering both land use and the height and bulk of buildings, was enacted in New York in 1916. Traffic studies brought electrically operated traffic lights to Detroit in 1916.[9]

The depression of the 1930's brought a halt to city growth and focused attention on urban problems. Attempts were made to develop slum-clearance and related programs to stimulate employment. Similarly, housing programs were undertaken to stimulate construction and thus add to employment. Both public and private housing projects were involved. A broad program of federal loans and subsidies for public housing was undertaken with the passage of the United States Housing Act of 1937. The approach of providing new houses for a limited number of slum dwellers, however, proved to be disappointing.

Illinois and New York passed legislation based on a broader approach. In New York, the Urban Redevelopment Corporation law enacted in 1941,

[8] See Raleigh Barlowe, *Land Resource Economics* (Englewood Cliffs, N.J.: Prentice-Hall, Inc., 1958), chap. x.

[9] See Miles L. Colean, *Renewing Our Cities* (New York: The Twentieth Century Fund, Inc., 1953), pp. 23–36.

and the Illinois Neighborhood Redevelopment Corporation law of the same year, made provision for property owners in a specific area to pool their interests, take shares in a redevelopment corporation which had the power of eminent domain, acquire properties, and redevelop them. Subsequently, New York made provision for insurance companies to invest in equities of redevelopment companies; and this brought such significant results as development of Metropolitan Life's Stuyvesant Town. Later, other states enacted various types of urban redevelopment legislation.

By 1943, legislation on the federal level for similar activities was proposed; and this resulted later on in the adoption of a broad-scale program under the provisions of Title I of the Housing Act of 1949. The Act provided loans and grants for local redevelopment purposes. Subsequently, emphasis was placed on the prevention of slum and blight conditions. Provision was made for federal assistance in financing long-range planning programs and for renewal demonstration projects. The Urban Renewal Administration was set up and its work expanded as more and more cities became interested in attacking problems associated with "near-in gray areas," various downtown problems, and also those related to urban "sprawl" and similar outlying area problems.[10] Subsequently programs of this type were revised and expanded including the Housing and Urban Development Act of 1965.[11]

Urban renewal as a term has been used to cover some three types of programs: rehabilitation, conservation, and redevelopment. Rehabilitation is the process of bringing structures that are substandard or in a deteriorating condition up to acceptable standards through the enforcement of codes and regulations. Conservation includes rehabilitation as well as spot clearance in order to upgrade an area. Redevelopment involves the demolition, clearance, and reconstruction of an entire area.[12]

The Federal Housing Administration's programs were expanded to provide for the insurance of loans to help finance private construction of redevelopment housing and to provide housing for those displaced

[10] See "Urban Renewal," *Law and Contemporary Problems*, XXV, No. 4 (Autumn, 1960) and XVI, No. 1 (Winter, 1961). In an introductory statement to Part I, David M. Walker says: "At the present time, the city core is the center of the renewal effort. . . . When urban renewal is viewed in the light of the more recent legislation as an attack on the problems of the city as a whole . . . the city center still requires immediate attention. . . . And yet, if we can depend on history to teach us any lessons for tomorrow, we must conclude that inevitably the suburban rings around our central cities will be adequate for, or incompatible with, twenty-first century living, and the urban renewal process will be moving into the suburbs before we are through with the central city."

See also William G. Grigsby, "Housing and Slum Clearance: Elusive Goals," *The Annals of the American Academy of Political and Social Science* (March, 1964).

[11] Public Law 89-117, 89th Congress, August 10, 1965.

[12] For more detailed discussions of these processes see U.S. Savings and Loan League, *Urban Renewal Manual*, 1963.

as a result of urban renewal projects. Various modifications and refinements have come along with almost every new session of Congress.

Of special significance was the establishment of the Department of Housing and Urban Development by the 89th Congress in 1965.[13]

The Federal Government and Public Housing

Public housing programs have generated a considerable amount of controversy over the years. The main justification for such programs has been the denial of access to housing markets of members of colored races or various religious groups. In some cases public housing is defended as a subsidy for lower-income groups.

Except for a limited venture into the housing field during World War I, the activities of the federal government in public housing date from the depression of the 1930's. Most of the early programs were designed to accomplish at least two objectives: (1) to stimulate recovery from depressed economic conditions and (2) to provide low-rent housing, usually through slum clearance projects. The programs included public ownership, subsidies, and to some extent tax exemptions, as well as other types of controls.

The earliest agency in this field was the Housing Division of the Public Works Administration. Attempting at first to operate by lending funds to limited-dividend corporations, the PWA soon proceeded to develop a program for the direct financing of government-owned housing.

Chief results of this program were the establishing of a few local housing authorities, experimentation in the mass planning and management of housing, and the development of support for additional public housing programs.

The United States Housing Authority established in 1937 provided for a system of finance and subsidy in which the federal government carried a substantial part of the load but allowed for the ownership and operation of projects by local governments. Federal grants were provided for local authorities. Usually occupancy in the projects was limited to families in the lower-income groups. In recent years local housing authorities have borrowed from private investors rather than the federal government. Some of the earlier government loans have been refinanced by private capital.

In general the USHA projects were less costly than those of the PWA, and the provision of a sort of federal-local government partnership brought about the establishment of numerous local housing authorities. These projects have competed to some extent with private properties, and probably have had the effect of retarding some private rental housing developments.

[13] Public Law 89-174, 89th Congress, September 9, 1965.

During World War II, the USHA was made a part of the Federal Public Housing Authority, which in turn was a subdivision of the National Housing Agency. The FPHA also financed the construction of temporary housing of many types during the war. The general social objectives which were largely responsible for the establishment of these agencies in the 1930's were supplanted by short-range wartime objectives. Following the war, the NHA was replaced by the Housing and Home Financing Agency, and the FPHA by the Public Housing Administration. Public housing activities have been relatively limited during most of the years since the end of World War II with only a small percentage of housing starts being due to public or publicly financed dwelling units.

A new type of approach to the provision of housing through public support was undertaken by the Housing and Urban Development Act of 1965. Under this act supplementary rental payments were authorized to private owners on behalf of tenants with low incomes. Programs arising under this legislation, although not public housing as such, will tend to serve the same purposes.

Public housing has been a highly controversial issue for a number of years. Of course, some public housing is essential, including housing for criminals, the insane, and other wards of the state. Also, provision is usually made for public housing for various governmental officials. Many college and university dormitories may be classified as public housing. The principal controversy, however, centers in the provision of public housing or, more recently, rent subsidies for people in lower-income or minority groups or both. It is hard to draw the line between those who can pay an economic rent and those who cannot. The extent to which one or another minority group may be denied access to the housing markets of the community may be diminishing. Even so, public housing and rent subsidies are likely to continue as important issues for some time.

Zoning and Building Regulations

On the local level of government, zoning and building regulations have a continuing influence on real estate decision-makers.

The zoning of land uses appears to be expanding. Now a commonplace practice in most municipalities, zoning has been expanding in use throughout the country. Increasingly zoning is carried out on a country-wide basis and to entire metropolitan areas in some cases.

We should recognize that zoning sets limits on competition and in effect establishes certain noncompeting areas as between types of land use. This is done because of the recognition that some land uses are incompatible and that orderly development cannot be relied upon to result from open market competition. Typically residential districts are designated and divisions may be made as between single-family and multi-family dwelling house areas; commercial areas are marked out as are industrial areas. One type of land use is not permitted to invade another.

Virtual monopolies may be granted and substantial gains may be had by getting certain land rezoned. Much land was rezoned to provide for shopping centers and apartment house developments in recent years. In some cases political influence and favoritism play a part in rezoning actions.

Successful zoning laws and planning regulations typically conform to the general pattern of city growth and do not run contrary to such patterns. Some flexibility, of course, is usually needed since none can be entirely sure of long-range land use needs.

In some cases zoning is used to serve the purposes of a special group. For example, "snob zoning," which typically requires three to five acres per residence, may protect existing exclusive communities and prevent development of new areas by builders for the general market. Builders sometimes seek out communities with lenient zoning laws.

Building codes which usually regulate quality and strength of materials, allowable stresses, and make provision for various sanitary and health considerations, have been subjected to a considerable amount of study and criticism in recent years.[14] Often they add unduly to construction costs. They usually fail to establish performance standards but rather impose a variety of detailed regulations and bureaucratic practices. They may be used to protect local workmen and business firms and often they delay the introduction of new construction materials and methods. Changes may be slow in coming, however, since numerous local special interests typically are involved.

Control by Use of Deed Restrictions

In addition to regulations set up by public authority, private owners can limit the uses to which property may be put, establish building restrictions, regulate land coverage, and control property in other ways. The usual manner of imposing such restrictions is to insert an appropriate provision in the deed by which property is transferred. Such restrictions may be special, applying to only one property, or general, relating to an entire area. Real estate decision-makers pay special attention to such arrangements.

Deed restrictions are usually supplementary to other controls; their potentialities for greater inclusiveness and differentiation between properties gives them additional value as control devices. Municipalities, of course, have no part in the enforcement of regulations of this type, such as they have in the enforcement of zoning laws.

[14] See for example, Hal Colling's article in *House and Home* (January, 1964), pp. 80ff.

Deed restrictions are of special importance in the planning of new subdivisions, since the developer may wish to impose much more strict and severe regulations than are contained in zoning laws, building codes, or other forms of regulation. For example, a subdivider may wish to control the price range of structures or the type of architecture, or in other ways impose restrictions which are much more detailed and involved than public regulations. We will have more to say about this in Chapter 15.

Deed restrictions belong to the law of contracts, and the legal presumption is always in favor of the free exercise of the right to contract. But this generalization is subject to two important limitations: (1) contracts may not be contrary to public policy and (2) they must not be unreasonable. The former test rests upon proof that someone is benefitted by the contract; the latter usually rests on the notion of being in accordance with the judgment of the average man.

Because of the attitudes of the courts arising from the long struggle to liberate land from feudal ties, there is a tendency to look with disfavor on too many restraints on the use and free transfer of landed property. Hence, when there is doubt about the meaning of a contract or the intent of the parties, the courts tend to construe in favor of the freer use of land. Despite these conditions, however, the latitude of control is still large. It is especially large if the restrictions form a part of a so-called general scheme for the regulation of a considerable area.

Deed restrictions may control the use of the land and indicate the types and uses of structures that will be allowed. The period of time for which deed restrictions are imposed varies widely, provision generally being made for an original term of from ten to thirty years or longer, and for extension beyond the original period. The time for which restrictions are imposed should conform to the requirements of the area, being determined by its probable life expectancy, the trends of city growth, attitudes of potential buyers, and similar factors.

Deed restrictions may be enforced by the seller, or they may provide that the restrictions run with the land and be jointly enforcible by seller and owner. Two general methods are available for enforcing deed restrictions. In the case of covenants running with the land, the usual remedy is a suit in equity to enjoin violations. In cases where the restrictions are in the nature of conditions upon which the deed is given, a reverter clause provides that the property is to revert to the seller if violations are claimed and can be proved.

In more recent years, property owners' associations or homes associations have been established to enforce restrictions, administer maintenance funds if any are set up, approve building plans, and promote community activities.

Other Forms of Private Regulation

Control over the development of new areas is important, of course. However, restrictions may also be used to control and preserve older residential neighborhoods. For example, neighborhood restrictive agreements may be set up which are quite similar to deed restrictions in a new area. The neighborhood restrictive agreement is a private contract entered into voluntarily by the owners of property in a given district for the purpose of establishing protections against blight. They may be as detailed and inclusive as the owners wish to make them, subject to the same limitations that surround deed restrictions. Also, they are mutually binding upon and enforcible by all owners who are parties. Often such agreements list the nuisances which are banned, specify duration and methods of continuance, provide for additions and alterations, authorize collection of funds for common expenses, and, in short, apply the techniques of deed restrictions to areas already built up. Restrictions can be broken by violations if no objections are raised.

Research and Information

The federal government carries on a number of research and informational activities which are of importance to real estate owners and users. The Bureau of the Census collects and publishes a large mass of materials pertinent to real estate problems, especially the information made available through the Census of Housing. The National Bureau of Standards and the Forests Products Laboratory carry on continuous research and publish much valuable information. The Housing and Home Finance Agency, the Federal Housing Administration, and the Federal Home Loan Bank system have conducted technical, market, and financial research on a continuous basis. Many of their publications have been useful to real estate owners and users as well as to subdividers, property managers, mortgage lenders, and appraisers.

In addition to the federal government, many states provide information about taxes, zoning and planning activities, and the like, while local governments provide, usually upon request, detailed information about construction and real estate activities. For example, a number of local planning boards have made real contributions to the literature of this field. Various private associations and firms publish house organs and reports, many of which are valuable. A number of university bureaus of business research and government research and planning publish special studies and periodic information about business and real estate conditions which are pertinent to real estate problems.

Future Regulations and Trends

As we suggested in the introduction to this chapter, those who make decisions regarding the ownership, use, leasing, development, marketing, or financing of real estate are influenced not only by current public and private regulations but also by the changes that are likely to take place in such regulations in the future.

We have tried to suggest some of the types of changes that may influence real estate decision-makers in the future. Other potential lines of development may also be noted. The growing complexity of our communities probably means more rather than fewer regulations in the future. The growing interdependence of land uses and the increasing importance of public land and public improvements for successful private developments must be recognized. The growing demand for public services probably means that taxes in general will tend to increase. How much this will affect real properties is an open question, but commercial, industrial, and apartment house properties are more likely to be affected than single-family houses.

The problems of the older parts of cities will require increasing attention if significant progress in urban renewal is to be achieved. Although various public and private efforts have been made toward finding solutions to these problems, much remains to be done, especially if private interests and capital are to be attracted into such programs to an increasing extent.[15] There is a possibility that the trend toward the suburbs may be reversed in some degree, but probably not to a major extent.

The growing attention being given by the executives of business firms to local community problems, local government, and the relationships between local government programs and the operations of business firms merits attention. Closely related is the growing interest of local chambers of commerce and other business groups in problems of this type. As a result, greater emphasis may be given in the future to the development of regulations and controls that stimulate the expansion and growth of real estate resources.

National-State-local Relationships

In attempting to estimate the impact of political and governmental trends, the real estate decision-maker finds it advisable to consider the potential effect of the program or policy under evaluation upon specific parcels of real property. He thinks in terms of the localization of income.

[15] Rosslyn, a suburb of Washington, D.C., provides an interesting example of successful private urban renewal programs.

For example, a general expansion of the federal highway program may have only indirect and limited effects on the real estate located in an area that is remote from any part of the expanded highway system. A reduction in federal taxes is likely to benefit some areas more than others. A space contract awarded to a firm in California is likely to have little impact on the value of real estate in a depressed area in the east.

In short, it is one thing to identify national or state-wide political or governmental trends of development and quite another to assess the impact of such trends on specific localities and on specific pieces of real estate. The impact of some national and state-wide policies may be fairly uniform as between localities; in other cases quite different effects may result.

Even within a local area the impact of governmental policies on different properties may be quite varied. We mentioned above some of the potentially variable impacts of changes in the property tax. Changes in the local transportation system may have quite different effects on various properties. Renewal programs may have a major impact on the properties in a specific neighborhood, somewhat lesser effects on properties in nearby areas.

The analysis of governmental and political trends is helpful to the real estate decision-maker to the extent that he can relate the results to the income production potentials of specific properties.

SUMMARY

Real estate is among the most highly regulated of all commodities; hence, governmental and political trends are important factors in real estate decisions. The extent of real estate regulations may be explained in part by the fact that government is the source of private rights in property, and in part by the impact of the use of one property on others. Real estate is affected by all levels of government through regulations ranging from local taxation to broad federal programs and policies. Government protection of private rights in property is an important basis of real estate value and potential changes in such arrangements are of major interest to real estate decision-makers. Private restrictions also may be important factors in real estate decisions.

Private property and a competitive economic order are generally accepted institutions in the United States, although their precise definitions and contents tend to change over time. Regulations or restrictions, whether public or private, inducive or coercive, may either supplement or supplant competition.

Taxation is particularly important to real estate decisions. Of growing importance also are federal agencies in real estate finance, urban renewal programs, and various changes in public ownership.

The growing complexity of our society indicates the growing importance of governmental and political trends for real estate decisions.

QUESTIONS FOR STUDY

1. Discuss the statement "things are not always as they seem to be" as it relates to governmental actions influencing real estate. Do you agree with the statement? Why or why not?
2. Make a list of regulations designed to maintain competition in real estate markets. Do the same for regulations that have the effect of reducing or supplanting competition in real estate markets.
3. Give examples of both coercive and inducive regulations.
4. Describe the probable impact on real estate of inflation and deflation in the future.
5. How would the elimination of depressions affect real estate decisions?
6. Do you believe that the federal government should promote home financing? Discuss the programs you would encourage to effect this goal.
7. List three ways by which the federal government subsidizes local government.
8. Explain how owners of real property would be affected by a reduction of taxes on real property.
9. Explain the procedure by which real-property taxes are determined.
10. If taxes on real property are uniform, what objection might property owners have to low assessments? What disadvantage or advantage would exist for the taxing body?
11. Evaluate the pros and cons of the arguments over public housing. Do you favor or oppose rent subsidies? Why?
12. What is the purpose of zoning regulation?
13. Explain the purpose of building codes. Do such codes tend either to restrict or to intensify competition?
14. What would you add to the discussion of "future regulations and trends" in Chapter 9? Do you agree with the hypotheses proposed?
15. Explain the chief uses of deed restrictions.
16. *Study Project 12.* What changes, if any, would you make in developing a summary of zoning regulations for your own city? Be sure to explain your reasons carefully. You may wish to note that in the sample regulations residential land uses are permitted in manufacturing zones.
17. *Study Project 13.* Choose as an example an urban renewal project with which you are familiar. How does this project fit within the general guidelines suggested? Discuss federal participation in your selected project and evaluate its contribution to local and national goals.
18. *Study Project 14.* Compare this discussion with the one presented in Study Project 13. Which position do you prefer? Why?
19. *Study Project 15.* Do you agree with the proposition that every urban community does not have an economic climate for renewing its central areas? Explain.

SUGGESTED READINGS

THOMPSON, WILBUR R. *A Preface to Urban Economics.* Baltimore: Johns Hopkins Press, 1965. Chaps. vii, x.

"Urban Revival: Goals and Standards," *The Annals of the Academy of Political and Social Science,* March 1964.

WEIMER, ARTHUR M. *Business Administration: An Introductory Management Approach.* Homewood, Ill.: Richard D. Irwin, Inc., 1966. Chap. vii.

10

Business Conditions and Industry Trends

Real Estate Decisions and Business Conditions

The general level of business activity has an important bearing on the income-producing capacity and potential of real properties and hence on real estate decisions. The real estate sector of the economy is greatly influenced by the economy as a whole and, in turn, influences general economic conditions in varying degrees.

Not only are general business conditions likely to influence real estate decisions, but conditions in specific industries, in regions, and in particular cities and local areas also have their impact. Conditions in specific industries or regions may be more favorable or less favorable than conditions in the economy as a whole. Although local economic conditions tend to parallel general economic trends, special local situations may bring substantial deviations from such trends.

Estimates of the future trends of economic activity for the economy as a whole, for an industry, for a region, or for a particular locality are far from easy to make. For the economy as a whole, estimates of future economic conditions involve predicting the decisions that will be made by some 60 million households, over 4 million farmers, and nearly 5 million business firms, as well as thousands of government officials on federal, state, or local levels. In some cases, it is necessary to anticipate the decisions of government officials in other countries, as well as the decisions of consumers, farmers, and businessmen abroad.

For a particular industry or line of business, it is necessary to anticipate changes in competitive conditions, market preferences, government
regulations, taxes, and many other related factors. Regional economic
trends often are hard to forecast due to possible changes in competitive
conditions and in regional economic opportunities. It is even difficult to
anticipate economic trends for a particular locality. A sudden shift in
government policies or the decisions of a major corporation to withdraw
its programs or investments may cause marked changes in the local economic outlook.

The Localization of Income

Those of us with interests in real estate administration have as much
concern with general economic trends, regional changes, and the prospects of various industries as those interested in other major fields of
business activity. In addition, our interest in real estate prompts us to
emphasize the localization of income, as we have pointed out at various
places in earlier discussions. The value of a particular piece of real
estate may be influenced by anticipations as to general economic or industry trends but it will be influenced especially by anticipated changes
in the stream of income flowing into a local economy. Even within a
local economy the effect of local economic trends on various parcels of
real estate may differ markedly.

In this chapter we consider various problems related to the analysis
of general business conditions and industry trends. In the following
chapter we discuss regional and local economic trends and their significance for the real estate decision-maker.

Long-Term and Short-Term Outlook

Real estate decision-makers are concerned both with potential changes
in the short run and in the longer term. Because of the long life of real
properties, long-term trends may be somewhat more important in the real
estate field than in others.

Thus, we pay special attention to projections of the longer-term future,
such as outlined in the excellent study, *Resources in America's Future*,
by Landsberg, Fischman, and Fisher.[1] This study projects potential
trends of development for the American economy as a whole and for
some of its principal sectors to the year 2000.

Similarly, we are particularly interested in the long sweep of historical
development. Often trends of development that have persisted for a long

[1] Hans H. Landsberg, Leonard L. Fischman, and Joseph L. Fisher, *Resources in
America's Future* (Baltimore: The Johns Hopkins Press, 1963).

time may give keys to future potentialities. Some interesting trends of this type are presented in *Balance Sheet of the U.S.* by Goldsmith and Lipsey, sponsored by the National Bureau of Economic Research.[2] A study sponsored by the Committee for Economic Development on *The Sources of Economic Growth in the United States and the Alternatives Before Us,* conducted by Edward F. Denison, identifies principal factors in past economic growth and points to their probable future effects. Denison emphasizes the education of the work force and the advancement of knowledge as major factors in economic growth along with a larger work force, increased use of capital, more efficient operations, and economies of scale. He says:

Whatever period we examine, it is clear that economic growth, occurring within the general institutional setting of a democratic, free-enterprise society, has stemmed and will stem mainly from an increased labor force, more education, more capital, the advance of knowledge, with economics of scale exercising an important, but essentially passive, re-enforcing influence. . . .[3]

Current Levels of General Business Activity

An understanding of the current status of business activity and its relation to previous trends is essential in studying business conditions. The decision-maker usually follows business activity regularly through trade journals, financial newspapers such as the *Wall Street Journal,* and general business magazines such as *Business Week.* However, he may wish to undertake a more detailed analysis. There are several general measures of business conditions, reported in current government publications, which will prove helpful.

One of the more important indicators of business activity is the level of industrial production. The Federal Reserve System makes monthly estimates of industrial production and publishes an index in the *Federal Reserve Bulletin.* This index is separated into various types of industrial activity which can be compared to each other or to the total.

Other general measures of business conditions which will prove helpful are the volume of employment and the level of personal income. Such information is published regularly in the *Survey of Current Business,* published by the Department of Commerce, the *Federal Reserve Bulletin,* and *Economic Indicators,* which we referred to in Chapter 1. Detailed data on population estimates are available in the Bureau of the Census' *Current Population Reports.*

[2] Raymond W. Goldsmith and Robert E. Lipsey, *Studies in the National Balance Sheet of the U.S.,* Vol. I (Princeton, N.J.: Princeton University Press, 1963).

[3] Edward F. Denison, *The Sources of Economic Growth in the United States and the Alternatives Before Us* (New York: Committee for Economic Development, 1962), p. 273.

What about business income? These same sources will provide information about corporate profits, proprietors' incomes, unincorporated business and professional income, and farm income. Information is also readily available in regard to business sales and inventories; manufacturers' sales, inventories, and orders; the number of firms in business; new firms started; and number of business failures—all of which are helpful figures when related to past levels.

The *Survey of Current Business,* in addition, publishes data on retail trade, advertising, securities and security markets, and industrial activities and product lines.

Types of Business Fluctuations

In considering the relationship of current busine   activity to that of preceding periods, three major types of changes in business activity may be distinguished: secular trends, seasonal fluctuations, and cycles.

A secular trend results from basic underlying forces, such as population growth or technological change, which exert a more or less steady influence on general business activity or on an industry over the long term. For example, in the United States during the last six or seven decades, the total output of all goods and services (called *gross national product,* or GNP), measured in constant dollars, has increased, *on the average,* by about 3 per cent a year.

Note that we said "on the average." Substantial fluctuations may, and usually do, take place around the trend line. These are the cyclical and seasonal fluctuations. It is sometimes difficult to distinguish between a fluctuation which is cyclical in character and one which represents a basic trend change. (In the late 1930's, for example, many people concluded that the long-term trend of American business had flattened out, and that the period of rapid growth had come to an end. Actually, they were confusing long-term trend and cyclical changes.)

There are various methods of identifying the trend line of a business series. Regardless of the mathematical technique employed, however, they all require the exercise of judgment. Unless we make proper allowance for the secular trend factor, erroneous conclusions may be drawn regarding business conditions and business prospects. For very short-term comparisons, however, trend can often be ignored.

With regard to seasonal fluctuations, little need be said. These are variations caused by factors associated with the calendar year cycle: the weather, the varying lengths of months, holidays, conventional vacation periods, and so forth. Almost any measure of business activity exhibits some seasonal fluctuation. More houses are usually built in the spring and summer than in the fall and winter, and the reasons for this are obvious (at least in the northern part of the United States).

Again, there are recognized statistical techniques for identifying normal seasonal variation, and the business analyst should know what to expect in the way of seasonal variation in studying any phase of business activity. Otherwise, he may be unduly disturbed (or encouraged) by

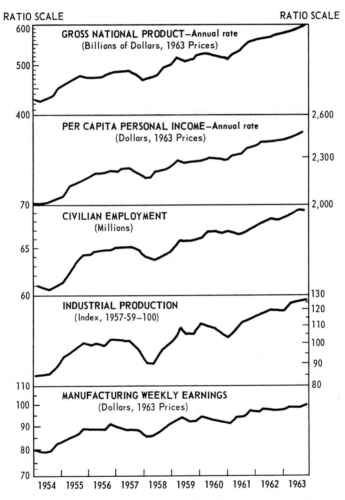

Fig. 10–1. Indicators of production and income. (Source: *Annual Report,* Council of Economic Advisers, 1964.)

what is, in fact, only a normal seasonal fluctuation. The business analyst should be on the lookout, however, for any changes in seasonal patterns. In recent years, for example, vacation periods and plant close-downs in July have become increasingly common. Any seasonal adjustment derived from past data is likely to undercorrect for this factor.

Assuming that proper allowance has been made for trend and seasonal variation, the main concern of the business analyst is with cyclical fluctuations.[4] We all know that the record of American business is one of ups and downs. At times, nearly all business firms have been prosperous and nearly all employable persons have been working. At other times, nearly everyone has found business poor, jobs scarce, and unemployment high. These swings in general business activity—through prosperity, recession, recovery, and prosperity again—are business cycles.

Before we go any further, we should dispose of the notion that there is anything rhythmical about business cycles. They have varied in timing from about two to about twelve years.[5] They vary even more in magnitude, all the way from the boom of 1929, followed by the deep depression of the early 1930's and the partial recovery of 1937, to the milder cyclical swings of 1948–49, 1953–54, 1957–58 and 1960–61. Unfortunately for the forecaster, each business cycle seems to be unique, and its length and amplitude are determined by a combination of forces never duplicated before and probably never to be duplicated in the future. In the past thirty years the amplitude of both business and real estate cycles has been less than previously largely because of the economic stabilizers.

Estimating Future Spending Patterns

It is not safe to project a trend into the future by purely mechanical means. It is necessary to analyze the fundamental forces at work and to draw some conclusions as to whether these forces will continue to operate in the future.

In an exchange economy, the level of business activity depends to a great extent on the volume of spending. The principal spending divisions are consumers, businessmen, and governments. Besides information on past and current levels of spending, some guides to the future intentions of each of these three major spending divisions are available.

Since consumer spending currently makes up over 60 per cent of the total expenditures in our economy, this area requires special consideration when estimating future levels of business activity. The Federal Reserve has sponsored various studies of consumer buying intentions and the general financial condition of consumers. The Bureau of the Census,

---

[4] Although a more detailed description might differentiate between major and minor cycles or between cycles and random fluctuations, we are using the term "cycle" in this general treatment of the subject to refer to the fluctuation remaining after removal of trend and seasonal factors.

[5] Wesley Mitchell, *What Happens During Business Cycles: A Progress Report* (New York: National Bureau of Economic Research, Inc., 1951), chap. iii; see also Homer Hoyt, *The Urban Real Estate Cycle—Performance and Prospects*, Technical Bulletin No. 38 (Washington, D.C.: Urban Land Institute, 1960).

the Survey Research Center at the University of Michigan, and various industry groups also carry on studies of this type. These surveys are, of course, subject to the usual errors of sampling and to the risk that consumers may change their minds after the surveys have been completed.

Of special interest to us are reports on plans for home buying, current levels of home ownership, home mortgage debt, owner equities, and related information. Such information may be related to current levels of consumer income, volume of employment, and the terms and availability of financing for such items as consumers purchase.

In recent years, total consumer spending has reflected fairly consistent growth, although there have been some shifts among various types of expenditures. Unusual events, such as war scares, have had far less pronounced effect than might have been expected. Even during the recessions of 1957–58 and 1960–61, unemployment rose and industrial production dropped, but consumer spending faltered only briefly.

Another major area for consideration is the volume of spending by business. Business spending for wages and salaries is of major importance with respect to the level of consumer incomes. Investment by business firms in plant and equipment is especially vital to anyone seeking to forecast future business conditions. Expansion of plant and equipment usually takes place when profit prospects are favorable and declines when they are not. Special programs such as tax adjustments by the government will also affect the volume of business spending.

The Department of Commerce and the Securities and Exchange Commission make a joint estimate of business plans for expenditures of this type, which is published in the financial newspapers and in the *Survey of Current Business*. McGraw-Hill Publishing Company also makes surveys of business plans for plant and equipment expenditures and reports them in *Business Week*. As in the estimates of consumer spending, of course, these estimates may be affected by any changes in plans. However, they have been very accurate during recent years.

In short-run analysis of business conditions, the level of inventories and inventory plans are of special importance. Low levels of inventory during periods of rapid expansion indicate the possibility of further advances in the volume of business activity. On the other hand, during a period of level or declining prices and income, a substantial rise in inventory levels may create instability because of pressure to reduce these levels. Information about inventories is reported regularly by the *Survey of Current Business* and also by the financial press.

It should be noted that improved methods of inventory control have enabled business managers to operate on relatively small inventories in recent years. Even so, inventories are an important factor in the short-run business outlook.

The third major area of spending is that of federal, state, and local governments. Information about the expenditure plans of state and local governments is not readily available, although past levels of expenditure are reported in the *Federal Reserve Bulletin* and the *Survey of Current Business.*

The earliest indication of future federal government expenditures is the President's Budget Message, submitted to Congress early in each regular session. The business conditions analyst must subsequently follow the appropriation and tax actions of Congress to determine whether they coincide with the original request.

After Congress has acted, the Bureau of the Budget prepares estimates of the timing and amount of receipts and expenditures of the federal government (summaries are reported in the financial news and in *Economic Indicators*). Funds are allocated by appropriations, but it is important to note expenditure plans, because the effect of federal government spending on business conditions depends largely on actual spending. A considerable period of time may elapse between appropriations and actual spending.

In addition to spending by consumers, businesses, and governments, spending in foreign countries, balanced against receipts, may at times be significant. Although in the United States these items do not claim the attention that they do in such countries as Holland and England, they are a factor of growing importance in estimating business trends.

Gross National Product

In order to make more detailed and complete analyses of business conditions, the gross national product (GNP) method has been developed by government economists. In this procedure, the major income and expenditure (product) accounts in the nation are grouped as shown in Table 10–1. The total is the sum of expenditures by the major groups just discussed. You will see summaries of the accounts regularly in the *Survey of Current Business* and in *Economic Indicators*. They are useful for short- and longer-term projections and often are useful in estimating trends in various industries or sectors of the economy.

Gross national product is the total value of all goods and services produced in the economy in any given period, usually a year. The method used by the Department of Commerce in calculating the official GNP figures avoids double counting by counting only the total value of final products and ignoring primary and semifinished products (except to the extent these add to business inventories). Calculated in this way, GNP indicates amounts actually paid in the market and therefore reflects price fluctuations as well as changes in physical output. Prices not otherwise available are estimated for goods and services wherever possible and are included in the GNP calculation. This includes assigning price values to government services, the output of self-employed persons, food produced on the farm for home consumption, and the imputed rental value of owner-occupied dwellings.

The items included in Table 10–1 are discussed briefly here so that you may understand their significance.

Table 10–1. Gross National Income and Product in the United States, 1965 (billions of dollars)

Income		Product	
Compensation of employees	391.9	Sales for personal consumption	428.5
Income of nonfarm unincorporated enterprises	40.3	Gross private domestic investment	104.9
Income of farm proprietors	14.3	Net sales abroad	7.2
Rental income of persons	18.6	Sales of goods and services to	
Corporate profits (adjusted before taxes)	73.1	governments	135.0
Net interest income	16.5		
(*Net*) *National Income*	554.6		
Plus: Indirect taxes	62.0		
Less: Adjustments *	0.3		
Net National Product	616.8		
Plus: Capital consumption allowances	58.7		
Gross National Income	675.6	*Gross National Product*	675.6

SOURCE: *Economic Report of the President,* 1966.
* Includes business transfer payments, statistical discrepancy, and current surpluses of government enterprises minus government subsidies.
NOTE: Detail will not necessarily add to totals because of rounding.

The right-hand side of this national account, as illustrated in Table 10-1, includes sales (or expenditures) for personal consumption, including food, clothing, haircuts, books, football games, and so forth. The term *personal consumption expenditures* excludes expenditures for capital goods —that is, things used in future production. This causes some problems. For example, an automobile bought for personal use is classified as a personal consumption expenditure, but it is considered a capital expenditure if bought by a company for business use. Houses are classified as capital goods, partly because so many of them are owned, as business ventures, by someone other than the occupant, and partly because of their long life, yielding property services over many years.

Gross private domestic investment includes, principally, expenditures by business for new capital goods—machines, factories, stores, locomotives, and the like. It also includes, as a plus or minus factor, net changes in

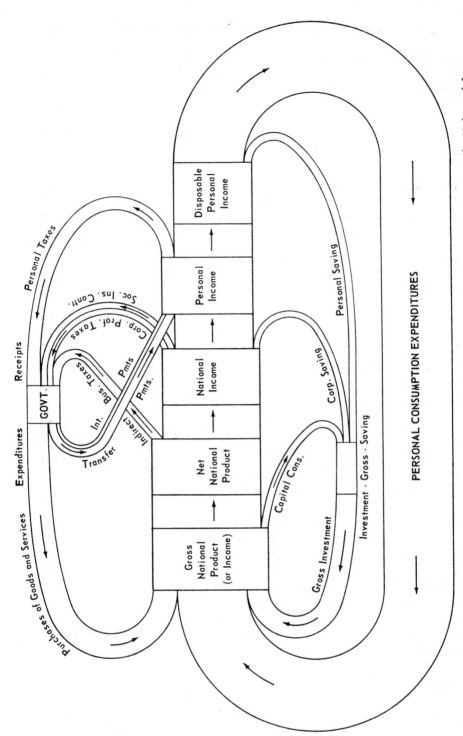

Fig. 10–2. The flow of money income and expenditures: the circular flow in a given time period. (Adapted from *America's Needs & Resources: A New Survey,* The Twentieth Century Fund.)

business inventories. Moreover, as noted above, it includes expenditures for new housing. An expenditure for an existing house simply reflects a shift of ownership. Nothing is added to total output.

Net sales abroad, more strictly termed *net foreign investment*, includes principally the excess of domestic output sold abroad over purchases by the United States of foreign output; it also includes certain other international balance of payment items.

Sales of goods and services to governments include all governmental units: federal, state, and local. Included are expenditures for compensation of employees (including military personnel) and government purchases of goods and services from business. Government investment in atomic energy installations or in other properties or capital equipment is also included.

These four general categories of expenditures, by consumers, business, and government, and of net sales abroad, together account for the total output, the gross national product (GNP), measured by what was actually paid for that output.

On the other side of the list of accounts set forth in Table 10–1, the same total of payments as is listed on the right-hand side is presented in terms of who receives them. These items constitute *gross national income.*

The sum of the first six items is called *net national income,* or usually simply *national income.* It represents the aggregate earnings of labor and property from the current production of goods and services in the nation's economy. In addition to national income, however, several other items must be included to account for the total of payments. One of these is indirect business taxes which are not received as income by any of the private factors of production. A second is capital consumption allowances, which consist chiefly of the charges made against current output for depreciation of capital goods. The item, *adjustments,* is a catch-all to cover certain minor adjusting factors, including the statistical discrepancy between gross national income as calculated from receipts and gross national product as calculated from payments.

So far we have been concerned with a static concept; an accounting of the nation's total income and output in a given, finite time interval. The dynamic concept of the moving, changing flow of income through the economy is shown in Figure 10–2. The chart is intended to illustrate not what happens in any finite time period, but rather the process of change from one time interval to the next.

Flow of Funds

Another important method of analyzing the economy and projecting future business conditions is the flow-of-funds approach, showing the relationship between GNP purchases and the nation's debt structure. This

Table 10–2.   Summary of Flow of Funds Accounts for Third

Sector	Consumer and non-profit organizations		Nonfinancial business sectors						Government sectors			
			Farm		Non-corporate		Corporate		U.S. Govt.		State and local	
Transaction category	U	S	U	S	U	S	U	S	U	S	U	S
A Gross saving..................		24.8		1.3		2.4		11.3		−2.9		−1.2
B Capital consumption......		12.6		1.1		2.3		8.0				
C Net saving (A−B)........		.12.2		.2		.1		3.3		−2.9		−1.2
D Gross investment (E+J)....	23.7		1.3		2.4		8.5		−2.4		−2.7	
E Private capital expenditures, net....................	16.9		1.4		3.9		10.0					
F Consumer durables........	11.7											
G Residential construction...	4.3				1.4		1.4					
H Plant and equipment......	1.0		1.2		.2.6		8.5					
I Inventory change.........			.1		−.1		.1					
J Net financial invest. (K−L)...	6.8		−.1		−1.5		−1.5		−2.4		−2.7	
K Financial uses, net..........	13.7		*		*		3.4		−1.6		−.3	
L Financial sources.........		6.8		.1		1.5		4.9		.8		2.4
M Gold and official U.S. foreign exchange..........												
N Treasury currency.........										*		*
O Demand deposits and curr.												
P Private domestic........	4.3						−.3				−1.0	
Q U.S. Govt...............	*								−2.4			
R Foreign.................												
S Time and svgs. accounts...	4.4											
T At coml. banks.........	2.0						.8		*		*	
U At svgs. institutions....	2.4											
V Life insurance reserves.....	1.1									*		
W Pension fund reserves.....	2.2									.1		.7
X Credit market instr........	2.1	6.2		.5	*	1.4	−.9	2.5	.9	.9	.7	1.7
Y U.S. Govt. securities....	1.6						−.8			1.5	.3	
Z State and local oblig.....	.2										*	1.7
AA Corp. and foreign bonds.	−.3							.5			.4	
AB Corp. stocks............	*							.1				
AC 1- to 4-family mtgs......	−.1	4.3						.4	−.1		*	
AD Other mortgages........	.8	.1	¤ .4			1.0		1.1	.1			
AE Consumer credit.........		1.6			*		.1					
AF Bank loans n.e.c........		.1		.1		−.1		.3				
AG Other loans............		.2		*		*	−.2		1.0	−.6		
AH Open market paper...						*	−.2		*			
AI Federal loans.........				*			.1		1.0			
AJ Security credit...........	*	.7										
AK To brokers and dealers..	*											
AL To others..............		.7										
AM Trade credit.............							.1	3.5	2.4	*	.1	*
AN Equity in noncorp. business	−.5		*	−.5		*						
AO Misc. financial trans.......	*		*		*		.3	*	−.1	−.3		
AP Sector discrepancies (A−D)..	1.1						.2.9		−.5		1.5	

SOURCE: *Federal Reserve Bulletin*, January, 1964.

approach was originally developed by Morris Copeland in 1952 [6] and was subsequently adopted and refined by the Federal Reserve System. Quarterly data is reported each month in the *Federal Reserve Bulletin*, with a lag of about four months.

[6] Morris A. Copeland, *A Study of Moneyflows in the United States* (New York: National Bureau of Economic Research, 1952).

Quarter, 1963—Not seasonally adjusted (In billions of dollars)

Financial sectors								Rest of the world		All sectors		Discrepancy	Natl. saving and investment	
Banking system		Savings institutions		Insurance		Finance n.e.c.								
U	S	U	S	U	S	U	S	U	S	U	S			
	.3		1.1		.2		-.1		*	37.2		4.9	37.2	A
										23.9			23.9	B
	.3		1.1		.2		-.1		*	13.3			13.3	C
.2		1.1		.9		-.1		.3		33.2		-.9	32.1	D
.1				.1						32.3			32.3	E
										11.7			11.7	F
										7.1			7.1	G
.1				.1						13.5			13.5	H
										.1			.1	I
.2		1.1		.8		-.1		.3		.9		-.9	-.3	J
3.6		4.3		3.4		1.9		.6		29.0			.4	K
	3.4		3.2		2.6		1.9		.4		28.2		.6	L
-.2								.2		*		*	-.2	M
	*									*		*		N
	-.3									.7	-.3	1.0		O
	1.7	-.2		.2		*				3.0	1.7	-1.3		P
	-2.1									-2.4	-2.1	.3		Q
	.1							.1			.1		-.1	R
	3.0									5.4				S
	3.0							.2		3.0			-.2	T
			2.4							2.4				U
						1.1				1.1				V
						1.4				2.2				W
3.4	*	4.8	.8	3.3		1.1	1.2	.2	.3	15.6	15.6	*	.1	X
-.7		.1		.4		.5		.1		1.5	1.5	*	-.1	Y
1.6		*		.1		-.1				1.7				Z
*				1.1		*	.4	*	.1	1.1			.1	AA
	*			.5		.1	.4	*	*	.5			*	AB
1.0		3.7		.5		.4				5.2				AC
.6		.7		.5						2.7				AD
.6		.3				.5				1.6				AE
1.0					*		.5	.1		1.0			.1	AF
-.7		*	.8	.3		-.1	-.1	.1	.1	.4	.4		*	AG
-.1		.1		.1		-.1	.1	*		-.1			-.1	AH
			.8					*		1.0				AI
.8						.7	.9			1.6				AJ
.7						.2	.9			.9				AK
.2						.5				.7				AL
					*					3.5	2.6	-.9		AM
											-.5			AN
-.4	.7	-.3				.1	-.2	-.1	.1	-.6	.4	1.0	.2	AO
*					-.7	*			-.3	4.0		4.0	5.2	AP

As compared to the income-statement form taken by the GNP data, flow-of-funds data are in the form of a "sources and uses of funds" statement. Instead of the three basic sectors in GNP data (consumers, business, and government) the flow-of-funds accounts system adds a fourth sector, that of financial institutions. One further sector, "rest of world," corresponds roughly to the "net sales abroad" in GNP statements. The accounts are developed for the entire economy, complete and consistent throughout, to show the interrelationships between these four sectors in their sources and uses of funds. A summary of the flow-of-funds accounts is shown in Table 10–2 as an example of the structure of this data.

Businesses and consumers make their spending decisions in light of the availability of credit, their own liquidity positions, and their plans for saving and investing. Government policy is also affected by anticipations of the future structure of monetary assets and liabilities. Although the assets and liabilities of any one sector need not balance, debt (liabilities) must be accounted for in the system as a whole. The holdings of such debt are recorded in the flow-of-funds accounts. With the financial sector added, considerable information on the activities of financial institutions is also provided.

There are many potential uses of these flow-of-funds accounts. For example, current quarterly information on the flow of mortgage funds is available through the accounts, showing both lender and borrower by sector. Economists have also used these accounts in an attempt to forecast interest rates and in making short-run projections of future credit demands.[7] Annual estimates are now available back to 1946 and quarterly data from 1952, so that historical perspective may be gained in an effort to understand present and future relationships.

Other Methods of Analysis

Efforts are being made constantly to improve the methods available for analyzing and forecasting potential changes in economic activity or to develop new approaches to these problems. In addition to gross national product and flow-of-funds, several other analytical methods are important, including "national wealth statistics," input-output tables, and balance-of-payments accounting.

National wealth statistics are set up in a manner that resembles an individual firm's balance sheet but pertains to the economic system as a whole. They provide measurements of the size and composition of the wealth of the entire economic system and record changes in them. The comprehensive study by Goldsmith and Lipsey referred to above is an outstanding illustration of this method of analysis.

Input-output tables trace the movement of goods and services between major industries of the economy. The method is attracting increasing attention. The Office of Business Economics of the U.S. Department of Commerce is increasing the amount of data that are needed for these

---

[7] Stephen Taylor, "Uses of Flow of Funds Accounts in the Federal Reserve," and William C. Freund and Edward D. Zinbarg, "Application of Flow of Funds to Interest-Rate Forecasting," *Journal of Finance* (May, 1963).

types of analyses.[8] Balance-of-payments accounting is used chiefly in measuring the volume and composition of a nation's international transactions.

Both input-output and balance-of-trade analyses have been applied in studying regional economies. Smaller countries, with somewhat homogeneous characteristics, might be considered regions for analytical purposes. In a country the size of the United States, with varying regional characteristics, comprehensive national income accounting such as GNP has proved more useful. However, in the following chapter we will see how the input-output and balance-of-payments methods, as they develop, can be used in regional analysis. Input-output analyses have been used also in various industry studies.

Long-Term Projections

One of the advantages of the GNP approach to economic analysis is its adaptability to long-term projections. As we have indicated above, real estate decision-makers often are more concerned with longer-run than shorter-run estimates.

The projections presented in the study *Resources in America's Future* are based in large part on the GNP approach. This study points out:

The most informative single measure of the size of the American economy is the gross national product, or the sum total of all the expenditures in a single year for all of the end products of the economy. . . . Yet because it is such a comprehensive measure of the multifarious activities that go to make up an economy, GNP is at the same time one of the least precise in meaning, . . . Despite conceptual and statistical shortcomings, the relationships between real GNP and a great many other economic series are remarkably consistent.[9]

The study projects the main components of GNP to the year 2000. By varying underlying assumptions, three projections (high, medium, and low) are developed. The totals are interesting, with medium projections indicating total output of slightly over a trillion dollars in 1980 (in constant dollars) and $2.2 trillion in the year 2000. But the components of the total are also interesting, giving us indications of the output of goods, services, and construction, as well as net exports, gross private domestic investment, government expenditures, and private consumption expenditures. Many of these categories can be broken down further; for example, hard goods and soft goods, durables and nondurables, or farm and nonfarm (the latter being industrial production). These also can be broken down into components and subcomponents.

[8] Wassily W. Leontief, "The Structure of the U.S. Economy," *Scientific American* (April, 1965), pp. 25–35; see also "The Interindustry Structure of the U.S.," *Survey of Current Business* (November, 1964).

[9] Landsberg, Fischman, and Fisher, *op. cit.*, p. 78.

Other types of long-term projections range from simple extrapolation of past trends and "rules of thumb" to carefully constructed assumptions about future trends. The GNP approach, however, has provided a useful model for both short- and longer-term estimates of economic developments.

Industry Analysis

Many studies that undertake to make short- or long-run projections of a particular industry start with GNP projections and relate potential industry developments to them. National markets, of course, are closely related to personal or business spending plans. In some cases, a given industry bears a fairly fixed relationship to one or another national measure of economic activity.

In many cases we have accumulated a substantial store of statistical information about an industry. The construction industry is a case in point. Good statistical data are available for new construction, both public and private, and for maintenance and repair activities. Estimates can be made for, say, a year ahead, or for the longer-term future. The study of *Resources in America's Future* projects principal categories of construction to 1980 and to 2000. See Table 10–3.

Table 10–3. Principal Categories of Construction, 1950, 1960 and
Medium Projections for 1980 and 2000
(billion 1960 dollars)

Category	1950	1960	Medium projection	
			1980	2000
Total construction	58.6	76.2	166.3	348.4
New construction	42.2	56.6	130.1	280.9
Maintenance and repair	16.4	19.6	36.2	67.5
of which for residential construction	6.2	7.2	10.8	14.7
Residential new construction incl.				
additions and alterations	19.6	22.6	54.7	126.4
Non-residential new construction	22.7	34.1	75.4	154.5
Private new construction	32.8	40.6	90.2	196.8
Public new construction	9.4	16.0	39.9	84.1
Components of public new nonresidential				
construction:	9.1	15.3	37.2	77.8
Schools and hospitals	2.3	3.2	5.0	7.4
Highways	2.6	5.5	16.1	34.6
Military & industrial	.6	1.8	5.1	12.3
All other (water, sewerage, etc.)	3.6	4.8	11.0	23.5

SOURCE: *Resources in America's Future*, p. 113.

Industry studies may attempt a forecast of costs, capital requirements, competitive factors, markets, and sales. Usually short-range estimates for a single business firm or an entire industry start with the basic projection of sales, which are related to some more-general measure of economic activity such as gross national product or disposable personal income. Past relationships are studied and the principal factors likely to cause variations are identified and analyzed.

The Department of Commerce has worked out relationships between disposable personal income and personal consumption expenditures for a variety of nondurable goods and services. The demand for nondurables tends to be easier to estimate because of the frequency of purchases and the short life of these products. Contrast this, for example, with housing or with automobiles.

In the case of automobiles, demand may fluctuate widely from year to year because of their durability. Hence, long-term, year-to-year, and seasonal factors all play a part in such projections.[10] In the case of housing or closely related industries such as furniture, short-term estimates can be based largely on demand factors, since supply is relatively fixed in a period of a year or two. Demand factors are likely to relate fairly closely to incomes and the terms and availability of financing in the short run. Over longer periods, population trends, the estimated rate of household formation, income trends, and the competitive position of housing relative to other goods and services bear careful study and consideration.

Some individual industries exhibit a cyclical movement which is more or less independent of general business cycles. However, as with general business cycles, the length and amplitude of the cycles are irregular. Some analysts claim to detect, for example, a cycle in real estate activity of roughly fifteen to twenty-five years in duration.

It is not our purpose here to outline even in a very general way the methods that are used in analyzing industry trends. Rather, we hope to indicate the importance of such studies, their relationship to the broader studies and projections of GNP and its components, and their implications in determining the values of specific parcels of real property.[11] The real estate decision-maker ultimately has to deal with specific, definite, practical problems related to particular properties and their income-producing potentials. We may be able to gain further insights into some of these relationships in the following chapter.

SUMMARY

The level of general business activity is an important determinant of income from real property. We are concerned with the localization of income. In many cases local business conditions tend to parallel general

---

[10] Carl A. Dauten, *Business Cycles and Forecasting* (Cincinnati: South-Western Publishing Co., 1961), chap. xxi.

[11] For an illustration of the use of input-output analysis in industry studies, see "Input-Output Relations of the Auto Industry," *Economic Review,* Federal Reserve Bank of Cleveland (March, 1965).

trends; in others local factors are of greater importance in determining the level of business activity. Industry trends and regional patterns of economic change also are important. Because of the impact of business conditions on real estate income, the analysis of such conditions provides a guide to decision-making. Such analyses are usually based on data related to employment, income, production, and prices. Such data and related information are published in *Economic Indicators, Survey of Current Business, Federal Reserve Bulletin,* and other government publications, and in the business and financial press.

Changes in business activity may be the reflections of seasonal, cyclical, or secular trend influences. Each of these may be analyzed.

The level of spending is an important determinant of total business activity. Consumer spending makes up the largest single element of total spending, although this in turn is dependent largely on business expenditures for wages and salaries.

The national income accounting system is an organized framework for measuring and analyzing economic activity. The most widely used measure of total activity is gross national product, which measures output in terms of expenditures on final products. Gross national income, which is equal to GNP, measures activity by the incomes received by producers of final products. Flow of funds, input-output tables, and other methods of analyzing business conditions also are in use. Industry projections often are related to GNP measures although other methods are also followed.

QUESTIONS FOR STUDY

1. Are real estate decision-makers more concerned with local or national business trends? Short or long-term trends? Explain your answers.
2. How do general business conditions affect the income-producing ability of real properties?
3. List the main indicators of current levels of general business activity.
4. What is meant by "gross national product"? How does gross national income differ from GNP?
5. Distinguish between secular trend, seasonal fluctuations, and cycles in business activity. Explain why each of these might be important to the analysis of real estate markets.
6. Explain the importance of each of the following to the level of general business conditions: (a) Spending by consumers. (b) Government spending. (c) Business spending for plant and equipment; business spending for inventories. (d) Spending by foreign countries for U.S. goods.
7. What types of information are included in the flow-of-funds accounts that are not available from national income accounts such as are used in GNP analysis?
8. Discuss the relationship between the construction industry and: (a) General business conditions. (b) Local business conditions.

9. How is the GNP approach used to project long-term trends in general business activity? What other methods might be used for a long-term projection? What advantage does the GNP approach have?

10. *Study Project 16.* Gather statistical data for the same period on general business conditions and compare this to the analysis developed in the Study Project. What conclusion, if any, can you draw from such a comparison? Explain your answer. Do you agree with the conclusion that "the possibility of serious outside shocks remains strong"? Discuss this possibility.

SUGGESTED READINGS

DAUTEN, CARL A. *Business Cycles and Forecasting.* Cincinnati: South-Western Publishing Co., 1961. Chaps. vi, xxi.

DENISON, EDWARD F. *The Sources of Economic Growth in the United States and the Alternatives Before Us.* New York: Committee on Economic Development, 1962 (Supplementary Paper No. 13). Chaps. xxiii–xxv.

HOYT, HOMER. *The Urban Real Estate Cycle—Performance and Prospects,* Technical Bulletin No. 38. Washington, D.C.: Urban Land Institute, 1960.

LEWIS, JOHN P., and Robert C. Turner. *Business Conditions Analysis* (rev. ed.). New York: McGraw-Hill Book Co., Inc., 1966. Part IV.

See also current issues of *Economic Indicators, The Federal Reserve Bulletin, The Survey of Current Business,* the President's *Economic Report,* and Federal Reserve Bank publications.

11

Regional and Local Economic Trends

Regional and Local Decision Influences

As we have suggested, the real estate decision-maker tends to be interested in the localization of income. Although economic activity in a region or locality may move parallel with general business conditions, there are often significant differences. For example, the Southwest and Southeast have grown substantially faster than the American economy as a whole in recent years.

Of major importance for most real estate decision-makers is the potential direction of economic activity in a particular locality—a metropolitan area or city or local rural community. Such decision-makers are also interested in the outlook for smaller sections of a local economy—in the market for the type of property under consideration and in the neighborhood or district in which the property is located. Again, we recognize that there may be variations between the growth rates of local areas and various types of markets within them.

In order to pursue our discussions in a somewhat orderly fashion, we consider in this chapter some of the factors related to regional and local economic analysis as a guide to real estate decisions. In Chapter 12 we take up various aspects of real estate market analysis and in Chapters 13 and 14 certain factors related to the analysis of land use patterns, neighborhoods, and districts.

desirable industrial sites; availability of capital and the ability to command it; and the presence of entrepreneurial, professional, technical, and related talent. In some cases such community resources as schools, utilities, governmental resources and services, and the like are also considered. These resources provide the general environment or climate in which growth may occur or fail to occur.

We should note that it is possible to study the markets for the major resources of a local economy and thus to gain insights into its economic growth potential. For example, the labor market,[4] the land market,[5] the capital market,[6] or the market for special talents such as entrepreneurship, research ability or leadership may be studied with varying degrees of intensity. Information about such markets may be related to the specific problems under consideration by decision-makers. For example, the efforts of various local communities to induce business firms to locate in their areas may be more rational than often is supposed if it is recognized that local community leaders may be interested primarily in the entrepreneurial, leadership, managerial, and research talent that may be gained.

In addition to studies of major local resources and their markets, *industry* studies may be undertaken, particularly of the more important industries in the local economy. Sometimes inventories of the assets and liabilities of a local economy may be developed and analyzed.

We might try to approach the regional or local economy as a subdivision of the national economy. For example, we might analyze local employment and income trends and make comparisons with national changes. Such indicators of economic activity as bank clearings, car loadings, electric power consumption, building permits and housing starts, and others may be analyzed and compared.

If we tried to make use of GNP analysis, however, or other types of analyses useful on a national basis, we would soon encounter difficulties largely because local and regional economies are "open" and not "closed." That is, there are no reasonably well-defined economic boundaries. Efforts are sometimes made to use regional accounts which resemble national income accounting; input-output analysis is attempted in some cases and flow of funds methods may prove to be useful. (See Chapter 10.) Most of these methods, however, are difficult to use because of inadequate data or because of the sweeping assumptions that typically are required.

---

[4] Wilbur R. Thompson, *A Preface to Urban Economics* (prelim. ed.; Washington, D.C.: Resources for the Future, 1963).

[5] Lowden Wingo, *Transportation and Urban Land* (Washington, D.C.: Resources for the Future, 1963) and Ralph Turvey, *The Economics of Real Property* (London: George Allen & Unwin Ltd., 1957).

[6] Harvey S. Perloff, E. S. Dunn, E. E. Lampard, and Richard E. Muth, *Regions, Resources and Economic Growth* (Baltimore: Johns Hopkins University Press, 1960).

Despite some theoretical and practical inadequacies, economic base studies have proved to be highly useful for the analysis of local economies. Tiebout defines economic base as follows:

The economic base of a community consists of those activities which provide the basic employment and income on which the rest of the local economy depends. An economic base study identifies the basic sources of employment and income and provides an understanding of the source and level of all employment and income in a community.[7]

Later in the chapter we consider the main elements in economic base studies and outline briefly the major features of input-output analysis. Before considering these topics it may be helpful to review some of the principal characteristics of local economies, primarily urban economies.

Location and Concentration of Economic Activities

The point at which a particular city will arise depends on factors which favor the establishment of activities which may give the city a competitive advantage over others. Usually topography has been the most important factor, although its effects have depended on whether military, political, social, or economic considerations were paramount.

In modern periods a specific city is established at a certain point and expands in importance mainly because opportunities to secure employment and income are available. The sites of many older cities were determined largely by defense factors. In a few cases social and religious factors have played a dominant part in determining city location. Sometimes political situations have determined the location of cities. For example, the location of Washington was the result of military and political factors. Most of our cities, however, grew up at points which gave them *economic* advantages. Economic advantages of various locations may result from one of the following factors or combinations of them:

1. Trade routes and transportation breaking points
2. Access to raw materials
3. Access to a rich hinterland or tributary area
4. Power resources
5. Climate

Some cities developed at transportation breaking points—for example, where land and water routes met. In such cases the availability of harbor facilities was the dominant factor. Cities often grew up at points where one type of water transportation met another—or where land trade routes intersected; air routes have tended to follow established locations but jet

[7] Tiebout, *op. cit.*, p. 9.

air travel has changed a number of old patterns. One writer has aptly stated:

> It is when the transfer of goods is accompanied by a breaking of bulk or by a change of ownership, there being then added the complex mechanism of commercial exchange performed by importers, exporters, wholesalers, retailers, insurers, brokers, and bankers, that wealth is accumulated and localized, with consequent power to control business for local benefit.[8]

Easy access to raw materials has often determined the location of a city because of the economies resulting from being near the sources of supplies. Generally, raw materials of great bulk which are costly to move have had more influence on the location of cities than other types of raw products. When such resources are exhausted, the towns which grew up near them decline, unless other economic opportunities develop.

Frequently, points which give easy access to a rich hinterland or tributary area form natural places for economic development. For example, the development of New York City was in part due to the fact that there was an easy route from the West through the Appalachian Mountains to the East. Similarly, Chicago's growth was based on the richness of its tributary area, the upper Mississippi Valley.

Power resources have accounted for the rise of cities at certain specific points, the "fall line" in the East having resulted in the establishment of various cities because of the available water power. In more recent times, other types of power, particularly electricity, which can be transmitted for considerable distances, have eliminated the dependence of machinery on natural power. When methods of using atomic energy are further developed, the importance of the location of power resources may be eliminated entirely as a factor in determining city location and development.

Climatic conditions also have been of importance in determining city location. Sometimes climate favors certain types of industry, the growth of cotton and woolen manufacture in areas with moist climates being a case in point. Space-age installations have largely gone to southern areas because of climatic factors. Climate usually has a more direct influence in determining the location of resort or amusement centers, such as Miami Beach or Atlantic City.

In general, no single factor accounts for the location of a city at a certain point. For example, the *exact* point where a town starts may be largely accidental, since any of a number of points in the vicinity might

[8] Richard M. Hurd, *Principles of City Land Values* (New York: The Record & Guide, 1924), chap. ii. See Study Project 20 for a discussion of the topic "Cities Do Not Always Grow." This material also provides some interesting comparisons of ancient and modern cities.

be equally desirable. New York's original location was due to a combination of advantages. And so was its phenomenal growth. As Raymond Vernon points out:

The disposition among historians is to lay New York's rise to the Erie Canal; to the ice-free conditions of the East River, kept clear by its churning tides; and to a comparatively unobjectionable sand bar at the mouth of New York's harbor—a sand bar more manageable than at the mouth of the Delaware. There is also a disposition to give credit to something in the fluid social structure of New York's life, an indefinable quality which even then attracted off-beat businessmen in search of their fortunes. At any rate, whether or not New York's social structure was part of the lure, its early growth was almost certainly based on a lead in foreign trade.[9]

The original site of Chicago was a swamp; but the point at which Lake Michigan and the Great Lakes system came closest to joining the Mississippi River and its tributaries was a natural trade center, originally for the fur trade and later for other types of markets. The decisive factor undoubtedly was the Illinois-Michigan Canal; otherwise, development might have occurred farther south.

Types of Cities

Cities may be classified in various ways. For our purposes it is desirable to classify them on the basis of the major employment and income sources represented. Such a classification might take the following form:

1. Industrial cities, including those involved chiefly in the manufacturing and processing of commodities
2. Cities devoted principally to commerce, which include seaports, lake ports, river cities, and railroad terminals and junctions
3. Political cities, including all those for which the activities of a state government or the Federal government provide the basic income source
4. Recreational and health resorts, as well as cities in which retired people reside
5. Educational, research and cultural centers

Many cities, of course, include all or nearly all of these major actiivties, although one or two types may be predominant.

Extractive industries ordinarily do not produce the largest cities. Our largest cities typically are those with superior transportation facilities which place them in the main currents of trade. Manufacturing generally has developed in larger cities to a greater extent than in smaller places, and such expansion has in turn contributed to further growth. It should be noted, however, that some cities have grown very large without be-

[9] Raymond Vernon, *Metropolis 1985* (Cambridge: Harvard University Press, 1960), p. 8.

coming great manufacturing centers. Kansas City, Denver, and Washington are cases in point.

Division of Labor and Size

At an early stage in the development of economic thought Adam Smith pointed out:

> The country supplies the town with the means of subsistence and the materials of manufacture. . . . We must not, however, upon this account, imagine that the gain of the town is the loss of the country. The gains of both are *mutual and reciprocal* and the division of labor is in this, as in all other cases, adjusted to all the different persons in the various occupations into which it is subdivided.[10]

Division of labor between town and country, region and region, industry and industry, and employment and employment continues to be a vital factor in explaining the character and direction of modern economic activity. Division of labor undoubtedly is the basis for the establishment of a local economy and the extent of its long-term growth. The economic base concept rests primarily on this principle, as we have pointed out.

After a local economy attains a certain size, however, it may be able to maintain its growth, if not to augment it, because it has the economic or political power to command further support. The assemblage of a pool of labor, particularly if special skills are represented, a supply of capital or the ability to induce it to come to a locality, a group of community leaders and hard-hitting entrepreneurs and politicians, highly trained professional people, experts and technicians all may help to assure ongoing economic activity and even some growth. Substantial additional growth, however, may depend on specialization and advantages in interregional trade.

Thompson suggests that an "urban-size ratchet" is at work, that once a locality attains a certain size and economic importance it can continue to grow and expand because of diversification, a "blending of young, mature and decadent industries," the influence of power politics, the large amount of sunk, fixed capital invested, the importance of the local market itself, and the chance that growth processes are stimulated in a city of some size—"a large urban area is more likely to give birth to new industries at critical points in its life cycle than is a small urban area." [11]

Whether the growth process is self-regenerative or the result of special factors, inside or outside the locality, remains an open question and the answer probably varies with the character of the local economy.

[10] Adam Smith, *The Wealth of Nations* (London: George Bell & Sons, 1908), III, p. 383. [Italics added.]

[11] Thompson, *op. cit.*, pp. 9–11.

Raymond Vernon points out in regard to the growth of New York:

In a pattern which will appear many times during this account, growth fed on growth. For a time, New York's unique scheduled sailings, its "ship brokers," and its wholesalers could be matched nowhere else. . . . During the middle decades of the century, though New York's role as the national gateway continued to expand, its own heavy dependence on the sea was already beginning to shrink. The Erie Canal had opened up a new route through which New York could tap the wheatlands and forests of the Middle West. Bits and pieces of rail line were also beginning to be put in place, adding another means by which raw materials could be shipped east and manufactured products could move west to the new territories.[12]

He points out further that activities that had sprung originally from the Port became independent; wholesaling took on the handling of domestic products as well as foreign trade; in finance, maritime insurance shifted to domestic property risks, foreign banking to domestic banking. In subsequent developments one type of growth gave way to another. New York's size probably aided in making these adjustments but explanations of these processes are not easy to nail down.

The growth of Chicago from a hamlet of fifty people in the early 1830's to a metropolis of more than six million in a century and a third can be explained by a wide variety of economic opportunities. As one of the authors has pointed out:

The advantage of the site of Chicago as a meeting place first of lake, river, canal, and wagon transportation, and then of lake and rail carriers in turn, made it the principal distributing and manufacturing center for a valley containing the richest combination of agricultural and mineral resources of the world that was being exploited for the first time. . . . The magnitude of the population was but the measure of the strength of the economic advantages of the site of Chicago, and of the economic resources of its hinterland—the Upper Mississippi Valley.[13]

And the growth of the Chicago region has continued, although at not as rapid a rate as for some other cities, notably in the South and West.

Factors Leading to Decline

While Chicago and New York were growing, some cities were declining in economic importance. Outstanding, of course, were certain mining and lumbering towns whose natural resources were exhausted. Some cities declined because others enjoyed an advantage in nearness to raw materials or markets, availability of labor and capital, climate, political preference, or the drive and dedication of local leaders. Certain smaller

[12] Vernon, *op. cit.*, p. 9.

[13] Reprinted from *One Hundred Years of Land Values in Chicago*, by Homer Hoyt by permission of the University of Chicago Press, pp. 279–84. Copyright 1933 by the University of Chicago.

cities lost their reasons for existence as improved transportation facilities enabled major cities to serve wider areas. Some cities were helped or hindered by governmental or administrative policies; e.g., differential freight rates and tax policies have had their effect on the growth of specific cities. In some cases the efforts of community leaders have stimulated city growth, while other cities failed of their potential because of inadequacy of local leadership.

As we suggested in the discussion above, an adequate supply of civic and social resources may help to stimulate economic growth. Thus, if a city possesses good local government, school system, hospitals and doctors, shopping facilities, and the like, new industries may be attracted to it. The lack of such facilities and services might repel business firms that are considering alternative locations for their new plants.

Thus, growth comes not only from the expansion of *present* sources of income and employment but from *new* sources as well. In the attraction of new income sources, the local environment may play an important role.

The real estate decision-maker is concerned with the entire complex of factors that enables a locality to provide goods and services on terms that will compete with those of other cities and localities—and hence, to hold, expand, or lose important sources of income.

We turn now to a consideration of economic base analysis as one way of estimating the potential of a local economy.

Concept of the Economic Base

The concept of the economic base was set forth by Werner Sombart in the 1920's and by Robert M. Haig as early as 1928.[14] Sombart pointed out the difference between "Städtegründer," which may be translated as *Town Founders* or *Builders,* and "Städtefüller," which may be translated as *Town Fillers.* Frederick Nussbaum subsequently used the terms "Town Fillers" and "Town Builders." Homer Hoyt, co-author of this book, refined the concept of the economic base in a variety of reports and articles from 1936 onward and dealt with some of the essential ideas in the concept of the economic base or economic background in his *One Hundred Years of Land Values in Chicago,* published in 1933.[15] The economic base concept has been criticised, re-evaluated, and refined by

[14] W. Sombart, *Der Moderne Kapitalismus, Dritter Band: Das Wirtschaftsleben im Zeitalter des Hochkapitalismus,* (2d rev. ed., 1927; 3d ptg.; Berlin: Duncker & Humblot, 1955), 413; also R. M. Haig, *Major Economic Factors in Metropolitan Growth and Arrangement,* Vol. I, *Regional Survey of New York and Environs,* Regional Plan Committee, 1928.

[15] Homer Hoyt, *One Hundred Years of Land Values in Chicago* (Chicago: U. of Chicago Press, 1933); "Economic Background of Cities," *Journal of Land and Public Utility Economics* (May, 1941), 188–95; "The Utility of the Economic Base Method in Calculating Urban Growth," *Land Economics,* XXXVII, No. 1 (Feb., 1961).

a number of students of the subject including Ralph W. Pfouts, Charles M. Tiebout, and Richard B. Andrews.[16]

Essentially, the economic base concept rests on international trade theory and on the multiplier effect of "export" activity. The locality or region is viewed in relation to other regions and its potential growth is considered as dependent upon "basic" sources of employment or income, that is, *those that command income from beyond its borders.* For example, manufacturing activity, since it usually leads to "exportable" products, is considered "basic" and the service trades as "nonbasic" or supporting activity. The impact of the former, however, is multiplied through the latter since basic income will support some service activity (ratios vary widely—1 to 1 or 1½ to 1 are not uncommon).

Nussbaum, for example, distinguished between "town building" and "town filling" activities. He said:

The principal constituent elements of the town are those who are able by power or wealth to command a means of subsistence from elsewhere, a king who can tax, a landlord to whom dues are paid, a merchant who makes profits outside the town, a student who is supported by his parents. These are "town builders." After them come what we call the "town fillers," those who serve the needs of the "town builders": the shoemaker who makes the king's shoes, the jeweler who depends on the purchases of the merchant's wife, the landlady from whom the student rents his room.[17]

Nussbaum's statement does not explain completely the variables involved but it does stress the division of labor on which a town or other local economy rests and its relationship to "outside" sources of income. The terms town "builders" and "fillers" are somewhat unfortunate since under some circumstances the "nonbasic" or "service" or "filler" types of economic activity may help to attract "basic" activities and thus play a leading rather than a supporting role in the local economy or region. In the Nussbaum quotation above, for example, the shoemaker might attract a tannery, the jeweler might be a factor in attracting a silversmith or metal working establishment, and the student might be so favorably impressed by the town that he later will set up a manufacturing plant there. Availability of outstanding service activities often helps to attract basic types of economic activities. Further, those who accumulate capital from either basic or service activity may invest it either locally or elsewhere and, if investing locally, thus further stimulate economic development.

---

[16] Ralph W. Pfouts (ed.), *Techniques of Urban Economic Analysis* (West Trenton, N.J.: Chandler-Davis Publishing Co., 1960); Charles M. Tiebout, "The Urban Economic Base Reconsidered," *Land Economics* (February, 1956). See also Tiebout's "The Community Economic Base Study" and Richard B. Andrews' various articles on economic base in *Land Economics* (May, 1953, to May, 1955).

[17] F. L. Nussbaum, *A History of the Economic Institutions of Modern Europe* (New York: Appleton-Century-Crofts, Inc., 1933), p. 36. By permission.

In any event, the essential factors in the economic base concept are (1) division of labor in the international trade sense, plus (2) the multiplier effect of "export" activity. Meyer has stated the concept this way:

Translating conventional international trade theory into regional terms, the "economic base" of a region is that group of industries primarily engaged in exporting from the region under analysis to other regions. An empirical multiplier is determined by observing the historical relationship between this export activity and total economic activity in the region. This empirical multiplier is then applied to estimates of economic base to forecast total economic activity.[18]

Outline of an Economic Base Analysis

For illustrative purposes we present here an outline of some of the major steps that may be taken in carrying out an economic base analysis of medium complexity. In summary these steps include: (1) determining the relative importance of major present and potential income sources; (2) analyzing each of the basic sources of income—manufacturing, trade, extractive industry, and other types; and (3) studying modifying influences—the size of the local market, quality of community facilities and services, governmental factors, and the general "climate" for local economic activities.

N.B.

Relative Importance of Basic Income Sources

1.

The sources of employment and income in a local economy are many and varied, but for convenience of analysis they may be combined into the following primary groups: (1) manufacturing, (2) extractive industry, (3) wholesale and retail trade, (4) special sources of income, such as political, educational, institutional, resort, or amusement activities. The stream of income brought into the city by people who receive pensions, rents, royalties, and interest from elsewhere should also be considered a part of the urban growth income. Few cities are supported by any one of these income sources alone; nearly all rely on a combination of various types.

Chicago, Detroit, Dayton, Hartford, Cleveland, Milwaukee, and Baltimore are predominantly industrial cities; while New Orleans, Minneapolis, Kansas City, Omaha, and Portland are predominantly commercial centers. Miami and Atlantic City are chiefly tourist resorts. Washington is supported principally by the activities of the federal government. In St. Louis, Boston, and Philadelphia there is a fairly equal division of employment and income between trade and manufacturing. In Springfield, Illinois, and in Oklahoma City there is an extraordinary diversity of sup-

[18] Meyer, *op. cit.*

port from manufacturing, extractive industry, trade, and state institutions. Ann Arbor, Michigan, is primarily an educational and research center.

2. Analyzing Basic Sources of Income

The first step in determining the economic potentialities of a city is to estimate the relative importance of each of the various sources of employment and income. Information concerning total employment, as well as the number employed in each of the main types of economic activity, can be secured from such sources as the Bureau of the Census, state employment services and their local branches, and chambers of commerce. Where more detailed information is desirable, assistance may be secured from the personnel departments of principal firms, and local labor unions. Information concerning payrolls is often available from census reports, local or state taxing authorities, and similar sources. From one or a combination of these sources, total employment can be obtained and the per cent of the total engaged in each of the major types of economic activity outlined above can be computed. Efforts should also be made to determine whether any new sources of income are likely to develop in the near future, and their relative importance.

By breaking down the employment of a city into its basic sources of income we can concentrate our attention on those types of economic activity which may be expected to have greatest influence on the future growth of the city. However, cyclical and seasonal variations in employment and income should be considered as well as general trends.

In order to forecast the employment and income trends of a city, each of the major sources of employment must be analyzed. In the analysis of each source of employment, it is important to note not only the future trend of the number of people who may be employed in various types of economic activity, but also the *level of wages and other incomes* and the meaning of these in terms of real income and purchasing power.

Analysis of Manufacturing

In forecasting the trend of manufacturing activities in a city as a source of future economic growth, each type of industry should be studied in some detail. Attention should be given to such factors as the nature of the products manufactured by each firm, the location of raw materials, principal markets, trends of demand for the products, and the competitive position of each of the major establishments. Such factors as the competence of management, the character of the labor supply, and special local advantages or disadvantages should be considered. In addition, tax burdens, the attitudes of local community leaders toward each firm, and the trends of local government policies generally merit consideration. Special atten-

ion should be given to competitive advantage of the location, diversification of industry, competitive position of the firm, and cyclical fluctuations.

From the standpoint of future effects on real estate values, it is important to determine whether the industries located in a city will remain,
advance in importance, decline, or move to another location. Among the
factors that tie an industry to a city are large plants, heavy fixed capital
investments in new and modern machinery, the availability of a large
body of skilled labor, favorable transportation rates, convenient access to
raw materials, proximity to markets, favorable attitudes of local community leaders, and taxes that are favorable relative to government services provided. In addition, it is important to determine whether any new
industries are likely to move into a city. The above factors will also have
a bearing on such probable developments.

There is always an element of risk if a city has great concentration of
industrial activity along one specific line. If half of the workers in a city
are employed in a single establishment, the whole structure of real estate
values may collapse if that establishment moves away. If there are many
establishments in the same industry, the risks are less; but the city may
suffer severely because of a decrease in the demand for the product or
the rise of a competing product. In addition, single-industry towns are
more likely to fall under the dominance of a relatively few businessmen
or labor leaders, with the result that real estate values may suffer from
shortsighted managerial policies or from prolonged strikes and industrial
disturbances.

The relationship of industrial plants in the city being analyzed to the
industry as a whole and to competitive plants in other locations is a matter
of basic importance. If a factory is located poorly, managed inefficiently,
uses obsolete equipment, or lacks satisfactory outlets, it will tend to lose
out in competition with other manufacturers unless these conditions are
typical of the entire industry. Under the latter conditions, the introduction
of laborsaving machinery may lead to less total employment, but may put
the plant in a much stronger competitive position, with the result that it
may play a greater part in the future economic life of the city.

Analyzing Income from Trade

The prospects for future employment and income from trade in any
city depend chiefly on the following:

1. The extent to which the city is expanding its trade area at the expense of competing cities or losing out in competition with such
   cities
2. The growth or decline of resources and purchasing power in the
   trading area
3. The potential growth or decline of population in the trading area

Diversification of types of trading activities and firms is not so important a consideration as in the case of industry, since we seldom find cities in which one or two stores serve all of the needs of a trade area. Similarly, cyclical fluctuations in trading activities are not likely to be so marked as in the case of industry, although such fluctuations may occur.

Analyzing Income from Other Sources

A forecast of employments and incomes which are dependent upon mines, oil wells, or timber resources requires an analysis of the probable future life of the natural resources involved and of the extent to which these resources can be utilized at prevailing or anticipated price and cost levels. Competition of the products of such extractive industries with other products of the same type should be considered, as well as the possibility for the development of substitute products.

Financial institutions such as banks, insurance companies, and savings and loan associations may play a key role in the economic life of a community, either because income is brought into the area or because various types of economic activity are facilitated.

Similarly, retail activities may add to local growth to the extent that trade is attracted from elsewhere. Cases in point include Neiman Marcus in Dallas and Marshall Field in Chicago.

For several decades employment in governmental agencies has tended to expand. Incomes of government workers have advanced. Since the seats of governments, such as state capitals or county seats, are relatively fixed, the possibilities of changes of location of such governmental activities are remote. However, cities with a large number of federal agencies may lose or gain income as the activities of such agencies are expanded or diminished or as changes of location are made.

The location and relocation of space and defense industries will be an important factor in the future of a number of cities, especially in the South and West.

Educational institutions are usually fixed in location and are not likely to move to other places unless exceptional conditions arise. Normally employment in such institutions is relatively stable; during recent decades, however, there has been a marked expansion of educational activity, and this general trend has been strengthened by higher income levels and population growth.

Employment and incomes derived from resort and amusement activities are subject to unusual fluctuations. The development of jet aircraft has changed the competitive pattern of resort areas. Such areas are affected considerably by the trend of general business conditions, since their incomes tend to decline sharply in recession periods. To the extent that a resort enjoys a prestige reputation or is endowed with exceptional natural advantages, of course, it will tend to be affected less by business recessions than will other resort centers.

In a number of towns and cities, retired people represent an important source of income. The extent and stability of such income depend on the sources from which it is drawn. As more and more people qualify for pensions or build up retirement funds, incomes of this type will play an increasingly important part in the economic fortunes of many cities, notably those in favorable climates.

Local Modifying Conditions

3.

The ratio between basic and service employment and income varies between local economies and in the same economy over time. Hence, it is usually necessary to make estimates of this ratio for each local economic base analysis. A 1 to 1 ratio is found in some cases and this is sometimes used as a "rule of thumb" guide. A ratio of 2 in basic to 3 in service employments is fairly common. Estimates can be made by allocating local employment into desired groupings on the basis of the data available. Other methods may be used as well.[19]

The degree of detail desired will influence the nature of an economic base analysis. Both export and local type industries may be analyzed in some detail by dividing their markets into sectors and subsectors such as business investment, housing investment, government purchases and investment, and the like.

Similarly, long-run analysis may require that consideration be given to the "multiplier" process. Some of the income earned by a manufacturing firm may be invested locally, some elsewhere; of that invested locally some may stimulate local activity, some may bring about further export activity. The "propensity to invest locally" can be estimated by developing assumptions on the basis of local data and experience.[20]

Conclusions tentatively reached in regard to the future growth of a city on the basis of a study of major income sources may be modified by favorable or unfavorable local governmental conditions; tax burdens in relation to public services provided; quality of the school system; adequacy of community facilities, such as hospitals and cultural and entertainment programs; quality of business, labor, and political leadership; and relative position with respect to other cities in the region or nation.[21]

[19] See Homer Hoyt "The Utility of the Economic Base Method of Calculating Urban Growth," *Land Economics* (February, 1961) and "A Method for Measuring the Value of Imports into an Urban Community," *Land Economics* (May, 1961).

[20] Tiebout, "The Community Economic Base Study," pp. 60–61.

[21] See "Guide to Making a Business Climate Appraisal," issued by Public and Employer Relations Services, General Electric Company.

Careful investigations may indicate which persons or organizations exercise the greatest influence and wield the major power in the local community. If it is possible to identify them, some estimate of their interest in the future of the city may be an important factor in predicting its potential growth.

Attention is usually given also to the size of the local market. The long-run marketability or salability of real property over a period of years depends in part on the strength of the economic base and on the growth potential of the city, but it depends also on the size of the market. Thus, if other things are equal, a property is more salable in a larger city than in a small one, simply because of the larger number of potential buyers. Also, the larger city often provides a more stable market, since the removal of an important plant or other installation usually will not have as much of an impact as if a plant of similar size moved away from a smaller city.

This is notably true of the market for owner-occupied homes. The market for investment residential (rental) properties may be broader than the city; and, of course, the market for business real estate may be regional or national or even international in scope.

As we have indicated, a heavy concentration of employment in one firm or one line of manufacturing may represent a risk factor. A one-industry town ordinarily is not considered to have as strong an economic base as a city with greater diversification of income sources, even if the income produced is approximately the same.

Also, the probability that a city may be able to resist adverse national or regional economic trends usually is a factor of strength. Thus, a political capital or an educational center may be fairly well insulated from changes in the general trend of business conditions.

It is desirable also to consider the potential impact of advances in technology and productivity. Such advances have greater significance for science-based and highly sophisticated industries than for many other types. As we have suggested also some growth may be locally generated. Tiebout very aptly points out:

Nothing here suggests that it is impossible for a community to grow without an expansion of exports. The world as a whole does not, as yet, export. Nevertheless, incomes have risen substantially. In like manner, an island community can increase its income even if it is isolated from the rest of the world. Increases in productivity and technological change are hallmarks of economic life. An increase in productivity of a locally oriented bakery will increase local income, even though exports do not increase. Nonetheless, this does not invalidate base theory. Base analysis, *qua* base analysis, does not focus on these changes. A base study, after all, cannot examine everything. All this means that changes in productivity, for example, can and should be introduced to modify any forecasts derived from a base study.[22]

[22] Tiebout, "The Community Economic Base Study," p. 75.

Input-Output Analysis

Input-output analysis has been adapted to the study of local economies; its future promise depends on the much-needed improvement in the accuracy and availability of data. This type of analysis revolves around the establishment of a model, in the form of a matrix, which highlights the sales of the output of each major producing sector to each major consuming sector of the economy, for example, the total dollar output of manufacturing which was consumed by the construction industry, by the power industry, and even by the manufacturing industry itself.[23] This table can be constructed in any desired detail, for example, the manufacturing industry can be broken into heavy and light manufacturing, or an even finer classification such as the chemical industry, the petroleum industry, the steel industry, etc. The degree of refinement depends on (1) the industrial make-up of the area in question, (2) the availability of detailed data, and (3) the potential value of added research effort to the problem under analysis.

From an input-output table, it is possible to determine the relative importance of a particular line of economic activity to the community and its impact in sustaining other lines by its purchases. The earnings and expenditures of governments can be included as sectors of the economy as can the receipts and spending of households. As a matter of fact, these two sectors are usually estimated independently and are used as inputs to the model. To understand how an input-output matrix is developed, we might look at the oversimplified 5×5 matrix depicted in Table 11-1.

---

[23] Fundamentals of input-output theory were developed by Wassily W. Leontief as early as 1936; see his "Quantitative Input and Output Relations in the Economic System of the U.S.," *Review of Economics and Statistics* (August, 1936). See also his *The Structure of American Economy, 1919-1939*, (New York: Oxford University Press, 1951); and *Studies in the Structure of the American Economy* (New York: Oxford University Press, 1953). Robert Dorfman outlined the concept of input-output in his article, "The Nature and Significance of Input-Output," *Review of Economics and Statistics* (May, 1954), as follows: "To set forth the bare bones, conceive of an economy as being divided into some number of sectors, say *n*. Suppose that the level of output of each sector depends on the level of some or all of the other sectors, and on nothing else. Then the formulas relating the output of each sector to the outputs of other sectors will form a set of *n* equations in *n* variables. If, further, these formulas are linear the equations can be solved by straightforward algebra. The result will be a set of sector outputs which are mutually compatible in the sense that each sector produces the quantity called for by the functional relationships assumed at the outset. What we have just sketched is simply a mathematical formalism; Leontief's task was to develop a set of economic concepts which would lead to this kind of mathematical structure and would invest it with meaning. This is just what input-output achieves. An input-output table or matrix is a set of linear formulas connecting the levels of activity in the various segments of an economy. Input-output analysis is the economic justification and interpretation of these formulas and their consequences."

Reading across Table 11–1 yields the sales of each industry to every other industry. Thus, the entry in the second column of the second row reflects the sales of the manufacturing industry to itself. The entry in the fifth column of the second row reflects the amount the manufacturing industry sold to households. Total sales of the manufacturing industry are shown in the total gross output column.

The figures gleaned from reading down the column depict the purchases of each industry from every other industry. Thus, the entry in the first column of the second row reflects the purchases of the agricultural sector from the manufacturing sector. Since every sale is at the same time a purchase, it makes little difference on which basis the figures are gathered.

Table 11–1. A Hypothetical Input-Output Matrix

Producing Sectors	Purchasing Sectors					Total Gross Output
	Agriculture	Manufacturing	Power	Construction	Households	
Agriculture	20	20	1	4	12	57
Manufacturing	5	30	2	3	45	85
Power	1	3	2	1	3	10
Construction	2	2	4	1	1	10
Households	32	50	6	11	4	103
Total inputs	60	105	15	20	5	265

In using this matrix for projective purposes, the household sector is usually considered as being exogenous to the model, that is, independent of the producing sectors, and is estimated first. The problem then resolves itself into estimating the production levels in each sector necessary to satisfy this household demand. This is accomplished by assuming that the production inputs will be combined in the same proportion in the future time period to produce a level of output as they were in the present period. Table 11–2 is a reconstruction of Table 11–1 in terms or these production coefficients which are then assumed constant.

Table 11–2 was derived by dividing each of the elements in a column by the column total. Thus, by dividing the element in the second row of the first column (5) of Table 11–1 by the column total (60), we get 0.08. This means eight cents out of every dollar produced by the agricultural sector is consumed by the manufacturing industry. Similarly, 53 per cent of agriculture's output goes to satisfy household demands.

With an assumed household demand in some future time period, estimated by some other method and used as an input to the model—that is, spending by households is considered their "production" and hence an input—the problem reduces itself to finding the levels of production necessary to satisfy this demand—recognizing the interactions of the model. Thus, an increase in household demand for food of 20 per cent will occasion something different than a simple increase in agricultural output of $2.40 ($12.00 × 1.20 = $14.40) to $59.40. An increase in agricultural output must be accompanied by increases in manufacturing, power, and construction output. These increases in output of manufacturing, power, and construction must in turn be supported by higher production of their various inputs. These latter increases in production are called the indirect effects as contrasted to the $2.40 increase in agricultural output occasioned by the increased household demand for food which is a direct effect. The procedure resolves itself into one of successive iterations performed on a computer. The process is stopped when the indirect effects are of such magnitude that they have no appreciable effect on the level of the various outputs, that is, they are within acceptable limits.

Table 11–2.   Direct Inputs per Dollar of Output

Producing Sectors	Purchasing Sectors				
	Agriculture	Manufacturing	Power	Construction	Households
Agriculture	0.33	0.19	0.07	0.20	0.18
Manufacturing	0.08	0.28	0.13	0.15	0.69
Power	0.02	0.03	0.13	0.05	0.05
Construction	0.04	0.02	0.27	0.05	0.02
Households	0.53	0.48	0.40	0.55	0.06
Total	1.00	1.00	1.00	1.00	1.00

Inadequate data often handicap the input-output analyst. There are also theoretical limitations, for example, the model must be considered one of stationary equilibrium so that time is of no consequence. This is because inputs, in reality, must be produced before they can be used for output and therefore current production in the model is connected not to current supply of inputs, but to previous periods of supply.

A problem also results from the fact that industries do not have identical production methods. Thus, output determines input only if the various firms expand and contract proportionally. Likewise, as firms within the industry produce multiple products, the theory must assume constant product mix for each industry as output expands. Furthermore, the use of production functions designating given outputs for given inputs is more naturally applied to mining, manufacturing, and utilities than it is to other sectors such as trade, finance, and the household. Estimation for the latter sectors may involve considerable approximation.

The theory also assumes that if output is given, the level of input is uniquely determined. Such a model does not take into account the possibility of input substitution; and this effect may be significant. In addition, there is a problem of distinguishing between inputs used for current output and those used for investment in plant and equipment.

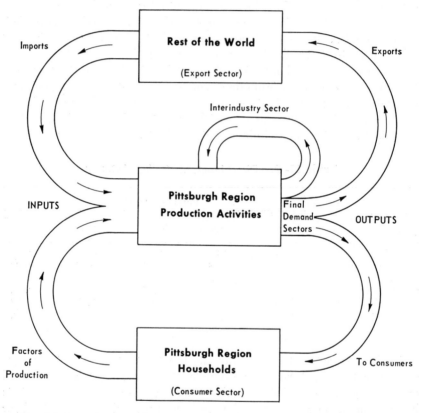

Fig. 11–1. Schematic flow chart of intersector relationships. [*Region with a Future,* Vol. III, p. 199; *Economic Study of the Pittsburgh Region* (Pittsburgh: University of Pittsburgh Press, 1963).]

Many of the advantages of an input-output matrix are statistical. It enables the analyst to record in a rather concise fashion a large amount of information about a regional economy and the interrelations of its sectors. Further, it imposes a statistical discipline on data collection assuring consistency in the approach. The table itself helps to reveal where there are gaps in the data and it may be suggestive of ways to fill them.

Recent study of the input-output technique has developed along the lines of improving the collection and estimation of data and eliminating some of the shortcomings of the assumptions. Some of these refinements have been complicating, for example, the use of dynamic models and linear programming. Others have been simplifying, for example, attempts to eliminate unnecessary and expensive detail or to develop short-cut methods of estimating data.

An interesting application of input-output analysis is provided by the *Economic Study of the Pittsburgh Region,* conducted by the Pittsburgh Regional Planning Association. Figure 11–1 presents a schematic flow chart of intersector relationships. It shows the division of the region's economy into three sectors: interindustry activity, exports, and production for local households.[24]

Other Techniques of Analysis

As we suggested in the introductory sections of this chapter, various other methods may also be used to facilitate the analysis of local economies, including regional accounts, balance-of-payments, flow-of-funds, location quotients, or proportionality techniques, as well as others. Each of these methods may be highly useful for particular purposes.

The intricacy of relationships between regions complicates the development of regional accounts. As we suggested earlier, regions are "open" rather than "closed" economies. Many of our large corporations may have headquarters in one region, do a major part of their business in others or internationally, and yet make no separation on a regional basis. Domestic and international separations typically are made. Federal government receipts and payments are also hard to assign to regions.

The Federal Reserve carries on a number of regional analyses and a variety of data have been developed on a regional basis. The various Federal Reserve districts have used regional balance-of-payment and flow-of-funds methods.[25] Studies of the flow of goods, services, and financial payments between regions have been developed from shipping and banking data and other sources. Although often lacking in various types of data, such flow studies often provide insights into the economic life of a region.[26]

[24] See Edgar M. Hoover *et al., Region With a Future* (Pittsburgh: University of Pittsburgh Press, 1963), p. 199.

[25] See for example, Norman N. Bowsher, J. Dewey Daane, and Robert Einzig, "The Flow of Funds Between Regions of the U.S.," *Journal of Finance* (March, 1958) and Guy Freutel, "The Eighth District Balance of Trade," *Monthly Review,* Federal Reserve Bank of St. Louis (June, 1952).

[26] See Frederick E. Case, *Real Estate* (Englewood Cliffs, N.J.: Allyn & Bacon, Inc., 1962), chap. v.

Location quotients sometimes are helpful. In such analyses the percentage of an activity in a particular location (region, state, county) is compared with the percentage of the same activity in the nation as a whole. The Department of Commerce has been making comparisons of this type using a proportionality technique to analyze various regional changes relative to the national economy. It is planned to develop data on a county-by-county basis and to make available continuing information annually on a number of comparative bases.

To date, these studies have undertaken in a preliminary way to differentiate between "industry mix" for states and major geographic regions and to analyze what is termed the "competitive effect" in employment changes. Computations are made, first, as to what employment changes would have been if an area had grown at the same rate as the national total; second, computations are made to determine how much more or less than this amount employment would have changed because the particular industries in the area grew more or less than the national average for those industries—this being called the "industry mix" effect; and third, the difference between actual growth and normal growth for the particular "industry mix" in the area is computed to determine the "competitive" effect.[27]

A number of students of local and regional economies are carrying forward a variety of work to improve both the theoretical and practical approaches to analytical and forecasting efforts. For example, efforts are made to study the multiplier effect in regional economic analysis.[28] There are continuing efforts to re-evaluate and improve economic base analysis. Mathematical model building is being tried in a number of cases. The net effect of all these efforts should be to provide real estate decision-makers with improved tools of analysis in the years ahead.

SUMMARY

Regional and local economic analysis provides valuable assistance to real estate decision-makers. Managers of multi-plant firms and chain store organizations can use such materials as well as investors in real estate properties, mortgage lenders, builders and land developers, and government officials. For these discussions, little effort is made to distinguish between regional and local economies since the purpose of the decision-maker is largely the governing factor. Our primary concern is with the problems of the real estate decision-maker and his decisions are related to factors influencing the localization of income. Natural factors and

[27] Robert E. Graham, Jr., "Factors Underlying Changes in the Geographic Distribution of Income," *Survey of Current Business* (April, 1964).

[28] Richard T. Pratt, "Multiplier and Economic Base Analysis," unpublished seminar report, Indiana University.

division of labor help to explain the location of economic activity along with local advantages that attract people of special competence—leaders, entrepreneurs, scientists, and the like—capital, and special facilities. These factors also help to explain expansion in one place as against another. In addition, once a certain size is reached an "urban-size ratchet" may go into operation.

The economic base method provides a useful approach to analyzing local and regional economies. It involves the application of international trade theory to local economic analysis. The relative importance of various local income sources is determined, their future potential analyzed, and local modifying factors considered in estimating the future growth potential of a local or regional economy by means of the economic base method.

Of other methods in use, input-output analysis holds considerable promise if required data can be made more readily available. Regional accounts, balance-of-payments, flow-of-funds, location quotients, or proportionality techniques are also used.

QUESTIONS FOR STUDY

1. List the purposes for which you might want to make a local economic analysis.
2. How can a region be compared to a city or urban area in terms of economic analysis?
3. How does regional analysis differ from an analysis of general (national) business conditions?
4. How can one city compete with another to encourage businesses to establish within its boundaries? Which of these methods are inherent advantages of a particular city and which may be developed?
5. What is the "urban-size ratchet" effect? Do you agree with the logic of this argument? Discuss.
6. Explain how you would analyze income and employment from trade in your hometown.
7. What is meant by "basic income sources" in the economic base model? What are the chief basic income sources for: (a) Your hometown? (b) The capital of your state? (c) The city in which your college or university is located?
8. What is meant by "urban service employment"? Can urban service employments contribute to city growth? Explain.
9. Is diversification of manufacturing desirable or undesirable in terms of its effect on the economic base of a city?
10. Assume that you are to present a talk to your real estate club on the topic "An Evaluation of Economic Base Analysis as an Aid to Decision-making." Prepare a brief outline of the main points you would want to make.
11. What are the advantages and disadvantages of the input-output analytic method?

12. Explain the use of location quotients for analysis of a locality. What special application might this have for the real estate decision-maker?

13. *Study Project 17.* (a) What qualifications does the author make about the value of applying such an input-output model? (b) What specific types of decision-making guides does the State of Mississippi anticipate will be developed from the proposed input-output analysis? (c) Of what value would the study be to businessmen? What specific information would be of special value to the real estate decision-maker?

14. *Study Project 18.* For the purposes of the problem you may assume that if the employment classification is predominantly basic, all the classification is basic; and that if the employment classification is predominantly nonbasic, all the classification is nonbasic. (a) What type of industry do you think the Chamber of Commerce should try to bring to Bel Aire? Why? How might industry be induced to locate there? (b) Assume that two manufacturing firms will locate in Bel Aire next year. One plans to employ 300 persons and the other plans to employ 200 persons. After the plants are in operation, what number of basic employees would you expect? Nonbasic employees? What would be the effect of such a development on total population? (c) What do you consider to be the long-range prospects for the marketability of real estate in Bel Aire? What are the principal factors in determining long-run marketability?

15. *Study Project 19.* (a) On the basis of the information provided by the quotation, and assuming you had an opportunity to invest in real estate in Hawaii, what kind of real estate would you choose? Defend your answer. (b) What type of additional information would you like to have to aid your decision? How would you develop such information?

16. *Study Project 20.* How do you account for the decline of these cities at various stages of their history? Can you explain the dominance of the world's largest cities at their particular time?

SUGGESTED READINGS

HOYT, HOMER. "The Utility of the Economic Base Method in Calculating Urban Growth," *Land Economics* (February, 1961).

ISARD, WALTER. *Methods of Regional Analysis: An Introduction to Regional Science.* Cambridge: The Massachusetts Institute of Technology Press, 1960. Chaps. v, vi, viii.

MEYER, JOHN R. "Regional Economics: A Survey," *American Economic Review,* LIII, No. 1, Part I (March, 1963).

PERLOFF, HARVEY S., *et al., Regions, Resources and Economic Growth,* published for Resources for the Future by The Johns Hopkins Press, Baltimore, 1960. Part III.

THOMPSON, WILBUR R. *A Preface to Urban Economics* (prelim. ed.). Washington, D.C.: Resources for the Future, 1963. Chaps. i, ii, iv.

TIEBOUT, CHARLES M. "The Community Economic Base Study." New York: Committee for Economic Development, 1962.

12

Real Estate Market Analysis

Market Factors in Decisions

Real estate decision-makers have a major interest in markets and locations since such factors have important influences on the income-producing potential of real properties and hence on their value. In this chapter we are concerned with market forces and with various suggestions for their analysis. In the succeeding two chapters we consider local location factors.

Market changes and potential market changes play an important part in the decisions of real estate owners, users, investors, brokers, managers, builders, appraisers, mortgage lenders, buyers, and sellers. Government officials engaged in planning, zoning, slum clearance, the administration of taxes and public finance, building codes, or the insuring and guaranteeing of mortgages are also influenced greatly by real estate market changes and trends.

Because of the diverse nature of real estate markets and the wide variety of factors that affect them, somewhat different approaches to the analysis of residential, commercial, industrial, farm, and special-purpose real estate markets often are required. Even so, there are a number of general guides to market analysis that are applicable to each of these types of real estate markets. We consider here some of the major characteristics of real estate markets, various analytical tools that may be used, kinds of data that are helpful, and the judgmental factors that often are highly important to the real estate decision-maker.

In all types of markets, including real estate markets, the major factors involved are those related to *demand, supply,* and *price.* Note that *price* is emphasized in our discussions along with supply and demand. Price is viewed broadly, however, to include rent, interest rates, special charges, and the like depending on the market sector under consideration.

The Market in Operation

A brief and general description of the forces operating in the real estate market, the principles explaining their relationships, and the functions which they perform may seem to imply that the competitive process brings about smooth adjustments between supply, demand, and prices. Such is not necessarily the case. Competition is the main regulative force, it is true; but the actual operation of the market is far from perfect or efficient. We pointed out some of the reasons for this condition in Chapter 6: real properties possess few of the characteristics which make it easy to carry on market dealings in them, the markets for many types of real estate are limited in extent, and there are no central exchanges to facilitate buying and selling. Furthermore, the real estate market is affected by the seasons, with spring and fall usually representing the active periods of the year. Likewise, variations in general or local business activity, the ease or difficulty of financing, and other special factors all have important effects. Government policies play a role of growing importance. The rapid industrial changes arising from scientific and technological advances are also having major effects on real estate markets.

As a result, the real estate market passes through periods of varying activity. At times a *seller's market* exists, which means that very few properties are available and a large number of users and potential users are demanding them. At othert imes a *buyer's market* exists—that is, the buyer can fulfill his needs at low prices and on advantageous terms.

Factors Conditioning Market Operation

The following are among the factors that condition the operation of real estate markets:

1. Each property is unique, since only one building can occupy a particular spot on the earth's surface. However, the degree of uniqueness varies. Row houses or town houses or standardized detached houses in a large homogeneous neighborhood are virtually interchangeable. In contrast, every 25 or 50 feet of land may change in value in a central business district. Also, we should note that a special-purpose building may be suitable for use by only one tenant.
2. Some properties are parts of estates or are involved in litigation, with restrictions on sale or lease so they cannot be sold or devel-

oped. Such properties, even though in desirable locations, are virtually out of the market.

3. Some owners have a sentimental attachment to their homes, farms, or other properties and refuse to sell for prices that reflect market conditions.

4. Some properties are leased for long periods and are not available for sublease or sale.

5. Buyers are often restricted to persons living in the city or neighborhood who are in a position to take advantage of bargains or the necessities of the seller.

6. Owners living outside of a city frequently are not familiar with local developments which may increase or diminish the value of their properties.

7. Prices are affected by the terms and availability of financing.

8. Oral agreements are not binding as in stock market or grain market transactions, so that a seller or buyer may not complete a transaction even though an obligation to pay a broker's commission may be incurred.

9. Whether the seller has a good title cannot be determined quickly as in the case of stocks or merchandise, so that a period of time must elapse before the title can be passed.

10. Real estate cannot escape local taxes as is often possible in the case of personal property.

11. The value of real properties is often affected greatly by changes in local zoning laws.

12. The value of any specific property is affected by the character of the neighborhood and the economic outlook.

13. Buildings are not standardized commodities like automobiles. They may have hidden defects or exceptionally favorable features.

14. There is no machinery for selling short in real estate markets.

15. While properties may turn over rapidly in periods of advancing prices, there may be long periods of low sales volume during periods of stagnation and decline.

16. Residential real estate has been subject to rent control in times of emergency, which checked the operation of normal market forces.

17. The value of real estate will be lowered by a high crime rate in the neighborhood. Property values depend on adequate police and fire protection.

18. Property values are affected by availability of water, sewer systems, utilities, and highways.

The nature of the real estate market is thus different from other types of markets. Yet its operation can no more be called exceptional than the operation of the stock market and the board of trade, which are themselves exceptional in the unusual homogeneity and standardized character of the articles in which they deal.

Minority Groups

In addition, the workings of the real estate market are sometimes modified considerably by the presence of certain elements of monopoly. One indication of monopoly elements is provided by the special market factors surrounding residential properties occupied by Negroes and other minority groups. In many of our larger cities such groups have been excluded from the sale and rental markets for a considerable portion of residential properties. Hence, the owners of properties in areas now occupied by such groups are placed in a monopolistic position. As a result of this position, it is possible to exact rents or prices higher than could ordinarily be obtained for equivalent accommodations in the broader and more competitive real estate market.

In some rural areas religious groups form closed communities in which land purchases are restricted to the members of a particular group or sect. Thus, such markets are limited.

It should be noted, however, that these higher rents or prices are secured usually by crowding the available accommodations to a greater degree than is typical of similar accommodations in the broader market. As a consequence, even badly deteriorated rental properties in such areas often produce handsome returns on the investment represented. Special efforts are sometimes made by investors in such preferred positions to protect themselves against further competition such as might arise from new housing developments designed for the occupancy of similar groups.

Market Variations

As we indicated in earlier discussions, real estate markets can be classified according to types of properties, scope, and whether dealings are concerned with the purchase and sale of properties themselves or the rental of the services of properties for specified periods. While the rental and sale markets for properties are not mutually exclusive, both forming parts of a larger whole, the rental market is not characterized by the wide variations which occur in the buying and selling of properties themselves. In part this is due to the fact that the rental market partakes indirectly of the nature of a consumers' goods market and the sale market of a producers' goods market. Usually variations of market activities in consumers' goods are not as marked as those in producers' goods.

However, the rental market influences selling prices and the rate of building. When a seller's market exists, prices may move high enough to bring about the production of new buildings. When new structures are made available, they remain on the market for long periods of time, since they usually last for many years. If more of these are produced than can be absorbed at prices characteristic of a seller's market, a long period of time is generally required for readjustments to take place.

An upward movement in the price of real estate services or rents and in the selling prices of real properties is normally the result of an increase in the demand for space. We have noted that in short-run periods, demand conditions are of greater importance than those of supply. The basic elements in demand are income and the terms and availability of financing. When such an increase in demand and prices occurs, the stage is set for an expansion of activity. Expansion of economic opportunities usually is necessary to attract people or to increase their incomes. Similarly, a loss of such opportunities tends to depress the real estate market.

People flock to a city from country districts, small towns, or other cities whenever new sources of income are established or old ones expanded. For example, Detroit grew rapidly after 1900 as a result of the amazing development of the automobile industry. In more recent years the Southwest and the Southeast grew rapidly as a result of the location and expansion of many defense and space industries in those areas.

A rapid increase in the rate of population growth does not of itself cause an advance in real estate activity, for it must be accompanied by buying power on the part of the newcomers. Buying power includes consumer and business incomes, but depends also on the terms and availability of financing. Likewise, the lack of any sudden population growth does not necessarily prevent an expansion from occurring if incomes advance and financing terms are liberal.

Wide variations in real estate activity can be explained largely in terms of the relative inflexibility of the supply of space. While people are willing to make a smaller amount of space go around in periods of depression by doubling up, they are unwilling to live under conditions such as this when their incomes increase. Also, business firms demand more and better space when their incomes advance. Under depressed conditions new construction will be at a standstill because it will not pay to build at the low existing rents. But, as the population and business firms expand in number and rent-paying capacity, the large supply of vacant units typical of depression periods is rapidly absorbed. When the percentage of vacant units reaches a low figure, rents begin to rise. Such an advance also forces up prices and values. The net rentals advance even more sharply than gross rentals because operating costs, interest charges, taxes, maintenance, and similar expenses are relatively fixed. Hence, the rate of profit is rapidly increased, and it becomes profitable to erect new buildings.

Market Expansion

In the early stages of expansion, construction of single-family houses predominates because many are constructed for their amenity values by those who have incomes sufficient to make down payments, even if the houses would not command rents sufficient to yield a normal monetary return on their cost. Similarly, business firms may expand plants or stores. As expansion progresses, however, it becomes profitable to construct apartment buildings, business blocks, industrial structures, shopping centers, and office buildings that are financed solely for pecuniary return. The period of construction usually begins with a period of easy credit. During such a period it may become quite easy to finance projects of various types.

As new buildings are erected, they absorb the vacant land; and a land boom results, with subdividing activity proceeding first at a slow rate and then gathering momentum if the pressure of building on land continues to increase. Large areas may be added to the supply of land available to the city. It should be noted that as outward movement from the city center occurs, the area available increases in a manner comparable to the square of the radius of a circle.

As we have pointed out, net rents tend to rise more rapidly than gross rents. Costs usually do not move up as fast as rental levels.

Expenditures for public improvements tend to increase at the same time that the volume of building and subdividing gains in momentum. Sometimes public improvements may be made in advance of current or immediate future needs.

Market Contraction

Some time in the course of this period of expansion, demand begins to fall behind the rapid additions to supply which are being made available. It becomes difficult for the operators to sell properties, and the sources of credit begin to tighten. The tightening of credit results in foreclosures; and unless the market continues to expand because of some increase in demand, an advance in the volume of foreclosures forecasts a period of decline. Many sectors of the real estate market may still maintain a peak level of activity. Construction of new apartments or stores may continue for some time at almost peak levels. There is as yet no marked decline in rents. Operating expenses are increasing, however, and foreclosures are likely to have an upward trend. The fact that almost all real estate is financed on a debt rather than an equity basis probably helps to intensify the variations that occur. In a sense, those who finance real estate can make or break the market.

If foreclosures mount in volume as credits are tightening, the entire market is affected. It becomes impossible to sell properties without cutting prices. Land values begin to decline. Just as net rentals rose more rapidly than gross rentals in the early period of expansion, they now fall more rapidly because of the fixed charges involved. Hence, profits are wiped out and market activity falls to low levels.

The rate of recession in the real estate market will be intensified if there is a simultaneous recession in business generally. In that event incomes of tenants will drop and vacancies will increase as some families double up and others leave the city. Prospective marriages will be deferred in many cases. Business firms will reduce the space used. The result will be a rapid decline in rents. Foreclosures will increase rapidly, first on apartment and office buildings, because rents decline faster than operating expenses and owners soon find themselves unable to meet interest even on their first mortgages. Then, if a long period of depression ensues, the foreclosures will extend to single-family residences and owner-occupied business properties. Many owners of single-family homes will struggle to the limit of their ability to hold their homes. Others, especially those with thin equities, will give up at the first sign of recession. As a result of this process of attrition, the prices of real estate holdings are forced down.

A large volume of foreclosures is characteristic of depressed conditions in the real estate market. As a result of the foreclosure process, properties are refinanced and the financial wreckage is cleared away. Thus the stage is set for another period of expansion, which does not come automatically but which awaits some special impetus resulting in an increase in the demand for real estate resources.

National and Local Market Activity

Although activity in many real estate markets follows general national trends of business conditions, there are significant local variations. Regional differences account in part for some of these variations. The rapid expansion of the Southeast and Southwest has resulted in the acceleration of activity in the real estate markets of those regions.

Differences in the "mix" of economic activities in cities often results in local market experience that differs from general national or even regional trends. Usually cities that are largely dependent on the production of producers' goods will have wider swings in real estate market activity than those that rely largely on the production of consumers' goods. Also, cities with a diversified economic base typically enjoy greater stability of real estate market operations than those with less diversification, especially one-industry towns.

Major booms in real estate market activity are likely to come during periods of general business prosperity. Some cities, however, may experience only moderate expansion in such periods, while in others market activity may attain boom proportions. Local, regional, and industry factors largely account for the differences.

The Cycle Controversy

There are widely divergent viewpoints as to whether there is a national cycle in real estate market activity. Some contend that such cycles can be identified, while others believe that local variations are so important as to make the concept of a national cycle meaningless.

Roy Wenzlick has been a major proponent of the concept of a national cycle; James C. Downs, Jr., and Homer Hoyt have stressed the importance of local market factors.[1] Hoyt points out, however, that general periods of prosperity and depression tend to affect all local markets but with varying degrees of intensity and the timing of the impact of general economic changes may also vary.

There does not appear to be any regularity of such cyclical variations in real estate prices or in the volume of real estate activity as can be identified. Studies of variations in real estate activity in Chicago showed intervals between peaks of activity of 20, 16, 18, and 35 years.[2] If activity peaks out in the mid-1960's, a forty-year interval will be involved since the last peak was reached in Chicago in 1925.

It is well to note also that real estate activity varies greatly at the same time in the same urban region between different sections of the region and types of property. For example, the 1890 boom in Chicago affected chiefly the South Side near the World's Fair grounds and some central office sites; the Chicago boom of the mid-1920's was largely an outlying business center, apartment, and suburban boom.

Basic changes in the American economy may reduce greatly if they do not virtually eliminate major business cycles and major real estate cycles. These changes include federal assumption of responsibility for economic conditions under the Employment Act of 1946, the guarantee of bank and savings and loan deposits, the guarantee and insurance of VA and FHA mortgages plus the widespread use of amortized mortgages, social security, unemployment insurance, pension funds, union wage policies, widespread use of time payments and consumer credit, the strengthening of the middle-income groups and the reduction of income extremes at both the higher and lower levels, plus others. Increased knowledge about the American and world economies and the factors of major importance in determining the direction of economic activity must also be included as an important factor in dealing with major cyclical movements of economic activity, including real estate activity.

[1] See various issues of Wenzlick's *Real Estate Analyst,* published by The Wenzlick Organization, St. Louis, Missouri.

[2] Homer Hoyt, "Effect of Cyclical Fluctuations Upon Real Estate Finance," *The Appraisal Journal* (April, 1947). See also Hoyt's *The Urban Real Estate Cycle—Performances and Prospects,* Technical Bulletin 38 (Washington, D.C.: Urban Land Institute, 1960).

As a result of these changes, the past three decades have seen only minor adjustments in comparison to some of the earlier changes.

Regardless of the merits of the cycle argument, we must recognize that real estate activity in almost any local market is likely to fluctuate markedly. There may be overbuilding especially of office buildings, apartment houses, and shopping centers. Maisel points out that housing production ranks among the most cyclically volatile industries; he says, "On an annual basis, movements of 30 to 40 per cent from peaks to troughs occurred three times between 1950 and 1962. Starts in the highest quarter exceeded those in the lowest by more than 50 per cent—a difference at annual rates of more than 600,000 dwelling units:" [3] Some local markets often exhibit even greater variations.

Future Market Variations

In more recent years real estate market activity has been somewhat more stable than it was a generation ago. Variations persist as we have pointed out, but market activity typically does not change violently in short periods of time. It may be that generally prosperous conditions in the American economy account for this. Or other factors may have contributed to a somewhat greater degree of stability including price support and subsidy programs as well as some gradual inflation.

The Employment Act of 1946, which committed us to the pursuit of full employment, and the policies that have evolved as a result of it have been important in this connection as have the built-in stabilizers such as unemployment compensation, progressive income taxation, and old age and survivors insurance. Heavy expenditures for defense and space exploration are important modifying forces. The role of the federal government in housing, with the insurance and guarantee of mortages, support of secondary mortgage markets, insurance of savings and checking accounts, and the development of nationwide mortgage financing systems through such programs as those of the Federal Home Loan Bank Board all have helped to provide increased stability.

Whether these and related developments will help in avoiding the extremes of booms and busts in real estate markets in the future remains to be seen. If a major business depression comes along it will undoubtedly bring substantial reductions in real estate activity of all types. Real estate has not been protected against speculative extremes in recent prosperous periods.

We should note, however, that during the postwar recessions of 1948–49, 1953–54, 1957–58, and 1960–61, real estate activity in general held up remarkably well. Indeed, government action in supporting the secondary

[3] Sherman J. Maisel, "A Theory of Fluctuations in Residential Construction Starts," *American Economic Review* (June, 1963).

mortgage market and in supporting insured and guaranteed mortgages resulted in house-building programs that had almost a contracyclical character in the 1957–58 recession and to a lesser degree in 1960–61.

Much has been said and written about the long-range demands for housing, for business structures, and for other real estate as a result of the population pressures that are increasingly in evidence. As we have pointed out, however, numbers of people have little significance in terms of market demand unless the people have good incomes and the ability to command credit. Currently, long-term income prospects appear to be favorable. Hence, demand for real estate resources may increase significantly during the years ahead.

There are numerous problems that may cause difficulties, despite these favorable general prospects. Some regions and some localities will fall far below national averages in terms of the growth that appears to lie ahead. Heavy taxation of real properties, the relatively slow introduction of improved construction methods and technology, labor problems, the growth of slum areas, the problems of the downtown areas, and the competition of many new goods and services for a portion of the income produced—all may cause difficulties. Beyond these, there is the general volatility of demand for real estate resources against relatively fixed supplies in short-run periods. These conditions continue to make possible variations in real estate market activity. The somewhat greater stability of general business conditions plus major efforts to control wide variations in economic activity, however, are bound to have their effect on real estate as well as other markets.

Types of Market Analysis

The National Association of Home Builders has distinguished two types of housing market analysis. The first is referred to as *trend analysis* which is intended to indicate the *direction* of the market. The second is called *quantitative market analysis* with efforts being made to break down the market by type of structure, location, and price brackets. The Association also distinguishes between *short-term* projections covering periods of less than twenty-four months and *longer-range* periods covering three, five, to ten years.[4]

Market analyses may also be classified by major area of interest: by type of property; new or existing structures; cost factors such as financing, construction materials, labor, and the like; geographic area, or in other ways. Classifications may also be made by purpose, degree of intensity of the analysis, and others.

[4] Uriel Manheim, *How To Do Housing Market Research:* Handbook for Local Home Builders Associations (Washington, D.C.: National Association of Home Builders of the United States, 1963), p. 3.

Purpose of the Market Analysis

As in the making of appraisals, the first step in the analysis of a real estate market is a careful definition of the problem. Why is the analysis being made? Is it to determine whether a builder should start a new project? Is an investor deciding on a major purchase or sale? Is a department store planning a new shopping center? Is a building manager trying to decide whether to raise rents? Is a mortgage lender planning to tighten financing terms? These questions and many others that might be raised suggest some of the variety of uses of market analyses.

The problems involved in making a market analysis generally will fall into two major groups: first, those pertaining to short-run objectives, and second, those pertaining to long-run objectives. For example, a builder may be concerned with whether he can sell the houses he builds within the next six months. An investor or a lending institution, by contrast, may be interested in the income potential and stability of properties over the next decade or two or longer. Planning commissions may be concerned with problems requiring that estimates be made for different types of land uses for as many as twenty or thirty years ahead.

Definition of purpose assists in determining whether short- or longer-run considerations should be given primary attention, the sector of the market that needs to be stressed, and the extent of the market that must be studied. For example, if several cities are located in close proximity, all of them may be included in a market analysis. On the other hand, a specialized problem may limit the analysis to a few areas or districts. Once purpose has been defined, we may proceed with a consideration of the principal factors bearing on market conditions.

Major Factors in Analysis

The main factors in the analysis of real estate markets may be listed as follows:

pp.267-276

1. The general level of business activity affects real estate markets. For example, the recessions of 1948–49, 1953–54, 1957–58, and 1960–61 affected real estate markets of nearly all types in varying degrees.

2. The level of local business activity also requires consideration. Local business activity, of course, may deviate from general national trends because of special local factors. Usually there is some relationship between local business conditions and real estate market trends.

3. Of major importance for all types of real estate are changes in the employment and income sources of the community. Expansion of existing economic activities such as may result from new factories, new government agencies, new tourist attractions, and the like tend to increase

market activity; the loss of employment and income has the opposite effect. Methods for analyzing changes of this type were outlined in the preceding chapter and are pertinent to nearly all types of real estate market analyses.

4. Financing terms and trends have a major influence on the demand for nearly all types of real estate. General and local mortgage market conditions form an integral part of almost every type of real estate market analysis.

5. While income and financing factors are of primary importance, population growth or decline tends to affect real estate markets. Not only are changes in the total population important, but also changes in the age distribution and composition of the population, as well as shifts of population within the market area. For example, a persistent movement to the suburbs may increase the demand for certain types of properties and bring a decline in the demand for other types, even though there are no changes in total population or in incomes.

6. Changes in the tastes and preferences of customers and potential customers may be highly important if they can be identified with reasonable accuracy.

7. The volume of building activity requires consideration, as well as construction cost levels and trends. Costs in relation to prices and rents have an important bearing on the rate at which additions will be made to the available supply. Also, the availability of improved lots and the cost of improving raw land usually require consideration.

8. Often the vacancy rate is the most important single indicator of real estate market trends. Rising vacancies usually indicate that the supply of existing space is greater than the demand for it. The rate at which vacancies are increasing or declining often provides the key to probable market changes. Closely related to vacancies in existing structures are the new structures that have not been sold or leased and remain on the market as an "overhang" for varying periods of time.

9. As we have suggested above, the interrelationship between prices, rents, and construction costs are important keys to market conditions and potential market changes. Wide differences between listing prices and final sales prices are especially significant.

10. The volume of market activity is reflected in the number of deeds recorded, the number of mortgages recorded, and the volume of foreclosures. Comparisons of present with past levels often provide good indexes of potential market changes.

11. Finally, all of the above factors must be studied in relation to each other and in relation to past developments. In this manner both short- and longer-range market trends may be identified and used as the basis for estimating future probable market changes.

General Business Conditions

We have pointed out in several connections that local forces exercise important influences on the real estate market. This is especially true of the markets for residential real estate. We do not wish to imply, however, that general economic trends have only limited influence on local real estate markets.

In many cases local markets will follow national trends rather closely. This is usually true when the major sources of local income and employment represent a typical cross section of the economy as a whole. In other cases local markets may deviate to some extent from national trends. This may be due to the types of employment and incomes represented or to special factors such as a rate of building that has been too rapid for local absorption, successful local efforts to bring in new industries, local financial policies that have unduly restricted building, unfavorable local government policies such as taxes, and many others.

Suggestions for analyzing general business conditions were outlined in Chapter 10. Estimates of general business trends usually precede the analysis of a specific real estate market. Then attempts are made to determine whether local conditions will follow closely or deviate significantly from general trends.

Local Business Conditions

The real estate market of a locality will be influenced by the trend of local business conditions, which may be influenced in turn by general economic trends. Of the many factors to consider in studying local business conditions, the most important is the trend of employment and incomes, as we suggested in the preceding chapter. Such information is generally available from local chambers of commerce and from state employment services as well as from the personnel offices of the major local employers. Frequently local chambers of commerce publish monthly data reflecting local business trends. Some universities publish monthly summaries of business conditions. In addition the various Federal Reserve Banks make available monthly reports covering business trends for the district served and for the more important cities in the district.

Besides showing employment and income, reports of these types frequently provide information on bank debits, department store sales, electricity production, newspaper advertising, car loadings, and similar information, as well as data on construction volume, real estate transfers, mortgages recorded, foreclosures, vacancies, and related materials more directly pertinent to the local real estate market.

While the conditions in the real estate market may at times be different from local business conditions, there is usually a close relationship between them. For example, real estate markets may be relatively inactive after a major local building boom even though other types of local business remain at high levels.

Employment and Incomes

As we have pointed out, an analysis of local economic trends is often the starting point for the analysis of the local real estate market or some sector of that market. This was discussed in the preceding chapter. Recent changes in employment or incomes have a vital influence on all phases of local real estate market activity. Of special significance, of course, are potential developments that are likely to strengthen or diminish the demand for specific types of properties. Such potential developments must be related directly to the specific market problem that is being studied. As the discussion in Chaper 6 indicates, income appears to be the primary factor in the demand for real estate. This point cannot be stressed too strongly in market analysis. If local incomes are good and income prospects are favorable, the real estate market is likely to be active (unless there has just been a great surge of building). Even though no new residents are attracted to the city, higher incomes will mean an increase in the demand for housing. Heavier spending will lead to greater demand for commercial property. Thus, demand for real estate can rise in a locality even though there has been no major increase in population. Similarly, demand will fall with a decline in incomes, even if there has been no loss of population.

As we pointed out above, information about incomes and income trends is often available from local or state government offices or the employment offices of larger enterprises. Such information is especially valuable in estimating short-run changes in the real estate market. Over the longer-run, prospects for increasing or decreasing employment and incomes are important in estimating the trend of real estate demand.

Population Changes

Analyses of the local economy often provide a helpful approach to the prediction of future population trends.[5] Past trends of population growth for census periods can be obtained from the U.S. Census of population.

The best single method of estimating the current population of most urban areas outside of central cities is to ascertain the total number of new dwelling units that have been added to the given area since the pre-

[5] See R. U. Tonsley, Eugene Clark, and Fred E. Clark, *Principles of Marketing* (New York: The Macmillan Co., 1962), chap. xxiv.

ceding census, as indicated by building permits. This total of new dwelling units may be multiplied by the average size of the family in the area in the last census to obtain the estimated additions to the population since that time. It may be preferable to secure data on the number of completed dwelling units since the preceding census from the electrical inspector's or assessor's office, but these figures on completed dwelling units are not universally available and they do not differ materially from building permit figures, since nearly all permits result in completed units. Allowance must always be made for vacancies, when the increase in population is estimated by new dwelling units. Conversions and doubling up may also be factors of importance in central cities.

Good alternative methods of estimating present population are based on the number of electric meters, since nearly every family has a meter, or on the number of water meters. The current population can be estimated by multiplying the present number of electric or water meters by the ratio of the population to the number of meters at the time of the last census.

It is very important in analyzing real estate markets, especially with respect to residential or shopping developments, to know what sections of the city are occupied by high, middle, or low income families. For cities of 50,000 population or over in 1950, data are available on the average monthly rent and the average value of owner-occupied houses as of 1960; for every census tract in a metropolitan area, the median family income is shown as well. To bring these figures down to date, it is necessary to increase such incomes by average increases that have prevailed since 1959, since that was the year for which income figures for the 1960 census were reported.

The best single method of estimating the current population of most urban areas outside of the central cities is to ascertain the total number of dwelling units which have been added to the given area since the United States Census of April, 1960, as indicated by building permits showing the number of new dwelling units. The number of occupied housing units for each block in each city or urban area with a population of 50,000 or more in 1950 is given in the United States Census of Housing for 1960 in the HC (3) series. Data for the number of occupied units in April, 1960, and median family income in 1959 are provided for every census tract in all standard metropolitan areas in the United States Census of Population 1960 in the PHC (1) series. The population and number of occupied units in April, 1960, the median family income, and other data are shown for each urban place of 2,500 population or more and for every county in all of the states by individual state bulletins by the United States Census of Population 1960 in the PC (1) A, B, C, and D bulletins. These bulletins, available in libraries or from the United States Depart-

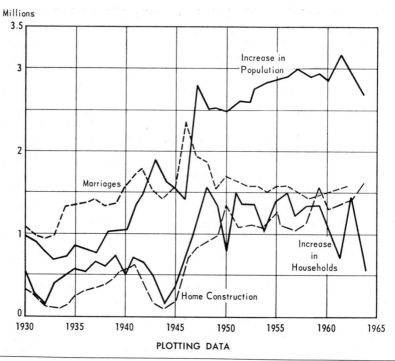

PLOTTING DATA

Year	Increase in Population	Marriages	Increase in Households	Home Construction
1930	1,418,000	1,126,856	542,000	330,000
1931	961,000	1,060,914	275,000	254,000
1932	800,000	981,903	167,000	134,000
1933	741,000	1,098,000	363,000	93,000
1934	795,000	1,302,000	504,000	126,000
1935	877,000	1,327,000	586,000	221,000
1936	819,000	1,369,000	562,000	319,000
1937	780,000	1,451,296	634,000	336,000
1938	1,008,000	1,330,780	595,000	406,000
1939	1,059,000	1,403,633	726,000	515,000
1940	1,094,000	1,595,879	504,000	602,600
1941	1,280,000	1,695,999	721,000	706,100
1942	1,458,000	1,772,132	600,000	356,000
1943	1,879,000	1,577,050	425,000	191,000
1944	1,658,000	1,452,394	225,000	141,800
1945	1,531,000	1,612,992	400,000	209,300
1946	1,461,000	2,291,045	711,000	670,500
1947	2,737,000	1,992,354	1,151,000	849,000
1948	2,505,000	1,811,155	1,582,000	931,600
1949	2,557,000	1,579,798	1,387,000	1,025,100

Fig. 12–1. Trends in population, marriages, households, and home construction, 1930–1964. (Sources: Bureau of the Census and *Economic Report of the President.*)

PLOTTING DATA. *Continued.*

Year	Increase in Population	Marriages	Increase in Households	Home Construction
1950	2,495,000	1,667,231	791,000	1,396,000
1951	2,677,000	1,594,694	1,017,000	1,091,300
1952	2,668,000	1,539,318	848,000	1,127,000
1953	2,618,000	1,546,000	830,000	1,103,800
1954	2,781,000	1,490,000	559,000	1,220,400
1955	2,853,000	1,531,000	895,000	1,328,900
1956	2,904,000	1,585,000	997,000	1,118,100
1957	3,055,000	1,516,000	758,000	1,041,900
1958	2,835,000	1,451,000	859,000	1,197,700
1959	2,948,000	1,494,000	900,000	1,531,000
1960	2,836,000	1,523,000	1,308,000	1,274,000
1961	3,166,000	1,548,000	681,000	1,337,000
1962	2,849,000	1,580,000	1,461,000	1,468,000
1963	2,687,000	1,651,000	537,000	1,613,000
1964	2,712,000	1,720,000	1,255,000	1,563,000
1965	2,464,000			1,518,000

Fig. 12–1. *Continued.*

ment of Commerce, Bureau of the Census, furnish the base point data for population, number of families, and family income as of April, 1960.

These data on occupied units can be brought up to date by the Construction Reports-Building Permits of the United States Department of Commerce, C 40-38, C 40-50 series entitled "Housing Authorized in Individual Permit-Issuing Places." There are annual summaries which show in detail the annual number of housing units for which permits were issued in every town, village, borough, city, and county in the United States which require building permits. These construction reports are also issued monthly and show the number of dwelling units as indicated by permits for most of the political subdivisions, excepting the very smallest, which had building activity for the latest month. By adding the total number of dwelling units shown by building permits issued from 1960 to the latest available month to the census figures for 1960, a fair approximation of the total number of occupied housing units at the latest date can be made for any given area. The construction reports provide no breakdown of the total number of dwelling units by census tracts or other political subdivisions within entire cities, but they do provide means of calculating the current number of dwelling units in suburban areas, where most of the new growth has taken place.

In using building permit data, allowances must be made for vacancies and unsold houses, and in central cities allowances must be made not only for vacancies but also for demolitions in slum clearance areas, as well as for new highways, conversions, and fire losses.

In calculating the number of households or the population in sections of central cities, use can be made of records of residential electric meters or water meters and records of local planning authorities; and these same data can be employed to check totals based on additions of building permit figures to census data.

The construction reports of the United States Department of Commerce are useful, not merely in estimating the total number of housing units, but also provide an accurate index as to what portions of a metropolitan area are experiencing the greatest building activity. The 1960 Census of Population shows the average number of persons per household in each census tract, city, borough, and county. The same ratio of persons per household can be used in estimating population for subsequent years.

The ratio between elementary school enrollment and population has fluctuated in recent years and varies greatly between city and suburban areas. School population is increasing more rapidly than total population in many areas, particularly in the newer suburbs, and less rapidly in older areas of cities.

Information about births and deaths for each year can be secured from city or county offices. Differences can be computed for each year, thus indicating population changes due to natural causes. Relating this to total population changes indicates net migration to or from the area. Often, local chambers of commerce or similar organizations have information of this type available. Visitation programs for new arrivals to the city may provide useful information. Also, rough estimates can be made through listings in telephone directories or numbers of gas or electric meters connected or disconnected.

While the general trend of population is important, some information should be secured about the marriage rate, since this indicates the rapidity with which new families are being established. Adjustments should be made for divorces, although a divorce does not necessarily lead to a reduction in the demand for housing. In many cases divorces lead to an increase rather than a decrease in the demand for space. Information about the number of marriage licenses and divorces can be secured from county offices.

Similarly, it is important to procure information on the extent to which doubling up or the sharing of dwellings by several families is taking place. Definite information seldom can be obtained, and estimates must be relied upon. Usually the extent of doubling up depends on general economic conditions. If there is much of it, a margin of vacant homes will appear even though no people leave the city. Hence, estimates of this type are necessary to supplement data on population changes.

Changes in Preferences and Tastes [6]

Consumers of real estate resources and services include the entire population and range from large corporations to single individuals. Within any real estate market, whether it is the market for industrial property in a certain city, the market for shopping center sites or subdivisions, or the market for rental housing, shifts may occur in the preferences and tastes of the customers involved. Such shifts may be very difficult to identify or to evaluate. Consumers of housing may be attracted by design or style changes; consumers of industrial real estate by efficient and convenient layouts of space; and consumers of retailing areas by ease of access and flexibility. At one time, one set of factors may be in favor; at another time, others will predominate.

Many real estate decision-makers rely on their own experience and observation of market changes to guide them with respect to changes in tastes and preferences. In some cases, surveys are conducted by means of questionnaires or interviews. Various types of controlled experiments may also be undertaken.

In many cases, however, the supplier of real estate resources and services anticipates trends in an almost intuitive way. Surveys of customers and potential customers may not reveal basic shifts in desires and preferences since people are not able to indicate preferences for things with which they are not yet familiar. Once available, however, customers may flock to buy. Ranch houses, split levels, and town houses have enjoyed popularity at various times but the determination of why or when has been a difficult process.

Financing Conditions

Next to incomes, the terms and availability of financing are the primary factors in determining the strength or weakness of demand for real estate. When financing is available on liberal terms and at low interest rates, the demand for property is strengthened. Rigorous financing terms tend to limit demand.

Financing conditions may vary between different sectors of the real estate market. Financing may vary between regions and cities. Generally, financing tends to be more readily available in eastern areas than in southern or western regions.

[6] For discussions of these and related topics see for example Kenneth R. Davis, *Marketing Management* (New York: The Ronald Press Co., 1961) or John H. Howard, *Marketing Management* (Homewood, Ill.: Richard D. Irwin, Inc., 1957). See also William G. Grigsby, *Housing Markets and Public Policy* (Philadelphia: University of Pennsylvania Press, 1963), pp. 171–73.

As we have pointed out, the mortgage market does not operate independently of the other capital markets. Hence, the availability of financing for real estate projects is dependent in part on the alternative uses for funds in other types of projects.

Information in regard to the terms and availability of funds for real estate financing may be secured from such sources as the Federal Reserve *Bulletin,* the publications of the regional Federal Reserve Banks and Federal Home Loan Banks, from financial newspapers and magazines, and from institutions which engage in real estate finance, such as insurance companies, banks, and savings and loan associations.

Construction Volume and Costs

The rate at which new additions to supply have been made during recent years should be studied by securing figures from city offices on the volume of construction and the number of demolitions. Such data are made available for a number of cities by the Bureau of Labor Statistics and by several commercial services.

Conditions in the building industry should be analyzed carefully. The availability of labor resources and of building materials and their prices require special consideration. The availability of building sites and the prices of available land need to be determined. Also, special attention should be given to changes and potential changes in building technology since this may affect construction costs. The quality and competence of architects often is a factor of importance and should be related to quality and competence of builders and developers.

Data on construction costs can frequently be secured from the city building department. Local real estate boards often assemble data of this type. Several federal agencies publish information on construction costs for a number of cities, and various commercial organizations also supply such data.

Construction costs must be related to selling prices and rents in order to determine future rates of building. When prices and rents are sufficiently above costs to allow a substantial profit margin, building proceeds rapidly. As the spread is narrowed, the rate of building slows down. Less efficient builders are eliminated. When costs exceed sales prices or capitalized rental income, nearly all building ceases.

One of the important elements in building and developing costs is land and the cost of improving it. When the available supply of improved lots has been exhausted, builders may face very large outlays of funds in order to develop new areas. If the market does not exhibit signs of substantial strength, such large-scale projects may be postponed.

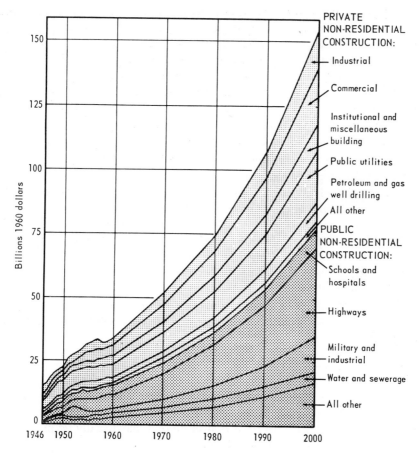

Fig. 12–2. Principal categories of nonresidential construction, private and public, 1946–1960, and medium projections to the year 2000. (Source: *Resources in America's Future*, p. 118.)

Vacancies

As we indicated above, the vacancy rate is one of the important indicators of real estate market conditions and trends. A surplus of vacant units will tend to retard price or rent increases even when demand is strong. Just what is meant by a surplus or deficit of vacant units cannot be defined exactly. The concept varies from one community to another and from one type of property to another. Normal vacancy for houses is usually considered as something less than 5 per cent, for apartments slightly over 5 per cent, and for business units it may run somewhat higher; but these are only rules of thumb which vary from one place to another.

Whenever the supply of vacant units exceeds a normal percentage, the market tends to be depressed. Competition of owners and sellers seeking tenants and buyers forces prices and rents downward and restrains new construction. When vacancies are increasing, the market must be watched closely, for an unsound situation may be developing because of either declining demand or overbuilding. If an increasing amount of vacancy is not checked, a collapse of rents, prices, and market activity may result. A decline in the vacancy ratio, on the other hand, may be reflected in an upward movement of rents and prices; but market activity will be limited because demand for space cannot be translated into sales and leases until a supply of space is made available.

Information about vacancies in various types of properties is frequently collected by local real estate boards. At times the Post Office Department conducts vacancy surveys in various cities. Often local public utility companies or departments will assemble data concerning vacancies, and the publishers of local directories may gather information of this type at periodic intervals. Conferences with important property managers often provide useful data. It is desirable that vacancy ratios be computed separately for different classes of property, for it frequently happens that one part of a market will have a shortage of space while another has a surplus.[7]

Price and Rent Trends

Any persistent changes in market prices or rents upward or downward reflect basic market conditions. Sometimes these movements are of short duration, but if they persist for a year or more it may usually be presumed that the trend will continue for a time.

On occasion real estate brokers test the market by advertising a popular type of property at a very reasonable price or rental. They are then able to gauge market conditions by the number of responses received to the advertisement.

Of special importance is the variation between listing and actual selling prices. Similarly the difference between the rental rate asked and finally paid is a reflection of the strength of the market.

The length of time new properties remain on the market before being sold or rented indicates the strength or weakness of demand. When long periods are required to dispose of property, the market is weakening. This assumes, of course, that prices have been set on a reasonably competitive basis.

---

[7] Manheim, *op. cit.*, p. 61. The types of data may be considered as direct, that is, a census survey, indirect such as idle electric meters or partial including listing of realtors, classified ads, FHA and Public Housing records, and others.

Market Activity and Trends

After the factors outlined above have been studied, it should be possible to make reasonably sound estimates of future market trends. This involves determining the present position of the market in relation to past conditions. Variations in market activity are reflected in the number of real estate transfers. Such information may be secured from the volume of deeds recorded in county recorders' offices. The number of mortgages recorded is available from the same sources, as is information about the volume of foreclosures.

Studies of these data covering fairly long periods of time are desirable. Data on deeds, mortgages, and foreclosures may be related to population trends; vacancy ratios; price, rent, and cost indexes; and the volume of construction. Such relationships provide a good indication of the present position of the market with regard to past periods.

Of major importance in studying market conditions and trends are *relative prices*. For example, construction costs may be rising, but rents and selling prices may be rising even more rapidly. Hence, further construction may be expected to take place despite the advancing costs. Furthermore, an upward or downward trend in prices and rents may cause buyers, investors, and property users to expect still further changes in the same direction and accentuate the trend that has been developing.

A reduction in financing charges may stimulate market activity, even though no other basic change has occurred. Favorable terms of sale, such as smaller down payments and longer periods in which to repay loans, may stimulate the market. Rising incomes may have only a limited effect if real estate rents and sales prices, as well as the prices of other goods and services, are moving up in proportion. In other words *real incomes* rather than monetary incomes deserve primary consideration.

It is well to remember also that real estate resources are in competition with other goods and services for a slice of the consumer's or the businessman's dollar. The real estate market does not operate in a compartment that is separated from other markets. It is an integral part of the entire economic system, and real estate market changes must always be considered in relation to other developments in the local or national economy.

Housing Market Analysis

The analysis of a housing market involves application of the pertinent factors outlined above to the residential rather than to other sectors of the real estate market. After careful definition of the specific problem under consideration, the analysis proceeds to a consideration of the major demand, supply, and price factors involved.

Expanding economic opportunities will bring people into a city from elsewhere and stimulate the demand for housing. Rising incomes even without expansion of employment may also lead to heavier housing demand. Thus, economic base and similar types of analyses are often helpful in housing market studies.

In relating income levels to housing demand, it is necessary to consider incomes in relation to house prices. As a rule, families cannot afford to pay more than about 2½ times their annual income for a house. Consequently, a good housing market analysis requires that an income distribution of the families in the area be secured. Data of these types are available from census materials by census tracts in metropolitan regions and for cities, towns, and counties. Such census reports also indicate the number of owner-occupied and rental units by price and rent brackets.

The supply of new dwelling units can be estimated on the basis of new building permits and the number of water meters or electric meters added. Data of this type can be broken down by districts and can be related to base periods such as those for which census materials are available.

A long period of strong building activity may indicate the possibility of a weakening market, especially if vacancies are rising and new houses are remaining on the market for long periods of time before being sold. Also, construction costs must be studied in relationship to current prices to determine whether it is likely to be profitable for builders to continue high volumes of construction activity.

Closely related to income, cost, and price factors are financing considerations. If financing is available on easy terms, demand may be maintained even though incomes are not advancing. Conversely, if financing terms are not favorable, housing demand may be reduced rapidly, even though incomes are steady or advancing. Changes in the terms of financing may have an even greater impact on the market than changes in incomes because of the large proportion of borrowed funds that go into most house purchases. For example, extending the term of the mortgage reduces the monthly payments of the home buyer.

Efficiency of building and low sales prices will stimulate demand. Larger builders, both those with large-scale on-site operations and prefabricators, have been able to stimulate demand in this way. However, whenever market prices fall below the amount for which the most efficient builders can and will construct houses, few will be added to the supply.

As we have suggested above, changes in design or style may appeal to changing tastes and preferences of house buyers. Changes in technology may make design and style changes possible.

Market Analysis for Shopping Centers

A market analysis to determine the soundness of a new shopping center requires consideration of special sets of factors in addition to those involved in the analysis of broader divisions of the real estate market. A general outline of a shopping center market analysis is presented below.

1. The size of the trade area is determined by the location of competing centers, by location of mass transportation routes, and by related factors. The time or distance from the center is not the vital factor. Families will drive long distances to reach a large shopping center if there is no similar facility near them. They will not drive even a short distance if they live within walking distance of a major shopping district. Most of the recently developed large regional shopping centers depend upon customers who arrive in automobiles. Families living near subways, elevated stations, or suburban railroad stations often prefer to shop in central shopping districts.

The size of the trade area varies with the type of center. It is broadest for a regional center with a large department store, smaller for a center with a junior department store, still smaller for a center with a variety store as the principal unit, and only neighborhood-wide for a center with a supermarket and drugstore as the chief units. The size of the trade area can best be determined by taking a sample survey of housewives to determine where they shop.

2. After determining the extent of the trade area, the next step is to estimate the number of families in each census tract, community, or district of the trade area. This is accomplished by adding to the number of dwelling units shown by the most recent United States Census the number of new dwelling units added since that time as reflected by building permits, electric meters, or water meters.

3. The average family income in each census tract or community is estimated on the basis of U.S. Census estimates of 1959 with adjustments for income changes since that time including the breakdown of family incomes for 1959 by $1,000 intervals from $1,000 to $10,000; $10,000 to $14,999; $15,000 to $24,999; and $25,000 and over by the U.S. Census for every census tract in every metropolitan area with a population of 50,000 and over. Adjustments for intervening years between 1959 and the date of the market analysis can be made by applying the average increase in per capita income for the state in which the center is located, using the midpoint of the income brackets as the average. Aggregate income of each community is determined by multiplying the number of families by the average income.

4. The next step is to estimate the volume of retail purchases for each type of store planned for the center as of the date of the survey. It is estimated that all families above the lowest income level spend about the same percentage of their incomes for clothing, shoes, furniture, and other fashion goods. The percentage of income which families spend in each metropolitan area in each type of store may be determined by relating total metropolitan area retail sales in each type of store to the total family income of the region or state as indicated by the U.S. Retail Census of 1963.

5. On the basis of questionnaires or sample surveys, an estimate may be made of the proportion of their income which families in the area will spend in each type of store planned for the shopping center in its first year of full operation.

6. The total sales of each type of store at the center being studied may be estimated by adding expected purchases from each segment of the trade area, taking into account the competition of other centers.

7. The store area required for the new center is estimated on the basis of expected average sales per square foot for each type of store. Parking area is calculated on a ratio of parking to store area.

8. The cost of constructing the center is estimated on the basis of current square foot cost for the number of square feet of store area required.

9. The rentals are estimated on the basis of percentages customarily paid by each type of store on the volume of sales.

10. The net return is estimated by deducting from the gross rents the annual charges for interest, maintenance of the buildings, real estate taxes, insurance, and allowances for vacancies and management fees.

11. The future sales at the center are based on estimates of the future growth of population and income of the trade area.

Market Analysis for Individual Stores

Surveys may be made for single stores as well as for shopping districts. For example, a survey may be made for the purpose of determining whether a new drugstore or hardware store can thrive in a specific location. In this case, the competition of other stores must be noted, the extent of the trade area from which the local neighborhood draws customers estimated, and the number of families and income of the families in that trade area determined. From these data, the total purchases for the type of store under consideration in the trade area will be estimated. Knowing the experience of their own type or a similar type of store in other neighborhoods with similar populations and incomes, the store company will decide whether sufficient volume of sales could be developed to warrant paying the rents for which stores could be obtained in the given location.

It is always necessary to estimate the potential growth of the trade area. An important factor is the amount of vacant land suitable for new homes in that area. It is desirable to ascertain the future program of builders for new home construction and to consult with telephone company and electric power company engineers as to their predictions for the future growth of the specific neighborhood or trade area.

Estimating Demand for Office Space

The potential demand for new office space in a city may be estimated by determining the number of occupied square feet of office space per capita for the metropolitan region. In large commercial and financial cities, 5 to 6 square feet of office space is needed for each person in the metropolitan area. This ratio must be determined for each city, since wide variations prevail. The amount of new office space potentially required may be estimated for each city on the basis of growth prospects and its prospects for development as a regional commercial and financial center.

Such general estimates, of course, should be related to current vacancy ratios, rents, construction costs, and the terms and availability of financing. Cycles in office building net income are of longer duration than those of general business. A period of overbuilding such as occurred in Chicago from 1923 to 1930 may produce a surplus of office space, which depresses rents and net income for a long time thereafter.

It has been estimated that 2 square feet of office space per capita is adequate for most "normal" requirements.[8] Thus, any space above such a figure indicates the extent to which a city is a national or regional office center. For example, San Diego has 2.2 square feet of office space per capita; New York, 16 square feet; and Chicago, 7.5 square feet.

Market Surveys of Industrial Space

In making surveys of available factory space, industrial buildings should be classified into one-story buildings and multi-storied buildings. The buildings should also be classified as to age, condition, and as to whether they have direct switch track connections. There may be a surplus of space in old multi-storied buildings but a scarcity of one-story factory buildings. Rental rates or sale prices of buildings offered for rent or sale should be obtained. Usually surveys of this type are made by the utility companies, such as the Commonwealth Edison Company of Chicago, with a view to attracting new industries to their region.

[8] See studies of Real Estate Research Corporation, Chicago.

Market Surveys for Renewal Purposes

In planning redevelopment or renewal of residential areas, surveys should be made to determine what types of dwelling units are preferred, how many rooms are desired in typical dwelling units, what proportion should be for sale or rent, and the potential demand in each price range. Interviews with a sample number of families in every census tract in a proposed renewal area are often helpful to ascertain how many families desire to move, the relation of the rent paid or the value of their homes to income, what type of dwelling unit is preferred by those who desired to move—row house, apartment, or detached house—whether they preferred to own or rent, and what rent or price they can afford to pay. Such surveys may be used as the basis for deciding what proportion of row houses, detached houses, and apartments should be built in the redeveloped area. Such surveys help to indicate the types of housing units in greatest demand and at what price or rental range. They also enable developers to avoid some of the mistakes that have been made in building large projects without analyzing local housing needs, preferences, and ability to pay. One author points out, for example:

In New York's East Harlem there is a housing project with a conspicuous rectangular lawn which became an object of hatred to the project tenants. A social worker frequently at the project was astonished by how often the subject of the lawn came up, usually gratuitously as far as she could see, and how much the tenants despised it and urged that it be done away with. When she asked why, the usual answer was, "what good is it?" or "who wants it?" Finally one day a tenant more articulate than the others made this pronouncement: "Nobody cared what we wanted when they built this place. They threw our houses down and pushed us here and pushed our friends somewhere else. We don't have a place around here to get a cup of coffee or a newspaper even, or borrow fifty cents. Nobody cared what we need. But the big men come and look at that grass and say, "isn't it wonderful!! Now the poor have everything."

This tenant was saying what moralists have said for thousands of years: Handsome is as handsome does. All that glitters is not gold.

She was saying more: There is a quality even meaner than outright ugliness or disorder, and this meaner quality is the dishonest mask of pretended order, achieved by ignoring or suppressing the real order that is struggling to exist and to be served.[9]

Careful analysis of the preferences of customers often helps to avoid error in a renewal program or in other types of real estate projects. Such analysis may point toward needs and wants that are not being adequately met by the market (including governmental as well as privately developed programs) and thus form the basis for creative advances over time.

---

[9] By permission from *The Death and Life of Great American Cities,* by Jane Jacobs, p. 15. Copyright, 1961, Random House, New York.

Surveys may also be conducted to determine whether there will be a demand for office buildings, hotels, and stores sufficient to warrant their inclusion in a renewal project. Current trends point to more and more large-scale, multipurpose renewal efforts.

SUMMARY

This chapter presents general guides to the analysis of various real estate markets including residential, commercial, and industrial types. It is essential to know the purpose for which any analysis is undertaken, and the purpose indicates whether long-run or short-run considerations will be dominant.

In the analysis of any real estate market, the following factors are usually applicable:

(a) general business conditions
(b) the level of local business activity
(c) changes in the economic base of the community
(d) income trends
(e) the cost and availability of financing
(f) population factors
(g) changes in tastes and preferences of customers
(h) the volume and costs of construction activity
(i) prices, rents, vacancy rates, and other indicators of market conditions.

These and related factors help to make estimates of future market changes. Factors related to income are of primary importance in estimating the demand for real estate; of almost equal importance are the terms and availability of financing.

Suggestions related to market analyses for housing, shopping centers, individual stores, office and industrial space, and also for redevelopment and renewal purposes are presented in this chapter.

QUESTIONS FOR STUDY

1. If demand in the real estate market rises, what will happen to prices and rents? Over the longer run what will happen to supply? Explain.
2. What relationship do you see between the volume of real estate activity and the level of local business conditions?
3. What reasons can you give to substantiate the argument that there is a national cycle in real estate market activity? Do you concur in this position? Why or why not?
4. Describe the processes of expansion and contraction in real estate markets.
5. How might greater stability be achieved in the real estate market?
6. What economic variables might influence a downturn in real estate activity on the national level?

7. List and explain the major factors to be considered in making a real estate market analysis.

8. Indicate the types of data in each of the following categories that you could profitably employ in making a market analysis: (a) Population. (b) Building costs. (c) Financing. (d) Incomes. (e) Employment. (f) Vacancies.

9. What is the relationship of economic base analysis to a real estate market analysis?

10. Prepare an outline for estimating population in the current year for the city in which your reference property is located.

11. Which special factors would you consider in making a market analysis for a shopping center? For an individual store in a shopping center?

12. How would you go about analyzing the demand for office space in your city? For industrial locations?

13. Why is market analysis important in real estate decision-making?

14. *Study Project 21.* Do you agree with the appraisal steps followed? With the estimate of value?

15. *Study Project 22.* (a) Explain the factors back of the weakening of prices for older buildings outlined in this article. (b) How do you interpret the evaluation of prewar buildings at "$100 billion dollars and probably much more"? (c) Explain how general price inflation might compensate for investment mistakes in the real estate field. (d) Would you agree with the assertion of some builders that "any overbuilding is temporary anyway"?

SUGGESTED READINGS

GRIGSBY, WILLIAM G. *Housing Markets and Public Policy.* Philadelphia: University of Pennsylvania Press, 1963. Chaps. ii, vii.

JACOBS, JANE. *The Death and Life of Great American Cities.* New York: Random House, 1961. Chaps. xi, xii.

MANHEIM, URIEL. *How To Do Housing Market Research:* Handbook for Local Home Builders Associations. Washington, D.C.: National Association of Home Builders of the United States, 1963.

Economic Indicators (published monthly by the Council of Economic Advisers). Washington, D.C.: Government Printing Office.

Survey of Buying Power (published annually in May by *Sales Management*).

Survey of Current Business (published monthly by the Department of Commerce). Washington, D.C.: Government Printing Office.

13

Location Analysis: Structure and Pattern of Land Uses

Location Factors in Real Estate Decisions

We have pointed out repeatedly that a real property may be thought of as a fixed but highly changeable point on a dynamic economic (and social and political) framework. This framework is made up of the property's immediate environment, its local economy and community, and the broader national and international environment.

The real estate decision-maker has a vital interest in a property's immediate surroundings and in its relationship to other parts of the local area and region, as well as in its broader environment. We usually refer to these various sets of relationships and particularly to those involving a property's immediate surroundings and its position relative to the local area and region as *location* factors. To a considerable degree, a property's income-producing potential is determined by location factors, conditioned, of course, by market changes and by trends in the local, regional, and national economy.

An urban property may be thought of as a share in the local economy or city and also as a share in a specific area or sector of the city. The economic strength of a city or local economy provides basic support for the values of all of the properties located there. If the local economy expands, however, all properties will not be affected in the same manner or to the same degree; some will benefit greatly, some slightly, and some may be affected adversely.

Similarly, a piece of real estate may be thought of as a share in the immediate neighborhood or district of which it forms a part. A variety of factors are at work constantly to bring about favorable or unfavorable changes in neighborhoods and districts and in major sectors of urban areas.

In this chapter, we consider location factors related to the general structure and patterns of land uses in the major sectors of cities; in the next chapter, we consider neighborhoods and districts.

Trends Affecting Structure of Land Uses

Although we have tried to emphasize the importance of location factors in dynamic rather than static terms, it may be helpful to consider briefly some of the forces that are likely to hold particular significance for the real estate decision-maker in the years ahead. As Lowdon Wingo pointed out:

Begin with the perspective that the city evolves to expedite the interactions of social and economic activities. The content of these activities is changing, and simultaneously a revolution is taking place in how these activities interact with each other. New organizational factors supplant earlier ones in the evolution of our cities, overcoming inertia and the resistance of entrenched (if vestigial) institutions—sunk capital in the physical plant of the city, legal institutions, behavior patterns. New forces are presenting us with new problems. . . .[1]

Wingo goes on to emphasize the anticipated rise in per capita incomes and the related implications for changes in expenditure patterns and in turn for future employment opportunities. Science and technology are bringing major changes in communication patterns. New machines, techniques, and processes are bringing new organizational relationships and hastening the obsolescence of existing plant and equipment which in turn hastens location decisions. Changes and potential changes in transportation patterns as well as in methods for bearing the costs of transportation are likely to have major effects. Less concentration of activity is required due to the nature of the transportation system, the influence of the automobile and improved roads, and related developments. More land can be used efficiently.

These factors and others related to them, all will have a bearing on the structure and pattern of future land uses. That urban growth will continue is almost beyond question although some slowing down in the rate

---

[1] Lowdon Wingo, Jr., "Urban Space in a Policy Perspective: An Introduction," in Wingo (ed.), *Cities and Space* (Baltimore: Johns Hopkins University Press, 1963), p. 11, by permission.

of growth may occur. It is interesting to note that the urban saturation point was almost reached in England by 1890 with 72 per cent of the population living in urban places of 2,000 or more. By 1960 the population in such places had increased further only to about 80 per cent of the total. In the United States 37 per cent lived in urban places of 2,000 or more in 1890, 86 per cent in 1960.[2]

The character of urban growth may change, and hence its effect on the values of different properties. Present trends suggest further expansion of urban areas with "urban sprawl" continuing as the settled areas spread out. More "interurbias" or "supercities" or new candidates for the designation of "megalopolis" may emerge as present urban areas grow together. Entirely new cities and towns are emerging such as Reston and Columbia City. There may be some tendency to reverse the outward trend as city centers regain some of their earlier appeal as a result of improved transportation and urban renewal programs as well as governmental changes which may spread some of the costs of the central city to outlying areas.

Competition Between Land Uses

Industrial and commercial locations have tended to spread more widely throughout urban areas in recent years. Residential land uses have become somewhat more fluid; apartment houses are now found mixed up with single-family houses; town houses or row houses are found in a variety of areas. Shopping centers are being scattered throughout urban areas; often a shopping center is a key factor in the success of a new subdivision. Increasingly, industrial developments, many of which are not incompatible with residential uses, are found at scattered locations throughout the urban area. Concepts of "inharmonious" land uses appear to be changing.

Downtown business locations compete with locations in outlying areas to an increasing degree.[3] Markets for land generally seem to be broadening as transportation facilities and the increasing use of the car and truck extend the areas over which various land uses can be located to advantage.

The role of the automobile undoubtedly will continue to be a major one in expanding urban land markets. The number of private passenger cars exceeded 70 million by the mid-1960's in comparison to slightly over 20 million in 1933; projections range up to more than 300 million by the end of the century.[4] Of course, a saturation point may be reached before

---

[2] Homer Hoyt, "The Growth of Cities from 1800 to 1960 and Forecasts to Year 2000," *Land Economics*, XXXIX, No. 2 (May, 1963).

[3] Arthur M. Weimer, "Investors and Downtown Real Estate" (Washington, D.C.: Urban Land Institute, Tech. Bulletin No. 39, 1960).

[4] Hans H. Landsberg, Leonard L. Fischman, and Joseph L. Fisher, *Resources in America's Future* (Baltimore: Johns Hopkins University Press, 1963), p. 131.

then or new technological advances may shift the demand from automobiles to something else. Jet aircraft will play an increasingly dominant role in determining land values in recreational areas. Locations that have jet airports and are at the crossroads of international travel routes like Oahu in Hawaii or Nassau in the Bahamas have developed extremely high land values while the land on other nearby islands has not advanced greatly.

Although zoning laws and deed restrictions, as well as other types of regulations, tend to limit competition and channel it into specific directions, there continues to be intense competition between land uses and within classes of land uses. To some degree, zoning laws and related forms of regulation have become another form of competition between land developers, investors, and users. Developers tend to seek those jurisdictions in a metropolitan area that have a minimum of zoning restrictions as to lot size, type of use, utility requirements, and tax levels.

In other words, competition may take social and political forms. Labor and political organizations sometimes provide the basis for competition between land uses and between neighborhoods. We should note also that all types of business competition cannot be explained by economic considerations alone.

The promotional activities of real estate developers and associations of business groups such as the merchants in a shopping center will continue to have a bearing on the competition between land uses. Intercity rivalries also will have an influence.

Related Land Use Factors

Governmental and political factors will exert growing influences on the future pattern of land uses. Their general character may change; for example, there may be a resurgence of interest in local governmental and political factors relative to broad national interests. But more pedestrian considerations will continue to be important. The effect of a heavier tax burden in one neighborhood than in a competing one will continue to merit the attention of the real estate decision-maker as will such factors as fire and police protection, control of traffic, location of traffic arteries, zoning laws, and the cost of local governmental services relative to their quality.

Social and cultural factors will surely play an important part in determining the future pattern of land uses, as we have already suggested. We have had a strong trend toward home ownership in recent years; this may be modified, of course, but we are fairly certain that home ownership will continue to be highly acceptable in most areas and that neighborhoods of home owners may represent relatively stable areas. Attitudes toward private property, home ownership, appropriate locations for various land uses, and many others are important in this connection. Prestige factors such as what is considered a "good address" change over time and their importance can easily be overlooked.

Social unrest and pressures are likely to expand. Primarily, these are related to the increased efforts of Negroes and Negro groups to gain wider access to housing in many types of neighborhoods; various other racial and, to some degree, religious groups also are involved. Increased leisure, broader social and cultural interests, longer life for many, and increased interest in political activities, notably on the local level, are likely to have effects on the location of various land uses.

Physical factors such as rivers, swamps, land contour, condition of soil and subsoil, and the like will continue to have a bearing on the location of land uses and the shifts that occur. Depreciation resulting from the physical deterioration of structures or from changes in use or fashion will have an influence, in part physical, in part social and economic. The existing transportation system has both physical and economic implications in regard to present and future land uses. Original locations may have been the result of political considerations as well as economic forces. Future changes or extensions will be the product of such factors but will be influenced greatly by the existing transportation system.

The tastes and preferences of people relative to real estate may undergo significant changes. The two-house family may become as popular as the two-car family in the not too distant future. Week-end cottages combined with "near-in" apartments appear to be competing effectively with some types of suburban residences. There may be some renewed interest in "near-in" locations in order to reduce commuting time. Many other changes may emerge as well.

Concepts of urban planning and renewal may undergo some changes. The challenging of previously accepted concepts of desirable neighborhood structure and renewal programs by such writers as Jane Jacobs may lead to significant changes. She says, for example, that she is trying to:

. . . introduce new principles of city planning and rebuilding, different and even opposite from those now taught in everything from schools of architecture and planning to the Sunday supplements and women's magazines. My attack is not based on quibbles about rebuilding methods or hairsplitting about fashions in design. It is an attack, rather, on the principles and aims that have shaped modern, orthodox city planning and rebuilding.[5]

All this suggests that the future structure and pattern of land uses will be determined by a wide variety of factors, as has been the case in the past. To some extent, past trends will be helpful, but it will be important to anticipate, if possible, the major forces that will affect land uses and interrelationships between them in the future.

[5] By permission from *The Death and Life of Great American Cities,* by Jane Jacobs, p. 3. Copyright, 1961, Random House, New York.

Stages of City Growth

As cities expand they tend to pass through certain stages of development. For example, a city in the initial stage of development is like a small country town.[6] Here there is little competition among various land uses. In general, the major business center is at the point of origin of the town, which may be a crossroads or a railroad intersection, the point at which a river meets the sea, or some similar focal point which caused original settlement there. A few light industries may grow up; if so, they are usually adjacent to the downtown business center. The homes of the merchants, professional groups, and those receiving higher incomes will be located near the stores and the downtown business area, while the homes of the workingmen will be located near the factories. Hence the town will represent a very simple sort of organization.

However, when expansion continues beyond this stage, the possible uses which may be made of the land increase in number and intensity. The area of the city will be expanded as a result of population growth, and the intensity of land use at various points will be increased. Various types of uses to which the land was originally put will give way to "higher" uses, or those which will yield a greater return per dollar of investment. For example, establishments which require relatively large areas in relation to business volume will tend to be crowded out of the central parts of a city because of the competition of other types of enterprises with greater rent-paying ability. Because the more powerful activities are able to force out other land uses, this competition for sites causes a constant movement within the city.

Such competition is most intense when the city is expanding. If a city is declining in economic importance, new demands for space are limited; and it is only the most favored locations which are able to earn substantial incomes. It is during periods of rapid growth that the most noticeable changes occur in the uses to which various parcels of real estate are put.

Methods of Urban Expansion

A city may expand (1) by growing vertically through the replacement of lower structures with higher ones, (2) by filling in open spaces between settled areas, or (3) by extending the existing settled area.

---

[6] Professor N. S. B. Gras has pointed out that the form of the village may either be "nucleated," that is, of a very compact form, which is sometimes called a "heap village," or it may be "nonnucleated," that is, spread out, the houses usually being some distance apart and near the field surrounding the village. One example of this is the so-called "long-street village," which is fairly common in Europe, also in Quebec, Nova Scotia, and Maine. See Gras, *An Introduction to Economic History* (New York: Harper & Row, Publishers, 1922), pp. 53–56.

When the settled area is expanded, growth may take several forms, the most important being (1) *concentric circle* or *ring growth* around the central nucleus; (2) *axial growth,* with prongs or fingerlike extensions moving out along main transportation routes; and (3) *suburban growth,* with the establishment of islands of settlements in advance of the main city area. These types of expansion are characteristic of most larger cities. Baltimore was for a long time a good example of ring growth, while New York, Chicago, and Detroit illustrate axial and suburban development.

A city located in the center of a level plain might be expected to grow outward in rings from the main point of origin. However, most of our cities were located at points where their growth was influenced by hills, rivers, and other topographical features. New York, located first at the southern tip of Manhattan Island, could expand only northward until ferries, bridges, and tunnels made growth in other directions possible. Chicago's growth to the east was stopped by Lake Michigan. In some cases the original topography of a site was changed by grading or filling when it became profitable to undertake such projects. For example, Boston was located on a rather narrow peninsula, but the filling-in of the Back Bay and similar areas provided space for expansion. The lake front in Chicago has been extended nearly a mile eastward from the Loop area. The original area of Miami Beach, Florida, was nearly tripled by pumping sand out of Biscayne Bay. In addition, topographical factors often govern the location of transportation lines, and these in turn influence the direction of city growth by accelerating axial and suburban developments.

When both ring growth and axial expansion occur, a star-shaped city structure results. As Hurd pointed out many years ago:

> In their methods of growth cities conform always to biological laws, all growth being either *central* or *axial.* In some cities central growth occurs first and in others axial growth, but all cities illustrate both forms of growth and in all cases central growth includes some axial growth and axial growth some central growth. Central growth consists of the clustering of utilities around any point of attraction and is based on proximity, while axial growth is the result of transportation facilities and is based on accessibility.[7]

Types of Land Use Patterns

Although we can distinguish central and axial growth in our cities today, a much greater variety and diversity of land uses and changes in land uses has emerged than appeared probable even at the end of World War II. Few of the earlier theories or explanations of city structure and land use patterns are adequate for current and future purposes although

[7] Richard M. Hurd, *Principles of City Land Values* (New York: The Record & Guide, 1924), pp. 58–59.

they give us some keys to understanding the processes that have gone on. It has been pointed out, for example:

In the era of the Greek cities in the fifth century B.C. a city was considered an artistic creation which should maintain its static form without change. To take care of population growth, the Greeks sent out colonies, like swarms of bees, to found new cities on the ideal model. Plato said that the ideal city should not contain over 5,000 inhabitants, although he, himself was the product of an Athens with 250,000 population. In the Middle Ages most continental European cities were surrounded by walls and many, like Milan, Italy, preserved an unaltered form for hundreds of years.[8]

The modern city tended to spread over wider areas as transportation made such dispersion possible. In the 1920's Burgess set forth his concentric circle theory in an effort to explain city form and structure. It is an interesting concept, though not too helpful today. Burgess said:

The typical process of the expansion of a city can best be illustrated, perhaps, by a series of concentric circles, which may be numbered to designate both the successive zones of urban expansion and the types of areas differentiated in the process of expansion.

He believed that each zone tended to invade the next one by a process called "succession." At the heart of his model was the "loop" with the financial and office district at the center and the central retail district surrounding and penetrating it. Beyond this, as he pointed out:

Encircling the downtown area there is normally an area in transition, which is being invaded by business and light manufacture. A third area is inhabited by workers in industries who have escaped from the area of deterioration but who desire to live within easy access of their work. Beyond this zone is the "residential area" of high-class apartment buildings or of exclusive "restricted" districts of single-family dwellings. Still farther out, beyond the city limits, is the commuter's zone—suburban areas, or satellite cities—within a thirty- to sixty-minute ride of the central business district.[9]

Burgess' explanation was made obsolete primarily by the automobile; but other factors were at work as well, including rising incomes, advancing technology especially in transportation and communication, the requirements for large amounts of space for single-story factory buildings, tax factors, and others. Noneconomic forces also played a part in this process.

The automobile made possible a wide dispersal of people over a metropolitan area, the wide separation of workers from places of employment, the rise of planned shopping districts with thousands being established

[8] Homer Hoyt, "Recent Distortions of the Classical Models of Urban Structure," *Land Economics* (May, 1964).

[9] Reprinted from *The City* by R. E. Park, E. W. Burgess, and R. D. McKenzie, by permission, University of Chicago Press, pp. 50–53. Copyright, 1925, by the University of Chicago.

following the end of World War II, the outward movement of manufacturing, as such land uses became more compatible with residential land uses, improved roads and freeways, and the general broadening of the urban land market.

The Sector Theory—Residential Neighborhoods

Another general theory of urban structure was developed by Homer Hoyt and set forth in 1939. This concept continues to have applicability at the present time although greater flexibility is required in making use of it. See accompanying maps showing high- and low-income areas in American cities.

If an entire city is thought of as a circle, and if the different residential areas are thought of as wedge-shaped sectors pointing to the center, the high-rent or high-price areas of the city will tend over a period of years to move outward to the periphery in the path described by one or more of the sectors. Similarly, if a certain sector develops originally as a low-rent or low-price area, the balance of that sector is likely to be occupied by low-rent or low-price residences as expansion proceeds outward. The same tendency is typical of intermediate rent or price sectors.[10]

The sector theory is based on the following general tendencies:

1. The various groups in the social order tend to be segregated into rather definite areas according to their incomes and social positions. While there are exceptions to this rule, it appears to have fairly general validity.

2. The highest-income groups live in the houses which command highest prices and rents, while the lower-income groups live in houses which are offered for the lower prices and rents. Generally the low-rent areas are located near the business and industrial center of the city and then tend to expand outward on one side or sector of the city, occupying the land which is not preempted by higher-rent residential areas or by business and industrial districts.

3. The principal growth of American cities has taken place by new building at the periphery rather than by the rebuilding of older areas. This means that some of our cities are beginning to resemble a hollow shell, with the major demands for land uses by-passing many of the "near-in" areas. In other cases these "near-in" areas become slums with little possibility of being rehabilitated through ordinary market processes. Heavy subsidies are usually required for renewal to occur.

---

[10] This theory was worked out by Homer Hoyt and first presented in a series of articles in the Federal Housing Administration's *Insured Mortgage Portfolio* (Washington, D.C.: Government Printing Office), Vol. I, Nos. 6–10. See also, his *The Structure and Growth of Residential Neighborhoods in American Cities*, (Washington, D.C.: Federal Housing Administration, 1939).

A detailed study of the movements of residential neighborhoods in American cities indicates that the high-grade neighborhoods of a city (measured by price or rent) tend to follow a definite path in one or more sectors of a city. In their expansion, high-grade residential areas tend to move outward along established lines of travel or toward other settled areas. Typically, such growth is toward high ground free from risk of floods. It may spread out into areas distinguished for their natural beauty; for example, along lake, bay, river, or ocean fronts. Growth proceeds toward open country and away from barriers to expansion. Real estate promoters and developers may at times bend the direction of growth. Outlying shopping centers and industrial uses may preempt some land that might otherwise develop into high-grade residences. In some cases, also, areas of blight may appear in what might be expected to develop as a high-grade area.

Changes will occur with the introduction of new traffic arteries and major road systems. It should be noted that the building of expressways and belt highways around cities has opened up large areas for residential development. In some cases new communities are developed on land areas that are large enough to establish their own character. For example, a high-grade neighborhood may be developed around a golf course. Developments of this type may be found at almost any point as the settled area expands, but more frequently are located beyond the original high-income sector.

The sector theory was a generalization based on the best data available in 1939. In 1959 the U.S. Census provided statistics on the number of families in each income group by $1,000 intervals up to $10,000, from $10,000–$14,999, from $15,000 to $24,999, and $25,000 and over. On the basis of these statistics Homer Hoyt in 1965 made a new study showing the location of households with incomes of $25,000 a year and over in the largest metropolitan areas in the United States.[11] Of 575,100 families with incomes in 1959 of $25,000 and over, 490,104 lived in urban areas and 66,236 in rural nonfarm areas. Of the total, 556,340 or 96.7 per cent lived in urban areas or on the fringe of urban areas. Of this total 314,000 lived in standard metropolitan areas with a population of 250,000 or over in 1960. In the metropolitan areas analyzed by Hoyt (as shown in Table 13–1), approximately half lived in concentrated areas where 10 per cent or more of the families had incomes of $25,000 a year or more in 1959, and usually over half had incomes of $10,000 a year or more. The other half with incomes of $25,000 a year or over were scattered throughout the metropolitan area.

As Figure 13–1 illustrates, there were very pronounced sectors of high-

[11] Hoyt, "Where the Rich People and the Poor People Live," Technical Bulletin No. 55 (Washington, D.C.: Urban Land Institute, 1966).

Table 13—1. Location of Families with Incomes of $25,000 or Over, 1959
(summarized)

	Number of Families Reporting Income	Number of Families with Income of $25,000 or Over	Per Cent of U.S. Total
United States total	45,128,393	575,100	100.00
Urban	31,940,104	490,104	85.22
Rural nonfarm	9,855,866	66,236	11.52
Rural farm	3,332,485	18,760	3.26
Standard metropolitan areas with population 250,000 or over	24,575,693	418,000	72.70
Estimated number of families in standard metropolitan areas of 250,000 or over living in areas in which 10% or more of the families have incomes of $25,000 or over	1,540,000	222,000	38.60
Estimated number of families in all standard metropolitan areas of 50,000–249,999 living in areas in which 7% or more of families have incomes of $25,000 or over	370,000	30,000	5.22
Total living in census tracts in which 10% or more of familes have incomes of $10,000 or over	1,910,000	252,000	43.82
Number living in rural areas or in city areas in which an average of 2% or less have incomes of $25,000 a year or over	43,218,393	323,100	56.18

SOURCE: Homer Hoyt, "Where the Rich People and the Poor People Live," Technical Bulletin No. 55 (Washington, D.C.: Urban Land Institute, 1966), p. 14.

income concentration in Washington, D.C., Houston, Kansas City, Indianapolis, Dallas, Baltimore, Chicago, Milwaukee, Omaha, San Antonio, Tulsa, St. Louis, Atlanta, and other cities. The pattern was more variegated in New York City which had clusters of high-income concentrations to the north in Manhattan, Westchester County, and Nassau County and lesser concentration in Bergen County and in the Oranges of New Jersey. Philadelphia and Boston while showing trends to the west and southwest respectively did not show such a distinct cleavage as some other cities. The data are now available for every student to make his own survey of income distribution within his own metropolitan area and to delineate the highest-level- and middle-income groups in his own area. Changes are always taking place in the growing cities and the student may note the value of new homes built since 1960 and check to see whether the old high-income areas are being extended in the same directions or new high-income areas are being created. With the development of new

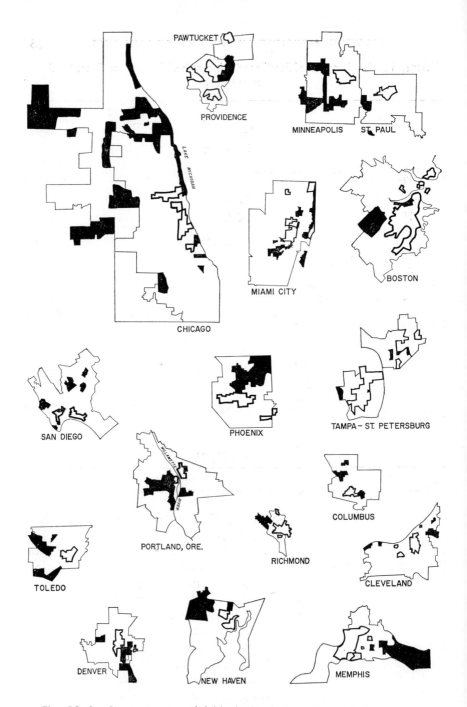

Fig. 13–1. Census tracts: solid black shows those in which 10 per cent or more of families had incomes of $25,000 or over and 50 per cent, $10,000 or over, in 1959; areas within black borders show lower-income areas—median family income under $5,000 in 1959.

296

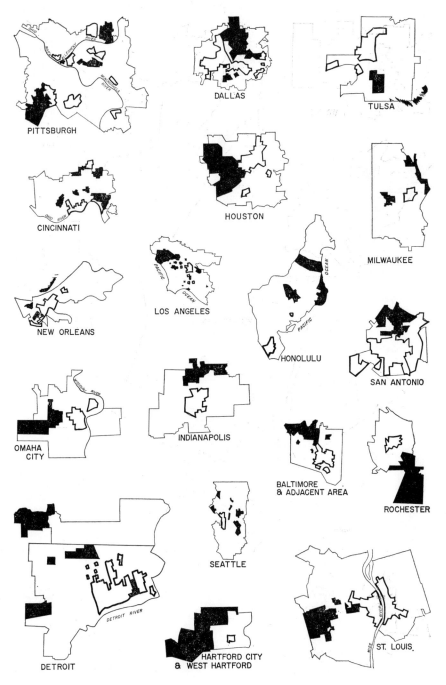

Fig. 13–1. Continued.

297

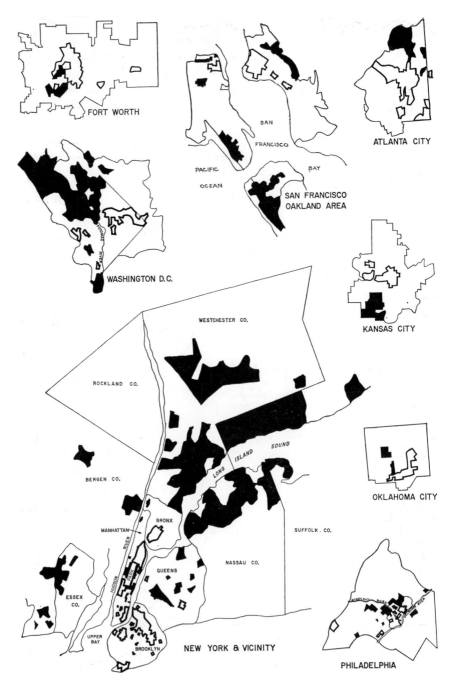

Fig. 13–1. *Continued.*

towns and the suburbs, there will undoubtedly be a change in old patterns as many high-income families will seek homes on golf courses or parks in the new communities. There probably is less concentration of high-income families in clusters now than formerly due to the egalitarian principles becoming more widespread, the avoidance of conspicuous display of wealth, and the leveling effect of steeply progressive income taxes.

The multiple nuclei concept was developed by Harris and Ullman as a modification of the sector theory. They stressed the clustering of land uses, especially business uses, and the impact of transportation, topography, and related factors. Family preferences and social customs were considered as major factors in the location of residential land uses.[12]

The great diversity of American cities makes it difficult to set forth general explanations of land use patterns. If the sector theory is viewed as a statement of general tendency rather than applied rigidly, it is often helpful in anticipating land use changes. We should remember that all shifts in the patterns of land uses result from the decisions of people either as individuals or as officials of business firms or governmental or institutional agencies. What motivates them at a given time may be hard to anticipate. They may react in one manner in one region and in another way elsewhere. Hence, the pattern of every urban region tends to have its own unique characteristics and is deserving of special study.

Land Use Patterns and Business Districts

The central business district of a city can expand in two ways: vertically and laterally. If the expansion is vertical, smaller buildings are replaced by taller ones. Such expansion generally takes place if the central business district remains in one place for a long time and is confined by some barrier and if the city is growing rapidly. The invention of the steel-frame skyscraper and the electric elevator facilitated vertical as against lateral expansion in many cities. However, lateral expansion of the central district has been of great importance, modified somewhat by the advent of the skyscraper and also by the growth of outlying business centers.

On the other hand, major shifts in the location of the central district sometimes occur. In such cases new buildings may be constructed at the edge of the main business district or at other points rather than on the sites of older buildings. In any case the expansion of the central business area forces out less intensive uses.

Although the central business districts in most cities have now declined in their rate of expansion, they continue to change and to move. The main

[12] Chauncey D. Harris and Edward L. Ullman, "The Nature of Cities," *Annals* of the American Academy of Political and Social Science (November, 1945) and Frederick E. Case, *Real Estate* (Englewood Cliffs, N.J.: Allyn & Bacon, Inc., 1962), pp. 53–54.

retail shopping center generally tends to move toward the best residential areas. For example, the stores in New York City moved up Fifth Avenue, following high-grade residential movement. The growth of Chicago, Washington, D.C., and Houston likewise illustrates movements of this type. In a similar manner the development of Miami Beach and the northeast section of Miami has attracted the central business section of the city.

Outlying business centers have developed at or near intersections between radial and crosstown transportation lines and the intersections of main automobile highways. Independent shopping centers tend to grow up on the periphery of large cities because it is difficult to reach the central downtown shopping area where traffic is congested. The extent to which such areas develop depends on the number of customers in the area and their current or potential purchasing power.

Each type of store has its own trade area and its own optimum size. A central department store with 100,000 square feet or more will have a trade area extending to that of another department store of similar or greater size. For example, the trade area of the Blass department store in Little Rock covers 41 Arkansas counties and is bounded by the trade area of Memphis on the east, Springfield, Missouri, on the north, Fort Smith on the west, and Texarkana on the south. The trade area of the Dayton department store in Minneapolis extends as far as Montana. On the other hand, the trade area of a variety store (such as Woolworth or Kresge) which has 10,000 to 20,000 square feet of floor area and which requires 10,000 to 15,000 families for its support extends only to the boundaries of the trade area of the nearest variety store with 10,000 or more square feet of floor area, which may be only two or three miles away.

Clothing stores in the popular-price lines usually tend to concentrate in central business districts or major outlying shopping districts, because women prefer to patronize a center which has a number of stores offering a wide variety of styles so that they can compare apparel as to quality and price. Fashionable women's stores such as Lord and Taylor, on the other hand, sometimes seek solitary locations in the midst of high-income neighborhoods such as in Westchester County, New York; Short Hills, New Jersey; or West Hartford, Connecticut. When several of these higher-price stores locate near one another the sales of all of them tend to increase.

Supermarkets, with floor areas as large as 20,000 square feet or even more, can be supported by neighborhoods with 5,000 families and can operate successfully in isolated locations with ample parking, because families buy food more frequently than clothing and tend to patronize the nearest supermarket that offers food comparable in price and quality to other supermarkets.

The development of large regional shopping centers has been one of the significant developments in urban land uses in the postwar years. The transportation network, the purchasing power represented in the present and potential market area, the types of goods and services offered at the center, and the parking spaces provided all have an important bearing on successful development.

The growth of these new regional shopping centers with ample parking has tended to curtail the expansion of existing central business districts. Many of these districts are seeking to hold their customers by building central parking garages, as in the case of the Lazarus store in Columbus, Ohio, and Foley's in Houston. Extensive public parking garages have been built in Chicago, Baltimore, San Francisco, and other cities for the purpose of aiding central retail districts.

The large department stores in central cities expanded both vertically and laterally on the same site by covering an entire block with a large building, such as Macy's in New York, Marshall Field & Company in Chicago, the J. L. Hudson Company in Detroit, and the Dayton store in Minneapolis. These large stores remained rooted at the same spot for long periods of time because of the convergence of mass transportation routes at their location. In New York there has been a movement of the higher-price women's apparel stores from 34th to 40th Streets on Fifth Avenue to the Rockefeller Center area near 50th Street and Fifth Avenue.

Land Use Patterns and Industrial Districts

In earlier years heavy manufacturing industries tended to be located in areas which were near the central retail district. In a few cases the industrial area completely encircled the business center of the city. Industrial locations were determined by transportation facilities such as wharves, docks, or railroad sidings, and by nearness to the labor supply. Hence, the early industries were obliged to locate near the centers of cities because the best transportation facilities were available at those points.

The present pattern of industrial land uses is frequently quite different from the earlier pattern. Henvy industries now tend to follow railroad lines, river valleys, or lake or ocean fronts in long bands of growth rather than to remain near the central business district. Frequently, industrial suburbs develop near the periphery of the city. In some cases a cluster of industries forms a specialized industrial section, such as Bush Terminal in Brooklyn, the Clearing District in Chicago, and the Trinity Industrial District of Dallas.

These changes have come about as a result of auto-truck transportation, which makes it possible for factories to locate at points which are some distance removed from central freight depots. Development of belt-line railroads and similar improvements in the transportation facilities also have played a part in these changes.

Industries are usually not able to occupy land which is of extremely high value. Areas which are located near the periphery of cities represent cheaper land, and the tax burden is usually lower. Hence, it is possible to use more land for storage space. Also, one-story buildings which permit continuity of factory operations can be used. Such structures are more economical than multi-story buildings for many types of manufacturing processes. They permit continuity of manufacturing operations, there is no use of space for elevators or ramps, heavy machinery can be installed in any part of the plant, railroad freight cars and trucks can enter the plant directly, overhead cranes can be installed, and expansion can be arranged more easily. Heavy industries may also locate in suburban areas now that workers' homes are more accessible and public transportation is no longer as important as in the past because of the widespread use of the automobile.

Unique *topographical features, transportation facilities,* and *lower-priced land* now appear to be the important factors in determining industrial locations within an urban area.

Analysis of Land Use Patterns

In order to make estimates regarding future probable changes in the land uses of a city, it is necessary to study past developments with some care. Changes in the internal structure of a city occur very slowly. Hence we cannot forecast future probable changes unless we can determine the major trends that have been in operation for a considerable period of time.

One method for collecting the necessary information is by the use of time interval maps. A photograph or a map of a city at a given moment of time fails to show the dynamic character of the city's growth. Several photographs taken at different time intervals or several maps for different periods reveal the processes of change. Thus, if the location of a certain type of area has changed from one period to another, it is possible to determine the direction and speed with which such movements have occurred by using devices of this kind.

Generally speaking, a period covering at least the time since the depression of the early 1930's should be studied. Another detailed description should be worked out for the end of World War II. These periods are suggested because they represent well-marked stages of city development. These situations should then be compared with current conditions.

If it is possible to undertake careful and intensive research, specific information can be secured from such sources as the Sanborn insurance maps, which show locations of individual structures in many cities for periods as far back as the 1880's. Also, valuable assistance can be secured from the United States quadrangular survey maps, which provide similar information. Older maps of cities can frequently be found that provide valuable data. City histories and old newspaper files often include accounts of the development of particular areas.

It is sometimes possible to compare recent aerial photographs of entire regions with those taken at a former period. Thus in recent surveys of the growth of the Washington metropolitan area, a comparison was made between aerial photographs taken in 1965 with those taken in 1958 and 1937. The marked growth in the urban settled area which had taken place in that period and the direction of growth were clearly indicated.

In the absence of such specific material, or if pressure of time necessitates the use of less refined methods, sufficient information can usually be secured by consulting older people who have a reputation for accuracy and good judgment and who are known to be well informed regarding the growth of the city. At least three different persons should be consulted. If there seems to be considerable disagreement among them, additional people should be questioned.

Regardless of the plan of attack adopted, a map (which may be referred to as a time interval map) for each period should be prepared which will indicate the areas occupied by (1) factories and heavy industries, (2) low-rent residential areas, (3) the chief central and outlying shopping or commerical areas, and (4) the more fashionable residental neighborhoods. From these maps a reasonably accurate picture can be secured of the major movements affecting each of these important types of land uses.[13]

Such general maps should then be compared with maps showing the development of the internal transportation system of the city. Maps showing the transportation system at various periods of time can usually be secured from city offices or from the offices of those who are in charge of the transportation system. Similarly, comparisons should be made with existing zoning maps which indicate the restrictions applying to various areas of the city.

When the movements indicated by the maps have been studied and analyzed, the forces of city expansion may be noted and the probable future structure of the city may be estimated. It is generally possible to assume that existing uses will expand outward in the same sector and that the trend of past development will be continued into the future, unless im-

[13] See Robert O. Harvey, "Land Uses in Bloomington, Indiana, 1818–1950," *Indiana Business Studies, No. 33* (Indiana University, August, 1951). See also Albert E. Dickens, "The Growth and Structure of Real Property Uses in Indianapolis," *Indiana Business Studies No. 17* (Indiana University, May, 1939).

portant and powerful forces are in existence or are likely to develop which will tend to cause a reversal of such trends.

Future Metropolitan Patterns

Recently, Kevin Lynch has suggested types of patterns for the metropolis of the future. One of these assumes that there may be a much greater spreading out of urban activities—what he refers to as a "dispersed sheet." He says:

The old center and most subcenters could be dissolved, allowing city-wide activities to disperse throughout the region, with a fine grain. Factories, offices, museums, universities, hospitals would appear everywhere in the suburban landscape. The low density and the dispersion of activities would depend on and allow circulation in individual vehicles, as well as a substantial use of distant symbolic communication such as telephone, television, mail, coded messages.[14]

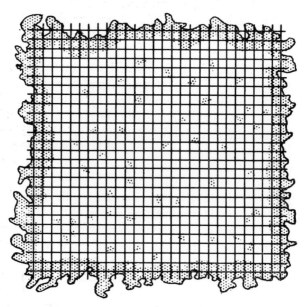

Fig. 13–2. The dispersed sheet. (Source: *Metropolis: Values in Conflict,* p. 98.)

This is essentially the Los Angeles pattern of the city and was apparently preferred by the late Frank Lloyd Wright. This pattern has high flexibility, independence, personal comfort, and the like, but its costs

[14] Kevin Lynch, "The Pattern of the Metropolis," in C. E. Elias, Jr., James Gillies, and Svend Riemer (eds.), *Metropolis: Values in Conflict* (Belmont, California: Wadsworth Publishing Co., Inc., 1964), p. 97.

would be high and distance would remain a major problem. Also, there would be little local identity and community participation might be limited. (See Fig. 13–2.)

A second type is outlined by Lynch as a "galaxy of settlements" (Fig. 13–3). Here, growth would not be dispersed evenly over a wide area as in the case of the "dispersed sheet," but would be bunched in relatively small units, each with high density at the center and with low density or no density between the units. It provides for many of the advantages of wider dispersion and solves some of the disadvantages.

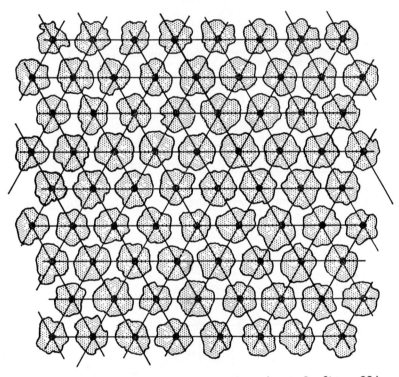

Fig. 13–3. The galaxy. (Source: *Metropolis: Values in Conflict*, p. 99.)

By contrast the "core city" would pack all urban activity in a small space with high density. As described by Lynch:

Parts of the city might become "solid" with a continuous occupation of space in three dimensions and a cubical grid of transportation lines. (The full application of this plan could cram a metropolis within a surprisingly small compass: twenty million people, with generous spacing, could be accommodated within a cube less than three miles on a side.) Most probably there would be a fine grain of specialized activities, all at high intensity, so that apartments would occur over factories, or there might also be stores on upper levels. The system of flow would necessarily be highly specialized, sorting each kind of traffic into its own channel. Such a city would depend almost entirely on public transport, rather than individual vehicles, or on devices that facilitated pedestrian movement, such as moving sidewalks or flying belts.[15]

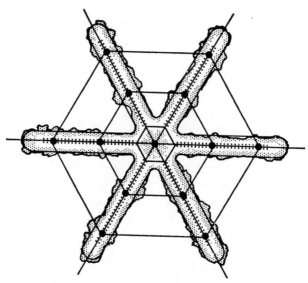

Fig. 13–4. The star. (Source: *Metropolis: Values in Conflict*, p. 103.)

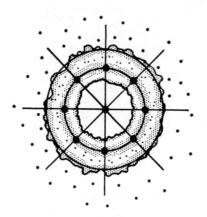

Fig. 13–5. The ring. (Source: *Metropolis: Values in Conflict*, p. 105.)

The plan would allow for combination with dispersion over the countryside, for example, week-end houses, long week ends with work concentrated in the "core" in three or four days per week. This type of

[15] *Ibid.*, p. 103 (by permission).

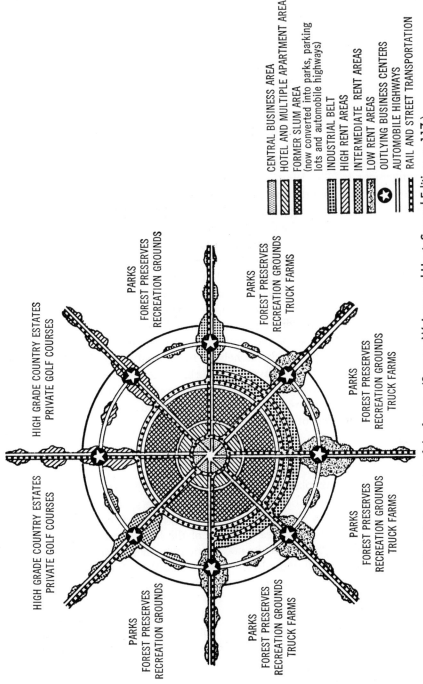

CENTRAL BUSINESS AREA

HOTEL AND MULTIPLE APARTMENT AREA

FORMER SLUM AREA
(now converted into parks, parking
lots and automobile highways)

INDUSTRIAL BELT

HIGH RENT AREAS

INTERMEDIATE RENT AREAS

LOW RENT AREAS

OUTLYING BUSINESS CENTERS

AUTOMOBILE HIGHWAYS

RAIL AND STREET TRANSPORTATION

HIGH GRADE COUNTRY ESTATES
PRIVATE GOLF COURSES

HIGH GRADE COUNTRY ESTATES
PRIVATE GOLF COURSES

PARKS
FOREST PRESERVES
RECREATION GROUNDS

PARKS
FOREST PRESERVES
RECREATION GROUNDS

PARKS
FOREST PRESERVES
RECREATION GROUNDS
TRUCK FARMS

PARKS
FOREST PRESERVES
RECREATION GROUNDS
TRUCK FARMS

PARKS
FOREST PRESERVES
RECREATION GROUNDS
TRUCK FARMS

PARKS
FOREST PRESERVES
RECREATION GROUNDS
TRUCK FARMS

PARKS
FOREST PRESERVES
RECREATION GROUNDS
TRUCK FARMS

Fig. 13–6.   A city of the future.   (Source: Weimer and Hoyt, Second Edition, p. 117.)

arrangement would contrast sharply with the "dispersed sheet" outlined above.

A fourth arrangement is designated as "The Urban Star" (Fig. 13–4). This would retain the dominant core of the city but would channel growth into axes outward from the center with open spaces between such settled areas. The radii might extend to other metropolitan centers; the dominant core would remain with secondary centers. Copenhagen follows this type of growth; it is the type that was emerging before the automobile upset older patterns of growth and it fits the patterns outlined earlier by Hurd and referred to above.

Combinations of the above may be made as well. One interesting arrangement is "The Ring," which would have a "doughnut" type of arrangement with low density in the center to make for easy access to the various parts of the ring or rings which would have high densities. This pattern could be combined with week-end houses and similar arrangements in the surrounding countryside (Fig. 13–5).

It is interesting to consider these types of arrangements as models. Some types of cities will fit one model and some others. Various combinations also exist. In the early editions of this book we presented our concept of the "City of the Future" and we reproduce it here again because it combines some of the arrangements outlined above. (See Fig. 13–6.)

General explanations of the structure and pattern of urban land uses, however, do not appear to be as helpful to the real estate decision-maker as was once the case. The diversity of urban life and the pattern of land uses seems to be increasing. Each situation requires careful analysis by the real estate decision-maker. He may be aided, however, by general concepts and models of the type outlined above.

SUMMARY

Location factors play an important part in real estate decisions; of these, the structure and pattern of land uses have special significance. A real property may be thought of as a share in the local economy and also as a share in a particular area or sector of the local community. When a city expands, all properties do not participate in the same degree; the reverse is also true. Factors likely to influence these interrelationships in future years include the anticipated rise in per capita incomes and resulting changes in expenditure patterns; the impact of science and technology on transportation, communication, and the obsolescence of plant and equipment; governmental changes, notably in allocation of costs and benefits; further expansion of the urban area; changing competitive patterns between land uses; social unrest and pressures; and the tastes and preferences of people.

Cities may expand by growing vertically, by filling in open spaces between settled areas, or by extending the settled area. Such expansion may take ring, axial, or suburban forms; and a variety of explanations has developed, including the concentric circle concept, the sector theory, and others.

Land use patterns may be analyzed by comparing changes over a period of thirty or forty years or more. Special maps may be prepared for this purpose.

Future metropolitan patterns may include the dispersed sheet, galaxy of settlements, core city, urban star, ring, or others. Diversity of urban life and land uses appears to be increasing and this makes it difficult to generalize.

QUESTIONS FOR STUDY

1. Why is location such an important factor in real estate decisions? In the determination of property income?
2. Explain this statement: "An urban property may be thought of as a share in the local economy or city and also as a share in a specific area or sector of the city."
3. List the urban trends that may affect the future structure of land uses. Which of these now has a major influence in your city?
4. Explain the changing character of the competition between land uses in recent years.
5. Which social and cultural trends may be expected to affect the pattern of land uses in the future? Which governmental and political factors? Which of these do you consider most important and why?
6. Explain the concentric circle theory of city structure set forth by Burgess.
7. Outline the principal features of Hoyt's sector theory.
8. Explain the application of the sector theory of city growth to the development of the residential neighborhood in which you live.
9. What are the principal developments affecting land use patterns in business districts? In industrial districts?
10. How do you account for the great diversity of land use patterns between cities?
11. What are time interval maps? Explain their use.
12. List factors that might cause a major change in the pattern of growth in your city.
13. Outline the concept of a "dispersed sheet" as a pattern for the metropolis of the future. The "galaxy of settlements" concept. The "core city." The "urban star." The "ring" concept. Which of these do you believe will be the most likely to emerge? Explain.
14. *Study Project 23.* (a) What important forces had come to bear in the development of Longview Valley through 1955? From 1956 through 1960? From 1960 through 1965? (b) What forces will encourage the future growth of Longview Valley? What forces will discourage the future

growth of the Valley? Describe the pattern of land uses in Longview Valley that you would expect to emerge by 1975. (c) Describe the programs you would favor for Longview Valley if you were: a city planner for the city of Metropolis; a home owner in Longview Valley; the chief executive of an industrial firm located in Longview Valley; a real estate broker in Longview Valley; a builder in Longview Valley; the owner of agricultural land in Longview Valley.

SUGGESTED READINGS

HARVEY, ROBERT O., and CLARK, W. A. V. "The Nature and Economics of Urban Sprawl," *Land Economics* (February, 1965).

HOYT, HOMER. "The Growth of Cities from 1800 to 1960 and Forecasts to Year 2000," *Land Economics*, No. 2 (May, 1963).

———. "Recent Distortions of the Classical Models of Urban Structure," *Land Economics* (May, 1964).

ISARD, WALTER. *Methods of Regional Analysis: An Introduction to Regional Science.* Cambridge: The Massachusetts Institute of Technology Press, 1960. Chap. ix.

LYNCH, KEVIN. "The Pattern of the Metropolis," in C. E. Elias, Jr., James Gillies, and Svend Riemer (eds.), *Metropolis: Values in Conflict.* Belmont, California: Wadsworth Publishing Co., Inc., 1964.

WENDT, PAUL F. *Real Estate Appraisal.* New York: Holt, Rinehart & Winston, Inc., 1956. Chap. v.

WINGO, LOWDON, JR. "Urban Space in a Policy Perspective: An Introduction," in Wingo, (ed.), *Cities and Space.* Baltimore: Johns Hopkins University Press, 1963.

14

Location Analysis: Neighborhoods and Districts

Purpose and Conditioning Factors

In order to analyze residential neighborhoods and business districts, it is essential first to determine the purpose for which the analysis is being made. We are concerned primarily with the use of studies of this type as an aid to business, governmental, institutional, and personal decisions. Every person, business executive or public official, however, may have specific objectives to achieve which will affect the type of analysis that is undertaken. It may be necessary to analyze a neighborhood or district in connection with the making of an appraisal, to aid in selecting a new location for a place of business, as a means of reaching a decision relative to the purchase of a home, as a basis for determining zoning law changes, or for many other purposes.

Purpose may determine the type and extent of the analysis that is undertaken. In some cases a quick inspection may be adequate. In others, careful studies of the more important factors bearing on the neighborhood or district will be required. Such analyses will include consideration of the relationships of the neighborhood or district to the structural pattern of land uses and the trends of land use expansion. Such analyses may also consider the impact of the growth potential of the city or region as an economic unit on specific neighborhoods and districts.

Having identified purpose, we should recognize that the specific locality may impose certain conditions that govern the analysis. For example, people who live in a country town may have different concepts of inharmonious land uses than those who live in larger cities. As the FHA points out in its *Underwriting Handbook:*

The relative importance of the component elements will also vary between communities as the market attitudes found in one differ from those of others. For example, the attitudes of the market in small towns toward land uses may differ from those in cities. Analysis of these attitudes of the varying markets is, therefore, important in determining the location rating criteria to be applied in a given community town or city. Error will occur if the criteria used in one city are applied arbitrarily in the making of location ratings in another.[1]

We should note also that the attitudes of people may change from time to time in matters of this type.

An analysis of a neighborhood or district should reflect the current attitudes and objectives of the persons for whom the work is being done rather than the points of view of the person or persons making the analysis. For example, the unwillingness of some groups in our population to live side by side may be a reflection of undemocratic attitudes but may also have an important bearing on the future of the specific neighborhood being analyzed.

Neighborhoods, Districts, and People

When we refer to neighborhoods and districts, we are likely to think in terms of land area, structures, and other physical factors. Although this is appropriate in a sense, we should remember that without people these physical factors would mean little. When we refer to neighborhoods and districts, we mean primarily the people who live or work in such places. The people may be influenced by their physical surroundings, but in a final analysis the people control the types of buildings and other improvements that are found in neighborhoods and districts. Thus, we are concerned with the factors that influence the decisions of people, either from a personal or a business standpoint, relative to real estate resources.

There is a tendency for us to think of impersonal forces as determining the future of specific localities. We refer to location factors, to market forces, political influences, and the like, often forgetting that when we do this we are really referring to the attitudes, points of view, interests, and objectives of specific persons. In combination, the opinions of large num-

[1] Federal Housing Administration, *Underwriting Handbook* (rev. ed.; Washington, D.C.: Government Printing Office, 1959), Sec. 71609.2.

bers of persons may appear to constitute an impersonal sort of force. Fundamentally, however, we are likely to reach false conclusions if we forget that real properties, neighborhoods, districts, the structure of cities or metropolitan areas all mean little or nothing unless we think in terms of the people who give importance to them. And it is the reactions, value judgments, hopes, and fears of people that finally result in the assignment of values to real properties, and that give one neighborhood a better reputation than another or give one business district an advantage over others.

In the discussions that follow we often refer to the physical characteristics of neighborhoods and districts. This should not obscure the fact that we are considering factors which are likely to influence the judgments and decisions of people in respect to real estate resources.

Types of Residential Areas

The largest proportion of the utilized land in our cities is devoted to residential purposes. However, these residential areas contain many different types of people, properties, and neighborhoods. Although the dividing lines between neighborhoods usually are not sharp, there are great differences between the deluxe residential suburbs at the one extreme and the slums at the other.

Neighborhoods might be classified by the types of people who live in them; by type, location, age, and condition of structures; or in other ways. Nearly all of these factors are reflected, however, in the level of rents or prices typical of the various neighborhoods of a city. Hence, the following classification is based on three general levels of rents or prices: high, intermediate, and low; in addition, types of structures and locations are reflected in the subclassifications. This is not a hard-and-fast classification, but will suggest the types of neighborhoods most generally found in our cities.

I. High-Rent or -Price Areas
  A. Apartment house or town house neighborhoods, located at desirable points
    1. On main mass transportation lines
    2. Near ocean, lake, or river fronts
    3. Near expressways
  B. Single-family neighborhoods
    1. Axial developments
      (a) Located along best transportation lines
      (b) Located along desirable water fronts
    2. Self-contained areas
    3. Suburban towns
    4. Country estates

  II. Intermediate-Rent or -Price Areas
      A. Apartment house neighborhoods
          1. New buildings
              (a) Garden types
              (b) Walk-ups
              (c) Elevator types
          2. Middle-aged buildings
              (a) Walk-ups
              (b) Elevator types
      B. Row-house or town house areas
          1. New developments
          2. Middle-aged areas
      C. Neighborhoods of two-family structures
          1. New developments
          2. Middle-aged areas
      D. Neighborhoods of single-family homes
          1. New developments
              (a) Suburban or peripheral developments
              (b) "Near-in" areas
          2. Middle-aged areas
              (a) Suburban or peripheral developments
              (b) "Near-in" areas
 III. Low-Rent or -Price Areas
      A. Multi-family dwelling areas
          1. Tenements
          2. Alley dwellings
      B. Old row-house or town house areas
      C. Old districts of two-family structures
      D. Single-family home neighborhoods
          1. Centrally located single-family houses in slums
          2. Areas of deteriorated intermediate single-family dwellings
          3. Shack towns on periphery
          4. Mill villages
          5. Lumber and mining towns
          6. Declining country towns

Density of Population

One of the factors of importance which is not indicated directly in the foregoing classification of neighborhoods is population density. Ordinarily we think of overcrowded conditions as being undesirable either from a social or an economic standpoint. In planning for the redevelopment of some of the slum areas of our cities, special efforts are made to decrease population density.[2]

[2] See, for example, M. Carter McFarland, *The Challenge of Urban Renewal,* Technical Bulletin No. 34 (Washington, D.C.: Urban Land Institute, 1958).

The density of population in cities depends on (1) the size of the total population, (2) the speed of the city's internal transportation system, (3) types of structures, and (4) land coverage.

In ancient Rome, for example, a population of 1,000,000 was crowded into an area of five square miles. Most of the residential buildings were 5 or 6 stories high, and the streets were only 8 to 10 feet wide. While the population density in the central portion of our larger cities is still high, improved transportation and more careful land planning have reduced density.

Some indication of the population densities likely to be found in residential neighborhoods may be secured from the following relationships. The population density is around 10,000 per gross square mile in neighborhoods of single-family houses where the lots are 50 feet wide and 100 feet deep and when half the land is allocated to streets, recreation areas, schools, shopping centers, and similar land uses. In row-house or town house areas under the same general conditions outlined above, the population density reaches 30,000 per gross square mile. In 3-story walk-up apartments with 4-room units and with 50 per cent of land covered by the apartment buildings, a density of 50,000 per square mile is reached. Population density ranges from 100,000 to 200,000 per square mile in areas of elevator apartments 8 to 22 stories high with 25 per cent land coverage.

Sometimes theoretical standards of population density are set up which ignore other important considerations. From the standpoint of light and air, conditions are worse in Chicago walk-up apartment areas, with a density of 70,000 persons to the square mile, where 3-story buildings are crowded together on the fronts of lots, than they are in New York developments which have 8- to 13-story apartment buildings on a 25 per cent land coverage with a density of 181,000 persons per square mile. It is not desirable, however, to impose uniform density rules on all locations. Sites near an express subway station are limited in area and tend to be occupied by families who want the maximum convenience in transportation. Hence, high-rise elevator apartments tend to develop in such locations. The ocean-front land at Miami Beach is limited in extent and tall hotels properly spaced are economically desirable there. Lower buildings can occupy less strategic areas.

Forces Causing Neighborhood Change

The forces which cause people to reach decisions that bring about changes in neighborhoods are of three main types: (1) physical and functional depreciation, (2) the development of more intensive land uses, and (3) changes of residence. Physical wear and tear and the introduction of new materials, designs, and equipment tend constantly to make existing structures less desirable places in which to live. As new houses are built, the older ones lose out in competition with them.

As more intensive land uses invade a residential area, there is a tendency for people to move to new locations. An apartment house development may be considered undesirable by the residents of a single-family area, who may move to some other neighborhood. Business uses sometimes invade residential areas. The relocation of an industrial district may affect a number of neighborhoods.

There is some tendency for families to move to more desirable quarters as income increases. As certain types of people move into a neighborhood, they may be absorbed without any significant change. On the other hand, the movement of some groups into an area will tend to replace others already living there. Some groups in our society will not consent to live side by side because of ingrained prejudices. Thus, the migration of families with certain characteristics into some neighborhoods frequently stimulates the emigration of earlier residents of the area.

As a result of the operation of these forces, people are drawn to newer or more desirable areas (as measured by their standards) and are driven from older or less desirable areas. Hence, a number of population movements are taking place more or less constantly in our towns and cities. Some families move into other apartments in the same building, others go next door, across the street, or around the corner. Still other families move long distances within the city or move to other parts of the country, while new individuals and families move into the city. It is estimated that each year about one family in five moves.

Neighborhood Stability

Those interested in real estate value changes sometimes observe that houses do not wear out but neighborhoods do. Residential neighborhoods pass through periods of early growth, of maturity, and of decline. A new neighborhood may be entirely built up by an operative builder, with all facilities complete and no intervening vacant lots. Where the area is subdivided and lots are sold to individual home builders, houses may be built on scattered lots. The development may be arrested for many years, with builders passing the area by to go to new areas where entire sections of new houses can be built. Widespread use of the automobile and buses has enabled these partially built-up areas to be skipped over. Sometimes the advantages of utilities and pavements in the older areas cause new houses to be built in the vacant lots at a later period.

There is no uniform rate of decline in neighborhood desirability. The Battery in Charleston, South Carolina, has maintained a high-grade residential character for over 200 years. Suburbs at a sufficient distance from the transition of uses maintain a high character for very long periods of time, if not indefinitely. Examples of this kind are Evanston, Oak Park Wilmette, Winnetka, and Lake Forest near Chicago; Scarsdale, Larchmont, and Bronxville in Westchester County, New York; Bethesda and Chevy Chase near Washington, D.C.; Shaker Heights in Cleveland; Roland Park in Baltimore; the Country Club District of Kansas City; and River Oaks in Houston.

When neighborhoods do decline, it is because the buildings become obsolete as to structure, architectural style, or lot area; because a succession of groups of people enters the area; or because the expansion of certain commercial or industrial establishments makes the area less desirable for residential purposes. Some families are greatly influenced by the types of children in the schools and move away from old neighborhoods when children of a different social or economic group constitute a majority.

Part of the cause of decline in the desirability of a neighborhood is the aging of the population. As children grow up to marriageable age, they may find it difficult to buy homes in the old neighborhood or they may prefer to move to newer neighborhoods where their friends are living. As the old residents die, a different social or income group may take their places.

One type of migration observed in a number of cities is the movement of a family from a central apartment to a suburban apartment, and then into a single-family home. When children reach school age, families tend to move from apartments to single-family homes, for it has been found in Arlington, Virginia, and other communities that while there are many babies in suburban apartments, there are only half as many children of school age as in single-family homes in the same area.

It cannot be assumed, however, that old residential neighborhoods have steadily declined in value after reaching maturity. Houses in old neighborhoods sometimes sell for higher prices than at the time they were built. But the general tendency is to lose out in competition with newer areas.

Frequently, the first members of a minority group to enter an area pay more for the houses and raise the market prices. In other cases, some residential neighborhoods are converted to higher uses by being absorbed in new commercial developments. This is rather infrequent, as most central business districts have ceased to expand laterally. The requirement for parking areas near existing shopping districts, however, is creating a demand for old houses near established commercial areas at prices high enough to absorb the cost of the structures.

Thus, there is no uniform rule as to the rate of decline in a neighborhood, and the analyst must study each neighborhood specifically and consider it in relation to the general pattern of residential land uses.

Hence, we consider chiefly the following items which are likely to influence decisions of owners, buyers, sellers, tenants, or investors:

1. Location of the neighborhood with respect to the structure of land uses and the main lines of city growth
2. Protection against blighting influences
3. The age of the neighborhood
4. The types of people in the area
5. The types of buildings and other improvements in the area
6. Transportation facilities available and rates charged
7. Nearness to schools, churches, shopping centers, amusement places, and places of employment
8. Tax burdens and special assessments
9. Utilities, conveniences, and services, and the rates charged
10. Special hazards and nuisances

In addition, attention should be given to the general social organization of a neighborhood and the attitudes and interests of the principal owners and investors in the area.

Land Use Structure and Main Lines of City Growth

The relation of each neighborhood to the main lines of city growth and to the structure of major land uses can be determined by inspection. In general, property values are likely to be more stable in areas which are in the main direction of city growth. Neighborhoods which are not likely to participate in such economic advance as is made by the city will tend to decline more rapidly than those which are located more favorably in this respect.

Protection Against Blighting Influences

Blighting influences include unfavorable land uses and inharmonious groups of people. As we have pointed out above, what is considered to be a blighting influence will depend in large part on the attitude of people living in the area. In some cases the building of apartment houses in a neighborhood of single-family homes will affect the area adversely, although some neighborhoods may be strengthened by such developments.

A neighborhood which is in the direct path of an inharmonious area is in danger of being blighted, especially if both are served by the same transportation lines. Frequently the presence of inharmonious groups in an adjoining area represents a threat to a neighborhood.

The extent to which blighting influences may affect a neighborhood depends in part on the protections which are set up against them. Zoning laws usually regulate the types of uses to which various areas in a city may be put. To be adequate they must not only indicate the permitted uses in a definite manner, but the uses allowed must be such as to promote harmonious and stable neighborhoods. In addition, attention should be given to the extent to which such regulations are enforced and the manner of their administration in the light of changing conditions. Height and area restrictions are also of importance, since they help to protect a neighborhood against overcrowding and the dangers likely to result from it.

As was noted in Chapter 9, regulations of these types are sometimes used by self-seeking groups for their own advantage rather than for the public purposes typically stated. As a result, zoning ordinances and similar regulations may give a false sense of security to home purchasers or investors.

Restrictive covenants, usually referred to as *deed restrictions*, represent another type of regulation. These are private covenants in the deed to property rather than public regulations. Hence, deed restrictions typically may be much more detailed and definite than zoning laws and may regulate such things as cost of buildings, types of structures, setback lines, and related matters.

Deed restrictions are usually set up at the time a new subdivision is started. Thus, much depends on the wisdom and foresight of the subdivider in such cases, as well as in his decisions with respect to lot sizes, land coverage, street locations, dedication of land to park and playground areas, and the like. Much depends also on the effectiveness of the administration of these restrictions.

An area which is entirely or almost entirely built up is less likely to change rapidly than one which is only partially developed, for in the latter case there is always the possibility of utilizing vacant land for purposes which do not harmonize with existing land uses. Hence, relatively undeveloped areas tend to be less stable than those which are more completely built up, unless adequate restrictions and regulations are in existence. The extent to which vacant areas may be a hazard to neighborhood stability varies somewhat from one city to another, depending chiefly on the rapidity with which the city is growing or changing.

Both natural and artificial barriers may protect a neighborhood against blighting influences. Public parks, hills, ravines, and similar barriers may be of great importance to the future stability of a neighborhood.

Neighborhood Age

In the case of both neighborhoods and people, age is a relative matter. Some age rapidly, others grow old gracefully. There are neighborhoods in some of our cities that are well over 100 years old but are still areas of desirable residences and stable property values. Other things being equal, newer neighborhoods which have been sufficiently built up to become established are more likely to be sound investment areas than older ones. However, other things seldom are equal in cases of this type. In analyzing neighborhoods, age should be considered only to the extent that it is likely to have a direct bearing on future property values.

Typically, age brings about deterioration of structures and increases the cost and difficulty of maintaining them. In addition, newer neighborhoods may be planned and developed in a more attractive manner than those which are older.

The Residents of the Area

Since future developments in a neighborhood will be determined to a large degree by the decisions of the people who live there, it is necessary to consider the principal characteristics of these people in the process of analyzing a neighborhood. Such questions as the following should be considered: What are the typical incomes of residents of the area? Are there wide variations of income? What percentage of the people own their own homes? Which occupations are represented? How frequently do people move into or out of the neighborhood? Does the general social organization and tone of the neighborhod make it a place where people like to live for long periods of time?

Typically, a high percentage of owner occupancy is indicative of a stable neighborhood, since owners tend to move less frequently than tenants. There also appears to be a tendency for those living in high-rent or -price areas to move less frequently than those in the intermediate-price and -rent and lower-price and -rent neighborhoods. Owners usually take great pride in their dwelling and do whatever they can to maintain and preserve the stability and appeal of the neighborhood.

Buildings and Other Improvements

Neighborhoods in which the structures are of the same general type and architectural style tend to be areas of relatively stable land values for long periods of time, provided the architectural design is appropriate for the community. This condition is strengthened if lot sizes are ample and relatively uniform, if the percentage of land covered by buildings is relatively low, and if setback lines are uniform or the buildings are arranged in accordance with an attractive pattern.

Typically, greater stability is assured if all of the buildings in a neighborhood are maintained in good condition. Obviously, houses which are kept in good condition last longer than those which are allowed to deteriorate, and hence there is less chance for depreciation.

Landscaping, gardens, walks, drives, and accessory buildings contribute to neighborhood advance or decline depending on their general character and maintenance. The nature of the topography and climatic and other natural advantages are all factors to be considered. The FHA *Underwriting Handbook* states:

> Few, if any, user groups are oblivious to good topography, pleasing views, wooded lots, broad vistas, and climatic advantages. Some groups may be more insistent in their demands for beautiful neighborhoods than others. . . . The absence of natural charm may be counterbalanced by pleasing landscaping, well-kept homes, grounds and streets. . . . Attractive street layouts, preservation of natural attractiveness, and other characteristics of good neighborhood design are conditions which minimize risk. Areas in which streets have been laid out with proper regard for drainage, land contours and traffic flow increase the desirability of the neighborhood to present and prospective owners.[3]

Transportation

Adequacy of transportation, like so many other factors involved in neighborhood analysis, is a relative matter. In small towns all neighborhoods may be within easy walking distance of schools, shopping centers, places of employment, and amusement points. In such cases transportation is of no significance in determining neighborhood stability. However, in most larger cities, transportation has a vital bearing on neighborhood stability, since neighborhoods which do not have access to desirable transportation facilities at reasonable cost suffer from the competition of those which are more favorably located. In all cases, transportation must be considered in relation to the present and prospective occupants of a neighborhood. If most of the families in a neighborhood have two cars, public transportation may be of relatively little significance. For many of the neighborhoods in our metropolitan areas, however, public transportation is of some importance to neighborhood stability.

The important point to remember in analyzing transportation is the comparison of services and costs between neighborhoods, since this factor is of major importance if it gives one area competitive advantages over others.

Civic, Social, and Commercial Centers

Neighborhood stability is increased if a neighborhood is served adequately by grade and high schools, shopping centers, churches, parks, playgrounds, hospitals, amusement places, and other civic, social, and commercial centers. If a neighborhood is served by schools of good reputation, there is competition among people to locate there, and property values are supported. In some cities the central downtown business district is capable of serving all neighborhoods adequately; but in our larger metropolitan centers, the services of outlying shopping centers are essential for most residential areas. Similarly, the location of the other com-

---

[3] FHA, *op. cit.*, Secs. 71617, 171618.

munity centers should be considered in relation to the requirements of the neighborhood under consideration, especially with respect to the major differences between competing neighborhoods.

Of special importance also is the extent to which civic, social, and commercial centers add to or detract from the general tone of the neighborhood. These intangible factors often have great significance.

Taxes and Special Assessments

The burdens of taxation often vary from one neighborhood to another in the same city because of the fact that the assessment process frequently results in the valuation of properties at different percentages of "true" value. If the properties in one neighborhood bear a higher proportionate tax load than those in other areas, instability may result. Thus, it is necessary to study assessment methods and to compare tax burdens in different neighborhoods in order to determine the extent to which uniformity or differences exist.

Property taxes constitute such a heavy burden on real estate owners that an unduly heavy tax load may militate strongly against neighborhood stability. The average tax burden on homes is high. A property owner is likely to pay in taxes over a period of years an amount equal to or more than the price of the building.

While it is always desirable that a neighborhood have adequate streets, sewers, sidewalks, and similar conveniences, their costs sometimes are excessive and are paid for over a long period of time. The special assessments levied for such purposes may be so heavy in a neighborhood that its stability will be endangered. Hence, it is always necessary to determine the payments which are outstanding and the length of time during which such payments must be made. In some cases each individual property owner is responsible for substantial payments over a long period, a situation which is bound to have an adverse effect on property values.

Utilities, Conveniences, and Services

The utilities, conveniences, and services which may be available in a neighborhood include electricity, gas, water supply, garbage disposal, street lighting, sewage disposal, drainage, street improvements, police and fire protection, and mail delivery. The types of services available and their cost to the user in comparison with other areas of the city should be analyzed carefully. In addition, the types of utilities, conveniences, and services available should be considered in terms of what is expected by the residents of the area.

As is true of many of the factors we are considering here, one area may have a competitive advantage over another if there are great differences with respect to the type, quality, and cost of the utilities and services available.

Topography, Hazards, and Nuisances

We have already pointed out how topographical factors may form natural barriers against blighting influences. Such matters as streets with steep grades, soil erosion, and hillside locations may be hazardous to persons and property. Low-lying areas may be subject to periodic floods; the condition of the soil may discourage lawns and gardens.

High-speed traffic thoroughfares create hazards for the residents of a neighborhood; high-tension electric lines involve some risks; locations near airports may be hazardous; nearness to industrial areas or railroad lines or yards may subject an area to noise and other nuisances.

The increase in airplane traffic to many airports may have caused some damage to the property values of residences located in close proximity to airports. The noise developed by large modern airplanes and the danger that there may be crashes in the adjacent areas are both factors of considerable importance in this connection. Just how much damage to property values may be caused by these developments is not too certain, but this is undoubtedly one of the factors to be added to the list of hazards and nuisances which affect residential properties.

Relative Marketability

All of the factors which we have discussed briefly in the preceding sections have a bearing on the marketability of properties in the area. As a summary of these factors, it may be desirable to consider the degree to which typical properties in the neighborhood will be salable over a period of years and whether they will be more or less salable than similar properties in other areas. We should remember that the high-price and -rent neighborhoods are not always the most stable areas in terms of the probable trend of land values.

As we have pointed out in the earlier part of this chapter, a careful analysis of the factors which have been discussed should give us a fairly reliable indication of the future trend of property incomes and values in a neighborhood and should provide a useful guide to real estate decisions. Such an analysis will be more reliable if proper allowances have been made for local applications of the general tendencies which we have outlined.

Types of Commercial and Industrial Districts

Although there are wide varieties of business (commercial and industrial) areas in our cities, they may be classified into five main groups.

Commercial districts include: (1) central business districts, (2) outlying business centers, and (3) isolated outlets and clusters. Industrial districts are of two main types: (1) those used chiefly for heavy industrial establishments and (2) those used principally by light industry. Industrial districts may also be classified by location.

The *central business district* is the functioning heart of the city. In it are concentrated the major retail, financial, wholesale, hotel, service, and governmental activities of the city. The specialized land uses in the central business district typically include the retail shopping area, office building area, hotels, theater and amusement section, banks and other financial institutions, government buildings, and, on the fringe, the wholesale district and the light manufacturing area. All modes of transportation lead to this center.

In the central business district the cost of doing business is high, competition is keen, good sites are at a premium, and there are chances for both great successes and great failures. Almost all kinds of business enterprise may be found there except those requiring large amounts of horizontal space or those dealing in commodities which are low in value in relation to bulk. The establishments with the greatest rent-paying ability obtain the choice sites, with the less desirable space going to other businesses. Generally speaking, the best parts of the central business districts are those with access to the greatest potential purchasing power, as measured by the quantity and quality of pedestrian traffic. Customers are drawn from all parts of the city and from its hinterland or tributary area, which may extend for many miles in all directions.

The types of business which can afford to locate in "100 per cent" business locations and pay the highest rents are department stores, women's apparel stores, shoe stores, men's clothing stores, jewelry stores, drugstores, candy stores, and variety stores. These stores can afford to pay 3 to 6 per cent of their sales in rent on sales volumes ranging from $80 to $200 or more per square foot of floor area, which yields returns of from $2.50 to as high as $15 per square foot in rents. Stores which cannot afford to pay the rents for ground floor locations in the heart of the central business districts include furniture stores (those whose sales rarely exceed $40 per square foot), hardware stores, barbershops, and food stores.

With the rapid development of large shopping centers, the downtown areas have suffered in varying degrees from this competition. Certain functions, however, appear to be performed best in central business districts. These include the functions of providing the greatest selection of retail merchandise, highly specialized activities, financial institutions, major office headquarters, theaters and other amusement places, and related activities.

Business uses may radiate out from the center of the city along one or more main traffic arteries. Businesses which require larger amounts of horizontal space, special parking facilities, or large quantities of land are found along these streets. New and used automobile and accessory dealers, filling stations, food marts, supermarkets, and larger grocery stores, farmers' markets, tourist hotels and motels, and the like are located on such streets. "Near-in" parts of such streets may be thought of as a part of the central business district; those farther out may be classified with outlying business centers.

Outlying business centers include a variety of districts which may be miniatures of the central business district, large regional shopping centers, smaller centers with parking facilities, or neighborhood business streets. Typically the outlying business center does not contain rapid transportation facilities or large terminals such as are found in the main center. Parking space and the presence of good feeder streets are of considerable importance to such a center.

Nearly all types of enterprises may be found in outlying centers. There has been a tremendous growth of large outlying shopping centers providing free parking and located away from mass transit lines. The choice sites go to the establishments with greatest rent-paying ability. Pedestrian traffic is much less significant than in the central area. Parking facilities are one of the major attractions in outlying centers.

Small neighborhood business centers may include only such establishments as appeal to the immediate needs of the people in the area, with little specialization of land use.

Isolated business outlets are single establishments doing business principally on a personal basis, as in the case of a delicatessen in the front of a residence or a beauty shop or dentist's office located in a part of a house or apartment. Increasingly, such stores as Sears Roebuck and various supermarkets occupy isolated locations. Isolated filling stations, restaurants, general stores, and repair garages are found on principal highways. Two or more such outlets may form a *business cluster* of establishments which complement each other, such as a drugstore, supermarket, and shoe repair shop. Typically they develop on small parcels of land which are designated by zoning regulations for commercial uses and are quite limited in extent. However, the small town or village business cluster is more like the central business district in embryonic form. It usually serves the village and the surrounding countryside, but the establishments located there are not highly specialized.

Heavy industrial areas are now being found to an increasing extent some distance from the central business district, with industrial suburbs developing to a marked degree. Areas of *light industry* may be found from the city center to the periphery.

Analysis of Business Districts

The more important forces to consider in analyzing a business district include the following: (1) probable changes in the internal structure of the city, (2) competition of land uses, (3) topographical factors, (4) transportation facilities, and (5) governmental policies.

The growth of the central business district will depend on the economic development of the area which it serves, including the city and its tributary region.

The strength of the central business district will depend to some degree on the type of city—whether an international, national, or regional capital is involved or whether the central district must compete rather directly with outlying business centers in the same area. Differences between office building and retail land uses should be noted. If a city is an international center such as New York, offices in the central district or districts enjoy some special advantages over outlying centers, and to some degree this is true of retailing. In another connection, one of the authors pointed out:

To an increasing extent, business is being done on a regional and also on a national basis. For example, businessmen in smaller cities now do their banking to an increasing extent in major regional centers. Many financial activities are tending to center in New York on a national basis.
All of this would tend to suggest that major office building developments will occur in a relatively few cities that will emerge as the principal regional economic capitals of the country. Only in them will it be economical to concentrate the highly specialized activities that result from a minute division of labor which is induced by large scale regional and national operations.[4]

Although financial activities and others that support major office building types of land uses are likely to be concentrated in the centers of principal regional cities, retailing has tended to move outward toward the outlying areas even in the larger regional and national economic capitals. Similarly there is little likelihood of manufacturing activities, except for some light types, seeing much further development in city centers, regardless of the type of city. The growth of the central business district also depends on the intensity of competition from outlying centers. Outlying business centers, however, may not participate in the general economic advance or decline of the city as directly as the central business district. If an outlying center serves a neighborhood in which many people draw their support from one industry, special attention must be given to this fact.

[4] Arthur M. Weimer, *Investors and Downtown Real Estate,* Technical Bulletin No. 39 (Washington, D.C.: Urban Land Institute, 1960).

Changes in the internal structure of a city are likely to affect all business districts within it. Generally the central business district tends to move in the main direction of city growth, although the location of main transportation terminals exerts great influence and usually anchors the central district to a fixed location. Parking difficulties have become one of the main disadvantages of central business districts. The growth or movement of outlying planned centers with free parking depends to a large extent on changes in the internal transportation system and on changes in residential areas. The continued decentralization of our cities indicates that many of the outlying planned business centers will develop markedly in the years ahead and that new ones will be established.

Other factors which have contributed to the growth of outlying business districts include the development of chain, department, drug, and variety stores adapted to such areas, and the opening in the outlying centers of branches of banks, savings and loan associations, and other financial institutions. Office buildings, sometimes of relatively large size, often develop in outlying districts.

Topography has a bearing on the growth of a business district, since most business establishments prefer locations on level land. Hence, a business district seldom moves uphill or down a steep incline. Topography also is an important determinant of transportation routes. Low-lying areas are often endangered by floods or require special protections which may be costly. The load-bearing qualities of the soil will affect the cost of building.

Taxation, zoning laws, transportation regulations, and other government policies have a major effect on business districts. Obviously, any decisions affecting the transportation system, including changes of main lines, rates, or related policies, will have a bearing on the future of business districts. Those tax policies are most important which result in different tax burdens for different districts. Frequently the central business district is required to bear an extremely high tax burden, and this may force certain business establishments to seek other locations. In some cases one outlying center bears a higher tax burden than others because of faulty assessment practices or because it is in a sewer or sanitary district or other special tax area which imposes high rates.

Land use regulations are not likely to affect central business districts to a marked degree, but are of major importance in determining the growth of outlying centers. Height and bulk regulations are of greater importance to central business districts.

Some types of business establishments are more successful if located near competing or complementary firms. Continuity of stores and shops contributes to the value of each of the stores because shoppers like to find a complete assortment of merchandise in one location and often want to compare prices. On the other hand, inharmonious uses will endanger the success of some establishments; for example, a retail store catering to a fashionable group will be affected adversely by the development of a low-priced entertainment and amusement center at a nearby location.

Pedestrian Traffic Counts

Estimates of the probable amounts of business which may be expected to develop at a downtown retail location are often based on traffic counts. In making traffic counts, sampling techniques are usually employed. A number of stations may be set up within each block on both sides of the street so that checkers can count the number of persons passing each point for five minutes during each business hour. Traffic intersections are not included, attention being centered at points where people are passing in front of stores. High correlations have been found between the number of pedestrians passing a point and the volume of retail sales, rents, and land values. While it is generally assumed that the average purchasing power of persons within the same business district is about equal, there are often marked differences between the crowds on the two sides of the same street. In some cases pedestrian traffic counts must be modified to allow for shopping by telephone and similar practices.

Analysis of Industrial Districts

The development of industrial districts is affected by (1) changes in the internal structure and pattern of land uses, (2) transportation facilities, (3) topography, (4) intensity of competition for land, and (5) government policies.

Like other types of districts, industrial areas will be affected by the general directions of city growth and by changes in the city's internal structure. Transportation facilities have always exercised great influence on the development of industrial districts; but with the development of truck transportation, light industry is no longer tied closely to main transportation lines. There has been a significant development of industrial plants along belt highways; for example, Route 128 in Boston, the Calument Expressway in Chicago, and the Pennsylvania Turnpike north of Philadelphia. This may be an important future trend.

Heavy industries still require adequate rail or water transportation, and their location and development continue to depend to a large extent on the transportation facilities available and their cost. Topography is of importance in this connection because it may control the development of new transportation lines and because industry tends to follow level and relatively low-lying areas rather than high ground, remaining near water fronts, or following valleys.

In most cities definite limits have been placed on the movement of industrial districts by city planning regulations and zoning laws. Usually, such laws and regulations are liberal in the amount of space allocated to present and potential industrial uses, but general limits are set. Some cities have allocated much more space to industry in their over-all plans for development than can ever be used in this way. Of the areas which could be used advantageously for industrial purposes, only limited portions typically are excluded from such uses by zoning laws.

Tax policies are of major importance in determining the future probable locations and developments of industrial districts. Tax burdens are one aspect of the whole problem of *competition for sites and the relative costs of land*. Usually, commercial establishments can outbid industries in their competition for space. Industrial establishments often require large ground floor areas, and only the light industries can operate economically in the upper stories of buildings. Hence, high land values are a handicap to heavy industrial development.

To escape high land values and high taxes, many industries have moved farther and farther from the centers of our cities, the movement occurring almost as rapidly as transportation facilities and plant investment have allowed. Industries now cover many parts of the countryside much as farms did in an earlier period. Formerly it was necessary to consider nearness to the homes of workers, but improved transportation and especially the increased use of the automobile have largely eliminated this consideration in determining industrial locations.

Industrial districts may be limited in their development by the amount of vacant land available. They may be influenced also by the rate of functional depreciation of industrial buildings, since some structures of this type are superseded by more efficient ones in a relatively short time.

SUMMARY

As with any investigation, it is essential to know the purpose for which neighborhood or district analysis is undertaken. Such analysis may be needed for business, personal, institutional, or governmental decisions. Purpose also helps to determine the type and extent of the analysis undertaken.

A number of classifications of neighborhoods may be employed. This chapter has presented a classification based on levels of rents and prices.

Neighborhood change is the result of the interaction of personal, business, and governmental decisions plus various historical or institutional factors. The primary forces behind these decisions are physical and functional depreciation, type and intensity of land use, and changes in residential patterns.

Many factors in the neighborhood environment will have important influences on decisions. They include location with respect to city growth, protections against blight, types of people and buildings in the area, availability of transportation, civic and social facilities, and taxes and similar factors which affect the income-producing potential of the area.

Neighborhoods tend to go through phases of growth, maturity, and decline. However, the time sequence of these phases is not fixed; some neighborhoods decline rapidly, whereas others remain as high-grade areas for long periods of time. There is no uniform rule as to the rate of decline of a neighborhood.

Neighborhoods of given price and rent levels usually are located in definite sectors of a city. Values tend to be most stable in those neighborhoods located in the main direction of city growth.

Commercial and industrial districts are classified in this chapter into five main groups. In analysis of these districts the following factors are of importance: (1) changes in the internal growth and structure of the city, (2) transportation, (3) topography, (4) competition for use of the land, and (5) governmental policies.

QUESTIONS FOR STUDY

1. Describe the principal forces causing changes in residential neighborhoods.
2. Make a list of the principal factors new affecting the neighborhood in which you live.
3. What blighting influences are likely to have greatest effect on your residential neighborhood in the next few years?
4. What are the main protections against blight? Which of these exist in the neighborhood in which you live?
5. How do population movements affect the future of a neighborhood? In analyzing a neighborhood, which population factors would you consider most important?
6. What effect does the condition of structures have on the future of a neighborhood? Does the age of structures have the same effect? Explain.
7. How important is the availability of public transportation for the future of a neighborhood?
8. As an investor, would you prefer to invest in industrial or commercial property? Explain.
9. *Study Project 24.* (a) What were the principal developments that set the stage for the emergence of the regional shopping centers? (b) Explain the chain store—supermarket—department store branch sequence and its significance for the regional shopping center. (c) What are the essential characteristics of the regional shopping center?

SUGGESTED READINGS

HOYT, HOMER. *Structure and Growth of Residential Neighborhoods in American Cities.* Washington, D.C.: Government Printing Office, 1939.

WEIMER, ARTHUR M. *Investors and Downtown Real Estate*, Technical Bulletin No. 39. Washington, D.C.: Urban Land Institute, 1960.

WENDT, PAUL F. *Real Estate Appraisal.* New York: Holt, Rinehart & Winston, Inc., 1956. Pp. 127–38.

Underwriting Handbook (rev. ed.). Washington, D.C.: Federal Housing Administration, Government Printing Office, 1959. Secs. 71601.1–71634.3.

WALKER, MABEL. *Business Enterprise and the City.* Princeton, N.J.: Tax Institute, Inc., 1957.

III

DECISION AREAS

15

Production: Subdividing and Land Development

Short- and Long-Term Decisions

The production of real estate resources is usually thought of in terms of the physical processes of land development, improvement, and building. These physical processes, while often intricate, have significance primarily because they provide people as individuals and as members of social groups with real estate resources and services. Thus, the developer of a large subdivision is in effect the developer of a community. The developer of a small subdivision creates at least a part of a neighborhood.

The manner in which land is subdivided, the size of the lots, the types of streets installed, the services and utilities provided, the quality and price level of the houses built, the community facilities provided, and related factors—all have a bearing on the kind of community or neighborhood that ultimately will result. Thus, early decisions have long-range impacts.

Typically, those who develop and sell land are interested primarily in providing properties that will be immediately attractive to potential buyers and hence readily salable. The concern of the real estate broker is similar to that of the original subdivider since his primary interest is in immediate sales. In both cases, however, the long-term success of these firms depends on the effectiveness with which the properties serve the needs of the buyers.

The interests of financial institutions and other investors are almost always of a longer-term nature. This is because the funds which are

335

advanced typically are repaid over a great many years. Similarly, the interests of property managers tend to be of a long-term nature.

Long-term investors and mortgage lenders are concerned that the properties developed and the communities and neighborhoods of which they are a part will continue to be desirable places in which to live and work over a number of years. The risks of financing properties that remain desirable over long periods of time are lower than those involved in financing other types of properties.

In this chapter and those which follow in Part III, we pay particular attention to the decision areas of production, marketing, and financing of real estate resources and their services. The decisions which are made at each of these stages of providing real estate resources and services for the community at large will be influenced by a wide variety of considerations.

Production of Real Estate Resources

If you were going to buy an automobile, you would probably visit one or more dealers, select the type and model you wanted, pay in cash or arrange the necessary financing, and drive the car away. You would hardly think of manufacturing it yourself or having it built entirely to your order.

If you wanted a house, however, you might consider these alternatives: you could go to a builder or a real estate broker and buy a house, either a used one or a new one, in somewhat the same way you would buy a car. Or you might buy a lot, install a water and sewage-disposal system, build a road, buy the necessary materials, and construct a house, either by your own efforts or by engaging a contractor to do the work for you. You might arrange for a prefabricated house dealer to put it up for you. You might buy a lot in a subdivision that had been carefully planned and in which all of the various utilities and streets had been installed. The developer of the subdivision might also be a builder and he might agree to build a house for you, either one planned by your own architect or one constructed from plans the builder had available.

Much the same type of situation would face a business firm wishing to develop its own place of business. A piece of land might be bought and a contractor engaged to erect the desired type of structure. Or a developed lot in an industrial district or a shopping center might be leased or bought and arrangements made for constructing a building.

In the real estate business the production of real estate resources is usually thought of as including only the processes of land development and building. Of course, in an economic sense the production of real estate resources or services includes all of the processes of developing the site and constructing the improvements, as well as financing, marketing, and property management. It involves the creation of facilities for the

PRODUCTION: SUBDIVIDING AND LAND DEVELOPMENT   **337**

production of income at fixed locations, whether these incomes are in the form of direct use of the property, as in the case of an owner-occupied home, or a place of business that is owned by the firm, or in the form of monetary returns to an investor.

Management of Subdividing and Building Firms

A wide variety of business firms are engaged in subdividing and land development activities. Frequently, such activities are combined with building operations. In some cases, an individual buys land and holds it for future development, sometimes subdividing it himself and installing the necessary facilities, sometimes selling it to others who do this. In some cases, several persons form a syndicate to engage in land development. Sometimes a real estate brokerage firm undertakes to develop land and sell the lots, or contracts with a builder to provide completed properties for sale.

Land development and building enterprises may be individual proprietorships, partnerships, or corporations. They may be operated as syndicates or trusts or in other ways.

Regardless of how they are set up, every firm engaging in subdividing or land development activities must perform the basic management functions of determining objectives, planning to achieve them, organizing resources, and controlling operations. Leadership is necessary to activate and set the process into motion.

Each firm must utilize the resources available to it, that is, the abilities of people, capital, capital goods, land, or other resources, in the process of producing and marketing the goods and services it provides. It must do this at prices in excess of costs if it is to remain in business very long.

In the case of enterprises in the field of subdividing and land development, as well as firms in construction activities, which are discussed in the next chapter, the products may be (1) raw land, (2) partially developed lots, (3) completely developed lots, or (4) developed lots complete with buildings and other improvements. These goods must be produced and sold. The firms may carry out all or parts of the production process; they may sell the product to the public or to other firms or individuals who will do this.

We should be careful to note, however, that whether a real estate firm is engaged in land development, building, brokerage, property management, or financing activities, it must perform production and marketing as well as financing activities. Although we refer to land development and building firms as being engaged in production activities, we use this term to refer to what they do for the community as a whole. Similarly, we refer to brokerage firms and property management firms as marketing enterprises because they perform marketing functions for the public. They must both produce and market their services, however, as well as arrange to finance their programs.

We are concerned chiefly with subdividing and land development in this chapter and with building processes and problems in the next. In recent years, large-scale developers have tended to combine subdivision, land development, and building operations. In some cases complete communities have been developed, including commercial and industrial structures as well as housing and community facilities.

Decisions Regarding Land Development

Although many of the decisions that are made in regard to land development and subdividing are based on hunches or intuition, others are the result of careful analysis, predictions, and postulates based on the best available information. Strategic considerations and value judgments also play a part in such decisions.

Of special importance in decisions related to land development are careful market analyses and the predictions of probable market changes based on them. Analyses of general and local business conditions often play an important part in such decisions. In addition, consideration is given to construction costs and trends, availability and cost of financing, price trends, government policies (especially as related to taxes), public improvements, and zoning and similar regulations. All of these factors will affect cost-return-risk relationships which are basic to decisions regarding land development.

Barlowe says, for example:

Several different types of costs are ordinarily involved in the development of land resources. Most important among these are the actual outlays of cash and human effort required to bring new land resources into use and to qualify partly developed resources for higher uses. Other significant costs include the social costs associated with individual and group sacrifices, the time costs which arise because of the time it takes to bring resource developments into use, and the supersession costs associated with our frequent practice of scrapping existing developments to make way for new resource uses.[1]

Strategic factors such as the timing of the development relative to competitive operations, the size of the effort, pricing policies, and the like will usually affect the decisions that are made. Attempts will be made to anticipate the decisions of competitors insofar as possible.

Decisions will turn finally on value judgments; and these are likely to be based on such matters as (1) the objectives to be accomplished by means of the project, (2) potential cost and return relationships, modified as necessary by tax considerations, (3) risk factors, (4) relationship of

[1] Raleigh Barlowe, *Land Resource Economics* (Englewood Cliffs, N.J.: Prentice-Hall, Inc., 1958), p. 229.

the project under consideration to others, and (5) the timing of the effort and the time required for it to pay out.

Steps in Development

The main activities essential to the developing of a real estate subdivision or other new development include the following:

1. Analyzing market conditions (determining the need for and the proper time for the proposed development).
2. Selecting an appropriate location.
3. Analyzing the principal features of the selected tract and developing preliminary plans and design.
4. Purchasing the location and establishing a method of financing. In the case of a shopping center, a leasing campaign will be carried on before financing is arranged.
5. Designing the layout of the area, locating the principal facilities, and determining relationship between public and private land uses; dividing the remaining portions of the land into parcels of such sizes and shapes as appear to be best adapted to the anticipated uses.
6. Securing approval of government authorities as required.
7. Arranging protections against risks by means of insurance and bonds.
8. Installing utilities, streets, and the various conveniences necessary for the development.
9. Establishing restrictions and methods for regulating land use.
10. Selling parcels or proceeding with construction.

Market Analysis

Prior to undertaking a new land development project, it is essential that the general conditions of the market be understood. In addition, the subdivider or developer needs information about the potential market for the specific types of products which he intends to sell. If he plans to sell lots, he needs to know something of the demand for lots of the type and price range he is considering. If he intends to subdivide and completely develop a tract of land, constructing houses, apartments, a shopping center, or other buildings on the lots, he will need information about their salability or rentability. Hence, the real estate developer will begin by considering the need for additional real estate resources. He will consider the available supply and current price and rent ranges in the light of potential demand. Land development calls for one of the specific applications of the market analysis procedures outlined in Chapter 12.

Generally, land development activity is greatest during periods of prosperity and high incomes. In depression periods relatively little activity is undertaken. History indicates that all too frequently land is developed during boom periods more rapidly than it can be absorbed by the market. For example, at the end of the boom of the 1920's, Chicago and its suburbs had enough lots to house over a million additional persons living in detached houses. Thus, the *timing* of a new subdivision or development is of basic importance to its success.

The heavy volume of land development in recent years has not meant that all of the old subdivisions were occupied. Many never will be because of poor locations, financial involvements, and other reasons. Premature subdivisions have created numerous problems, not only for the subdivider himself but for the community at large. Careful market analyses should help to prevent such occurrences.

These analyses should include a consideration of the principal demand, supply, and price factors having a bearing on the specific project under consideration. The principal demand factors are the trends of employment and incomes of the potential customer group and the terms and availability of financing. From the standpoint of supply, the availability of competing facilities and the potential development of competing projects are of prime importance. Relative prices and rents for old and new accommodations of a similar size and type need careful consideration. Costs of development require careful study.

As the FHA points out, "Every proposed residential development first must pass the basic test of whether or not there is a demand in the immediate neighborhood for the proposed properties." [2]

One should always remember in making analyses of this type that relatively long-range predictions are required. Only in exceptional cases is a subdivision completely developed and sold in the space of one or two years. In most cases the process goes on over a longer period of time.

The FHA says also:

Where a tract of land . . . exceeds the current needs of the market, or is obviously beyond the capacity of the sponsor to develop in the near future, it is desirable to develop the tract by sections and install land improvements only to the extent needed for the current building program. . . . The development of the tract continues on a sectional basis until the tract is completely developed or until such time as it is determined . . . that the market will not absorb additional properties. . . . This method of handling large tracts tends to prevent the speculative sale of lots, beyond current market need or demand.[3]

Location

Just as poor timing may result in unsuccessful developments, improper locations lead almost inevitably to developments which fail to become

[2] *FHA Underwriting Handbook* (Washington, D.C.: U.S. Government Printing Office, 1959), Sec. 70413.2.

[3] *Ibid.*, Sec. 70414.1.

desirable additions to our real estate resources. The proper location of new real estate developments leads to the orderly expansion of the urban pattern rather than to a wasteful dispersion of services and population, with the heavy individual and community costs which result.

The successful development of a new area requires a careful study of the past trends of city growth and structure and the location of competing or complementary areas. The discussions in Chapters 13 and 14 are applicable to problems of this type.

Location factors of special importance in decisions relating to a new housing development typically include the following:

1. The site should be favorably located with respect to urban growth for the type and class of development planned.
2. The site should not require undue development costs and be free from natural hazards.
3. Protections should be available in the form of natural barriers, zoning, or deed restrictions; if not available, they should be set up.
4. The site should be reasonably accessible in terms of time and cost of travel.
5. The location and planned development should put the properties in a favorable competitive situation relative to competing developments in terms of general attractiveness, lot sizes, utilities and conveniences, roads and streets, and parks and other public areas.

The factors which are of major importance in the location of commercial and industrial real estate developments are: (1) available transportation facilities, (2) topography and the nature of the soil and subsoil, (3) the relationship of the area to other parts of the city, and (4) the location and character of competing sites.

In most cities the location of commercial and industrial developments is limited by zoning laws. Recently, however, the location of such developments at points far removed from the center of cities has often placed them beyond the control of zoning regulations. While this gives the developer greater flexibility of operations, he will usually consider the relationship of a new commercial or industrial subdivision to the probable future pattern of the city and to the way in which the transportation network is likely to develop.

Analyzing the Selected Tract

Experienced developers make careful analyses and surveys of tracts prior to reaching decisions to purchase them. It is necessary to determine the usability and marketability of *all parts* of the area. Substantial losses can be avoided if advance consideration is given to the less desirable portions of a tract. A competent engineer or land planner should study the area and prepare layouts of the tract.

One student of the subject says:

Marketing subdivisions may be compared to marketing beef. The butcher pays so much a hundred for the carcass, and the subdivider pays so much an acre for his land. When the butcher retails, he charges according to the choiceness of the cut. He must charge enough for the porterhouse and tenderloin to take care of the waste and the cheap cuts.[4]

It should be noted also that the first properties marketed may have to be priced somewhat lower than those sold after the area has been partially developed. The earlier purchasers frequently require a price inducement for bearing a portion of the risk of a new project.

Cost of development must be studied with great care. Such costs vary widely. Flat land, of course, requires less preparation than rough terrain. An area which is to be densely settled requires heavy streets and sidewalks and large water mains and sewers. Less densely settled areas require only light streets, and sidewalks may not be needed. Utility lines, however, will need to be longer in proportion to the number of people in the area.

Improvement costs should be related to traffic load, number of families per acre, and the character of the layout of lots and devices. The buying power of the residents must be considered with care.

The largest elements in the improvement bill are the costs of streets and walks. Costs of sanitary sewers (and, except in areas of very low density, storm sewers) and water mains are added; costs of grading, draining, and landscaping, as well as the cost of engineering service. The cost of gas and electric service requires advance payments, but usually is reimbursed as the service is put into use.

Factors of importance in studying both costs of development and marketability include (1) topography; (2) limitations established by zoning ordinances and other regulations; (3) accessibility to places of employment, to schools, and to shopping, amusement, and civic centers; (4) location with respect to high-quality neighborhoods ("good addresses") and special attractions such as golf courses; (5) taxes; (6) potential special assessments; and (7) future probable management, financing, and maintenance costs.

Purchasing and Financing

The purchase of land for a new development is similar to the buying of other real estate. Options may be bought; in some cases land may be purchased on contract; or it may be bought outright. The usual complex legal formalities are involved as in all real estate transactions. Of course, it is especially important to the land developer that title matters be defi-

[4] Statement by Seward Mott.

nitely settled and that as much red tape as possible be eliminated if parts of the development are to be sold.

Brokers are often commissioned by developers to find suitable tracts or to assemble land where diversity of ownership is involved. The difficulty of assembling tracts of sufficient size for economical development has been one of the main factors preventing the redevelopment of "near-in" areas and has accelerated the trend toward city decentralization.

One of the characteristics of the financing of real estate developments is the limited amount of equity capital investments. Although provision has been made by several states whereby large institutional lenders may develop and own real estate projects, such activities have been limited chiefly to the projects of several of the larger life insurance companies. Most operators rely on borrowed funds to a large degree, usually tying in the financing of the development with mortgage arrangements. The insurance of mortgages by the Federal Housing Administration and the guaranteeing of mortgages by the Veterans Administration have helped to make money available for residential subdivision and related development projects.

Division of the Tract

The decisions reached in regard to the number of lots to be laid out, the areas to be used for business purposes, land dedicated to public use, the utilities and conveniences to be installed, and the restrictions to be established all involve detailed study of numerous factors. For example, the type and extent of street improvements are limited on the one hand by minimum essentials for decent urban living and on the other by the amount which prospective buyers or tenants can pay over and above such minimum requirements.

Local customs, climate, and soil conditions play a large part in determining the types of roads and streets constructed. The general plan for developing the tract will determine the road and street pattern. Courts or cul-de-sacs with proper turning space help to reduce traffic hazards; adapting the road system to the topography of the area not only adds to the attractiveness of many lots but also helps reduce costs.

The size and shape of the lots will be dependent on the anticipated land uses, on topographical features, on local planning regulations, on the income levels of prospective purchasers, and on the proposed price or rent scale. In earlier years many developers attempted to subdivide an area in such a way that the greatest possible number of lots would be obtained. Present-day practice dictates the division of an area into the greatest number of *readily salable lots*. Land planners and engineers have made real progress in solving problems of this type.

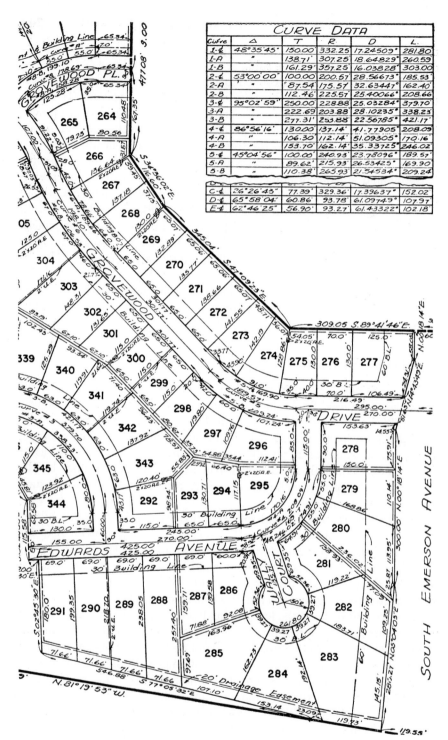

Fig. 15–1. Subdivision layout. (Courtesy Paul I. Cripe, Inc.)

The inclusion of park and playground areas in the plan of a subdivision adds greatly to the attractiveness and salability of many lots. The extent to which land in a tract will be dedicated to parks and playgrounds will be influenced, of course, by the nearness of the development to established facilities of this type. Also, provision should be made for shopping center sites, schools, churches, and related facilities.

The following suggestions serve as guidelines for neighborhood planning:

1. Heavy through traffic should be discouraged.
2. Extension of major streets should be planned in advance.
3. Traffic should flow toward thoroughfares.
4. Minor streets should enter major streets at right angles.
5. Avoid planning of dead-end streets. (Courts with adequate turning space, however, are often desirable.)
6. Streets should fit contours of irregular land.
7. Short blocks are not economical.
8. Plan commercial sites where needed.
9. Provide school and church sites.
10. Parks are a definite community asset.
11. Preserve natural features of site for improved appearance.
12. Deep lots are wasteful.
13. Plan lots of adequate width.
14. Avoid sharp-angled lots.
15. Plan wider corner lots.
16. Make lot lines perpendicular to street.
17. Plan lots to face desirable views.
18. Protect lots against adjacent nonconforming uses.
19. Protect residential lots against major street traffic.

Securing Government Approvals

With few exceptions, it is necessary to secure the approval of various government agencies before subdividing programs may be carried out. State and local planning regulations typically require that plans for each new subdivision be approved. Detailed plats and working drawings for a proposed subdivision showing the lots; position of streets; type and quality of streets, curbs, and sidewalks; land dedicated to public use; and related matters are presented to the proper authorities for approval. In some cases modifications are required. Sometimes approval is denied. Tax matters must be cleared in some cases.

State governments typically require the submission of plans for provision of water and for sewage disposal in order to safeguard public health. Approval must be secured to gain access to state roads. Some states require the submission of evidence of ability to deliver title to lots and in other ways undertake to protect the public against fraud and misrepresentation.

Federal regulations usually do not apply to subdivision development unless federal highways, taxes, or similar matters are involved or unless FHA or VA financing is desired. Approval must be secured for the proposed development from appropriate FHA and VA offices if such financial plans are to be used. Federal regulations may be involved if a subdivider needs to gain access to federal roads or if there are liens against the property resulting from a failure to pay federal taxes, or if the project involves use of the federal urban renewal program.

Protections Against Risks

Before any work is undertaken in the development of the physical subdivision, various protections usually are arranged against such risks as injuries to persons or property. Usually this is done through insurance coverage under a "manufacturer's and contractor's liability" policy. Also it is customary to arrange for performance bonds if contracts are let for such work as grading, utility installation, and the like. Such bonds provide a guarantee through an insurance company that work will be completed according to the contract that has been arranged.

Huebner and Black point out in this connection:

As the name implies (Contract Bonds), these bonds guarantee performance of construction, road-building, and other contracts between private parties or between such parties and government. . . . The nature of the guarantee is that should the principal fail to perform the contract in strict accord with its terms and specifications, the surety will be responsible either to have the contract completed or pay the resultant cost, up to the penalty of the bond, which in amount is usually the full contract price. Such a bond is termed a "performance" bond.[5]

Utilities and Conveniences

The problems involved in the provision of utilities and conveniences vary so widely from one development to another that it is difficult to make general statements about them.

In the long run, the use of sanitary sewers is more desirable than the use of septic tanks. City water is to be preferred over individual wells. In some cases there is no way to avoid such alternative arrangements, however. Sometimes community water or sewerage systems may be established and operated by the property owners in the area.

Telephone and power companies usually extend their services to a new development without cost to the developer. Other utility companies usu-

[5] From *Property Insurance*, 4th ed., by S. S. Huebner and Kenneth Black, Jr., pp. 435–36. Copyright © 1957, Appleton-Century-Crofts, Inc., New York.

ally make an installation charge with provision for refund if a sufficient number of users move into the area. Installation of underground utility mains and laterals prior to street surfacing helps to reduce costs. However, installation far in advance of needs should be discouraged.

Walks are usually required when there is a density of five houses or more per acre. Finished grading, lawns, and suitable planting help to enhance the appeal of a new development. If there are railroads, heavy traffic arteries, or other features likely to be objectionable to residents of the new area, screen planting or the construction of solid fencing or walls may be desirable. The developer should give consideration to provisions for street lighting, fire protection, and electrical, telephone, and gas services. Underground wiring adds greatly to the attractiveness and long-term appeal of an area.

Usually contracts are let for the various types of work that are necessary. Generally this will be done by entering into one contract for grading, another for road or street installation, another for sewer installation, and the like. Sometimes a general contract is let and the general contractor may sublet parts of the work.

Regulations

The establishment of restrictive covenants and plans for regulating a new development should be considered as an essential part of the developer's functions.

The types of restrictions established will depend on the extent to which zoning laws and land planning provisions regulate land uses, as well as on the character of the new development. In some places new developments are regulated by master plans established by local planning authorities. Standards for new subdivisions and developments may be established by such authorities. Zoning laws are usually the most important method for carrying into effect the master plan of a local authority. In some cases, however, this method is inadequate. The protection afforded by suitable covenants is of primary importance in the areas which lack the benefit of adequate and effective zoning. In properly zoned areas protective covenants are an important supplementary aid in maintaining neighborhood character and values. The extent of zoning protection is limited to governmental exercise of the police powers of maintaining and promoting public health, safety, and welfare. Protective covenants, being agreements between private parties, can go much further than public regulations in meeting the needs of a particular development and in providing maximum possible protection.

Usually the developer needs to establish more specific and detailed regulations than are set up by public bodies if he is to assure the orderly and stable development of the new area. Deed restrictions are the most effective means for accomplishing this purpose. They may control land uses, lot sizes, design and size of structures, position of structures on lots, nuisances, price ranges, land coverage, architectural factors, utility easements, and related matters. Deed restrictions should provide suitable enforcement provisions, be recorded in the public land records, and be superior to the lien of any mortgage that may be on record prior to recording the protective covenants. In some cases a "homes association" or "property owners' maintenance association" is organized to administer such regulations.

As the FHA points out:

Protective covenants should provide suitable enforcement provisions, be recorded in the public land records and be superior to the lien of any mortgage that may be on record prior to the recording of the protective covenants. The proper form of protective covenants varies in the different states. A generally acceptable and enforceable form is a written declaration by the owner of the entire tract which is recorded in land office records. Sometimes in small developments, the covenants and conditions are stated on the recorded plat. When a separate declaration is made, it is good practice to record it simultaneously with the recordation of the subdivision map.[6]

Protective covenants may also contain various special conditions such as regulations governing individual water supply and sewage-disposal systems, for example, requiring conformance to stated standards; protection of sites for community facilities such as parks, schools, and shopping centers; and related matters. Occupancy restrictions, of course, may not be enforced by the courts.

Marketing

The process of marketing a new development depends on the types of properties established and the objectives of the developer. If the subdivider wants to sell lots directly to users, quite a different marketing program will be set up than for a large-scale housing development or other type of project.

In the case of a subdivision it is considered good practice to develop and market one part of the area at a time. Relatively few subdividers today follow the practice which was common a generation ago of simply dividing raw land and selling unimproved lots on an indiscriminate basis. Orderly development almost never resulted from such practices. Today the subdivider typically installs streets and roads and makes provision for essential utilities as a minimum. He may also build houses or other structures on the lots, either for sale or for rent.

[6] FHA, *op. cit.*, Sec. 70440.2.

When houses are built for sale, good practice dictates that houses be grouped rather than scattered. "Model houses" and "open houses" are often employed as selling devices. Auctions of lots were typical of practices a generation ago, but in relatively few cases are they used as a marketing method today.

In case a subdivision is only partly developed and the developer finds it difficult to complete his project, he may improve his chances for success if he places new restrictions on the land through the cooperation of the property owners, resubdivides into lots of proper size to fit the current market, vacates unnecessary roads, and eliminates insofar as possible objectionable features.

If a rental housing project is developed, the marketing process is quite different, since house services rather than the houses themselves are being sold. Marketing operations are discussed in greater detail in Chapters 17 and 18.

Recent Trends in Land Development

Most of the new single-family homes built in the United States since the end of World War II have been constructed in new subdivisions on the periphery of existing cities or in vacant interstices between the older residential communities. Developers have had the opportunity to lay out a new design of streets and a different lot size from the old pattern. Winding streets and cul-de-sacs often replaced the old rigid design of streets and lots. Planning the new subdivisions created an extensive field of activity for land planners.

The widespread demand for larger houses made it necessary to provide wider lots with frontages of 75 to 100 feet or wider. The old narrow-lot subdivisions with frontages of 30 to 50 feet have become obsolete.

Vacant land on the edge of cities becomes ripe for house building when sewer and water mains are extended from the central city or its principal built-up suburbs. Most of our new housing developments have been constructed in areas closely adjacent to the older settled areas and have been a mass extension of urban growth from the main urban body.

Houses in higher-priced residential developments have been constructed on larger lots of one or more acres, in areas separated from the concentrated urban mass by green belts. These developments have been dependent on wells and individual septic tanks. Some entire communities have been built, as in Pittsburgh, which are in open areas, and which have their own sewage-disposal system and water system. Other communities have relied on individual septic tanks, which have sometimes, under certain soil conditions, become objectionable, if the density is greater than a few houses to the acre. Many cities, villages, and counties in the

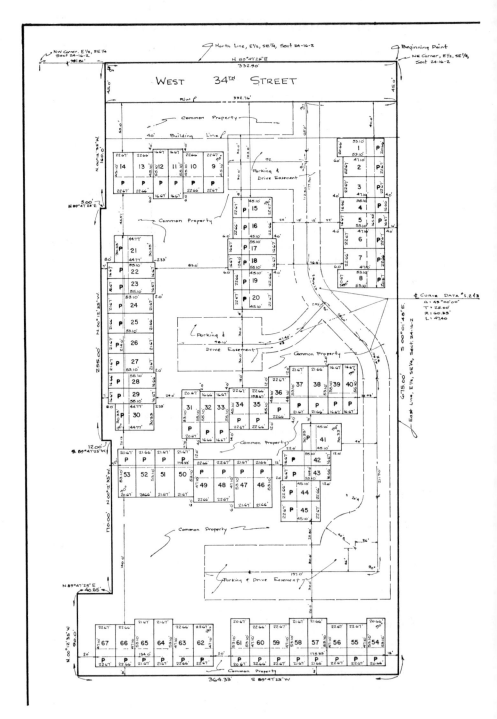

Fig. 15–2. Tara Town House on the Green addition—section 1.

I hereby certify that the within plat is true and correct and represents a survey of a part of the East Half of the Southeast Quarter of Section 24, Township 16 North, of Range 2 East in Marion County, Indiana, being more particularly described as follows:

Beginning at the Northeast corner of said Half Quarter Section, running thence South 00 degrees 01 minutes 48 seconds East upon and along the East line of said Half Quarter Section a distance of 675.00 feet to a point; running thence South 89 degrees 47 minutes 25 seconds West and parallel with the North line of said Half Quarter Section a distance of 364.33 feet to a point; running thence North 00 degrees 12 minutes 35 seconds West a distance of 90.00 feet to a point; running thence North 89 degrees 47 minutes 25 seconds East a distance of 40.55 feet to a point; running thence North 00 degrees 12 minutes 35 seconds West a distance of 170.00 feet to a point; running thence South 89 degrees 47 minutes 25 seconds West a distance of 12.0 feet to a point; running thence North 00 degrees 12 minutes 35 seconds West a distance of 255.0 feet to a point; running thence North 89 degrees 47 minutes 25 seconds East a distance of 5.00 feet to a point; running thence North 00 degrees 12 minutes 35 seconds West a distance of 160.00 feet to a point on the North line of said Half Quarter Section a distance of 991.81 feet North 89 degrees 47 minutes 25 seconds East of the Northwest corner of said Half Quarter Section; running thence North 89 degrees 47 minutes 25 seconds East upon and along said North line a distance of 332.90 feet to the place of beginning, containing 5.214 acres, more or less.

The area designated as "Common Property" contains 3.244 acres ±.

This subdivision contains 67 lots, numbered 1 thru 67 inclusive and "Common Property" as indicated. The size of lots and widths of streets are shown on this plat in figures denoting feet and decimal parts thereof.

This survey was made by me during the month of May, 19--.

Witness my signature this   day of   , 19--.

James E. Dankert
Registered Land Surveyor #4028

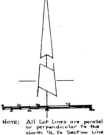

NOTE: All Lot Lines are parallel
or perpendicular to the
North 1/2, 1/4 Section Line
P = INDIVIDUAL PATIO
ON EACH LOT

TARA TOWN HOUSE
ON THE GREEN ADDITION
SECTION ONE

Fig. 15–2. Continued.

351

United States have sought to regulate density of residential development by requiring minimum lot sizes.

As a result of the heavy suburban building activities of the last decade, there is a growing scarcity of vacant sites for new single-family homes that are close to sewer and water lines in some of the larger metropolitan areas. The travel time between home and work has gradually been lengthening as the distance to new suburban developments increases and as automobile traffic congestion continues to rise. This has been responsible in part for the increased demand for apartments which are located near places of employment. Apartments have also become a part of various outlying suburban developments.

Large-scale, carefully planned developments are being undertaken to an increasing degree. Often, 600 to 1200 or more acres are involved. Such developments may include single-family units, garden and high-rise apartments, and town houses. Provision is made for recreation areas, shopping centers, schools, and related facilities.[7] In some cases entire cities are being planned from the beginning. The projected Columbia City will have 150,000 residents when development is complete. The site for this development is a 14,500 acre tract of land between Baltimore and Washington, D.C., which is projected to become a "new town." [8] Developments in the Washington-Baltimore area include King's Park West, 500 acres; Colton, 1,600 acres; and Reston, another "new town," 7,000 acres.

Problems of Land Development and Urban Growth

Subdividers and land developers have sometimes been criticized for lack of foresight in arranging for the orderly expansion of urban areas, for premature subdivisions, for the poor planning of new areas, for attempts to make excessive profits, for unsound financing plans, and for failure to establish sound regulations and controls.

Although land developers have contributed their share to present-day problems of land utilization, governments have been relatively inactive until recently in establishing the regulations necessary for orderly developments and in setting up a realistic framework within which competitive forces could operate.

Some progress has been made in recent years. Planning has been extended to cover metropolitan areas in some cases. Carefully developed plans for long-term growth have been worked out for a number of localities including both urban and rural areas. In some cases zoning may prescribe lot sizes of from one to four acres, and this is permissible if for health or safety purposes; however, if large areas are set up as a require-

[7] See John L. Schmidt and Arthur S. Goldman, "Design and Construction Advances Need Lender Support," *Savings and Loan News* (September, 1963).

[8] See statement by developer James W. Rouse in *Savings and Loan News* (May, 1964), pp. 40–41.

ment in order to limit growth, such regulations may be unconstitutional. Despite the progress that has been made, much remains to be done in this field.

Higher standards are being followed in many subdivision developments. These include larger lots, wider streets, better curbs and gutters, and improved storm and sanitary sewers and water mains. Increasing restrictions are being placed on private wells and sewage-disposal systems. The importance of larger-scale developments to reduce costs is being stressed, as well as reduction in the scattering of developments, and the need for expansion of community facilities to keep up with land needs. Regional planning and the coordination of public facilities on a metropolitan basis are being accorded increased attention.

The improvement of land development in the future will require the very best efforts of both public and private business administration. Recognition must be given to the development of a sound division of labor between government and private enterprises. Possibly new governmental devices will have to be developed in order to provide a sound framework within which the private developer can operate.

On the other hand, private practices must improve. We can hardly expect this to happen unless the necessary inducements are present. Private business practices respond more definitely to promises of profits and sound investments than to preachments by public-spirited citizens. Realistic recognition of this should help city planning commissions and other public bodies in their work.

Advancement in the field of land development will result chiefly from a many-sided attack on current problems by private enterprises and public agencies. In addition, the demands of the consumers as a result of higher housing and business standards will exert continuous, even though often indefinite, pressure toward better land development.

The importance of the consumer as a force toward improved standards is emphasized in this statement:

And there's still another direct influence to better land planning, design and the expanded use of newer and better materials, an influence that is already pushing the trend toward better quality construction. The influence: Today's buyer isn't being *forced* to buy a home. The shelter shortage is a thing of the past. Today's buyer demands higher quality and better design. If he doesn't find it one place, he'll look somewhere else. Tomorrow's home buyer will be no different. He'll also demand a bigger and better property for his dollar.[9]

SUMMARY

The terms *subdividing* and *land development* describe the activities of those firms and individuals engaged in the production of real estate resources. Decisions at this stage of operation have long-range importance,

[9] Schmidt and Goldman, *op. cit.*, p. 68.

since the manner in which these functions are performed has considerable impact on the eventual character of the property and of the community or neighborhood of which it forms a part. Developers and builders usually are interested in immediate or early sale of the properties involved, and their outlook is essentially short run. Users, investors, and property managers, however, typically take a longer-range view, since their interests are tied in with the development of the community and the future income-producing potential of the properties.

Although subdividers and developers are engaged in the production of real estate resources, each firm must arrange the financing of its own operations and the marketing of its own products. These products may be raw land, partially or completely developed lots, and perhaps buildings and other improvements. The timing of development and subdividing is of extreme importance in determining a project's success, and therefore should be based on careful market analysis.

Location, timing, and costs all are important factors in the production of real estate resources. Because of the typical reliance on borrowed capital, financial institutions and other investors exercise much influence on decisions to produce real estate resources. Governmental approvals also are important, particularly with respect to building permits, zoning laws, and insuring or guaranteeing of mortgages through FHA or VA if such arrangements are desired. Approvals also are required to insure conformity with local use and occupancy regulations and with public health requirements. The influence of the consumer of housing is highly important in developing improved standards.

QUESTIONS FOR STUDY

1. Suppose that you are planning the introduction of a proposed "Woodland Acres" subdivision. What market factors would you consider in determining whether or not this new subdivision might be successful?
2. What factors would be most important in determining the location of this subdivision?
3. Should you include commercial, residential, and recreational sites in the plan for the "Woodland Acres" subdivision?
4. Would you plan to include land for apartment houses as well as for single-family homes? Explain your position.
5. In your planning for the subdivision, what allowances should you make for traffic patterns? If the land is irregular in contour, how should the streets be laid out?
6. Outline the principal regulations that would help to assure the orderly development of a subdivision.
7. Why is timing so important in new land developments?
8. Make a list of the important costs involved in developing land.

9. Are greater public controls needed over private subdivision developments? Give reasons for your position on this question.

10. Are the interests of a land developer typically of a long-term or short-term nature with respect to a specific project? Explain.

11. What factors determine the way in which a tract of land should be subdivided into lots?

12. What are the most important items that should be included in protective covenants?

13. *Study Project 25.* (a) On what basis do you think the officials of the Flamingo Development Company decided that this land was ripe for subdivision? (b) Which of the three alternative land patterns would you choose? Explain your choice. (c) Would your choice of land patterns be any different if you were going to build instead of just subdivide? Explain. (d) How much would each lot cost under each of the three alternatives? (e) How many acres would you develop at one time: 10 acres, 20 acres, or all 40 acres? How would you decide? (f) Which additional deed restrictions would you include? Which deed restrictions would you exclude? Why?

SUGGESTED READINGS

CASE, FRED E. *Real Estate.* Englewood Cliffs, N.J.: Allyn & Bacon, Inc., 1962. Chap. xxvii.

FEDERAL HOUSING ADMINISTRATION. *Underwriting Handbook* (rev. ed.). Washington, D.C.: U.S. Government Printing Office, 1959. Sections 70401, 70494.

U.S. SAVINGS AND LOAN LEAGUE. *Construction Lending Guide.* Chicago: The League, 1964.

16

Production: Building

Relation of Building to Land Development

In the preceding chapter we considered the functions and some of the problems of the land developer and subdivider. We pointed out that in many instances building and land development were integrated operations, while in others they were carried on separately. Obviously, the completed product is composed of land and buildings, hence the best results are often achieved when the processes of land development and building are integrated and there is close coordination between them.

New real estate resources are the result of at least six processes: (1) *initiating*, (2) *planning*, (3) *land development*, (4) *building*, (5) *financing*, and (6) *marketing*. As we pointed out in the preceding chapter, all of these processes except building are involved in land development even if a project is undertaken solely for the purpose of marketing lots. When we include construction, however, many of these activities become more complicated.

The building process itself requires the performance of these principal functions: (1) *planning*, including the design and engineering of the building (this is chiefly the responsibility of the architect in order to meet the program requirements of the developer); (2) *financing*, including construction loans and financing the sale of the final product; and (3) *construction*, including purchase of the materials and equipment, employment of labor, and assembling and installing the materials and equipment. This is largely the work of the contractor and subcontractors and may be thought of as a fabricating or manufacturing process.

Construction Enterprises

The business firms engaged in construction range all the way from very small organizations to large companies operating on a regional, national, and in a few cases an international basis. General contractors and subcontractors are included. Lumber and building supply dealers form a part of this industry. Prefabricated house manufacturers and the manufacturers of building materials and equipment play a major role in the construction field. The firms in this industry, as in others, may be individual proprietorships, partnerships, or corporations. Syndicates may be set up for large projects.

Each of these business firms must establish its own objectives and manage its resources as effectively as possible in trying to attain its objectives. Its owners and managers must establish plans to achieve objectives, organize resources, and control operations. Leadership plays a big part in the success of enterprises in this field. Even in small enterprises, large amounts of money are involved. Hence, owners and managers must be able and willing to undertake the big risks that typically are involved. This often requires courage of a high order plus good judgment and organizing ability as well as a sense of timing.

Construction Decisions

As we suggested in the preceding chapter, a number of complicated factors are involved in decisions to undertake new land development programs. Such programs frequently include building as well as land development. Primary decisions are made by the owners of the land. Those who lend money to owners almost always play a major role in such decisions. Since long-term commitments usually are necessary, it becomes extremely difficult to estimate potential costs, returns, and risks with any degree of accuracy. Sometimes developments contemplate relatively quick sale and recapture of investment as in the case of a small subdivision and building operation with all properties designed for sale. In other cases, long-term investments are involved as in the case of an apartment house, shopping center, or office building.

Typically, the firms engaged in building activities have only a short-run interest in these projects. Such firms may have a general or a special contract for a construction project. But even in short-run periods many uncertainties exist. Costs may vary widely in the space of a few months. There may be sudden changes in weather conditions. Labor problems may cause expensive work stoppages. It may be impossible to get delivery of key materials. These are all parts of the risk undertaken by the building contractor when he assumes responsibility for a project.

In some cases, a builder will take a part of his compensation in stock of the new development. He then has both a long- and a short-term interest in it, the length of the term depending on the type of development. The interests of brokerage firms and bonding companies, however, is almost always short term in character.

Initiating

A real estate development may be initiated by an individual for the sole purpose of providing himself with a place to live. He will probably buy a lot, consult an architect, arrange financing, and make arrangements with a contractor, who will secure the necessary materials, equipment, and labor. Or the initiator may be an operative builder who is undertaking a new development for the purpose of building and selling houses or building and renting houses or apartments. An industrial firm may initiate a project such as an addition to existing plant facilities or the erection of new plants. A merchant may want to build a store. A private investor may develop a shopping center or an apartment house. A carpenter may decide to build a few homes for sale. Almost anyone with savings or credit may initiate a building project.

The size of the operation may range from a single house or the conversion of an old dwelling into several efficiency apartments to the development of an entire community. The resources available, condition of the market, risks, cost-return relationships, and objectives of the developer—all will affect the scope of the project. The Levitt organization, for example, has developed entire communities in Long Island, eastern Pennsylvania, and New Jersey. An entire town has been developed as a retirement community at Sun City, Arizona, by Del Webb. The developers of the Irving Ranch in California are creating a major city of some 93,000 acres. "New towns" such as Reston and Columbia City represent an important new trend in the building industry.

During recent years, prefabricated home manufacturers have become an important part of the building industry. They have been of major importance in the housing field but have also engaged in shopping centers and related developments. Building materials and equipment manufacturers have influenced the methods of both large- and small-scale on-site builders. Through research programs they have made improvements in the use of materials and in the efficiency of building processes.

Regardless of who initiates a building project, plans must be made, financing arranged, and construction carried out. In some instances the initiator may perform all of these functions himself. In projects of any size, however, specialists usually perform various parts of the process.

Planning the Building Operation

Planning is usually the work of the owner or developer and the architect designer or engineer. The developer determines the type, price range, and quality of structure. On the basis of this information, the architect plans the building. This includes the following activities: (1) schematic design including preliminary sketches and estimates of probable construction costs and time; (2) design development which comprises preliminary design drawings, outlining specifications, and probable cost estimates; (3) preparation of construction documents—working drawings, specifications, and all documents necessary for bidding and construction; (4) construction with the architect providing general supervision and project inspection.

The preliminary sketches which an architect prepares are diagrams of the building which give a clear picture of the proposed arrangement, showing the location and size of the rooms, the general appearance of the structure, the equipment to be included, and the position of the structure on the lot. Preliminary cost estimates are often made on the basis of these sketches. After definite agreement has been reached on all points between the developer and the architect, working drawings are prepared which show the exact size and location of all walls, partitions, and rooms, the material to be used at various points, and all details of construction. Specifications are then written which supplement the drawings, establishing the quality of materials and workmanship, and indicating how the work is to be executed.

Generally speaking, building operations fall into two categories: (1) those accomplished by a builder-developer-contractor employing an architect or a designer either on a fee basis or as a member of his staff; and (2) those accomplished by an individual who lets the work to a contractor but employs an architect to administer the contract for the owner, as in the case of a custom-built house project.

Letting Bids

Bids are usually invited from several general contractors, although contracts may be let without competitive bidding. If bids are invited, the contract is normally awarded to the lowest bidder, unless his figure is so low that there is doubt about his ability to do a satisfactory job. Bids may be taken on the following bases:

1. A fixed price for the entire project.
2. Cost plus a percentage for profit (usually 10 per cent).

3. Cost plus a profit percentage, say 10 per cent, but with a maximum limit established.
4. Cost plus a percentage with a maximum upper limit, with provision for dividing any savings between contractor and developer.
5. Cost plus a fixed fee.

Other methods may be used as well, but the above arrangements are typical. The fixed price method is used very widely. Contracts for mechanical work may be let separately with a general contract covering the rest of the project.

The Building Process

A single contract may be awarded to a general contractor, or various contracts may be let for specific parts of the project. If the former plan is followed, the general contractor typically parcels out certain phases of the work among subcontractors. In the case of some large projects, all of the work may be sublet. In either event, the construction process is seldom carried out by a single organization. The types of work for which subcontracts may be let include roofing, plumbing, lathing, painting, tiling, heating, electricity, and structural iron work. The general contractor usually reserves for himself such work as he is equipped to handle. This may be excavating, putting in foundations, masonry, carpentry, or other work. Figure 16–1 illustrates some of the interrelationships in building operations.

A subcontractor may be a building supply jobber or dealer, but more frequently such suppliers sell materials to the general contractor or to one or more subcontractors. Many materials are originally processed by building supply manufacturers, who sell them directly to contractors or through supply dealers. Restrictive practices sometimes surround these operations, as we shall see in a later section.

After all contractual agreements have been arranged and provision has been made for the required materials, the necessary labor force is hired and the actual work of construction is carried out. Many different types of labor are required even in the construction of a single-family dwelling. From twenty-five to forty-five crafts may be involved in relatively simple house-building operations. As many as eighty occupational groups may be engaged in a large-scale building project.

Because of the high degree of organization typical of building labor, the contractor and subcontractors frequently arrange for the necessary labor through a union official. Since the degree of labor organization varies from city to city, workers are sometimes hired directly. Contractors seldom maintain anything resembling a permanent work force, although a skeleton organization may move from job to job. Usually other laborers are recruited as needed for each job.

1. Most Typical Builder-Developer Arrangement

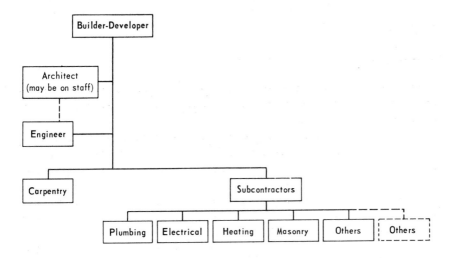

2. Custom-House Arrangement

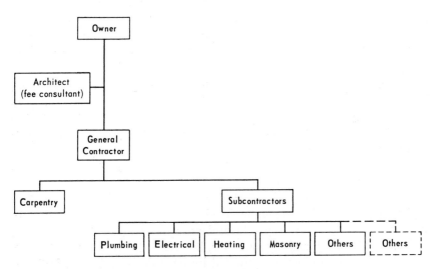

Fig. 16–1. Organization of building operations.

It has been estimated that skilled labor accounts for more than 70 per cent of all building labor. This is due in part to the fact that many workers are classified as "skilled" even though they may not perform skilled operations.

The building process is completed when the owner or developer accepts the structure as finished and final payments have been made. The period between the letting of contracts and the completion of construction may be as short as several weeks in the case of prefabricated operations. It may cover several months or even a year or two or longer for large projects.

Building Costs

Except for such prefabrication of structural parts or equipment as takes place, the "manufacturing" of a building occurs at the site. Hence, costs vary with local situations.

Architects' fees usually are 6 to 8 per cent of the cost of a structure, except on very small projects where the percentage is higher. Fees vary with services performed. When an architect performs "full services" and handles the job for a client, a fee of 8 to 10 per cent may be quite reasonable. In some cases an architect may be engaged on the basis of a one-time development cost plus royalties if the designs are to be repeated. A 1 to 1½ percentage of cost may be a reasonable fee in such cases.

Building costs vary widely between localities because of differences in the local availability of materials and resulting transportation costs. Furthermore, building costs vary greatly due to differences in climate. Not only do insulating and heating costs vary greatly from one part of the country to another, but so do the requirements for foundations, glazing, roofing, and many other items. In general, however, the market tends to accept those materials found locally.

The contractor may buy his materials and supplies in several ways. Usually the channels for distributing building materials are similar to those of many other products: from manufacturer to wholesaler or jobber to retailer and then to the consumer, who in this instance, however, is represented by the contractor.

In some cases manufacturers maintain control of the distribution process down through the retailing level; in others they sell to wholesalers who distribute through their subsidiaries or sell to independent dealers. The typical lumber dealer generally handles a wide variety of materials, though usually there are separate dealers in hardware, paint, wallpaper, and similar items. Plumbing materials, linoleum, tile, heating equipment, and electric wiring often are installed by local dealers. Larger builders, however, may absorb these functions.

Although the dealer serves the contractor in numerous ways, such as maintaining his inventory for him and frequently promoting business and helping to arrange financing, there are numerous instances of special arrangements which favor the more substantial builders or which limit in various ways the introduction of certain new products into a local market.

All types of labor in the building trades usually receive high wages on an hourly or daily basis. Approximately half of the cost of most structures is required to pay the labor bill. Because the degree of labor organization varies widely from locality to locality, there are wide differences in labor costs.

The actual cost of materials in place depends upon the efficiency of labor. When building is at low ebb, bricklayers tend to lay more brick than when jobs are plentiful. Some contractors, such as Levitt, subcontract all or nearly all work, putting it on a price basis; and the resulting in-place costs are often low even though the weekly wages of workers on such projects are among the highest in the building trades.

Other expenditures typically incurred in the usual construction project include costs of construction loans; building permits; workmen's compensation; liability, unemployment, and other types of insurance; social security taxes; sales taxes; contractors' overhead; and the maintenance of equipment. In some instances the payment of "side money" and bonuses represents substantial amounts.

Prefabrication and Industrialization

Recent years have seen rapid advances in the application of standardization and large-scale production methods to the building industry. There are three principal types of developments which are tending toward the industrialization of building. They are (1) simplification and standardization of parts by manufacturers; (2) adaptation of factory methods to production at the site by large-scale contractors and operative builders; and (3) prefabrication of virtually complete structures for assembly at the site.

Standardization of house plans and designs has been progressing for some time and has brought economies through reduction in costs of design and increased efficiency of labor.

A number of preparatory operations are now carried on away from the site with manufacturers preparing precut lumber, roof framing, stairs, prehung doors and windows, cabinets, and similar items. In addition, much equipment assembly is completed prior to delivery to the site.

The standardization of plans, designs, and materials, as well as more manufacturing of parts away from the site, has brought economies to nearly all types of builders. In addition, large-scale and operative builders have adapted factory methods to production at the site, and prefabricators manufacture virtually complete units for assembly.

Large-scale builders now arrange for workers to move from one operation to another, organizing the work with a relatively high degree of efficiency. In part, this has been made possible by the introduction of a number of laborsaving devices including power excavating, grading, and hoisting machinery; electric saws and drills; concrete, mortar, and plaster mixers; spray guns for paint; and power sanders. The introduction of some of these laborsaving devices, however, has been resisted by the unions, as has the use of precut and prefabricated materials which are delivered to the site for assembly.

Prefabrication has made significant progress in the recent years. Economies of substantial proportions have been achieved both in production and distribution processes. Great progress has also been made in purchasing materials and equipment on a large scale for assembly in factories and delivery as a more or less complete package. Prefabrication has probably led to greater mechanization of traditional building processes as well, not only for houses but also for large-scale projects such as office buildings.

During the period of postwar shortages, prefabricated houses gained a wider acceptance than they had previously. With the solution of various manufacturing problems, greater emphasis is being given to the marketing and financing of prefabricated houses. It is highly probable that prefabrication will dominate the small-house field in the future unless very substantial progress is made in construction at the site. Many local building codes do not now exclude prefabricated houses. Some union rules, however, tend to cancel the economies resulting from these production methods.

Marketing Practices of Prefabricators

Local dealer representatives have become the primary method of marketing prefabricated homes. This permits local acquisition of land and the utilization of and adaptation to local labor and supply conditions. It also aids in the developing of local sources of financing. The future of prefabrication both in terms of advance in the production process and in distribution will depend to a large extent on the development of financing arrangements which meet the requirements of this industry.

Specific arrangements for local dealerships vary widely. Some manufacturers control them very closely, and others have rather informal working relationships with their dealers. Integrating of manufacturer and local dealer activities is especially important in connection with advertising and sales promotional campaigns. Considerable progress has been made in overcoming consumer resistance; additional advances will be required in this area.

One of the major problems of local dealers in the prefabricated housing industry arises from the fact that land cannot be prefabricated. As we saw in the preceding chapter, the costs of acquiring and developing land are often very great. Sometimes the financial requirements for land development are beyond the resources of local dealers and beyond their ability to command the necessary credit through traditional channels. Hence, a few prefabricated house manufacturers have established special financial programs to assist local dealers in their programs of acquiring and developing land.

Financing

Ordinarily the contractor does not finance construction. Usually he provides only the working capital for current operations either from his own funds or from bank or individual loans. In some cases a pool is made up by the builder and other private investors, with profits being divided and the arrangement dissolved at the completion of a project. In most other manufacturing processes, of course, the producer finances the operation. In the case of construction, however, the owner or developer and the ultimate consumer may both become involved in the financing of production.

A fairly typical arrangement is that of the construction loan under which a financing institution agrees to advance funds at various stages of the building process. Upon completion of building, the construction loan is typically supplanted by a mortgage. In other cases the permanent mortgage is recorded and payments are disbursed at various stages of construction. In some cases a commitment is given with provision for merging of short-term construction loans and long-term financing.

In the case of residential building, the operative builder usually arranges for individual mortgages for his houses and assigns the mortgage to the purchaser. Many lending institutions engage in construction financing in the hope of securing mortgages. The use of FHA "conditional commitments" to insure loans usually provides the owner or developer with sufficient credit to enable him to finance all or substantial portions of construction. Commitments from the Veterans' Administration for loan guarantees are often used in a similar manner.

Industrial plants are usually financed by the firms who own or intend to use them. Commercial properties may be financed by private investors or by owning or using enterprises. Insurance companies are gaining in importance in this field. Again, there is often a fusion of construction and long-term financing. The sale and lease-back arrangements have been used widely as a method of financing commercial properties.

Some larger financial institutions, such as insurance companies, now develop properties and rent them. In such cases they finance the entire operation from start to finish. Except for the latter type of arrangement, most of the financing of construction is cumbersome. This is due chiefly to the fact that the property rather than the credit of the developer or contractor is the principal security. Laborers and subcontractors are protected by mechanics' liens, an arrangement which also reflects this situation. Thus, financial institutions can exert great influence on construction operations because of their dominant position in providing the necessary credit advances.

Building Industry Trends

Despite its problems the building industry has made progress in a number of directions in recent years. Of special importance are advances in (1) technology, (2) engineering and architecture, and (3) management. Problems persist, however, in a number of areas including labor, materials distribution, and government-business relationships.

Technological advances include the development of new products, improved uses of old products, and more efficient production methods resulting from new machinery and prefabrication. Product changes range all the way from better heating and lighting equipment, air conditioning, and cooking and other kitchen equipment to improved uses of glass, better insulation, and the use of aluminum covering for exteriors. Technology may soon give us even better basic systems of construction, improved finishes for both interior and exterior application and such mechanical devices as automatic cleaning equipment, luminous walls, and "instant cooking." Even the sewerless toilet may not be too many years away.

Engineering and architectural advances include improved space planning, more efficient layout of buildings, better combination of building materials, and many related developments. Even prefabricated houses in the lower price ranges have been given the benefit of good architectural design and planning.

Management has improved the processes of planning, organizing, and controlling operations. Longer-range planning has characterized the activities of subdividers and builders. Seasonal fluctuations have been reduced by careful scheduling of work so as to allow for colder weather operations. The increased diversity of materials and products used in construction has necessitated better managerial planning and scheduling. Many builders have been able to improve their organizational arrangements through better division of work and more effective supervision. Controls have improved in part because of rising costs and in part because of tax considerations. Inventory controls have been improved in the construction industry but also there have been advances in inspections, in cost accounting, and in budgeting.

In the earlier postwar years, the building industry probably suffered from too much prosperity. As competition became more intense, greater emphasis was placed on improved products and methods and on cost cutting. Still, much remains to be done. The industry suffers from restrictive building codes, restrictive labor practices, and from its dependence on the development of regional supporting facilities by government to allow for new land development. Many builders, of course, continue to follow outmoded practices. Informal agreements sometimes result in price fixing and the reduction of competition.

Because of restrictive practices, the introduction of new products and methods often is retarded. There has been some tendency to revise building codes in order to introduce greater flexibility, but many localities follow requirements that are unduly restrictive. Building operations have been limited by the slow rate at which local governments and other agencies have constructed new streets, roads, water and sewer systems, and provided schools and other community facilities.

Although problems persist, the building industry can take credit for significant advances in recent years. It holds numerous opportunities for young people who have energy, imagination, and a willingness to pioneer.

Labor Problems

Building labor is highly organized in most cities. Many organizations continue to follow craft rather than industrial lines, although war and post-war experience has brought some modifications in this respect. Jurisdictional disputes are among the more difficult problems of the building industry and at least some of these would be eliminated if labor were organized on a different basis.

The attitudes of labor unions in the building trades have been traditionally antagonistic toward laborsaving machinery and devices. There has also been insistence that production be limited to prescribed speeds. Featherbedding rules are common. While one can hardly blame the individual worker for resisting the introduction of laborsaving machinery and for not wanting to work himself out of a job, union leaders have been slow to recognize that these policies are shortsighted and not in the ultimate interests of the workers. In the long run, the earnings of workers are limited by their productivity. Laborsaving devices aid in the process of increasing output per worker. If this were not the case, China and India would have the highest wage levels in the world, since they have few laborsaving devices in use and the proportion of labor to capital employed in production is high.

Professor Sumner Slichter once made the following comment in regard to labor organizations in the construction industry:

Powerful unions have existed in the building trades for well over a generation, but no important thinking on the difficult problems of housing has originated with unions in the building industry. Few officers of these unions have taken the lead in bringing about modernization of building codes, in fostering city planning, or in sponsoring better municipal government—all needed to encourage the construction industry.[1]

This statement is still substantially true today.

Developers and contractors are largely at the mercy of labor because of the nature of the building process. The success of a construction project depends to a large extent on the efficiency of labor. It is not difficult to sabotage a job. Physical property offers an easy target for destruction or threats of destruction in order to enforce demands.

The building trades have succeeded in establishing high hourly or daily wage scales. In part this is an attempt to compensate for seasonal and cyclical variations in construction activity, and in part it is the result of a high degree of labor organization and the strategic position of building labor which enables it to enforce its demands.

Limitations on the number of apprentices who are trained, the relatively disorganized condition of some employers, the small scale of a number of building operations, and the policies of trade-unions in resisting the introduction of laborsaving devices all help to explain the success of labor organizations. Not only are wage scales high, they are relatively inflexible downward. Even during depression periods, wage rates tend to be maintained at high levels. Productivity of workers, however, tends to increase in such periods.

It is probable that considerable benefit would result from a more flexible wage scale, both for labor and for the builder and consumer. It may be that some form of annual wage arrangement is the answer to these problems. The nature of employment in the building trades, however, with laborers moving from one job to another as projects are finished, is a real obstacle to the establishment of an annual wage.

Improved labor relations would be highly beneficial to the construction industry. Ordinarily the number of wage disputes is higher in this field than in most others, and the elimination of some of the lost time and the added risks which result would benefit worker and employer alike.

Materials Distribution Problems

The materials distribution system now results in highly competitive pricing. The emergence of "cash and carry" lumberyards and builder-dealer merchandising connections contribute to the intensity of competition. Because of his dominant position in many local communities, the materials dealer must be reckoned with by manufacturers and builders

[1] Sumner H. Slichter, *The American Economy* (New York: Alfred A. Knopf, Inc., 1948), p. 61.

alike. In some cases dealers organize and establish more or less fixed prices and working agreements, thus reducing competition. The combination of the functions of dealer and builder in recent years, however, has led to some progress. In this arrangement, the owner or developer deals with only one firm rather than with a number. Such an arrangement is often favorable to the individual home builder.

Government and Building

As we have suggested, the building codes of a number of cities make excessive requirements and hinder the introduction of new structural materials. In addition there are fire-prevention, elevator, and related codes, as well as occupancy regulations. Codes are seldom changed as often as necessary to keep abreast of industrial developments. Also, the administration of building codes frequently leaves something to be desired.

Licensing laws for architects, contractors, engineers, and even workmen in certain building trades are in force in a number of states. While their objectives are desirable, they often lead to restraints and virtually monopolistic practices. The property standards and minimum construction requirements set up by the FHA have had desirable effects, but have also added to the regulatory problems faced by the building industry. The Federal government has influenced building through improvement of financing practices as a result of the work of the Federal Home Loan Bank System, the Federal Housing Administration, the Veterans' Administration, and the Federal National Mortgage Association. The Bureau of Standards and the Forest Products Laboratory have helped to develop and improve materials. They also establish better criteria for judging the performance of materials. The Housing and Home Finance Agency, the FHA, Department of Commerce (especially the Bureau of the Census), and the Federal Home Loan Bank System have prepared much information about housing markets. The recently established Department of Housing and Urban Development has major opportunities in this field.

Relatively little has been done toward eliminating restrictive and monopolistic practices in the building industry. Local zoning laws and city planning regulations also affect building activities, and local tax burdens must be reckoned with constantly. The laws governing the sale, transfer, and marketing of new real estate developments often are not adapted to present-day requirements.

Place of the Building Industry in the National Economy

The building industry is one of our largest, and is mainly responsible for the quantity and quality of our real estate resources. A number of other industries are dependent wholly or partially on building, such as

Table 16–1.   Principal Categories of Construction, 1950, 1960 and
Medium Projections for 1980 and 2000
(billion 1960 dollars)

Category	1950	1960	Medium Projection 1980	Medium Projection 2000
Total construction	58.6	76.2	166.3	348.4
New construction	42.2	56.6	130.1	280.9
Maintenance and repair	16.4	19.6	36.2	67.5
of which for residential construction	6.2	7.2	10.8	14.7
Residential new construction including additions and alterations	19.6	22.6	54.7	126.4
Nonresidential new construction	22.7	34.1	75.4	154.5
Private new construction	32.8	40.6	90.2	196.8
Public new construction	9.4	16.0	39.9	84.1
Components of public new non-residential construction:	9.1	15.3	37.2	77.8
Schools and hospitals	2.3	3.2	5.0	7.4
Highways	2.6	5.5	16.1	34.6
Military and industrial	.6	1.8	5.1	12.3
All other (water, sewerage, etc.)	3.6	4.8	11.0	23.5

Source: Resources in America's Future, Appendix Table A4–3.

lumber, cement, steel, brick, building stone, glass, hardware, and others. The solution of many of our housing problems must await improvements in the building industry. Building activity is one of the main determinants of prosperity and depression and is an important index of general business conditions. Because of the importance of the industry in our economy, great advantages would result from improvement in the efficiency of its operations and from a lessening of the cyclical and seasonal fluctuations to which it has been subject in past years.

Changes That Lie Ahead

A recent statement prepared by John L. Schmidt and Arthur S. Goldman summarizes some of the major changes that are going on in the building industry, particularly as it relates to housing. Among other statements, the following is especially significant.

American home building has progressed more in the last decade than it did during the first 50 years of the 20th Century. But even though we today enjoy the highest standard of housing in the world, we still stand at the threshold of a whole new era of better housing. We stand at this threshold today, but we have not crossed it because technology is far, far ahead of practice.

Admittedly, successful home builders are introducing new materials and new building methods. But still, home building remains the most fragmented industry in the country, one that is hamstrung by zoning ordinances, building codes, labor difficulties and the inertia of habit. The result—a gap between what architects and engineers know *how* to do and what builders are *permitted* to do.

The gap between knowledge and practice also is widened by the paradox of poor public acceptance. Here we find a typical house buyer who "demands" newer, better and more economical methods and materials, yet one who tends to label new and better materials or methods as "cheap or flimsy substitutes." But one thing is encouraging—the search for cost savings. The search for cost savings is probably home building's greatest motivation to change; we can be thankful that this is a never-ending search.

The attack on costs during the next 10 years will focus on the untapped potential efficiencies of conventional construction and on development of other systems of building.

How and in what ways will this attack on building costs take place? We can expect significant changes on three fronts: The ways we use land; the methods used in construction; and the quality and character of design.[2]

Is the Building Industry Having Its Industrial Revolution?

The large amount of experimentation going on in the building industry may be comparable to the experiences of other industries during the earlier phases of their industrial revolutions. As a result of this experimentation, the building industry has already taken on quite a different appearance in the past decade or so. This is probably the most important reason for optimism in regard to the potentialities of this field.

As Lyle C. Bryant has pointed out,

Industrial revolutions are never accomplished overnight. As we look back over industrial history, however, the striking fact is that almost every industry has had its "revolution," each heralded by a period of seething unrest and experimentation much like what we see in the building industry today.[3]

SUMMARY

The building process consists of the planning, financing, and construction of buildings upon improved land. Land development and building operations often are combined. Construction firms range in size from very small to very large builders. Construction is a risky business, involving substantial sums of money.

Almost anyone with savings or credit may initiate a building project, whether he is an individual desiring a residence or a large operative builder. Whether the project is a single residence or an entire community, it must be planned, financed, and constructed. Various specialized parties such as architects, contractors, and subcontractors are involved in the physical operation, while financing usually is arranged through one or another type of financial institution. Decisions about construction are

[2] John L. Schmidt and Arthur S. Goldman, "Design and Construction Advances Need Lender Support," *Savings and Loan News* (September, 1963), p. 67.
[3] Lyle C. Bryant, unpublished manuscript.

made primarily by property owners and developers, subject to the veto of lenders and the influence of various specialists, notably architects and engineers.

In recent years, the building industry has realized advances in technology, engineering and architecture, and management. Of particular importance has been the development of simplification and standardization, the use of factory methods of production at the building site, and prefabrication of materials for assembly at the site. Materials distribution, governmental factors, and labor relations remain as critical problem areas. In labor, extensive organization of the building trades into many different craft unions, and the instability of employer-employee relationships have tended to result in jurisdictional disputes, featherbedding, and resistance to technological advance. Significant changes may be anticipated in methods of using land and carrying out construction as well as in quality and character of design.

QUESTIONS FOR STUDY

1. What are the main processes involved in the development of new real estate resources?
2. Describe the principal steps in planning for the construction of a single-family residence. Would the planning be any different in the case of an apartment building?
3. What are the two principal types of building operations in terms of the role of the architect?
4. What is the relationship of the subcontractor to the contractor? Why does the contractor sublet parts of his contract?
5. Why do building costs vary between regions of the country?
6. Explain the important advantages of prefabrication; the main advantages of large-scale on-site construction.
7. Indicate ways in which the marketing practices of prefabricated housing manufacturers differ from those of other builders.
8. How might labor practices in the building industry be improved?
9. Would you favor the establishment of an annual wage in the building industry? Why or why not?
10. What are the principal advantages of building codes? In what ways may building codes hinder construction activities?
11. Can you suggest ways in which the financing of building construction might be improved?
12. Outline the principal current trends in the building industry. What are the principal changes that appear to lie ahead?
13. *Study Project 26.* A discussion in the *Architectural Forum* presents a variety of construction projects that have been planned. They are indicative of recent trends in architecture and in building construction. After studying these projects, outline the trends in building and real estate development that you believe are exemplified by these projects.

14. *Study Project 27.* Do you agree that house building is no longer a "one man show"? Explain your position.

SUGGESTED READINGS

KRATOVIL, ROBERT. *Real Estate Law* (4th ed.). Englewood Cliffs, N.J.: Prentice-Hall, Inc., 1964. Chap. xxii.

LANDSBERG, HANS H., LEONARD L. FISCHMAN, and JOSEPH L. FISHER. *Resources in America's Future.* Baltimore: The Johns Hopkins Press, 1963. Chap. iv.

MARTIN, PRESTON. *Real Estate Principles and Practices.* New York: The Macmillan Co., 1959. Chaps. iv–v.

NATIONAL AERONAUTICS AND SPACE ADMINISTRATION. Conference on Space Age Planning, Chicago, 1963. Section 23, "The Prime Contractor's Role in the National Space Program," by John Leland Atwood.

U.S. SAVINGS AND LOAN LEAGUE. *Construction Lending Guide.* Chicago: The League, 1964.

17

Marketing: Brokerage and Promotion

Decisions in Real Estate Marketing

The basic decisions in regard to the marketing of real estate are made by present and prospective property owners who must decide whether to buy or sell, at which prices, on what terms, and at what time. Sellers or buyers may be individuals, business firms, or governmental or institutional agencies. The motives behind decisions to buy or not to buy, or to buy more or less, or to sell or not to sell, or to sell more or less may arise from a variety of sources.

Of major importance are objectives, which in turn may vary widely. For example, the owners and managers of a business firm may decide to buy land to allow for future expansion, an individual investor may be concerned with increasing the return on his capital or with improving his tax position, or the head of a family with providing a better home for his wife and children. The same objectives may motivate both purchases and sales, as for example a business firm may sell to another in order to move to a new location, but at the same time both may thus assure space for future growth. Of course, opposing objectives may also lead to purchases and sales.

Other factors that may influence decisions of this type may include: (1) Anticipated changes in the trend of general and local business conditions; for example, differences of opinion may exist about trends of expansion or contraction or the rates at which either may occur. (2) Anticipated changes in real estate markets or in specific sectors of such markets may lead to decisions as to property purchase or sale. (3) Prospective changes in money market conditions may have a strong impact on such decisions. (4) Probabilities of change in location influences may be important—for example, belief in the rapid expansion of a new subdivision or in the future of a new shopping center may lead to decisions to buy; belief in no expansion or slow expansion may lead to decisions to sell. (5) Finally, there is always the matter of the alternatives open. A property owner may be forced to liquidate his holdings quickly in order to meet pressing personal or business problems. A business firm may be forced to buy a particular property because it is the only one which will allow it to expand at its location.

Other factors may play a part as well, including probable changes in government or political conditions, anticipated changes in technology, possible population movements, international uncertainties, and the like. Those we have outlined give some indication of the factors that are likely to play a major part in decisions to buy or sell real property.

Because the processes of buying and selling real estate are complex and the market is not well organized, the decisions of prospective buyers and sellers often are facilitated, influenced, and translated into action by brokers and sales personnel. We pay special attention to their work in this chapter. Our attention will center on such topics as the major characteristics of real estate marketing, real estate brokerage and sales organizations, listing procedures and arrangements, relationships between owners and brokers, processes and methods involved in the selling of real estate, promotion programs including advertising and public relations, sales contracts, financial factors in sales, title transfers, and various possibilities for improving the marketing of real estate.

Characteristics of Real Estate Marketing

The marketing of real estate involves all of the processes of bringing together buyers, sellers, and users of real properties or property services. It frequently includes assistance in making financial arrangements to carry out sales or leases. Often provisions for the management of properties are involved as well. Buyers and sellers, lessors and lessees, of course, can negotiate directly and often do. Brokers, however, play a major role in many real estate transactions—serving, essentially, as negotiators and counselors.

Real estate brokers play a more important part in the marketing of real estate than do brokers and middlemen in many other fields. In part this is due to the relatively disorganized character of real estate markets. It is often difficult to bring buyers and sellers together, and the broker performs an important service in facilitating this process.

Because of the nature of the market there is wide room for bargaining, since prices are not set with the same precision as in many other types of markets. The original asking price of a seller of property may be much

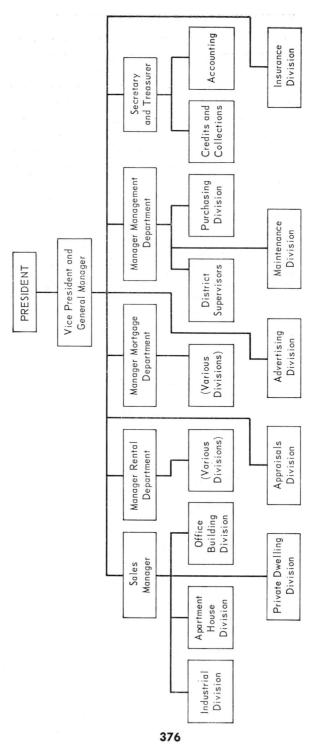

Fig. 17-1. Organization of a large real estate company.

higher than any bids that can be secured. Gradually the broker works out adjustments. He tries to find the potential user or investor who can secure maximum advantage from the property. He informs the seller of sales prices or rents for comparable space. In some cases he may be careful to keep the potential buyer and the seller apart until the final closing. In other cases he will bring them together and skillfully guide the interview.

Since it is often difficult for sellers and buyers alike to secure adequate information about property values, current prices and rents, financing arrangements, and the like, the broker performs the function of supplying such information. In addition, the broker helps to avoid errors in the complicated process of selling real property. As Hoagland has aptly pointed out:

> It is sometimes thought that all a real estate broker needs to start him in the business is a fairly presentable automobile and a decent suit of clothes. It is true that many enter the business with little more than this. Their exit is likely to be as easy as their entrance. The successful broker knows the city in which he operates and particularly the neighborhood in which he hopes to make sales. It is axiomatic that he cannot know too much about the property he has for sale or rent. On occasion he may say too much, but he can never know too much. He must have the capacity for winning the confidence of those with whom he deals. Few buyers or sellers of property know its value or can acquire the facility of learning it. They must lean heavily upon the representations of the broker. They will not do this unless they trust him.[1]

Many large corporations include real estate departments in their organizations for the purpose of arranging for the use and management of the properties that are needed for their operations. Such departments often work with local real estate brokers in making arrangements for the sale, purchase, leasing, or financing of real properties. The bulk of the work of brokers, however, is carried out for individuals, families, small businessmen, and small investors. Because of their knowledge of the local market, familiarity with properties, and skill in negotiating, brokers are usually able to market properties to greater advantage than those who own them. The work of brokers may range from simple transactions such as the sale of a single-family home to complicated arrangements involving the sale, financing, and leasing of large blocks of properties.

Selling Organizations

The organizations engaged in real estate brokerage include many types, ranging from one-man offices to brokerage departments of large real estate firms. A large real estate firm will usually have brokerage, management, leasing, insurance, mortgage, and appraising departments. In addition there may be separate departments for advertising, collections, accounting, and legal work. (See Fig. 17–1.) Both the brokerage depart-

---

[1] By permission from *Real Estate Principles*, 3d ed., by Henry E. Hoagland, p. 286. Copyright, 1955, McGraw-Hill Book Co., Inc., New York.

APPROVED STANDARD FORM
INDIANA REAL ESTATE ASSOCIATION, INC.
2625 N. Meridian St.   Indianapolis 7, Ind.

LISTING CONTRACT

To ..Neighborhood Realty Co...............................August 5..............19....

In consideration of your listing for sale and undertaking to find a purchaser for the real estate described on the reverse side of this contract, I or we hereby grant and give you the exclusive right and authority to sell or exchange the same for a period from August 5......19....to....November 3........19....., and represent that no other exclusive agreement is now in force with any other realtor or broker.

In the event you find a purchaser ready, willing and able to buy said real estate, or should said real estate be sold by or through you, ourselves or otherwise, during said time price or terms and upon the terms named on the reverse side of this contract, or for any other price or terms or consideration acceptable to me or us, I or we hereby agree to pay you as commission a sum equal to five per cent of the sum for which said property is sold or exchanged; but not less than $100.00, and you are hereby authorized to accept an earnest money deposit with any offer to purchase said real estate. Said deposit may be retained by you until settlement is made. Should purchaser fail to complete said purchase said earnest money deposit shall be applied first to your advertising and other expense and the balance shall be divided equally between us. I or we also agree to do and to perform all that may be necessary to enforce the contract made with the purchaser for the property described herein and collection of any money due.

It is agreed that you, or your representatives and all prospective purchasers shall at all reasonable times have access to said premises and appurtenances located thereon for the purpose of inspecting the same.

I or we agree the price stated herein includes all mortgages, unpaid special assessments and any balances due for furnaces, or miscellaneous equipment now on or attached to the premises.

If said real estate is sold or exchanged within four months after the expiration of the term of this agreement to any person, firm or corporation with whom during the exclusive period of this listing you, your representatives or myself or ourselves had negotiations relative to the purchase of said property for said price stated herein, I or we agree to and upon terms acceptable to me or us, I or we agree to pay you a commission equal to five per cent of the gross sales or exchange price thereof, provided, however, that this extension clause shall not be applicable and binding during the term said real estate is relisted with some other licensed realtor under an exclusive listing contract upon or after the term of this listing agreement.

This contract is enforceable without relief from valuation and appraisement laws and with attorney's fees.

I or we also agree to furnish a complete abstract of title showing a good and merchantable title to said real estate, or a Title Insurance Policy for the sale price of said real estate. I or we also agree to execute and deliver a good and sufficient warranty deed or land contract for the same to whom you direct. To induce you to enter into and accept this contract I or we hereby warrant that the undersigned is or are the sole and only owner or owners of the property above described and that the within mentioned encumbrances are the only and all encumbrances against said above described property. I or we further represent that the statements on the back hereof are made by me or us and that the same are true and are a part of this agreement. I or we have read the foregoing contract and thoroughly understand the contents thereof, and having received a duplicate thereof, and agree to give possession on or before........30........days after final closing of transaction. You are hereby authorized to put a "FOR SALE" sign on said real estate.

This contract is binding also upon my or our heirs, administrators, executors or assigns.

....
Joe Doakes............................Owner

....
Mary Doakes............................Owner

The undersigned accepts this authority to sell and agrees to the terms of said contract

this....5th....day of....August........................19....

Neighborhood Realty Co.

By:..........Realty..............., Salesman

Approved Form — INDIANA REAL ESTATE ASSOCIATION, INC.

IMPROVED PROPERTY

Street No. 3420 North Delaware .... City Indianapolis

Legal Description Lot 58 in John Platt's Addition to the City of Indianapolis, as per plat thereof in Plat Book 29, Page 112, in the Office of the Recorder of Marion County, Indiana.

Size of Lot 100 x 200	Kind of Roof Shingle Foundation Cement Block
Which Side of Street West	Front Porch Yes Rear Porch Yes
Type of Home 1-story Bungalow	Bath, Kind 1 Full
Built of Frame with Wood Siding	Heated by Oil Cabinet Type
When Built 1925	City Water Yes Gas Yes Electric Yes
Kind of Floors Hardwood	Septic Tank No Sewer City
Kind of Trim Yellow pine with fir doors	Garage Rear Storm Windows Yes
Built-in Features Kitchen & Breakfast Room Cabinets	Front Drive Conc. Walks Kind Cement
Fireplace in Living Room	Insulation Ceiling Yes Water Heater 30 gal. gas
Plaster or Yes Dry Wall	Street Paved Yes Water Softener No
Open Stairway to Basement	Assessed Value $6,750.00
Rooms, 1st Floor Bed Rms.	Taxes per Annum $386.40
Rooms, 2nd Floor None Bed Rms. None	Mortgage $7,650.00 Int 5½ %
Closets, 1st Fl. 4 2nd Fl. None	Monthly Mgt. Paym'ts $85.00
Venetian Blinds Yes Screens Yes	Mortgage The Indiana National Ban(k)
Decoration Painted	Bal. Due on Land Contract $ None
Sleeping Porch None	Principal None Interest None
Attic None Basement Full	Paym'ts on Land Contract None
Grade Entrance Yes	Holder of Land Contract None
Will Exchange for No exchange	Fire Insurance $15,000., Exp. Jan. 1,
Terms of Possession 30 Days	Price $18,000.00
May we put up a sign? Yes	Terms Cash or cash to balance
REMARKS:	of mortgage which may be assumed.

Listing Agent Neighborhood Realty Co.

ment of a larger organization and the one-man office perform the functions of securing listings, advertising, selling properties, arranging for the closing of deals, and related activities. In the smaller organization the broker, often with the aid of a secretary or assistant, will perform all of these functions himself. In larger organizations the broker will have a number of salesmen in addition to office personnel; and he may have specialists in charge of legal, advertising, and appraising work. The salesmen may work under the direction of the broker or a sales manager, and they may specialize in residential, business, or industrial properties.

Usually we refer to the owner of a real estate agency as a *broker*, and to those who assist him in the marketing of properties as salesmen. A Realtor is a member of a local real estate board which is affiliated with the National Association of Real Estate Boards. The term *Realtor* is copyrighted by this organization and may be used only by authorized persons.

Listing

Whenever an owner of real estate employs the services of another to assist him in the sale of a property, he enters into an agency or brokerage agreement in which he lists the property for sale. The legal rules governing the relationship between an owner and a broker are a special branch of the law of agency—every broker being an agent, although not every agent is a broker.

The relationship between the owner and broker is established by an agreement between the parties. Such agreements may be oral or they may be written contracts. (See Fig. 17–2.) In a majority of states, agreements between principal and broker need not be in writing, although written agreements are preferable and some states have set up definite statutes requiring that such agreements must be in writing.

The authority given to a broker by the owner may be of a general or a special nature; for example, if the broker is to manage an apartment or office building for the owner, the agency will be general, but if the owner lists a piece of property with the broker for sale, the agency is usually special. Ordinarily, the duty of a broker is merely to find a purchaser who is ready, willing, and able to purchase in accordance with the terms laid down by the owner.

Other authority may be given, such as the right to show the property, to put up signs, to advertise, or even to sign the contract of sale. If the agent departs from his authority, the owner may be liable; nevertheless,

---

Fig. 17–2. Listing contract. (By permission from *Indiana Supplement to Law of the Real Estate Business,* by Harold F. Lusk and George F. Bloom, Bureau of Business Research, Indiana University, 1959—approved by the authors, 1966.)

if the principal or the agent has acted in such a manner that his action would be reasonably believed to have been authorized, as interpreted by persons in the community where the agent acted, or even though the agent has exceeded his authority and there has been no reliance, the principal is responsible if he ratifies the agent's act. If the owner does not ratify, the broker may be responsible to the third party.

The broker is expected to act in good faith always and to exercise reasonable care and diligence. If higher prices are offered than are asked, the agent is obliged to indicate this fact to the owner and not to use such knowledge to his own profit. A universally accepted rule of agency is that an agent cannot serve two principals. This rule applies to brokers. Thus, a broker cannot represent both the buyer and the seller unless both know of the arrangement and consent to it. Then the broker must act with absolute impartiality.

Types of Listing Agreements

The agreements which are drawn up between an owner and a broker may be of various types, the most important being (1) open listing, (2) exclusive agency, and (3) exclusive right to sell contracts. In addition, an arrangement called "multiple listing" exists in some cities.[2]

Such agreements, when entered into, will usually include, in addition to the parties to the contract: a sufficiently accurate description of the property to make it possible to prepare a sales agreement, and the terms of the sale, including the broker's commission, the length of time for which the property is listed, and any special conditions to be fulfilled.

In an open listing contract the owner may employ as many brokers as he chooses. A time limit may or may not be set. The broker making the sale collects the commission; but the owner may sell the property himself, in which case no commission is paid. If a contract is drawn up in which the designated broker is the only agent of the owner, an exclusive agency agreement exists. In such cases the broker receives a commission if sale takes place as a result of the efforts of anyone but the owner. A third type of agreement is provided in the exclusive-right-to-sell contract. Under such an agreement the broker is the only person who may sell the property (except for the owner) during the period of the agreement, and he ordinarily is entitled to a commission even if sale results from the efforts of the owner himself.

Multiple Listing

While most owners prefer to dispose of their properties as quickly as possible, they often find it difficult to decide between an open listing,

[2] See Harold F. Lusk, *Law of the Real Estate Business* (rev. ed.; Homewood, Ill.: Richard D. Irwin, Inc., 1965), pp. 7–11.

ML # 2120	MUNICIPALITY Rumson, N.J.	ADDRESS 20 Ross Place	SECTION

NAME Harrison Rhodes & Helen D.	PHONE 842-2222	B.R. & B. 5 3½	PRICE $60,000

CONST. Brick & Frame	STYLE Colonial		AGE 6 years
L. B. Listing Broker's Name	LOT FR. 200 SIDE 200 REAR 200		AC Approx. 1

ROOMS	LOWER LEVEL	1ST FLOOR	2ND FLOOR	3RD FLOOR		
					GAR. Attached CAR. 2	
					HEAT Hot Water Baseb'd FUEL Oil COST $400	
HALLS		8x26			F. P. In Living Room & Den	
L. R.		15x26			LAUNDRY Off Kitchen	
D. R.		15x15			SCR. Combin. Aluminum S. S.	
KIT.		14x18			APPLIANCES Electric Range, Wall Oven, Dishw'r	
DEN		15x18			PERS. PROP. Carpeting in L. Rm.	
GAME RM.	15x22				TAXES $1,265 YR. 19	
SUN RM.					MTGEE Local Bank BAL. $30,000	
M.B.R.			15x22		RATE VA - FHA - CONV.	
2nd B. R.			12x16		PAYT $214.94 (pr.&int.) REM. YRS. 20	
3rd B. R.			12x14		WHY SELLING Relocating	
4th B. R.			10x12		POSSESSION 60 Days	
ADD B. R.		Maid's			OPEN HOUSE 10/5/	
BATHS		1½	2 Tile		APPRAISERS (Note: Usually 3 brokers chosen)	
PORCH		14x20			CONDITION Excellent	
PATIO		12x20			KEY AT Lock box (Call first) EXP. DATE 1/4/	

BASEMENT Full and Dry

Owner's Address If different from above:

REMARKS: Master bdrm. has dress. rm., 2 closets; game rm. is panelled; patio is flagstone & has new awning. House is fully air-conditioned. Kitchen has breakfast area. Grounds are beautifully shrubbed; many tall trees.

LOT 4 BLOCK 20 MAP Borough of Rumson	ASSESSED LAND $9,000 IMPROV. $36,000

IN CONSIDERATION of the services to be performed by the undersigned REALTOR, herein called Broker, a participant in the RED BANK AREA MULTIPLE LISTING SERVICE, and/or by other participants in the said Service, the undersigned owner, herein called owner, does hereby authorize and give to Broker the exclusive and irrevocable right to sell the above described property at a price of $ 60,000   and further agrees to pay the member selling said property a commission of six per cent of this or any other price accepted by the undersigned.   In the event said property is sold, traded or exchanged through any source during the term of this agreement, the undersigned agrees to pay the aforesaid commission to the member listing said property or his nominee.   The authority to sell shall automatically terminate six months from the date hereof. Commission will be due and payable at title closing. Above member reserves the right to cancel this contract if the listed price is 15% or more above the evaluation made by said members.

The undersigned hereby acknowledges receipt of this agreement and receipt of the New Jersey Attorney General's interpretation of the Fair Housing Act.

DATE: June 1 .... 19......

George Bassett   _Harrison Rhodes_ .... L. S.
(Witness)   (Owner)

Accepted by: _Francis Doakes_   _Helen D. Rhodes_ L. S.
(Listing Broker)   (Owner)

It is mutually agreed that no FOR SALE signs shall be displayed during the term of this agreement.

Fig. 17–3. Multiple listing form. (Courtesy Red Bank Area Multiple Listing Service, Red Bank, New Jersey.)

which engages the interest of a large number of brokers, and an exclusive-right-to-sell agreement, which places responsibility on a specific broker and assures him a reward for his efforts. In order to secure the major advantages of both methods, some real estate boards have set up "multiple listing" systems. Where such arrangements exist, the broker with whom a property is listed also lists it with other members of the organization. If he sells the property himself, he receives the full commission; if another sells it, the commission is split on a predetermined basis between the selling broker and the one with whom the property was listed. In some cities, multiple listing systems are compulsory for registered brokers or those who are members of a local association or board—that is, every member of the board is required to list all properties with the organization. More generally, however, an optional system exists. The use of the multiple listing system preserves many of the advantages of the exclusive-right-to-sell contract, and at the same time extends the scope of the market by including as many brokers as possible.

Fred E. Case has said in this connection:

> One of the oldest and most successful multiple-listing agencies is the Southwest Branch of the Los Angeles Realty Board established in 1921 and in continuous operation since that time. In any particular year, depending upon market conditions, this board may have anywhere from 3,000 to more than 15,000 listings from which its members can make sales. The volume of business transacted through this board runs into millions monthly since the board estimates their average listing value at $10,000. The Board bases its success on the following principles: (1) a listing must be submitted in writing within thirty-six hours after it is signed, (2) no listing may be reported sold and removed from the active sales list until both the buyer and seller have signed, (3) listing terms cannot be changed if they increase the difficulty of selling, (4) no listings can be canceled in less than forty days unless the owner pays the full commission rate, (5) the board cannot interfere in the operations of any member's operations, and (7) all brokers must deal directly with the owner and not through the multiple board.[3]

Broker and Owner Relations

Except where a broker's employment is definitely indicated as exclusive, it is assumed that a nonexclusive agreement exists. In such cases as many listings may be made with as many brokers as the owner wishes, all being terminated in various ways, such as the destruction of the property, bankruptcy, insanity, or death of either party, and by mutual consent or by revocation. Thus, in most situations, the owner may revoke the broker's authority without incurring any liability, unless he does so in order to avoid paying a commission after the broker has introduced him to a prospect.

In cases where there is doubt of the broker's right to a commission, it is necessary for him to show that he was actually employed; that he was the "procuring cause" of the sale; that he exercised good faith; that he produced the customer on the seller's terms; that the customer was ready, able, and willing to buy; that the contract was consummated within

---

[3] Fred E. Case, *Real Estate* (revision of *Modern Real Estate Practice*) (Englewood Cliffs, N.J.: Allyn & Bacon, Inc., 1962), p. 376.

the time limits, if any were set; and that a completed transaction was brought about if the contract required it.

Securing Listings

A real estate broker must have listings before he can sell any property. The listings may be thought of as his merchandise, as the stock of goods on the shelves of his store. In ordinary periods, relatively little difficulty may be encountered by a broker in securing listings. His business acquaintances, the owners of property with whom he has dealt, and former customers may provide him with an adequate stock of merchandise. There are times, however, when brokers must make special efforts to secure listings, especially when the market is active.

Brokers may advertise, indicating their desire for listings; they may call on or write letters to property owners who may be willing to dispose of their properties; they may canvass management firms to determine whether rental properties are for sale; they may canvass financial institutions who hold foreclosed properties or who have clients with properties for sale; and they may engage in numerous other related activities. In some cases, brokers have carried on house-to-house canvasses inquiring whether home owners are interested in selling their properties. There has been much argument among brokers as to the effectiveness of this doorbell ringing technique.

Some real estate firms combine brokerage with property management. In such a combination the property management activities of the firm may yield a number of listings for the brokerage department. Since the firm is serving the owners through the management of properties, the owners are very likely to ask the same firm to sell such properties as are to be placed on the market.

All the above suggests that a broker's acquaintances in the business community, his reputation for efficient service, and the quality of his advertising are of major importance in securing listings. These same factors are also of basic importance in the selling of properties once they are listed with him.

Terms of Listing Agreement

It is not only important for the broker to secure listings; he must also obtain them under favorable conditions. If an owner lists a property at a price which is far above the market, there is relatively little chance for the broker to market it, regardless of how much effort and money he spends. Real estate brokers often say, "A property well listed is half sold." By this they mean that the property is listed at a price and on terms which are reasonable in relation to current market conditions.

Sometimes also they mean that the period of the listing is long enough to allow the broker to carry out a careful sales campaign.

In some cases, brokers accept listing on terms that are not realistic. As a result, the properties cannot be sold; later, negotiations have to be carried on with owners and prices and terms adjusted to levels that should have been worked out originally. Some brokerage offices refuse to accept listings unless prices and terms are realistic. This saves the time of salesmen, eliminates renegotiations, and speeds up the turnover of property listings. Other offices will accept listings on almost any terms in order to prevent competitors from getting them, then renegotiate if possible before the end of the time involved in the original listing agreement. The first type of policy is probably to be preferred. The latter works reasonably well in a period when markets are expanding rapidly but in other periods properties listed on nonrealistic bases can waste sales effort and advertising expense, and result in painful renegotiations and general frustration.

The obtaining of listings under favorable conditions is often the primary factor in the success of a real estate brokerage organization. In some cases, a broker may ask several of his salesmen to give an independent estimate of the price that can be secured for a property before it is listed for sale. The salesman who calls on the owner to arrange the listing is armed with this information. Records of sales in the area in which a property is located and information about sales prices for comparable properties are usually considered before a listing is arranged. The public records may be checked to determine if possible the amount that the owner paid for the property. In these ways brokers are often able to avoid delays in the sale of property because the original asking price is too high.

Brokers sometimes arrange for an independent appraisal in order to establish a reasonable asking price. Some real estate boards set up committees for this purpose in order to facilitate the work of brokers. Brokers prefer that properties be listed under exclusive-right-to-sell agreements for periods of at least ninety days. In the case of special-purpose property a longer period may be desirable. Typically the broker's commission is 5 or 6 per cent of the sales price, although a lower percentage is sometimes paid in the case of more expensive properties.

The Process of Selling Real Estate

In boom periods the selling of real properties may amount to little more than taking orders. When demands are high and brokerage offices have long lists of live prospects who are anxious to secure desirable space, relatively few sales problems are encountered. Such periods are relatively rare, however, and even in boom periods there may be many people who would like to buy but who are unable to meet the prices demanded by owners.

Usually, therefore, every brokerage office will maintain a list of prospects. These are secured from answers to advertisements, from acquaintances of the broker or his salesmen, from tenants in buildings managed by the firm or others, from financial institutions, and from other business firms. Prospect files are kept alive by frequent analysis in order that dead cards may be eliminated and live ones substituted.

The primary job of the real estate broker or his salesmen is to match properties and customers. Only in the case of new construction can the property be tailor-made to fit the customers' needs, whether a residence, a store, or a factory building is involved. Matching properties and customers requires a detailed knowledge of the property on the one hand and the needs of the customer on the other. It is important to recognize that *exchange must be a mutually beneficial proposition if an enterprise system is to function.* Too often people think that in a business transaction one of the parties must gain an advantage. Or salesmanship is thought of as a series of hocus-pocus procedures and mumbo-jumbo phrases whereby the customer is forced to act contrary to his wishes or best interests. Both of these ideas are fallacious.

Exchange must be mutually beneficial; both the seller and the buyer must gain or expect to gain, otherwise no exchange will take place. The buyer must want the property more than the money and the seller must want the money more than the property. The broker's job is to arrange a meeting of minds between buyer and seller, and basically that means finding a property suitable to the buyer's needs at a price that is mutually agreeable to both parties.

In some cases other factors also are involved. For example, the broker may find it necessary to help the buyer arrange for financing; legal difficulties may require solution; tax problems may complicate the seller's or the buyer's situation; it may be necessary to arrange for extensive alterations or repairs; or special arrangements may be necessary for closing the deal, such as escrow agreements and the like. In some cases, because of emergencies, it may be necessary to buy or sell quickly.

Qualifications of Brokers

This brief summary of the processes involved in selling real estate suggests that a broker and the salesmen who work for him need a broad knowledge of a number of subjects and a detailed knowledge of real estate and the factors which have a bearing on real estate values. A broker should be able to analyze properties in terms of their adequacy for the uses which a prospective customer may wish to make of them. Similarly, he should be able to analyze the customer's needs and match these with appropriate properties. He needs a detailed knowledge of real estate financing, subdividing and land development, building activities, the local real estate market, and general and local economic trends which bear on real estate values. He should know enough real estate law to recognize those situations which require competent legal advice. In addition, he needs a knowledge of office organization and procedure, commercial correspondence and business communications, advertising media and methods, and related information.

Much has been said about the importance of a pleasant personality for a real estate broker. While tact, good humor, and the ability to persuade are important, there are many successful brokers who have less than the average share of these qualities. Tact and good humor cannot take the place of knowledge, judgment, imagination, organizing ability, and hard work.

Selling Methods

What we have said above may suggest a low regard for salesmanship. This is not the case. The right kind of salesmanship has a very important place in the equipment of the broker and in the whole process of marketing real estate. By the "right" kind of salesmanship we mean the correct analysis of properties and customers' needs, the presentation of *facts* rather than opinions about properties, and the exercise of enough imagination to help the customer see the possibilities of the properties under consideration.

As has been indicated, selling starts with listing. Realistic pricing and related sales terms are a primary factor in real estate sales. Following listing, a selling strategy needs to be worked out. The broker or a member of his staff needs to think in terms of potential buyers, people who may lead to potential buyers, competitive properties, alternative plans for developing sales, the selection of the alternative offering most promise, and then action in terms of advertising, sales promotion activities, brochures, sales kits, and the like.

Basically, the selling of real properties involves exactly the same processes used in selling other types of goods and services. Specific methods vary widely, depending on the type of property being marketed, the personality of the salesman, and the kind of customer. To a large extent selling is a psychological process about which it is difficult to generalize. Methods that are successful if employed by one salesman will fail if used by another. Every successful salesman must study himself as well as the property and the customer. He must determine in advance how he can best bring about a meeting of minds.

Methods which will help to bring about the sale of one type of property may be ineffective if used in connection with another. Also, the types of selling methods which will produce desired effects in the case of one group of customers often fail if used in dealing with another group. Probably the only statement with general validity is that adequate information, carefully and honestly presented, is the most useful selling device available.

For the real estate salesman, adequate information about the subject property includes a knowledge of the exact location, size, and shape of lot and detailed data about the building or buildings involved, especially with respect to such items as age, type of construction, number of stories, floor area, and potential monetary or direct returns. He should be acquainted with the district in which the property is located and understand the relationship of the district to the growth and structure of the city. In addition he should be familiar with sales which have recently been made of similar types of property, the values of competing properties in the area, and the trends of prices and rents for properties of the type under consideration. All of this information has little value, however, unless the salesman applies it to specific sales problems. Basically, this means property analysis with a view to matching the customer's requirements.[4]

Presenting the Information and the Property

The steps in a sale are sometimes listed as (1) attention, (2) interest, (3) belief, (4) conviction, and (5) action. In some cases a sixth, satisfaction, is added. Sometimes these steps are reduced to (1) attention, (2) interest, (3) desire, and (4) action.

Regardless of how divided, the sales process is not really a series of separate steps. It is a continuous process in which the customer's mind may have passed through the earlier steps listed above before he sees the salesman. The good salesman directs the interview with the customer, but only in rare cases will he undertake to dominate it. He will try to lead the customer to a final decision by suggestion, by providing additional information, and by answering objections.

He may lose his leadership in a sales interview if he fails to keep up with the customer, turns the interview into an argument, or lets it become a visit. Analysis of the customer will help to avoid such mistakes. Another cause of failure in selling is losing the confidence of the customer. Misrepresentation of facts, attempts to conceal undesirable features rather than admitting them frankly, and exaggeration, all lead to loss of confidence. Such simple things as failure to keep appointments may undermine confidence. Loss of confidence also results if the salesman is unable to

---

[4] For a more detailed discussion of this topic see *Portraits of Success* (Chicago: The National Institute of Real Estate Brokers, 1964).

provide adequate information. This is often avoided by the use of property briefs and sales kits.

Ordinary courtesy and good manners are essential to the successful salesman. Lack of consideration, overbearing attitudes, and the like may be very costly. For related reasons, every salesman should use nontechnical language. Even businessmen are not familiar with all of the technical language used in real estate transactions. The house buyer may be puzzled by such terms as *equity, elevation, cubic content, masonry construction, amortization,* and many other terms which are used commonly by those associated with real estate. The avoidance of technical language prevents confusion in the mind of the customer and facilitates the selling process.

The Property Brief

Some brokers follow the practice of preparing a folder which presents pertinent information about a property. This folder is usually referred to as a *property brief.* After a customer has been shown or told about a property, this brief may be left with him in order than he may study it at his leisure. Property briefs may be simple or elaborate, depending on the type of property involved. Usually such a brief will contain one or more photographs of the property; a diagram of the floor plan; the dimensions of the building or buildings and the lot; descriptions of the equipment in the buildings; information about income and operating expenses, including especially data on taxes, insurance, and special expense items; information about the condition of the structure, its age, and probable economic life; information about the neighborhood or district; and financial information including the price, the terms of the sale, mortgages outstanding, and the like.

A property brief is designed to answer questions in the customer's mind after the first or an early sales interview has ended. In addition, such a brief may keep alive the interest of the customer, or he may show it to someone else who may become a prospect in turn.

The Sales Kit

The sales kit contains the essential information about the properties which a broker has for sale. It may be thought of as a series of property briefs. However, the information is designed for the use of the salesman rather than the customer and may not be presented in as elaborate a manner as in the property brief. In some cases, duplicate information sheets are prepared for a sales kit so the customer may be provided with a copy.

In addition to information about specific properties, a sales kit (which may be nothing more than a loose-leaf notebook) may contain maps of the city or of specific neighborhoods or districts, information about tax rates, data on insurance rates, types of financing plans, amortization tables, indexes of construction costs, and other information which may be valuable to the salesman.

Promotion

We use the term "promotion" to include all types of activities and programs intended to aid the sales process. In the real estate field this will encompass advertising, open houses, displays and related efforts, and public relations programs. We emphasize particularly the areas of advertising and public relations in these discussions.

Advertising and public relations serve the dual purposes of securing listings of properties to sell or rent on the one hand and of facilitating the selling or renting processes on the other. In most types of enterprises advertising and public relations activities are used primarily as an aid in selling. In the real estate business such efforts also help to secure the merchandise for the broker to market. Similarly, a real estate financing institution by its promotion efforts will appeal to both savers and borrowers.

Effective public relations programs require two-way communications between a firm and its public. It is important for the firm to know what the public thinks of it and its programs. Then proper steps can be taken to correct undesirable impressions or to add to points of strength. In all types of promotion programs it is well to remember that ideas have wide appeal and that originality is often the key to success.[5]

Evaluation of public relations programs is extremely difficult. If coupons are used in advertising, it is possible to estimate the impact of the advertisements involved. In most cases, however, it is not possible to measure very closely. In a final analysis, success depends on the total volume of business generated over a period of time.

To be effective, promotion programs should be planned with a view to furthering the objectives of the organization. Formulation of effective programs requires careful analysis of the firm's business and its market. It is necessary also to budget carefully the resources that will be allocated to the various phases of the programs that are evolved. In short, a careful *promotion strategy* is needed. This will cover such factors as the type of programs to be undertaken, the size of the effort, relationships between programs, and relations to the competitive situation. For example, if it

[5] See Jean C. Halterman and Bert C. McCammon, *Individuality in Retail Advertising*, Small Business Administration, Small Marketers Aid No. 23 (Washington, D.C.: Government Printing Office, 1957).

is anticipated that a competitor will expand his promotion efforts, it may be desirable to expand even more and to start sooner. Or expansion of a competitor's advertising program, for example, may be countered by a reduction in advertising effort but by expansion of direct sales programs. As is true in other fields, promotion strategy depends to a considerable extent on anticipated changes in market conditions, public attitudes, governmental influences, and programs of competitors.

The fundamental questions of *what* is to be sold, *where,* and *to whom* require analyses of the properties that are for sale or rent, the services that may be provided by the firm, and the markets in which the firm will compete. Careful market analysis, as outlined in Chapter 12, often is helpful in planning promotion programs. Different types of programs may be indicated depending on whether the market is expected to advance, decline, or continue at the same level.

The economic soundness of promotion programs and especially of advertising has been debated for some time. Some economists have taken a highly critical position relative to advertising and to many other forms of promotion. False and misleading advertising, of course, is harmful. All types of promotion, however, should not be condemned on this account. New products could hardly be introduced and brought to a wide market without promotional efforts. The function of informing customers and potential customers about a product is important. In some cases people appear to prefer the glamor and reassurance of advertising programs to cheaper prices.

Types of Real Estate Advertising

Real estate advertising may be classified according to purpose, media used, and the form in which it is presented. In terms of purpose, three main types may be distinguished: primary institutional, name, and specific.

Primary institutional advertising pertains to real estate in general and has for its chief purpose the creation of favorable public attitudes toward real estate, investments in real estate, or the people engaged in the real estate business. From a competitive standpoint every type of commodity is in competition with every other type for a slice of the consumer's dollar. Institutional advertising is designed to aid real estate in this competition. Such organizations as the National Association of Real Estate Boards, local real estate boards, the American Bankers Association, the U.S. Savings and Loan League, the Mortgage Bankers Association, and various associations of builders carry on advertising of this type.

Name advertising has for its main purpose the popularizing of the name, activities, and reputation of a specific real estate firm.

Name advertising is designed to appeal to the owner who may wish to list his property for sale or rent, to the saver and borrower, to the contractor and property buyer or user. Such advertising may include spot announcements on radio programs, business cards in the classified advertising columns of newspapers, or the sponsoring of special publicity programs.

For example, a firm may distribute quarterly or monthly "Letters" containing comment on economic and business conditions. Such letters may form the basis for news releases as well.

Specific advertising pertains to individual properties and property services. Its purpose is to aid in the selling or renting of a specific property. The most widely used type is classified newspaper advertising, which usually combines name and specific appeals.

Hoagland points out, however, that some advertising which appears to be specific may in fact pertain to several properties. He says,

What appears to be a presentation of facts about some specific property may be only a blind advertisement, the contents of which could apply to any one of several parcels listed with the broker. In answer to inquiries which may be generated by the advertisement, a quick-thinking broker may decide which of several properties he wishes to show the prospect.[6]

Advertising Media

The principal advertising media for most realtors to consider are newspapers, radio, television, signs, posters, direct mail, streetcar or bus cards, office displays, and a miscellany of items such as blotters, matchbooks, calendars, letterheads, and so forth.

Since the market for many types of real estate is local in nature, the newspaper fits such advertising requirements rather specifically. Newspapers reach a heterogeneous group of readers. The reading life of a newspaper is very short; usually it is read as soon as received and then discarded. The average time spent in reading it is about twenty minutes.[7]

Magazines have a longer reading life than newspapers and are often read more carefully. However, few magazines are directed toward a specific local market, and hence products which are sold in national or regional markets are more likely to be advertised in this medium.

Thus, industrial properties are likely to be advertised in magazines that reach various industry groups, farm properties in farm journals, and resort and recreation properties in magazines stressing outdoor activities, sports, and recreation. Advertisements relating to properties that may appeal to retired people are found in a number of magazines.

[6] Hoagland, *op. cit.*, p. 324.
[7] C. H. Sandage and Vernon Fryburger, *Advertising: Theory and Practice* (5th ed.; Homewood, Ill.: Richard D. Irwin, Inc., 1958), pp. 440–45.

Display and classified advertising are the two main kinds which appear in newspapers and magazines. Real estate firms use classified advertising to a predominant extent, although in special cases display advertisements are used. Preferred space in a newspaper is usually considered to be the right-hand column on the right-hand page, the front or back page of a section, and the positions next to reading matter. Such spaces often command extra rates.

There are various advantages and disadvantages to advertising in morning or afternoon papers or in daily or Sunday editions. Much real estate advertising is concentrated in the classified sections of Sunday editions, since greater circulation may be provided, readers have more leisure time, and in the case of residential properties much of the "shopping" is done on weekends. The Sunday editions combine many of the advantages of the newspaper and magazine media for the real estate advertiser.

Direct mail advertising includes letters, folders, booklets, cards, leaflets, and the like. It is the most selective of all types of advertising.[8] However, it is relatively costly in terms of cost per reader, but selectivity may make such costs relatively low. Effectiveness of direct mail advertising depends on the copy used and especially on the mailing list which is prepared. In some cases direct mail is sent to persons of influence such as financial executives and others who are in a position to refer customers.

Mailing lists may be based on prospect files, names of people visiting open houses, respondents to advertisements, city directories, members of civic clubs, and the like. In some cases mailing lists for specific purposes may be purchased.

Radio and television are the most recent major media, with the latter currently achieving phenomenal results for many advertisers; but both are less selective than newspapers.[9] Television affords the additional power of demonstration. Short announcements or spots on local stations are preferable for most real estate purposes. Programs, especially on television, quickly reach prohibitive costs. Use of either or both of these media should be carefully coordinated with other advertisements for maximum effectiveness.

"For Sale" or "For Rent" signs on properties are among the oldest forms of real estate advertising. They have been generally successful. Usually they carry the broker's name, office location, and telephone number. "Sold" signs are sometimes used to attract future listings. A suburban operator north of Chicago found signs pointing to, and briefly describing, his subdivision were his most effective media.

Posters are used in connection with the sale of subdivisions or the renting of space in larger buildings. Car or bus cards are often used to advertise a real estate firm rather than specific properties.

---

[8] Albert W. Frey, *Advertising* (3d ed.; New York: The Ronald Press Co., 1961).
[9] Sandage and Fryburger, *op. cit.*, pp. 424–35.

Displays are not used widely in the real estate field. Some brokers display in their offices photographs of properties which they are marketing. A few use window displays. Often displays at home shows or other occasions are utilized. These types of advertising may be effective, but they reach limited audiences and hence may be relatively costly.

Many real estate firms use calendars as a form of name advertising. Some make use of novelties, blotters, and similar devices.

Motivation Research

In recent years, advertising specialists have given considerable attention to motivation research as a means of finding out why some advertising messages are more effective than others. Through motivation research, attempts are made to determine why prospective buyers react as they do to products or services or to the advertisements used in attempting to sell them. For example, are people more interested when considering the purchase of a home in shelter, comfort, conveniences, or in the prestige of home ownership? Why have colonial style houses had such a strong appeal over many years? Is this because many people think of a little white house in an attractive location, perhaps with a white fence around it, when they think of a home? Through motivation research, attempts are made to answer questions like this about consumer preferences.

A recent example of the utilization of motivation research in the real estate field is found in "A Report on Attitudes of Realtors, Home Owners and Prospective Home Owners." [10] This study, conducted late in 1963, revealed that the home owners of today differ in some respects from those of yesterday. Home ownership is currently viewed as an investment rather than in terms of a permanent, deep-rooted family association. Although the home has kept the traditional values of thirty years ago such as security, shelter, privacy, independence, pride of ownership, and the like, the owner tends to view his home today more as an investment, a form of saving, and a means of building an equity.

Motivational research techniques were used in this study to uncover ways to understand the ultimate consumer of real estate better and to gain a better perspective on his feelings toward the purchase of a home and the assumption of a mortgage, as well as his attitudes toward lending institutions.

Public Relations

The term "public relations" may be used in such a broad sense as to include almost every type of activity that a firm or the members of its

[10] Study conducted by Marplan, a division of Communications Affiliates, Inc., of New York and sponsored jointly by the Savings and Loan Foundation and the U.S. Savings and Loan League.

staff may undertake. Many public relations programs try to develop a broad understanding between the business firm and the public it serves or the public at large. Such understanding requires that two-way communication be established and maintained between the firm and its public and the public and the firm.

As a result of such a program, those who operate a real estate firm should be able to determine what the public thinks of it, where its points of strength and weakness may lie, and the types of programs that will add to its strength and shore up its weaknesses.

The primary purpose of most public relations programs is that of winning the approval of the community and the public. This may be done in a variety of ways. In the real estate field, special attention is often given to community activities, especially those that are likely to lead to community betterment such as work on the solution of tax or other government problems, assistance in land planning or zoning programs, or help in the improvement of schools, parks, and other community facilities. Those in the real estate business usually have information and experience of a type that enables them to make real contributions to the solution of such community problems. Such efforts may bring favorable public reaction to the firm, develop close association with community leaders, and generally assist other aspects of the firm's promotion programs.

Publicity Programs

A real estate firm may be able to publicize many of its activities or those associated with it through the news columns of newspapers or radio or television news broadcasts or in related ways. A regular program of providing news releases may be very productive if carried out with imagination and efficiency. The following events may have news value if stories are prepared properly for release:

1. The sale or lease of an unusual property
2. Announcement of a new building program
3. Special or unusual arrangements for financing sales
4. Office expansion or announcement of a new location for an office
5. Promotion of personnel
6. Firm activities designed to recognize unusual services of its personnel
7. Volume of sales or rentals for a quarter or a year
8. Personal activities of staff members, especially of a professional type, such as attending conventions, study groups, special courses, institutes, and real estate board or other trade association activities
9. Community service of officers or staff members
10. Sponsorship of home shows

11. Modernization and repair programs
12. Any activities relating to the improvement of housing or living conditions

Best results are secured if the job of preparing and releasing publicity is assigned to one member of the staff or if the broker makes it a special part of his own activities. Whoever handles publicity must become acquainted with the editors, financial editors, or real estate editors of local papers and those who prepare and present the news programs of local radio and television stations. Sometimes local and national trade association publications provide outlets for publicity releases as well.

Contracts

When a buyer and seller are brought together, the broker's function may be completed. However, he may be authorized to act for either party in drawing up a contract of sale, or he may give advice during this stage of the transaction. Once such a contract has been drawn up, the broker may collect his commission even though the transaction is not completed.

After the broker has brought seller and buyer together, a purchase-and-sale agreement is usually drawn up. Of course, a sale of real estate may be made without a preliminary contract, the seller executing and delivering a deed and the buyer paying the purchase price; but in practice such transactions are rare. In some cases the agreement is a land contract or a contract for deed, which may be a method of selling real estate on the installment plan. Sometimes the buyer secures an option to purchase, which is an agreement to buy a stipulated property at a certain price within a designated period. For this option the buyer pays a certain sum, which is usually applied on the purchase price if the transaction is completed. In some cases exchange agreements are drawn up in which properties are traded, rather than sold for money. Exchange agreements differ little from ordinary contracts of sale; but they are double in form, and the price is paid in whole or part by property.

Buyers and sellers may also be brought together by auction sales, which may be voluntary or involuntary. In voluntary auction sales, the terms of sale are written in advance. After the property is sold to the highest bidder, the transaction becomes a private matter between him and the owner. Involuntary auction sales usually result from the desire to satisfy a lien. Such sales must be public, adequate notice must be given, and various legal formalities must be satisfied.

The drawing up of a sales agreement is an important step in the selling process, since it is the first evidence of a meeting of minds between the buyer and seller. Contracts should be carefully drawn. It is always wise to arrange a written statement which contains all of the items about which

APPROVED STANDARD FORM
INDIANA REAL ESTATE ASSOCIATION, INC.
Marott Hotel Arcade—2625 North Meridian Street—Indianapolis, Indiana

OFFER TO PURCHASE REAL ESTATE

To___Neighborhood Realty Co._____, Realtor

___Indianapolis_____, Indiana

September 3_____, 19___

The undersigned, hereinafter called purchaser, hereby agrees to purchase from the owner, hereinafter called the seller, through you as broker, the real estate known as No.___3420 North Delaware_____.___St., in the City (or town) of_____Indianapolis_____, County of_____Marion_____, State of Indiana, the legal description of which is:

Lot Numbered Fifty-eight (58) in John Platt's Addition to the City of Indianapolis, as per plat thereof in Plat Book 29, Page 112, in the Office of the Recorder of Marion County, Indiana,

and to pay as the purchase price therefor the sum of

Seventeen Thousand and 00/100 -DOLLARS ($_17,000.00___)
payable as follows:
One Thousand and 00/100 -DOLLARS ($_1,000.00___)
as earnest money deposited with the broker herewith, which shall be applied on the purchase price at the closing of this transaction, and the balance of the purchase price shall be payable in accordance with Paragraph___2___as hereinafter set forth:

PARAGRAPH 1 (SALE BY DEED) The balance of the purchase price shall be paid in cash upon delivery of warranty deed.

PARAGRAPH 2 (SALE BY DEED ASSUMPTION OF MORTGAGE) A down payment of
Nine Thousand Three Hundred Fifty and 00/100 - - - - - - - - - - -DOLLARS ($_9,350.00___),
of which the earnest money is a part, subject to a mortgage now of record in unpaid amount as of___June 30,___19___ of
Seven Thousand Six Hundred Fifty and 00/100 - - - - - - - - - - - DOLLARS ($_7,650.00___),
interest at_____-%, monthly payments of $__85.00___, including principal and interest_____,
which the grantees agree to assume and pay at date of closing.

PARAGRAPH 3 (SALE BY CONTRACT) The balance of the purchase price shall be paid as follows:

A down payment of_____DOLLARS ($_____)
of which the earnest money deposit shall be a part, and the balance of

_____DOLLARS ($_____)
shall be paid under the terms of the approved Indiana Real Estate Association, Inc., form of LAND CONTRACT to be executed by the parties at the closing of the transaction, the interest rate therein to be_____%. Monthly payments of $_____

PARAGRAPH 4 (SALE ON OTHER BASIS) If neither Paragraphs 1, 2, or 3 is applicable, then upon the following terms:

Purchaser shall have complete possession on__or before 30 days after delivery of a General Warranty. Deed. Failure by seller to surrender possession on date of delivery of deed or land contract shall not make the seller a tenant of purchaser, but in such event seller shall be obligated to pay purchaser $_10.00___ per day as liquidated damages for each day seller holds over, and this provision shall not deprive purchaser of any other legal or equitable remedy available under the law.

Rents, if any, and interest on mortgage indebtedness, if any, shall be prorated as of date of closing.

Insurance shall be (prorated) (cancelled) as of date of closing.

Taxes shall be prorated as of the date of closing, that is to say, seller shall be charged with and pay taxes on said real estate payable in the current year and for that portion of taxes payable the following year calculated as of the date of closing, and purchaser shall pay all taxes subsequent thereto. Seller shall be charged with and shall pay all delinquent payments on assessments for public improvements, if any, and all payments on such assessments currently due. Purchaser shall pay all assessments for public improvements becoming payable and becoming a lien after date of closing.

Purchaser shall be furnished, at seller's expense, a complete and merchantable abstract of title continued to date as quickly as the same can be prepared, said abstract to show a merchantable or insurable title to said real estate in the name of the grantors who will execute and deliver a general warranty deed (or contract of sale if so specified herein) conveying said real estate (or in the case of a contract of sale, agreeing to convey) in the same condition as it now is, ordinary wear and tear excepted, free and clear of all liens and encumbrances except as stated herein and subject to easements or restrictions of record, if any. However, if sellers have Owners Title Insurance, in that event purchasers shall be furnished, at sellers' expense, an Owners policy of Title Insurance in the amount of $_17,000.00___. Should additional time be required for making or continuing such abstract, or for correcting defects of title, reasonable extension of time shall be given.

This transaction is to be closed within___10___days after said abstract showing merchantable title or binder for title insurance is delivered.

This offer is void if not accepted in writing on or before 12:00 o'clock noon of___13th___day of___September___, 19_.

This purchase includes such lighting fixtures, window shades, venetian blinds, curtain rods, linoleum cemented to floors, storm sash, screens, awnings, fences, clothes poles, laundry tubs, shrubbery, traverse rods, drapery cranes, water heater, gas burner, oil burner, stoker, heat regulator, water pump, sump pump, pressure tank, water softener, towel racks and bars, door bells or chimes, lattices, television tower, antenna and rotor now installed or in use on the premises. Seller guarantees that all of the above accessories or appliances are fully paid for or will be fully paid for, at the final closing of this transaction, unless otherwise herein stated.

The risk of loss or damage to improvements on said real estate or a substantial portion thereof by fire or otherwise, until delivery of deed or contract, is assumed by seller, and if all or a substantial portion of said buildings are so destroyed or damaged prior to execution of said deed or contract of sale, this agreement at the election of the purchaser shall not be binding upon the purchaser, and in such event any earnest money deposited shall be returned to the purchaser.

The said earnest money deposit above mentioned shall be returned in full to purchaser promptly in event this proposition is not accepted. In the event this proposition is accepted, and purchaser shall, without legal cause, fail or refuse to complete the purchase of said real estate in accordance with the terms and conditions hereof, said earnest money deposit shall be retained by the broker under his listing contract with said seller and shall be applicable to the broker's and the seller's damages, but seller may also sue for specific performance or pursue any other legal remedy available to seller under the law.

the parties have agreed. (See Fig. 17–4.) Such an agreement is preliminary to a sale; if consideration is given, an option contract is formed which may bind the parties for a period of time during which various matters may be investigated. In some cases an escrow agreement is made.

A contract for sale should cover at least the following items: (1) the parties, (2) legal description of the property, (3) the price and financial arrangements, (4) title, (5) time and place of closing, and (6) various special items. As in all other contracts, the parties must be legally competent and capable of entering into contracts. For example, the capacity of married women is usually defined by statute. Similarly, the ability of a corporation to contract is indicated by its charter. In real estate contracts it is always wise to require signatures by both husband and wife in order to remove any doubts about dower rights. Also, if purchasers are to take title as *joint tenants* or *tenants in common*, it is necessary to indicate this fact. Good practice dictates that both parties to a contract should sign it in duplicate, each retaining a signed copy.

While a property is usually designated by street and number during the early stages of a transaction, it is usually necessary to describe it more exactly in the sale contract. The description need not be as detailed as it is in the deed, but it must be accurate. Property may be located by metes and bounds, that is, with reference to certain landmarks, roads, rivers, streets, corners, or other designated points, and then described by a certain number of feet in various directions from a starting point. In most cities property may be located by a plat or subdivision map which is filed in the land records office. Lots and blocks are numbered on such a plat and descriptions can easily be made. Property may also be designated with reference to government land surveys; that is, with respect to north and south lines or *principal meridians*, east and west lines or *base lines*, townships, and sections, as outlined in Chapter 5.

Financial Arrangements

The financial arrangements between the buyer and seller must be set forth exactly in the contract of sale. Of greatest importance are the following: (1) price, (2) the deposit on contract, (3) the amount of cash to be paid on closing, (4) existing mortgages and purchase money mortgages, and (5) miscellaneous items.

Usually the purchaser is required to make a deposit at the time the contract is drawn up. This deposit is called *earnest money* and is used

---

Fig. 17–4. Offer to purchase real estate. (By permission from *Indiana Supplement to Law of the Real Estate Business,* by Harold F. Lusk and George F. Bloom, Bureau of Business Research, Indiana University, 1959; approved by the authors, 1966.)

to bind the transaction. Typically, it represents 5 to 10 per cent of the purchase price, the amount varying according to the agreement between the parties. In case the buyer fails to perform the terms of the contract, this amount may be forfeited to the seller, who may then use it to pay any commission which he owes a broker.

The amount of money to be paid to the seller at the time the deal is closed should also be designated in the contract. Sometimes the exact form of payment is indicated. For example, a certified check may be required. It is necessary to indicate specifically the amount to be paid at the time closing takes place in order to make certain that there has been a complete understanding between the buyer and seller.

Since most real estate is mortgaged, it is necessary to make some arrangement regarding the mortgages, if any, which are in force. A recorded mortgage is an encumbrance on the property, and the purchaser takes the property subject to it. The mortgagee may proceed against the land after sale to a third person. The third person, however, does not subject his personal assets to the payment of the mortgage unless he assumes it. If he does, it is important that the contract of sale indicate in detailed form the terms of existing mortgages.

In some cases real estate is sold subject to a *purchase money mortgage* —that is, the seller agrees to take back a mortgage for a certain part of the price. In such a mortgage the general rules governing all mortgage transactions regulate the relationship between the parties. Ordinarily such mortgages are subordinate to any existing mortgages in force.

Various miscellaneous items governing the financial arrangements between the buyer and the seller should also be indicated. For example, taxes may be delinquent or payable at some future time, and there should be a definite agreement regarding the amounts which each party shall pay. Also, arrangements must be made regarding special assessments, rents, insurance, water charges, and other similar matters.

In order to guard against uncertainty, it is desirable that a complete statement be drawn up indicating the purchase price, the amount to be paid on deposit, the amount to be paid at the time the transaction is closed, the presence of existing mortgages and the method of their disposal, agreements regarding purchase money mortgages, and an itemized statement of any other financial arrangements which are involved.

Title Problems

Before a piece of real estate can be transferred, it is necessary to determine the condition of the title. Because of the many uncertainties surrounding the title to a piece of property, careful investigations must be conducted before a transaction can be completed. A contract of sale usually provides that the seller shall furnish a good, merchantable title. It may also require the furnishing of a complete abstract or summary history of the *chain of title,* which includes all deeds and other instruments of record since the original grant of land by the government. The buyer may require some form of title insurance or a certificate of title. Typically, all of these matters are indicated in the contract, together with certain defects or encumbrances which the buyer is willing to waive.

Also, the contract usually specifies the form of deed which the seller will deliver, indicating whether a warranty, quit-claim, bargain-and-sale, or other type of deed is to be given. In ordinary transactions the buyer demands a full covenant warranty deed in which the seller takes all responsibility for the validity of the title. In some cases a bargain-and-sale or special warranty deed is all that can be demanded; for example, this would be the case in purchasing from a trustee or the executor of an estate. Such a deed limits the personal liability of the seller. It is seldom used in a free conveyance, for most purchasers are unwilling to buy a title that may be valueless. Usually the party who is to draw the deed and pay the expenses is indicated in the contract; otherwise the seller cares for these matters.

While it is not necessary to indicate the time and place of closing, it is desirable to include such provisions in the contract. In addition, contracts often include clauses in regard to the payment of broker's commissions, loss or damage by fire, limitation of seller's liability in case of defective title, provisions allowing the purchaser to assign the contract, as well as provisions regarding fixtures and personal property, making time the essence of the contract, leases, and various other subjects.

Closing of Title

After the contract of sale has been signed, each party must comply with its conditions. If the property does not comply with its description or the title is not as the vendor agreed, he must see that the conditions of the contract are met. A check of the property description may indicate that it does not coincide with the tract which the buyer specified. Similarly, encroachments may be discovered; that is, a building on the land may be partially located on adjoining land, or a building on adjoining land may encroach on the seller's property. Any substantial difficulty of this type may render the property unmarketable. On the other hand, slight encroachments may be of little consequence. Where one property is separated by a party wall, that this actually bounds the property must be determined.

Of greater difficulty, however, is the problem of determining the status of title. The buyer usually requires a title search to be made as soon as a contract of sale has been entered into so that he may know the status of the title. The seller may be required to furnish an abstract of title, a guarantee policy, or a certificate of title. An abstract will present a complete history of the property, and an attorney's opinion is made on this to the buyer. However, a title company may make a search and, upon the

APPROVED STANDARD FORM
INDIANA REAL ESTATE ASSOCIATION, INC.
2625 N. Meridian St.   Indianapolis 7, Ind.

CLOSING STATEMENT

October 10_____, 19____

Seller(s)__Joe Doakes and Mary Doakes_____Buyer(s)__Jack Byers and Betty Byers__

Address__3420 N. Delaware St.__Phone ME 1-1451__Address__1846 Lark Avenue__Phone ME 1-1775

FINAL CLOSING STATEMENT

ADDRESS OF PROPERTY 3420 N. Delaware St.Lot No.__58__Addition John Platt's City__Indianapolis

• • • • •

	Buyer	Seller
Purchase Price		$17,000.00
Unearned Insurance Premium____yrs.____mos.____days		41.50
Escrow deposits, Taxes, Insurance,		
Earnest money deposit____September 3____, 19___	$ 1,000.00	
Additional down payment, if any, _____, 19___		
Balance 1st mortgage held by The Indiana National Bank	7,310.00	
Interest 1st mortgage from July 1, 19 to October 10, 19	115.63	
Balance _____, 19___		
Interest from____to____		
Real Estate Taxes—Spring____Fall__19__ Taxes	193.20	
Prorated Rent, from January 1, 19 to October 10, 19	298.64	
(Note: In this example purchaser is given credit for the pro-rated taxes. In other sample closing statement taxes are treated as an expense.)		
Balance due sellers	8,124.03	
	$ 17,041.50	$ 17,041.50

SELLERS EXPENSE

Cash received by Neighborhood Realty Co. Realtor		$ 1,000.00
Continuation of abstract by Brown Abstract Co. Co.	$ 52.50	
Documentary Stamps	11.00	
Funds, if any, advanced to Seller(s)		
Brokerage Commission Neighborhood Realty Co. Realtor	850.00	
Balance due Sellers	86.50	
	$ 1,000.00	$ 1,000.00

Conditions:

Possession to be given buyers on or before____November 9,_____, 19__

Abstract of Title delivered to____Buyers____

_____keys for premises delivered to Buyers.

_____copies of survey given to Buyers.

Assignments of Insurance sent to____Sam Actuary____19_____Agent

$15,000.00 Insurance, Term 3-year , Expires July 20, /, Premium $160.57 Co. American Mutual Insurance Co.

Assignment of Escrow Deposits sent to_____, 19__.

Next payment on Mortgage due by Buyers____November____, 19____, Amount $____.

Next payment of Real Estate taxes due from Buyers _____, 19____.

Notice to tenant, if any_____, 19____ Rent due_____, 19____ Amt. $_____

Accepted by   Accepted by

Jack Byers
Jack Byers   **Buyer**   *Joe Doakes*
                                                  Joe Doakes   **Seller**
Betty Byers
Betty Byers   **Buyer**   *Mary Doakes*
Neighborhood Realty Co.   Mary Doakes   **Seller**
_____Realtor   By   *Bill Darr*
                                                                          Salesman

400

A closely related problem arises from the increasing number of people who are required to move from one city to another because of changes in their work assignments. Some companies guarantee certain managerial employees against loss if they are required to move to conform to company programs. Usually an independent appraisal is made and if the owner of the house who is forced to move finds it necessary to sell for less than the appraised value, the company makes up the difference. If a national network could be developed in some manner which would permit the turning in of a property in one city to a broker for sale and the purchase of a house in another city from another but perhaps affiliated broker with appropriate arrangements to tie both transactions together, the transfer of people between locations would be facilitated.

SUMMARY

Basic decisions in real estate marketing are made by present and prospective property owners who are motivated by a variety of factors. Brokerage and promotion play a large part in real estate marketing due to the difficulties of bringing buyers and sellers together. Selling organizations vary in size and degree of specialization. Listing of properties for sale often is the key to successful sales; listing agreements of various types may be arranged. Multiple listing systems are expanding in popularity. Processes of selling real estate resemble those in other fields but knowledge of real estate resources is essential. Special aids such as property briefs and sales kits are often used.

Promotion includes all types of activities and programs that help and support the sales effort. Advertising, displays, open houses, public relations programs, and related activities are all parts of promotion. Publicity programs often are used to good advantage by brokerage firms.

Upon completion of a sale, a purchase-and-sale agreement usually is drawn up pending final arrangements. Financing often is worked out by the broker. Title problems sometimes create difficulties. When all matters are worked out, a final closing statement is set up. In some cases escrow agreements are used. Contracts finally arranged may be enforced specifically or alternative arrangements may be worked out.

QUESTIONS FOR STUDY

1. Why do brokers play such an important role in the marketing of real properties?
2. What is meant by "listing"? How does a broker obtain listings?
3. How do you interpret the statement "a property well listed is half sold"?
4. Differentiate among the various types of listing contracts employed by brokers. If you were a broker, which would you prefer? If you were a

small manufacturer desiring to sell your property, which type of listing contract would you prefer? Why?

5. The ABC Corporation is transferring its local plant manager, Mr. Carson, to the home office in another state. He has to dispose of his home within 30 days, and asks you to sell it for him. Mr. Carson wants $27,500 for the property. After inspecting the property, you decide that it will not bring more than $25,000 in the current market and may have to be sold for even less in order to complete a sale within 30 days. What action would you take under these circumstances?

6. "Exchange must always be a mutually beneficial proposition." Why? Is this statement consistent with the attempt of a firm to maximize its profits? Explain.

7. Indicate ways in which the selling of real estate differs from the selling of other commodities.

8. Distinguish between a property brief and a sales kit.

9. Define "promotion" as it pertains to real estate sales. What is meant by a "promotion strategy"?

10. Prepare illustrations of the principal types of real estate advertising. Which types of advertising would be most effective for residences, investment property, industrial property?

11. Distinguish between public relations and publicity.

12. If the seller of a certain real property changes his mind after signing a sales contract, what remedies are available to the buyer?

13. What essential items need to be covered by a contract for the sale of real estate?

14. *Study Project 28.* (a) How might the "six great motivaters" be applied to the public relations program of a real estate brokerage firm? (b) Compare the discussion of motivation research in this study project with that presented in the present chapter.

SUGGESTED READINGS

CASE, FRED E. *Real Estate.* Englewood Cliffs, N.J.: Allyn & Bacon, Inc., 1962. Chaps. xxii, xxiii.

LUSK, HAROLD F. *Law of the Real Estate Business* (rev. ed.). Homewood, Ill.: Richard D. Irwin, Inc., 1965. Chaps. i–ii, xii–xiii.

MARTIN, PRESTON. *Real Estate Principles and Practices.* New York: The Macmillan Co., 1959. Chap. viii.

OTTESON, SCHUYLER F., WILLIAM G. PANSCHAR, and JAMES M. PATTERSON. *Marketing: The Firm's Viewpoint.* New York: The Macmillan Co., 1964. Pp. 539–42, 556–62.

18

Marketing: Property Management

Meaning of "Management" and "Property Management"

The terms *management* and *administration* are used in relation to all types of organized activities. As we suggested in our discussions in the introductory chapters, we use these terms interchangeably in most situations to identify the processes of using resources effectively in the attainment of desired objectives. In this broad sense, the term *management* may be applied to all types of business and to all aspects of the real estate business.

The term *property management*, however, has come to have certain special connotations in the real estate business.[1] Although the owner of a property might manage it himself, the term *property management* usually is applied to situations in which someone other than the owner performs the management function. Because of this type of usage that has grown up in the real estate field, we tend to use the term *administration* in relation to broader managerial processes and the term *management* in the specialized sense of property management as indicated above. Although we use the term *property management* in the customary narrow sense, it will be understood that when an individual owner or a business firm manages a property, the principles and methods of the property manager may be applied.

[1] Durand Taylor, "The Functions of a Property Manager," *Journal of Property Management* (Winter, 1962).

The increasing complexities of many problems associated with the managing of real properties, together with the fact that some owners know relatively little about real estate principles and practices, accounts in large part for the development of this specialized branch of the real estate business. Absentee ownership, use of trustee arrangements, tax factors, technological developments, and growth of the corporate ownership of real property have contributed to the development of property management. In addition, it is often difficult for some owners to maintain favorable income-expense relationships for their properties.

Special Characteristics of Property Management

Certain conditions create special types of problems for the manager of real property. The durability of real estate necessitates managerial planning over longer periods of time than is necessary for many other types of business. Furthermore, real properties are economically inflexible —that is, once they are improved their uses are relatively fixed for long periods. Hence, to a large extent the manager is called upon to operate properties so as to get as large a return as possible from relatively fixed resources.

Current expenses are only slightly more flexible than the basic investment. Many important operating expenses, such as taxes, insurance, and interest charges, are usually beyond the control of the property manager. Hence, a slight decline in gross income usually means a considerably larger decline in net returns.

As we have said before, the fact that real properties are fixed in location means that the manager cannot move a property to those who desire its services; rather, they must be induced to come to it. For the same reason, the property cannot escape adverse developments affecting a city or a neighborhood or district.

While property management is a specialized branch of the real estate business, a knowledge of the basic principles which explain the utilization of real estate is helpful in developing a successful operation. Thus, good management requires adequate information about the economic base and future prospects of the city in which a property is located. Knowledge of the structure of the city and its characteristics of growth and development are extremely helpful in the planning of long-range management programs. The manager should understand the forces affecting the specific districts or neighborhoods in which properties under his management are located. In addition, he should be familiar with the forces affecting the market for the types of real estate he is managing. Market information is needed almost constantly and should be kept up to date and analyzed currently. With such knowledge, the property manager can adjust rental schedules and certain types of expenditures in accordance with changes in the market.

Apartment houses, office buildings, loft buildings, stores, and dwellings are the types of property most frequently operated under the direction of specialized property managers. Farm management has grown in importance in recent years. Some shopping centers and industrial districts are operated by management organizations. Each type of property involves special problems of management, but the general principles of management are the same for all.

Relation of Management to Ownership

The relationship between managers and owners has been well summarized by Harold F. Lusk as follows:

The real estate manager is the agent of the owner. His legal position is similar to that of the manager of a branch office or branch store. He is a general agent—that is, an agent vested with general power involving the exercise of judgment and discretion. He is usually empowered to transact all business connected with the property entrusted to him. The property manager is generally authorized to negotiate leases, collect rents, make ordinary repairs, keep the premises in a rentable condition, pay taxes, and perform many other additional services. He is a fiduciary and must use his best efforts to further the legitimate interests of his principal. The principal is liable for the acts of his manager, done within the scope of his authority.

The manager may be authorized to keep the property insured, take care of tax matters, such as attending hearings on tax assessments. However, in all his activities, he must comply with the instructions of the owner. The manager cannot lawfully substitute his judgment for the judgment of the principal (owner).

The manager owes a duty to keep accurate accounts and to make an accounting to the owner at such periods as have been agreed upon, and also at any time the principal requests one. The manager owes a duty not to commingle the money of the owner with his own money. He should keep a separate account for money handled for each owner. If he does not keep separate accounts, he makes himself personally liable to the owner for all money of the owner coming into his hands.[2]

Frequently, the property manager's relationship with the owner is defined by a specific contract. When such a contract is drawn up, it includes a description of the property to be managed, the length of time for which the agreement is to run, removal and cancellation provisions, the amount of compensation to be paid the manager, and the duties and powers given to him. As in all other contracts, the parties must be legally competent; and all terms of the agreement must be stated definitely and

[2] Harold F. Lusk, *Law of the Real Estate Business* (rev. ed.; Homewood, Ill.: Richard D. Irwin, Inc., 1965), p. 34. See also Robert Kratovil, *Real Estate Law* (4th ed.; Englewood Cliffs, N.J.: Prentice-Hall, Inc., 1964), chap. x.

exactly. Since the manager is the owner's agent, the general law of agency governs such relationships, but the use of a specific contract eliminates many special problems.

Typically, such contracts are drawn up for specific periods with provisions for renewal, the owner often reserving the right to cancel the agreement by giving the manager adequate notice of such intention. Management contracts should present a complete list of the functions to be performed by the manager and should provide for complete centralization of authority in the manager with respect to all work undertaken in connection with the property. Sometimes management contracts are set up with a trial period of three or six months.

Compensation is usually computed on the basis of a percentage of gross collections, 5 to 8 per cent being a "normal" management fee, although other arrangements are not uncommon. The amount of compensation and the manner of computing and paying it should be specified in the manager's contract.

The management functions may be performed by individual agents of the owner or by a management company which operates a number of properties for many different owners. Frequently a real estate office conducting a general brokerage business will include a property management department in its organization. Some economies are effected by this arrangement, and the selling process is often facilitated if a buyer knows that the firm making the sale is willing to manage the property. While the average property management department seldom produces large revenues, it is a source of steady income, a factor of considerable importance to real estate firms during periods of limited market activity.

The Management Organization

In order to perform the manifold functions required of management, various employees must be hired; where the scope of operations is broad, a complete organization must be set up. (See Fig. 18–1.) If a number of buildings are involved, superintendents may be hired for each one of sufficient size to require a full-time person. Of course, janitors must be hired and supervised, as well as other laborers, including repair and maintenance men and others. In larger management organizations, special functions, such as collecting rents and hearing complaints, may be delegated to specific people. Similarly, advertising may be handled by one department, tenant selection by another, and legal matters by a third department. Accounts always require special attention, and accounting departments are normally provided in all offices of any size.

The management of a property often involves certain responsibilities which cannot be departmentalized and which are on the borderline be-

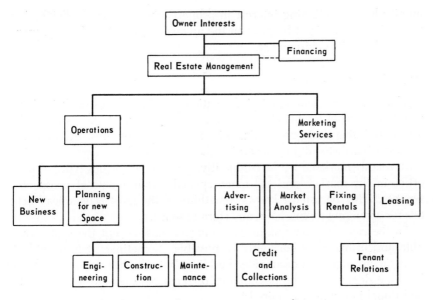

Fig. 18–1. Real estate management diagram.

tween the functions of the manager and the owners. In some cases, these are handled in part by attorneys.

Property Management Functions

The functions performed by property managers include the general management processes of establishing objectives, planning to achieve them, organizing resources, and controlling operations. The property manager also performs the functions of (1) planning space, (2) marketing property services, (3) conserving the property and its surroundings, and (4) supervising the operation of the property, which will include among other things the maintenance of accurate records and accounts. The manager is expected to keep the owner informed regarding the property and its operation and to consider with him any significant changes in policy.

In the performance of his functions the property manager must consider the interests of three parties: the owner, the tenants, and "the party of the third part," the members of the community in which the property is located. The owner is concerned with potential changes in the value of the property and is interested especially in securing a reasonable return on his investment. Tenants are interested in the space and equipment provided, their condition and maintenance, their cost to them, and the special services and conveniences which may be provided. The community has a continuing interest in property management policies, since they will have a direct bearing on the advance or decline of the property involved and its environment.

Planning Space

If a manager has adequate information about the local market, his advice to the owner, architect, and builder will be of great value in planning a new building or in modernization and repair programs. A competent manager is able to advise concerning the type of building accommodations most readily marketable, the competitive position of various types of properties in the market, and the many special requirements of prospective tenants. Also, he usually knows something of the most economical methods for arranging rooms, halls, and storage space.

In the case of older buildings, managers must accept the space available and utilize it as efficiently as possible. Sometimes it is possible to alter the arrangement of an older building, but whether or not this should be done depends on the possibilities of securing adequate return on the additional investment required.[3]

Establishing Rental Schedules

Once a building, regardless of type, is constructed, the manager must fix a rental schedule and enter the market. Fixing a rental schedule calls for an accurate knowledge of such matters as the character of competing space, rents currently charged, the nature of the potential demand, the special requirements of prospective tenants, and the various advantages and disadvantages of the location. A general level of rents is determined first, from which the manager is able to develop a rental schedule for the individual quarters. Specific rates, however, are determined in view of market conditions. If net income is to be maximized, rents must be adjusted carefully. For example, if rents are too low, all of the space will be rented; but the total return will be less than what might be realized under a higher rental schedule. On the other hand, if rents are too high, the increase in the number of vacancies will reduce income. The determination of a rental schedule for a building is one of the basic functions of a manager, and to a large extent his success or failure depends on the care with which this work is done.[4] Also, the process of adjusting rental schedules is never complete—rents must follow the market, rising when the demand for space is strong and diminishing when demand falls off.

---

[3] James C. Downs, Jr., *Principles of Real Estate Management* (8th ed.; Chicago: Institute of Real Estate Management, 1964), chap. v.

[4] The Sheridan-Karkow formula is often used to determine the rental value of office space.

Constant analysis of all factors affecting the market is essential in the performance of this function.

Selling Space

With the establishment of a rental schedule, it becomes necessary for the manager to secure tenants. Promotion programs as outlined in the preceding chapter may be helpful. If the building is new, it may be necessary to advertise and solicit for tenants. A new building opens with a competitive advantage, for it usually makes available all of the newest facilities. The opening of a new building is always detrimental to existing buildings, even if it is only a small structure. When a large new office or apartment building is opened, the existing structures must face stiff competition. Tenants of existing buildings are made conscious of the advantages of the new building through advertising and systematic solicitation. If special concessions are offered by the new building or if rental schedules compare favorably with those of existing structures, there will be a tendency for tenants to move from their old quarters to the new building.

The process of advertising space requires great care, for it is easy to waste funds on improperly directed advertising. If the management organization is sufficiently large, this function may be performed by a special person or department. If not, it is often wise for the manager to employ outside assistance in this work.

In established management organizations, the number of prospective tenants who will call at the office in search of accommodations is frequently large. This is especially true in the case of people seeking residential space, particularly if the management office has developed a reputation for fair dealing and courteous treatment of tenants over a period of time.

In the process of attracting tenants, the wise manager is careful to consider both short- and long-range factors. To a large extent, the condition of the market will govern the specific procedure followed—a buyer's market calls for a different program from that suitable in a seller's market. The original rental campaign continues until complete or nearly complete occupancy is achieved. Thereafter, the problem of management is to hold tenants and to meet the competition of other buildings, both old and new.

Selecting Tenants

It is very important that the character of tenants be investigated carefully at the time a building is being opened for occupancy, especially in the case of large apartment houses and office buildings, since tenants give a building the reputation of being either desirable or undesirable. If a manager can secure a highly desirable group of tenants in the first instance, many of his renting problems will be solved for some time in the future. Downs lists the following factors as being of major importance in selecting residential tenants: stability, housekeeping ability, child care, living habits, tenant compatibility, and social responsibility.[5] The housing of more than a dozen families under one roof requires exceptionally careful selection of tenants. Hence the apartment house manager often requires a signed application for a lease, accompanied by a deposit, in order to allow time for investigation. Then the actual lease is signed later.

The manager of an office building faces a number of special problems in selecting his tenants. He must always be on the alert against certain types of tenants, especially those whose businesses are likely to involve unethical practices. He must decide whether he desires a few large tenants or a number of small ones, a specialized tenancy or a general one. Usually, property managers prefer to have enough leading firms operating in a certain line of business to create a "center," but not so many that the exodus of such a group will result in the loss of a large percentage of the tenants. In connection with the selection of commercial tenants, attention should be given to such factors as the ability, aggressiveness, and progressiveness of the firms under consideration as well as tenant reputation, service requirements, and expansion requirements.[6]

Medical buildings, because of their particular physical requirements, are an exception. In larger cities, physicians tend to congregate in certain buildings and expect the property manager to enforce high standards in the selection of tenants.

With the expansion of its activities, the federal government has become an important customer in the market for office space. Its leasing requirements and policies differ somewhat from those of the average tenant. For example, annual rent may not exceed a fixed percentage of the fair market value of space leased, and the cost of repairs and alterations may not exceed a stated percentage of the first year's rental. Leases are made on a government form. Sometimes a 30-day cancellation clause is required in order to permit a move to governmentally owned space if it becomes available, and the time of the lease seldom runs longer than the end of the fiscal year (June 30).

The successful manager is familiar with current vacancy rates in various types of properties in the city. There is probably no such thing as a normal vacancy, although a vacancy ratio of around 5 to 8 per cent for office buildings and 5 to 10 per cent for apartment houses is generally considered normal. A manager's own vacancy situation is always significant, since it helps to determine policy changes.

[5] Downs, *op. cit.*, chap. ix.
[6] *Ibid.*, chap. xix.

Leasing Practices

Property managers ordinarily arrange all leases for the space they operate. However, leases are not used for all types of property, and the extent of their use varies from one part of the country to another, depending on the statutes of various states. About 50 per cent of the management offices which operate residential buildings require tenants to sign leases for at least one year. In some states leases for one year or longer must be in writing to be valid; in others, oral leases are valid for as long as three years. In many cases residential space is rented on a month-to-month basis, and the tenants are free to move or the owner or manager can request tenants to move if either party gives appropriate notice.[7]

It is not customary to require the tenant to post any security when leases for residential property are signed. A lease ordinarily binds the owner and manager very effectively because the property serves as security and guarantees performance of the terms of the contract. But unless the tenant is financially responsible and has assets which can be attached if the lease is broken, it is difficult to enforce a lease of this type.

When leases run for periods of longer than a year, which is common practice in the renting of stores, loft building space, or offices, definite lease agreements are usually drawn up, with liquidated damage provisions for failure to perform the contracts. Since business firms usually possess more financial responsibility than individuals, property owners and managers have greater protection in such cases. When leases run for long periods of time, they are usually considered to involve many special problems not normally a part of the functions of property management.

From a legal standpoint, a lease is a transfer of possession and the right to use property to the tenant for a stipulated period, during which the tenant pays rent to the owner. At the end of the period the right of possession reverts to the owner of the fee. It is a contract containing various terms and conditions, the most important being the agreement to pay rent. To be valid, such a contract must be entered into by parties who are legally competent; and it must describe the property, the term or period of the lease, the rent, and special covenants of the contracting parties completely and exactly.

Special problems which may be anticipated in the lease include such items as the exact dates on which the lease begins and ends, arrangements governing the agreement in case of damage to the space, such as may result from fire, and termination of the lease in case of complete destruction of the building or the relationship which shall exist between tenant and owner in case a new building is constructed.

[7] Subject to rent control regulations, if in force.

X 48—Form of Apartment Lease Approved by the Committee on Real Property of The Association of the Bar of the City of New York.

JULIUS BLUMBERG, INC., LAW BLANK PUBLISHERS 80 EXCHANGE PLACE AT BROADWAY, NEW YORK

Lease, made the 12th day of December 19 , between John Land 400 West 66th Street, Manhattan, New York hereinafter called the Landlord, and Robert Money 5000 Riverside Drive, Manhattan, New York hereinafter called the Tenant.

WITNESSETH: The Landlord hereby leases to the Tenant, Apartment 5B on the Fifth floor, in premises, 400 West 66th Street Borough of Manhattan , City of New York, hereinafter called the building, to be used as a private dwelling apartment, and not otherwise, for a term to commence January 1st 19 and to end December 31st 19 unless sooner terminated as hereinafter provided, at the annual rent of $ 1800.00 payable in equal monthly installments of $ 150.00 each in advance on the first day of each calendar month during the term, the first of said installments to be paid on the signing of this lease.

The parties hereto further agree as follows:

1st. The Tenant will pay the rent as herein provided.

2nd. The Tenant will take good care of the leased premises, fixtures and appurtenances, and suffer no waste or injury; make all repairs to the leased premises, fixtures and appurtenances necessitated by the fault of the Tenant, his family, guests, servants, assignees or under-tenant; conform to all laws, orders and regulations of the Federal, State or Municipal governments, or of any of their departments, and regulations of the New York Board of Fire Underwriters, applicable to the leased premises, but shall not be required to make any expenditure to comply therewith unless necessitated by his fault; and save harmless the Landlord from any liability arising from injury to person or property caused by any act or omission of the Tenant, his family, guests, servants, assignees or under-tenants; repair at or before the end of the term, all injury done by the installation or removal of furniture and other property; and at the end or other expiration of the term, surrender the leased premises in as good condition as they were at the beginning of the term, reasonable wear and damage by fire or other casualty excepted.

3rd. The Tenant will not, without the Landlord's written consent, make any alteration in the leased premises and will not deface or permit the defacing of any part of the leased premises; will not do or suffer anything to be done on the leased premises which will increase the rate of fire insurance on the building; will not use any shades, awnings, window air-conditioning units or window guards, except such as shall be approved by the Landlord; will not keep or harbor any animal in the leased premises without first obtaining the written consent of the Landlord; will not permit the accumulation of waste or refuse matter; and will not assign this lease or underlet the leased premises or any part thereof without the Landlord's written consent, which consent the Landlord agrees not to withhold unreasonably.

4th. The Tenant will observe and comply with such reasonable rules as the Landlord may prescribe on written notice to the Tenant for the safety, care and cleanliness of the building, and the comfort, quiet and convenience of other occupants of the building.

5th. The Landlord shall furnish, insofar as the present facilities of Landlord provide, the following services: (a) Elevator service; (b) Hot and cold water in reasonable quantities; (c) Heat at reasonable hours during the cold seasons of the year; (d) Air-conditioning during the warm seasons of the year.

6th. The Landlord shall have the privilege of furnishing the electric current consumed at the leased premises, and current so furnished shall be paid for by the Tenant at the rates charged for similar consumption by the local public utility company. If the Landlord furnishes the Tenant with telephone service, the Tenant shall pay for each call at the rate established by the Landlord, but the Tenant shall not be precluded from obtaining telephone service direct from the telephone company. Charges for electric current and telephone service shall be deemed additional rent, and for non-payment of same the Landlord shall have the same remedies as for non-payment of the fixed rent.

7th. In case of damage by fire to the building, without the fault of the Tenant, if the damage is so extensive as to amount practically to the total destruction of the leased premises or of the building, or if the Landlord shall within a reasonable time decide to rebuild, this lease shall cease and come to an end, and the rent shall be apportioned to the time of the damage. In all other cases where the leased premises are damaged by fire without the fault of the Tenant, the Landlord shall repair the damage with reasonable dispatch, and if the damage has rendered the premises untenantable, in whole or in part, there shall be an apportionment of the rent until the damage has been repaired. In determining what constitutes reasonable dispatch consideration shall be given to delays caused by strikes, adjustment of insurance and other causes beyond the Landlord's control.

8th. If the leased premises, or any part thereof, are taken by virtue of eminent domain, this lease shall expire on the date when the same shall be so taken, and the rent shall be apportioned as of said date. No part of any award for the leased premises, however, shall belong to the Tenant.

9th. If the Tenant defaults in the performance of any of the covenants or conditions herein contained, other than the covenants to pay rent, or if any conduct of the Tenant or occupants of the leased premises shall be objectionable, the Landlord may give to the Tenant ten days' written notice thereof, and if such default has not been cured or the objectionable conduct stopped within said ten day period, then at the expiration of said ten days the Landlord may give the Tenant five days' notice of the termination of this lease, and at the expiration of said five days' notice the term of this lease shall expire, and the Tenant shall then surrender the leased premises to the Landlord, but the Tenant shall remain liable as hereinafter provided. In case of default by the Tenant in the payment of rent, or if the ten day notice above provided for shall have been given and the ten day period shall have elapsed without curing such default or stopping the objectionable conduct, and the five day notice above provided for shall have been given and the five day period shall have elapsed, or if the leased premises become vacant or deserted, the Landlord may at any time thereafter resume possession thereof by any lawful means, and remove the Tenant or other occupants and their effects, by dispossess proceedings, or otherwise, without being liable to prosecution or damages therefor, and hold the premises as if this lease had not been made. In any such case, the Landlord may at the Landlord's option relet the premises or any part thereof as agent of the Tenant or otherwise, and receive the rent therefor, applying the same first to the payment of such expenses as the Landlord may have incurred in connection with said resumption of possession and reletting, including brokerage, cleaning, repairs, and decorations, and then to the payment of rent and performance of the other covenants of the Tenant as herein provided; and the Tenant agrees, whether or not the Landlord has relet, to pay to the Landlord the rent and other sums herein agreed to be paid by the Tenant, less the proceeds of the reletting, if any, as ascertained from time to time, and the same shall be payable by the Tenant on the several rent days above specified. The Tenant hereby waives all right of redemption to which the Tenant or any person claiming under the Tenant might be entitled by any law now or hereafter in force.

10th. The failure of either party to insist in any instance on strict performance of any covenant hereof, or to exercise any option herein contained, shall not be construed as a waiver of such covenant or option in any other instance. No modification of any provision hereof and no cancellation or surrender hereof shall be valid unless in writing, and signed by the parties.

11th. If this lease is assigned by the Tenant, or the leased premises are underlet or occupied by anybody other than the Tenant, the Landlord may collect rent from the assignee, under-tenant or occupant, and apply the net amount collected to the rent herein reserved, and no such collection shall be deemed a waiver of the covenant herein against assignment and underletting, or the acceptance of such assignee, under-tenant or occupant as Tenant, or a release of the Tenant from further performance of the covenants herein contained.

12th. This lease shall be subject and subordinate at all times to the lien of existing mortgages and of mortgages which hereafter may be made a lien on the premises. Although no instrument or act on the part of the Tenant shall be necessary to effectuate such subordination, the Tenant will, nevertheless, execute and deliver such further instruments subordinating this lease to the lien of any such mortgages as may be desired by the mortgagee. The Tenant hereby appoints the Landlord his attorney in fact, irrevocably, to execute and deliver any such instrument for the Tenant. If any underlying lease to which this lease may be subject shall terminate, the Tenant shall attorn to the owner of the reversion.

13th. All improvements made by the Tenant to the leased premises which are so attached to the freehold that they cannot be removed without material injury to the premises, shall become the property of the Landlord.

14th. Any notice by either party to the other shall be in writing and shall be deemed to be duly given only if delivered personally or mailed by registered or certified mail in a postpaid envelope addressed (a) if to the Tenant, at the building in which the leased premises are located, and (b) if to the Landlord, at the address, if any, noted on the lease, or, if none, then to the building, provided, however, that if either party admit, either in writing or under oath, the receipt of notice, evidence of service in accordance herewith shall not be necessary.

15th. The Landlord shall not be liable for damage or injury to person or property occurring within the leased premises, unless caused by or resulting from the negligence of the Landlord or any of the Landlord's agents, servants or employees, in the operation or maintenance of the leased premises or the building.

Fig. 18–2. Lease form. (Prepared by The Association of the Bar of the City of New York. Published by Julius Blumberg, Inc., New York.)

16th. If the making of repairs or improvements to the building or its appliances, or to the leased premises, other than those made at the Tenant's request or caused by the Tenant's negligence, shall render the leased premises untenantable in whole or in part, there shall be a proportionate abatement of the rent during the period of such untenantability.

17th. Interruption or curtailment of any service maintained in the building if caused by strikes, mechanical difficulties, or any other cause beyond the Landlord's control, whether similar or dissimilar to those enumerated, shall not entitle the Tenant to any claim against the Landlord or to any reduction in rent, nor shall the same constitute constructive or partial eviction, unless the Landlord shall fail to take such measures as may be reasonable in the circumstances to restore the service without undue delay.

18th. During the four months prior to the expiration of the term, applicants shall be admitted at all reasonable hours of the day to view the premises until rented; and the Landlord and the Landlord's agents shall be permitted at any time during the term to examine the leased premises at any reasonable hour; and workmen may enter at any time when authorized by the Landlord to facilitate repairs in any part of the building; and if the Tenant shall not be personally present to permit any such permissible entry into the premises, the Landlord may enter same by a master key, or forcibly, without being liable in damages therefor and without affecting the obligations of the Tenant hereunder.

19th. Neither party has made any representation or promises, except as contained herein, or in some further writing signed by the party making such representation or promise.

20th. The Landlord covenants that the Tenant, on paying the rent and performing the covenants hereof, shall and may peaceably and quietly have, hold and enjoy the leased premises for the term herein mentioned.

21st. The provisions of this lease shall bind and enure to the benefit of the Landlord and the Tenant, and their respective successors, legal representatives and assigns. The Landlord shall be released from, and the Landlord's grantee shall be liable for, all liability of Landlord hereunder accruing from and after each grant of the reversion.

22nd. The Landlord acknowledges receipt from the Tenant of $150,00as security for the performance of the Tenant's obligations under this lease. To the extent that said sum shall remain unapplied to such performance after the date fixed as the end of the term or after the earlier expiration of the term pursuant to paragraphs 7th or 8th hereof, said sum shall be returned by the Landlord to the Tenant if the Tenant shall have surrendered possession of the leased premises to the Landlord as herein provided.

IN WITNESS WHEREOF, the parties hereto have signed this instrument, the day and year above written.

In the presence of:

John Land
Landlord

Robert Money
Tenant

Fig. 18–2. Lease form (reverse).

Other points which are often included in the lease are these: (1) reservation by the manager of the right to enter upon the premises for inspection, (2) specific uses to which the property may be put, (3) restriction or regulation of subleases, (4) control of the placement of signs and other things which may affect the appearance of the building, and (5) definition of the rights of the tenant in case of condemnation proceedings.[8]

The rents fixed in a lease may be of several types: (1) a flat rate for the period covered; (2) a graded or step-up rental; (3) a percentage rental varying with the amount of tenant's gross or net income; or (4) a rental which is adjusted by reappraisal of the property at certain times.[9] Also, various combinations of these types of leases may be worked out. For example, a lease on a business property might be drawn up which provides for a minimum flat rent, plus a percentage of the tenant's gross business receipts if they exceed a certain stipulated amount. In the case of long-term leases, such an arrangement is often desirable to guard against important changes in the value of money.

[8] For a discussion of leases see Lusk, *op. cit.*, chap. xviii, and Kratovil, *op. cit.*, chap. xxix. On percentage leases see Downs, *op. cit.*, chap. xvii.

[9] Reappraisal leases have seldom worked out advantageously, since it is difficult to secure an adjusted appraisal which will be acceptable to both landlord and tenant.

Concessions or special services provided by the owner may be such as to create a wide gap between the real and the nominal money rent. Thus, a rental may be set at $125 per month for an apartment, with a concession of one month's rent, which means in fact that the real charge is $114.58 per month. Managers often make such arrangements instead of cutting rents, because they believe that it will be easier, when the market warrants a return to the old level, to raise rents by eliminating concessions than by reinstating a schedule previously abandoned. The provision of special equipment, or, in some cases, the payment of moving expenses in order to get the tenant in are other examples of concessions.

Duration of Leases [10]

Different provisions are to be found respecting the duration of the lease:
1. Tenancies for a fixed or definite term
2. Tenancies for a periodic term, subject to termination upon notice (tenancy "from month to month" or "from year to year")
3. Tenancies for an indefinite period, subject to termination with notice (tenancy at will)

Sometimes leases hold over—that is, the tenant stays after the expiration of the lease. If this happens, as a general rule the owner has the option of either taking proceedings to dispossess the tenant or of assuming that the lease has been renewed for another term.

Once a lease has been drawn up and signed, it may be terminated by expiration of the agreement, by eviction of the tenant by the owner, forfeiture of the lease by the tenant, or voluntary surrender and acceptance. Each of these methods of terminating the lease, except the first, is governed by detailed legal regulations.

Express and Implied Covenants

As in the case of most real estate contracts, leases contain certain express and implied convenants, the landlord or lessor guaranteeing possession and quiet enjoyment and promising that the property will be suitable for use. The lessee guarantees to pay rent, to use the property in a stipulated fashion, and to care for the premises. In accordance with the latter agreement, the lessee is usually required to carry certain insurance for the protection of the property, although this varies with the type of property involved. In the case of business property the lessee is often required to assist in the payment of taxes if they reach a certain point. Such an agreement in a lease is called a *tax participation clause*.

[10] Lusk, *op. cit.*, pp. 376–77.

Conservation of Property

The property manager is responsible for the maintenance of the property so that its economic life may be as long as possible. This means that he must follow a regular program for making repairs and replacements. At times modernization will be undertaken. For example, older office buildings have frequently been able to compete effectively with new buildings because their managers have devised modernization programs giving them many of the desirable features provided by newly produced structures.[11] The complete interior modernization of an older building represents a huge outlay, but it may be carried out on a piecemeal basis over a period of time. Thus, special attention may at one time be given to a particular floor that seems to have "gone dead," at another time to the space which is being rented to new tenants, and at still another time to that occupied by important tenants whose leases are up for renewal. When such a program is carried out over a ten- or twelve-year period, no great outlay is necessary at any one time; and the program can often be financed out of increased earnings resulting from the changes themselves. The operation of office buildings has been virtually revolutionized by automatic elevators, air conditioning, increased use of electrical equipment, and improved office layout and design.

The careful planning of repair programs over a period of time, and the proper allowance for such work in the budgetary setup of the organization, are important functions of good property management. In apartment house management it is usually safe to allocate one month's rent per year to normal repairs and decorations. Another 5 per cent of the income is usually set aside for painting, roofing, renovation of heating equipment, and other types of repairs which do not arise every year but must be paid for over varying periods of time.

Successful conservation of a property requires that attention be given not only to the physical condition of the structure, but also to the quality of the tenants and to the properties and people in the surrounding neighborhood. Property managers frequently have real opportunities for the up-grading of an area by the careful and systematic selection of tenants as well as by following adequate maintenance and modernization programs. Neither a property nor its environment can be thought of in connection with management programs without giving careful consideration to the people living or working in the property and in the area.

Thus the property manager is involved with processes of *community organization* even though he seldom thinks of himself in such a capacity.

[11] See for example the January–February, 1964, issue of *The Journal of Property Management,* Chicago, Institute of Real Estate Management.

Physical facilities take on meaning only in relation to people and the various interrelations between the people who may be involved. The property manager can benefit from the work of the sociologist and social psychologist as well as that of the engineer and architect.

Building Operation

The day-to-day and month-to-month operation of a building involves a multitude of activities. The competent manager constantly checks receipts and outlays in order to maintain a proper relation between different income and expense items, such as upkeep, conservation, and improvement of the property. Such a ratio will vary with conditions in the market, the age of the property, and the special objectives of the management program.

Building operation includes the jobs of collecting rents, caring for insurance and taxes, and purchasing and using supplies, in addition to many related activities. Valuable information on this subject and related management problems will be found in the publications of the Institute of Real Estate Management of the National Association of Real Estate Boards, especially the *Journal of Property Management*.

Collecting Rents

It is necessary to collect rents in order to obtain income in the case of a leased property. While the large majority of tenants will pay promptly if asked punctually and in a proper manner, at least 10 per cent of the potential collections are likely to cause problems. Many collection systems fail because threats are made and never carried out. The making of threats is a last resort of the manager and is used as a collection device by the careful manager only after all others have failed. Informal reports from property managers indicate that the best collection procedure is simply to demand what is due at the time it is due; follow-up notices after a five-day interval often are helpful and if not heeded another notice requesting a call at the management office may be effective. Managers for the most part appear to believe it is wrong to have the tenant feel that a collector will be sent if payment is not made; rather the tenant should feel that it is his obligation to handle the payment.

It is common knowledge that many tenants of residential properties take offense at being asked to pay their debts, regardless of how adroitly they are handled. Insofar as possible, the wise manager will try to determine whether or not difficulties of this kind are likely to arise before the tenant is accepted. Credit reports and careful analysis of references are useful in this connection, and in some cities real estate boards or property managers' associations maintain files of information covering a large number of tenants. Some delinquency always will develop, since a few people follow the policy of moving every few months, to the chagrin and loss of managers and owners. An average rental loss of 5 per cent is not uncommon. Of course, the management office can create a great deal of good will by granting extensions of time for payment when they are honestly deserved. In order to grant such favors, however, it is necessary to secure a considerable amount of knowledge regarding the tenants involved.

Collections are not such a difficult problem in the case of business properties or office buildings, since the tenants are more likely to pay their obligations in a prompt and businesslike manner. Even here the . collection problem sometimes becomes burdensome and must be handled firmly and tactfully, unless it is apparent that the tenant is unable to pay. Then steps are taken to obtain possession of the property without delay.

Insurance [12]

The property manager may be responsible for placing insurance and paying for it regularly. Normally, fire insurance in an amount equal to approximately 80 per cent of the replacement cost of buildings is carried (80 per cent coinsurance). Sometimes in the case of large buildings this is supplemented by use and occupancy insurance—that is, insurance against the loss of rent resulting from destruction of a building.

Public liability insurance typically is carried for all buildings. Also, boiler and plate glass insurance are necessary in some cases; and if rent collectors are employed, good practice requires that they be bonded. Insurance against theft, tornadoes, and other hazards is also carried by many management organizations. Good management often can effect substantial savings in insurance by eliminating various risks or by the use of coinsurance, thus securing the benefits of reduced insurance premiums.

Taxes and Other Fees

The payment of taxes and special assessments, as well as of local license and inspection fees, requires careful and prompt attention by a property manager. In some instances, where the taxes on a building appear to be out of line with those on similar structures, the management can effect savings by calling this fact to the attention of the proper tax officials. Errors are sometimes made by tax officials who may estimate the value of a building by its external appearance rather than by its earning power. This is especially true of large office buildings or apartment houses. The

[12] See J. Edward Hedges and Walter Williams, *Practical Fire and Casualty Insurance,* (7th ed.; Cincinnati: National Underwriter Co., 1961). See also Downs, *op. cit.,* chap. xxx.

preparation and submission of accurate statistical materials to the proper tax officers, presenting data on earning power, is often a helpful method of attacking this problem. Problems of this type often arise in connection with older buildings which have been assessed at high values during years when their earning power was great, but for which tax adjustments were not made as income-producing ability declined.

Tenant Relations

The basic opportunity available to every property management organization for building good will arises from its numerous relationships with the tenants. Such good will is an important asset—one that can be created only over a period of time. As one management official has said, "Unlike the broker, the property manager does not sell the prospect once; he must keep him sold." [13] The effectiveness with which this selling process is carried out is a good measure of tenant-landlord relations.

Many managers follow the practice of writing or visiting every new tenant within 30 days after he has moved into a building in order to let the tenant know that his welfare is being considered and to provide him with an opportunity for bringing any complaints to the attention of the manager. This is done in the belief that hunting for trouble will lead to fewer demands on the part of tenants. However, many managers do not share this view. Much depends on the type of tenant involved. Some managers write to desirable tenants who have moved from a building, thanking them for their considerate treatment of the property and for their patronage. Such letters often lead to favorable indirect advertising.

In the management of a large building, it is necessary to follow the principle of seeking the greatest good for the greatest number. Frequently, there will be tenants who will not recognize the rights of other occupants of the building and who will not take proper care of the quarters they are renting. When this happens, it is best to request the removal of such tenants as soon as possible, for they can quickly destroy much of the good will the management has built up.

Complaints and requests from desirable tenants require a sympathetic hearing, even when they are unreasonable, as is often the case. Impatient treatment of minor complaints often results in the loss of a desirable tenant. The policy of establishing general rules to which exceptions cannot be made has provided many managers with a convenient device for refusing impossible or difficult requests. General rules also help to avoid the charge that the management is playing favorites. Especially in office or apartment buildings, any special concessions are soon discovered. Tenants resent any appearance of favoritism on the part of management and are likely to demand similar concessions themselves.

[13] Statement made by Graham Aldis, Aldis & Co., Chicago.

In the management of office buildings special devices for creating good will are frequently employed. Among these are found the provision of safety vaults, parking accommodations, libraries and conference rooms, and even the publication of a house organ. Many such devices are beyond the resources of the average building; but every manager, by the exercise of foresight and imagination, can find many ways of cultivating the good will of tenants.

Management Records and Accounts

In order to control operations effectively, a manager needs adequate records of all transactions and accurate accounts of all operations. Probably no single aspect of property management requires more attention. Without adequate and accurate accounting methods, it is impossible for the manager to render the proper reports to the owner. Without proper accounting he cannot determine the success of the policies he is following and he will lack precise knowledge of the points at which savings can be effected.

The type of accounting system which a manager will use depends in large part on the magnitude of his operations, the size of the building or buildings under his supervision, and the characteristics of the manager. Bookkeeping machines and the use of addressograph plates for rent bills, employees' names, and Social Security numbers are often justified in larger offices.[14] Possible short cuts, such as the elimination of various forms, must always be considered from the standpoint of savings secured and effects on standard accounting procedure.

Some managers follow a policy of requiring the preparation of data periodically on the basis of unit costs—for example, rental rates per square foot or per room, cost of heating per cubic foot, annual expenses per unit, per room, or per square or cubic foot, and similar reductions of various items of income and expense to unit bases. Such records are often useful in determining efficiency of operations, but their value depends in part on the records available and the uses to which they can be put. If sufficiently extensive data are involved and they can be put to a variety of uses, a computer may prove to be desirable.

Reorganized buildings often have special requirements in their trust indentures calling for the allocation of a certain portion of the net income to specific accounts, such as bond retirement. Certain items such as net income, extraordinary expenses, and others are frequently defined in such indentures in a manner that does not conform to customary management or accounting procedure. This creates special problems. Again, institutional owners, such as insurance companies and banks, often require

[14] John G. Held, "Property Management Through Automatic Bookkeeping," *Journal of Property Management* (Fall, 1963).

the use of accounting forms designed for general uses which do not fit the needs of specific buildings.

Professional Management Organization

The chief professional organization in the property management field is the Institute of Real Estate Management. It was established in 1933, first as an organization of management firms but later (1938) as a professional society of qualified individuals.[15] Membership is limited to those who can meet stated experience, educational and ethical standards, and can successfully pass designated examinations. Those selected for membership may make use of the designation CPM (Certified Property Manager).

The Institute has done much to further the development of the property management field. It publishes *The Journal of Property Management* and various other reports and studies. It provides for a ready exchange of experience among members. It stimulates educational programs and encourages the continuing personal and professional development of its members. In addition, it helps to present the entire field in a favorable light with respect to the investing and renting public, thus performing a highly valuable public relations function.

SUMMARY

Property management refers to the performance of the managerial function with regard to real estate resources by specialized individuals or firms rather than by the owners of properties. It is increasing in scope and importance because of the growing complexity of tax, legal, and managerial factors. Although property management refers to a specialized activity, its principles and methods may be applied successfully by those who manage their own properties.

The property manager, who may be part of a brokerage firm, has the legal status of general agent for principals who are the property owners, and therefore seeks to achieve the objectives of the owners, which usually means obtaining the best possible return from the relatively fixed resources of land and buildings.

The primary functions of property management include planning space, marketing property services, conserving the property and its surroundings, and supervising the operation of the property. These functions include such activities as establishing and adjusting rental schedules; selecting tenants and collecting rents; repair, maintenance, and building operation; arranging for insurance; tenant relations; and the keeping of accounts and

[15] Frederick E. Case, *Real Estate* (Englewood Cliffs, N.J.: Allyn & Bacon, Inc., 1962), pp. 428–29.

records. The property manager should be cognizant of developments within the community or neighborhood which affect the income-producing ability of his principal's property.

QUESTIONS FOR STUDY

1. How do you explain the growth of property management in recent years?
2. In what ways may the following factors create problems for the property manager? (a) The durability of real property. (b) The economic inflexibility of real properties. (c) Inflexibility of operating expenses. (d) Fixity of location of real property. (e) Uniqueness of each piece of real property.
3. Assume that you are managing the Hilltop Apartments, owned by the widow of the late J. Randolph Hilltop. (a) Make a list of your specific duties as manager of this property. (b) What are your obligations to Mrs. Hilltop, as owner of the property? (c) How would you expect to be compensated? (d) What factors would you consider most important in establishing the rental schedule for the building?
4. Suppose that you take over the management of an office building and find that the rents being charged there are approximately 10 per cent above the rents of comparable properties. Vacancy rates, however, have been about the same. Would you conclude that this rental schedule was too high? Why or why not?
5. Give reasons why you believe that it is or is not desirable to establish general rules for all the tenants in a building.
6. What is meant by "hunting for trouble" in connection with tenant relations? Indicate reasons why this is or is not a sound management practice.
7. Evaluate the inspection and tenant relations policies described as follows: The firm of Applegate and Smith, Property Managers, follows the practice of making an annual inspection of each property under the firm's management, to determine the general conditions of each. The tenants are not interviewed at the time of the inspection, as tenants are prone to ask for a large amount of repair and renovation work. Mr. Smith states: "Given the slightest opportunity, most tenants will ask for almost anything; yet if they have to call at the office or write a letter asking that certain things be done, fewer complaints come in. In fact, many tenants will do minor repair jobs themselves rather than make a complaint."
8. Differentiate between flat rate, graded, percentage, and reappraisal leases.
9. The small office building that you are managing has a replacement cost of $400,000. How much insurance should be carried on this building? If more than one type of insurance is necessary, list the different types and reasons why each should be carried.
10. As manager of the property in question 9 you discover that the taxes are apparently higher than taxes on similar properties. What action would you take? Is it your responsibility as property manager to take any action at all?
11. List the factors you would consider in selecting tenants for an apartment building. In what ways can careful selection of tenants help lengthen the economic life of the building?

12. Describe the action you would take in the following situation: The Acme Realty Company has followed the practice of hiring its own repairmen for the properties under its management. Several landlords complain that the management company is making extra money from these repair operations and recommend that all repair work be done on a contract basis, with bids let to the most favorable bidder and with the landlord charged on the basis of such bids. Would you agree to the change of policy recommended, or continue in the practice of hiring your own repairmen? Why?

13. *Study Project 29.* The Omnibus Realty Company has decided to expand operations to include property management. The various members of the firm have recommended alternative policies and have given a brief statement of the advantages of each of the alternative policies. Read the Study Project carefully, and then answer the following questions: (a) Which of the suggested policies would you recommend? (b) Explain your reasons for each of your policy recommendations. Do you agree that all arguments presented for each of the alternative policies were valid? Explain. (c) Have you made any implicit assumptions as to the type of property that the property manager department would be handling? If so, what are these assumptions?

14. *Study Project 30.* (a) Explain why owners rent single-family dwellings. (b) How can the property manager best serve the needs of the owners of single-family houses who put them on the rental market? (c) Why is vacancy such an important problem in this field? (d) What are some of the by-products in the management of single-family homes? (e) Why does the author recommend a minimum fee rather than a percentage of gross? (f) What are the principal "fringe benefits" of this type of activity?

SUGGESTED READINGS

Downs, James C., Jr. *Principles of Real Estate Management* (8th ed.). Chicago: Institute of Real Estate Management, 1964.

Kratovil, Robert. *Real Estate Law* (4th ed.). Englewood Cliffs, N.J.: Prentice-Hall, Inc., 1964. Chap. xxix.

Lusk, Harold F. *Law of the Real Estate Business* (rev. ed.). Homewood, Ill.: Richard D. Irwin, Inc., 1965. Chap. xviii.

19

Financing: Methods
and Instruments

Characteristics of Real Estate Finance

In this chapter and the two which follow, we consider the subject of
real estate finance. This chapter deals with the methods and instruments
used in the financing of real estate resources and projects; Chapter 20
with the principal institutions and agencies operating in this field; and
Chapter 21 with mortgage lending programs and risks.

As we have pointed out repeatedly, the terms and availability of financing play a major role in decisions affecting the development, marketing,
ownership, and use of real estate. For example, most purchasers of real
property, whether they are business firms or individuals, must borrow a
part or all of the funds needed to pay for the desired property. Similarly,
most builders, land developers, and subdividers must borrow a part or
all of the funds needed to finance construction and land development.

Like most other commodities that have economic value, real estate
resources may be pledged as security for loans. Although the principles of
finance involved are similar to those explaining other types of financing
decisions and programs, the major characteristics of real properties, particularly their long life, fixed locations, and relatively limited marketability,
have brought about the development of numerous special practices and
policies.

Of the various characteristics of real estate finance the following are of
major importance:

1. The terms and availability of credit in the real estate field depend in
part on conditions in the general capital markets. Real estate is in compe-

tition with other types of investment opportunities for the funds with which to finance the purchase, development, or use of real estate resources.

2. While some short-term financing is used, especially in the case of construction projects, most of the financing in the real estate field is long term in character. Real properties and even repairs on real properties last for long periods of time and investments in them are relatively fixed.

3. Loans typically are made against the security of real properties, and mortgages or similar instruments are used to pledge the borrower's interests. The processes required to mortgage real estate are complex and technical.

4. Because of the long-term nature of real estate financing, special risks are involved. These arise from changes and anticipated changes in business conditions, government programs, local economic conditions, location factors, the property itself, consumer preferences, market changes including interest rates, legal factors, and administrative arrangements.

5. Real estate resources and projects may be financed by means of equity (owner's) or borrowed funds. Or leases may provide for the use of property without the necessity of financing ownership.

Equity Funds

Whenever fee ownership is to be acquired, the prospective buyer faces several alternatives. If he can pay the entire purchase price out of savings or other funds, no financing problem is involved. Conversely, when the seller is willing to sell "on contract" without down payment, no equity funds need be raised. In most cases the buyer will have available some portion of the purchase price and will borrow funds for the remainder. Sometimes he is unable to provide the necessary down payment from his own resources and is faced with the problem of assembling sufficient equity funds.

Thus the buyer of a house may borrow against his life insurance or his automobile, or use personal credit to raise funds from relatives or other sources to assemble the necessary equity funds. A business firm may borrow by pledging other real properties or other assets. It may issue securities to raise funds for this purchase and for other purposes. Or other available funds may be used.

The equity for real estate developments such as apartment houses, office buildings, and shopping centers is often secured by organizing a corporation and selling stock. In some cases, the services of architects, engineers, and builders are paid for in whole or in part by means of stock. Sometimes the owner of the land will take all or part of his payment in the form of stock.

Partnerships, syndicates, and trusts may also be formed to provide for the assembly of equity funds for real estate developments. Estates, foundations, unions, and limited dividend corporations have also engaged in the equity financing of a number of housing projects, many of which have had a long record of success.

In more recent years life insurance companies and mutual savings banks in a number of states were given authority to make equity investments in residential income-producing housing. Such investments are owned outright, with no mortgage financing being involved. In addition, life insurance companies are authorized in all but a few states to make equity investments in nonresidential income properties. Such investments have expanded rapidly in recent years. Under certain conditions various savings and loan associations may acquire land for development.

Borrowed Funds

The borrowing of funds for the purpose of financing fee ownership of real estate is accomplished largely by the use of the mortgage, the trust deed in the nature of a mortgage, bonds, and land contracts. Other arrangements are also possible but are of less importance. Construction financing may be accomplished by a short-term loan or under various types of mortgage arrangements. Property improvements may be financed by the use of open-end mortgages or by the use of personal credit. The purchase of equipment is sometimes financed by means of a "package mortgage," as well as by the use of personal loans or installment credits. Of major importance, however, is the mortgage, and we shall give special attention to the processes of mortgage financing.

The Mortgage [1]

A mortgage creates the existence of a debt and requires a pledge of property to secure it. Technically the mortgage note admits the debt and contains an agreement to repay it in accordance with specified conditions. The mortgage pledges the property as security for the obligation. The note makes the borrower personally liable for the obligation, and he cannot simply abandon the property to avoid payment of the debt. It is possible, however, to create a mortgage without the mortgage note; and in that case the borrower has no personal liability.

At common law a mortgage amounted to a conveyance of an estate to the mortgagee, which conveyance became void upon the performance of the terms of the mortgage. Today it is considered more in the nature of a

[1] For a more complete discussion, see Harold F. Lusk, *Law of the Real Estate Business* (rev. ed.; Homewood, Ill.: Richard D. Irwin, Inc., 1965), chap. xv.

lien upon the estate to secure the performance, normally a money payment, specified in the instrument. The term *mortgage* is commonly used to denote the instrument by which such interest in property is transferred. Any instrument or legal form which conveys an interest in property for the purpose of giving security is in effect a mortgage, regardless of its form.

Several of the terms used in the above definition require further clarification. We have already pointed out that a *deed* is an instrument that conveys title to real property. A *conveyance* is a transfer of the interest in property from one person to another. In mortgage transactions the debtor or borrower is called the *mortgagor*. The creditor or lender is called the *mortgagee*. The period for which the mortgage is made is called the *term*.

In order that a conveyance of the type required in a mortgage transaction be valid, it must be in writing, must be executed by the mortgagor with all the formality prescribed by the statutes of the particular state in which the property lies, and must be delivered to the mortgagee. The laws of the state in which the property is located govern the mortgage transaction.

In the earlier stages of the development of the law of mortgages, the actual possession of property, as well as the title to it, passed to the mortgagee or lender during the period of the loan. If the debt was not paid in full and in accordance with all of the requirements on the day it became due, all of the rights of the mortgagor or borrower were forfeited. As mortgage transactions developed, experience indicated that the possession of the property was not necessary in order to secure the lender against loss. Consequently, the law was changed to permit the mortgagor to retain possession as long as the mortgage was not in default.

At the present time some states provide that the title, as well as the possession of the property, is kept by the mortgagor, the mortgage being regarded merely as a lien and not as an actual conveyance of title. These are called lien theory states, as contrasted with title theory states, in which the law more nearly resembles the earlier concept.

The arbitrary forfeiting of all rights in the property by the borrower in case he defaulted on the debt worked considerable hardship on the mortgagor, particularly in those cases where the value of the property was considerably greater than the debt. This aspect of the earlier law of mortgages was also changed. At the present time, all states require that some legal steps be taken by the mortgagee after default of the debt before the property can be proceeded against for debt payment. Such legal steps are called *foreclosure,* and this may take a number of forms. There are still wide variations between the states. Usually this process provides for the public sale of the property under the foreclosure laws, with the mortgagee securing repayment from the proceeds of the sale and the mortgagor being allowed to keep any surplus which remains. If a sufficient amount is not realized, the lender may secure a deficiency judgment against the borrower. (This is not the case in all states, however.)

Types of Mortgages

Mortgages may be classified by *degree of priority* and by *method of repayment*. Any mortgage which is subordinate to a mortgage or mortgages on the same property is a *junior mortgage*. The degree of priority is usually indicated by referring to the instrument as a first, second, third, and in some cases fourth mortgage; but the public records must always be consulted to determine which claims against the property have precedence. Also, a junior mortgage may become a senior lien if prior claims are paid. Obviously, junior mortgages typically contain more risk than senior mortgages, and consequently they usually yield a higher rate of return and are not written for long periods.

Various methods of repayment may be provided in a mortgage agreement. If no payments on the principal are made during the term of the mortgage, it is called a *straight term* mortgage. If repayment is made in accordance with a definite plan which requires the repayment of certain amounts at definite times so that all of the debt is retired by the end of the term, the mortgage is *amortized*. If parts of the debt are repaid during the term of the mortgage and part remains to be paid when the debt falls due, it is called a *partially amortized* mortgage. Various combinations of straight term and amortized mortgages may be used; for example, a straight term mortgage may allow amortization in part or in entirety according to the terms of the instrument; or an amortized mortgage may be converted into a straight term agreement under certain conditions. In some cases mortgages "balloon out" with a big final payment at the end of the term.

There are cases where a deed in the form of an absolute conveyance is used to transfer the title to the property. It may contain no reference to any debt or condition, indicating that it is really given as security for a debt. Such a legal instrument may be a mortgage in legal effect if it is actually given for the purpose of securing a debt and if this fact can be proved in the courts.

Mortgages may also be classified as to purpose. For example, a *blanket mortgage* may be issued against a subdivision with individual mortgages granted on specific projects and released from the blanket mortgage as sales are made. In many instances the seller of a property will take back a purchase money mortgage in partial payment. In this respect he helps to finance the project. Other types include open-end mortgages, which allow for additional advances during the life of the loan, and package mortgages, which allow for the inclusion of equipment and fixtures of various types.

With the rise of the Federal Housing Administration's program of mortgage insurance and the Veterans' Administration guarantee of mortgages, such financing is often distinguished from other mortgages by referring to the former as *insured* or *guaranteed* and to the latter as *conventional* loans.

The Package Mortgage

Because of the increasing amount of equipment used in homes and the special problems arising from financing the purchase of such equipment, a number of financial institutions make use of the so-called *package mortgage*. Practices vary between states, but usually provision is made for financing the equipment under the mortgage which is set up to finance home purchase. The various items of equipment included must be designated exactly and made a part of the mortgage agreement. Usually, only equipment which has a relatively long, useful life is included in such arrangement. The Federal Housing Administration insures mortgages of this type and has developed an extensive list of equipment which is considered to be eligible for inclusion in mortgage agreements. Such items of equipment as the following are included: plumbing accessories, air-conditioning systems, awnings, blinds, cabinets and bookcases (not built in), dishwashers, fireplace accessories, floor coverings, garbage disposal units, laundering equipment, radiator covers, ranges, refrigerators, screens, storm doors, and the like.

The Open-End Mortgage

If an ordinary mortgage is set up with provisions for securing future advances to the borrower, an *open-end* mortgage is created. In recent years such arrangements have been made by various mortgage lenders in order to allow the borrower to secure funds for the maintenance and improvement of the mortgaged property. Some legal difficulties may arise in case other liens or judgments are placed against the property before additional funds are requested under the open-end provision. However, many mortgage lenders have adopted this type of mortgage in order to discourage the borrower from using short-term loans to finance necessary improvements to the property. Such loans may impair his ability to carry his regular mortgage obligations. At the same time the improvements may be desirable to maintain the property in good condition. The use of the open-end mortgage appears to be gaining in popularity.

CONSULT YOUR LAWYER BEFORE SIGNING THIS INSTRUMENT—THIS INSTRUMENT SHOULD BE USED BY LAWYERS ONLY.

THIS MORTGAGE, made the 1st day of   May   , nineteen hundred **and**

BETWEEN   JOHNATHAN. WHITE, residing at 711 Front Street,
in the City, County, and State of New York

, the mortgagor,

and   WILLIAM W. JONES, residing at 115 Lenox Hill Avenue,
in the City, County, and State of New York

, the mortgagee,

WITNESSETH, that to secure the payment of an indebtedness in the sum of ********************
TEN THOUSAND ($10,000)** dollars,

lawful money of the United States, to be paid on or before the 1st day of May, 19 ,

with interest thereon to be computed from the date hereof, at the rate of   6   per centum
per annum, and to be paid on the   1st   day of   May   19   , next ensuing and semi-
annually   thereafter,

according to a certain bond,
note or obligation bearing even date herewith, the mortgagor hereby mortgages to the mortgagee

ALL that certain plot, piece or parcel of land, with the buildings and improvements thereon erected, situate,
lying and being in the Village of Lyons, in the County of Wayne, State of
New York, and bounded and described as follows:

BEGINNING at a point on the southerly side of One hundred and
seventh Avenue (Wayne Avenue) distant forty feet westerly from
the corner formed by the intersection of said southerly side of
One hundred and seventh Avenue with the westerly side of One
hundred and thirty-fifth Street (Clinton Avenue) running thence
southerly parallel with One hundred and thirty-fifth Street one
hundred feet; thence westerly parallel with One hundred and
seventh Avenue forty feet; thence northerly parallel with One
hundred and thirty-fifth Street one hundred feet to said southerly
side of One hundred and seventh Avenue and thence easterly along
said southerly side of One hundred and seventh Avenue, forty feet
to the point or place of beginning.

SUBJECT to covenants, restrictions and reservations contained in
former instruments of record and to encumbrances of record.

TOGETHER with all right, title and interest of the mortgagor in and to the land lying in the streets **and**
roads in front of and adjoining said premises;

TOGETHER with all fixtures, chattels and articles of personal property now or hereafter attached to or **used**
in connection with said premises, including but not limited to furnaces, boilers, oil burners, radiators **and**
piping, coal stokers, plumbing and bathroom fixtures, refrigeration, air conditioning and sprinkler systems,
wash-tubs, sinks, gas and electric fixtures, stoves, ranges, awnings, screens, window shades, elevators, motors,
dynamos, refrigerators, kitchen cabinets, incinerators, plants and shrubbery and all other equipment **and**
machinery, appliances, fittings, and fixtures of every kind in or used in the operation of the buildings standing
on said premises, together with any and all replacements thereof and additions thereto;

TOGETHER with all awards heretofore and hereafter made to the mortgagor for taking by eminent **domain**
the whole or any part of said premises or any easement therein, including any awards for changes of grade **of**
streets, which said awards are hereby assigned to the mortgagee, who is hereby authorized to collect and receive the proceeds of such awards and to give proper receipts and acquittances therefor, and to apply **the**
same toward the payment of the mortgage debt, notwithstanding the fact that the amount owing thereon **may**
not then be due and payable; and the said mortgagor hereby agrees, upon request, to make, execute **and**
deliver any and all assignments and other instruments sufficient for the purpose of assigning said awards **to**
the mortgagee, free, clear and discharged of any encumbrances of any kind or nature whatsoever.

Fig. 19–1. Mortgage form. (Courtesy The Title Guarantee Company, New
York.)

AND the mortgagor covenants with the mortgagee as follows:

1. That the mortgagor will pay the indebtedness as hereinbefore provided.

2. That the mortgagor will keep the buildings on the premises insured against loss by fire for the benefit of the mortgagee; that he will assign and deliver the policies to the mortgagee; and that he will reimburse the mortgagee for any premiums paid for insurance made by the mortgagee on the mortgagor's default in so insuring the buildings or in so assigning and delivering the policies.

3. That no building on the premises shall be altered, removed or demolished without the consent of the mortgagee.

4. That the whole of said principal sum and interest shall become due at the option of the mortgagee: after default in the payment of any instalment of principal or of interest for fifteen days; or after default in the payment of any tax, water rate, sewer rent or assessment for thirty days after notice and demand; or after default after notice and demand either in assigning and delivering the policies insuring the buildings against loss by fire or in reimbursing the mortgagee for premiums paid on such insurance, as hereinbefore provided; or after default upon request in furnishing a statement of the amount due on the mortgage and whether any offsets or defenses exist against the mortgage debt, as hereinafter provided. An assessment which has been made payable in instalments at the application of the mortgagor or of the premises shall nevertheless, for the purpose of this paragraph, be deemed due and payable in its entirety on the day the first instalment becomes due or payable or a lien.

5. That the holder of this mortgage, in any action to foreclose it, shall be entitled to the appointment of a receiver.

6. That the mortgagor will pay all taxes, assessments, sewer rents or water rates, and in default thereof, the mortgagee may pay the same.

7. That the mortgagor within five days upon request in person or within ten days upon request by mail will furnish a written statement duly acknowledged of the amount due on this mortgage and whether any offsets or defenses exist against the mortgage debt.

8. That notice and demand or request may be in writing and may be served in person or by mail.

9. That the mortgagor warrants the title to the premises.

10. That the fire insurance policies required by paragraph No. 2 above shall contain the usual extended coverage endorsement; that in addition thereto the mortgagor, within thirty days after notice and demand, will keep the premises insured against war risk and any other hazard that may reasonably be required by the mortgagee. All of the provisions of paragraphs No. 2 and No. 4 above relating to fire insurance and the provisions of Section 254 of the Real Property Law construing the same shall apply to the additional insurance required by this paragraph.

11. That in case of a foreclosure sale, said premises, or so much thereof as may be affected by this mortgage, may be sold in one parcel.

12. That if any action or proceeding be commenced (except an action to foreclose this mortgage or to collect the debt secured thereby), to which action or proceeding the mortgagee is made a party, or in which it becomes necessary to defend or uphold the lien of this mortgage, all sums paid by the mortgagee for the expense of any litigation to prosecute or defend the rights and lien created by this mortgage (including reasonable counsel fees), shall be paid by the mortgagor, together with interest thereon at the rate of six per cent. per annum, and any such sum and the interest thereon shall be a lien on said premises, prior to any right, or title to, interest in or claim upon said premises attaching or accruing subsequent to the lien of this mortgage, and shall be deemed to be secured by this mortgage. In any action or proceeding to foreclose this mortgage, or to recover or collect the debt secured thereby, the provisions of law respecting the recovering of costs, disbursements and allowances shall prevail unaffected by this covenant.

13. That the mortgagor hereby assigns to the mortgagee the rents, issues and profits of the premises as further security for the payment of said indebtedness, and the mortgagor grants to the mortgagee the right to enter upon and to take possession of the premises for the purpose of collecting the same and to let the premises or any part thereof, and to apply the rents, issues and profits, after payment of all necessary charges and expenses, on account of said indebtedness. This assignment and grant shall continue in effect until this mortgage is paid. The mortgagee hereby waives the right to enter upon and to take possession of said premises for the purpose of collecting said rents, issues and profits, and the mortgagor shall be entitled to collect and receive said rents, issues and profits until default under any of the covenants, conditions or agreements contained in this mortgage, and agrees to use such rents, issues and profits in payment of principal and interest becoming due on this mortgage and in payment of taxes, assessments, sewer rents, water rates and carrying charges becoming due against said premises, but such right of the mortgagor may be revoked by the mortgagee upon any default, on five days' written notice. The mortgagor will not, without the written consent of the mortgagee, receive or collect rent from any tenant of said premises or any part thereof for a period of more than one month in advance, and in the event of any default under this mortgage will pay monthly in advance to the mortgagee, or to any receiver appointed to collect said rents, issues and profits, the fair and reasonable rental value for the use and occupation of said premises or of such part thereof as may be in the possession of the mortgagor, and upon default in any such payment will vacate and surrender the possession of said premises to the mortgagee or to such receiver, and in default thereof may be evicted by summary proceedings.

14. That the whole of said principal sum and the interest shall become due at the option of the mortgagee: (a) after failure to exhibit to the mortgagee, within ten days after demand, receipts showing payment of all taxes, water rates, sewer rents and assessments; or (b) after the actual or threatened alteration, demolition or removal of any building on the premises without the written consent of the mortgagee; or (c) after the assignment of the rents of the premises or any part thereof without the written consent of the mortgagee; or (d) if the buildings on said premises are not maintained in reasonably good repair; or (e) after failure to comply with any requirement or order or notice of violation of law or ordinance issued by any governmental department claiming jurisdiction over the premises within three months from the issuance thereof; or (f) if on

Fig. 19–1. Mortgage form (*sheet 1 reverse*).

application of the mortgagee two or more fire insurance companies lawfully doing business in the State of New York refuse to issue policies insuring the buildings on the premises; or (g) in the event of the removal, demolition or destruction in whole or in part of any of the fixtures, chattels or articles of personal property covered hereby, unless the same are promptly replaced by similar fixtures, chattels and articles of personal property at least equal in quality and condition to those replaced, free from chattel mortgages or other encumbrances thereon and free from any reservation of title thereto; or (h) after thirty days' notice to the mortgagor, in the event of the passage of any law deducting from the value of land for the purposes of taxation any lien thereon, or changing in any way the taxation of mortgages or debts secured thereby for state or local purposes; or (i) if the mortgagor fails to keep, observe and perform any of the other covenants, conditions or agreements contained in this mortgage.

15. That the mortgagor will, in compliance with Section 13 of the Lien Law, receive the advances secured hereby and will hold the right to receive such advances as a trust fund to be applied first for the purpose of paying the cost of the improvement and will apply the same first to the payment of the cost of the improvement before using any part of the total of the same for any other purpose.

16. That the execution of this mortgage has been duly authorized by the board of directors of the mortgagor.

Strike out this clause 16 if inapplicable.

This mortgage may not be changed or terminated orally. The covenants contained in this mortgage shall run with the land and bind the mortgagor, the heirs, personal representatives, successors and assigns of the mortgagor and all subsequent owners, encumbrancers, tenants and subtenants of the premises, and shall enure to the benefit of the mortgagee, the personal representatives, successors and assigns of the mortgagee and all subsequent holders of this mortgage. The word "mortgagor" shall be construed as if it read "mortgagors" and the word "mortgagee" shall be construed as if it read "mortgagees" whenever the sense of this mortgage so requires.

IN WITNESS WHEREOF, this mortgage has been duly executed by the mortgagor.

IN PRESENCE OF:

Deborah Behrmann   Johnathan White (Seal)

STATE OF NEW YORK, COUNTY OF New York **ss:**
On the 1st day of May 19 , before me personally came Johnathan White
to me known to be the individual described in and who executed the foregoing instrument, and acknowledged that executed the same.

(Seal) Christopher Robin
Christopher Robin
Notary Public, State of New York
No. 00-0000000
Qualified in New York County
Commission Expires March 30, 19

STATE OF NEW YORK, COUNTY OF New York **ss:**
On the 1st day of May 19 , before me personally came Deborah Behrmann the subscribing witness to the foregoing instrument, with whom I am personally acquainted, who, being by me duly sworn, did depose and say that he resides at No. 12 Mockingbird Lane, New York, New York; that she knows Johnathan White to be the individual described in and who executed the foregoing instrument; that he, said subscribing witness, was present and saw him execute the same; and that he, said witness, at the same time subscribed her name as witness thereto.

(Seal) Christopher Robin
Christopher Robin
Notary Public, State of New York
No. 00-0000000
Qualified in New York County
Commission Expires March 30, 19

Fig. 19–1. Mortgage form (*sheet 2*).

Guaranteed Mortgage

When a mortgage company, bonding house, government agency, or other organization or person assures the payment of interest and principal of a mortgage in case the mortgagor defaults, a *guaranteed mortgage* results. The value of the guarantee depends on the soundness of the organization providing such additional security. Private mortgage guarantees were in use in the 1920's. Thereafter, little use was made of such guarantees until the late 1950's, when there was some revival of interest in them. The Mortgage Guarantee Insurance Corporation (MGIC, often referred to as "magic,") is a case in point. The setting up of the Federal Housing Administration in 1934 resulted in widespread use of federal mortgage insurance, which is a form of guarantee. The guarantee of mortgages by the Veterans' Administration after World War II had a marked effect on mortgage financing. The FHA and VA will be discussed in greater detail in the next chapter.

The general character and cost of residential construction has been influenced somewhat by the guaranty of loans by the Veterans' Administration and the insurance of mortgages by the FHA. The making of loans on a high loan-value ratio by savings and loan institutions, banks, and insurance companies has had important effects on our housing markets. Most families when buying homes think chiefly in terms of the monthly payments they will be required to meet, if they can raise the down payment. Lowering the down payment and lengthening the period of amortization (which lowers monthly payments) almost always broadens the market. The majority of young families are unable to make large down payments; hence the market is greatly restricted if such payments are required.

The financing of apartment buildings was stimulated under the FHA program during the early postwar years. Under this program, the government insured mortgages on such projects on fairly liberal terms. Less liberal terms were provided in the 1950's, and for a time apartment house construction and financing declined in importance in relation to other types of residences. More recently there has been a revival of such activity, in part because cooperative apartment house projects have increased in imporance, but also because of the condominium form of ownership and the expanded interest of conventional lenders in apartment house projects.

The Process of Mortgaging Real Property

Two basic elements must be present in order for a mortgage to exist: a *debt* and *a pledge of property to secure the debt.* If either of these elements is lacking, no mortgage agreement exists. The debt may have been incurred prior to making the agreement or simultaneously with it, or it may come into existence after the date of the agreement.

A mortgage which is given to secure a debt already in existence is subject to prior mortgages and liens, even though these are not recorded. This is due to the fact that the lender did not rely upon mortgage security at the time the loan was made. Hence, the law holds that he has not been injured by any failure to record such prior claims and will not protect him against them.

If a mortgage is given to secure advances to be made in the future, the amount of such loans need not be stated in the mortgage and may be at the option of the mortgagee. However, it is customary to fix a maximum amount in such an agreement. There is no question regarding the validity of such mortgages, but the rights of subsequent mortgagees and others who secure claims against the property differ widely from one state to another.[2]

In order for anyone to mortgage a piece of property, he must actually possess a stated interest in the property he is offering as security. In general, any interest in real property which can be sold or assigned can be mortgaged. But, as we have already pointed out, the interests that one may own in real property are many and varied. Thus, the mortgagee must always be certain that the mortgagor actually possesses the title to the property which he claims to have.[3] His title may be clouded and he himself may not be aware of it. Taxes, special assessments, prior mortgages, mechanics' liens, attachments, judgments, or court orders may leave little actual ownership for the borrower to mortgage. Similarly, private or public restrictions may so limit the use of a property that it is incapable of earning the type of return which is expected of it. Rights of dower and curtesy, easements, reservations, encroachments, prior liens, and rights of tenants are all possible claims that may interfere with the setting up of a satisfactory mortgage agreement. Such matters must always be determined by a competent lawyer or title company. Further, a careful and accurate description of the property is of major importance, since this eliminates uncertainties regarding the location or extent of the property which is mortgaged. Usually it is sufficient to describe the property by referring to it in the same way that it is described in the deed or as the number of a lot shown on a recorded map, but personal investigation and inspection help to avoid mistakes and misunderstanding. Surveys by competent engineers should be made whenever questions arise which are likely to create future problems.

[2] In general, the law states that the making of such advances is optional with the mortgagee, and if those who hold junior liens against the collateral notify the mortgagee of their claims and direct him not to make further advances, then such advances will be inferior to the junior claims.

[3] Under certain circumstances a mortgage will be held to convey an interest which the mortgagor or borrower did not own at the time the agreement was made. For example, the mortgage might contain a provision by which the mortgagor stated and guaranteed that he had good title to the property. If he did not have such title and later acquired it, the law will hold that such title actually passed to the mortgagee or lender at the time the agreement was made. This is permitted because it would be unjust to allow the borrower to benefit by his own wrong.

In general, the property should be designated with accuracy, the amount of the debt indicated, the terms of repayment, the exact conditions under which the conveyance is made, and any special promises or agreements that are a part of the contract.

Foreclosure

The legal steps that must be taken by the mortgagee or lender for the purpose of having the property applied to the payment of a defaulted debt are called *foreclosure*. Legally there is a distinction between *strict foreclosure* and *foreclosure by sale*, although the latter method has come to be used so generally that most people have this in mind when they speak of the process of foreclosure.

One of the early developments of the law of mortgages relieved the borrower from forfeiting his property through failure to pay within the time set, provided he paid within a reasonable time thereafter. The time was determined by a court of equity. This process made it necessary for the mortgagee to institute a court action in order to determine that a reasonable time had elapsed. In case sufficient time has been allowed, he was able to secure a decree foreclosing or terminating all rights and interests of the mortgagor in the property. Such an action by a court constitutes strict foreclosure. The decree given by the court under strict foreclosure proceedings does not order a sale of the property but confirms the absolute title to it in the mortgagee or lender.

Strict foreclosure is still used in many states, but is permitted only under special circumstances. For example, this method may be proper in cases where the value of the property does not exceed the debt and the mortgagor does not contest the action. It is also proper in cases where the mortgage is in the form of an absolute deed without any written condition or agreement to reconvey. As we have indicated, however, the method most generally used in this country to collect a defaulted mortgage debt is foreclosure by sale. There is considerable variation from state to state in regard to the methods and practices followed.

In most states the mortgagee has several remedies from which he may choose the one best suited to his purpose. Where there is no prohibition by statute, he may pursue all of his remedies, concurrently or successively. He may sue for judgment on the note, which can be collected out of other property owned by the debtor, and at the same time start foreclosure proceedings. In some states a judgment for the debt may be taken in the foreclosure action and will stand against the debtor to the extent that it exceeds the amount realized from the foreclosure sale. In other states separate court action must be brought to make up any deficiency.

Foreclosure by Sale

The two methods of foreclosure by sale most commonly used are (1) foreclosure under power of sale contained in a mortgage or deed of trust, and (2) foreclosure by court action resulting in a decree of sale.

If the mortgage instrument expressly authorizes the mortgagee or trustee to sell the property in the event of default, the laws of many states permit him to do this so long as he follows the procedure prescribed by statute. Whether or not the mortgagor has the right to redeem the property within a certain period after sale depends entirely upon the laws of the state in which the property is located. Some states allow no redemption after a sale of this type. Others provide that the mortgagor may redeem the property within a certain period after sale if he pays the costs of the sale and the full amount of the debt.

Many states require that all foreclosure sales must result from court action even though mortgages and deeds of trust contain powers of sale. Under this arrangement a suit is brought by the mortgagee against the mortgagor and all parties who have acquired an interest in the property subsequent to the mortgage.

The law provides that the rights of no person shall be affected by a decree unless he is before the court. Because of this regulation, it is important for the mortgagee to search the record carefully in order that all persons who have acquired rights in the property may be made parties to the proceedings and properly served with summonses or otherwise brought before the court.

Usually the decree directs the sheriff to sell the property to the highest bidder after public notices of the time and place of sale as prescribed by statute. The purchaser at the sale may receive a deed from the sheriff conveying an absolute title, or he may receive merely a sheriff's certificate which will become a conveyance of the title within a specified period if the property is not redeemed within that time.

Redemption

The interest of the mortgagor in the property prior to foreclosure is frequently called the *equity of redemption*. This should not be confused with the *statutory right of redemption*, which is a legal privilege recognized in certain states. In some states the mortgagor, and frequently junior lien holders as well, are given the right to redeem the title upon payment of the redemption price within a certain time after the foreclosure sale. This redemption period ranges from six months in some states to two years in others. Some states allow the mortgagor to retain possession of the property during the redemption period, while others give possession to the purchaser and allow him to retain it unless the property is actually redeemed within the time allowed.

In some cases a mortgagor is unable to pay his debt but is willing to convey the property to the mortgagee in order to satisfy the claim. By doing this he is relieved (if the mortgagee agrees) of personal liability, the danger of future deficiency judgments, and the unpleasant publicity frequently associated with foreclosure proceedings. Such a proposal is often agreeable to the mortgagee, for it relieves him of the expenses and delays connected with foreclosure proceedings. Under some conditions, the lender may even pay the borrower a sum of money for title to the property. However, a deed of this type must be considered carefully by the mortgagee before he accepts it because of the fact that its validity depends upon the intention of the parties involved and on other special circumstances.

Trust Deed

The *trust deed in the nature of a mortgage* [4] is an instrument which provides for the conveyance of title to a third party who holds it *in trust* as security for the payment of an obligation by a borrower. The creditor is called the *beneficiary*, the *legal holder* or the *mortgagee*. The party holding the title for the period of the loan is called the *trustee*. The trustee, then, is holding the stakes, with instructions to reconvey title to the debtor when the debt is repaid or to sell the property in event of default. Sales proceeds are applied to the payment of the debt, with any surplus remaining payable to the borrower. In a few states, this instrument has virtually supplanted the mortgage, and it is commonly used the country over in transactions involving substantial amounts of funds. In a number of states, the trust deed can be foreclosed by trustee's sale without any court proceedings. However, in most states, the trust deed is virtually identical to the mortgage and is legally considered as such.

Mortgage Bonds

When several persons or a group of persons lend money on the security of a property, mortgage bonds may be issued. A customary procedure is to give a mortgage or a trust deed to a trustee, who holds it for the benefit of the bondholders. In such cases, the mortgage is accompanied by a trust

---

[4] The trust created for holding a trust deed in the nature of a mortgage should not be confused with the "naked" or "dry" trust. The latter is created solely to hold title to property and is not associated with any debt. In fact, it performs no functions other than to hold title for the convenience of the transferror. The "naked" trust is common in Illinois and a few other states.

agreement, which sets forth in detail the rights of the bondholders in the security and the duties of the trustee. For example, a corporation may wish to borrow an amount which is greater than any one person wishes to lend. In such a case the corporation may convey its property to a trustee and provide for the issuance of bonds against it. Such bonds can then be sold to the public generally and the debt distributed among a great many persons. In cases of this type, the trustee acts on behalf of all of the bondholders. If foreclosure and sale become necessary, the trustee pays over to each bondholder his share of the proceeds.

The Land Contract

The *land contract,* or contract for a deed, is a written agreement by which a property is sold to a buyer who agrees to pay in installments the established price with interest over a specified period of years. Generally a down payment is required, although the amount is usually nominal, 10 per cent or less of the purchase price being common. Under the land contract, the seller retains title until the agreed payments have been made by the purchaser. Frequently, however, the agreement provides that when the installment payments have reached a specified percentage of the purchase price (for example, one half), the seller will give a deed or transfer title under a regular mortgage as security for the remaining payments. The most appealing factor to the purchaser is probably the generally low down payment required. Buyers can sometimes secure property under land contract where the down payment necessary under a conventional mortgage would obviate the transaction. Retention of title makes it relatively easy for the seller in most states to avoid the cumbersomeness of conventional mortgage procedure in enforcing the terms of the contract. The land contract, however, poses certain dangers for the unwary purchaser. Generally the contract is not recorded; hence the purchaser may lose this protection. He may lose his equitable interest, as well as use and occupancy upon default. It is also possible that the seller may lose, through foreclosures of prior liens, the right to convey title before the purchaser is in a position to demand it.

Financing Construction

Individuals and firms engaging in the development of real estate, whether the task be road building or house building, rarely have sufficient funds to carry a job to completion without some form of financing. Personal or company capital is supplemented with loans, advances from purchasers, and credit from material suppliers and subcontractors. The various sources of financing can be combined in many ways, and, of course, not all of them are used in every building venture.

Construction financing varies according to the requirements and characteristics of the participants in a particular building project. In the same construction job, the originator or sponsor and subcontractors may require financing for themselves, but may also provide financing for others. For example, an individual or firm for whom a structure is being built might obtain a loan to finance the project and also make personal advances to the builder, who in turn, operates between advances on a commercial line of credit and credit from subcontractors and material suppliers.

The most common type of construction financing is the construction loan granted to the originator or sponsor of the building project in which the proceeds of the loan are disbursed as construction progresses. A construction loan may be either one or a series of short-term notes which are drawn at intervals during the construction and refinanced when the project is completed, or a single long-term loan in which the principal is advanced in installments. Thus, construction financing may be either interim financing or an integral part of long-term financing.

Many different construction-loan disbursement schedules are in use. They are not influenced by whether the loan is long or short term. Some systems permit payouts as certain phases of the project are completed; for example, 25 per cent of the loan is paid out when the foundation is completed, 25 per cent when the structure is under roof and rough plumbing and wiring are installed, 35 per cent when the structure is completed and ready for occupancy, and 15 per cent after the period for filing mechanics' liens has elapsed. Other payout systems permit the borrower to draw loan funds in amounts equal to a certain percentage of the cost of the work completed for which payment has not already been made. The final balance of the loan is disbursed upon completion. Some systems simply require the builder to submit all bills to the lender, who in turn pays them and gives the builder the balance of the loan account upon completion. The Federal Housing Administration and the Veterans' Administration require three inspections during construction on residential units which are to be eligible for insurance or guaranties, so the payouts on FHA and VA projects are usually related to the required inspections.

A short-term construction loan is not necessarily a mortgage loan, although the long-term loans are nearly always secured by a mortgage on the real estate being improved. Established building firms frequently obtain construction financing through an unsecured line of credit, just as other types of firms borrow on their general credit. Individuals or companies having special structures custom-built for them, such as residences or stores or factory buildings, typically have to pledge the property being developed in order to obtain construction funds.

Whether construction financing is interim financing or a part of a long-term loan depends on the policies of the lender granting the loan and the financial and operating characteristics of the borrower. For example, national banks are not permitted to loan on the security of real estate unless improvements have already been placed on the land. National banks are permitted, however, to grant loans for construction purposes without regard to mortgage security provided that the term of the loan does not exceed six months. Fewer complications are encountered by national banks, and more liberal loans may be granted if construction financing is carried out with short-term loans.

Federally chartered savings and loan associations, in contrast, are permitted to grant loans on the security of real estate which is to be improved with the proceeds of the loan. Therefore, a federally chartered savings and loan association can finance construction with ordinary mortgage loans in which the principal is advanced during construction.[5]

Some lenders and some borrowers are not interested in long-term mortgage financing. Commerical banks are often willing to finance building operations as a commercial venture but do not care to invest in long-term mortgage loans. Other lenders may be willing to finance construction on a short-term basis so that they can temporarily avoid committing funds on a long-term basis. Building firms engaging in custom construction are often not concerned with long-term financing but only with financing the project during the construction period.

Material suppliers and subcontractors participate in construction financing by granting credit to builders and owners while a project is being brought to completion. Credit from suppliers and subcontractors can be used either to supplement or to replace construction loans.

The Use of Leases in Lieu of Financing

As we indicated previously, property users in some instances make use of leases in order to avoid the financing problems arising from fee ownership. In some cases the line of demarcation between certain forms of leasing agreements and various mortgage agreements is barely discernible, although from a strictly legal standpoint distinctions do exist. Many business firms have made use of leases in acquiring the use of various types of properties in recent years. Leasing has been used to an increasing extent by chain store organizations. Industrial and public utility firms have also made use of such arrangements. Probably the most important reason for this development has been the need of business firms while they are expanding to conserve capital for current uses rather than to commit it to long-term fixed uses. Rising prices and high income taxes may also con-

[5] See for example the U.S. Savings and Loan League's *Construction Lending Guide*, Chicago, 1964. It covers such topics as land planning, design, construction, appraising, and construction loan procedures.

tribute to the need for current capital. Under leasing arrangements no fixed debts are created and no debt is reflected upon the financial statements of a firm. In addition there are some income tax advantages in the leasing arrangement, since rent is considered a business expense while repayment of the principal of a mortgage is not. Interest on a mortgage, however, is considered a business expense.

Types of Leases

A number of types of leases are in use, ranging from the ordinary short-term lease, in which a business firm or individual rents an existing property and pays periodic rentals for the duration of the lease, to long-term amortized leases. Under long-term amortized leases, a business firm may arrange to have a site purchased and improvements constructed for it by an individual or a company for lease back to the firm. Under this type of arrangement, the rentals will often completely amortize the investment and also provide a return to the lessor. At the end of such a period, title to the property vests in the lessee. In this instance the lease is almost identical, from an economic standpoint, with the purchase of a property with a 100 per cent loan amortized in a given period. In legal terms, of course, this is not the case.

Different types of business organizations follow various arrangements in regard to leases. For example, a grocery chain organization ordinarily will not lease an outlet in an outlying shopping center for more than five or ten years. However, arrangements are usually made for renewal at the option of the chain store organization. Some department and variety stores have leased outlets in so-called "100 per cent" retail locations for 30 years or longer; but even in such locations, shorter terms are used with increasing frequency. Leases for long terms often include provisions for payments based upon a percentage of the dollar volume of business. This arrangement is commonly called a *percentage lease*. Sometimes there are *graded* or *step-up leases,* with the rental moving from one level to another in accordance with the specific agreements that have been made. When the lessor has the responsibility for taxes, insurance, and property maintenance, the arrangement is called a *gross lease,* in contrast to a *net lease,* in which the lessee assumes that responsibility.

The Buy-Build-Sell Lease

Sometimes a property which is needed by a business organization is not available at the time and in the location desired. In such instances business firms may buy land in the desired location, build the type of structure and other improvements that are needed, and then sell the property to individual or institutional investors, arranging to lease it back after the sale. This is known as a *buy-build-sell lease*. Such plans provide properties of exactly the type desired, and only temporary financing needs to be obtained by the business organization wishing to use the property. Safeway Stores pioneered this type of arrangement.

In some cases arrangements are made whereby the property may be repurchased by prearrangement. Usually this arrangement is called a *rejectable offer*. The lessee states that the lease is to be cancelled and offers to repurchase on the basis of the original arrangement. If the offer to repurchase is not accepted by the lessor, the lease is cancelled.

The Sale-Leaseback Arrangement

The buy-build-sell lease outlined above is a specialized type of the sale-leaseback arrangement, which is more commonly associated with the sale of existing properties with arrangements for leasing them back. Such arrangements enable a business firm to raise funds for working capital purposes without surrendering the use of the property which has been owned up to that point. Many of the early sale-leaseback arrangements were made with educational institutions, foundations, and charitable organizations, which enjoyed tax exemptions. However, changes in the revenue laws provided for the taxation of such organizations at full corporate rates on rentals received from properties that were leased to the extent that borrowed funds were used.

Life insurance companies have acquired the right to invest in income properties, and they have been one of the more important sources of funds for arrangements of this type. More recently, pension funds have played an important role in this field. Many of the earlier sale-leaseback arrangements contained options to repurchase; but because questions were raised regarding the tax status of such arrangements, repurchase agreements are not currently being used to any great extent. Renewal provisions, however, are almost always used.

The Long-Term Ground Lease

The ground lease system dates back to English and colonial procedures. Ground leases once played an important part in the development of business properties, and are still employed in a few localities, particularly in Pennsylvania, Hawaii, and Maryland, as a means for real estate financing. The long-term ground lease usually runs for 99 years and may be renewable forever. It applies only to the land, and arrangements are usually required for improving the land within a specified period of time. Such improvements then serve as security for the lease and insure continued occupancy by the tenant. These leases are almost always "net" in form. Because of difficulties that arose with arrangements of this type during the depression years, most business firms have tended to prefer package deals that secure both land and building under a single long-term lease.

SUMMARY

Because of the high unit value of real properties, most parties in the real estate field rely heavily on borrowed funds to accomplish the development, construction, or purchase of real estate. Thus, the terms and availability of financing are important factors in real estate decisions.

Like many other economic goods, real estate may be pledged as security for borrowed funds. Because of fixity of location, long life, and limited marketability of real estate, special practices and instruments have been developed for use in the financing of real properties.

This chapter emphasizes the method of financing through use of mortgages and related instruments like trust deeds in the nature of a mortgage, bonds, and land contracts. Mortgages, which are evidences of debt and pledges of property as security, are classified by degree of priority, method of repayment, and purpose.

The most common course of action in the event of default on a mortgage is foreclosure by sale. Most states make allowance for the interest of the mortgagor by establishing redemption provisions.

Various types of leases may be employed by users of real estate resources who do not care to undertake the financial responsibility of ownership.

QUESTIONS FOR STUDY

1. How are the terms and availability of real estate credit related to conditions in the general capital markets?
2. Over the past year assume that conditions in the mortgage markets, particularly for single-family homes, have been highly competitive. Business expansion is increasing the demand for funds for plant and equipment expenditures. What effect do you believe this is likely to have on the home mortgage market? Explain your position.
3. List the chief sources of equity funds for investment in real estate.
4. Differentiate between each of the following pairs: (a) A first mortgage and a second mortgage. (b) A senior mortgage and a junior mortgage. (c) A conventional mortgage and an insured or guaranteed mortgage. (d) An amortized mortgage and a straight term mortgage. (e) An open-end mortgage and a package mortgage.
5. Indicate the various types of action available to mortgagees in the event of default on a mortgage.
6. Describe the process of financing a construction project.
7. Explain the difference between the buy-build-sell lease and the sale-leaseback arrangement.

8. Why do some firms prefer leasing arrangements to the alternative of financing ownership of the real estate resources they employ?
9. Which of the various types of lease arrangement would you prefer, and in each case give reasons to explain your preference, if you were in business as: (a) A real estate manager for a chain of grocery stores? (b) A property manager for a shopping center? (c) A physician leasing office space? (d) A general manager of a small, single-plant manufacturing firm?
10. In purchasing a new home for your family residence, would you prefer to assume a "conventional" mortgage or an "insured" mortgage? Why? Explain the relative advantages and disadvantages of each.
11. *Study Project 31.* (a) Why is the mortgagor suing the purchaser? (b) What facts most influenced the decision of the judge in this case? (c) What is meant by purchasing a property "subject to the mortgage"? (d) Do you see any hazards in purchasing a property subject to a mortgage? Explain.

SUGGESTED READINGS

CASE, FRED E. *Real Estate.* Englewood Cliffs, N.J.: Allyn & Bacon, Inc., 1962. Chap. xix.

MARTIN, PRESTON. *Real Estate Principles and Practices.* New York: The Macmillan Co., 1959. Chap. ix.

U.S. SAVINGS AND LOAN LEAGUE. *Construction Lending Guide.* Chicago: The League, 1964.

20

Financing: Institutions and Agencies

Types of Institutions

In the preceding chapter we considered some of the more widely used methods and instruments of real estate finance. We turn now to a review of the principal institutions and agencies operating in this field: commercial and mutual savings banks, savings and loan associations, and life insurance companies. We consider briefly individual lenders, mortgage brokers and companies, pension funds, real estate investment trusts, and other sources of funds for real estate projects and programs.

The principal institutions engaged in real estate finance are organized either on a stock or on a mutual basis. Thus there are stock and mutual life insurance companies, mutual and stock savings and loan associations, and mutual savings banks; nearly all commercial banks are organized as stock companies. Virtually all of the institutions in this field are organized as corporations, but in the case of mutuals ownership rests with members —that is, policyholders in the case of mutual life insurance companies, savers in the case of mutual savings and loan associations and mutual savings banks.

Regardless of how organized, most financial institutions must secure special federal or state charters in order to do business. Thus, they are granted at least a limited monopoly position. This is not true, of course, of individual investors and certain mortgage and investment companies that are also real estate lenders.

Financial institutions are influenced in their decisions and programs by public agencies and policies to a greater extent than most other business organizations. Thus financial institutions in the real estate field are influenced by Federal Reserve and Treasury policies just as are all financial institutions. In addition, there are a number of agencies that affect real estate financing programs rather directly, particularly in the housing field. These include the Federal Home Loan Bank System; the Veterans' Administration; and the Department of Housing and Urban Development, which includes the Housing and Home Finance Agency, the Federal Housing Administration, Community Facilities Administration, Urban Renewal Administration, and the Federal National Mortgage Association. Also, the Federal Land Banks and several other agencies are important in farm financing, and the Small Business Administration is of some importance in the financing of real estate projects for business firms.

Savings and Loan Associations

Savings and loan associations, referred to in various parts of the country as homestead associations, building and loan associations, savings associations, and cooperative banks, are one of the most important sources of funds for real estate financing, especially in the field of home ownership. These institutions typically make over 40 per cent of the nonfarm mortgages of $20,000 or less and hold about the same proportion of the total mortgage debt on one- to four-family nonfarm homes.

These institutions specialize in residential mortgage financing. A large majority of their loans are made on the security of single-family houses, although they also finance multi-unit residential structures and, to a more limited extent, smaller commercial, industrial, and institutional properties. They have authority to invest to a certain extent in the obligations of municipalities and to make loans to finance college education. Besides mortgages, their investments typically are limited to United States government bonds and home improvement loans. In some cases they may own and develop subdivisions.

Originally patterned somewhat after the building societies of England, the early organizations of this type started as small mutual benefit societies, typically being dissolved whenever all members had acquired homes. This terminating arrangement was supplemented gradually by other plans, until today there is no necessary relationship between the members of the associations who save and those who borrow. In terms of actual operating procedures, however, savings and loan associations now more nearly resemble mutual savings banks than the old mutual benefit societies from which they developed. Some states provide for stock or guaranteed stock types of organization, as well as mutuals.

The growth of savings and loan associations was encouraged considerably by the establishment of the Federal Home Loan Bank System in 1932 and the system of federally chartered institutions in the following year. In addition, the establishment of the Federal Savings and Loan Insurance Corporation, with the insurance of savings accounts, first to $5,000 and later to $10,000, was of major importance to the growth of these associations. Their growth in the postwar period has been exceptionally rapid, total assets rising from 8.7 billion dollars in 1945 to over $130 billion dollars in 1965.[1] There are some 6,000 savings and loan associations in operation. Of these, slightly less than a third have federal charters; over two-thirds have state charters. However, the state-chartered institutions hold less than half of total assets. Some 70 per cent of all savings and loan associations qualify for insurance of savers' accounts through the facilities of the Federal Savings and Loan Insurance Corporation.

Partly as a result of their growth and pressure from competitive institutions, and partly because of the heavy governmental demands for funds, savings and loan associations were subjected to corporate income taxes in 1951. Prior to that time they had qualified for tax preference as cooperative societies. Another substantial change in tax provisions took place in 1962.

Savings and loan associations generally limit their lending operations to local areas. They were early pioneers in the development of the amortized mortgage. They may buy mortgages originated in other areas or sell local mortgages to lenders elsewhere. These associations, however, pride themselves on being local thrift and home-financing institutions. Many of them have attained large size, with several exceeding a billion dollars of assets. The general trend is toward a smaller number of associations of larger than current average size.

In some states branch operations are authorized. Generally these are states in which banks also have authority to establish branches. A few associations operate over entire regions, such as Farm and Home Savings and Loan Association of Nevada, Missouri, with branches in Texas and the Pacific First Federal of Tacoma, Washington, with branches throughout Washington and Oregon.[2]

Mutual Savings Banks

Although savings and loan associations have developed throughout the country, mutual savings banks have been concentrated largely in the New

---

[1] For detailed information, see *Savings and Loan Fact Book* (annual) (Chicago: U.S. Savings and Loan League). See also, *Savings and Loan Principles* (2d ed.; Chicago: American Savings and Loan Institute Press, 1960) and Leon T. Kendall, *The Savings and Loan Business* (Englewood Cliffs, N.J.: Prentice-Hall, Inc., 1962).

[2] For an estimate of the growth potential of the savings and loan business see Edward E. Edwards and Arthur M. Weimer, "A Second Look at the Decade of the Sixties and its Challenges for the Savings and Loan Business," Chicago, U.S. Savings and Loan League, 1963.

England and Middle Atlantic states. These banks are especially important in Massachusetts, New York, and Connecticut, with more than one-third of all mutual savings banks in the country being in Massachusetts. They are also important in a few widely scattered cities such as Philadelphia, Minneapolis, and Seattle. Most of these banks are old and firmly established institutions with a long record of experience in real estate investments covering, in some cases, more than a century. Real estate investments ordinarily represent a considerable proportion of their total assets. Mutual savings banks, with their emphasis on thrift, have been well adapted to the requirements of real estate financing, since time deposits represent a large proportion of their total deposits. These institutions hold about 13 per cent of the total mortgage debt on one- to four-family nonfarm homes.

Commercial Banks

Commercial banks have always been an important source of funds for real estate financing, and they have extended their activities in recent years. Banks have always been regulated rather closely in regard to mortgage lending, the principal limitations being on the ratio of the loan to the appraised value of the property and/or the term of the loan. National banks may lend for terms up to twenty-five years and advance amounts up to 75 per cent of the appraised value of property if mortgages are amortized. Straight term mortgages are limited to 50 per cent of property value and to terms of five years. However, if the mortgages are guaranteed by the Veterans' Administration or insured by the FHA, these provisions do not apply.

State banks are also regulated with respect to their mortgage practices. As a practical matter, state laws do not vary so widely with respects to mortgage practices as was once the case. The activities of the federal government in specifying practices for national banks have tended to iron out many variations. In addition, banks have become more interested in real estate mortgages and have played an increasingly important part in such financing.

Mortgage lending, however, is relatively less important for commercial banks than for some of the other types of lending institutions. Typically, the mortgage lending activities of a bank are carried on by its mortgage loan department. The size and complexity of such a department varies with the volume of business.

The importance of commercial banks in real estate financing is greater than would be indicated by their direct mortgage investments. They play a significant role in the short-term financing of building operations, where frequently permanent financing is often assumed by some other type of lending institution upon completion of construction. Commercial banks also extend credit to other financial institutions, which then supply long-term real estate credit. Thus, commercial banks in such instances finance the mortgage inventories of other institutions. In some cases they engage in "warehousing" operations, holding mortgages for short terms under agreements with other lenders to repurchase them. Also, many banks

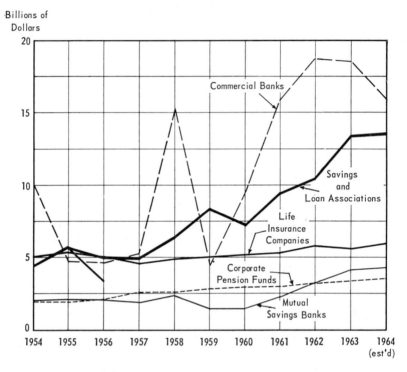

Fig. 20–1. Selected sources of funds, 1954–1964, in billions of dollars.

acquire mortgages on real estate security in the exercise of trust functions; these loans do not appear on the banks' records of assets. Trust funds are sometimes invested in junior mortgages. In terms of direct investments, the real estate mortgage portfolios of commercial banks have increased rapidly in recent years.

Life Insurance Companies

Life insurance companies are one of the important sources of real estate mortgage credit. The mortgages held by life insurance companies typically represent about one fifth of total mortgages outstanding in the United States. While some life insurance companies prefer to finance larger projects, the operations of many of them have been extended into the field of small-property financing as well.[3]

In general, insurance companies have followed cautious and conservative lending practices and hence their mortgage interest rates are often relatively low. Usually their loans are made through local mortgage brokers or correspondents who act as their representatives. In some cases the insurance companies make loans through their own representatives who are direct employees of the companies which they represent. Many insurance companies buy mortgages, leaving the servicing to be done by local brokers or originators of mortgages who receive a commission for this work.

Mortgage Brokers and Companies

Mortgage brokers and mortgage companies are more important as facilitating agencies in the processes of real estate financing than as direct sources of funds. As Saul B. Klaman has said:

The modern mortgage company is typically a closely held, private corporation whose principal activity is originating and servicing residential mortgage loans for institutional investors. It is subject to a minimal degree of federal or state supervision, but has a comparatively small capital investment relative to its volume of business, and relies largely on commercial bank credit to finance its operations and mortgage inventory. Such inventory is usually held only for a short interim between closing mortgage loans and their delivery to ultimate investors.[4]

Mortgage brokers usually represent an insurance company or other financial institution. Mortgage companies may deal with a number of institutions and agencies. Usually these organizations place funds of lenders or originate mortgages and sell them, retaining a servicing fee. Servicing includes collecting interest and principal payments and often the disbursement of funds for taxes and insurance on the mortgaged properties.

In some cases, mortgage companies deal heavily in second mortgages and other junior liens, often originating such loans and selling them to private investors.

Mortgage companies have helped to channel funds between short- and long-term capital markets and have facilitated the movement of funds between primary and secondary mortgage markets. In many ways their operations resemble those of bond dealers.

---

[3] For detailed information about the lending activities of life insurance companies, see *Life Insurance Fact Book* (annual) (New York: Institute of Life Insurance).

[4] Saul B. Klaman, "The Postwar Rise of Mortgage Companies," *Occasional Paper 60* (New York: National Bureau of Economic Research, Inc., 1959), p. 1.

Table 20–1. Sources and Uses of Funds in the United States Money and Capital Markets, 1956–1966
(in billions of dollars)

	1956	1957	1958	1959	1960	1961	1962	1963	1964	1965[e]	1966[e]
Sources of funds											
Life insurance companies	5.0	4.7	4.9	4.9	5.1	5.2	5.7	5.9	7.1	7.6	8.2
Savings and loan associations	4.9	4.9	6.3	8.3	7.2	9.3	10.3	13.2	11.0	9.6	10.0
Mutual savings banks	2.0	1.7	2.4	1.5	1.5	2.2	3.3	3.6	4.3	4.3	4.5
Noninsured pension funds	2.5	2.9	3.0	3.6	3.8	3.8	4.0	4.2	4.6	5.0	5.3
Commercial banks	3.9	4.5	14.7	4.0	9.2	14.6	18.4	17.0	20.0	27.0	25.0
Federal Reserve Banks	0.1	−0.7	2.1	0.3	0.7	1.5	1.9	2.8	3.5	4.1	3.9
State and local funds	2.0	1.9	1.7	3.0	3.2	3.1	3.6	3.6	3.4	5.0	5.0
U.S. investment accounts	2.3	1.2	−0.9	−0.7	1.4	−0.6	1.0	2.4	2.7	3.0	5.0
Federal loan agencies	0.9	1.6	0.6	2.5	1.5	1.0	0.9	−0.6	0.5	1.1	1.5
Nonfinancial corporations	−1.7	2.5	4.1	10.4	−2.3	2.5	5.1	3.8	6.0	2.6	4.7
Fire and casualty companies	0.5	0.7	0.8	1.5	1.1	1.3	1.2	1.2	1.1	1.0	1.1
Foreigners	0.5	a	a	4.5	1.0	0.6	2.2	1.0	0.5	−1.4	1.2
Individuals and others	8.8	8.1	1.7	12.2	5.4	3.4	5.3	7.5	13.1	14.3	14.6
Total sources	31.6	34.1	41.4	55.9	38.9	47.6	63.0	65.4	77.7	83.2	90.0
Uses of funds											
Corporate bonds	4.7	7.1	5.9	4.1	5.0	5.2	4.9	5.6	6.6	8.5	9.0
Corporate stocks	2.5	2.7	2.1	2.4	1.7	2.6	0.7	−0.2	1.4	0.3	0.5
State and local government issues	3.1	4.6	5.4	4.7	3.9	5.2	5.6	7.0	6.3	7.2	7.4
U.S. Government issues	−4.1	−1.7	8.0	7.9	−0.6	6.1	7.5	6.1	8.7	3.0	8.5
Federal agency issues	0.5	2.2	−0.5	2.2	a	0.7	1.6	1.5	0.4	2.2	2.5
Mortgages: 1–4 family	10.8	8.6	10.1	13.2	10.4	11.8	13.4	15.7	15.4	14.5	15.0
Other	3.8	3.5	5.2	5.8	5.6	7.7	11.9	13.5	15.2	15.0	16.0
Business credit	7.2	3.9	2.9	7.4	6.2	4.1	8.3	6.6	12.4	17.7	16.6
Consumer credit	3.5	2.6	0.2	6.2	4.5	1.6	5.5	6.7	6.9	9.0	9.0
All other credit	−0.4	0.5	2.1	2.1	2.2	2.5	3.6	3.0	4.3	5.8	5.5
Total uses	31.6	34.1	41.4	55.9	38.9	47.6	63.0	65.4	77.7	83.2	90.0

a $50 million or less.   [e] Estimated.   *Note:* The uses of funds measure the net changes in outstanding loans and securities; the sources of funds measure the net changes in ownership. Because of rounding, components may not add to totals shown.

Source: Courtesy of James J. O'Leary, Vice President and Director of Economic Research, Life Insurance Association of America, from *1965 Record of Life Insurance Investments*, p. 42.

Pension Funds

In recent years various pension funds have become a source of support for the financing of real estate projects. Usually such funds are administered under a trust arrangement. Their principal purpose is to finance retirement programs for participants. Such trusts may be administered by an official of the company under which the program is operated. In some cases, funds of this type are administered by insurance companies under appropriate annuity contracts. In such cases, of course, the funds are invested by the insurance companies. Often commercial banks administer pension funds for the companies involved.

While the bulk of the investments of pension funds has tended to center in government and corporate bonds, mortgage investments have been growing in importance and probably will continue to do so. Usually mortgages are purchased that have been originated by banks, mortgage companies, and other lenders. Nearly all of the mortgage investments of pension funds to date have been in FHA-insured and VA-guaranteed loans.

Real Estate Investment Corporations and Syndicates

The real estate investment trusts are well known among the intermediaries that have developed to allow investors to channel funds into the real estate market. In addition to the investment trusts, the real estate investment corporation and the syndicate are fairly widely used. The real estate investment corporation may be a builder and developer or may be a corporation that has a special interest in the real estate field and offers its securities to the public for purchase.

Syndicates are limited partnerships in which the principal participants are usually the general partners and have unlimited liability, but provision is made for limited partners who may receive and share proportionately in profits but have no voice in day-to-day operations. Their liability is limited to their investment.

Examples of the former include Tishman Realty and Construction Company, and City Investing Company; the latter types have been promoted by such organizations as Glickman and Apache Realty.

Real Estate Investment Trusts

Real estate investment trusts have a long history, being started more than 100 years ago in Massachusetts. The development occurred because Massachusetts law did not allow corporations to hold real estate for investment purposes, but trusts were permitted to make such investments.

The early trusts were closely held but subsequently offered shares of beneficial interest to the public. They expanded beyond the New England area and prospered until a Supreme Court decision in 1935 determined that they should be taxed as regular corporations thus removing an earlier tax advantage. Federal regulations effective January 1, 1961, gave real estate investment trusts an advantage equal to that of the regular investment company or mutual fund. The development of rules and regulations provided that the trusts should comply with detailed regulation by the Treasury Department and they became in essence closed-end investment trusts with major investments in the real estate field. As has been pointed out,

To qualify for preferred tax treatment, the trusts must: (1) pay out 90 per cent of their net income to shareholders; (2) have at least 100 shareholders; (3) permit no more than 50 per cent (in value) of their outstanding stock to be owned by or for five or less individuals; (4) be investors and not merchants of real estate; (5) derive 90 per cent of their gross income from rent on real property, interest, and gain on the sale of securities and real estate; and (6) derive 75 per cent of their gross income from real property interest, gain on the sale of real property, and shares of other trusts and "other" real estate sources. The last clause allows 15 per cent of gross income to come from dividends and the sale of other securities, and 10 per cent to be derived from any source permitted by the other requirements.[5]

Individuals

The lending practices of private individuals vary so widely that only the most general statements can be made about them. Often private individuals take greater risks than could be accepted by lending institutions. Sometimes noneconomic considerations govern the actions of private individuals, as in the case of a father who sells his son a house and takes back a mortgage on generous terms. Regardless of their methods, or the motives behind their actions, private individuals are an important source of funds for real estate financing. This is especially true of junior financing arrangements, particularly in the residential field.

Other Sources of Funds

Trust funds, colleges, universities, and other institutions often invest in real estate mortgages. Some institutions of this type have invested large amounts of money in this manner. In addition, cooperative societies and cooperative credit unions have some importance in this field.

[5] Glen S. Taylor and E. Norman Bailey, "Real Estate Investment Trusts," *Business Horizons,* VI, No. 2 (Summer, 1963), 74.

State and local governments have not occupied a place of major importance in the provision of funds for real estate financing in this country. However, several states have made special provisions for home loans for veterans. Provision has been made for local public housing authorities, redevelopment activities, and similar arrangements by state and local governments. Loans and subsidies of various types are made to local authorities by the Public Housing Administration for various purposes such as redevelopment, slum clearance, and public housing programs.

The Federal Government and Real Estate Finance

In some degree, the federal government has had an interest in real estate finance from the time of its establishment. Early programs for the disposition of the public domain included many financing problems. The Homestead Act included financial features. Other programs might be cited as well.

The enactment of the Federal Farm Loan Act in 1916 marked the beginning of the government's present activities in the financing of farms. Although the United States Housing Corporation operated during World War I, it was subsequently liquidated; and present federal programs in the housing field date largely from the early 1930's. World War II, the Korean War, and extensive defense programs since that time have all influenced federal programs in the housing field.

It is not our intention to review all of the federal activities in housing and related areas, but rather to concentrate on those that have a primary bearing on real estate finance.[6]

General Monetary and Credit Policies

Financial and other lenders in the real estate field are influenced greatly by general money market conditions and by Federal Reserve policies. The Federal Reserve may influence the availability of funds by pursuing policies designed to produce varying degrees of easy or tight

---

[6] We do not cover, for example, the activities of the PWA Housing Division, the Resettlement Administration, various activities of the WPA, TVA, and the U.S. Housing Authority. Also, we do not include discussions of war housing programs or those of the National Housing Agency, the RFC, or the RFC Mortgage Company. And although the history of the HOLC (Home Owners' Loan Corporation) is highly interesting and was a most successful operation of the Federal Home Loan Bank Board, it is more of historical than current interest and will not be included here. Those interested in this agency may wish to refer to Rosalind Tough, "The Life Cycle of the Home Owners' Loan Corporation," *Land Economics* (November, 1951). For a good summary of various federal activities in housing prior to 1950, see Miles L. Colean, *The Impact of Government on Real Estate Finance in the United States* (New York: National Bureau of Economic Research, Inc., 1950).

money market conditions. The impact of such policies often is uneven as between different money markets and financial institutions.[7] Mortgage interest rates typically respond rather slowly to general money market changes. Insured and guaranteed loans have carried fixed interest rates, thus necessitating the use of discounts or premiums to adjust to market changes. Therefore, when yields on government and corporate bonds rise, there is a tendency for funds to move out of the mortgage market into such investments; when bond yields decline, funds tend to move back into the mortgage market.

Because the Treasury Department is such a large user of funds, the policies followed in borrowing either for new purposes or to refinance older bond issues, including interest rates offered, maturities of bonds, and the like, are bound to affect money markets generally and the mortgage market as well. Thus, those who lend funds to finance real estate projects attempt to anticipate changes in money markets and in Federal Reserve and related monetary policies. The impact of such changes is felt rather directly by financial institutions and through them by borrowers.

The Federal Home Loan Bank System

The Federal Home Loan Bank Act was passed in 1932 and had important consequences for urban real estate finance.[8] This Act set up a system of twelve regional banks (later changed to eleven, then back to twelve) administered under a board of directors (a commissioner during World War II), and allowed membership to all state and federally chartered financial institutions, other than commercial banks, which engaged in long-term home financing and conformed to certain requirements. The large majority of the membership in the ensuing years was comprised of savings and loan associations. The various Federal Home Loan Banks, which in a sense serve as reserve banks in their regions for their members, may make loans directly to their member institutions but not directly to private investors. While the government subscribed to a substantial block of the stock of these banks originally, provisions were set up for the retirement of these subscriptions over a period of years through the purchase of stock by member institutions. Since 1951, the

---

[7] Although it is not our purpose here to discuss the impact of monetary policies in any detail, there have been some interesting discussions of the impact of such policies on commercial banks and other financial institutions by John G. Gurley and E. S. Shaw. See, for example, their articles in the *American Economic Review*, XLV (September, 1955), 515–38; *The Journal of Finance*, XI (May, 1956), 257–76; and *Brookings Institution's Reprint No. 13* (1956). See also, Commission on Money and Credit, *Impacts of Monetary Policy* (Englewood Cliffs, N.J.: Prentice-Hall, Inc., 1963).

[8] Approved July 22, 1932, Public Act No. 304, 72d Congress. See also *Savings and Loan Principles*, *op. cit.*, chap. xviii, and Josephine Hedges Ewalt, *A Business Reborn* (Chicago: American Savings and Loan Institute Press, 1962).

capital stock of the Federal Home Loan Banks has been owned entirely by their member institutions.

The main idea back of the establishment of the Federal Home Loan Bank system was the forming of a central pool of funds which might be used for mortgage purposes and which would tend toward the development of a national mortgage market. It was patterned somewhat after the central mortgage financing institutions of Europe, such as the Swedish Town Mortgage System. The stated objectives of the system were to relieve financial strains on home owners and financial institutions during the depression emergency, to assist in the revival of home construction, and to strengthen the institutions specializing in the financing of home ownership.

As a part of the Home Owner's Loan Act of 1933, provision was made for a system of Federal Savings and Loan Associations. Such associations are incorporated under federal law, being chartered by the Federal Home Loan Bank Board either as new associations or as converted state-chartered institutions. They are required to become members of the Federal Home Loan Bank System. The basic purpose of this legislation was to meet a need in many communities for more adequate home financing facilities by providing for local institutions throughout the country which would operate under a uniform plan incorporating the best operating principles and practices of savings institutions specializing in home financing. These "federalized" institutions have access to funds, in addition to those provided by their own members, by borrowing from the Federal Home Loan Bank of their region either on their own unsecured notes or on the security of mortgages or from other sources.

Provision was made in 1934 for the insurance of the savings and investment accounts in saving and loan associations by Title IV of the National Housing Act. Under this legislation, savers' and investors' accounts were insured at first up to $5,000 and later up to $10,000. Membership in the Federal Savings and Loan Insurance Corporation is compulsory for federally chartered institutions and is optional for state chartered institutions.

Membership in the Federal Home Loan Bank System consists primarily of savings and loan associations plus a few savings banks and a handful of insurance companies. Of the savings and loan association members there is an almost equal division between federally chartered and state chartered institutions.

VA Loans

Under the Servicemen's Readjustment Act of 1944, the Veterans' Administration was authorized to guarantee veterans' loans secured by real property. Subsequent amendments included various other veterans.

Varying arrangements were made from time to time as to amounts and terms of the loan guarantees. Currently, a financial institution is guaranteed against loss on loans to honorably discharged veterans up to 60 per cent of the property's value, or $7,500, whichever is less. Loan limits are thirty years for homes, forty for farms.

Mortgage loans of this type are made by all types of financial institutions as well as by private lenders. Interest rates have been fixed at various levels. Considerable interest in flexible interest rates, however, has been expressed from time to time.

Mortgage lenders often prefer loans guaranteed by the Veterans' Administration to those insured by the FHA because in case of default, and after all reasonable efforts to make adjustments have been exhausted, the lender may file a claim for the full amount of the guaranty to be paid in cash by the Veterans' Administration.

Experience with VA loans has been highly favorable. The fixing of interest rates, often at levels well below those dictated in the competitive market, has caused these loans to be sold at substantial discounts, and at times to be virtually nonmarketable. The special assistance programs of the Federal National Mortgage Association have been used to provide marketability at such times.

Department of Housing and Urban Development

In 1965 Congress authorized the establishment of the Department of Housing and Urban Development.[9] Provision was made for an Under Secretary and four Assistant Secretaries as well as a General Counsel. One of the Assistant Secretaries was designated to head the Federal Housing Administration which was transferred to the Department. Provision was made for a Director of Urban Program Coordination for close liaison with state and local governments as well as other federal departments and agencies. Also transferred to the Department were the functions, powers, and duties of the Housing and Home Finance Agency, the Public Housing Administration, and the Federal National Mortgage Association. The President was directed to undertake studies in order to make recommendations for the transfer of other functions to or from the new Department. Hence, some changes are likely to occur in its scope and operations. Pending such changes we will review the programs of those organizations that have been a part of the Housing and Home Finance Agency and related agencies.

The Housing and Home Finance Agency was established in 1947 for the purpose of coordinating various federal activities in the housing field. The Federal Home Loan Bank System, which was a part of this agency

[9] Public Law 89–174, 89th Congress, September 9, 1965 (79 Stat. 667).

originally, was subsequently restored to its position as an independent agency. Constituent agencies of the HHFA have included the Federal Housing Administration, the Public Housing Administration, the Federal National Mortgage Association, the Urban Renewal Administration, and the Community Facilities Administration.

In addition to coordinating the activities of its constituent members, the HHFA has undertaken to coordinate its efforts with those of other agencies such as the Federal Home Loan Bank Board, the Veterans' Administration, and various other government departments and agencies with an interest in housing and home finance.

The Federal Housing Administration

The Federal Housing Administration was set up by authority of the National Housing Act of 1934. While the original provisions of this Act have been modified by subsequent legislation, the main functions of this agency have followed a rather uniform pattern. Basically, FHA is an insurance agency of the government, insuring lending institutions against loss in the financing of mortgages and loans made in accordance with the requirements of the National Housing Act and the administrative regulations of the FHA. While the FHA program has been altered from time to time to meet changing conditions, insurance of mortgages as provided in the original Act is generally continued. The continuing activities of the FHA include property-improvement loan insurance or Title I loans, home mortgage insurance on one- to four-family dwellings or Title II loans, the insurance of mortgages on rental housing projects, and related programs. Special arrangements have been made to facilitate the construction of housing in defense areas. Provisions have also been made for the insurance of mortgages on cooperative housing, mortgages on publicly owned housing, farm housing, and for the insurance of loans for other purposes.

The mortgage insurance system established by the FHA enabled commercial banks to engage more heavily in real estate financing than had been possible prior to the provision of such insurance. In addition, the mortgage lending activities of many other types of financial institutions were facilitated. All lending institutions that wished to participate in the FHA program, however, were required to become approved mortgagees and to meet the standards established by the FHA for such approval.

The Federal National Mortgage Association

In the National Housing Act of 1934 provision was made for the establishment of national mortgage associations to serve as a secondary mortgage market. Further, in 1935, the RFC Mortgage Company was established to provide an agency within the Reconstruction Finance Corporation which could enter directly into the mortgage field by purchasing mortgages on various types of property and by lending directly on mortgage security. Until 1938, no national mortgage associations had been established; hence the Federal National Mortgage Association was set up in that year as a subsidiary of the RFC, with funds provided by the RFC Mortgage Company. The FNMA ("Fanny May") provided a market for insured mortgages and enabled smaller institutions to sell their mortgages, retaining the servicing fee.

With the liquidation of the RFC Mortgage Company under 1947 amendments to the RFC Act, the FNMA became the sole government agency serving as a secondary mortgage market. It was made the sole possible national mortgage association in 1948. The Housing Act of 1948 authorized the FNMA to purchase not only mortgages on one- to four-family houses insured by FHA but also FHA-insured mortgages on rental property and mortgages guaranteed by the Veterans' Administration.

In 1954 the FNMA was rechartered as part of HHFA to help provide a continuing secondary mortgage market. In 1965 it was made a part of the Department of Housing and Urban Development, as we indicated above. Lenders selling insured or guaranteed mortgages to this agency are required to conform to its regulations. From time to time, FNMA may sell mortgages as well as buy them.

The FNMA also operates certain special assistance activities which permit it to buy with government funds mortgages that are not typically marketable such as mortgages in disaster areas, on military housing, on minority group housing of certain types, various types of "middle-income" housing, and on relocation housing in connection with slum clearance and urban renewal programs.

Other Housing Programs

The Public Housing Administration administers federally aided low-rent public housing programs. Such projects are built and operated by local housing authorities with financial assistance from PHA. Funds are secured by selling bonds and long-term notes and by borrowing from the Treasury.

The Urban Renewal Administration has been involved in programs for slum clearance and urban renewal. It was set up in the Housing Act of 1954 to administer the programs established by this Act as amended in subsequent legislation as well as those established under the Housing Act of 1949. These programs included planning advances, loans, and grants made to localities for projects to clear and redevelop slum areas, as well as to rehabilitate areas to prevent the development of slums. Included also were programs to develop, test, and improve techniques to prevent slums and blight.

Federal Farm Programs

Various federal programs for the provision of assistance in financing farms and farm homes and other buildings have been carried on since the enactment of the Federal Farm Loan Act of 1916. Under this act, the federal land banks were established to provide financial assistance for farmers by means of loans made through national farm loan associations for periods of five to forty years on the basis of first mortgages on farms. The borrower is required to purchase stock in the Land Bank that makes the loan in the amount of 5 per cent of the loan that is arranged.

Joint stock land banks were also set up in 1916 but were discontinued in 1933. At that time, the Federal Farm Mortgage Corporation was established to administer Land Bank Commissioner loans. These were discontinued in 1947. The Farm Security Administration was set up in 1937 and subsequently was replaced by the Farmers Home Administration. Direct loans are provided through this organization to farmers for acquiring ownership and for constructing and repairing farm homes and other farm buildings but only in case financing cannot be arranged through other sources. The Farmers Home Administration also provides for the insurance of certain farm mortgages.

SUMMARY

This chapter describes the nature of the more important institutions and agencies operating in the field of real estate finance. Particular attention was directed to the activities of commercial and mutual savings banks, savings and loan associations, and life insurance companies. Individual lenders, mortgage brokers and companies, real estate investment trusts, and pension funds also may be important suppliers of funds.

Financial institutions are subject to extensive influence and control exercised by governmental agencies. To some extent this results from the partial-monopoly nature of financial institutions which must obtain special permission in order to operate. Much governmental influence is indirect, resulting from the effect of Federal Reserve and Treasury policies on the supply of funds and the level of interest rates.

Government activity in the housing field has led to the establishment of a number of agencies, all of which influence or regulate private real estate decisions to some extent. These agencies include the Federal Home Loan Bank System, the Veterans' Administration, and the new Department of Housing and Urban Development, with its component parts.

The programs and policies of private financial institutions and of governmental agencies are important factors in determining decisions in the real estate field. These institutions and agencies influence, among other factors, the availability of real estate credit, the desirability of alternative investments, and the methods by which real estate is financed.

QUESTIONS FOR STUDY

1. Who are the principal borrowers in the real estate mortgage market? Who are the principal lenders?
2. Describe the functions performed by mortgage brokers in the financing of real estate. How important are these functions?
3. Which financial institutions are most important in real estate finance? What reasons can you give to explain their importance?
4. Describe the purpose and primary operations of the constituent agencies included in the Department of Housing and Urban Development.
5. Explain the roles played by insurance companies, savings and loan associations, mutual savings banks, and commercial banks in the financing of real estate. Do commercial banks have any particular advantages or disadvantages as compared with other institutions engaged in real estate finance? Explain.
6. Which of the financial institutions involved in the real estate field are likely to enjoy most rapid growth in the next decade? Why?
7. Explain the relationship between Federal Reserve policies and the availability of mortgage funds. How is the supply of mortgage credit related to general money market conditions?
8. In what way can the operations of the Treasury Department affect the terms and availability of mortgage funds?
9. Describe the structure and organization of the Federal Home Loan Bank System. How do its activities influence the financing of real estate?
10. Are there any significant differences between FHA-insured mortgages and VA-guaranteed mortgages? If so, explain what these differences are.
11. Do you think the federal government will play a larger or smaller role in the area of real estate finance in the years ahead? Are there likely to be marked differences between urban and rural real estate in this regard?
12. *Study Project 32.* (a) Contrast the role of government as related to the savings and loan business in the 1950's and 1960's. (b) Do you believe housing will increase or diminish in importance from a political standpoint? (c) How important do you believe liquidity to be in the savings and loan field? (d) How do you think it can best be provided for?
13. *Study Project 33.* (a) How much larger would Federal Home Loan Bank have to be in order to be comparable to Federal Reserve Banks in their field of operation? (b) Would you wish to see the Federal Home Loan Bank System expand substantially? Why or why not?

SUGGESTED READINGS

COMMISSION ON MONEY AND CREDIT. *Money and Credit.* Englewood Cliffs, N.J.: Prentice-Hall, Inc., 1961. Chaps. i, vi, vii.

EDWARDS, EDWARD E. "Some Thoughts on Liquidity and Other Essays," Bloomington, Indiana: Bureau of Business Research, Indiana Business *Information Bulletin No. 35,* 1959.

KLAMAN, SAUL B. "The Postwar Rise of Mortgage Companies." *Occasional Paper 60.* New York: National Bureau of Economic Research, Inc., 1959.

MAISEL, SHERMAN J. *Financing Real Estate: Principles and Practices.* New York: McGraw-Hill Book Co., Inc., 1965. Chaps. i–v.

SAVINGS AND LOAN PRINCIPLES (rev. ed.). Chicago: American Savings and Loan Institute Press, 1961.

TAYLOR, GLEN S., and E. NORMAN BAILEY. "Real Estate Investment Trusts," *Business Horizons,* VI, No. 2 (Summer, 1963).

21

Financing: Mortgage Lending

Importance of Mortgage Credit

Although we may ordinarily think of finance as a matter of borrowing and lending, it is important to recognize that nearly all types of decisions in the real estate field have important financial aspects. Decisions to buy, build, lease, sell, improve, and use real estate all involve financial considerations. Thus, the administration of real estate finance is almost as broad a field as real estate administration in general.

One way to narrow the concept of real estate finance is to center attention primarily on two ways of viewing the subject: (1) how to finance the use of real property, and (2) how to invest in real estate without responsibility for the use of it. In connection with the first point, the arrangements that are made many range from complete equity ownership on the one hand to leasing arrangements on the other. Some type of mortgage arrangement, however, is the most widely used method of financing the use of real estate.[1]

In connection with the second point made above, a wide variety of methods of investing in real estate may be employed without being responsible for its use, including complete equity ownership of leased property, various equity and debt combinations of leased property, savings and loan accounts, Federal Home Loan Bank obligations, and others. Again, however, various types of mortgages represent the most widely used method of

[1] Suggested by Edward E. Edwards, Fred T. Greene Professor of Finance, Indiana University. Professor Edwards points out that nonfarm mortgage debt rose from $30 billion in 1945 to $260 billion in 1963. In 1945 the mortgage debt was 12 per cent of the publicly held federal debt; in 1963 it exceeded the federal debt. See his article, "Changing Character of Real Estate Mortgage Markets,"' *Journal of Finance,* XIX, No. 2, Part I (May, 1964).

investing in real estate without incurring responsibility for the use of the real estate.

Since we cannot cover the entire range of methods of financing the use of real estate or investing in it, we will center our attention in this discussion on mortgage credit and the administration of mortgage risk. In mortgage transactions, we always have a borrower and a lender. Their decisions will be influenced by the objectives they hope to achieve, anticipated relationships between costs and returns, degree of risk involved, and the alternative arrangements that may be available.

The mortgage lender is concerned with the soundness of the projects he finances and the conditions under which he may carry the risks involved. The lender's decision to advance funds will be affected by his estimate of the income prospects of the borrower, the market trends likely to affect the property, and the return on the investment relative to the risk involved and probable yield on other investments. When general and local prospects appear to be favorable, the lender will tend to be more liberal in his financing than when the outlook is more uncertain. At times virtually no credit may be available for mortgage financing because lenders are much more interested in liquidity than in yield.

The borrower's decision to use mortgage credit will turn primarily on his estimate of the return he can earn on the borrowed funds relative to their cost and the risks involved. In some cases, of course, he must borrow to protect an earlier position he has taken.

Problems of mortgage financing are important to the public as well as to borrowers and lenders. The public at large is interested in the proportion of savings going into real estate projects and in the efficiency with which such savings are used. Mortgage lending plays a major role in channeling savings into real estate projects.

Mortgage Lending Policies

The lender is primarily concerned with the repayment of his loan with interest over a number of years. While liberal financing terms facilitate the programs of the developer, broker, owner, or user of property, conservative financing terms may prevent them from undertaking unsound ventures. In many respects the lender with his long-range point of view thus serves as a stabilizing force in the real estate market.

However, the lender faces numerous conflicts in his own policies. Ultraconservative practices usually limit his earnings. Liberal financing may lead to numerous foreclosure problems. The overoptimism of a boom period may lead him to extend credit on terms that are too liberal for the life of the mortgages which he makes. Such overoptimism, moreover, may cause booms to run to greater extremes than would otherwise

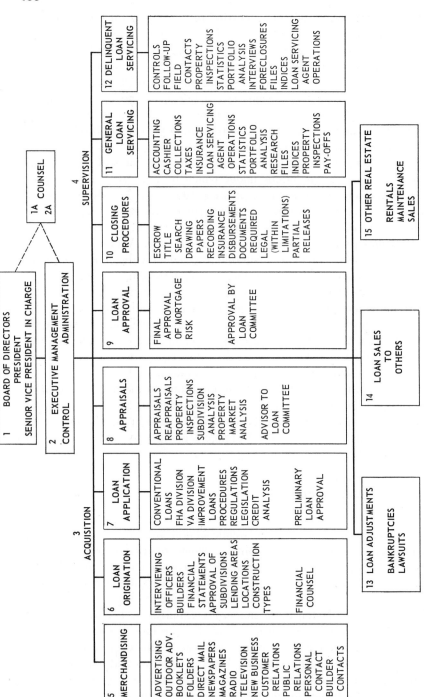

Fig. 21-1. Functional organization for mortgage lending. (By permission from *Mortgage Lending*, by Willis R. Bryant, p. 63. Copyright, 1956, McGraw-Hill Book Co., Inc., New York.)

be the case. By contrast, highly conservative practices in boom periods may limit developments which are needed for the orderly progress of his community. Also, ultraconservative practices during the depths of a depression may prolong the agony of such a period.

The mortgage lender who is financing new real estate projects is helping to create competition for properties which stand as security for mortgages that he has already made. If a new type of construction is being featured by a builder, the mortgage lender who finances him may find that such properties are not marketable if foreclosure becomes necessary. Or, if successful, such a project may produce properties that cause rapid obsolescence of properties that the lender is already looking to as security for mortgages. On the other hand, if the mortgage lender fails to finance a progressive builder, he may cut himself off from a good market for his investment funds.

The mortgage lender tends to object to government regulation during prosperous times; yet he cannot object too strongly because he frequently finds it necessary to rely on the support of the government when the cold wind of a depression paralyzes his operations.

The mortgage lender, whether he is a banker, a savings and loan association official, a representative of an insurance company, or a private investor, thus provides an interesting study of contrasts and conflicts. His policies often contrast sharply with those of others in the real estate field. His own objectives and policies are often in serious conflict with one another. Yet he is one of the key figures in the real estate business. His decisions have important long- and short-range effects, both on real estate in general and on the success or failure of specific projects for the development, marketing, ownership, and use of real properties.

Management Problems of Lenders

Like other business firms, the owners and managers of the institutions engaged in real estate finance must determine objectives, develop plans to achieve such objectives, organize resources effectively, and control operations to assure conformity with plans. Of special importance in the successful management of such institutions is the care with which the risks involved in mortgage financing are estimated and the effectiveness of the programs developed to carry these risks.

The various institutions engaged in mortgage finance have essentially the same management problems. (See Fig. 21–1.) It is necessary to attract savings, and at costs that permit successful lending operations. The required personnel must be selected, hired, trained, and organized into an effective work team. Proper locations must be selected and developed for the place of business. It is necessary to generate the required loan volume, and more specifically to select the risks to be underwritten. After loans have been made, they must be serviced, and all mortgage loans as a group, or the *portfolio*, must be administered in a manner that makes the total loan program successful. The decisions and programs undertaken in order to accomplish these things will be influenced by anticipated changes in business conditions, in money markets, in real estate activity, and in government policies.

Like the managers of other types of business activities, the managers of mortgage lending institutions have the general problem of securing the required resources on sufficiently favorable terms to carry on the programs believed to be essential in achieving selected objectives. In our discussions here, we will not undertake a review of all of these topics. Our attention will center primarily in the management of the risks that are involved in mortgage financing.

Lending Risks

The individuals and institutions engaged in lending funds on the basis of real estate mortgages assume various types of risks. The successful administration of these risks is a complicated process. Although individual investors who finance real estate projects may make their decisions in regard to the risks they assume on informal bases, institutional lenders have developed rather definite procedures for arriving at decisions and for carrying them out.

The following steps typically are involved. After an application for a mortgage loan is made, a preliminary analysis is undertaken. If the results are favorable, the property to be pledged as security for the loan is appraised. The credit status of the borrower is determined. Final decisions are then reached, often being made by a loan committee. Once the loan becomes a part of the portfolio of the institution, it must be serviced throughout the period of its life. That is, interest and amortization payments are collected, and taxes and insurance payments are arranged.

Sometimes the loans are refinanced, and this may be a source of risk. If refinancing occurs early in the life of the loan, the costs of servicing the mortgage may exceed returns. Hence, some mortgage loans contain prepayment penalties. Refinancing usually results if competitive conditions change. Thus, it is desirable that loans be well adapted to the needs of the borrower and to his financial ability on rates and terms that are likely to be competitive at least for a reasonable period of time.

Sources of Risks

The risks involved in mortgage financing vary widely from one project to another, but they tend to arise from essentially the same sources. These sources affect both the borrower and the lender. Both must assume various risks. The borrower may lose his property and the income it may bring, plus (in some cases) other resources as well. The lender may lose yield on the funds advanced and may even lose all or part of the principal amount. The borrower has to decide how much he can afford to pay for borrowed funds in relation to the return he expects to receive from using them, recognizing the risks that are assumed in pledging his property. The lender has the problem of adjusting risks to the cost of funds and the return secured as a result of lending them. Although we pay special attention to the risks of the lender in this discussion, it is important to note that the risks of both the borrower and the lender arise from the same general sources.

First, there is the danger that the borrower may be unable to meet his obligation under the mortgage loan. This will bring him losses, of course, and may also bring losses to the lender. The yield on the investment may be impaired. Second, the property pledged as security for the loan may decline in value, and as a result the amount realized from its sale may not be adequate to cover the unpaid balance of the loan plus foreclosure and related costs. Finally, the lender runs the risk that the other assets of the borrower may not be adequate to make up the difference.

In its Underwriting Handbook, the Federal Housing Administration defines mortgage risk as follows:

Risk is present in every mortgage transaction because of possible future occurrences which may cause loss to either or both of the parties to the transaction. The risk in any particular case may increase or decrease from time to time during the life of the loan but it continues in some degree throughout the period. The mortgagor takes the risk of losing the property which he pledges as security for the loan. The mortgagee takes the risk of sacrificing all or a portion of the interest which the amount loaned might be made to earn and the possible loss of all or a portion of the principal amount of the loan.[2]

The lender thus has the problem of estimating the risk involved in a mortgage loan in relation to the return that may be realized. If risks are considered to be high, it may be possible to make adjustments by charging higher interest rates or lending for a short period of time (although in some cases this may increase rather than reduce the risk), or lending a relatively small amount in relation to the value of the property. In some cases, of course, the risks may be considered too great to make adjustments to them. Also, some lenders have fairly standardized lending plans and will only select those loans that fit these plans, rejecting others which might be acceptable under proper conditions by other lenders.

---

[2] Federal Housing Administration, *Underwriting Handbook* (rev. ed.; Washington, D.C.: Government Printing Office, 1959), Sec. 70203.1.

In order to estimate the risks involved, most lenders analyze (1) the borrower, (2) the property, (3) the market, (4) legal rules and regulations, and (5) problems of administering the loan.

Some risks can be insured. For example, the hazards of fire, windstorm, public liability, and similar uncertainties can be transferred to a major extent to appropriate insurance companies. Certain hazards in defects to title to property may be shifted to a title insurance company. Credit life insurance may be used to help meet the risk of the borrower's death or disability. Almost all other types of risks, however, must be assumed by the lender in advancing funds on the basis of real estate security unless mortgage insurance or guarantees (public or private) are used. Thus, the risks of the lender on real estate security, are numerous and complex.

Lines of Defense

Against these various types of risk there are several lines of defense. The first of these is the borrower's income-producing ability. If this is sufficient, the pledge of property need not be used. If not, or if the original borrower sells his property to a less desirable credit risk, the property becomes the second line of defense. In some cases a foreclosure of the property does not recompense the lender for the entire amount of his advance. Such conditions frequently arise where property is foreclosed during periods of depression. The mortgagee may then sue the borrower and receive a deficiency judgment, the value of which depends on the borrower's assets. (Its value varies also from state to state.)

The deficiency judgment forms the third line of defense. In cases where the borrower's assets are sufficient, such deficiency judgment is valuable security, since it cannot be evaded except by bankruptcy. Of course, if a deed is given in lieu of foreclosure, the third line of defense is not available to the lender. We should remember, also, that forced sales usually occur during depression periods when deficiency judgments are most likely to be valueless. In a final analysis, high levels of economic activity both nationally and locally help greatly in carrying mortgage risks.

Borrower Risks

All lenders of money are vitally interested in the individuals or companies that obligate themselves to repay a loan, even though a property is offered as security— ". . . the aim of mortgage lending policy and practice should be to avoid, if possible, recourse to forcing a sale of the mortgaged property in order to satisfy the debt of a defaulted mortgagor."[3] While individuals and companies may borrow for various pur-

[3] *Ibid.,* Sec. 70202.

poses, two main groups may be designated: (1) individuals wishing to finance the ownership of homes, and (2) individuals and companies financing real estate projects for business and income-producing purposes.

Analysis of risks arising in connection with the first group of borrowers requires that attention be given to the following: (1) the borrower's personal fortune, (2) his income, (3) the type of work in which he is engaged, (4) his future prospects for economic advance or decline, (5) his health, (6) his age, (7) the number of people dependent upon him, and (8) the extent of his various obligations or potential obligations of a personal and business nature. Certain personal characteristics require consideration, including his reputation for fair dealing and prompt payment of obligations and his ability to manage his personal affairs.

Analysis of risks arising in connection with the second group of borrowers designated above necessitates a consideration of (1) the financial status of the person or company involved, and (2) the income-producing ability of the project which is to be financed. If the borrower is a corporation, the lender has no recourse to the incomes or assets of individuals, and hence attention must be directed to the condition and earning capacity of the company and the economic soundness of the project involved.

An interesting illustration of the specific items which may be investigated in analyzing the risks arising from borrowers is presented by the methods devised and used by the FHA. Both individual and commercial borrowers are analyzed with respect to the following items:

1. Credit characteristics of the mortgagor
2. Motivating interest in ownership of the property
3. Importance of monetary interest to mortgagor
4. Adequacy of available assets for the transaction
5. Stability of effective income
6. Adequacy of effective income for total obligations [4]

Property Risks

Analysis of the uncertainties arising in connection with the pledge of a specific percel of real estate as security for a mortgage requires a consideration of all the factors likely to affect its value during the period of the loan. In addition, it is necessary for the mortgagee to consider such questions as: (1) the value of the property in relation to the amount of the loan requested; (2) the property's economic life, structural soundness, and durability in relation to the term of the loan; (3) its inherent income-producing ability in relation to the amount of the loan, plus interest and servicing charges; and (4) its present and prospective competitive position in the market. Basically, the lender tries to make certain that the market value of the property will exceed the unpaid balance of the loan throughout the life of the mortgage.

[4] *Ibid.,* Sec. 70215.

The economic life of a property is a function of its location, design, structural soundness, and marketability. Analysis of the income-producing ability of a property requires a consideration of its adaptability to the uses to which it is put and the potential demand for the type of services it is yielding in relation to the probable future supply likely to become available. An estimate of potential income-producing ability, however, is of little value unless considered in connection with the amount of the loan plus interest and servicing charges during the period of the financing contract. Like so many other problems of this type, it is difficult to consider a single factor except in relationship to others. For example, property changes will affect the borrower. A sudden decline in a property's value may cause the borrower to sell or to abandon his interest in it.

Market Risks

Since investments in real estate typically are not liquid, the degree of marketability is an important risk element. For example, special purpose buildings are generally not so easy to market as other types, and hence involve a greater amount of uncertainty. Similarly, expensive residences are often hard to sell for amounts that even approximate the original investments in them. Also, their degree of marketability is usually limited in small cities. The competitive position of the property in the market at the time and under probable future market conditions is of primary importance in the analysis of mortgage risk.

Sudden declines in markets have a profound effect on mortgages made just prior to such changes. Such mortgages have not been *seasoned*— that is, reduced in value by amortization payments. When a borrower has reduced the principal on a high loan-value loan only slightly, he may be inclined to abandon the property if the amount still due on the mortgage is greater than the current market price of the property. Thus, greater risks of loss appear to be concentrated in the early years of the life of a mortgage. We should note, however, that the nature of the security has a great deal of bearing on risk. For example, a 30 per cent loan on a vacant lot might go into default while an 80 or 90 per cent loan on a well-built and properly located house that the borrower wanted to keep as his home might prove to be highly successful.

Legal Risks

We have pointed out that the laws regulating real estate finance are much more complex and involved than those regulating many other types of transactions. For example, the lender must determine whether the borrower is capable of mortgaging the property, whether he actually owns it or such interest in it as he claims to possess, and the extent of all preceding claims outstanding against it. In some cases zoning laws or deed restrictions may limit the uses to which a property may be put and seriously impair its earning power.

Further, mortgage moratorium laws create risks in many states. In some parts of the country foreclosure laws are very favorable to the borrower and foreclosure costs are high. In others, such laws favor the lender. For example, in the metropolitan area of Kansas City, Missouri, foreclosure is accomplished by the exercise of the power of sale after three weeks' notice by publication in a newspaper, with a deed being given immediately to the purchaser at the sale; while in Kansas City, Kansas, the mortgagor is allowed from six to eighteen months to redeem his property after sale.

The variations of foreclosure regulations between states emphasize the need for uniform mortgage laws that will result in reasonably similar types of mortgage forms and foreclosure proceedings. The great diversity in the mortgage and foreclosure laws of the different states is a major obstacle to the development of a national or even a regional mortgage market. The Federal Home Loan Bank System, the Federal Housing Administration, the Federal National Mortgage Association, and the Veterans' Administration loan program have helped to enlarge the mortgage market; but such development will be limited so long as the laws governing mortgage practice very widely.

Administrative Risks

In drawing up a loan agreement, the lender assumes various risks of an administrative nature. Allowances for such risks can be made in numerous ways, no one of which is completely separated from the other. The ratio of loan to value, the interest rate, the term of the loan, the method of repayment, and the amount of initial or continuing servicing charges must be adjusted to each other in specific situations if allowances for administrative risks are to be made.

Traditionally, a low loan-value ratio was believed to be sufficient protection against most risks. However, difficulties often arise because values are frequently overestimated. For example, a loan-value ratio of 60 per cent might afford little protection to a lender if the transaction were entered into during a boom period when the value of the property was estimated at a high figure. Shrinkage of value might soon result in a loan-value ratio of 70 or 100 or even 110 per cent or more.

Again, a low loan-value ratio might bring about a situation in which the borrower was forced to resort to second- or third-mortgage financing, the costs of which might be high enough to impair his ability to meet the obligations of all the mortgages; or the borrower might refinance his mortgage at an early date, with the result that the mortgage would not have earned enough to pay the cost of putting it on the books. Similarly, a low loan-value ratio might afford slight protection against various uncertainties if the loan had an extremely long term, during which no repayments of principal were made, but during which the property depreciated rapidly.

The interest rate must also be considered in relation to other factors and with respect to the possibilities of price level changes during the term of the loan. For example, if provisions were made in a mortgage which allowed the interest rate to fluctuate with general price level changes, this problem would be minimized. Variable interest rates are used by a few mortgage lenders in this country and are used rather widely in England.

The term of the loan represents similar problems. Unless the term is considered in relation to the method of repayment, it has little significance. Risks may be guarded against to some extent by the plan of repayment. Thus a twenty-year loan on an amortized basis may contain less risk than a ten-year straight term loan, depending on the rate of amortization. It should be noted in this connection that an amortization plan which provides for large payments during the earlier years of a loan usually contains less risk than one providing for a uniform rate of repayment or one requiring larger payments during the later years of the term. Also, a lender may think that liberal loans are justified during boom periods if they are amortized. Hence he may increase his risks simply because he thinks he has a device for meeting them.

Again, conservative appraisals, in the minds of some lenders, may be balanced by liberal loans, or high interest rates by longer-term loans. Thus every device for reducing risk may become a risk element itself if the administration of a mortgage lending program is weak. Rising foreclosure rates in the mid-1960's may be attributed at least in part to deficiencies in the administration of mortgage lending programs. Risks were not being assessed with sufficient accuracy to provide protections against them.

Amortized mortgages are not sound risks simply because they are amortized. Like other risk elements, amortization must be adjusted to all of the factors bearing on the probable success of the mortgage arrangement. Further, it is always necessary to bear in mind that real estate credit is of a long-term character, and therefore a financing transaction may fail because the loan agreement was not adjusted to the longer-range risk factors in a specific situation.

Portfolio Management

Obviously the risks assumed in one mortgage loan may offset in part the risks assumed in another. There is thus somewhat less total risk in an entire loan portfolio than in all of the loans individually. Typically, all of the loans made will not go into default at one time. Loans made at an earlier period that have been partially amortized may help to carry the risks of recently made loans.

Nevertheless, the management of the mortgage loan portfolio requires constant attention. In some cases it may be desirable to sell loans in order to meet current demands or to improve yield on the entire portfolio. Or in other cases buying loans may be indicated. Sometimes geographic spreading of risks may dictate the sale or purchase of loans, especially if the institution may only originate loans in a given area.

In some cases it may be advisable to undertake the financing of new developments by providing construction loans in the interest of securing from such activities a volume of mortgage loans that may remain in the portfolio for a long time.

A mortgage loan portfolio cannot be managed without regard to the over-all programs of the institution. For example, provision of adequate liquidity may at times necessitate the sacrifice of yield by shifting funds from mortgages to government bonds or other securities that have the desired liquidity. In some cases considerations of this type may dictate the distribution of loans between conventional, insured, and guaranteed mortgages.

Anticipated changes in money market conditions, in real estate activity, or in government policies or programs may also influence the decisions taken in the management of a mortgage loan portfolio. For example, if money markets are expected to become tight with rising interest rates, lending volume may be restricted in the hope of securing higher yields later.

Life insurance companies have emphasized portfolio management because of their wide choices between mortgages and other investments and the wide geographic areas over which many of them carry on mortgage lending operations. Usually life insurance companies establish a standard pattern for a mortgage loan and then select carefully the regions, cities, communities, neighborhoods, and types of properties that will qualify for mortgage financing. From time to time changes may be made in the basic mortgage pattern. The proportions of funds channeled into mortgages or into other investments may be altered. Changes may also be made in the regions and localities that are considered qualified for mortgage lending activity. Also, the types of properties considered desirable as security may be redefined from time to time. For example, at one time there may be preferences for residential mortgages, at others for mortgages on shopping centers, on farms, or on office buildings.

All of these decisions tend to reflect the objectives that the company is trying to achieve. The mortgage portfolio is managed in a manner that will best achieve such objectives. Additions to the portfolio will be made on this basis, as will decisions to sell mortgages.

SUMMARY

Primary decisions in real estate finance are made by borrowers and lenders. Although their objectives differ, both borrowers and lenders assume risks, and need to administer their financial programs so as to carry such risks.

The borrower runs the risk of losing his property and the income it produces, and perhaps other resources as well. His decision concerns the estimate of the return he can earn on borrowed funds and whether this exceeds the costs, with appropriate allowance for risks.

Lenders must assume several noninsurable risks. The lender may lose all or part of the principal sum, as well as the interest income. There is the danger that the borrower will not be able to meet the obligation, that the mortgaged property may decline in value and not be adequate to cover the unpaid balance, and that the borrower may not have sufficient assets to make up the deficiency. The lender is concerned with the return on his investment relative to the risk involved and the returns on alternative investments. Once the loan is made, his primary interest is in the repayment of the principal amount, with interest, within the specified time.

The risks assumed by both borrowers and lenders arise from the same general sources. These sources are the income producing ability or other resources of the borrower, the value and income-producing ability of the property, and the uncertainties of market conditions. Legal and administrative risks also may be important.

Financial institutions engaging in real estate finance have the additional problem of attracting the savings of individuals and business firms on terms that will permit profitable lending. They also have the problems of managing mortgage portfolios as well as the usual types of management problems common to most business enterprises.

QUESTIONS FOR STUDY

1. List the principal sources of risk to lenders in the financing of real estate. Can these risks be avoided? Explain.
2. List the factors you would consider in evaluating an individual borrower. Which factors would you consider most important?
3. Would the same factors be important in analyzing a commercial borrower? Explain any additional factors that should be considered in the case of the commercial borrower.
4. If you were planning to purchase a tract of vacant land in order to subdivide and develop it, where would you go to secure financing? List the risks that you, as borrower, would encounter in this project.
5. To what extent would the mortgage lender make use of the following in adjusting to the risk involved in a real estate financing transaction? (a)

Loan-to-value ratio. (b) Term of the loan in relation to the life of the property. (c) The interest rate. (d) The rate of amortization.

6. If real estate values decline sharply, can any of the adjustments outlined in the preceding question prevent a mortgage from going into foreclosure? Please comment.

7. Give reasons why most real estate transactions involve small equity and heavy reliance on borrowed funds. Is this a desirable state of affairs? Explain.

8. What is meant by a "seasoned mortgage"? Explain any differences in risk between seasoned and unseasoned mortgages.

9. Outline the possible conflicts of interest involved in the lending policy of financial institutions in the real estate field. How may these conflicts be resolved?

10. What are the principal ways in which lenders can adjust to differences in risk as between alternative lending opportunities?

11. Suggest some of the different forms that legal risks may take. What should be the lender's attitude toward legal risk?

12. Are amortized mortgages less risky than straight term mortgages? Why or why not?

13. If a financial institution pursues a policy of conservative lending but makes liberal appraisals, would you consider this an inconsistent policy? Why or why not? What reasons could you advance in defense of such a policy?

14. What is the reasoning behind use of the loan-value ratio as a protection against risk?

15. *Study Project 34.* Study the mortgage application as presented by Mr. Smith and then answer the following questions: (a) Should this loan be approved? Why or why not? (b) If you recommend approval, would you be willing to lend more or less than the amount requested? How might adjustments be made to take account of the risks involved? (c) Does the appraisal give adequate information? Explain. (d) Is there other information about this loan application that you would need in order to reach a sound decision? Explain.

16. *Study Project 35.* Prepare a 500-word comment on Professor Edwards' statement that you would be willing to present in a public appearance.

17. *Study Project 36.* Explain why the condition of the local real estate economy is such an important factor in determining the quality of mortgage credit. How does this concept differ from conventional approaches to the analysis of mortgage credit? Why is *time* such an important factor in the analysis of mortgage risk?

SUGGESTED READINGS

EDWARDS, EDWARD E. "Changing Character of the Real Estate Mortgage Markets," *Journal of Finance*, XIX, No. 2, Part I (May, 1964). (See Study Project XXXV.)

FEDERAL HOUSING ADMINISTRATION. *Underwriting Handbook* (rev. ed.). Washington, D.C.: U.S. Government Printing Office, 1959. Sections 70202–70212.

KENDALL, LEON T. *Anatomy of the Residential Mortgage.* Chicago: U.S. Savings and Loan League, *Occasional Paper No. 2*, 1964.

MAISEL, SHERMAN J. *Financing Real Estate: Principles and Practices.* New York: McGraw-Hill Book Co., Inc., 1965. Chaps. vi–xi.

IV

SPECIAL PROPERTIES AND PROBLEMS

22

Residential Real Estate and Housing Problems

Residential Real Estate Market

The market for residential real estate may be subdivided in several ways. One important division is between properties themselves and the services that the properties provide. The demand for properties themselves arises from two general sources: first, those who buy in order to occupy and use the property, and, second, those who buy for investment purposes in order to market the property services to tenants.

The scope of the market is substantially different if considered from the standpoint of investors as against owner-occupants or tenants. The investment market is broader, since investors from one city may purchase apartment houses or other properties in another. Except for resort property, or "second homes," owner-occupants and renters of residential real estate almost always are residents of a particular community or are planning to move to that community soon.

Another division of the market may be made between new and used properties. Builders and developers of new properties operate over a broad area. The market may be regional or even national in scope.

To prefabricated housing manufacturers, for example, the market will be at least regional in scope, and it is beginning to take on national and international aspects for the larger concerns. Large-scale conventional builders often operate on a regional or national or, in a few cases, an international basis. To the local agent or dealer-builder for a prefabricated housing manufacturer, the market is typically a local one, as is the case for the smaller-scale conventional builder.

Thus the residential real estate market can be understood best if subdivisions of this type are kept in mind. The scope of the market is different from the standpoint of the supply and demand sides; it is one type of market from the standpoint of the builder or investor, another type from the standpoint of the home owner or tenant.

Supply of Residential Real Estate

In contrast to most other goods and services, the amount added to the supply of residential real estate in a single year generally represents only a small percentage of the total. With over 60 million dwelling units in the total housing supply, the addition of a million and a half units in a year means a 2½ per cent addition. This is due to the long life of most single-family homes, doubles, duplexes, and apartment houses. It means that in any short-run period, as we noted in Chapters 6 and 12, major market changes are almost always the result of changes in demand rather than supply factors.

We should note that in a given locality the supply may be increased by significant amounts in the course of a year, although additions constituting as much as 10 per cent of the dwelling units are rare. In any given year there may also be wide variations between the type and quality of housing constructed in various localities.

Despite the long life of housing units of all types, changes in the supply are going on more or less constantly. The supply is being increased by the construction of new dwelling units—single-family homes, duplexes, doubles, three- and four-unit structures, town houses, and apartment houses, and projects of larger size. The supply may also be increased by the conversion of larger single-family homes into doubles, duplexes, or small apartment houses. In some cases, stores and other buildings may be converted to residential uses.

The supply of housing is being reduced constantly by demolitions or as a result of destruction by fire, windstorm, or flood. Sometimes demolitions occur to make room for new residential uses, in other cases for commercial or industrial uses. Renewal and redevelopment programs and highway and other projects may bring about demolitions.[1] During the 1950's some 200,000 units were demolished on the average annually. In the mid-1960's this figure moved upward to more than 250,000 units.

Significant changes are taking place almost continuously in the *quality* of the housing supply as well as in quantity of dwelling units. Physical

[1] For a summary of recent changes in the housing inventory, see U.S. Bureau of the Census, "Components of Inventory Changes 1957–1959," *1960 Census of Housing* (Washington, D.C.: Government Printing Office, 1963), Vol. IV, Part II.

depreciation goes on day by day and year by year. Newer and better housing units bring obsolescence to those in the existing supply. Remodeling, repair, and modernization programs counteract these tendencies to some extent. The extension of sewer, street, and water facilities benefit some residences at the expense of others. The same thing is true of the construction of new schools and other community facilities. Blighting influences are turning some neighborhoods into slums at the same time that renewal programs are rescuing others from such a fate. Thus, despite the apparent permanence of the housing supply, it is undergoing constant change.

The Demand for Housing

Housing demand is primarily a reflection of (1) incomes and income prospects, (2) terms and availability of financing plus anticipated changes in financial terms, (3) preferences of consumers for housing or for other goods and services or for savings, (4) population factors, including age distribution as well as numbers, location, and other characteristics, and (5) cost and price factors, including materials, labor, land, financing, and others.

The demand for housing involves more than the desire and willingness to pay for shelter, comfort, and privacy. It includes prestige factors, particularly in the case of home ownership. Prestige factors, however, may also be of importance in regard to rental housing, especially in the higher rental ranges.

It is important to recognize the interrelationships between the factors outlined above. For example, incomes and income prospects may be indicative of a strong demand for housing but may be offset by unfavorable financing terms or by high costs and prices. Similarly, recent and projected population growth suggests that housing demand will be strong in the late 1960's and 1970's. If incomes do not expand, however, or if financing is not available on favorable terms, there may be little expansion in housing demand despite the pressures of population. Or again, people may prefer to spend more or less on travel, automobiles, amusements, education, or other things than on housing.

Personal Incomes

Of major importance to an understanding of the changes in the demand for residential real estate in recent years is the rising level of personal incomes, both in monetary and in real terms. In 1929, income per capita, after taxes, measured in terms of 1964 dollars, was $1,273. By 1933, it declined to $938 (again in terms of 1964 dollars), or a drop of 26 per cent. In 1964, per capita disposable (after tax) income was $2,248. Thus, even a decline in income from 1964 levels of the proportions experienced in the depression of the early 1930's would still leave incomes well above their 1929 levels.

The significant advance in incomes that has taken place in recent years has had at least several effects on housing demand. Income advances probably account to a considerable extent for the rise in home ownership, the movement to suburban areas, greater preference for single-family detached houses, usually of the one-story or split-level variety, and the increase in the popularity of higher-quality apartments such as are found in garden-type or high-rise developments. In short, *as income levels move upward, the luxury and qualitative aspects of housing tend to increase in importance.* Conversely, as incomes decline, the utilitarian aspects of housing demand tend to increase in relative importance.

When real incomes are high and tending to go higher, the demand for all types of residential real estate, with the possible exception of that renting at very low levels, must be analyzed in terms of its luxury aspects. In a sense, of course, nearly all housing as we know it today is a luxury. All of the people in the country could be provided with shelter in barracks for a small fraction of the investment that is represented by our current housing supply and for a small fraction of the annual costs of the housing services that we enjoy. When incomes are high, however, people are not satisfied with modest housing accommodations.

When incomes are high and consumers stress the qualitative and luxury aspects of housing, the rate at which dwelling units grow obsolete increases. Hence there is a tendency for older houses to lose out in their competition with newer accommodations. Considerable emphasis at such times is placed on modernization and repair programs for older properties.

During periods when demand is unusually strong and before building programs can add appreciably to the available supply, the prices of older houses and the rents for older apartments move up along with the prices and rents for newer accommodations. As the number of dwelling units increases, however, older houses begin to lose out in competition with newer, more modern structures. Hence the prices and rents of older properties level out and begin to move downward before newer properties are affected.

Eventually, if there are great additions to supply or if incomes begin to move downward, some of the older properties may be able to compete more effectively as consumers try to reduce their living expenses. Often older properties are not encumbered with heavy carrying charges and gain in relative competitive position. As newer properties are refinanced or other adjustments are made to cyclical changes, they will move into a more favorable competitive position relative to older structures.

Table 22–1. Selected Characteristics of American Families, 1962

	Number of Families (millions)	Per Cent of Total
Total	47.0	100
Age of head:		
14–24 years	2.5	5
25–54 years	30.4	65
55–64	7.3	16
65 years and over	6.8	14
Education of head: [1]		
8 years or less	16.3	35
9–11 years	8.6	19
12 years	12.2	26
More than 12 years	9.3	20
Sex of head:		
Male	42.3	90
Female	4.7	10
Labor force status of head: [2]		
Not in civilian labor force	8.4	18
Employed	36.9	78
Unemployed	1.7	4
Color of family:		
White	42.4	90
Nonwhite	4.6	10
Children under 18 years of age in family:		
None	18.8	40
One to three	22.7	48
Four or more	5.5	12
Earners in family:		
None	3.8	8
One	21.1	45
Two or more	22.1	47
Regional location of family: [3,4]		
Northeast	11.5	25
North Central	13.1	29
South	13.5	30
West	7.0	16
Residence of family: [4,5]		
Rural farm	3.3	7
Rural nonfarm	9.9	22
Urban	31.9	71

SOURCE: Robert C. Turner.
[1] Based on 1961 income (1962 prices).
[2] Labor force status relates to survey week of March 1963.
[3] Based on 1960 residence and 1959 income (1962 prices).
[4] Data are from 1960 Census and are therefore not strictly comparable with the other data shown in this table, which are derived from *Current Population Reports.*
[5] Based on 1959 residence and 1959 income (1962 prices).

Trend Toward Home Ownership

Preferences for single-family owner-occupied homes are usually a reflection of higher incomes along with easy financing and some tax advantages. In 1920, owner-occupied homes represented 41 per cent of all nonfarm dwellings. Prosperous conditions in the 1920's brought this percentage up to 46 by 1930. The depression brought owner-occupied homes down to 41 per cent of the total nonfarm dwelling units by 1940, approximately the same percentage as in 1920. The prosperity of the 1940's (and

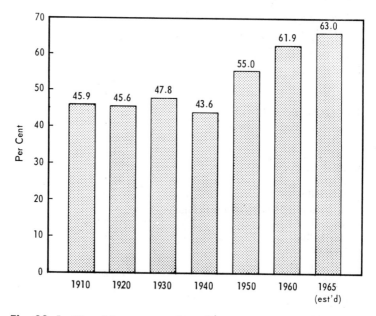

Fig. 22–1. Rise of home ownership. (Source: Bureau of the Census.)

controlled rents, which limited access to rental properties) resulted in the most rapid gain of home ownership for any decade in our history, and, by 1950, over 53 per cent of the nonfarm dwellings were occupied by owners. By 1964, this proportion had advanced to around 63 per cent (see Fig. 22–1). The number of nonfarm families who own their homes increased from 17.3 million in 1947 to 25.5 million in 1956 to 32.9 million in 1960 and is expected to increase to 38.4 million by 1970.[2]

A decline in incomes, or even in income prospects, undoubtedly would slow down the trend toward home ownership. When incomes move down-

[2] See "The Savings and Loan Business at $100 Billion" (Chicago: U.S. Savings and Loan League, 1963).

ward, consumers are reluctant to take on the long-range obligations that are involved in home ownership. Also, they may prefer not to be tied too closely to one area, since greater economic opportunities may develop elsewhere. In addition, houses are hard to sell during periods of recession and most people attach great importance to the liquidity of their investments during such periods.

For most families, home ownership is advantageous when prices are rising, since the investment involved is hedged against inflation and against rising costs. Indeed, home ownership is one of the main ways by which a family of moderate means may protect itself against inflationary developments.

In a period of declining incomes the opposite is true; and consumers tend to favor rented rather than owned space, since rents tend to decline while the major costs of home ownership, such as taxes and mortgage payments, do not decline or do not move downward as rapidly as rents.

Table 22–3.   United States Population and Trends in Housing Tenure

Year	Population	Occupied Dwelling Units	Owner-occupied Dwelling Units	Percentage Owned	Percentage Rented
1890	62,948,000	12,690,000	6,066,000	47.8	52.2
1900	76,094,000	15,429,000	7,205,000	46.7	53.3
1910	92,407,000	19,782,000	9,084,000	45.9	54.1
1920	106,466,000	23,811,000	10,867,000	45.6	54.4
1930	123,077,000	29,322,000	14,002,000	47.8	52.2
1940	131,954,000	34,855,000	15,196,000	43.6	56.4
1950	151,288,000	42,826,000	23,560,000	55.0	45.0
1960	179,983,000	53,021,000	32,796,000	61.9	38.1
1961	183,043,000	53,760,000	33,385,000	62.1	37.9
1962	185,822,000	54,499,000	34,225,000	62.8	37.2
1963	188,500,000	55,238,000	34,855,000	63.1	36.9
1964	191,000,000	55,977,000	35,222,000	63.0	37.0

SOURCES: Bureau of the Census, *1960 Census of Population;* Housing and Home Finance Agency; Senate Subcommittee on Housing; United States Savings and Loan League, *Savings and Loan Fact Book* (Chicago: The League, 1965), p. 29.

Pattern of Home Ownership

In general, home ownership is more common in the smaller towns and cities than in the large metropolitan communities. Less than half of the families own their homes in metropolitan communities, while over two-thirds are home owners in small towns and rural areas. There is some variation between large cities as well, however, with Detroit ranking much higher in terms of home ownership than New York. The lower percentage of home ownership in New York and Chicago than in other cities probably is due to the availability of a large number of apartment buildings in these larger cities.

Home ownership tends to be higher among older than younger families. Only a small percentage of the families headed by persons 25 years or less are home owners, while around two-thirds of the families headed by persons 65 and over fall in this group. Frequency of home ownership increases most rapidly among families in the 30 to 44 age group, suggesting that strongest demand is found among families in this age range.

According to a study conducted by the U.S. Savings and Loan League in 1963, the average age of the buyer of the typical single-family house who uses savings and loan financing is about 41 years. Of the heads of households buying homes and using conventional mortgage financing provided by savings and loan associations, 14 per cent were under 30 years of age, 16 per cent between 30 and 35, 17 per cent between 35 and 40, 17 per cent between 40 and 45, 15 per cent between 45 and 50, and 10 per cent between 50 and 55. Thereafter, the percentages of buyers dropped sharply, with only 11 per cent over 55 years of age.[3]

Relative income affects home ownership, with more concentration in the higher brackets than in the lower-income levels. Home ownership varies somewhat with occupation; managerial and self-employed rank higher, and unskilled and service personnel lower than the average for all groups. Whether this is simply a reflection of incomes or whether occupation also has a bearing is not definite.

The bulk of owner-occupied homes are single-family, detached structures. In doubles, duplexes, and structures with three or four dwelling units, owners often occupy one unit and rent out the remaining space. Only a small percentage of the structures with five or more units are owner-occupied. Probably most of these are cooperatively-owned apartment buildings. The trend toward the ownership of individual apartments has been rising, especially in the higher price ranges since the condominium arrangement has become more generally available.

Rental Housing

The upsurge of rental housing represents one of the significant housing developments in recent years. In 1956, multi-family housing (much of which is intended for the rental market) comprised only 8 per cent of total housing starts. By 1964, this percentage had advanced to 37 and may remain at or near this level for some years. More apartments were

---

[3] Leon T. Kendall, *Anatomy of the Residential Mortgage* (Chicago: U.S. Savings and Loan League, 1964). See also H. E. Riley, "From Slums to Suburbia," in *How American Buying Habits Change*, U.S. Department of Labor (Washington, D.C.: Government Printing Office, 1959).

A Decade of Change in Housing, 1960-1970

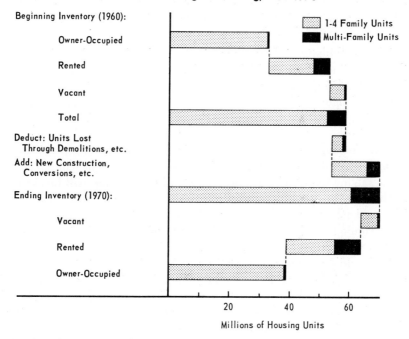

Fig. 22–2. A decade of change in housing, 1960–1970. [Source: Edward E. Edwards and Arthur M. Weimer, *A Second Look at the Decade of the Sixties and its challenges for the savings and loan business* (Chicago: U.S. Savings and Loan League, 1963), p. 18.]

actually constructed in 1905 and 1906 than in 1956.[4] Annual expenditures for multi-family units are expected to rise to more than $8 billion in 1970.

The majority of the apartment house developments are of the garden type currently—one- to three-story buildings—but the volume of high-rise, elevator apartments has also been growing.

Factors that account for the rapid growth of interest in the apartment house field include, according to Winnick, the following:

. . . a shortage of land, changes in consumer tastes; some disillusion with the suburbs; a remarkable surge of funds into equity apartment investment; and finally the broader market brought about by the changing demographic composition of the American people. . . . But I would single out the last factor—the demographic—as having a significance greatly exceeding all the rest combined. It was close attention to historical trends in the age structure of the population, so importantly related to birth and marriage rates and so impor-

[4] Louis Winnick, "Rental Housing: Problems for Private Investment," *Proceedings, Conference on Savings and Residential Financing*, (Chicago: U.S. Savings and Loan League, 1963).

tantly influenced by wars and the business cycle, that led to insights as to why apartment construction was so relatively strong in the '20s, so weak in the mid-'50s, and was likely to become strong again by the end of the '50s and for an indefinite period thereafter.[5]

These population influences are indicated by the number of persons in the 20 to 24 age group, which will advance by around 6 million between 1960 and 1970 and from which will spring between 2.5 and 2.75 million additional households. Four out of five of these households are likely to be renters in their earlier years. Similarly, there will be a gain of 2.75 million in the 25 to 29 age group in this period, many of whom will be renters. By contrast, the numbers in the 30 to 39 age group will decline by around 2 million and this has been the age group in which first-time home buying tends to be strong. Eventually, this group will be expanded as those in the 20 to 29 bracket move into the 30 and above age groups. This will not mean a diminution of the 20 to 29 year group, however, since coming after them are still larger numbers—one and a fraction for every one in that group now.

It should be noted also that the number of people in the age groups above fifty will expand by around 8 million by 1970 and by 13 million by 1975. Again, this is a group that will tend to expand the demand for rental housing, even though the number of home owners in this age bracket continues to be high.[6]

Home ownership has lost some of its appeal as the market for used houses has become more competitive in a number of localities. In a period of rising real estate prices home ownership offers definite advantages over renting; in a period of falling prices the reverse is true. Even stable prices cause home ownership to lose some of the appeal it had during periods of rising prices. In addition, real estate taxes have tended to rise rapidly in a number of localities.

Condominiums and Cooperatives

Garden apartments tend to employ the same general construction and materials as single-family dwellings. As in the case of town houses, garden-type apartments may be rented or sold directly or through a condominium arrangement. About two out of three apartments constructed in the early 1960's were of the garden type. High-rise, elevator apartment buildings usually have concrete or steel-frame structures. Many are of the luxury type. They may be rented or sold through cooperative or condominium arrangements.

[5] *Ibid.*
[6] See Edward E. Edwards and Arthur M. Weimer, *A Second Look at the Decade of the Sixties and Its Challenges for the Savings and Loan Business* (Chicago: U.S. Savings and Loan League, 1963).

Cooperatives and condominiums are similar in that they both involve an ownership concept. In a cooperative the occupant acquires ownership by purchasing shares in a corporation that owns the building. Ownership of such shares gives him a preferred position as against nonshare holders. He may be required to offer his shares to the corporation in case he wishes to sell, and he typically will need to get approval for improvements and changes he may wish to make.

The condominium provides for the individual ownership of a specific apartment together with ownership of an undivided interest in the land and other parts of the structure in common with other owners. Thus, an owner has the same general ownership rights in an apartment that he might have in a single-family home, except that he shares the ownership of land, hallways, lobbies, garages, swimming pools, and similar improvements.[7] The buyer has a deed to his apartment; he can mortgage, sell, or bequeath it. This form of ownership has increased the attractiveness of apartments to a number of families. Previously, ground level occupancy had been much more attractive than other arrangements.

The Suburban Trend

The movement to the suburbs and away from the central parts of cities has been one of the significant social developments of recent times. This movement may be explained in part by rising incomes and living standards. It is a reflection also of major changes in consumer preferences in regard to housing. The single-family detached house and the garden-type apartment have become increasingly popular. Such housing typically is more expensive to build than other types. More land area is required. Although land in outlying areas has been readily available, prices have tended upward rapidly in recent years. Spreading out in terms of land use is also becoming increasingly expensive in terms of utility lines, streets, sewers, water mains, and other facilities.

Lower tax rates in outlying areas, the availability of favorable financing terms, increased automobile ownership plus improved streets and roads, especially limited-access highways and freeways, the desire to "escape" from the downtown city and related developments—all played a part in stimulating the suburban trend. The outward movement of people has been accelerated by the development of large shopping centers in suburban and rural areas and by the establishment of numerous industrial installations in such areas.

Important apartment house developments along major expressways at some distance from downtown centers are growing in importance. Such

[7] See Robert R. Milroy, "The Condominium," *Business Horizons* (Spring, 1964), pp. 51–52.

LEGEND
SUBURBAN
SELF-CONTAINED TOWN
AGRICULTURE - HOMESTEAD
PUBLIC PARK - PARKWAY
CONSERVATION
INDUSTRY
GOVERNMENT
ADJACENT COMMUNITIES
EXISTING HIGHWAY IMPROVED
NEW HIGHWAY

Fig. 22–3. General plan for the growth of Fairfax County.

492

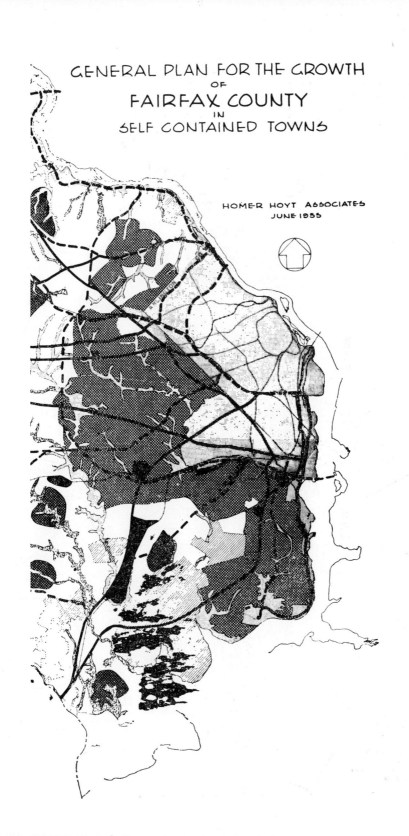

GENERAL PLAN FOR THE GROWTH
OF
FAIRFAX COUNTY
IN
SELF CONTAINED TOWNS

HOMER HOYT ASSOCIATES
JUNE 1955

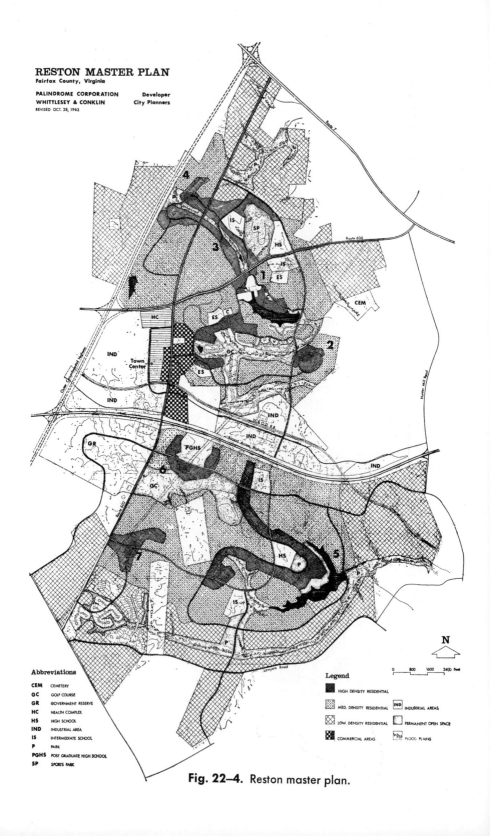

RESTON MASTER PLAN
Fairfax County, Virginia

PALINDROME CORPORATION   Developer
WHITTLESEY & CONKLIN   City Planners
REVISED OCT. 28, 1963

Abbreviations

CEM CEMETERY
GC   GOLF COURSE
GR   GOVERNMENT RESERVE
HC   HEALTH COMPLEX
HS   HIGH SCHOOL
IND INDUSTRIAL AREA
IS   INTERMEDIATE SCHOOL
P   PARK
PGHS POST GRADUATE HIGH SCHOOL
SP   SPORTS PARK

Legend

■ HIGH DENSITY RESIDENTIAL

▨ MED. DENSITY RESIDENTIAL   IND INDUSTRIAL AREAS

▨ LOW. DENSITY RESIDENTIAL   ▨ PERMANENT OPEN SPACE

▨ COMMERCIAL AREAS   ▨ FLOOD PLAINS

Fig. 22–4. Reston master plan.

housing units provide ready access to places of employment either in the downtown or outlying areas as well as to downtown or regional shopping centers. New and projected expressways, including the belt highway around Washington, D.C., the network of expressways and tollways in Chicago, the Gulf Freeway in Houston, the expressway around Atlanta, and many others will present opportunities for apartment house developments of this type.[8] Of special interest are the "new towns" that are being developed. Examples include Reston in the Washington, D.C., area, a completely new community on 6,750 acres (see Figs. 22–3 and 22–4), Columbia City of about the same size, and the Irvine Ranch development in California on 93,000 acres.[9]

There appears to have been some disenchantment with the suburbs in recent years. It may be that the difficulty of developing land still farther from the center of cities will increase costs to the point of discouraging the outward movement of people. Young married couples or older people whose children have grown up often prefer to live closer to their places of work and to the facilities of the downtown area. Certain occupational groups, such as TV and radio workers, need to live close to their places of work. Renewal and redevelopment programs have brought about the development of new housing facilities located near the center of cities. Such facilities may offer attractions not generally available in rental properties in such locations now, including parking areas, such recreational features as swimming pools and bowling alleys, convenient shopping centers and services, and others.

As William H. Whyte, Jr., has said, "There are definite signs of a small but significant move back from suburbia. There is also evidence that many people who will be moving to suburbia would prefer to stay in the city—and it would not take too much more in amenities to make them stay." [10]

Nevertheless, we should recognize that the attractions of suburban and rural areas are strong. It will take powerful forces to reverse the outward movement of people from the older areas of cities.

Financing and Housing Demand

Since few home buyers have the funds to pay for a house when it is bought, financing terms and conditions play an important role, especially

[8] Homer Hoyt, "Expressways and Apartment Sites," *Traffic Quarterly* (April, 1958).

[9] See Arthur M. Weimer and Norman Strunk, *Quarterly Letter,* U.S. Savings and Loan League, Chicago (Summer, 1965). See also Robert Tannenbaum, "Planning Determinants for Columbia, a New Town in Maryland," *Urban Land* (Urban Land Institute), XXIV, No. 4 (April, 1965).

[10] William H. Whyte, Jr. (ed.), "Are Cities Un-American?" in *The Exploding Metropolis* (New York: Doubleday & Company, Inc., 1958), p. 24.

in the demand for single-family homes or for apartments under cooperative or condominium arrangements. Thus when down payments are low, terms of mortgages are long, and interest rates and costs are low, a tremendous stimulus is given to the demand for owner-occupied homes. The buyer uses a small amount of his own funds and a major amount of a financial institution's or other lender's funds to make the purchase.

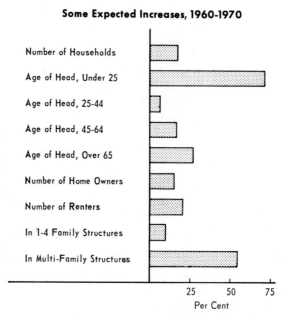

Fig. 22–5. Some expected increases. [Source: Edward E. Edwards and Arthur M. Weimer, *A Second Look at the Decade of the Sixties* and its challenges for the savings and loan business (Chicago: U.S. Savings and Loan League, 1963, p. 19.]

When money markets are tight and funds for home financing are not readily available, the demand for single-family homes declines more or less sharply, even though incomes may continue to be high. At such times the demand for rented living accommodations may increase. Builders may wish to shift to the construction of doubles, small apartments, or large apartment houses; but the financing of residential income properties follows somewhat the same pattern as that of single-family dwellings. Promoters and developers will expand their operations when financing terms are favorable and reduce their activities when credit is not readily available. Typically, when credit is available for one type of construction or investment activity in the residential field, it is also available for others.

The financing of home ownership, however, either for new or for used houses, has somewhat more stable characteristics than the financing of larger-scale operations. This is due in part to the role that savings and loan associations play in the home financing market. They specialize in this type of business and do not tend to move into and out of the mortgage market as conditions in the other financial markets change. Insurance companies and savings and commercial banks, which enjoy broader investment powers, tend to shift their activities between the various capital markets as yields and investment opportunities change.

Not only do conditions in the mortgage and other capital markets affect the financing available for residential real estate, but also the methods of financing available have some effect. For example, the advent of mortgage insurance by the Federal Housing Administration and the guarantee of loans by the Veterans' Administration undoubtedly stimulated the demand for owner-occupied homes. The availability of mortgage money under FHA insurance for large-scale apartment house projects brought numerous investors, promoters, and developers into this field.

Population and Housing Demand

When incomes are stable or rising, population growth tends to stimulate housing demand. It should be noted, however, as we have pointed out earlier, that population growth alone will not increase housing demand. If incomes are falling, housing demand will decline even though population may be increasing. Thus, the rapidly rising population is not in and of itself an assurance of strong housing demand in the future. It is indicative of a strong demand if economic growth continues and is strong enough to cause per capita incomes to advance.

Not only is total population growth important, but its distribution between age groups and geographic locations also has a bearing on housing demand. As we have indicated above, rapid gains in the younger age brackets are now being made, and this indicates strong demand, at first for rental housing, later in all probability for single-family homes. As the accompanying chart (see Fig. 22–6) indicates, significant gains during the 1960's will be made in the age groups under 25, with some gains in the 25 to 34 age bracket. The 35 to 44 age group will decline somewhat in numbers, while some gains will be made in the age groups 45 and over, and particularly in the 65 and over group. It appears that birth rates are beginning to decline, and this may have significant effects on population distribution by age groups later on.

The trend toward larger families in recent years has stimulated the demand for three- and four-bedroom housing units relative to the smaller sizes. The movement of people to larger metropolitan areas and toward

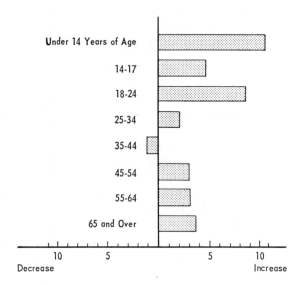

Fig. 22–6. Population changes, 1960–1970. [Source: Edward E. Edwards and Arthur M. Weimer, *A Second Look at the Decade of the Sixties* and its challenges for the savings and loan business (Chicago: U.S. Savings and Loan League, 1963), p. 17.]

the suburbs has had significant effects on housing demand, as we have noted. Similarly, the trend of population movements toward the South and Southwest seems likely to continue, assuming that economic opportunities go on developing in those regions.

Consumer Preferences and Expenditures

Consumer tastes and preferences in the housing field shift as they do in other areas. Reasons for the shifts are not always easy to find. Indeed, the consumers themselves may not understand them.

Consumers are spending relatively smaller proportions of their incomes for housing. This does not mean that housing is of poorer quality—far from it. The quality of housing was never better. Nor does it mean less expenditure of dollars per year in total on housing. What it does reflect is growing over-all prosperity plus the tendency toward smaller proportions of a typical family's income being spent for housing. A half century ago about a fifth of a consumer's dollar went for housing; now it is around an eighth. At that time about two-thirds of consumer spending went for food, clothing, and shelter; today about half goes for these items.

Reflecting the demand for improved quality of housing, only one house in three is now built with only one bathroom; fifteen years ago a large majority were built with only one bath. Increasingly, air conditioning, built in facilities of many types, and increased mechanization reflect the improved quality of housing. Better design and materials of construction also are generally in evidence.

What will be the trends of consumer preference in regard to housing in the future? How will such preferences be determined?

Consumer opinion surveys and similar types of investigations can determine with reasonable accuracy which types of properties and property services appear to be most readily marketable in the near future. Greatest contributions to progress, however, have been and always will be made by those who are able to provide the public with housing of higher quality and at lower costs than has been available in the past. If the original pioneers in the prefabricated house industry, for example, had relied on market opinion polls, it is very unlikely that many prefabricated houses would have been produced. But such pioneers in new building methods, designs, and marketing practices have made important contributions to the provision of greater house services per dollar of cost.

An interesting analogy may be drawn from the automobile field. Market studies by major companies in the postwar years resulted in a striking similarity of styles. Relatively little pioneering was done. As a result many foreign cars began to gain in popularity and in turn have begun to influence domestic styles.

Second Homes

Another development that appears to have long-term significance is the trend toward a "second home." More and more American families now own a second home, just as they own a second car; and the trend increases with rising incomes. In many families, especially large ones, a second home is an economical means of providing family vacations in favorite recreation spots. In some cases a vacation home is a "second" at the time of purchase but is intended eventually to serve as a retirement home.

The size and cost of a second home varies widely, but wealth is no requisite. Low-cost do-it-yourself or premanufactured units are often chosen. In some cases, the cost of a land site in popular recreation areas may exceed construction costs.

While lake cottages, beach bungalows, and more elegant summer homes have been on the American scene for years, more and more vacation homes are built with the same year-round facilities that are found in permanent residences. The family can then spend extended periods out of the city, perhaps with the head of the family commuting into the city.

The same factors that are encouraging the growing trend to second homes—improved highways, faster airplane schedules, increased leisure time, higher incomes, and crowded cities—are also factors that should assure a vigorous resale market for second homes. In fact, families tend to "trade up" on second homes as they do with their permanent homes and their cars. With greater accessibility, marketability, and year-round construction, financing of vacation homes is becoming easier.

The number of vacation homes in the total housing stock of the United States is difficult to estimate. The 1960 Census reported 1.7 million "seasonal vacant" housing units, up about 600,000 from the 1950 Census. While this figure includes cabins and houses reserved for loggers, herders, or migratory farmworkers who occupy the quarters during periods of employment, approximately 300,000 additional housing units are classified as "held for occasional use." In addition, many vacation dwellings are mobile homes, travel trailers, house boats, or other accommodations that the Bureau of the Census does not count as housing units unless occupied as permanent residences.

The stock of "homes" in the United States used exclusively as a second place of residence seems to be rising continuously. It has been estimated that by the end of the decade 200,000 houses and apartments will be constructed each year for the second home market.

Much of the apartment building in resort areas definitely can be classed as for the second home market. Many of the new apartments are being rented on an annual basis, even though the tenants use them for only a few months of the year. Subleases frequently permit other families to have a second home at other seasons of the year.

At least some of the demand for apartments in lieu of a house reflects the desire for a second home in a suburban or resort area. Weekend commuting and closing up the home for summer or winter vacation present fewer complications in the case of apartment living.

The travel-trailer industry reported record sales of 83,310 units in 1964. About 60 per cent of these units are bought for hunting, fishing, and camping trips; most of the rest are intended for travel and vacations.

In the 1960 Census of Housing 766,565 trailers were counted as housing units, or 1.3 per cent of the housing supply of 58.3 million units. Although not considered a housing unit by the Bureau of the Census when used for vacation purposes, trailers fill a genuine demand for vacation housing. In 1964 over 10 per cent of the nonfarm housing units started were mobile homes. House cars, land yachts, and self-propelled self-contained vacation houses by other names are also gaining rapidly in popularity.

"Filtering Down"

Since housing tends to lose value as it ages, there is a tendency for it to "filter down" to lower-income groups. Thus, it may be contended that even though new housing is not usually available to those in the lower-income strata, used houses, either for owner-occupancy or rent, will become available by the filtering-down process. The situation is somewhat similar to the automobile market.

One indication of the operation of the filtering process is the large number of single-family homes in the rental market. A very large percentage of these were constructed originally for owner-occupancy As they lost out in competition with newer homes for owner-occupants, they tended to be shifted to the rental market.

"Doubling Up"

The sharing of dwellings by families, or doubling up, is quite widespread during periods of acute housing shortages. Doubling up also occurs during depression periods, when families move in with relatives in order to economize on living costs. Even in prosperous periods there is some doubling up for various reasons. For example, a young married couple lives with in-laws until an apartment or house is found. An elderly couple lives with a son or daughter in order to help look after children so that both of the younger people may be employed. For the most part, however, doubling up is a reflection of low incomes or acute housing shortages.

Technological Advances

Improvements in construction operations have influenced the supply of residential real estate greatly in recent years. Of special importance in this connection are (1) development of large-scale on-site building operations; (2) more prefabrication of housing parts used in conventional building, such as doors and windows; (3) the growth of the prefabricated housing industry; (4) modular planning; (5) improved heating, air conditioning, and other mechanical equipment.

All of these trends will affect residential real estate in the future. The advent of television has placed new requirements on room arrangements. Air conditioning is gaining in importance and popularity. Folding walls and the use of walls with built-in features have increased in importance.

The result of these developments is to increase the rate of obsolescence of older residences. Greater premium will undoubtedly be placed in the future on modernization programs for older properties. Those which cannot be modernized will lose out rapidly in their competition with others.

An analogy may be drawn from the automobile industry. The "low-priced" car of today costs substantially more than it did thirty years ago. In terms of performance, however, the modern car far exceeds its earlier counterpart. It may be that new trends in dwelling construction will follow a similar pattern, with emphasis on improved services rather than on lower unit prices.

Marketing Changes

There is increasing recognition that land development holds the key to most successful house-building operations and to stable future residential neighborhoods. It may be that greater gains in the future will be made in the areas of land development and in marketing than in any other phase of residential real estate.

The combination of land development, building, and marketing has been helpful to both conventional builders and prefabricators. The careful coordination of these activities, plus assistance provided for the local dealer by the manufacturer of prefabricated homes in land assembly and planning, market analysis, scheduling of building programs, and financing, have been of major importance in the success of prefabrication. Large-scale on-site builders have also provided many of these advantages.

There continues to be great need for the simplification of real estate transfers. This would benefit especially the residential market, with its numerous small transactions and its relatively uninformed buyers and sellers, especially in the owned-home field. With the great progress that has been made in other areas, it is to be hoped that the transfer of title, insurance of title, abstracting, and the many other phases of the process of property transfer may be simplified in future years.

Other marketing developments of importance include the increased role being played by property managers, and the development of programs for trading in houses.

As we indicated above, more and more residential properties are being managed by professional property managers. The success of the property manager in increasing returns on investments in residential properties has led to a substantial expansion of this type of activity. The growing complexity of business practices, particularly with respect to government regulation and taxation, also explains the increasing importance of this phase of residential real estate marketing.

Trade-in Problems

Many builders and brokers have been trying to develop satisfactory arrangements to facilitate the trading in of houses. If home owners could trade in their houses much like they trade in automobiles, they would be able to improve their housing conditions more rapidly than is now the case; and, of course, housing market activity would be stimulated. Some builders have worked out trade-in programs and operated them on a limited basis. A few financial institutions have provided programs of loan commitments to facilitate the trade-in process. But much remains to be done.

One of the difficult problems is that of making trade-in arrangements to facilitate moving from one city to another. For example, if Mr. A has been assigned to a new job in a new location by his company, it becomes necessary for him to sell his house in one city and buy another house in the city to which he will move. A service that would facilitate such location changes is needed. It would have to operate on at least a regional basis and preferably on a national basis. A number of companies provide guarantees for key personnel to protect them against loss from the sale of their homes in the case of company-directed moves from one location to another.

Another problem is that of carrying an inventory of unsold traded-in houses. The financial commitments involved soon exceed the resources of most house builders and brokers. Also, many houses need reconditioning and often remodeling before being resold. This takes time and further financing. Also, houses vary widely in quality, even after being reconditioned. The house buyer needs some sort of assurance of quality such as is provided by the "O.K. Used Car" programs.

SUMMARY

The market for residential real estate includes both new and used housing. Demand for residential real estate may arise from the desire and economic capacity for owner-occupancy or for investment purposes. From the viewpoint of the owner or tenant, the market is localized; from that of large builder or the investor, it is much wider and may be regional or national or, in some cases, international in scope.

Because of the long life of houses, only small additions to the supply can be made in any period as short as a year. New construction and conversion of older structures may add to the supply, while destruction or demolition take units from the market. Thus, short-run market changes result primarily from changes in demand. While the total supply of housing is relatively stable in the short run, constant changes take place in its quality. Depreciation and obsolescence reduce the quality of existing housing; this is offset in part by repair and modernization programs.

The demand for housing depends primarily on incomes and conditions of financing, but also on consumer preferences, the number, characteristics, and location of people, cost and price factors, and prestige considerations. As incomes rise, the luxury and quality aspects of housing increase in importance. There has been a strong trend toward increasing home ownership, including both single-family houses and apartments.

Population changes alone will not necessarily stimulate or retard demand. If income prospects and conditions of financing are favorable, population growth and movement can be an important influence on the amount and type of housing required. If income prospects and funds for financing are not favorable, population changes are likely to have limited effects on housing demand.

Technological developments such as prefabrication of houses and parts, large on-site building operations, modular planning, and improved mechanical equipment also have been significant in recent years. Marketing methods have improved; but there is need for a simplified process of property transfer, and a workable system of trade-ins in the market for residential real estate.

QUESTIONS FOR STUDY

1. List the ways in which the supply of housing may be increased or decreased within a given year.
2. What has been the greatest influence on residential housing supply in your community in the last five years? What do you anticipate will be the greatest influence in the next ten years?
3. Explain how changes in the quality of our housing stock occur.
4. Give an example of the interrelationship of factors affecting demand for residential housing.
5. In what way is housing a luxury? How does this affect the demand for houses?
6. How do you account for the trend toward home ownership throughout American history? Do you think that public policy has favored home ownership?
7. Explain the relationship between age of household head and home ownership. Would you expect a change in this relationship in the future? Why or why not?
8. What has caused the upsurge of rental housing?
9. Explain the similarities and differences between condominiums and cooperatives.
10. Discuss the advantages and disadvantages of the suburbs for residential housing. Do you foresee a decline in suburban living for the future? Why or why not?
11. Would it be desirable to have a system whereby existing houses could be traded in on new houses? Explain your reasons. Explain how you think such a system should work. What possible difficulties do you see?
12. Explain the relationship between financing arrangements and the demand for housing.
13. What is meant by "filtering down"? By "doubling up"?
14. How could the market for residential real estate be made more efficient?
15. *Study Project 37.* (a) What are the principal bearish aspects of the economic future arising from population changes? (b) What are the principal implications for consumer demand in the population changes that appear to lie ahead? (c) How would you interpret the impact of the population

changes that are in the offing on the demand for apartment houses? The demand for single-family homes?

16. *Study Project 38.* (a) The question asked in the survey was: " 'If you could do as you please, would you like to live closer to the center of (. . . Metro Area . . .) or farther from the center or just where you are?' " What factors other than consumer aspirations will affect their decisions regarding location of housing? (b) On the basis of this article, do you predict an increase in suburban living during the 1960's and 1970's? Does this differ from your answer to question 10 above? How and why? What factors other than those mentioned in the Study Project should be considered before predicting the suburban trend?

17. *Study Project 41.* (a) Why do some U.S. corporations find themselves in the residential real estate business? (b) Outline the principal problems involved in serving in effect as a landlord for management personnel. (c) Do you think that there is any future for companies that would enter the business of handling employee transfers? Why or why not?

SUGGESTED READINGS

ANDERSON, MARTIN. "Fiasco of Urban Renewal," *Harvard Business Review* (January–February, 1965).

EDWARDS, EDWARD E., and ARTHUR M. WEIMER. *A Second Look at the Decade of the Sixties and its Challenges for the Savings and Loan Business.* Chicago: U.S. Savings and Loan League, 1963.

KENDALL, LEON T. *Anatomy of the Residential Mortgage.* Chicago: U.S. Savings and Loan League, 1964.

MAISEL, S. J., and L. GREBLER. "Determinants of Residential Construction," Research Study 4 in Commission on Money and Credit, *Impacts of Monetary Policy,* Englewood Cliffs, N.J.: Prentice-Hall, Inc., 1963.

WINNICK, LOUIS. "Rental Housing: Problems for Private Investment," *Proceedings, Conference on Savings and Residential Financing.* Chicago: U.S. Savings and Loan League, 1963.

23

Business Real Estate Decisions: Commercial and Industrial Properties

Decisions on Business Real Estate

The scope of the markets for commercial and industrial real estate varies; but in most instances it may be thought of as regional, and in some cases national and even international, in extent. Decisions related to these types of properties are affected by national, regional, and local factors. The leasing of a retail store is likely to involve virtually a national market if the tenant prospects are chain organizations. The extent of the interest of chain organizations in purchasing or leasing the store, however, will depend on local conditions, on the strength of the local market, and on the competitive position of the property under consideration in that market. Space in an office building may be leased by organizations operating on a regional or national basis, but their interest in a specific space will be influenced greatly by local market factors. Much the same thing is true of the market for industrial real estate.

Decisions to purchase or lease commercial and industrial real estate are generated by prospects for returns from the use of the properties that fit the needs of particular firms. The users of such real estate may own or rent. Investors may purchase for lease to users. Builders, promoters, and speculators may develop new properties for lease or sale to business firms. Decisions to buy or lease commercial and industrial real estate depend in part on the present level and future prospects of general business conditions, on the relative prosperity of the particular line of business activity involved, and on local real estate market conditions. As in the case of residential real estate, income and income prospects, plus the terms and availability of financing, play a major role in determining the strength of demand.

Administration of Real Estate

In some business firms the decisions relating to real estate are made by one or another of the top officials. Only an occasional decision of importance is necessary. Between such decisions, real estate involves largely housekeeping activities that are parceled out to one of the operating divisions of the company.

For a growing number of business firms, however, real estate is of sufficient importance to call for full-time management direction and a specialized staff. This is notably true in chain store organizations, firms in the rubber industry and in petroleum, organic chemicals, and paper products.[1] Of course, for firms in the construction field or in land development and subdividing, real estate is of basic importance to top management. Lumbering companies, public utilities, railroads, and various other transportation lines pay special attention to real estate functions.

In many cases the real estate manager of a company reports to the vice president and treasurer. In some cases the treasurer or assistant treasurer performs the required real estate functions in addition to his other duties. In a few instances there is a vice president for real estate because of its importance in the company's program.

Retail Business Property

Before considering the factors that affect decisions related to retail business property, it is necessary to consider the structure of retail land uses. Of major importance are the central business district, the outlying center on main transportation lines, the new type of regional business district with automobile parking, the neighborhood convenience center (with or without parking facilities), and the isolated store cluster. These types of retail locations were considered briefly in Chapter 14.

In the central retail district are located the largest department stores and the greatest concentration of stores selling women's and men's apparel, shoes, and jewelry, as well as variety stores. These stores are usually grouped together within a few blocks, within walking distance of each other in what is known as the "100 per cent" retail location.

[1] National Industrial Conference Board, Inc., *The Conference Board Business Record,* XVI, No. I (January, 1959), 46–56.

This concentrated business district is usually at the converging point of mass transportation lines leading to all parts of the metropolitan area, such as State and Madison Streets in Chicago, 34th Street and Sixth Avenue in New York City, and 8th and Market Streets in Philadelphia. In smaller cities this center is often located at the intersection of the two principal traffic arteries.

This main business district has the highest pedestrian traffic count in the city. The store rentals and the land values are the highest in the metropolitan area. Although this business district frequently does not occupy more than 1 per cent of the area of the city, it may represent from 10 to 25 per cent of the total real estate value.

The basic reason for the concentration of all of these stores in fashion goods lines is the desire of shoppers to compare styles and fashions as to quality and price. It has been found that competing stores in apparel lines sell more merchandise per square foot when they are grouped together than when they are isolated. It is thus not merely the convenience and accessibility of the central business district to residents of the entire metropolitan area, but its ability to offer a complete range of styles and fashions that causes the volume of sales to reach the highest levels in these central areas. This is largely what prompts business decisions to locate there. Department stores cannot thrive on neighborhood trade because they cannot afford to offer a sufficiently large stock of merchandise to such a limited market. Such stores can operate successfully, however, in the larger outlying shopping centers.

The central business district often includes the central office building area or the financial district of a city, so that the office workers contribute to retail sales. It often serves also as the entertainment and cultural center. In the central business district there may also be located state, city, county, or federal office buildings and the courts. In the larger centers, international offices, both private and governmental, are often found as well.

Space Demands in Central Locations

The store managers or chain operators who bid for space in the central business district and pay the high rents for a position in the "100 per cent" location do so because of the opportunity to obtain a high volume of sales. They would locate on side streets or in outlying neighborhoods if their volume of business would be as great as on "Main Street." In fact, as we shall see, some types of stores, like supermarkets, can do a record volume of business in neighborhood centers and do not need to pay the premium for central business locations. Other types of stores, like furniture stores, with a low volume of sales per square foot, are located on the fringe of the central business districts where rents are lower, or on the upper floors of buildings in central business districts.

The greatest magnets in the central business district are the large department stores, which consist in effect of many stores under one roof. However, practically 60 per cent of their sales consist of apparel. These stores frequently occupy whole blocks, such as Macy's in New York, Marshall Field's in Chicago, and Hudson's in Detroit. The largest stores have 2 million square feet of floor area in a single building and have huge annual sales totals.

Department stores usually own the land and building occupied by the store, or lease it on a long-term basis. The department store is a specialized building and can usually be used only by another department store. Chain department store organizations have grown in importance; for example, Allied Stores operate some ninety stores, each under an individual firm name, and have aggregate sales of nearly $1 billion. This organization has bought independent stores in many cities. Many department stores operate branches, which are usually located in the same metropolitan area; thus they can obtain the benefit of advertising in the local newspapers and use the same warehousing facilities. Other chain department stores include the May Company, Macy's, Federated Department Stores, Lord & Taylor, and others. The latter limits its operations to locations within a 250-mile radius of New York.

The sale or purchase of department stores as real estate does not occur frequently. The usual transaction is the purchase of the store with its land and buildings, fixtures, stock of goods, and good will by a national chain department store organization such as Allied or Federated Stores.

Department stores typically generate demands for nearby space on the part of specialty apparel, shoe, and variety stores. Such firms often seek locations near a department store, which attracts customers from all over the metropolitan area by its advertising.

National chain organizations have discovered, from analyzing their own sales experience, the conditions under which they can thrive best. When they are selling merchandise in a certain price range, they seek locations where shoppers in that income group congregate. They know which types of stores complement each other. Many chain stores prefer to locate between two of the largest department stores.

Lease Information

Prospective lessors or lessees of space often rely on brokers for information to guide their decisions. The broker who specializes in commercial leases hence must secure all the information available regarding the terms of leases in the area in which he is operating.[2] These leases are

---

[2] See *Nathan Nirenstein's Real Estate Atlases of the Central States* (Springfield, Mass.: Nirenstein National Realty Map Co., 1958). See also Homer Hoyt, "Effect of Rents, Operating Expenses, and Construction Costs Upon Net Income of Regional Shopping Centers," *The Appraisal Journal* (January, 1963).

usually recorded, but the rentals paid are not always revealed in the recorded instrument. Representatives of insurance companies and other brokers usually have knowledge of leases in which they have participated and can exchange information.

Retail store leases now are usually made on the basis of a percentage of sales, with a minimum guarantee. These percentages vary with the volume of sales per square foot and the type of store building required. The owner is of course primarily interested in the number of dollars per square foot he receives in rent. Supermarkets usually pay only 1 per cent of sales as rent, but they have sales volumes of from $150 to $350 a square foot, so that the rent per square foot would vary from $1.50 to $3.50.

Most apparel stores will pay 5 per cent of their gross sales as rent, and with sales volumes of from $50 to $100 per square foot, they would be paying $2.50 to $5 a square foot. Furniture stores have a lower volume per square foot because of the large area required to display davenports, tables, beds, and other bulky items. Their sales might not exceed $30 a square foot, so that on a 5 per cent basis they would not pay much over $1.50 a square foot in rent.

Determination of Prices and Rents for Retail Space

How much rent does the owner have to get in order to pay the interest, taxes, depreciation on his building, and maintenance expenses? Stores in old locations are rented for whatever they will bring in the market. An empty store building brings nothing, and an owner will take anything that affords him a surplus above actual maintenance costs. A developer will not build a new building, however, unless he is guaranteed a sufficient rental to cover interest and amortization on the mortgage which is often at an 8 per cent constant rate. Of this 5¾ to 6 per cent may be interest charges and the balance amortization. Ordinarily 2 per cent is estimated for real estate taxes and insurance.

A supermarket type of building on one floor can be built in many localities for $10 a square foot. Thus, the owner would have to be guaranteed $1 a square foot in rent to cover the annual charges on the building alone, with nothing for the land or servicing the parking areas. Usually the owners or developers of such projects demand $1.50 a square foot as a minimum guarantee. Department stores usually offer to pay only 2½ per cent of gross sales as rent, and they often demand two-level buildings with escalators and air conditioning, which are very expensive to construct. Department stores are the essential magnet in the regional shopping center. Developers often make special arrangements to attract such stores.

Percentage leases in high-volume stores located in central business districts, which yield $5 to $15 a square foot in rent, cover not only interest, depreciation, and real estate taxes on the building, but also a return on the high land value. The land value is determined by capitalizing the amount that remains after deducting the annual charges on the building and real estate taxes on the land.

Retail store leases are usually executed for a term of ten years or more if a new building is being constructed for the tenant. Shorter terms may be employed for stores already in existence. These leases often provide for an option to renew on the part of the tenant.

In practically every lease in a planned shopping center, provision is made not only for a minimum guarantee but also a rental based on percentage of sales. Rents paid above the minimum guarantee are often referred to as overage rents. The minimum guarantees of strong tenants such as national chain organizations are the chief factor in providing security for mortgage loans.

Percentage leases are sometimes on a sliding scale, with the percentage declining after a certain volume of sales is reached. In negotiating the leases the prospective tenant often asks for extras in the form of special store fronts, air conditioning, mezzanine floors, finished basements, and sometimes even the store fixtures. Consequently the real estate broker negotiating the lease must have a thorough knowledge of every element of construction and equipment costs.

National chain stores frequently offer the store owner a percentage which is fixed on a national basis. Extra percentages, however, may be obtained in centers which provide special features, such as air conditioning, underground delivery facilities, or expensive store fronts. A regional shopping center with large department stores is often in a better bargaining position than a shopping center without a key tenant. For this reason the builders or developers often will give inducements in the form of a low minimum or low percentage lease to a key tenant such as a department store.

For certain types of stores, such as barbershops or small types of businesses that do not keep accurate books, the rental usually is set on a fixed monthly basis rather than on a percentage of sales.

The guarantee of a minimum rental is necessary for securing financing from insurance companies or other financial institutions for new stores. If a high minimum is obtained, however, it is usually at the sacrifice of a lower percentage of sales.

These general principles of leasing apply to outlying regional locations as well as to central business districts. There are a number of old-established retail districts with department and clothing stores seven to ten miles from the central business district, such as 63rd and Halsted Street in Chicago, 69th Street in Philadelphia, and Fordham Road in New York. There are hundreds of outlying centers in the United States which have a group consisting of a variety store, such as a Woolworth or Kresge store, some apparel stores, drugstores, supermarkets, and local convenience shops. National chain store operators now prefer locations in planned shopping centers with ample parking rather than in the older style shopping centers.

The trend away from the small grocery store to the large supermarket of 20,000 to 40,000 square feet of store area, with a free parking lot adjoining, has caused hundreds of isolated locations to develop. On the average a family spends over $1,000 a year for food. Thus, 5,000 families will support a large supermarket. These stores seek locations with enough vacant land to afford free parking to their customers, and they may select an area where there are no other stores in order to secure such a tract. Such stores can do a record volume of business without supplementary establishments, since most families do not combine food purchasing with apparel or other shopping.

Changes in Shopping Center Pattern

The almost universal ownership of automobiles has caused a revolution in the shopping center pattern. This change has taken place largely since World War II and is still going on.

The prewar shopping center was usually located on mass transportation lines. The land at streetcar intersections, subway stations, and suburban railroad stations rose to a high price level. Usually no space was left for the parking of automobiles. The automobile opened up a vast new territory for shopping center locations. Any tract of vacant land, five acres or more in extent, with sufficient buying power in the surrounding area and with reasonably good access roads, became a shopping center possibility.

The basic problem in developing such a center almost always is *zoning*. The old zoning laws usually provided for narrow commercial strips not over 125 feet deep along the principal thoroughfares. The new type of center requires a rectangular plot with a depth of at least 400 to 500 feet. It is frequently difficult to secure rezoning in established residential neighborhoods because of objections of the property owners. Because of the great opportunities open, thousands of plans for shopping centers have been projected in recent years. At the end of 1963, over 8,000 shopping centers of various types were reported in operation. Further developments appear likely.[3] It is probable that too many of these new centers have been promoted in some localities. Generally, these centers do not increase the total retail business but only divide it. In some cases, of

---

[3] See *Directory of Shopping Centers in the U.S. and Canada,* 1964 edition, (Chicago: The National Research Bureau, Inc., 1963). See also S. F. Otteson, W. G. Panschar, and J. M. Patterson, *Marketing: The Firm's Viewpoint,* (New York: The Macmillan Co., 1964), pp. 322–42.

course, a metropolitan area may expand its trade area at the expense of smaller towns or by competing effectively with other metropolitan areas.

Some centers are being developed with elaborate central facilities such as air-conditioned malls and attractive public areas and the like. This adds new dimensions to the competitive situation both in terms of costs on the one hand and attracting customers on the other.

Changing Character of Retail Sales

The impact of shopping centers is illustrated by the following comparative figures. Between 1954 and 1958 merchandise sales outside central business districts in major American cities advanced by 54 per cent. In the period from 1958 to 1963, gains of 89 per cent were registered. Absolute losses on general-merchandise sales in the central business core were reported in a substantial number of metropolitan areas. In 1958 general-merchandise sales in the central business districts dropped below the sales of stores outside central business districts for the first time. By 1963 the sales of stores in the central business district were only half of those reported for areas outside the central business district.[4]

Types of Shopping Centers

Whether there are too many or not enough shopping centers in any community depends in part upon the type established. We have classified them into four types: [5]

1. The *large regional center* typically includes a department store of 100,000 square feet or more as the principal store, supplemented by numerous women's and men's apparel stores, shoe stores, household appliance stores, furniture stores, drugstores, and supermarkets with a total store area of 250,000 to 1,000,000 square feet on a 35–100 acre site. Around 200,000 people are required to support this type of center.

2. The *community center* usually has a junior department store such as a J. C. Penney or W. T. Grant store as its principal tenant. This main store typically has 25,000 or more square feet, and the center has an overall store area of 100,000 to 400,000 square feet on a 15–40 acre site. Supermarkets, drugstores, variety stores, and some apparel stores are found in such a center. A trade area of around 100,000 people is required to support a center of this type.

[4] Homer Hoyt, "U.S. Metropolitan Area Retail Shopping Pattern," Part I, "Exodus of the Department and Apparel Stores," *Urban Land* (March, 1966); Part II, "Planned Shopping Centers," *ibid.* (April, 1966).

[5] Hoyt, "Classification and Significant Characteristics of Shopping Centers," *The Appraisal Journal* (April, 1958), pp. 214–22. See also Hoyt's article "Appraisal of Shopping Centers," in *Encyclopedia of Real Estate Appraising* (Englewood Cliffs, N.J.: Prentice-Hall, Inc., 1959), pp. 281–95.

Table 23–1.   Sales of General Merchandise, Central Business Districts and All Areas Outside, 1963 and 1958

| SMA[1] | Sales (in thousands) | | | | | | Number of Regional Centers[3] | Per Cent of Increase Outside CBD |
| | Total | | CBD[2] | | Outside CBD | | | |
	1963	1958	1963	1958	1963	1958		
New York	$2,106,346	$1,493,509	$908,859	$849,801	$1,197,487	$643,708	21	86.02
Los Angeles	1,488,618	914,490	130,951	141,062	1,357,667	773,428	14	75.15
Chicago	1,327,204	940,491	288,728	288,011	1,038,476	65,480	22	59.15
Philadelphia	756,803	573,450	220,808	259,136	535,995	314,344	14	70.53
Detroit	833,027	578,422	151,683	165,471	681,344	412,951	24	65.00
San Francisco–Oakland	622,257	414,291	203,995	191,011	418,262	222,280	10	87.37
Boston	564,205	422,996	205,430	201,702	358,759	221,294	13	62.12
Pittsburgh	457,966	386,756	176,968	208,852	280,998	177,904	8	165.47
St. Louis	446,285	340,906	110,783	126,232	335,502	214,674	6	56.28
Washington, D. C.	517,069	317,261	128,310	133,418	388,759	183,843	13	111.46
Cleveland	484,555	354,056	156,453	185,230	328,102	168,826	14	94.32
Baltimore	368,415	243,140	80,426	93,321	287,989	149,819	13	92.24
Minneapolis–Saint Paul	377,675	260,565	171,686	167,913	205,989	92,652	11	110.94
Buffalo	242,392	192,675	53,094	61,279	189,248	131,396	9	44.07
Houston	319,572	190,047	78,831	80,901	240,741	109,146	6	120.57
Miami	218,966	137,547	46,886	47,820	172,080	89,727	9	91.79
Milwaukee	267,880	200,039	69,154	71,628	198,726	128,411	5	54.76
Dallas	253,301	185,142	68,591	81,524	184,710	103,618	14	77.80
Seattle	252,894	205,597	106,743	103,959	146,151	101,638	5	43.80
Cincinnati	243,488	178,411	106,863	110,766	136,625	67,645	8	101.97
Atlanta	263,101	189,516	104,054	116,389	159,047	73,127	7	117.49
Kansas City (Mo. and Kan.)	227,223	155,615	53,632	64,884	173,591	90,731	8	91.24
San Diego	229,845	115,676	19,211	37,903	210,634	77,773	7	170.83
Denver	224,554	167,531	56,276	69,869	168,278	97,662	11	72.30
Total	$14,057,256	$9,707,061	$4,049,798	$4,197,383	$10,007,458	$5,509,678	277	81.63

[1] Standard metropolitan area.   [2] Central business district.   [3] Planned regional centers with sales in excess of $10 million in 1963.

Fig. 23–1. Southgate Center, Cleveland, Ohio. (Courtesy Aerial Surveys, Inc.)

3. The *large neighborhood center* in which a variety store such as Woolworth or Kresge, with 10,000 to 20,000 square feet, is usually the principal unit, with a total store area of 50,000 to 100,000 square feet on a site of 10 to 20 acres. A supermarket, a drugstore, and local convenience stores are typical. About 35,000 persons in the trade area are required to support such a center.

4. The *neighborhood center*, in which a supermarket of 20,000 to 30,000 square feet is the largest unit, with total store area of 50,000 square feet or more, will usually include a drugstore and local convenience stores. Such a center can be supported by 5,000 families, or around 17,500 persons, in its trade area.

The largest regional centers often duplicate the central business district, with several of the leading department stores represented in the location. However, rivalry between department stores has prevented such developments in a number of cases. In Philadelphia, Baltimore, Washington, New York City, and St. Louis, each principal department store has tended to develop its own location instead of joining with other department stores in the establishment of one large center. As a result a number of medium-size centers have evolved in such cases, each with a small following of other stores rather than one super center.

In Milwaukee, however, Marshall Field's and Gimbel's have occupied Mayfair center. In Westchester County in New York, Wanamaker's and Gimbel's have stores in the same center; in Evergreen Plaza, south of Chicago, The Fair, Montgomery Ward, and Carson Pirie Scott & Co.; North Shore of Boston, Jordan Marsh and Filene's; and in Lennox Square in Atlanta, Rich's and Davison & Paxon. Negotiations are under way in other cities to bring the leading department stores together in one center.

This new retail pattern is still in the process of evolution; but, as large investments are made in store buildings, this pattern will assume a fixed form and will not be changed easily. As these centers are built, operating experience regarding the volume of sales in different types of centers and different combinations of stores will become available.

Parking

Free automobile parking for the shoppers is the indispensable requirement for the new type of shopping center. The amount of land that should be set aside for parking varies according to the proportion of shoppers who come on mass transportation lines and the number who live within walking distance. For centers in which most of the shoppers come by private automobile, a 4-to-1 ratio between parking and mall areas and net selling area is considered sufficient. It is not necessary to take care of the peak load of Christmas shoppers, as parking areas used for this peak load would be idle eleven months of the year.

It is estimated that an average car space should produce an annual sales volume of $10,000 worth of general merchandise and $15,000 worth of food. The necessity of providing a large parking area means that even a small neighborhood center should have 5 acres of land, and a large regional shopping center 50 to 100 acres. A developer planning a shopping center usually has to find this amount of land under one ownership or in a few ownerships, because he does not have the power of condemnation and may have to pay prohibitive prices in acquiring a number of separate parcels. Since 80 per cent of the land must be made available for free parking, an extra-high land cost makes such projects unprofitable.

Location of Outlying Retail Centers

Some developers have followed the old-style retail pattern and located their centers at major highway intersections. This creates a problem of traffic congestion, because the shoppers' traffic is added to that of the through traffic. It is desirable that the shopping center location be on a major thoroughfare such as a radial highway and near a circumferential highway going around the periphery of the city. It is not necessary or even desirable that a center be located at a cloverleaf intersection, if it is somewhere near the point of traffic interchange. Frequently, the ideal location is not available because it is already filled in with houses, so the largest available tract under one ownership is selected.

The location must have a sufficient number of families and buying power within a reasonable driving-time distance to support it, with allowances for competing centers of the same type. The trade area cannot be measured entirely in terms of driving-time distance in all directions, however, because shoppers will often drive halfway across a state in rural areas to reach an outlying regional center, while they will not come from a downtown area only a few miles away.

Traffic volume on existing highways must be considered in planning a shopping center. The problem of crossing any heavy streams of traffic must also be studied. It is desirable to have as many access roads into the center as possible, so that a large number of shoppers can drive into or out of the center without creating undue congestion.[6]

In the future the location of new shopping centers is likely to be influenced considerably by the federal highway program, with its provision for limited-access roads between major cities and with belt highways around cities. Instead of building shopping centers on the edge of the old cities, as in the case of the early postwar developments, new centers are likely to be located at central points between a number of large and small cities. A case in point is the Allied Stores' North Shore Center at Peabody, Massachusetts, 20 miles north of Boston, with access to a trade area with a population of 1,500,000 people.

Hoyt has summarized the trend of probable development in this way:

> In the future, as in the past, the means of transportation from home to shopping centers with ample selection of fashion goods will be the governing factor in the location and composition of the regional center. In the automobile age, highway access, ample free parking, and a complete selection of merchandise are and will continue to be the decisive elements in the creation of successful regional shopping centers.[7]

The Department Store

The department store originated in Paris and was introduced into the United States in the 1860's by Marshall Field in Chicago, Wanamaker in

---

[6] For various methods used for selecting retail locations, see Richard L. Nelson, *The Selecting of Retail Locations* (New York: F. W. Dodge Corp., 1958).

[7] Hoyt, "Classification and Significant Characteristics of Shopping Centers," p. 222. See also his "The Residential and Retail Patterns of Leading Latin American Cities," *Land Economics*, XXXIX, No. 4 (November, 1963).

Fig. 23–2. Northland Shopping Center, Southfield, Michigan. (Courtesy Urban Land Institute.)

Philadelphia, and Stewart in New York. With the development of mass transportation beginning with horse-drawn streetcars in the 1860's, cable cars, elevated lines, and electric surface cars in the 1890's and subways in the early years of the twentieth century, downtown locations increased significantly in importance. All the various types of transportation converged in the central business district and created high land values at central locations such as State and Madison streets in Chicago, 34th Street and Sixth Avenue in New York, and Broad and Market streets in Philadelphia. Department stores sought out such locations expanding both laterally and vertically. Macy's in New York, Hudson's in Detroit, and Marshall Field's in Chicago developed into huge establishments of 2 million square feet or more area and reached sales in peak shopping periods in excess of a million dollars a day.

The department store continued to play a major role in retailing despite the decentralization of retail activity. In 1963 68 per cent of general-merchandise sales in retail distribution were attributable to department stores. They became the chief magnets for outlying shopping centers just as had been the case in downtown business districts.

The decentralization of retailing activities started after World War I. It was characterized at first by the rise of outlying centers at streetcar intersections or streetcar transfer corners, subway stations, and suburban railroad stations. The downtown area was not affected very much except in the larger cities.

The automobile brought further decentralization, extending the process. This process of decentralization, however, proceeded at a leisurely rate. There were 27 million cars in the United States as early as 1929 but they had only little impact on the pattern of retail distribution. For example, the Country Club Plaza in Kansas City was built in 1920 and was the first large shopping center that did not depend on mass transportation but relied on private automobiles. Some other centers of this type began to make their appearance, but it was not until after World War II that the shopping center became a major force in the retailing pattern. Early centers of this type included Silver Spring in the Washington, D.C., area, Cameron Village in Raleigh, North Carolina, and Utica Square in Tulsa, Oklahoma. These were built on vacant tracts of land near the center of the city and at the edge of built-up areas.

As the highway network around cities expanded, opportunities for shopping centers multiplied rapidly. Northland in Detroit, Old Orchard in Chicago, North Shore north of Boston, Southdale in Minneapolis, and many others were built on large tracts of land on or near expressways in trade areas with a large total population and income, but often there were relatively few families in the immediate vicinity.

The first of the mall-type centers with stores in the center of a large tract surrounded by parking was Northgate in Seattle. It was designed by John Graham and opened in 1950. The first types were open malls. The closed, heated and air-conditioned malls which have become very popular were first developed in the late 1950's and early 1960's. Examples include Ward Parkway in Kansas City (1958), Cherry Hill in New Jersey (1961), and Sharpstown in Houston (1961).

The Discount House

In recent years the discount house has played a growing role in the retailing field. Such stores as Korvette, Zayre's K-Mart, Woolco, and others are important in this connection. Often these stores were built in solitary locations, either with their own food stores or adjoining a super-market. They are self-service stores with the customer waiting on himself, paying cash, and taking his merchandise away in his own car, or paying a delivery charge. These stores are often large units with 100,000 square feet or more of store area and carry a huge number of lines of merchandise.

A number of variety stores moved into the discount area, for example, Woolworth into Woolco and Kresge into K-Mart. J. C. Penney moved from junior to full-scale department stores, that is, from stores with 40,000 to 60,000 square feet to stores with 150,000 square feet or more.

Future Retailing Trends

The late 1960's and 1970's are likely to witness another surge in urban growth. This will be the time when those who were products of the baby boom following World War II will have children of their own reaching school age. This is likely to bring rising demands for single-family homes with yards and for garden apartments in outlying locations. Thus the urban area is likely to be extended farther, and probably a new group of shopping centers will rise to serve this outlying population belt.

Developments of this type will not eliminate retailing activities in the central cities. Central city sales may not expand rapidly and may even stabilize at levels near those of 1965. Improvements in mass transportation may revitalize many of the downtown areas, however, and add growth potential to the retail establishments located there. New downtown developments that combine hotels, stores, offices, and apartments in one aggregate like Bunker Hill in Los Angeles, Atwater Park Plaza in Montreal, the Church Street Redevelopment in New Haven, Penn Square in Philadelphia, and others will provide highly attractive centers. Many of these will include closed malls for shopping that will compete effectively with these types of developments in outlying regional centers. As one of the authors has pointed out:

These new urban redevelopments based on bringing together functions that must have a central meeting place for face to face contacts would create new headquarters centers of great beauty and great economic efficiency. The central shopping goods stores will probably never regain the dominant position they once held in the urban pattern, but they will tend to regain some of their lost position and to become a part of new and better integrated urban central focus if property owners, city, state and Federal agencies combine to assist in analyzing the functions of a metropolis and concentrate in bringing together those functions which thrive best in the central market place.[8]

The Retail Brokerage Field

Emphasis has been placed upon the new-type shopping centers because this will undoubtedly be one of the major fields of commercial brokerage and lending activity in the future. These new-type centers are usually owned by one proprietor or developer. All the tenants are granted joint rights in the parking area and, as a result, a single store cannot readily be sold. However, the leasing of stores in these new centers and the management of the centers is creating a new field of real estate endeavor. These new developments will require that adjustments in the older business districts be made. Tenants who move to the new outlying centers often are supplanted by others who find advantages in central locations.

The Modern Office Building

The modern office building evolved as a result of the need for bringing business executives, brokers, lawyers, investors, and others within walking distance of each other so that they could meet quickly in face-to-face contact. The early office buildings prior to 1880 did not exceed six stories in height, except in a few rare instances. Taller buildings were not practical because the walls of a solid masonry building would be so thick at the base that they would absorb most of the ground floor rentable area. The invention of the steel-frame skyscraper in Chicago resulted in the construction of the Home Insurance Building in 1884. The development of the hydraulic and then the electric elevator contributed further to the development of the modern skyscraper. The early office buildings in Chicago, such as the Tacoma Building, the Capitol Building, and the Masonic Temple, built in 1889–90, did not exceed 16 to 22 stories in height. After 1923, a revision of the zoning ordinance in Chicago permitted towers as high as 44 to 47 stories. New York City has had the tallest office buildings, the Empire State Building having 102 stories, the Chrysler Building 73 stories, and the Woolworth Building 58 stories. In more recent years the "baby skyscraper" has increased in popularity, notably in New York. The tallest building in the world, the John Hancock Center, is being developed on Chicago's near north side.

[8] Hoyt, "U.S. Metropolitan Area Retail Shopping Pattern."

Supply of Office Space

Most of the larger office buildings that have ever been erected in this country are still in existence. The office building supply is a result of an accretion to a large, existing stock of building space. Office buildings have been built in a series of waves. Periods of overbuilding in which more office building space was constructed than could be absorbed were followed by years of complete cessation of office building. Office building

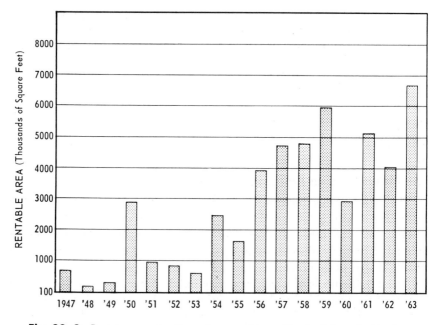

Fig. 23–3. Postwar construction of competitive office buildings in Manhattan, 1947–1963. (Source: Office Building Construction Surveys Research Department, The Real Estate Board of New York, Inc.)

in Chicago reached peaks in the early 1890's, from 1910 to 1914, and from 1923 to 1930. Office building in New York City followed a cyclical pattern which was somewhat different from that in Chicago. Recent years have witnessed another great period of expansion of office building construction. There are indications that the peak in office building construction in the current period of expansion was reached in 1964 in New York City, Houston, Washington, D.C., and some other cities. Office building in New York City was accelerated by the desire to initiate projects before the imposition of projected changes in zoning laws.

As a result of the periods of overbuilding of office space, office rents and net incomes tend to decline after such periods and may remain depressed for long periods, even if general business conditions are good. There was practically no office building construction in Chicago after the Field Building was completed in 1930 until the new Prudential Insurance Building was constructed in 1953. It required a period of twenty-three years to absorb the excess supply of 8,500,000 square feet of vacant space that was created during the 1920's. In rapidly growing cities in Texas and California, the construction of office buildings has been almost continuous since the end of World War II. There has been a substantial volume of construction in New York City in recent years (see Fig. 23–2). Certain cities tend to develop as office building centers and there is no direct relationship between population and the amount of office building space.

Office Rentals

The rent for modern office building space normally includes heat, cleaning service, janitor service, electricity, and water. Consequently the increasing cost of these services has compelled property managers to secure higher rents for space in new buildings. Because of the cost of these services, office building net income may decline rapidly when vacancies increase. The mortgages on all Chicago office buildings, except one, were foreclosed after 1929; and there were widespread foreclosures in other cities. The combined effect of high vacancies and low rents reduced the income below the point that was sufficient to meet interest payments and taxes.

The office buildings in the United States erected prior to 1930 still constitute a significant proportion of the existing supply. A large number of these buildings were sold at foreclosure and refinanced with lower mortgages. Consequently these buildings have been able to carry the interest on the refinanced mortgages as well as operating costs and still rent for around $3 to $4 a square foot. New buildings erected at current costs must in most cities secure a rental of at least $6 per square foot, often more. Consequently new office buildings are at a disadvantage in their competition with office buildings constructed at much lower cost levels. Their many attractive new features, however, enable them to compete to advantage.

In many cases new buildings are located in areas of heavy demand, as in the uptown section of New York. As protection against possible decline in rentals below high break-even points, a large part of the space in these new office buildings sometimes is leased to large corporations for long terms.

Types of Office Building Occupancy

Most office buildings have been erected for multiple-tenant occupancy. This means that a number of small offices are rented to a variety of tenants on every floor. In this type of occupancy the building manager must provide all services. Public hallways cannot be rented. When an entire floor is rented to a single company, however, all the floor area will produce an income.

Office buildings located in central business districts frequently contain retail stores on the ground floor. In financial districts, banks often occupy the ground floor of an office building which they own, and rent the space in the upper floors. In a few cases, such as the Terminal Building in Cleveland and the Carew Tower in Cincinnati, a hotel and department store are combined with the office building. In St. Louis, large department stores typically occupy the lower floors of office buildings, with offices on the upper floors. The Merchandise Mart of Chicago has offices on the five lower floors and manufacturers' representatives occupy the space on the upper floors. In office buildings on such main retail streets as State Street in Chicago there are numerous dentists' and doctors' offices. In other buildings, retail stores are found on upper floors, intermingled with offices. These office buildings with mixed types of uses involve special problems of management and accounting.

Types of Office Building Locations

Office building districts may be concentrated, as in the Chicago Loop, or scattered in a number of sub-office building locations, as in New York. In the course of time, office building districts tend to move. In Chicago the office building area of around 1890 was located at the south end of the Loop. After 1920 new office buildings were developed on North Michigan Avenue. In New York there is a movement away from the downtown Wall Street areas to the uptown areas, where 75 per cent of the corporation managers now maintain their offices. There has been, however, some recent construction in the Wall Street financial district; but most new office buildings are being erected in the uptown area. Some office buildings have been developed in outlying locations, thus stimulating further the suburban trend. In some cases, office buildings are developed in conjunction with larger regional shopping centers, Northland in Detroit and Ward Parkway in Kansas City being cases in point. Of special importance are medical and dental clinics, real estate offices, and the home offices of various corporations. Parking is of growing importance. A one-to-one ratio of parking space to office space is considered adequate and often necessary to get financing. Redevelopment programs have been important factors in office building development in such cities as Pittsburgh and Philadelphia. In nearly all cities new office buildings tend to be located in the direction of high-income areas; for example, to the northwest in Washington, D.C., to the north in New York City, to the south in Houston, and to the northwest in Los Angeles (see Fig. 13–1).

Advantages of Various Office Building Locations

Tenants seek offices at points of maximum convenience from the standpoint of their own particular lines of business. Brokers typically want offices near the Stock Exchange, lawyers near the courts or title companies, insurance men near the insurance company offices, and the like. Specialized office building districts tend to develop, such as the financial district in LaSalle Street in Chicago, the fire and casualty insurance center in New York, and the advertising, radio, and television center in uptown New York. Convenient transportation to residential areas is also important. The uptown area of New York has the advantages of the Pennsylvania and Grand Central stations, with their suburban trains and the subways; the Loop in Chicago is at the point where suburban railroads, elevated lines, busses, and subways converge.

Some organizations, particularly insurance companies, maintain large office buildings for their own use. Here face-to-face contacts with other companies are not important and there is no need for them to be near other office buildings. The large insurance companies in New York—the Metropolitan Life Insurance Company, the New York Life, the Equitable, and the Mutual—probably maintain central offices because at the converging points of subway lines they can secure a large number of employees from all the boroughs of New York City. The Prudential office building in Chicago derives similar advantage from its central location.

In other cases, however, insurance companies, such as those in Hartford, Connecticut, have located their offices away from the central business district. In Houston, Texas, the Prudential Insurance Company recently completed a twenty-story office building that is located on a 26-acre tract opposite the Shamrock Hotel, five miles from downtown Houston. The large ground area permits ample free parking and a large outdoor swimming pool. Most of the workers live in the vicinity of the office building.

The Demand for Office Space

The decline in office building construction after 1930 created the impression that the total demand for office space in the United States was declining. In Chicago, however, there has been a constant increase in the per capita use of office space. The amount of office space needed varies in different cities. On the average, about 2 square feet of office space per capita will serve the needs of the residents of an area. More is needed for regional, national, and international centers. New York's requirements may be over 15 feet per capita (excluding North Jersey), Chicago, 7 to 8 feet, and so on. The demand for office space reflects the general level of business activity and conditions in special lines of business.

Table 23–2. The Demand for Land in Central Urban Areas

Central Business District Office Space in Selected Cities

City	Metropolitan Area Population 1960	Occupied Net Usable Square Feet of CBD Office Space	Square Feet of Office Space per Capita
New York	10,694,633	171,300,000 (est.)	16.0
Chicago	6,220,913	46,370,000 [a]	7.5
Boston	2,589,301	20,000,000 [b]	7.7
St. Louis	2,060,103	10,898,603 [b]	5.3
Washington	2,001,897	10,300,000 [b,c]	5.1
Minneapolis	1,482,030	7,469,200 [a]	5.0
St. Paul	1,482,030	3,363,098 [b]	2.3
Buffalo	1,306,957	4,563,269 [b]	3.5
Cincinnati	1,071,624	7,839,886 [b]	7.3
Kansas City, Mo.	1,039,493	4,930,200 [b]	4.7
San Diego	1,033,011	2,234,449 [a]	2.2
Denver	929,383	7,149,800 [a]	7.7
New Orleans	868,480	4,903,600 [a]	5.6
Louisville	727,139	4,586,200 [b]	6.3
Dayton	694,623	2,208,676 [b]	3.2
Fort Worth	573,215	2,096,450 [a]	3.7
Syracuse	563,781	2,249,200 [a]	4.0
Hartford	525,207	4,683,859 [a]	8.9
Honolulu	500,409	1,155,850 [a,c]	2.3
Toledo	456,931	2,236,720 [b]	4.9
Des Moines	266,315	4,011,000 [a]	15.1
Little Rock	242,980	2,153,550 [a]	8.9
Portland, Maine	120,655	1,548,000 [a]	12.8

[a] Real Estate Research Corporation surveys 1958–1962.
[b] Planning departments and commissions surveys, 1953–1960.
[c] Excludes most government buildings.
Courtesy Real Estate Research Corporation.

The Owners of Office Buildings

Tall office buildings are the outstanding landmarks of most American cities. Because of the prestige attached to their ownership, banks, large insurance companies, and other financial institutions often own the buildings in which they occupy quarters. In the 1920's, office buildings were often financed by bond issues, with the equity retained by promoters. When these mortgages were foreclosed, new investment groups bought control, usually by acquiring the bonds far below par value. Recent office building construction has been financed largely by loans from insurance companies and not by sales of bonds to the public. The equity has often been retained by the builder or developer.

Problems of Office Building Management

The manager of an office building attempts to set rates for space that allow for differences in the desirability of various areas in the building. The most desirable space is that with direct outside light on floors at elevator express stops. An ideal depth for most offices is 40 feet, which allows for a 20-foot reception area space and 20 feet for interior offices.

In selecting tenants, preference will usually be given to companies of outstanding prestige that may attract other desirable tenants to the building. It is necessary to consider the needs for expansion and, if possible, to have sufficient leeway to be able to meet the potential needs of desirable tenants.

The office building manager has the job not only of selecting tenants but also of employing service workers and supervising maintenance and repairs. Building managers' associations exchange information on operating experience, study relationships with building employee unions, and cooperate on other problems affecting the industry.

The Industrial Real Estate Market

The market for industrial real estate is affected by factors substantially different from those which have a primary bearing on the markets for retail or office space. The most desirable sites for factories, in nearly all instances, are no longer found near the center of metropolitan areas but in outlying suburban or even in rural locations along railroad lines or highways, or near sources of raw materials. While the trend of demand for retail space has moved outward from the center of the city, and that for office space has moved outward to some extent, the demand for central locations for such uses remains stronger than in the case of industrial real estate.

At one time industrial uses also competed for central locations, since only in such areas could the combination of factors involving rail or water transportation, nearness to sources of power, and nearness to workers' homes be found. With the development of truck transportation and belt lines, power transmission over wider areas, and the general use of automobiles by workers, industry has moved outward from city centers.

In general, industries seek sites that are not congested and are easily accessible for materials and workers. Emphasis is placed on relatively low land costs and attempts are made to minimize tax burdens. The increasing use of single-story factory buildings, permitting continuity of operations on the same level, has emphasized the need for low-priced land. Industries engaged in heavy manufacturing or those with highly specialized requirements usually own the space they use. Others often lease or make use of the sale-leaseback device.

Demand for Industrial Space

Decisions affecting real estate in the industrial field tend to reflect general company policies with respect to expansion programs, preferences in regard to adjoining or new locations in the same or in other cities, the use of branch operations, and the like. Tax burdens, freight rates, labor relations, local government attitudes, transportation facilities, power, water supply, and related factors all have a bearing.[9] Typically, an industrial organization is not interested in local economic conditions to the same degree as a retail establishment. Indeed, some industries seek out locally depressed areas in order to take advantage of an available labor supply. The regional movement of industry to the South, for example, has been influenced by labor market conditions.

As a general rule, processing plants which increase the bulk of products, or make a fragile or perishable product, prefer to be near their customers; while plants which reduce the bulk of products, or make them less perishable, do not regard nearness to the consumer as particularly vital. Since a very large portion of all material going into factory production has already been processed by another factory, the supplier groups tend to locate near the industries which they serve. As a result there is a heavy concentration of industry on the New York–Chicago axis. There is more production of this type within 100 miles of New York than in the eight southeastern states, and within 100 miles of Chicago than in all of the western states excepting those on the Pacific Coast.

Selection of Industrial Locations [10]

In selecting a factory location, business managers typically analyze (1) the general region in which the factory is to be built, (2) the particular city within the region, (3) the selected area within the metropolitan region, and (4) the specific site. The basic purpose of selecting the location is,

[9] See "Guide to Making a Business Climate Appraisal," The General Electric Co. See also Paul Starrett, "Appraising Industrial Properties," *The Appraisal Journal* (January, 1959), pp. 54–61, and Mabel Walker, *Business Enterprise and the City* (Princeton, N.J.: Tax Institute, Inc., 1957).

[10] Discussions of this topic are presented in Walter Isard, *Location and Space Economy* (New York: John Wiley & Sons, Inc., 1956), and Edgar M. Hoover, *The Location of Economic Activity* (New York: McGraw-Hill Book Co., Inc., 1948).

of course, to find the site in which the industry can operate to maximum advantage, where production costs will be lowest, and the costs of marketing at a minimum.

1. *The Region.* Most types of industries can operate economically only in definite regions. However, these regions may be rather broad in extent. Thus, the steel industry must be situated at the most economical meeting place of coal and iron ore. The steel industries in Chicago, Pittsburgh, and Cleveland are based on the accessibility to coal by rail or river and to the iron ore of the Mesabi Range, which is available by cheap water transportation on the Great Lakes. The increasing dependence on imported iron ore caused the building of the Fairless Steel Works on the Delaware River near Trenton and the doubling of the capacity of the Bethlehem Steel Plant at Baltimore. Many steel-using industries find it necessary to locate near the primary steel plants. Industries refining bulky materials must also be located near the source of supply. Thus, the concentration plant of the Kennecott Copper Corporation's Utah mine is located at Bingham Canyon at the source of supply, because the copper-bearing rock has only 1 per cent copper and it would be uneconomical to transport this bulky material great distances.

Proximity to markets is also an important consideration in factory location. Many industries are located in the northeastern part of the United States because of the nearness to the great concentrations of urban population in that region.

The electronics industry and related activities have been less directly tied to raw materials and markets than some of the older industries. Also, research and development programs of various firms often are located in favorable environments such as university towns or in pleasant climates. We should note too that political factors may play a part in the location of various defense and similar types of contracts.

2. *The Specific City Within the Region.* It sometimes happens that the maximum advantages of location in a region can be obtained in only one specific city. Thus, industries depending upon ocean shipments must be located near ports, such as New York, Baltimore, New Orleans, or San Francisco. Where it is important to be at the center of the railroad network, the Chicago area is to be preferred. In other cases, the specific industry must be located near others of the same type or near complementary industries. Women's ready-to-wear manufacturers find it desirable to be in the New York fashion center, because styles change quickly. Manufacturers of cameras prefer to be near Rochester, New York. The leading automobile firms obtain advantages by being close to the automobile-parts manufacturers in Detroit.

In many cases, however, an industry could be located to almost equal advantage in any of five, six, or more cities. The decision as to which city is selected is often governed by the availability of a site or factory building, by the preference of the factory manager for a certain city as a place of residence, by the promotional activities of the local chamber of commerce, by the tax situation, by the characteristics of the labor supply, or by the railroad, trucking, and other transportation facilities of a given city.

3. *The General Area Within the Metropolitan Region.* As we have indicated, new plants are now more frequently located in outlying suburban areas than in the central business districts as was formerly the case. The chief cause of this move has been the growing preference for the one-story industrial building as compared with the multi-story type. The one-story plant requires extensive ground areas which usually cannot be found in central locations. It has been found in a number of cases that factory operations can be carried on in these single-story buildings at a saving of 25 per cent in cost compared with the same factory processes in factories with several floor levels. The advantages of one-story factory buildings located in suburban or rural areas include the following:

(a) The factory process is continuous without the necessity of interrupting manufacturing operations at each floor level.

(b) There is no waste space for elevators or ramps and no cost of elevator operation.

(c) Heavy machinery can be installed in any part of the building, with the foundations resting on bedrock, so that the building is not jarred by vibration.

(d) Railroad freight cars and trucks can enter the plant directly, which results in a saving in handling costs.

(e) Overhead cranes can be installed and the plant can be equipped with conveyor belts for moving goods in process through the building.

(f) The one-story plant is far more flexible and can be more easily expanded to meet the growth of any particular department. If there is ample ground area and the building is constructed with curtain walls, any part of the building can be pushed out to meet the needs of growth.

(g) The factory grounds usually include ample areas for the parking of the workers' cars.

(h) There is more room for recreation areas on the ground and it is easier to provide cafeterias and restrooms within the buildings.

(i) The cost of one-story buildings is often less per square foot than the multi-story type.

(j) The land cost is lower in outlying locations than in central areas.

(k) Real estate taxes are usually lower in suburban tracts.

(l) The workers' homes, particularly those of the skilled workers, are often near these factories because of residential decentralization.

Some factory sites have been selected because of their proximity to the homes of their workers, although this is not a factor of major consideration currently.

(m) Because of widespread automobile ownership, workers prefer to work in pleasant modern factories with ample parking areas rather than in congested central-city areas. Workers can reach these locations more quickly on the highways encircling the metropolitan areas than they can the central districts with their heavy traffic.

(n) Suburban locations are more convenient for interstate trucks, which are now widely used. Downtown traffic congestion can be avoided. Suburban plants also are more conveniently located with respect to outlying railroad belt lines.

(o) Industrial districts in which a group of factories of the nonnuisance type can obtain advantages by operating as neighbors also can be created more easily in suburban locations than in downtown areas.

4. *The Specific Site.* Having narrowed the choice down to one specific city and to a general area within the metropolitan area of that city, it is necessary to select the exact site. The following factors will be weighed by plant managers in this process:

(a) In reviewing all the sites, it is necessary to find those that are zoned for industry and which will permit the location of the specific type of industrial plant proposed. If not actually zoned, opinions can be secured from zoning authorities as to what zoning is possible.

(b) It is often desirable to have a location with direct access to a railroad from which a railroad siding could be constructed into the site at reasonable cost. It is often desirable also to be near a major highway for truck transportation.

(c) Sites with bus transportation to the homes of the workers may be preferred, as some auxiliary transportation often is desirable even though most of the workers have cars.

(d) The site should have sewer and water connections, particularly in the case of a small industry. Some large industries install their own sewage-disposal plants and develop their own water supply. In the case of such industries the availability of a source of water is important. It is also necessary to ascertain whether there is a stream in which the effluence of the sewage treatment plant or the factory wastes can be discharged.

(e) Tracts of sufficient size for the type of operation under consideration must be selected. Consideration is often given to room for expansion. An area under one or at most two ownerships must usually be found.

Fig. 23–4. Sixty-fifth Street, Clearing Industrial District, Chicago, Illinois. (Courtesy Clearing Industrial District, Inc., Chicago, Illinois. Photo by Chicago Aerial Industries, Inc.)

(f) When there are a number of different local municipalities or townships in the metropolitan area, the sites in the one which will do most to facilitate the location of the new industry are preferred.

(g) The factory should be located on a site most convenient to the homes of the present workers or to the areas where most of the future labor supply may be located.

(h) Access to power lines is necessary.

(i) If all other advantages are equal, the site which can be obtained at the lowest price will usually be purchased.

Manufacturing Districts

Of special importance in the market for industrial real estate are manufacturing districts. Such developments as the Central Manufacturing District and the Clearing Industrial District in Chicago, the Trinity Industrial District of Dallas, and the Bergen County Terminal in New Jersey are typical (see Fig. 23–4). Organizations of this type provide industrial facilities with rail service, financing arrangements, fire and police protection, heat, light, gas, water, and other services. Space is available for purchase or rent on varying bases. The Trinity Industrial District of Dallas is located within five minutes of the downtown area on property that was reclaimed from flood land. Levees were built and channels straightened so that industrial locations could be provided. Many other industrial districts are located in suburban areas, however, where cheap land and low tax rates provide advantages. In many instances, industrial districts serve best the needs of the lighter industries, since heavy industry often requires special-purpose construction and equipment.

Trends in Industrial Construction

With greater specialization, emphasis has been given to the development of facilities which serve the needs of specific industries. Some plants are referred to as "controlled conditions plants," providing ideal operating and working conditions with control of light, temperature, humidity, and noise.

Many plants are designed so that the interior arrangements may be as flexible as possible. Larger bays are being used, typically running up to 100 feet, in contrast to 50 to 60 feet in older plants. Building heights are being raised in order to allow for conveyor operations; greater emphasis is given to low-cost maintenance; and the exteriors of plants are being given greater attention, with carefully maintained grounds, landscaping, neat lawns, and recreational areas.

Wholesale and Storage Warehouses

Wholesale and storage warehouses are often located near central-city areas. As a result of the direct delivery of merchandise from the manufacturer to the retailer, the wholesale function has declined. Large warehouses were once stored with merchandise near the Loop of Chicago and the downtown areas of other cities. Now frequent door-to-door deliveries are made by trucks from factories to stores. Cold storage warehouses still remain near central business districts, and department stores and other stores still maintain warehouses for distribution of goods within the metropolitan area.

The Merchandise Mart, in Chicago, once designed for wholesale use, is now highly successful as a headquarters for manufacturers' representatives. For example, one entire floor may be devoted to furniture, another to women's apparel, and so on. The Furniture Mart is the leading furniture wholesale market. Buyers come here only at certain seasons.

The supply of central warehouse and storage space probably is adequate for most future needs because many factories have moved away from the multi-story buildings to outlying one-story plants. Space in such multi-story buildings often is well designed for warehouse or storage use.

SUMMARY

This chapter deals with factors influencing decisions with regard to real estate used by business enterprises. This market may be regional, national, or even international in scope. Income factors and the terms and availability of financing remain major determinants of the level and intensity of demand.

Real estate administration may occupy various positions in the organization of a firm, depending upon the importance of real estate to the firm's operations. Major real estate decisions usually are made at top levels of management.

The highest land values and store rentals for retail property are found in the central business district of a city, where pedestrian traffic density is greatest. Large department stores, central offices, and financial institutions usually form the nuclei of the district. Space in the central business district usually is leased for long periods, and percentage leases with a fixed minimum rent, or sometimes a sliding scale, are commonly used. Key tenants may be given special rent concessions because of their ability to attract other firms to the building or area.

The increased use of automobiles has led to the development of outlying shopping centers, ranging from large regional centers to smaller neighborhood outlets. Parking space is an essential feature of the larger centers, and a ratio of parking to store space of 4 to 1 is common. This greatly increases the amount of land needed by retail establishments. The location of new centers is influenced by the pattern of the developing highway system.

The modern skyscraper office building serves the preference of the executives of business firms to be located within easy access of each other. The skyscraper was made possible by the advent of steel-frame construction and the electric elevator. Office buildings historically have been built in waves; when overbuilding occurred, rents have been depressed for long periods, regardless of the trend of general business conditions. The supply of office space is relatively fixed in the short run. High occupancy rates typically are needed to make office buildings a financial success. Demand for office space depends to a considerable extent on the level of general business activity.

Improved transportation has allowed more decentralization of industry, and manufacturing firms now tend to seek uncongested sites readily accessible for suppliers and employees. Thus, they can make use of locations where land prices and tax burdens are lower. Industrial location depends also on such important factors as the nature of the product, the location of raw materials and markets, and the supply of power and of labor. A growing preference for one-story buildings has increased the demand for land for industrial purposes. Some areas have seen the development of industrial parks or districts.

QUESTIONS FOR STUDY

1. How do the markets for commercial and industrial real estate differ from residential real estate markets?
2. Where do you think the real estate function should be placed in the firm's organization? Explain. To what extent will this depend on the nature of the firm's business?
3. What is meant by a "100 per cent" retail location?
4. Why have fashion goods stores tended to concentrate in the central business district? Do you think they will continue to concentrate there? Explain.
5. Why has the large department store been an important inhabitant of the central business district? Will this be true in the future? Explain.
6. Describe typical leasing agreements for each of the following: (a) Supermarkets. (b) Apparel stores. (c) Furniture stores.
7. Do you think that the policy of national chain organizations in establishing percentages on a national basis is sound? Why or why not?
8. Define and describe each of the principal types of shopping centers.
9. Explain the importance of parking facilities to: (a) The outlying shopping center. (b) The downtown department store.

10. How do you explain the popularity of large, centrally located office buildings?
11. Have office buildings tended to be decentralized in the manner that has characterized residential and retail developments? Why or why not?
12. Describe the major factors determining rentals of office space.
13. Explain the advantages and disadvantages of: (a) Single-tenant versus multiple-tenant office buildings. (b) Specialized-tenant versus generalized-tenant occupancy of office buildings.
14. Who owns office buildings? Why?
15. What are the principal characteristics of the market for industrial real estate?
16. Why is there a heavy concentration of industry on the New York–Chicago axis? Do you anticipate any change in this pattern in the future? Why or why not?
17. Indicate the main factors involved in selecting a site for an industrial location of: (a) The general region. (b) The choice among cities. (c) The site within a specific city.
18. Describe the main characteristics of industrial districts.
19. *Study Project 39.* (a) About when did the home and the office begin to be separated? (b) How can you account for such separation? (c) How do you explain the statement that "in the post World War II era, we have building because of controls"? (d) Comment on this statement: "Reuse in the complete sense of the word is exemplified by downtown Manhattan."
20. *Study Project 40.* (a) Do you see advantages or disadvantages in the Skidmore, Owings & Merrill design for the new Macy store outlined in this study project over the traditional shopping center? (b) Would you expect more developments of this type? Explain.

SUGGESTED READINGS

ANDREWS, RICHARD B. *Urban Growth and Development.* New York: Simmons-Boardman Publishing Corp., 1962. Chap. iv.

HOOVER, EDGAR M. *Location of Economic Activity.* New York: McGraw-Hill Book Co., Inc., 1948.

HOYT, HOMER. "Effect of Rents, Operating Expenses, and Construction Costs Upon Net Income of Regional Shopping Centers," *The Appraisal Journal* (January, 1963).

MAISEL, SHERMAN J. *Financing Real Estate: Principles and Practices.* New York: McGraw-Hill Book Co., Inc., 1965. Chaps. xiv, xv, xvi.

NELSON, RICHARD L. *The Selecting of Retail Locations.* New York: F. W. Dodge Corp., 1958. Chaps. i, ii, v.

24

Farms and Other
Rural Real Estate

Types of Rural Real Estate

Classification is almost never easy and broad land use classifications present some special problems. The line between "rural" and "urban" becomes increasingly difficult to draw. If we consider as urban only the land in cities of 2,500 people or more, including city parks, 21,400,000 acres were used in this way in 1960; estimated needs move up to 32 million acres in 1980 and to 45 million acres in the year 2000.[1] Clawson emphasizes the importance of land *withdrawn* from other uses to serve urban purposes, since a third to a half of urban land is not in actual use but awaiting development.[2]

The remainder of the land, nonurban land, includes farmland and ranch land such as crop land along with pasture and grazing land and nonproductive farmland; commercial forest land; land used for recreation, excluding reservoir areas and city parks; land used for transportation purposes; wildlife refuges; reservoirs; and finally, a residual classification. It is not our purpose here to consider each of these types of land use. Rather we center our attention on land uses that we believe to have special significance for real estate purposes and more or less arbitrarily have selected farms and ranches for primary consideration, plus presenting a summary discussion of land used for forestry and for rural, or rather,

[1] Hans H. Landsberg, Leonard L. Fischman, and Joseph L. Fisher, *Resources in America's Future* (Baltimore: Johns Hopkins Press, 1963), chap. xviii.

[2] Marion Clawson *et al.*, *Land for the Future* (Baltimore: Johns Hopkins Press, 1960).

nonurban, recreation. Such nonurban land as is used for residential purposes (rural nonfarm) was considered in Chapter 22.

Dynamic Agricultural Situation

Despite growing demands for agricultural products, the number of
farms has declined from around 7 million in the mid-1930's to approximately half that number in the mid-1960's. At the same time, the average
size of farms has increased. Farms with a thousand acres or more (less
than 4 per cent of the total) account for approximately half of all farmland. The top 3 per cent of the farms account for more farm production
than the bottom 78 per cent.[3]

About 15.6 million Americans lived on farms and ranches in 1960. This
number was reduced to 13.4 million by 1963 and appears to be declining
further each year. Not all of these people derive their main incomes from
agriculture; many are industrial workers who farm part time or retired
persons or others not primarily dependent on agriculture.

Agriculture has been going through a revolution characterized in general by a shift toward a business and managerial type of operation with
increasingly heavy emphasis on relatively large-scale programs and large
blocks of capital investment. Scientific and technological advances have
been back of these changes including improved feeds and fertilizers, more
effective plant and animal breeding, better agricultural implements and
power, as well as improved roads and trucks, and related developments.
There have been marketing as well as production changes; contract farming has increased in importance as have the efforts of various farm
cooperatives. Throughout these many changes, government programs
including various controls and supports have played an important role.

The Market for Farms

Agriculture, with individual units varying through a wide range of
productivity, size, and capital requirements, presents a real estate market
with its own peculiar problems and characteristics. To lump all farms
together in considering the characteristics of the farm real estate market
is no more correct than to lump all factories or all retail stores together.

As in the case of other types of real estate, there is no organized market
for farmland. Systems for grading and classifying farmland leave much

---

[3] For a discussion of agricultural trends, see John H. MacMillan, Jr., "Farm Sur-
pluses: How to End Them," *Business Horizons*, II, No. I (1959); Murray R. Benedict,
Can We Solve the Farm Problem? (New York: Twentieth Century Fund, 1955); *An
Adaptive Program for Agriculture* (New York: Committee for Economic Develop-
ment, 1962); and Edward Higbee, *Farms and Farmers in an Urban Age* (New York:
Twentieth Century Fund, 1963).

to be desired. Furthermore, the principal buyers of farmland usually are found in the immediate locality. In some instances farms are purchased by outside investors.

Soil fertility, the condition of buildings and other improvements, accessibility to roads, schools, churches, electric power lines, and shopping centers, as well as community ties, family sentiment, and the like, all have a bearing on the market for farms. Many of the factors are subjective in nature.

Farmland is sold by the acre and is ordinarily priced in terms of so many dollars per acre, with the value of farm buildings and other improvements included in such a price.

Farm real estate brokers usually operate within a single community and seldom cover an area that extends much beyond a county. Many real estate brokers specialize in farmland, and in some cases include farm management as a part of their business activities.

The practices followed by farm brokers are little different from those followed by the real estate brokers in urban communities. As in the case of urban real estate, income plus the terms and availability of financing are of major importance in determining the intensity of demand for farm real estate at any given time.

The Demand for Farms

The demand for farm real estate, just as is true of the demand for most other types of capital goods, is a derived demand. It is derived from the demand for the goods or services in the production of which the capital goods are used. Thus, an understanding of the demand for farm products is basic to understanding the demand for farms themselves.

The income-producing ability of farms depends on the production of crops and livestock and on the market for these products. Of course, farms are sometimes bought for essentially noneconomic reasons, such as the wish to pursue a rural way of life, sentimental attachments to a particular farm or locality, the desire to follow a hobby, such as the raising of a special strain of cattle or conducting special experiments, and for similar reasons. In most instances, however, the demand for farms arises from their ability to produce economic returns.

Although the supply of farm products varies with weather and market conditions, the demand for them fluctuates even more widely. The greatest fluctuations have occurred as a result of the shifting demands during war periods. In addition, however, the consumers of farm products adapt their purchases to their income situations. When incomes are high the demand for farm products is strong, particularly the demand for foods of higher quality. When incomes are low the demand for such foods as bread and potatoes does not tend to decline greatly, but the demands for foods of higher quality move downward. Under high standards of living the demand for many types of food partakes of the nature of a luxury demand, with the result that substantial downward adjustments may be anticipated whenever incomes decline.

As a result of these conditions the prices which farmers have received for their products have fluctuated widely between the different stages of the business cycle. These fluctuations in prices and incomes tend to be reflected in the prices of farms.

There are other areas of demand for farms that should be mentioned. One of these is the investor who is in the higher income brackets. People of this type may try to buy run-down farms, spend heavily for development purposes and then sell the farms for a capital gain.

In some cases investors buy farms as a long-term hedge against possible future inflation. Of course, there are always investors who buy land near settled areas in the hope of sale for urban rather than rural purposes. Whenever the yield on government bonds and similar investments moves downward, the interest of investors in farms tend to advance.

Factors Affecting Rural Land Values

Like other real property, the value of rural real estate depends upon its ability to produce income. The value of a producing farm is derived by capitalizing the anticipated future net income. Suburban land on the fringe of cities often derives its value from the anticipated urban use. Consequently, its present value is based on the value of urban land uses, discounted by the length of time it will take for such land to be utilized in that way. When sewer or water mains are extended into such areas, the price of land advances rapidly.

The level of net farm earnings depends upon relationships between prices received by farmers and production costs, which will be affected by the quality of farm management, technological developments in production, changes in the efficiency of marketing agricultural products, real estate taxes, financing charges, government programs, and related factors.

The principal physical factors affecting the value of farmland are soil fertility, rainfall, and the length of the growing season. Other factors include buildings and other improvements available, location in the community, and accessibility to markets, schools, churches, shopping centers, and power lines. Buildings and other improvements are becoming increasingly important on the modern farm. Buildings are more important for some types of farming, such as dairying and poultry, than for other types, such as beef cattle ranching.

The value of farmland depends also upon its suitability for different types of crops (see Fig. 24–1). The cheapest land is found in arid or semiarid regions. Its uses are limited to grazing. The value of such land may be related to the number of acres required to support one steer and the value added in the increased weight of the steer, minus labor and feeding costs. Other low-grade rural land includes that used for the production of pulpwood. Such a crop can be produced in around seven years where there is a long growing season. A slightly higher type of land is that improved with permanent pasture in areas with abundant rainfall. In Florida, for example, there are areas of this type which will support one steer per acre.

Such rural land uses contrast with the rich farmland of the Middle West. This rich land, in an area provided with adequate summer rainfall and a growing season long enough to mature corn, produces high yields. Much of the land in this region is sufficiently level to permit the widespread use of tractors, harvesters, and similar mechanical equipment. Rainfall diminishes in the areas west of Iowa in the Dakotas, Nebraska, and Kansas. Wheat is the principal crop in these regions, as it is in Canada.

The highest farmland values result from orchard crops, especially citrus fruits. Oranges and grapefruit can be raised only in a subtropical climate where the temperature does not fall below 25 degrees or if it falls below such levels does so only for short intervals. Some cool weather is required, however, for the production of the best quality of fruit. Consequently, commercial citrus fruits cannot be produced to any extent in the tropics. Citrus groves require eighteen to twenty years before they reach the full bearing stage. However, they have a bearing life of over seventy-five years. Because of the long life and heavy capital investment required, extended periods of overproduction and low prices result when too many orchards are developed. Of special interest in connection with the growing of citrus fruits is the use of frozen concentrates, which permits the absorption of a much larger supply than formerly.

Apple orchards, peach orchards, grape vineyards, pecan groves, tung groves, and walnut groves share some of the characteristics of citrus farming, but each has its own peculiarities. Among these are greater annual fluctuations in yields and a shorter bearing life.

Cotton requires a longer growing season than corn, but a shorter one than various types of orchards. Cotton has long been one of the principal crops of the southern states, although its relative importance has diminished in more recent years.

At the present time, tobacco acreage is limited by government control. Consequently the right to use specified acreage for tobacco production

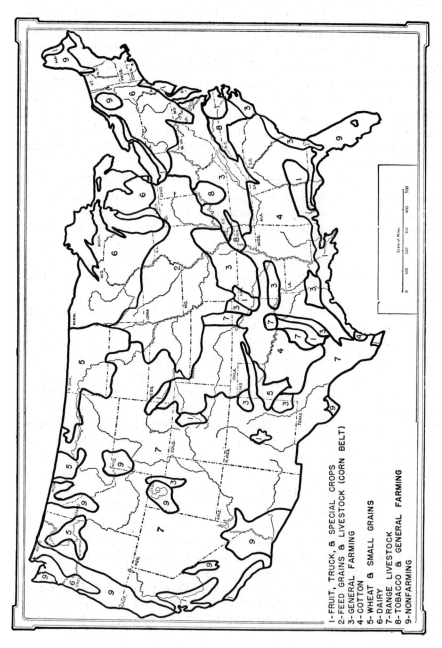

1- FRUIT, TRUCK, & SPECIAL CROPS
2- FEED GRAINS & LIVESTOCK (CORN BELT)
3- GENERAL FARMING
4- COTTON
5- WHEAT & SMALL GRAINS
6- DAIRY
7- RANGE LIVESTOCK
8- TOBACCO & GENERAL FARMING
9- NONFARMING

Fig. 24—1. Agricultural products of the United States.

adds to the values of the land involved. Tobacco is raised in a number of states, largely in Kentucky, Virginia, and the Carolinas.

Timberland is valued on the basis of the estimated value of board feet of standing timber of saw-log size. Its value tends to fluctuate with the price of lumber. While scientific forestry has not been practiced extensively in the United States, there have been significant developments in more recent years. The adoption of sustained-yield management methods holds promise of adding to the value of timberlands.

In summary, the valuation of an individual farm requires consideration of (1) the fertility of the soil; (2) climatic factors, especially rainfall and the length of the growing season; (3) topography; (4) the amount of land under cultivation and the amount used for woodland or grazing; (5) accessibility to hard roads; (6) character of the houses, barns, and other improvements; (7) quotas allowed for raising certain crops; and (8) specific location possibilities for conversion to urban uses.

Appraising Farms

While there are many rules of thumb followed by farmers, real estate brokers, and investors in estimating the value of farms, more refined techniques of appraisal have been developed in recent years (see Fig. 24–2). The steps in a farm appraisal may be outlined as follows:

1. The legal descriptions are checked against the farm boundaries. Aerial photographs are being used to an increasing extent in this process. They are often available in the county offices of the Department of Agriculture.
2. An inventory of the soil and farm improvements is made. Soil augurs are used to test the quality and depth of the soil. Estimates are made of the remaining useful life of the buildings and their current condition.
3. An estimate is made of the normal net rental income of the farm. Estimates are based on normal prices for the crops produced on the farm. A schedule of normal annual expenses is established, including building depreciation.
4. The estimated net income is capitalized at a rate which reflects the going rate for investments of this type.
5. Adjustments are made as required to fit the specific situation, giving added value to farms that are especially well located and deducting for improvements that need to be made immediately.
6. Sale prices of similar farms in the community are determined from county files, newspaper files, and real estate brokers and appraisers. Comparisons are made with the farm being appraised and an estimated value is derived by correlating the value as determined by both the income and the comparative methods.

F.L.B. 4-308
Rev. 10-63

APPRAISER'S REPORT
TO THE FEDERAL LAND BANK OF LOUISVILLE

Bureau of the Budget
Form No. 108-R019.1

Federal Land Bank Association of _____ Application No. _____
                                         CITY OR TOWN   STATE

I have made a personal examination of and identified the property described in above numbered application made
by_____of_____
for a loan of $ _____ and report as follows:

A. LOCATION, TYPE, AND QUALITY OF FARM

                                   Civil District or

1. State _____ County _____ Section ____ Township _____ Range ____ Total Acres ____

2. The farm is located ____ miles ____ from ____ ; ____ miles ____ from ____
                       (DIRECTION)   (NEAREST TOWN)   (DIRECTION)   (COUNTY SEAT)

3. Farm is on _____ miles ____ from nearest highway _____ Type of farming
   (KIND, NUMBER, AND CONDITION OF ROAD)   (DIRECTION)   (GIVE NUMBER AND TYPE)

4. in community is _____ Conveniences available are (v) _____
                                            (RFD, SCHOOL BUS, MILK ROUTE, POWER LINE, TELEPHONE, ETC.)

5. This farm _____ in _____ drainage or levee district.
         (IS-IS NOT)   (NAME)

6. Adequacy of drainage _____ Overflow hazards _____

7. Adequacy of water supply (describe) _____

8. A comparison of this farm with the average in the community is: Location _____ ;

9. soils _____ ; Improvements _____ ; General desirability and salability _____

10. The general condition of farm is _____
                         (EXCELLENT, GOOD, FAIR, POOR)   (BEING MAINTAINED, IMPROVED, NO CHANGE, DEPRECIATING—DISCUSS)

11. The farm is a class ____ farm . It is in a class ____ area. Land ____ in a mineral area. (Discuss in Par. I)
                (A-B-C-D-E)   (1-2-3-4-5)   (IS-IS NOT)

B. PURCHASE DATA OF FARM

1. Applicant acquired this farm _____ by _____
                        (YEAR)   (PURCHASE OR INHERITANCE)

2. The purchase price was, without personal property, $_____ ; with personal property _____ $_____

3. Cash payment .... $_____ Changes since purchase (describe) _____

4. Contract .... $_____ _____

5. Mortgage .... $_____ _____

6. Trade .... $_____ _____

7.   TOTAL $_____

8. Remarks _____

C. PLAT

1. The legal description given in the application _____ correct. Indicate corrections, if any, on plat and explain in remarks.
                                         (IS-IS NOT)

2. Extreme care should be used to ascertain location of corners if buildings are close to line. Indicate points of compass and show scale of map. Designate section number at section centers.

D. DESCRIPTION OF BUILDINGS

No. and Kind	Rooms	Size	Type of Construction	Type of Foundation	Type of Roof	Condition-Improvements and Adaptability to Probable Use for the Next Few Years. Also Any Other Features That Enhance or Reduce Salability, Including Conformity with Community Standards	*Value For Insurance Purposes

* Present cost of replacement less depreciation, including obsolescence   TOTAL |$

Fig. 24–2. Farm appraisal report form.

E.   DESCRIPTION OF LAND

Normal Use	Acres	Type and Quality of Soil; Topography; Crop Adaptability; Ease and Economy of Operation; Any Other Important Features.
TOTAL		

F.   EARNING POWER OF FARM (Typical Operator - - Usual Conditions)

Crop	Acres	Average Yield Per Acre	Average Total Production	Unit Value (Normal Price)	Average Gross Value	Average Normal Sales	Value Landlord's Share
				$	$	$	$
Pasture		Units for mos. @ $					
TOTALS				$	$	$	

Rentability of this farm is _____

Usual rental terms are _____

Estimated normal net outside income of typical operator $_____

Sources and dependability of outside income under usual conditions (discuss)_____

G.   INCOME AND EXPENSE   Typical Operator   Rental

	Typical Operator	Rental
Sale of crops	$	$
Sale of livestock (pltry)	$	$
Sale of livestock products	$	$
Sale miscellaneous products	$	$
R: Cash $_____ Share $_____	$	$
Total Gross Income	$	$
Cash operating expenses	$	$
Feed	$	$
Real estate taxes	$	$
Personal property taxes	$	$
Drainage O&M costs	$	$
B. & I. pymts. for____yrs.	$	$
Building upkeep	$	$
Repair & replmt. equipmt.	$	$
Ins. on bldgs. & per. prop.	$	$
Int. on short term credit	$	$
Total Expenses	$	$
Net Return	$	$

H.   VALUATIONS AND ACCEPTABILITY

Normal agricultural value of farm $_____

Normal market value of farm $_____

Present market value of farm $_____

1.   Consideration has been given to total taxes, O&M, and B&I charges of $_____per acre and project debt liability of $_____against this land.

2.   Any shortage in the acreage of this farm that may be developed upon examination of the title and verification of the plat which does not exceed _____percent of the total acreage shown in my report and which is not caused by the exclusion of a specified part of the property will not affect my estimate of the normal agricultural value.

3.   This property _____ (IS-IS NOT) satisfactory security for a loan not to exceed _____ years subject to the following requirements being fulfilled: _____

4.   Without the foregoing requirements being fulfilled the NAV is $_____ PMV is $_____. it is a class _____ (A-B-C-D-E) farm, and _____ (is-is not) satisfactory security for a loan not to exceed_____Years.

I.   REMARKS   (Explain any unusual features not sufficiently covered elsewhere. If security is not acceptable or if the term is limited, give reasons.)

Compared to   benchmark _____

Located in _____ County _____

Location: _____

Soils: _____

Improvements: _____

Overall: _____

Benchmark NAV_____ PMV_____

This farm NAV_____ PMV_____

(Per acre if so calculated)

The above report is true and correct to the best of my knowledge and belief.

1.   Date appraised_____ 19____

2.   Date written _____ 19____

3.   Date mailed _____ 19____

4.   Date received by FLBA _____ 19____

LAND BANK APPRAISER

Fig. 24–2. Farm appraisal report form (reverse).

Size of Farms

The size of farms is usually measured in terms of acres of land. The acre is not an entirely satisfactory unit of measurement, since it includes the surface area only. It does not reflect the quality of farmland, and quality varies widely. While some standards have been developed for grading the quality of agricultural land, additional progress is needed. In terms of acres the average size of farms in this country has been increasing, rising from slightly over 200 to around 300 acres in the past 10 years. The basic reason for this is the increased mechanization of agricultural production. In all probability, many farmers could utilize more acres than they do now.

At the present time, however, it is not a simple matter to extend the acreage which a particular farmer has under cultivation. Farmland may usually be purchased or rented only in relatively large quantities. For example, a farmer may wish to add twenty-five acres of land to a farm. Such a block of land, however, is not likely to be available. He must ordinarily buy an entire farm, including a set of farm buildings for which he would have little or no use. As a result of this situation, many farmers have expanded their scale of operations, not by adding more land, but by using more capital in the cultivation of the land available to them. There are often problems of fitting available machinery to a particular size of farm operation. Often the availability of improved machinery will virtually force an expansion in the size of an operation. Because of this and related factors, it appears probable that the acreage of land in the average farm will tend to rise in future years.

Farmland Tenure

A system of farmland tenure may be defined as the sum total of the arrangements by which land is owned, rented, leased, used, exchanged, and transferred. All nations have struggled with the problem of devising satisfactory rules, laws, and other arrangements for controlling these matters. For example, feudalism was a system of agricultural land tenure. There have been many other systems as well. The land practices followed in this country from Revolutionary times have had the objective of widespread ownership of farms by those who operate them. By the mid-1960's, only about a quarter of all farm operators in the United States were tenants. About three-fifths of farm operators were full owners, and the ramainder were part owners. The latter group owned part of the land they operated and rented some additional land.

The proportion of tenancy in the United States rose to 42 per cent in the early 1930's. By 1950 there were relatively fewer tenants on American farms than at any time since 1890. High prices for farm products in World War II and the postwar era enabled many farm tenants to become farm owners. The growing interest of investors in farms, however, may make it more difficult for tenants to become owners than was the case in the earlier postwar years.

Capital Requirements

Total assets of American agriculture were estimated at $230.5 billion on January 1, 1965. About 85 per cent of this represented equity capital.

The value of all farm real estate in 1965 was estimated at $158.5 billion. This was over two-thirds of total farm assets. Outstanding against this was an estimated real estate debt of $18.7 billion. This means that farmers have close to a 90 per cent equity in their land.

The rate of capital turnover in agriculture is typically slow. Although many farmers had a capital turnover (length of time required for receipts to equal total capital invested) of three to four years during World War II, the normal length of time is now more likely to be six to eight years in the Midwest. Time required varies with type of farm, level of prices, and related factors. Dairy and poultry farmers turn their capital over more quickly than beef cattle farmers, for example.

Table 24–1. Balance Sheet of American Agriculture, 1965

Item	January 1, 1965 (Billion Dollars)	Estimate January 1, 1966
Assets		
Physical assets:		
Real estate	159.4	170.0
Non-real estate	57.3	61.4
Financial assets	21.1	21.8
Total	237.8	253.2
Claims		
Real estate debt	18.9	21.1
Non-real estate	18.6	20.0
Equities	200.3	212.1
Total	237.8	253.2

SOURCE: *Economic Report of the President, 1966.*

Farm Financing

As in the case of other real estate uses, the purchase of fee ownership with the use of both equity and debt funds, plus the leasing of properties, constitute the major methods of acquiring rights to use farm real estate. Funds for the financing of farms are made available by institutional

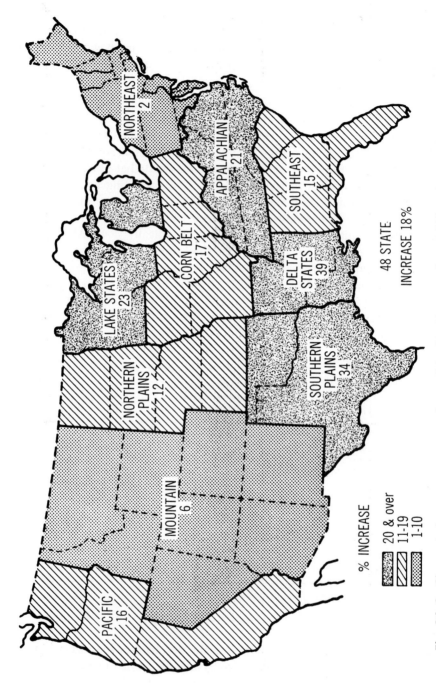

Fig. 24—3. Change in farm mortgage recordings: all lenders, January–June, 1962, to January–June, 1963. (Source: U.S. Department of Agriculture.)

lenders, particularly commercial banks and insurance companies, by individuals (especially retired farmers), by cooperative credit agencies, and by the government. During prosperous periods, banks and insurance companies are of major importance as sources of farm credit. During periods of depression and low farm incomes, the major burden of financing shifts to government agencies or to government guaranteed loans.

Of the $18.8 billion farm mortgage debt outstanding at the beginning of 1965, life insurance companies held about a fifth, banks a tenth, Federal Land Banks a sixth, Farmers Home Administration about 3 per cent, and individuals and others nearly a third. During the postwar years federal agencies declined in relative importance in the field of farm financing, insurance companies and commercial banks increased in relative importance, and individuals and others maintained about the same relative position.

Government Programs

For over thirty years we have had a system of government supports of the prices of farm products. Details of the system have varied from time to time, but the basic principles have remained much the same. Support programs of some type seem likely to continue. There are indications, however, that the interests of the consumer will be accorded increased attention. This was evident in the changes made in wheat and cotton supports in the 1964 legislation. The political balance seems to be shifting away from the farmers.

Three basic questions are involved in a system of government support of farm prices: first, which prices shall be supported; second, on what level; and third, by what means. Government supports have tended to be on a selective rather than on a uniform basis. Originally, only the so-called basic products—wheat, corn, cotton, rice, and peanuts—were supported. From time to time others have been added to the list and some have been dropped.

The basic principle determining the level at which prices are supported has been the concept of "parity." Parity is defined as the ratio which prevailed between farm prices and nonfarm prices during the period 1909 to 1914. This period is considered to be one in which a "normal" ratio between these two sets of prices prevailed. Several methods have been used to maintain parity, the most important being the "loan and storage" system. For example, the farmer stores wheat at an approved storage facility and offers the stored wheat as collateral for a nonrecourse loan from the government on the basis of the support price. If the farmer sees fit, he may repay the loan, redeem his wheat, and sell it on the open market. If he does not, the government takes the wheat as payment for

Table 24–2. Farm Mortgage Debt by Principal Lender

	Outstanding Loans Reported By							
Year	Federal Land Banks $1000	Federal Farm Mortgage Corporation $1000	Joint-Stock Land Banks $1000	Farmers Home Administration $1000	Life Insurance Companies $1000	Commercial and Savings Banks $1000	Other Farm-Mortgage Debt $1000	Total Farm-Mortgage Debt $1000
1940	2,009,820	713,290	91,726	32,178	984,290	534,170	2,220,925	6,586,399
1945	1,209,676	347,307	5,455	195,519	938,275	449,582	1,795,101	4,940,915
1950	906,077	58,650	270	193,301	1,172,326	937,144	2,311,510	5,579,278
1955	1,266,953	12,834	–	287,171	2,051,784	1,210,676	3,415,860	8,245,278
1960	2,335,124	–	–	439,269	2,819,542	1,631,271	4,857,203	12,082,409
1965	3,686,755	–	–	619,492	4,295,228	2,668,535	7,634,470	18,904,480

SOURCE: U.S. Department of Agriculture, *Agricultural Finance Review.*

the loan and the transaction is concluded. In fact, such a loan is a sort of conditional sale to the government at a "pegged" minimum price. Other methods which the government has used to support prices include outright purchase in the open market, subsidized exports, market quotas, acreage restrictions, and the Soil Bank program.

Farm Trends

In all probability, the trend toward larger and fewer farms will continue as farm management improves and as technology advances, thus making possible increased use of machinery and improved seeds and fertilizers. Farms are likely to take on to an increasing extent many of the characteristics of large-scale manufacturing operations. Fewer people will get their incomes from farming. As recently as a hundred years ago over half of our people made their living by farming. Now, less than one in ten derives his income from farms. In a few years this ratio may decline to one in twenty. Larger farms and more machinery will require increasing capital investment per farm and for agriculture as a whole. Hence, it will become somewhat more difficult to enter the business of farming than was formerly the case. Furthermore, educational requirements will increase, not only in terms of a knowledge of agricultural methods and techniques, but also of administration and management.

Those who now attempt to operate marginal farms will gradually move into other occupations. Some farms of this type will be absorbed by larger commercial farms. Others may be used for reforestation and recreational purposes.

The federal highway program is having significant effects on farming. Many farms are being brought closer to markets. More farm families may live in suburban homes and commute to farm operations. This is already true of much crop farming, as in the case of the wheatlands of Kansas.

The number of owner-occupied farms may tend downward if the interest of high income investors in farms continues or increases. Because of them it may become increasingly difficult for farm tenants to become owners.

Of course, there is no way of knowing the long-term impact of scientific and technological research on farming. It may be that in the not-too-distant future many of our food requirements will be produced in the laboratory and factory.

Timberland

A large portion of land in the United States is covered with timber. Not only is this a source of lumber, but also of a great many by-products, such as turpentine, resin, and camphor. Timberland produces both human and animal foods, such as nuts, acorns, and wild fruit. It acts as a watershed, helps to support wildlife, and also provides certain recreational resources. At least three different types of land may be used for forests: (1) that where forests now exist and which is well adapted to the continuation of such use, (2) land where forests previously existed and which is better adapted to the growing of trees than to any other use, and (3) land which was previously in cultivation and might have been kept in cultivation if proper protective measures had been taken in time, but which now can be best utilized for the growing of trees.

Sustained Yield Management

Land which is now in timber and for which this is its proper use can best be kept in such use by *sustained yield management.* This means that the timber should be managed in such a way that it will yield a relatively uniform crop year after year, or at least at frequent intervals rather than only a single crop once every generation, half century, or longer. For many years most of our timberland has been "mined" rather than cropped. Sustained yield management involves selective cutting, taking only the mature trees for commercial lumber production. It also involves the cutting of malformed, diseased, and "weed" trees to give appropriate room, light, and plant food to the more desirable types. By this general process a forester can improve the quality of his timber in much the same manner that a livestock breeder improves the quality of his herd. Frequently the returns from the lower-grade products are sufficient to cover labor costs incurred in the process of sustained yield management. The trees that are cut, of course, must be replaced either by planting seedlings grown in nursery plots or by resetting certain trees which have been left standing for the purpose.

Adequate replacement can rarely be achieved if the woodland is grazed by domestic livestock. Cattle and hogs, especially the latter, destroy almost all young growth in a forest. In addition there is the need of protecting timber from fire, which is the ever-threatening enemy of woodland. Much progress in the field of fire prevention and protection has been made in recent decades, but highly destructive forest fires continue to occur.

Reforestation

In cases where cutover land has not proved to be suitable for agricultural use, programs for reforestation may be undertaken. In the northern parts of the country, unfortunately, a period of fifty to one hundred years is often required for the growing of trees from the seedling to the saw-log stage. Because of the long waiting period, interest on the investment, taxes, and risks from many sources, programs of this type are not always attractive to private persons or business firms. In the South, particularly along the lower Atlantic and Gulf coastal plains, where the growing season is long and the rainfall is heavier, the rate of tree growth is sufficiently rapid to be attractive to private developers and investors. In this area trees may grow to sufficient size for commercial lumber products in twenty to thirty years. There is also some possibility of income from turpentine and other naval stores in the meantime. Tax arrangements have been made somewhat more favorable to developments of this kind in recent years.

Recreational Land

Factors which impart recreational values to rural land include the following: (1) favorable climate; for example, cool summers, mild winters, large percentage of sunny days, snow for skiing, and the like; (2) scenic beauty; for example, bodies of water, mountains, and forests; (3) a relative abundance of wildlife, with opportunities for hunting, fishing, nature study, and photography; (4) facilities for water sports, including swimming, boating, and related activities; (5) historic or antiquarian interests, such as battlefields, relics of pioneer settlements, and the like.

Obviously a piece of land does not need all of these characteristics to have recreational value; any one of them alone may be sufficient to merit some degree of recreational use of land. Rarely are all of the characteristics listed above found in combination, but it is not unusual to find several of them available at a given site. New England, the northern lake regions, and parts of the Rocky Mountains attract people because of their cool summers. Florida, the Gulf coast, and parts of Texas, New Mexico, Arizona, and California attract people because of their relatively warm winters. The Adirondacks, the White Mountains, and Sun Valley in the Rockies appeal to smaller numbers of more active people for skiing and other winter sports.

Traditionally, hunting and fishing have been the most common forms of recreational use of rural land. Private and public hunting preserves have been developed. Lakes and streams have been stocked with fish in recent years. It is estimated that more people go fishing than engage in any other form of recreation.

The attractiveness of lakes, streams, and ocean beaches for water sports is closely related to the almost universal search for favorable climates. More and more people have been taking regular vacations. To a large degree these are concentrated in the summer months, but winter vacations are growing more popular. As a result, the incomes of winter resorts have tended to expand. Jet aircraft are changing somewhat the pattern of preferences for various resort areas.

Almost all of us are to some extent interested in our history. Old battlegrounds, ghost towns, relics of early settlements, and similar points of historical interest have a wide appeal. While this country lacks the old castles and other romantic ruins of Europe, we do have a number of interesting relics of both Indian and early American culture.

The use of rural land for parks has been growing in importance. Some of the large national parks and forests, such as Yellowstone and Glacier National parks, are famous throughout the world. In recent years a number of states have developed systems of state parks. Those of Indiana, such as Brown County, Turkey Run, and McCormick's Creek, are cases in point. In addition the private development of parks has progressed. Usually such parks are located in accessible areas and tied in with such sports as hunting, fishing, horseback riding, and related activities.

Growing Importance of Recreation

With the growth of population, higher incomes, and increased leisure time, the demands for recreational facilities of all types have tended to expand. Outdoor recreation has attracted vastly greater numbers of people in recent years than in the period prior to World War II. This is due in large part to the increased mobility of our people. Widespread ownership of automobiles; favorable airline, bus, and boat fares; improved highways; and more widespread and longer vacations have all contributed to the growing interest in outdoor recreation. Furthermore, there are more retired people who have both leisure and independent incomes.

In all probability such factors as growing population, rising incomes, greater leisure time, and increased mobility will continue to operate in the years ahead. Consequently, recreation activities in general and outdoor recreation activities in particular seem likely to grow in importance.[4]

SUMMARY

Rural real estate includes land in use for farms and ranches, forestry, recreation, nonfarm residences, and other uses. Of these, agriculture is the most important.

The income-producing ability of most rural real estate is influenced by natural resources and characteristics of the land more than by specific location, as in the case of urban real estate, although location is of

---

[4] For a discussion of outdoor recreation, see Marion Clawson, *Outdoor Recreation* (Washington, D.C.: Resources for the Future, Inc., 1958). See also Dennis Gabor, *Inventing the Future* (New York: Alfred A. Knopf, Inc., 1963).

importance. The market for rural real estate is largely localized, and not highly organized. Rural real estate is sold by the acre, and prices are quoted in dollars per acre. Some brokers who deal in rural real estate also offer farm management services.

The demand for agricultural land is a derived demand, depending upon the demand for and prices of farm products. Some demand reflects the interest of investors in the income tax advantages of farm ownership and development, and some reflects the speculative hope that the land may be required for urban expansion in the future. The major determinants of demand are incomes and the terms and availability of financing.

The price support programs which have been in operation over the past three decades have been an important influence on product prices and therefore on rural real estate values.

A recent trend, reinforced by technological improvements, is toward fewer farms, and these of larger unit size. The higher capital requirements for modern farming tend to make entry into farming more difficult. This, plus the interest of large investors in agricultural properties, may retard the trend toward more widespread ownership of individual farms by farm operators.

Timberland represents an important sector of rural real estate. Sustained yield management and tax advantages have tended to attract investors into timberland in recent years.

Recreation of all types appears to be a growing influence in American life. Demands for outdoor recreational facilities are growing; this indicates a substantial expansion in the use of various lands for recreational purposes.

QUESTIONS FOR STUDY

1. Explain why agriculture has shifted toward managerial-type operations. What effect has this had on land uses and values?
2. How does the market for farms differ from the market for other types of real estate? Why?
3. Explain why the demand for farms is a derived demand.
4. Do practices of farm real estate brokers differ from those in urban areas? Explain.
5. Explain the major factors that determine the value of rural land. Which of these is most important? Why?
6. Explain how farm operations can be expanded by using capital instead of additional land.
7. What factors explain the increasing average unit size of farms? What advantages do you see in this trend? If there are any disadvantages, explain why and for whom.
8. Why might investors not directly interested in farming desire to own farm property?

9. Compare and contrast the financing of farm and of residential real estate. Identify and define the financing agencies that are most important in rural real esate.

10. What is your evaluation of farm price-support programs? How do these programs affect the income-producing ability of rural real estate? What is their effect on the values of rural real estate?

11. What are the major determinants of demand in the market for timberland? What are the major determinants of supply?

12. What is sustained yield management?

13. Is the amount of land devoted to recreational activities likely to increase or decrease in the years ahead? Why?

14. *Study Project 42.* (a) State whether you are in general agreement or disagreement with the CED farm program proposal and explain your reasons. (b) What would be the impact on land values if the CED programs were implemented? Explain. (c) To what extent is your opinion of the CED proposal based on strictly agricultural considerations? What other considerations may be important in evaluating the proposals?

SUGGESTED READINGS

CLAWSON, MARION. *Outdoor Recreation.* Washington, D.C.: Resources for the Future, Inc., 1958.

———, *et al. Land for the Future.* Baltimore: Johns Hopkins Press, 1960. Chaps. iii, vi.

COMMITTEE FOR ECONOMIC DEVELOPMENT. *An Adaptive Program for Agriculture.* A Statement on National Policy by the Research and Policy Committee, New York, July, 1962.

HIGBEE, EDWARD. *Farms and Farmers in an Urban Age.* New York: Twentieth Century Fund, 1963. Chap. iv.

25

International
Real Estate Trends

World Urbanization

The growth of cities at a more rapid rate than the surrounding rural areas is a worldwide phenomenon. London was the only metropolitan area approaching 1 million population in 1800; in 1964, there were 133 metropolitan areas in the world with a million or more residents. The number of cities with a population of 100,000 or more increased from 36 in the year 1800 to 1,128 in 1960. The total urban population of the world increased from 45 or 50 million in 1800 to over 1 billion in 1964. If the present population explosion continues, urban population may increase to around 3½ billion by the year 2000.

This growth of cities is the consequence of a transition from a society dominated by agriculture to one with an increasing development of manufacturing, which began in England and then successively took hold in Germany, the United States and Japan, and the Soviet Union and Red China. Industrialization is in its incipient stages in India, Brazil, Mexico, and in many other countries.

Relative Importance of Real Estate as an Investment

It may be a matter of surprise that in many foreign nations real estate is a larger medium of investment than all other investments combined. Despite the more than $300 billion in real estate mortgages in the United States in 1964, of which over two-thirds were in single-family homes, there is a tremendous opportunity for investment in stocks and bonds in the

United States which does not exist in undeveloped nations. In many nations, land has been the chief medium of investment because of the lack of industries offering their securities on the market.

Investment by Europeans or by Nationals of Other Countries in American Real Estate

There is a recent trend toward investment by Europeans and other foreigners in income properties in the United States. These investments are prompted by a variety of motives: (1) vanity, or the prestige of owning property in Manhattan or some other American center; (2) fear of either confiscation in their home lands or discriminatory taxes on their own real estate; and (3) possibility of capital gains or tax advantage in investing outside their own nations. American brokers are becoming familiar with the problems involved in securing real estate investments from other nationals, such as getting authority from their governments to transfer funds, foreign exchange rates and practices, and financing and property management.

Ground Plan of Foreign Cities Contrasted with American Cities

Aerial views of foreign cities often disclose an irregular street pattern, with densely packed buildings, which gives the appearance of a giant organism. On the other hand, most American cities, excepting Boston, were surveyed and built on a rectangular pattern. The newer suburbs of American cities built since 1934 during the automobile age, reveal a pattern of curving streets, which distinguish them from the rigidly straight lines of the old cities based on streetcar transportation.

Latin American cities have followed the design laid down by the Spaniards and the Portuguese, in which the central plaza is bordered by square blocks. Washington, D.C., is an example of a city planned from its inception with radial streets intersecting the rectangular street pattern. In Brasilia, a planner's ideal has been realized by the creation of super blocks of 2,500 population with an elementary school at the center and with four super blocks constituting a community large enough for a high school. In Brasilia there is a rigid separation between government buildings and office areas and the residential areas, and there are no grade intersections at street crossings. Other planned capital cities are Canberra, in Australia, and Islambad, the new capital of West Pakistan.

Ownership

The discussions of real estate decisions set forth in this text have application chiefly to nations in which (1) real estate properties are privately owned, (2) there is no fear of total or partial confiscation of private property by the state, and (3) inflationary tendencies are limited.

The laws of property in the United States were first developed by the English common law, and the real estate principles observed in the United States are almost equally applicable in England and the British dominions of Canada and Australia, and in nations where English laws and principles were established as in South Africa and East Africa.

At the opposite pole are Soviet Russia and Communist China, where the state owns practically all of the land, and where private ownership is limited to the right to use and occupy a single house or a small garden. It is obvious that the freedom to buy and sell buildings or vacant lands at prices determined by bargaining between a buyer and seller in an open market cannot exist where the right to buy or sell is denied, the movements of the buyer and seller are regulated, the prices of all building materials are controlled by the state regardless of cost, and where the state, by its own fiat, determines where new industries, apartment developments, and new cities shall be located. In Russia rents bear no relationship to cost of construction. Consequently, American principles of real estate value and real estate decision processes could not be applied to the Soviet Union without great modification.

Of course, private real estate ownership in the United States is subject to public control of various types such as zoning, building regulations, financing arrangements, real estate taxes, and sometimes and in some places by rent control. Nevertheless, the United States is the outstanding example of a nation of private property ownership by millions of individuals, business firms, and independent institutions. The United States possesses the advantage, not only of a wide distribution of ownerships of all types of property, but also of a division of ownership into tolerably efficient economic units. There are few large tracts under one ownership except in grazing areas; on the other hand, there are few individually owned farms too small to be operated by machinery.

Between the private ownership of the United States and the state ownership of Russia, there are numerous mixed types. In a number of countries there has been expropriation of large land holdings and redistribution among small farmers. In present-day Finland and in Sweden the state owns large tracts of land for control purposes.

Fear of Confiscation

In any nation which has enjoyed protection of private property rights but which fears that a change of government will reduce the value of real estate either by (1) outright confiscation, (2) condemnation at a low price, (3) rapid increase of real estate taxes, or (4) special advances in wages of building workers and operators, activity in the real estate market will be virtually suspended. This was true in Nairobi, Kenya, in the summer of 1962, when the knowledge that Kenya would be granted independence and given over to native rule within a year threw the real estate market into a tailspin. No loans could be obtained on real estate at that time.

Surveys and Recording of Deeds

The transferability of real property and the ability to value parcels of real estate in the market depend upon accurate land surveys which identify each parcel, and upon protection of the title. As we pointed out in Chapter 5, in the United States, government land surveys established the base boundary lines for areas west of the Alleghenies, dividing most of this vast area into square mile tracts. Deeds to lands are recorded in the county courthouses, so that the names of titleholders are a matter of public record. Title guarantee companies, or lawyers examining the abstracts showing the chain of title, or the Torrens system, assure the purchaser that he is securing a merchantable title to the land described in the deed.

In contrast to this, in some of the new nations of Africa like Ghana, there are no accurate land surveys. The land, as in pre-Columbian North America, is owned by the tribe.

In many nations of Europe, land in small strips has been owned by the same family for generations and is constantly subdivided further by inheritance. In some village economies, as was the case in Czarist Russia, the village elders redistribute the land among the villagers at stated intervals.

Inflation

A relatively stable currency has been important to the ownership and use of real estate in the United States. Although our dollar has lost value rapidly in two world wars, and at a slower pace in recent years, our recent large-scale construction activities have been made possible through long-term financing. Insurance companies, banks, and savings and loan institutions have been willing to make loans repayable thirty years or longer in the future in terms of fixed dollars. In Brazil in 1963 it was impossible to secure a loan for five or ten years, even at a *monthly* interest rate of 5 per cent, because the cruzeiro had been losing its value at an even greater rate. This inflation did not curtail but, rather, accelerated the urge to build or to buy land, because of the desire to invest the money as fast as possible in land or buildings. It was necessary to pay cash and to sell each floor of these buildings on a condominium basis as fast as they were erected.

Distribution of Income

The most important differences between the scope and magnitude of the real estate market in the United States and most other nations are those resulting from the high family incomes and the high proportion of families in the middle income brackets in the United States. The average per capita income in the United States is the highest in the world—$2,248 after taxes during 1964. In 1958, when the per capita disposable income in the United States was nearly $2,000, the per capita income in the United Kingdom was estimated at $1,000; that of West Germany at $725; and the U.S.S.R. at $575. The annual per capita income of the United States has been running about ten times that of Brazil, Mexico, Portugal, and Spain, which ranged from $200 to $280, and forty times that of India, Pakistan, and Indonesia, which was $53 to $60 annually.

Not only was there thus a very high level of income in the United States, but there was also a very large middle class, with 52 per cent of all families earning over $5,000 a year in 1960, compared with but 8 per cent in 1945. The affluence of the United States cannot be compared to other nations solely in terms of money income. We know, however, that a much larger proportion of the families in the United States have sufficient purchasing power above the bare necessities of life to buy automobiles and single-family homes with all modern utilities, as well as furniture, television sets, and household appliances, than in other parts of the world. In 1964, there were 36 million owner-occupied housing units in the United States, or 61.9 per cent of the total number. The construction, financing, and selling of new housing units at the annual rate of around 1,500,000 has created a tremendous real estate market in the United States.

The situation in the United States may be contrasted sharply with that of nations where there is only a small middle class and where there is a vast gulf between the relatively small number of wealthy families and the great majority of the poor. In these nations there are huge landed estates owned by the highest-income families, and operated by tenant farmers on the one hand, and thousands of small rural plots owned by poor families which cannot be operated efficiently by machinery on the other. Transfers of real estate by deed are infrequent in these societies since property is usually passed on from father to sons by inheritance. Obviously, the scale of activity in the real estate market and the real estate brokerage and management business in such nations is greatly restricted compared to our own.

Transport: Ownership of Automobiles

The relatively high incomes of families in the United States make possible the almost universal ownership of automobiles. In 1964, there were 66 million privately owned automobiles in the United States and 12 million trucks. The widespread ownership of a private means of transportation has had a far-reaching effect in promoting the growth of suburbs, at a distance from the central business district, and it has brought about the creation of a new type of shopping center and a widespread dispersal of factories and even office buildings to the periphery of cities.

In 1955, while the United States had 339 cars per 1,000 population, Canada had 181 and Australia 183. In that year, Northern European nations had from 58 to 111 cars per 1,000 population, and Argentina and Uruguay had 32 cars per 1,000 population. Most Asiatic, African, and South American nations had less than 15 cars per 1,000 population.

The number of automobiles has recently shown marked gains in Northwestern Europe, increasing from 58 to 122 per 1,000 persons in West Germany between 1955 and 1963, from 92 to 120 per 1,000 persons in the United Kingdom, from 60 to 106 per 1,000 persons in Belgium, and from 111 to 140 per 1,000 persons in France in the same eight-year period. These figures may be compared to 351 per 1,000 persons for the United States in 1963.

Where only a small proportion of the population owns private automobiles, the predominant form of transportation is by bus or train. In some great cities like London, Paris, Berlin, Moscow, Tokyo, and Buenos Aires there are subways in addition to buses and trains. Since mass transit lines cannot operate economically to thinly settled single-family housing areas, the majority of dwelling units in the great cities of Asia, Latin America, and Continental Europe are in apartment buildings, which are concentrated in bands along mass transit lines or bus lines, or in suburban clusters served by mass transit as in Moscow and Helsinki. Apartment units are also cheaper to build than single-family houses, and occupy far less ground area.

Mass transit lines leading to the center of the city also sustain the central business district. There has been relatively little decentralization of cities abroad. The central business districts of Rotterdam, Cologne, London, and other European cities, bombed out in World War II, were rebulit in their old locations. In most cities outside the United States, the central areas contain the chief attractions of urban life—the parks, palaces, museums, ancient monuments, national capitols, as well as hotels, theatres, and restaurants. The Parthenon on the Acropolis is near the center of Athens; the Arche de Triomphe, the Louvre, and Notre Dame are at the center of Paris; Buckingham Palace, Westminster Abbey, the Houses of Parliament, and St. Paul's are in the center of London. The Ginza district of Tokyo—its shopping and amusement district—attracts throngs at night. The principal cathedrals, museums, the capitols, and monuments of Bogotá, Lima, Buenos Aires, Rio de Janeiro, and Quito, as well as the tallest office buildings and the leading stores face or are located near the central plaza. In these foreign cities the central areas are continually rebuilt and renewed, and there is no typical slum or blighted area resulting from shifting land uses or out-migration of the population.

Similarities Between the United States and Other Nations

Although there are thus-marked differences between land use patterns and real estate practices in the United States and other nations, there are also some tendencies in other countries to move in the direction of our patterns and practices. Some of these may be noted in the following discussions of the sector theory, shopping centers, tall office buildings, and soil qualities.

Sector Theory

The rise of the middle class in many nations and the increased ownership of the automobile will make it possible for more and more families to live in single-family detached houses on the periphery of the city. This has already taken place in Latin America. Wealthy families have tended to move from patio type dwellings on the central plazas to homes or apartments on the outer fringe of one sector of the city, as in Bogotá, Lima, La Paz, Quito, Santiago, Buenos Aires, Montevideo, Rio de Janeiro, and Caracas.

Shopping Centers

The increased ownership of automobiles will also lead to the establishment of outlying shopping centers with free automobile parking. Canada and Australia already have many planned shopping centers similar to those in the United States. There is a limited number of these shopping centers in other nations, such as the Amstel Center in Amsterdam, Rosebank in Cape Town, South Africa, and others now being proposed in Europe. Sears Roebuck has a number of stores in Latin America in midtown locations but most of these are solitary stores.

The practice of making leases, not only with minimum guaranteed rent, but also with rents based on a percentage of sales seems to be unknown in most countries. Difficulties may also be experienced in other countries in securing commercial zoning for a sufficient area of land to provide free parking areas.

Tall Office Buildings

New tall office buildings have broken the old sky lines in London, Paris, and Milan, as well as in Rio de Janeiro and Mexico City. Thus, the uniform height of buildings so long maintained is giving way to the irregular sky line of American cities.

Soil Qualities

In all parts of the world are found agricultural areas in which the composition of soils, rainfall, length of the growing season, and suitability for crops are similar to some areas in the United States, and they are measured and defined by soil scientists as in the United States. Differences in the values of crop lands or grazing lands in other nations compared to the United States would result from lower labor costs, lower selling prices if there is no price support of crops, and import restrictions or tariff duties of the other nations buying the crops.

Foreign Investments in Real Estate

Foreign investors have recently made large investments in United States planned shopping centers, office buildings, and apartments. In addition to income property, thousands of lots in Florida resort developments have been sold to Europeans.

Appraisals and Real Estate Valuations

Where the titles to real estate are not jeopardized by confiscation, the value of real estate properties based on comparable sales, reproduction cots, and net income would be computed in a similar manner to that in the United States. The formula would be the same, but the figures in it would be different. Thus, in Johannesburg, South Africa, elevator office building costs of construction would be approximately $6 per square foot, due to partial use of native labor, compared with $18 to $22 per square foot in the United States, but office rents would be only $2 per square foot annually compared to $6 or $7 per square foot here.

Rent control in Brazil has the same depressing effect on values as in the United States. In Brazil, France, and other nations where rent control is applied to existing apartments, new apartments have been built and sold on a condominium basis.

SUMMARY

World urbanization represents one of the significant developments of recent years. This reflects the increased industrialization of many parts of the world. With this has come a growing interest in real estate, notably in urban and urban-related areas. In recent years international investments in real estate have risen in importance. In many foreign countries real estate is a relatively more important medium of investment than in the United States because of the importance of the securities market in this country. Investments of other nationals in the United States have tended to rise and opposite trends are also to be noted. Differential yields on investments, differences in tax treatment, and the desire for a spreading of risks are all factors in these processes.

The private ownership of real estate varies greatly as between countries around the world, as does the legal system which regulates such ownership. Fear of confiscation is an important factor in stimulating foreign investment on the part of many nationals. A closely related factor is the fear of inflation. The ownership of real property is influenced greatly by the distribution of income that prevails in particular countries. The large middle class in the United States is a significant factor in widespread real estate ownership.

Trends toward suburban developments are less extensive abroad, even in Western Europe, than in the United States, because of the lower per capita ownership of automobiles. This situation, however, is changing rapidly in Western Europe. As a result, there is likely to be an expansion of shopping centers and tall office buildings in such countries.

QUESTIONS FOR STUDY

1. Why does real estate tend to be a relatively more important form of investment in foreign countries than in the United States? How would this affect the real estate markets of those countries?
2. Contrast the typical ground plan of U.S. and foreign cities. What factors account for the principal differences?
3. Why are investors from other countries acquiring interests in income-producing property in the U.S.?
4. How does the fear of confiscation affect the ownership of real estate? The trend of land values?
5. How is inflation likely to affect real estate ownership and investment? How important is a stable currency for real estate investors? Explain.
6. In which ways may income distribution affect real estate markets?
7. As mass automobile ownership extends to countries beyond the U.S., what changes in city structure would you anticipate for those countries?

8. Cite an example of changes already created by automobiles in foreign countries and explain their effects on real estate values.
9. Contrast real estate appraisals in the U.S. and abroad.
10. *Study Project 43.* (a) Assume you are one of the realtors going to Europe to promote investment in U.S. real estate. Outline a promotional approach, including the advantages of such investments. Include, also, a summary of trends in this type of foreign investment and the reasons encouraging such trends. (b) Assume you are a foreign investor to whom the above approach has been presented. What disadvantages do you see in investing in U.S. real estate? Do they outweigh the advantages? Which factors do you think will be most significant in making your final decision?

SUGGESTED READINGS

UNITED NATIONS. *Demographic Year Book.* New York: United Nations, 1962.

GINSBURG, NORTON. *Atlas of Economic Development.* Chicago: University of Chicago Press, 1961.

GOTTMAN, JEAN. *Economics, Esthetics and Ethics in Modern Urbanization.* New York: Twentieth Century Fund, 1962.

HOYT, HOMER. *World Urbanization,* Technical Bulletin #43. Washington, D.C.: Urban Land Institute, April, 1962.

The Worldmark Encyclopedia of the Nations. New York: Worldmark Press, Harper & Row, Publishers, 1962.

26

Real Estate and Economic Growth

Economic Growth Potentials

We have referred at various points in earlier discussions to growth projections of the American economy. We have paid attention particularly to various estimates made by Resources for the Future, Inc. Median projections indicate that gross national product at the level of one trillion dollars will be reached by 1980 or possibly sooner (this is in terms of 1960 dollars). By the year 2000, median projections suggest the possibility of GNP somewhat more than doubling again. Both family and personal incomes will also rise, and despite the larger population, per capita income will continue to show advances. As was pointed out by the study,

The average U.S. citizen, young or old, now has at his disposal a personal income of a little less than $2,000, roughly 50 per cent higher, in real terms, than at the start of World War II. The prospects are for another 50 per cent rise over the next twenty years and a similar one in the twenty years after that. This Medium projection comes out, in money terms, to about 3,000 of today's dollars in 1980 and 4,300 in 2000. Our Low projection is $2,600 in 1980 and $3,500 in 2000; and our High, $3,200 for 1980 and $5,300 for 2000.[1] [For 1964 this figure was above $2,200.]

Expansion of this magnitude will require better decisions relative to the utilization of existing resources as well as in the development of new resources.

[1] Hans H. Landsberg, Leonard L. Fischman, and Joseph L. Fisher, *Resources in America's Future* (Baltimore: Johns Hopkins Press, 1963), p. 80.

What part will real estate resources play in the economic growth of this country? Will their role be of greater or lesser importance than it has been in the past?

Answers to these questions depend in part on the number of people, their incomes, their locations, and their changing standards; for example, how much of their incomes they wish to spend for real estate resources and services in relation to other things. Answers will depend in part on the relative cost of providing real estate resources and services in comparison to the costs of other goods and services. This will depend on the rate at which technological advances are made in the real estate field in comparison to advances in other areas and on the quality of the decisions determining the effectiveness with which resources are managed in the real estate field and in other fields. Much will also depend on the nature of changes in transportation that accelerate or retard new real estate developments.

Because we add only a small percentage to the total supply of real estate resources each year, much depends on the efficiency with which existing resources are used. This in turn depends in part on conservation and renewal programs. For a short period of time, real estate requirements could be met by more intensive use of existing properties. Over a longer period, the destruction and deterioration of a portion of the available supply would require the provision of some new facilities even with a static population with static incomes and standards. Every year some real estate resources are taken out of use as a result of demolition, fires, windstorms, or other causes. Also, some properties are highly specialized and pass out of use through obsolescence. The multi-story factory building is a case in point.

We have been adding new housing facilities at a rate of about 3 per cent of the total supply per year. Even if we moved this rate up to 4 per cent per year, within a ten-year period we would add only a little over a third to our present housing supply. Much the same thing may be said of the development of commercial and industrial real estate.

Decisions as to the rate of building or the conservation and renewal of older properties will be made in part by private individuals and the executives of business firms and in part by public officials reflecting the points of view of the electorate. If real estate resources are taxed on a more favorable basis than is now the case, for example, this will have an important effect on their future role; if people wish to add to or reduce various subsidies to real estate, it will affect the rate of development or redevelopment of these resources.

In terms of the population pressures that have been generated, there is little doubt that space demands will increase in the years ahead. In view of the prospect for rising incomes, there may also be a demand for higher quality of real estate resources and resource services. The location of economic opportunities and, hence, the location of the homes of people will change. Thus, there may be a surplus of real properties in some places at the same time that there are shortages in others.

Varying Impact of Growth

In a discussion of this type, distinctions need to be made between various types of properties. Changing technology and transportation patterns will undoubtedly alter the types of industrial real estate that will be most useful in the future. Recent rates of technological change suggest that industrial real estate resources will tend to grow obsolete rather rapidly in the years ahead. To a significant degree the same statement applies also to commercial real estate. The advent of regional shopping centers, supermarkets, and other new store arrangements has already brought rapid obsolescence to many commercial real estate resources. Obviously, new developments in the future will have similar effects.

The shopping habits and preferences of people in recent years have tended to favor outlying as against downtown locations. The continuation of this trend will have important effects in the future; a reversal of this trend, or a partial reversal, would affect the rate at which various types of commercial real estate would be required.

Residential real estate resources have undergone important changes in recent years, as we have seen in our previous discussions. The earlier preference for single-family suburban living has been modified to a degree by the rising demand for apartments. In some cases people are tending to prefer downtown or "near-in" locations for their regular residences, but are combining such living arrangements with relatively nearby weekend cottages and other resort properties. The years ahead, thus, may see the emergence of more and more two-house families just as recent years have seen a rapid increase in the number of two-car families.[2]

Rural land uses have undergone rapid changes as we have seen in Chapter 24. Farmers are now living and working in what is essentially an urban society.

Power can be transmitted over wider areas than formerly. The new federal highway program is bringing a redistribution of both rural and urban land uses. Pipelines, new waterway developments, jet aircraft, and changes which we cannot as yet foresee will continue to bring shifts in land uses and in the intensity of land uses.

[2] See Norman Strunk and Arthur M. Weimer, *Quarterly Letter* of the U.S. Savings and Loan League (Summer, 1964).

Requirements for New Resources

In Chapter 6 we suggested some of the types of demands that might affect our requirements for real estate resources in the future. Of course, general estimates may be wide of the mark. But we are fairly sure that (1) population will continue to grow; (2) there will be more people in the 25 to 35 age group in the years immediately ahead, an age group that usually influences considerably the rate of family formation and the birth rate; (3) incomes will continue upward—not consistently, but with general improvement over time; and (4) the long-term growth potential of the American economy is very great.

If these assumptions are reasonably correct, we may expect substantial expansion in our requirements for real estate resources of nearly all types in the years ahead. We may not need more farmland, for example, but will probably use present agricultural land resources more intensively. We may expand somewhat the land area used for forests. We may see more land used for recreational purposes. And especially are we likely to see a major increase in the land used for various urban and suburban purposes.

Demands for new dwelling units may average from 1.4 to 1.6 million per year for some time. This reflects an increase in formation of new households at a rate of around a million per year, rising family incomes, plus the demolition of older houses.

We should note that there will be considerable variation in the demands made on real estate resources, however, from year to year, region to region, and city to city. Growth in the South, West, and Southwest is expected to be more rapid than in other parts of the country. Growth of some cities, whether in the North, East, West, or South, will be more rapid than that of others. New real estate resources will be developed in response to demands, and such demands will vary greatly from region to region and city to city. Also, growth is more likely to occur somewhat irregularly from year to year than to follow a consistent pattern.

We should recognize also that growth will not proceed at the same rate in different parts of cities. The suburban and interurban trends undoubtedly will continue and affect greatly the demand for new real estate resources in the years ahead. Outlying areas probably will provide the major portion of new developments, not only in terms of single-family homes, but also retail space, one-story factory buildings and industrial parks, research parks, schools, churches, and even many office buildings.

Apartment house construction has increased recently in central and "near-in" areas and probably will do so in the future. Also, many new office buildings and stores are projected for the downtown and nearby areas. Thus, there may be a better balance between growth in central areas and outlying areas in the 1960's and 1970's than was true in the 1950's.

Central and "near-in" areas may see more renewal and new real estate resource development than has been typical of the earlier postwar years. Some downtown areas will serve as the central meeting points and headquarters for entire regions and a few for the entire continent. Developments like Rockefeller Center in New York and Penn Center in Philadelphia, however, have demonstrated the importance of substantial open spaces, even at the core of cities. Thus, new developments are likely to follow new patterns.

New Towns

As we pointed out in our earlier discussions, a number of completely new communities are likely to be developed in the next decade or two.[3] They may be surrounded by green belts and cover wide areas around present metropolitan centers. Many of these will be "new towns"—complete communities with an independent economic base. Some of these new communities will be essentially "dormitory towns" without the customary economic base. Their residents will derive incomes from nearby commercial and industrial centers, but their towns will be independent of other cities in physical and local political terms. The essential economic basis for the new "dormitory" communities will be their community facilities—sewage-disposal plants, water systems, and electrical, gas, and related facilities. They will have their own schools, hospitals, recreational areas, and other community services. Most of them will have a balance between single-family residences and apartments so that the needs of young families and retired persons can be met as well as those of families with growing children. (See Fig. 26-1.)

Developments of new towns and communities are not likely to create a shortage of land for urban purposes. The land area used by urban and rural nonfarm structures currently is only about 25 million acres, or 1.3 per cent of the land area of the continental United States, excluding Alaska. Even with the most lavish use of land for urban purposes, it is unlikely that twice this amount will be needed for a long time.

The new federal highway system and related road developments will open up great areas of land within easy commuting distance of central places of employment. Thus, new patterns of urban development are likely to emerge that have relatively limited relationships to the older structure of cities.

[3] See "New Towns of America," *House and Home* (February, 1964).

Fig. 26–1. Prospective town center, Columbia City, Maryland. (Courtesy Ezra Stoller Associates.)

Development Methods and Costs

As we suggested in our discussion of building and subdividing in Chapters 15 and 16, significant advances have been made in these fields in recent years. Still, costs have advanced substantially, and generally have risen more than in other fields. If the methods of land development can be improved, and if we can continue to come up with new products and processes, there undoubtedly will be rapid expansion of real estate resources. Except for historical buildings and sites, we are likely to continue our preference for new resources in contrast to the conservation, renewal, or redevelopment of older resources.

What happens will depend on the effectiveness of management and administration as well as on improved technology in the fields of land development and building and the rate of improvement in these fields in comparison to others. Public policy, of course, will also play an important part. The quality of land planning methods and techniques will have an important bearing on the development of new real estate resources in the years ahead. While it is never possible to anticipate with great exactness the ways in which various areas should be developed, increased research and study undoubtedly will lead to the development of improved planning and better zoning in the years ahead. Expanded research and development programs may prove useful in the public policy areas as well as in the managerial and technological fields. Indeed, the invention of new social, political, and economic relationships would appear to be essential to enable various agencies of local and state government to function with sufficient effectiveness to meet future requirements.

Conservation and Renewal

As we have pointed out, the real estate resources required in the future will be provided in part by the continued use of the resources now available. The effectiveness of such use will depend on the care with which these resources are used and managed, and on programs for redeveloping, rehabilitating, or renewing properties, neighborhoods, and districts—in short, programs that will lengthen the economic life of real properties.

Good housekeeping, both on a private and public basis, will be important in this connection. The development and enforcement of higher standards of land use and building occupancy will also play a part, as will the impact of tax burdens, land planning programs, and the like. In brief, the conservation of existing resources will affect the type and quality of the services they can provide and will influence the rate at which new resources are developed.

Throughout our history we have tended to stress the development of new resources rather than the conservation and renewal of the old. Typically, it was more expeditious to use up our forests, minerals, and similar resources as we needed them than to conserve them for future use. In part this resulted from the abundance of natural resources available and the continued discovery of new resources. In part this point of view represented a faith in the continuation of scientific and technological advances which provided substitutes for many natural resources. For example, weather control and the production of agricultural products in laboratories in future years, both distinct possibilities, would change greatly our interest in conserving the fertility of agricultural lands.

Even in the case of urban real estate resources it has often been more convenient and probably more economical to develop new areas on the periphery of cities than to conserve, renew, or redevelop older areas. Also, the automobile and improved roads and streets reduced dependence on specific locations and increased greatly the amount of land area that could be used effectively for urban purposes.

The way in which a given piece of urban real estate is used, however, may have a considerable impact on other real properties. This is especially true of adjacent or nearby properties. Thus, we often find it necessary to clear a slum or renew a blighted area in order to prevent the deterioration of properties in a nearby area.

The renewal problems of the downtown area are especially complex. The present functioning heart of the city can in some cases be supplanted by reliance on other downtown areas, particularly if larger interurbias emerge; in some cases, outlying business centers may absorb many of the functions typically performed by the downtown center. But in many cities it will be necessary to conserve, renew, and redevelop the downtown area.

There are also the "near-in" areas—slums near the center of the city and other "gray" areas. Their blight may affect other districts and neighborhoods adversely. Often the social costs of delinquency and crime generated in such areas become a drain on municipal governments. In some cases, slums may be converted to other uses. In the future, much of the land near the center of the city may be used for automobile parking and for recreational facilities. Higher-priced apartment projects are being developed in some localities of this type.

In many cities there are slum areas on the periphery which may lead to the deterioration of present attractive suburbs. Failure to provide for adequate zoning in advance of expansion often results in an urban sprawl that creates problems of inharmonious land developments.[4]

[4] See William H. Whyte, Jr. (ed.), "Urban Sprawl," in *The Expanding Metropolis* (New York: Doubleday & Company, Inc., 1958).

Priority of Urban Problems

A few years ago the Committee for Economic Development asked a number of economists to identify the most important economic problem to be faced by the United States in the next twenty years. Of the 48 papers dealing with this subject published in Volume I of the CED report, *Problems of United States Economic Development,*[5] four stressed the subject of urban problems—congestion, renewal, and related problems. Professor Alvin Hansen said, in discussing the great prospective wave of urban growth, "This tidal wave will throw up economic, fiscal and social problems the like of which we have scarcely caught a glimmer. . . . The central *economic* problem springing from this development will be that of finance. The tidal wave of urban growth will push to the foreground as never before the problem of federal-state-local fiscal relations."[6]

Luther Gulick, President of the Institute of Public Administration, said in this connection, ". . . at the moment of our greatest prosperity we find ourselves confronted with an evil that threatens to throttle a large part of our business activity and to rob us of the fruits of our ever-advancing technology. That is, the stagnation and dry-rot which has attacked our great metropolitan centers."[7]

Today, the problems of the urban community are even more pressing than they were a few years ago. Few areas of American life present more difficult problems. Dr. Dennis Gabor pointed out recently in his book, *Inventing the Future,* that three major problems now face the human race:

Our civilization faces three great dangers. The first is destruction by nuclear war, the second is overpopulation, and the third is the Age of Leisure.

If the first happens, people will know what to do. Most of civilization may be destroyed, but not all mankind; even some pockets of white people will survive here and there. This will face the survivors with a familiar problem. One can perhaps call it an archetypal situation for which man is psychologically well prepared. As a beetle which has dropped into a glass seems to gather new strength every time that it slips back to the bottom, man will start scrambling up vigorously towards what will then appear as a lost paradise. . . .

If the world is stricken with overpopulation, people will also know what to do. It will be a harsh world, with hard work and strict discipline, and with very little freedom. But though such a crippled life runs contrary to some of man's basic instincts, we know (alas!) that men can survive as slaves. As long as the daily bread is a daily victory there will be enough incentive left to survive.

[5] *Problems of United States Economic Development* (New York: Committee for Economic Development, 1958).

[6] *Ibid.,* pp. 326–27.

[7] *Ibid.,* p. 317.

Only the Age of Leisure will find man psychologically unprepared. Leisure for all is a complete novelty in human history. There have been small earthly paradises before, such as Samoa, Burma, or Bali, where people worked little and were satisfied with what they had. The new technological paradise in which the work of a small minority is sufficient to keep the majority in idle luxury is an entirely different matter. It is not yet with us, but it is coming towards us with rapid strides.[8]

We are not as yet vitally concerned with the problems of "the Age of Leisure," but if they materialize, they will be largely urban problems and their solutions are likely to be found in cities and improved ways of urban living.

Conserving and Renewing Values

In considering conservation and renewal programs, we must be careful to think in terms of uses and *values* rather than in terms of physical resources. It is difficult to justify the redevelopment of a slum area for residential purposes if people no longer wish to live there. Some other use, however, may give value to the area and also benefit other areas. Although we usually think in economic terms about resources and their uses, it is necessary also that social costs and returns be considered, especially with respect to programs such as those designed to redevelop slum areas. In some cases aesthetic considerations may play a part in the value judgments that are made. From an economic standpoint, programs of conservation usually relate to the appropriate rate of discount of the future income to be derived from real estate or other resources over the period of their economic life. In terms of social costs and returns or aesthetic considerations, the problems become much more complicated and decisions more difficult to reach. Some sort of total value concept or present total value concept may be applied to a group of interrelated resources.

It is helpful, also, in considering conservation and renewal programs to consider the differences between various types of resources. First, there are *nonrenewable* resources. For example, a natural recreational area may not be subject to renewal. The same thing is true of coal, petroleum, and natural gas. Second are the *renewable* resources, which are subject to replacement either through natural processes or through human decisions and programs. Basic soil fertility may be destroyed but is also subject to renewal. The productivity of renewable resources can be increased, maintained, or diminished as a result of individual, business, or public decisions.

[8] Dennis Gabor, *Inventing the Future* (New York: Alfred A. Knopf, Inc., 1964), pp. 3–5.

Public Facilities

Our machinery for channeling significant portions of our savings into investments in community facilities and services appears to be inadequate. Savings institutions are being given broader powers to invest directly in new community facilities. Much remains to be done, however. Financial institutions, such as savings and loan associations, mutual savings banks, and life insurance companies, are now performing important services by the direct development of new housing projects and related facilities within the limits of their present authority. Broader powers for investment in redevelopment projects on the part of such institutions may also produce substantial benefits.

Local governments need to project and plan their needs for community facilities and services for a number of years into the future. Many projects of this type take a long time in the planning stage. Often they are undertaken at times when many other types of expansion are going on, with the result that financing charges are usually high. If such projects could be financed in periods of "easy" rather than "tight" money, substantial savings might result. Also, there might be savings in bidding for the materials and labor that may be required if the timing of such developments can take advantage of changes in general and local business conditions.

Not only longer-range but more inclusive plans for urban expansion and renewal are needed. The complicated system of multiple local governmental units creates some problems in this connection. But local government reorganization may not lead to improved long-range planning for community facilities unless there is strong public support for such programs. Current trends suggest that such support will gain strength in the years ahead.

Improvements in Administration

In which respects may real estate administration be improved in the years ahead and thus facilitate economic growth processes? It would be difficult to give direct answers to this question. We may indicate, however, some of the areas in which improvements are probable.

One possibility is the improvement of management and administration generally. Real estate administration is not separated from other aspects of business administration. The same principles of management apply in this field as in others. As our knowledge of decision-making increases, real estate administration will benefit along with other fields. As we improve our capacity to implement decisions in any area by better planning, organizing, and control processes, we may make use of such developments in real estate. Special adaptations may be required, of course, since decisions and programs for implementing decisions in the real estate field must be related to fixed sites, to long-term commitments, to large fixed investments, to special market conditions, and to other factors that pertain to the localized nature of real property income.

A second possibility for improved administration in the real estate field may arise from better administration of real estate by the owners and users of real estate—business firms, individuals and families, and various agencies and institutions. For example, many business firms are paying increased attention to the effective use of the real estate resources that are available to them. Private consumers of real estate and especially home buyers and owners are growing more sophisticated with respect to their use of real estate and their investments in it. At one time the objective of the home buyer appeared to be the achievement of debt-free home ownership. Today home owners tend to view their equity in a home as they do other types of investment. They borrow against their equity to finance a variety of family needs.

A third area from which improvements in administration may come is the real estate business itself. Business firms in the real estate field may be managed more effectively. Improvements may be made in the processes of land development and building, real estate marketing, or the financing of real estate ownership and use.

A fourth field in which there may be progress is in the general environment or climate in which real estate decisions are made and implemented. Of special importance are government programs and regulations relating to business in general and to the real estate field in particular. Restraint of inflation or deflation, extension of highway systems, better systems of local government, improved land planning and zoning, more equitable taxation, more imaginative renewal and redevelopment programs, and better systems of facilitating the financing of real estate, to mention a few possibilities, would have a decided impact on the administration of real estate.

Improvements in the various areas listed above may come about in part from research. They may arise from new insights developed by businessmen or by students of business administration. Or improvements may come from sources that we cannot now foresee. The universities and independent research agencies may make important contributions. Business executives and private individuals may point the way to improvements. Also, government agencies, trade associations, and other organizations may contribute to improvements in a number of ways.

Knowledge of Administration

Our knowledge of administrative theory, principles and practices has expanded greatly in recent years. The business firm has been viewed to an increasing extent as a key social institution and both the internal and external responsibilities of its management have been subjected to careful study. Management decision-making has been given major attention by practicing managers and by students of business administration. Quantitative analyses have been used to improve decision-making. Attempts have been made to draw on the social and behavioral sciences to find new insights into problems of management leadership and human relations.

Still, we have a long way to go. As Robert D. Calkins has pointed out:

> It is rather astonishing that we know so little about administration in view of the very extensive literature on the subject and its prevalence and importance in nearly all aspects of modern life. This state of affairs is to be traced in part to the variety and complexity of the process we call administration. It is equally perhaps a result of the fact that no satisfactory framework has been found from which we may view the subject systematically and usefully for both the scholar and the practitioner.[9]

University schools of business and various other areas of specialization in our universities, notably the behavioral sciences, have been giving increasing attention to the development of this type of framework as have various practicing business executives. As our knowledge of administrative theory expands, we may expect practices to improve, both in the real estate field and in others.

Long-Range Planning

In connection with the implementation of managerial decisions, increasing emphasis has been given to long-range planning as one of the more important tools of management. Some managers have shied away from the term "planning" and prefer to think of "anticipations," "expectations," and "forecasts." Planning or whatever the process is called is of special importance in the administration of real estate resources because of their long economic life and the large investments that are represented.

[9] Robert D. Calkins, "The Decision Process in Administration," *Business Horizons* (Fall, 1959). Calkins also says: "The contributions of sociology, social psychology, anthropology, political science, and the behavioral sciences generally to an understanding of organization, group behavior, motivation, leadership, strategy, game theory, role playing, and the like can no longer be ignored by those seriously interested in understanding the art of administration. Nor can these subjects properly be avoided in the development of administrative skills." "The Art of Administration and the Art of Science," *Indiana Business Report No. 29* (Indiana University, 1959), pp. 10–11.

Winston Churchill pointed out, for example, that while we control the planning and production of buildings, once constructed they tend to control us. Every business establishment, institution, and family is controlled to some degree by the real estate resources it uses. Thus, careful planning in order to anticipate future real estate requirements is highly important for business administration in general, but it acquires special significance in connection with real estate resources. For example, the growth of many business firms has been severely limited by the failure to anticipate space, equipment, and location needs.

Business managers and private individuals have tended to rely heavily on architects and engineers for assistance in planning the development or redevelopment of real estate resources. Such specialists, however, are able to do this type of planning effectively only as the owners and users of real property can outline realistically their potential needs for space and facilities. This is a planning responsibility of business management that is coming to be recognized to an increasing degree. Long-range planning for the development and use of real estate resources probably will be facilitated by improved projections of long-term economic trends as well as by better projections of the future potential of specific industries, localities, and areas.

Individuals and families are giving more attention to their real estate requirements over time. Typically, however, they do not have the degree of control over their locations nor can they translate future plans into action with the same degree of effectiveness as the owners and managers of business firms. To some extent this is true also of government agencies, since programs of government may change rapidly with shifts from one administration to another or with changes in the preferences of the electorate in regard to public programs.

Organization of Resources

Marked improvement has been made in the ability of business managers to organize resources and operations. Managers have been giving real estate resources increasing attention, as we have seen. Many firms are establishing real estate departments or paying greater attention to allocating responsibility for real estate decisions. The proper mix of real estate and other resources in the organization of a business firm's operations is not always easy to determine. It appears that improvements are being made; and there is little question of the increasing concern of business firms with the role of real estate resources in influencing the effectiveness with which other types of resources may be utilized.

The relationship of real estate resources to others in the business firm depends to a considerable extent on whether the firm is primarily engaged in manufacturing, marketing, or service activities. It is probable that more changes will be forthcoming in the service lines than in others, in part because greater advances have already been made in the manufacturing and marketing fields.

Control of Operations

Significant improvements have been made in control processes in many lines of business. There has been more widespread use of budgeting in management planning and control operations. Cost accounting has contributed much to improved controls. High-speed computing equipment has broadened the types of records and controls that are feasible. Increased attention has been given to the establishment of realistic standards as a basis for measuring performance.

In the real estate field, rapidly changing values, both upward and downward, have required that careful controls be imposed to adjust for insurance requirements, tax obligations, and refinancing possibilities. More careful controls of modernization and repair programs have also been stressed in order to preserve property values.

Leadership and Entrepreneurial Ability

The magnitude of the potential requirements for real estate resources suggests that leadership of a high order will be essential to formulate and carry out the necessary programs. Such leadership will come in part from those now engaged in business administration or more particularly those engaged in one or another part of the real estate business. Such leadership will come also from younger people, many of whom are now preparing themselves for careers in the business world. You may be among them.

In the business world, leadership and entrepreneurial abilities often are combined. The distinction is far from easy to make. One may be a leader without being an entrepreneur if his leadershp role requires him largely to execute programs and policies that are originated by others. But the more effective leaders often have "entrepreneurial minds." By this we mean that they have the capacity to think creatively, to innovate, to develop new ideas and concepts, and to apply them in the solution of programs. In this respect the entrepreneur and the artist may have much in common.

Traditionally, economists have also associated entrepreneurship with risk taking. Whether this is an essential requirement may be open to question. Also, risks may take a variety of forms; reputations may be risked as well as money. The entrepreneurial mind may be found among public officials as well as private businessmen. Indeed, the close relationship between public and private programs in the real estate field suggests that leadership and creative talents of a high order will be required in the public agencies related to real estate in the years ahead if substantial progress is to be achieved.

Often progress depends on the general environment in which programs are carried forward to a much greater extent than on the effectiveness with which programs—public or private—are managed. The general environment in which real estate resources are developed, utilized, owned, financed, or marketed depends to a considerable extent on public policies and programs and on the leadership of public agencies.

Efficiency of Real Estate Firms

It is probable that those who develop, finance, and market real estate are as capable, work as hard, manage as carefully, and in general try to operate as efficiently as those in other fields of business. While the numerous small organizations that are typical of this field may result in some inefficiencies and lack of coordination, there are many other fields in which enterprises are also small and not closely coordinated. Consider many of the service lines, for example.

It may be that such inefficiencies as exist are due to the nature of the commodity in which the real estate business deals and the institutional framework surrounding its operations. The long life of real properties, the fact that they represent relatively large economic units, and their fixity of location create special problems, as we have noted. Possibly, larger enterprises could deal with these problems more efficiently than those which now are typical of the field. Yet the mere fact of size is no guarantee of efficiency. We know from the experience of recent years that a large builder may be able to do more in the way of applying sound principles of land planning and reap some of the economies of large-scale operations from a project. There is always the danger, of course, that he may overexpand, interpret market demands incorrectly, or make other mistakes to which the smaller operator may be less susceptible. Even so, there is little doubt that larger-scale operations are paying off in the land development and building field.

With respect to real estate marketing, we might raise several questions suggested by the development of chain stores. Is there any basic difference between selling real properties or their services and selling groceries? Are the arguments against large-scale operations in the real estate brokerage field comparable to the arguments of the small, independent retailer against the chain stores?

Suppose we consider also the internal organization of our real estate enterprises. It has been suggested that the small brokerage offices, for example, cannot provide much for their employees in the way of training programs, opportunities for promotion, or provisions for retirement and the like. On the other hand, the independence of these smaller enterprises may offer great incentives through opportunities for achieving ownership of a small concern, and this may in large measure counterbalance the personnel programs of larger organizations. If the owners and operators of small business firms were accorded special tax treatment, the appeal of the small enterprise might be increased. For example, if the owners of small business firms could pay low taxes on, say, the first $50,000 of annual income, managerial talent might move to small business firms rather than to the larger corporations as is often the case.

There are also other advantages in the organization of a small establishment. The individual proprietorship or partnership form of organization may be used to a larger extent. Small organizations are more flexible, less cumbersome, and more easily adapted to changes in market requirements.

We should note that a number of techniques have improved in recent years. Appraising is an area in which real advances have been made; the same thing may be said of mortgage risk analysis.

The educational programs of a number of universities and colleges have contributed to improved practices. Special mention should be made of the institutes, short courses, and correspondence study programs sponsored by a number of the trade associations in this field.

Yet, much remains to be done. When we compare many real estate enterprises with those in other fields, the differences are not always in favor of the former.

Individuals and Families

The individuals and families owning and using real estate resources often are unable to bring to their management problems the degree of knowledge and experience that can be provided by business firms. There is little doubt, however, that home buyers and owners have become more sophisticated with respect to real estate matters in recent years. In part this is due to a rather widespread improvement in the availability of economic and business information. In part it results from the rising incomes of individuals and families.

Despite these developments, the opportunities for improving the utilization of real properties by individuals and families are great. More information and a wider dissemination of knowledge about housing would undoubtedly improve our consumption of this commodity. More information about real properties and the problems related to their ownership and use probably would help those rather large numbers of small investors who buy and sell, own, manage, lease, and finance real properties.

If families were able to plan their housing needs throughout the family cycle, it is possible that housing would be utilized more effectively. During the family cycle original housing requirements are small; as the family expands, the requirements increase; then, as children grow up and leave home, the requirements decline, until finally the housing needs are somewhat similar to those at the time the family was established. Relatively few families, however, are able to adapt easily to these changes in their housing requirements. Some developments in this area may be noted, however, as more families acquire a "second home." (See Chapter 22.) Usually this is done at first for week-end recreational and vacation purposes. Later on, such properties may serve as retirement housing.[10]

Often those who own their homes or who are small investors in real estate fail to take advantage of possibilities for refinancing with changes in money market conditions. Or they fail to take tax law changes into proper consideration.

It is probable that we should develop means for reducing the risks of home ownership. One of these is the risk of loss of the home through mortgage foreclosure. There may be a need for a system of mortgage insurance that protects the home buyer rather than the lender. The FHA and private mortgage insurance now provide protection only for the lender. Some financial institutions make provision for a grace period in case borrowers maintain a good payment record on their mortgages or make some payments in advance of current schedules. The extension of such practices or some related protections for uncertainties of this type might be highly useful.

Another risk of home ownership is that of liquidity. It is often difficult to convert the equity in a home into cash, especially in a short time. Provision for cashing-in equities through a trade-in system or through some other means undoubtedly would be a valuable facility to many present and potential home owners.

Environmental Factors

As we suggested above, the environment in which real estate is developed and utilized, owned, financed, and marketed determines to a considerable degree the progress that may be made. This environment is a product in part of our total history. It is determined by our historical

[10] See Strunk and Weimer, *op. cit.*

traditions, values, standards, and accepted ways of doing things. This aspect of our environment can be changed relatively little even in a generation or two. Environment is also a matter of the social, economic, and political framework within which business and other activities are carried forward. We can, of course, change laws from time to time. We even amend the Constitution now and again. Usually public policies and programs do not change rapidly unless major emergencies require prompt action.

Much depends on how our private and public agencies are administered from day to day and week to week. The attitudes and points of view of public officials and private business men has much to do with setting the tone and in determining the day-to-day working environment. Willingness to experiment, ready acceptance of change, adaptability, creativity—these terms describe the kinds of attitudes that appear to be most helpful in accomplishing progress in any line of economic activity.

The successful administration of real estate resources depends to a considerable extent on the ability of administrators to adapt to changing economic, social, political, and governmental conditions. Improved economic forecasting undoubtedly will be helpful in adapting to changing business conditions, although we must recognize that sudden changes, such as the outbreak of war, substantial deterioration of international relations, or irresponsible domestic programs that result in rapid inflation or deflation, might alter greatly the expectations of business analysts and of business managers.

Probably the environmental factors that have closest relationship to real estate administration are the laws and regulations under which real estate is owned, used, developed, marketed, and financed. Broader areas of public policy, of course, are also involved, as we have suggested.

Our system of legal arrangements for the ownership, transfer of title, and mortgaging of real properties is cumbersome. A number of forms and processes that had their origin in medieval times are still in use, even though it is difficult in many instances to justify them by the requirements and standards of the modern market. If it is possible to buy the stocks or bonds of a corporation located in another part of the country by making a telephone call, why must we be burdened by the legal formalities and processes that are a part of every real property transfer? Is the real estate business carrying a part of the legal profession on its back because of these cumbersome legal formalities?

The processes of searching titles and of bringing abstracts up to date are difficult and time consuming. Would it not be possible, by the more widespread use either of private title insurance or of the Torrens system, to simplify these processes? Why should we not have a system of title insurance which insures against all defects in titles rather than against unknown defects only? Or is this more properly a government function?

Because many real estate enterprises are relatively small, should government undertake a greater amount of research for these establishments? Since larger corporations have their own research departments, is it proper for government to give special aid to small businesses in this manner?

While there is generally little question about the desirability of land planning and zoning regulations established by local governments, many of these laws need revision. In the process of making such revisions, would it be desirable to include provisions also for controlling the indiscriminate subdivision of lands? If such a step is considered desirable, how should new subdivisions be regulated?

While we should recognize that taxation is always a point of friction between government and business establishments, do the facts of the situation call for a substantial revision of real property taxation? Should real estate taxes be frozen at current levels? Should taxes be used as a device for promoting developments which are considered to be in the public interest?

To what extent is government responsible for the improvement of business practices? Undoubtedly the activities of the Federal Home Loan Bank System and the FHA have made for such improvement. In the field of agriculture, government has assumed far-reaching responsibilities for the improvement of farm practices. Should it assume similar responsibilities in the real estate field? Do we need an extension service for real estate and other small businesses similar to the programs in the field of agriculture?

Do we need changes in the Federal Home Loan Bank System, the FHA, or other government agencies operating in this general area? How should the new Department of Housing and Urban Development help us to cope with some of the rapidly expanding problems of the urban community and the impact of these problems on our real estate revenues? Is private mortgage insurance likely to replace the FHA? Or are new types of mortgage insurance programs likely to emerge? Is it desirable to have competing government systems of real estate finance? Despite some of the arguments for greater centralization of such agencies, there are real advantages in competition, even among government agencies.

What kinds of real estate decision problems are likely to emerge with the next depression? Can we expect the numerous changes that have been made in the past three decades to carry real estate through the next depression with less difficulty than the last one?

In a final analysis, the standards to which real estate enterprises and real properties must conform are set by the public through the customs and traditions followed—the casting of dollar votes in the market place or ballots at the political elections. In addition the general pressures of public opinion establish requirements to which real properties and those in charge of business enterprises generally, or real estate firms in particular, must conform.

SUMMARY

Long-term economic projections indicate substantial growth and hence the need for the best possible decisions in regard to the utilization of existing real estate resources and the development of new resources. Long-term economic growth will have a varying impact between town and country, major regions, and various local communities. Some brand new communities and towns will be developed to meet the requirements for additional resources. Improved conservation and renewal programs will also play an important role. Public facilities will need to expand in proper proportion in order to make the private real estate facilities useful. Real estate administration is likely to improve in part because of the general advances being made in management and administration and in part because of more widespread knowledge on the part of those who produce, finance, market, and use real estate resources. Leadership and entrepreneurial ability will be especially important in bringing about improved administration and in adding to the efficiency of real estate firms. Of special importance, however, will be the environment in which real estate is utilized, owned, developed, financed, and marketed. In part this environment is a product of our total history; but in part it will depend on a dynamic social, economic, and political framework, as well as the manner in which public and private agencies are administered. The major changes will reflect the standards that are set by the public at large.

QUESTIONS FOR STUDY

1. Do you consider the long-term economic projections that are outlined in these discussions to be unduly conservative or optimistic? Justify your position.
2. Contrast the ways in which long-term economic growth may affect the major regions of the country. How is long-term economic growth likely to affect your community?
3. Certain assumptions regarding population, incomes, and long-term growth potential were made in these discussions. Do you agree or disagree with these assumption? Explain.
4. Do you agree that new cities will be built in the years ahead? Why should this type of development occur rather than additions being made to existing communities?

5. What role do you see for conservation and renewal programs in terms of long-range economic growth? Indicate the types of natural resources that you believe should be given special attention in terms of conservation.

6. Why is it important to think in terms of conserving values rather than in terms of physical resources?

7. Do you agree with Dr. Dennis Gabor's identification of the three major problems now facing the human race? Explain your position.

8. Explain why public facilities have to expand in a proper relationship with private real estate developments. In your judgment is the proportion between public and private investment likely to change? Explain.

9. Indicate the principal ways in which real estate administration may be expected to improve in the years ahead.

10. How may the efficiency of real estate firms be improved in the years ahead? Which of these developments do you consider to hold greatest promise?

11. How do you define entrepreneurial ability? How is this particular type of ability likely to bring about improved real estate administration?

12. Why is the environment in which real estate is utilized, owned, developed, financed, and marketed so important in terms of future developments? What types of environmental changes do you believe will be of greatest importance during the next 15 to 20 years?

13. Do you believe that the administration of public agencies may be improved as well as that of private agencies? Explain your position.

14. *Study Project 44.* (a) How do you explain the author's idea that if the quantity of land had been 1 per cent larger the national income would have been 0.030 per cent larger? (b) How would land compare with labor in this respect? (c) Refer to the table in this study project. How do you account for the steady decline of the percentage of the national income related to land in comparison to that related to labor or reproducible capital goods?

15. *Study Project 45.* (a) Do you agree or disagree with the general point of view presented by Professor Edwards? Explain the reasons for your position. (b) How does he distinguish between long-range and short-range plans? Is this a defensible definition? (c) How do you explain the statement that "savers are willing to invest their money at four, five, or six per cent, and even less, but business firms will not proceed with investment opportunities unless they promise 10, 12, 15 per cent and higher returns"? (d) Why does Professor Edwards believe that depressions must be avoided? Explain.

16. *Study Project 46.* (a) Do you agree with Mr. Lippmann's statement that "the need and the ability to rethink and to relearn is the hallmark of a free society"? Explain your position. (b) Do you agree with the description of our government as being one that is essentially operated by reflection and choice? How would this contrast with other types of government? (c) Do you agree with Mr. Lippmann's identification of the primary problems that have emerged in the quarter-century since the beginning of World War II?

SUGGESTED READINGS

GABOR, DENNIS. *Inventing the Future.* New York: Alfred A. Knopf, Inc., 1964. Chap. i.

KUZNETS, SIMON. *Economic Growth and Structure: Selected Essays.* New York: W. W. Norton & Co., Inc., 1965.

LANDSBERG, HANS H., FISCHMAN, LEONARD L., and FISHER, JOSEPH L. *Resources in America's Future.* Baltimore, Md.: The Johns Hopkins Press, 1963. Chaps. iv, xviii.

McCLELLAND, DAVID C. *The Achieving Society.* Princeton University: Van Nostrand Co., Inc., 1961. Chaps. i, vi, x.

SCIENTIFIC AMERICAN. "Technology and Economic Development." New York. Alfred A. Knopf, Inc., 1963. Pp. 3–19, 70–85.

STUDY PROJECTS

STUDY PROJECT 1

REFERENCE PROPERTY

This study project is intended to familiarize the student with a specific parcel of real property. The student should select a "reference property" for himself and prepare a similar analysis.

(a) *The Property.* This property is a single-family, one-story, frame residence located at 1776 N. Upton Street, Eroica, Illinois. The lot has a frontage of 50 feet and a depth of 150 feet. It is on the west side of a paved street. The house is 34 feet by 30 feet and contains six rooms and a bath. There is a half-basement and a front porch. A frame one-car garage is located near the back of the lot.

The exterior walls are of cypress lapsiding over building paper and yellow pine sheathing. There are oak floors in the living rooms, linoleum over pine in the kitchen and bathroom. The plastering is in fair condition; however, the bathroom should be replastered at an early date. The half-basement has a concrete floor and cement block walls. There is an unfinished utility room for washer and dryer off the half-basement. The windows are double-hung and weatherstripped. Storm windows and screens are available, as are combination doors. The roof is of asphalt shingles and is in good condition.

The grounds are well maintained. There are several good-sized shade trees. A concrete drive leads from the street to the garage. There is a concrete walk to the front porch and a gravel walk along the side of the house to the rear entrance.

(b) *Legal Description.* The legal description of the property is lot number 76 in Eroica's subdivision, Section 10, Township 12 North, Range 9 West, City of Eroica, Sunrise County, State of Illinois. (Known as 1776 N. Upton Street.)

(c) *Location.* This property is located in a neighborhood of small homes, most of which are 30 to 40 years old. Approximately two-thirds of the houses are occupied by owners. The property is three blocks from a shopping center and within five blocks of a grade school. There is a high school ten blocks away, and there are a number of churches in the area. The downtown district may be reached by bus in approximately 20 minutes. The bus stop is three blocks away. Eroica is a small city of 75,000 people. From the early 1930's to the start of World War II there was little business expansion. The war brought a revival of economic activity and several new industries were established. Business conditions continued to be favorable and currently are good.

(d) *Ownership.* This property is now occupied by its owner and his family. He purchased it in 1951 for $15,000 with a down payment of $3,000. The seller took a mortgage for the balance. This mortgage was paid off in 1957.

(e) *History of the Property.* The land was originally subdivided in 1928; but the lot was not sold until 1929, at which time it brought $300. The house was built in 1938 at a cost of $13,500. Special assessments for street improvements totaled $171 and were paid off prior to 1942.

(f) *Income and Operating Expenses.* Since the house is owner-occupied, no money income is being earned by the property. However, comparable houses are renting for $150 per month. Taxes amount to $445 per year, maintenance and repairs have averaged around $100 per year for the past three years, and insurance costs $55 for a three-year policy.

STUDY PROJECT 2

CODE OF ETHICS OF THE NATIONAL ASSOCIATION OF REAL ESTATE BOARDS *

Preamble

Under all is the land. Upon its wise utilization and widely allocated ownership depend the survival and growth of free institutions and of our civilization. The Realtor is the instrumentality through which the land resource of the nation reaches its highest use and through which land ownership attains its widest distribution. He is a creator of homes, a builder of cities, a developer of industries and productive farms.

Such functions impose obligations beyond those of ordinary commerce; they impose obligations of grave social responsibility and patriotic duty to which the Realtor should dedicate himself, and for which he should be diligent in preparing himself. The Realtor, therefore, is zealous to maintain and improve the standards of his calling and shares with his fellow-Realtors a common responsibility for its integrity and honor.

In the interpretation of his obligations, he can take no safer guide than that which has been handed down through twenty centuries, embodied in the Golden Rule:

"Whatsoever ye would that men should do unto you, do ye also unto them."

Accepting this standard as his own, every Realtor pledges himself to observe its spirit in all his activities and to conduct his business in accordance with the following Code of Ethics:

Part I. Relations to the Public

Article 1: The Realtor should keep himself informed as to movements affecting real estate in his community, state, and the nation, so that he may be able to contribute to public thinking on matters of taxation, legislation, land use, city planning, and other questions affecting property interests.

Article 2: It is the duty of the Realtor to be well informed on current market conditions in order to be in a position to advise his clients as to the fair market price.

Article 3: It is the duty of the Realtor to protect the public against fraud, misrepresentation or unethical practices in the real estate field.

He should endeavor to eliminate in his community any practices which could be damaging to the public or to the dignity and integrity of the real estate profession. The Realtor should assist the board or commission charged with regulating the practices of brokers and salesmen in his state.

* Adopted by the National Association of Real Estate Boards, June 6, 1924, and revised June 22, 1928, with subsequent amendments.

Article 4: The Realtor should ascertain all pertinent facts concerning every property for which he accepts the agency, so that he may fulfill his obligation to avoid error, exaggeration, misrepresentation, or concealment of pertinent facts.

Article 5: The Realtor should not be instrumental in introducing into a neighborhood a character of property or use which will clearly be detrimental to property values in that neighborhood.

Article 6: The Realtor should not be a party to the naming of a false consideration in any document, unless it be the naming of an obviously nominal consideration.

Article 7: The Realtor should not engage in activities that constitute the practice of law and should recommend that title be examined and legal counsel be obtained when the interest of either party requires it.

Article 8: The Realtor should keep in a special bank account, separated from his own funds, monies coming into his possession in trust for other persons, such as escrows, trust funds, client's monies and other like items.

Article 9: The Realtor in his advertising should be especially careful to present a true picture and should neither advertise without disclosing his name, nor permit his salesmen to use individual names or telephone numbers, unless the salesman's connection with the Realtor is obvious in the advertisement.

Article 10: The Realtor, for the protection of all parties with whom he deals, should see that financial obligations and commitments regarding real estate transactions are in writing, expressing the exact agreement of the parties; and that copies of such agreements, at the time they are executed, are placed in the hands of all parties involved.

Part II. Relations to the Client

Article 11: In accepting employment as an agent, the Realtor pledges himself to protect and promote the interests of the client. This obligation of absolute fidelity to the client's interest is primary, but it does not relieve the Realtor from the obligation of dealing fairly with all parties to the transaction.

Article 12: In justice to those who place their interests in his care, the Realtor should endeavor always to be informed regarding laws, proposed legislation, governmental orders, and other essential information and public policies which affect those interests.

Article 13: Since the Realtor is representing one or another party to a transaction, he should not accept compensation from more than one party without the full knowledge of all parties to the transaction.

Article 14: The Realtor should not acquire an interest in or buy for himself, any member of his immediate family, his firm or any member thereof, or any entity in which he has a substantial ownership interest, property listed with him, or his firm, without making the true position known to the listing owner, and in selling property owned by him, or in which he has such interest, the facts should be revealed to the purchaser.

Article 15: The exclusive listing of property should be urged and practiced by the Realtor as a means of preventing dissension and misunderstanding and of assuring better service to the owner.

Article 16: When acting as agent in the management of property, the Realtor should not accept any commission, rebate or profit on expenditures made for an owner, without the owner's knowledge and consent.

Article 17: The Realtor should not undertake to make an appraisal that is outside the field of his experience unless he obtains the assistance of an authority on such types of property, or unless the facts are fully disclosed to the client. In such circumstances the authority so engaged should be so identified and his contribution to the assignment should be clearly set forth.

Article 18: When asked to make a formal appraisal of real property, the Realtor should not render an opinion without careful and thorough analysis and interpretation of all factors affecting the value of the property. His counsel constitutes a professional service.

The Realtor should not undertake to make an appraisal or render an opinion of value on any property where he has a present or contemplated interest unless such interest is specifically disclosed in the appraisal report. Under no circumstances should he undertake to make a formal appraisal when his employment or fee is contingent upon the amount of his appraisal.

Article 19: The Realtor should not submit or advertise property without authority and in any offering, the price quoted should not be other than that agreed upon with the owners as the offering price.

Article 20: In the event that more than one formal written offer on a specific property is made before the owner has accepted an offer, any other formal written offer presented to the Realtor, whether by a prospective purchaser or another broker, should be transmitted to the owner for his decision.

Part III. Relations to His Fellow-Realtor

Article 21: The Realtor should seek no unfair advantage over his fellow-Realtors and should willingly share with them the lessons of his experience and study.

Article 22: The Realtor should so conduct his business as to avoid controversies with his fellow-Realtors. In the event of a controversy between Realtors who are members of the same local board, such controversy should be arbitrated in accordance with regulations of their board rather than litigated.

Article 23: Controversies between Realtors who are not members of the same local board should be submitted to an arbitration board consisting of one arbitrator chosen by each Realtor from the real estate board to which he belongs or chosen in accordance with the regulations of the respective boards. One other member, or a sufficient number of members to make an odd number, should be selected by the arbitrators thus chosen.

Article 24: When the Realtor is charged with unethical practice, he should place all pertinent facts before the proper tribunal of the member board of which he is a member, for investigation and judgment.

Article 25: The Realtor should not voluntarily disparage the business practice of a competitor, nor volunteer an opinion of a competitor's transaction. If his opinion is sought it should be rendered with strict professional integrity and courtesy.

Article 26: The agency of a Realtor who holds an exclusive listing should be respected. A Realtor cooperating with a listing broker should not invite the cooperation of a third broker without the consent of the listing broker.

Article 27: The Realtor should cooperate with other brokers on property listed by him exclusively whenever it is in the interest of the client, sharing commissions on a previously agreed basis. Negotiations concerning property listed exclusively with one broker should be carried on with the listing broker, not with the owner, except with the consent of the listing broker.

Article 28: The Realtor should not solicit the services of an employee or salesman in the organization of a fellow-Realtor without the knowledge of the employer.

Article 29: Signs giving notice of property for sale, rent, lease or exchange should not be placed on any property by more than one Realtor, and then only if authorized by the owner, except as the property is listed with and authorization given to more than one Realtor.

Article 30: In the best interest of society, of his associates and of his own business, the Realtor should be loyal to the real estate board of his community and active in its work.

Conclusion

The term *Realtor* has come to connote competence, fair dealing and high integrity resulting from adherence to a lofty ideal of moral conduct in business relations. No inducement of profit and no instructions from clients ever can justify departure from this ideal, or from the injunctions of this Code.

The Code of Ethics was adopted in 1913. Amended at the Annual Convention in 1924, 1928, 1950, 1951, 1952, 1955, 1956, 1961, and 1962.

STUDY PROJECT 3

CAUSATIVE THINKING *

Business administrators, charged with the responsibility of leadership for the success of enterprises, have tried in several ways to divine or to assess the future. By the practice of haruspicy in ancient times, skilled individuals sought to predict future events by inspecting the entrails of sacrificial victims such as rams or bulls. Later refinements included interpretations of the flights of birds or the chains of lightning. Oracles and crystal-gazers once had the same function and respect as modern economic forecasters. Historically, executive leaders have attempted to predict the future and react to unfolding environmental conditions through rational, short-range decisions.[1]

Long-range planning among business executives was not popular until after World War II. Prior to that time, planning for long-range objectives was considered to be of little value because of the futility of trying to divine the future. Subsequently, a change has occurred in the attitudes of a growing number of businessmen and the place of long-range planning in their value system.

The most enlightened administrators are now challenged by the possibilities of designing or shaping desired future events and company achievements. Past practices have allowed events to happen that resulted in having to react to unfolding environmental conditions, thereby always allowing the past and the present conditions to shape their future. Long-range planning permits an administrator to meet the contingencies of the future—not by predicting it, but by being aware of the need for change and the need to prepare for changing conditions in the market, or the political climate, or technological progress in the economy.

* John F. Mee, "IDEAtional ITEMS from the desk of John F. Mee." By permission from *Business Horizons* (Summer, 1963).

[1] As late as 1941, a research study of management policies and practices of a group of leading industrial corporations, conducted under the auspices of the Stanford University Graduate School of Business, disclosed that few companies attempt to plan their operations beyond a twelve-month period. See *Top-Management Organization and Control* by P. E. Holden, L. S. Fish, and H. L. Smith (Stanford: Stanford University Press, 1941).

"Causative thinking" is a mental process that some administrators have found useful in facilitating their long-range planning activities. Many of the important happenings that are advancing the theories and practices for business administration are the product of causative thinking by intent. They depend upon a more scientific understanding of cause and effect on human actions and events. They indicate that today's events are at least a partial causative factor in determining future situations and that human achievements consist of something more than some interaction of blind forces and a hope for an acceptable outcome.

Causative thinking depends upon the gift of creative imagination in the human mind. If a business administrator can imagine a situation that has not yet taken place, he also can creatively fashion a series of prior events that can fulfill his desired purpose and satisfy his objectives. By thinking backward from such imagined future situations, an enterprising individual may conceive of a series of related events by which a present situation can be converted into the desired future situation. Thus, the imagined future effect becomes a causative factor in the chain of events that results in the final desired effect. Administrators, corporate planners, or project managers can do more than plan for desired future results. They can follow courses of action, with each action changing the existing environment according to the previously conceived series of events, until the desired result becomes a reality.

Causative thinking presents an approach to the understanding of time relationships involved in causes and effects. To some extent, the imagined future reality is made the cause of each action event, and the future determines the events preceding it. Causative thinking reverses the general notion that cause and effect always move in a conventional time sequence. The concept of imagined time is introduced as a contrast to real time. Limitations of causative thinking may be attributed to human errors, dull imaginations, or the low degree of understanding of the administrative leaders in the total situation.

Causative thinking is a means for making events happen to shape the future of an enterprise instead of adapting to a future that unfolds from blind forces. Inasmuch as many new concepts and techniques in the business community give evidence of the application of causative thinking, an awareness and understanding of some of them may be of interest to anyone concerned with the responsibility for achieving long-range objectives by long-range planning.

Illustrations of business practices that employ causative thinking are: PERT (Program Evaluation Review Technique), rhochrematics, synectics, information retrieval systems, and general systems theory.

1 Probably the most familiar of the above techniques is PERT, which was first applied in 1958 to the Polaris program. Similar techniques are known as the critical path method, least cost estimating and scheduling, automation by network systems, and resource allocation for multiple projects. Through PERT, an administrator can visualize the desired end and then establish the sequence and relationship of all essential work events in planning its achievement. Uncertainties in achieving the objective are identified as well as pertinent time and cost considerations.

2 Rhochrematics offers a scientific approach to the management of material flows. Its concept requires the abandonment of the traditional idea of employing skilled personnel to supervise minor functions as autonomous units. Rhochrematics requires the construction of a composite conceptual framework for the integration of the management of the flow of all materials from their original sources through production facilities to final consumers. The flow of goods in the production pipeline is accelerated and the total cost of materials is reduced.

3 Synectics means the joining together of different and apparently irrelevant elements. According to William Gordon, author of the first book on the subject, synectics theory involves the integration of diverse individuals into a problem-stating and problem-solving group. The objective of the synectics research to date has been to develop and test an operational theory of human creativity. An industrial synectics program can be directed toward product improvement and development to assist in bridging the gaps between basic research and the application of its findings in the market economy.

4 Information retrieval systems encompass the total process by which information is recorded, organized, stored, and recovered when required. The process includes more than the intellectual routines, procedures, and techniques required to screen, index, and identify information placed into a collection. It also involves the principles, systems, and equipment necessary to facilitate the storage and recovery of information economically and in accordance with the needs of those who wish to use it.

5 In the general systems theory concept, emphasis is on the over-all objectives of a business firm and its role within a larger system in society. The systems concept provides an administrator with a way of thinking about the process of managing an enterprise or any portion of it. A conceptual framework is designed for the visualization of internal and external factors as an integrated whole operating system with all functioning subsystems in their proper place in relationship with each other. Business systems are recognized as parts of larger systems—a company, an industry, or a society.

New concepts, new techniques, and new methods for business administration in a changing business environment usually are produced by a new combination of existing concepts or elements. They rarely if ever appear *de novo*. Although the illustrations described are refinements and combinations of older concepts and techniques, they indicate the increasing use of causative thinking by a growing number of administrators.

STUDY PROJECT 4

COMPLETE GUIDE TO SHOPPING A NEW HOUSE *

How to Use This Article

You'll need a note pad. As you read, jot down all points that are important to you. Some will be completely personal. For example, whether or not you want a family room—and, if so, where in the house. Other points are basic to every quality house—such things as equipment, construction, materials. When you come to discussions of these in the article, you may want to clip and keep them in your note pad. This way you can have your own tailored shopping list, simple enough to use for on-the-spot rating of every house you see.

Start your model house shopping by seeing as many subdivisions and areas in your city as possible. Don't limit yourself to a narrow price range. Builders are offering more house per dollar than ever, and you may be surprised to find that a house you thought was over your budget is actually within range. Also,

* By the Editors of *Better Homes and Gardens* (May, 1964). © *Meredith Publishing Co., 1964. All rights reserved.* By permission.

seeing a few over-budget houses may lead you to ideas you can incorporate into a lower priced home.

Even as you walk through some of the houses, you will be able to rule them out. At this point, you may want to eliminate some houses because of location.

Look around now for signs of the future in any area you consider. Is strip zoning along major access streets allowing a layer of cheap, commercial eyesores to develop? You may be sure it will get worse if it has already started. Look for the trend in the area; is it, and will it be an area you'll be proud of? Note the environment within the subdivision, too. Look for varied houses, curved streets, pleasant vistas.

The right choice of options always pays off. You'll be making dozens of decisions as you zero in on the right house. The majority of good builders today offer many variations and extras for each of their standard models. You'll be better off to buy from a builder who does offer these choices. First, of course, because you'll end up with more of what you want. And secondly, because the other houses around you will reflect the individuality and differences that good neighborhoods should have.

Generally, the extra-cost options mean only a little extra down payment and a small addition to monthly charges. When you split the cost this way, it's possible to have the equipment and facilities that make for better living right at the start. (It is surprising how soon your family will want that extra bath.)

Almost every "extra" costs more to install later than when the house is being built. When you add the higher costs of short-term financing to future improvements, you'll soon discover many bargains in any list of options. In today's resale market, it's the house with the desirable extras that sells quickly and returns the best percentage of your investment.

Make Sure the Floor Plan Fits the Way You Live

Your best evaluation of a model's floor plan can be made when you and your family are alone in the house—not when it is filled with other shoppers. When a house looks right to you—and meets all the qualifications—make an appointment to spend a half hour or so in it by yourselves. Sit down, relax, get the feel of the house. The wrong floor plan creates problems and inconvenience; the right one helps your family live the way you choose.

Zoning. Divide the house into sleeping, living, and working zones—the three should be separated in all but the very smallest homes you'll see. Bedrooms should be quiet and private. It's best not to be able to look down the bedroom hall from the living areas. The living room should be separated enough from the kitchen work areas so that the dishwasher's hum is unobtrusive.

Buffer areas between each zone help peace and quiet. The bedroom wing should be buffered from other zones by closets, dressing room, or baths. If it isn't, consider adding sound-deadening insulation board to the wall construction. There should also be a door to close the bedroom wing from the rest of the house.

To check the sound control built into a house, take along a portable radio. Turn it on and then walk through other rooms to listen to the noise level. Rate the house high if the radio's noise is confined to the room where you place it.

Traffic patterns. While you're in the house, trace the routes your family will be taking for these trips:

Front door to family room

Front door to kitchen
Kitchen to bedroom wing
Back door to closet bath
Garage or parking area to kitchen

If the traffic is well-organized, you won't cross the center of any other rooms for these trips. In any of these cases, you should rate the house lower if the traffic crosses the main furniture grouping.

Check other routes your family takes. You'll want to be certain the floor plan lives up in this respect, too. Keep in mind that plan organization will determine the number of wasted steps you take each day you live in the house.

If the house has a basement, note the stairway and the ease of getting heavy things down from outside. Best access is by a separate stairway that opens outside, but a straight inside stairway near a door is workable.

Get the right kind of a plan. Put the house through a week day. Where will the family gather after work and school? Is there space for hobby activities? Then plot your weekend habits in the house. Where will the adults relax when another family drops in on Sunday afternoon—and where will the children get together? Will the house make entertaining a pleasure or a problem?

If the house has a family room, be sure it will serve the functions you want. You may find it placed near the living room and this is fine for families who frequently entertain many people at once. In this case, the fact that the two areas flow together can be an advantage. On the other hand, your family may get the most good from a detached game-room type of family room that is not connected to either the kitchen or living room. Or you may prefer a family room closely related to the kitchen—for all-day use by small children.

Some houses offer you a floor plan with all the bedrooms located in one wing. Others separate the master suite in another part of the house. Either of these plans can be good—if the house measures up in other respects. But you should analyze your family's needs before you make the decision.

Furniture arrangement. Most models you'll be visiting will have furniture in them. You'll get good decorating ideas while you're there, but you should also look for flexibility and other possible arrangements—especially if you're satisfied with the furniture in your present home and won't be adding much to it. With the brochure in hand, look all around the living areas to see where furniture will work best for you.

In each bedroom, check to see that beds and storage furniture can be arranged for maximum use of the floor space.

Expandability. Even if you are almost certain that you'll never want to add to your new house, make sure an addition is possible. If the house doesn't have a family room, look for a logical place to add one. Or, if it has only two or three bedrooms, consider what a bedroom addition would mean. Your situation may change in a few years—or the expansion possibilities may appeal to a prospective buyer.

Concentrate Next on the Kitchen

That kitchen is very important, so take time to evaluate it carefully. Look beyond the shiny newness to see whether or not there is real efficiency.

Five major work centers. Check each of the following: Cooking center should have 24 inches of heatproof counter surface next to the cook-top. Serving center needs 24 inches also; mixing center requires 42. An 18-inch refrigeration counter should be on the opening side of the refrigerator door. The cleanup center needs 36 inches at the right of the sink and 30 inches at the left. These dimensions are in addition to the space taken by the appliances or the sink; but counter space can add up as two work centers.

Storage capacity. Count up the capacity of all the cabinets. Your best reference point here is your old kitchen. If you are short in your present home, be sure there is enough more to take care of all your needs.

Also look for adjustable shelves in both lower and upper cabinets. Pull out the drawers to see that they operate easily and stop before they fall out. Rate the kitchen up if the cabinets are equipped with accessories to fit specialized needs; rate it high, too, if cabinets have a baked-on finish. If the kitchen has a large, pantry-type storage unit, the shelves should be adjustable and organized to make every inch of space convenient.

The kitchen should also have a handy place for the wastepaper basket and towel rack. And, if there is a baby's highchair in your family, look for a place to put it.

Appliances. When you look at the appliances, be sure to note them all. In a comparison between two new houses, you'll want to know how both the number and quality of appliances stack up. The majority of builders offer a choice of appliances—different brands and different models of each brand. The stripped-down models sometimes used in new homes are generally less desirable. From the standpoints of present convenience and long-range investment, you do much better to put your money into better models.

Turn on the food waste disposer to check for noise and vibration. Check to be sure the switch isn't located where it's likely to be turned on accidentally.

Look at the ventilating fan for an Underwriters' Laboratories label and the cubic foot per minute rating: it will tell you how big a kitchen the fan was designed to handle.

Discuss warranties with the builder's salesman for each appliance and find out what you should do if service is needed after you buy.

Space and traffic. The generality of "the bigger, the better" doesn't always hold true in the kitchen. The added roominess may impress you at first, but the many steps between each job soon can change your mind. The main working area should be large enough to be comfortable and no more; and traffic into the house from the back door should not cross through this area. If there is eating space in the kitchen, it should be at least 7x8 feet in order to seat four people around an adequate-sized table comfortably.

Lighting and electrical outlets. Even during daytime, you can check on lighting in the kitchen. If you find only one ceiling fixture, the lighting is inadequate. There should be light sources that make all the surfaces at the five major centers bright. These fixtures might be mounted on the ceiling or under the soffits or wall cabinets.

Look for electrical outlets to serve all the counter-top surfaces—you'll be needing them for the small appliances you have now—and for some future ones. You should also check for an outlet near the eating area.

Some negatives to watch for. The oven door should not open into a through-traffic lane. This inconvenience can make tempers flare.

The cooking-top should not be right next to a separate wall oven—you'll need counter space between. Heat-proof stainless steel or ceramic tile is best.

Wood counter surfaces or built-in chopping blocks are great, but not next to the sink. Moisture can ruin them.

Windows above the sink should be high enough to keep curtains and sills from being splashed; turn the faucet on full blast and see.

Never Skimp on Mechanical Equipment

Heating and cooling system. You'll be better off if the furnace and air conditioner have a brand name you recognize. Discuss servicing with the builder and check the reputation of the subcontractor who installs the heating-cooling equipment.

If the heat is a warm-air system, look for a cold air return in every room (except baths and kitchen). The speed of the blower fan should be adjustable. Run the fan for a noise check, and be sure the filters can be changed easily. In all systems, the heat should be supplied to outside walls.

Heating and cooling controls. Check the thermostat to see if it is made by a manufacturer with a reputation for quality. Then check the furnace/air conditioner; the controls there should also be a quality name you recognize.

Water heater. Look at the brand name, capacity, warranty, and recovery rate. You'll want one whose manufacturer will be able to back a long-term warranty. The smaller the capacity of the tank, the higher recovery rate it should have. The recovery rate indicates the unit's speed in bringing the water to the desired temperature. A 40-gallon gas unit's recovery rate should be about 35 for a 4-person, 2-bath household; a 30-gallon heater should have a recovery rate of 45. Any heater you buy should have a corrosion-resistant lining and a pressure relief valve.

Water softener. The capacity you need is determined by the hardness of the water in your area and how much water you use. A phone call to the water company will help you determine if a softener has the proper capacity. You'll see units ranging from fully automatic to manual. All types do the same job; the difference is in the attention they require.

Electrical service. Look at the entrance panel for the amperage capacity. Anything under 100 amps is inadequate. Then count the number of circuits and compare this number with other houses you've seen. You should have a circuit for the heating system, the air conditioning system, laundry, kitchen, and—depending on the size of the house—more than one circuit for other outlets and for lighting. Also look for grounded outlets in all below-grade areas and in the kitchen. The grounding gives you extra protection.

Local codes usually give you an adequate number of outlets in living areas. But check to be sure you'll have convenient outlets for any special needs. These include hobby areas, outdoor needs, garage, and unfinished areas like a basement. You'll save a lot by having all outlets and light sockets installed at the beginning, even when there is an extra charge. Adding them later costs much more.

Telephone and music. One mark of good planning is concealed wiring for your telephones. The wires are placed in the walls like the electrical wires— with outlets wherever you might want to place a telephone.

If you have—or plan to have—a stereo or high-fidelity music system, you may want to ask the builder to install the wires for piping the music to other rooms, too.

Plumbing fixtures and fittings. Quality here means satisfaction for a long time. Tubs should have a flat bottom and be made of enameled cast iron or high-quality enameled steel; they should be rigid and have an acid-resistant finish.

Best quality lavatories are solid vitreous china. Ask if they have acid-resistant finishes. Water closets with an elongated bowl are generally better than those with a round bowl. The flushing action is important too; a siphon-jet action is best, but reverse-trap operation closets are good, too. The wash-down system is generally not acceptable. Top-quality models often have antisweat liners or mixing valves to take the chill off the water.

Try out the faucets and other fittings—the new single-control faucets will give you good service and they are easy to clean. New interchangeable valve units (instead of washers) operate easily, and rarely need attention. The best fittings are an alloy containing brass—and the more brass in them the better. Look for shut-off valves on the water supply lines to lavatory, water closet, and kitchen sink. You should also find an easily removed panel for access to the bath tub drain and faucets.

You Can Get the Storage You Need

The need for more and better storage alone can be a good reason for looking for a new house. Excellent storage is being planned into many good houses, and you should insist on it for your family. Storage space itself is part of the answer; good, convenient organization is the rest. Take a "storage walk" through each room—or through the floor plan sketch in the brochure. You should see all the following types of storage in qualities large enough for your family.

Bedroom area. Look for large clothes closets, well organized to use all the space inside. Children's rooms should also have space for toys and other possessions. Compare the linen closets to what you have in your present home. The master bedroom should have a wealth of clothes storage facilities; rate the house up if there are special facilities for shoes, hats, purses.

Point-of-use storage. Look for good solutions to the everyday type of storage problems. There should be one centrally located closet for cleaning equipment. This closet should accommodate your vacuum, brooms, mops, small cleaning supplies so any item can be reached easily. Rate a house low if the entry closet is small. It should be large enough to handle all "front door" coats for your own family, plus space for your guests' use. You'll need storage in the family room—and plenty of it. Good planning here will give you a couple of closets or a storage wall for toys, games, card tables, snack tables, and all the other things you'll want to keep handy. Look for built-in storage facilities in the living and dining rooms, too. Keep in mind, however, that good storage furniture also can do this job.

Bulk storage. You should find space to store trunks and all the other large items every family has. If the house has a basement, part of the space there should be allotted for this use. If it is a basementless house, look for an out-of-the-way area to handle this job. Convenient access and organization are not quite so important here, but the space should be large enough to fit your needs.

Specialized spaces. Hobbies take space and any member of your family who has such interests will put a premium on the house that provides a good working area. Family life gets a lot smoother and the investment lasts a lot longer when there is a special closet set aside for photography equipment, guns and hunting clothes, or easels and paintbrushes. You may not find your exact needs in the model; but you should find an extra closet or space you or your builder can adapt.

. . . .

[Look for low upkeep materials, notably siding, roofing, insulation, windows and glass, doors and hardware, and paint. Will the house help with house-keeping? Note particularly items related to easy floor care, washable walls, and laundry area.]

The Lot is Part of the House

When you're purchasing a new home, you're paying for much more than just a structure. The lot is one of the highest priced parts of your total investment —and you should be able to get plenty of use from the land.

Outdoor Living. If the house you're looking at has a patio, note the size (it should be at least as big as a small living room) and the accessibility (it should open from the living room, family room, or kitchen, preferably at about the same level). You should also check the patio for privacy, expandability, and shade—either existing or to be added.

In many lower-priced homes, you'll have to add the patio later yourself. This usually is no handicap, since the cost is about the same whether a patio is built at the same time as the rest of the house or if it is built a year or two later. But the house should be planned so that the addition of outdoor living will give comfort and convenience.

Parking and car approach. Rate a house high if it offers a generous amount of convenience for car storage and off-street parking. Good planning today includes adequate facilities for at least two cars per family—plus parking for guests so the first arrivals can leave without waiting for the late-comers to go home first.

Landscaping and trees. Shrubs, lawn, and other plantings are all as much a part of your new home as furniture and built-in appliances. You should know before you buy exactly what amount of landscaping and what size plants the price tag includes. If there are no old trees, you should discuss new ones with the builder, too. He often can provide extra plant materials at reasonable cost —and all plants will get off to a good start. Often these extras can be included in the mortgage.

Outdoor storage. You can expect a convenient storage area for lawn equip-ment, snow blowers and shovels, outdoor toys, ladders, and tools that won't crowd your cars out of their allotted spaces. If you're looking at a house that has no separate storage unit for these items, make sure the garage is big enough to store them *and* your cars.

STUDY PROJECT 5

A LAST MESSAGE FROM A FRIEND *

When John F. Kennedy died on November 22nd, the arts in America, in-cluding architecture, lost the best friend they had had in the White House since Thomas Jefferson.

Less than a month before his death, President Kennedy delivered a brief address at Amherst College, at a ceremony honoring the memory of Robert

* *Architectural Forum* (December, 1963).

Frost. The President's words had to do with the place of the artist in American society, and some of those who heard Mr. Kennedy at Amherst felt that those words were among the finest spoken by him since his inauguration.

"The men who create power," said the President, "make an indispensable contribution to the nation's greatness. But the men who question power make a contribution just as indispensable . . . Art establishes the basic human truths . . . The artist . . . becomes the last champion of the individual mind and sensibility against an intrusive society and an officious state." One wonders what other chief of state, anywhere, has recently defended and upheld the artist against "an intrusive society and an officious state . . ."

The President continued: "The great artist is thus a solitary figure. He must often sail against the currents of his time. This is not a popular role . . . Yet, the artist's fidelity has strengthened the fiber of our national life . . . If art is to nourish the roots of our culture, society must set the artist free to follow his vision wherever it takes him."

He had no doubts about where the artist's vision might lead our country. "I look forward to an America which will not be afraid of grace and beauty," the President continued; "(an America) which will protect the beauty of our natural environment, which will preserve the great old American houses and squares and parks of our national past, and which will build handsome and balanced cities for our future . . . I look forward to an America which commands respect throughout the world not only for its strength but for its civilization as well."

And the President added: "In serving his vision of the truth the artist best serves his nation. And the nation which disdains the mission of art invites the fate of Robert Frost's hired man—'the fate of having nothing to look backward to with pride and nothing to look forward to with hope.'"

Thanks to the words and the works of John F. Kennedy, the artists and architects of this nation—and, indeed, all their fellow-Americans—have something to look backward to with pride and much to look forward to with hope.

STUDY PROJECT 6

HEISLET v. HEISLET *

10 Utah 2d 126, 349 P.2d 175 (1960)

This was action by Annie Ray Heislet (plaintiff) against Nadine Heislet (defendant) to quiet title to certain real property. Judgment for Nadine Heislet and Annie Heislet appealed. Judgment affirmed.

Annie Heislet acquired, through conveyance and inheritance, a five-ninths interest in a house and lot. Nadine Heislet acquired a four-ninths interest by inheritance. Annie and Nadine owned the property as tenants in common. In 1945, Annie and her husband moved into the house, and during the years they lived there they improved it by constructing a fruit and furnace room, a utility room and stairway to the basement, by remodeling the bathroom and kitchen, rewiring the electrical system, painting the inside and outside of the house and blacktopping the back yard at a cost of $4,075. They paid the taxes on the property. Although Nadine knew that the improvements were made, she was not asked nor did she offer to contribute for them or for taxes.

* Harold F. Lusk, *Business Law: Principles and Cases* (7th ed.: Homewood, Ill.: Richard D. Irwin, Inc., 1963), pp. 700–702.

After Annie's husband died in 1951, she continued to live in the property until 1958 when she sold it for $10,500. Annie and her husband, during the time they had possession of the property, rented it to third persons for a period of 17 months and collected and used the rent money collected. The court found that the fair rental value of the property during this period was $75 per month. Annie claims ownership of the property by adverse possession. Nadine claims that she is the owner of four ninths of the property and asks an accounting for the rents collected and the rental value of the house during the time Annie occupied it. Annie in turn claims the right to contribution for the improvements made.

WADE, JUSTICE. Annie contends that the court erred in failing to find that her possession of the property was adverse to Nadine. The court found that at no time prior to the commencement of this action did Annie inform Nadine that she claimed to be the owner, nor did Nadine seek possession of the property involved herein. In *Clotworthy* v. *Clyde* this Court quoted with approval the test laid down by this Court in *McCready* v. *Fredericksen* to the effect that in order for a tenant to adverse his cotenant he must "bring it home" to his cotenant and by the most open and notorious acts show to the world that "his possession is intended to exclude, and does exclude, the rights of his cotenant."

Since the court found that Annie's possession was not adverse to her cotenants this Court will not disturb such finding unless it was clearly against the weight of the evidence or unless the court has misapplied the principles of law or equality. The mere fact that Annie paid the taxes would not be such an act as would unequivocally inform her cotenants that she was claiming adversely because as we pointed out in *McCready* v. *Fredericksen,* unless the interest of each tenant is assessed separately it is the duty of one tenant as much as the other to pay all of the taxes and when he does so it is for the benefit of all and the only right he has is for contribution. The further fact that extensive improvements were made while Annie was living on the property also are not inconsistent with cotenancy. As this court stated in *Sperry* v. *Tolley:*

". . . It is likewise true that the repairs and improvements made in the dwellings, buildings and fences are acts normally consistent with a tenancy in common and not adverse to it."

In the instant case the repairs and improvements were such as a person in possession would make for one's own convenience and satisfaction and would not necessarily show an intent to oust cotenants of their rights or rebut the presumption that they were made for the benefit of all the cotenants. This being so this Court will not disturb the District Court's finding that Annie's possession was not adverse to her cotenants.

Nadine has cross-appealed, contending that the court erred in deducting from her interests in the property her proportionate shares of the moneys expended by Annie and her husband for taxes and improvements and not offsetting against these expenditures the reasonable rental value of the property for the number of years in which they had sole possession of it. In *Utah Oil Refining Co.* v. *Leigh* we approved the doctrine that ". . . a tenant in common is not chargeable with rents by his cotenant for taking exclusive and sole possession of part of the property, as long as he does not take and hold more than his just proportion. . . ." However, even though Nadine is not entitled to her proportionate share of the reasonable rental value of the premises because she was not ousted or excluded from possession of her portions had she desired to take such possession, the question of whether Annie is entitled to contribution from her for improvements made is a difficult one. As stated in 14 Am. Jur., Cotenancy, ¶ 49, commencing on page 115:

While contrary doctrines have been enunciated and the question is conceded to be one of great difficulty, it appears to be generally agreed that a cotenant who has made improvements upon the common property without the assent of his cotenants is not ordinarily entitled to contribution and cannot, as a matter of right, charge them with the value or costs thereof or maintain any action that would result in a personal judgment against them. . . . Compensation for improvements is allowed, however, where the other cotenants have stood by and permitted him to proceed to his detriment.

. . . .

"It follows that in passing on a claim for contribution arising out of the erection of improvements, all the circumstances of the case should be taken into consideration. Where it appears that the cotenant making the improvements has acted in good faith, without any design to injure or to exclude his cotenants . . . the court may allow him the amount which represents the increase in the value of the estate. . . .

. . . .

"Although there is authority to the contrary, the great weight of authority holds that compensation may be awarded where the improving tenant acted in the bona fide belief that he was the sole owner of the property. . . ."

Taking into consideration the fact that there is no evidence that Annie did not act in good faith and in the further belief that she was the sole owner of the premises when the improvements were made, the circumstances are not such as to make the District Court's decision inequitable that Nadine in the furtherance of justice should contribute her proportionate share for the improvements.

STUDY PROJECT 7

DAMAGE DUE TO POLICE POWER EXERCISED IN CONJUNCTION WITH A TAKING *

The problem of police power in connection with condemnation appraisals is one which presents itself much more frequently in these days in which the construction of highways with some measure of access control or traffic channelization is the rule rather than the exception. The problem is most often confronted in cases where an existing highway or street is widened with additional right of way being taken, and where there is included in the widening project the construction of a median strip, or the channelization of entrances to commercial establishments which regulate access and often eliminate parking on the right of way which the property owner has enjoyed for some time. The slight additional taking may have very little effect upon what the property will bring if offered for sale, whereas the construction of the median strip may substantially reduce the traffic available to the property and in the case of commercial property, greatly lower the price that the property will bring on the market.

The problem resolves itself into two major aspects: the legal and the practical. Although confusion exists in both, the legal or theoretical may well be the simpler problem with more easily found answers. In approaching the problem from the legal point of view, it is necessary first to distinguish between

* Harrison Lewis, *The Appraisal Journal* (October, 1961), pp. 481–88.

that construction on a particular project which is done under an exercise of the police power and that which is done under an exercise of the power of eminent domain. This is often not an easy task and is a complicated subject in itself. For the purposes of this discussion we will assume that the police power involved had been held to be a valid and justified exercise of this power.

By way of review and since it is a part of the over-all problem, it might be well to state the general distinction between police power and eminent domain. Nichols states it as follows:

> In the exercise of eminent domain, property or an easement therein is taken from the owner and applied to public use because the use or enjoyment of such property or easement therein is beneficial to the public. In the exercise of the police power, the owner is denied the unrestricted use or enjoyment of his property, or his property is taken from him because his use or enjoyment of such property is injurious to the public welfare. Under the police power the property is not, as a general rule, appropriated to another use, but is destroyed or its value impaired, while under the power of eminent domain it is transferred to the state to be enjoyed and used by it as its own.[1] [See references on page 615.]

The difficulty in distinguishing between the two is discussed by Nichols as follows:

> . . . the police power embraces regulations designed to promote the public convenience or the general prosperity as well as the public health, safety or morals. . . . In one sense, the police power is but another name for the power of government.
> When injury is inflicted upon the value of a particular piece of real estate as an incident of a general regulation of a restrictive character, enacted in behalf of the public health, safety or morals, the courts are slow to consider such injury an exercise of the power of eminent domain requiring compensation. . . . However, it is always a question of degree. . . .[2]

Or, as it is stated by the United States Supreme Court in the Pennsylvania coal case: [3]

> One fact for consideration in determining the limits of the police power is the extent of the diminution. When it reaches a certain magnitude, in most if not all cases, there must be an exercise of eminent domain and compensation . . . so the question depends on particular facts.

Highway Authorities Use Police Power

Although the distinction may be a difficult one at times and leads to much of the confusion concerning compensability, since one generally thinks of the various highway organizations as operating under eminent domain, nevertheless highway authorities do exercise the police power and many of their activities have been held to be a valid exercise of this power. A few of these which have been so held and which are encountered most often in conjunction with a construction project are:

1. The conversion of a two-way street into a one-way street.
2. The prohibition of left turns and U-turns.
3. The construction of curbs which restrict access to abutting property.
4. The construction of a median strip in the center of a highway.
5. The prohibition or regulation of the size and type of driveways.
6. The regulation of parking immediately adjacent to abutting property.
7. The rerouting or removal of traffic from in front of the abutting property.

If the highway authority imposes some of these restrictions without taking additional property, it is universally held that this valid exercise of the police power does not give rise to any right to compensation.[4] If this is true, then there should be no problem. It should follow that an exercise of the police power, whether in conjunction with a taking or alone, is *damnum absque injuria*.

Joint Use Clouds Issue

However, confusion does arise in the minds of appraisers, lawyers and courts, first, in distinguishing between police power and eminent domain when they are exercised at the same time; second, in the application of the before and after rule of damages; and third, in the concept of market value. In the minds of many, once a taking has occurred the doors are thrown wide open. This comes in part from the measure of damages as stated by the courts. In many states the measure of damages for a partial taking is the difference in the fair market value of the entire property immediately prior to the taking, and the fair market value of the remaining portion immediately after the taking, which difference includes the value of the part taken and damage to the remainder, offset by benefits. Since it is obvious that an exercise of the police power can materially affect the price of a given piece of property in the market, this exercise of police power when done in conjunction with the taking can actually substantially lessen the after value.

Therefore it would appear that an inconsistency would exist between those cases which, on the one hand, say that an exercise of police power is not compensable, and those cases, on the other hand, which state that the measure of damages for an exercise of the power of eminent domain in a partial taking is the difference between the before and after market value. This inconsistency cannot be explained by the rationale that the police power is not exercised until some time subsequent to *immediately* after. In most jurisdictions it is proper to consider the project in a completed state for the purpose of estimating damages and benefits to the remainder.[5]

Attitude of the Courts

Let us examine what has been done in courts which have dealt with this specific problem. It appears that there are few cases in which the question has been directly presented. There are, however, four cases of interest. One which discusses the question at some length is the Fox case,[6] in which the State condemned right of way across the property of respondents for construction of a limited-access highway. The taking consisted of a strip of respondent's land having an approximate area of two-tenths of an acre. A service road was constructed across respondent's property giving access to the limited-access facility. A median strip installed between the east and west lanes of traffic on the limited access highway prevented respondents from making a left turn into the west-bound traffic lanes of the limited-access highway. The State appealed, assigning as error testimony that concerned loss of value to the remainder of respondent's property, due to the construction of a median strip that prohibited left-hand turns on the highway in front of respondent's property. The Supreme Court of the State of Washington, in reversing the decision of the lower court, stated:

The State's assignments of error must necessarily rest upon the proposition that, concurrent with a compensable taking in a condemnation proceeding, the State may exercise the police power for traffic control and public safety for which there can be no compensation, even though it affects the method of ingress and egress.

The crux of respondent's argument is: The State cannot extract one feature of an overall plan and label it an exercise of the police power in order to reduce the compensation payable to the property owner in a condemnation proceeding. . . .

The Court then continued:

As indicated in *Walker* v. *State*, 1956, 48 Wash. 2d 587, 592, 295 Pac. 2d 328, we find nothing in the limited-access facilities statute that shows a legislative intent to surrender or modify the right of the highway commission to install and maintain such traffic control devices under the police power.

The statutory process by which an existing highway becomes a limited-access facility is a combination of the exercise of eminent domain and of police power. *Carazalla* v. *State*, 1955, 259 Wisconsin 593, 70 N. W. 2d 208, 71 N. W. 2d 276. The State must compensate for property rights taken by eminent domain; damages resulting from the exercises of police power are not compensable. *Walker* v. *State, supra.* Hence we cannot subscribe to respondent's contention that the State does not have the right to show the category under which a particular aspect of the limited-access facility plan falls. This is permissible for the purpose of fixing the award for those items that are compensable as a matter of law, not for the purpose of reducing the compensation payable to the property owner in the condemnation proceeding.

Although *Walker* v. *State, supra* was not a condemnation action, the abutting property owner sought compensation for diminution for his right of ingress and egress. The opinion deals only with the right of the highway department, under the police power, to prohibit left turns across a four-lane highway by the installation of a concrete center line curb. Therein the court said:

". . . We have found no authority, nor has any been called to our attention, which allows to the abutting property owner damages allegedly arising from statutes or ordinances (a) establishing one-way streets; (b) forbidding U and left turns; or (c) authorizing the use of other suitable traffic control devices deemed necessary by proper authorities to warn, regulate, and guide traffic upon public thoroughfares.

Although an abutting property owner may be inconvenienced by one-way traffic regulations immediately in front of his property, he has no remedy if such regulations be reasonably adapted to the benefit of the traveling public. The property owner must point to illegality, fraud, or arbitrary or capricious conduct."

Since the instant proceeding is a combination of the exercise of the power of eminent domain and the police power, it follows that the law of the Walker decision is apposite to the instant case.

We conclude therefore that the court erred when it admitted testimony that concerned loss of value to the remainder of respondent's property due to the construction of a median strip that prohibited left-hand turns on the highway in front of respondent's property. *Blumenstein* v. *City of Long Beach*, 1956, 143-Cal. App. 2d 264, 299 Pac. 2d 347.

On Access Limitation

The second expression of opinion, found in the Blumenstein case (cited in the Fox case), is interesting in that the taking in itself might well have been held to be an exercise of police power. The case is usually cited on this point; however it also contains the points in which we are interested.

Respondent owned a parcel of land in Long Beach lying and fronting on the north side of Anaheim Street. Defendant in construction and extension of the Long Beach Freeway constructed an island in Anaheim Street which ran past respondent's property. That part of the street which lay north of said island and upon which respondent's property fronted became an outlet of the Long Beach Freeway carrying traffic in a westerly direction only and depriving respondent of access to Anaheim Street. Respondent brought this action in inverse condemnation to recover damages. The court awarded damages and the city appealed. The court, in holding that there was a taking of access by converting a part of Anaheim Street into the freeway, and affirming as to the issue of liability, based their decision on the Ricciardi case.[7] On the point with which we are concerned the court said:

Notwithstanding respondent's right of recovery as established, we find it impossible to affirm the judgment by reason of the unsatisfactory nature of the evidence which is emphasized by the appellant's motion to strike the estimate of plaintiff's only expert witness upon the damage which had been done to the plaintiff's easement of access by the construction of the improvement. The estimate of the witness was that the market value of the respondent's property had declined to the extent of $15,000 as a result of the improvement, the property's highest and best use now being industrial rather than commercial. The motion was based upon the admission by the witness under cross-examination that he had let factors influence his determination of the decline in market value such as a presumed future loss of vehicular parking in front of such property due to an anticipated exercise of police power and the diminution, diversion, and rearrangement of traffic in front of the subject property because of the construction of the improvement. Furthermore, the witness indicated that circuity of travel in attempting to reach southerly portion of plaintiff's property as caused by existing traffic regulations was a factor in his determination of market value.

The problem of the measure of damages for a properly compensable injury to easement of access to an abutting highway is fully and completely covered in *Rose* v. *State of California*, 19 Cal 2d 713, 737 et seq., 123 Pac 2d 505, in which the facts are substantially the same as those present in *People* v. *Ricciardi, supra.* It was there held that although diminution of market value of the subject property caused by the construction of the complained of improvement is in general a proper measure of damages in condemnation actions, direct or inverse, *the decline of market value must be tempered by an exclusion of loss of value due to noncompensable injury.* Appellate decisions of the State have made it clear that damages resulting from mere diversion of traffic or inconvenience resulting from circuity of travel . . . are noncompensable.

This case is important in reconciling the differences between the police power cases and those that state the before and after rule.

On Divided Highway

In the Ensley case,[8] the State took some of the owner's land for purpose of widening the contiguous highway but also created a divided highway compelling customers of the condemnee approaching from one direction to travel to a street intersection beyond the property, make a left turn onto such street, and travel half a block to reach an entrance to the property therefrom. The Court held that this impairment of access was wholly unrelated to the land taken, and since it merely created some circuity of route, did not constitute a taking within the meaning of the eminent domain statute. The Court applied the conventional principle that there is no property right in the free flow of traffic past an abutter's property, disallowing compensation although it occurred concurrently with a taking.

The Smith case [9] held that in connection with the construction of a divided highway, the property owner was entitled to compensation for an unreasonable restriction of the number of access entrances to the property, but that traffic regulations prohibiting the crossing of the highway, the making of left turns, and the making of U-turns except at designated points where there were no raised "jiggle" bars (which had the effect that traffic on the opposite side from defendant's gas station could not enter it directly), did not constitute a taking of defendant's property within the law of eminent domain. The court stated that such regulations were almost universally regarded as reasonable in that they facilitated travel, and virtually eliminated collisions between vehicles going in opposite directions. The court also said that the defendant had no vested right to the continuance of existing traffic past his establishment, and that the requirement that he cross the highway only at designated places was imposed alike upon all members of the public and were not compensable.

There may be other cases on the subject but nowhere has the writer found any case which held that an exercise of the police power was compensable whether exercised concurrently with a taking or separately. It is true that the courts at times have discussed injuries imposed by police power which were called compensable. However this appears to be a mixing of terminology, and what the courts are really saying is that the action cannot be sustained under the police power but is in fact an exercise of eminent domain.

Problem—Before and After Rule

Since it appears that the courts which have been squarely presented with the question of compensability of an exercise of police power in conjunction with a taking, have held it to be noncompensable, where does the problem lie? The problem arises out of a misunderstanding of the before and after rule, and in its application. Fair market value for the purposes of condemnation seems to be a hypothetical concept. I doubt seriously if a piece of property ever traded at the legal definition of a before fair market value, and I am certain that one never traded at an after fair market value. Market value is hypothetical in that it assumes an unreal set of facts. It assumes a willing buyer and seller, neither under any compulsion to buy or sell, and in most jurisdictions, conversant with all the facts surrounding the property. If all this actually existed there would be little motivation for the exchange of property. There are also items which affect the price of the land but cannot be considered in estimating this market value. In before market value it is improper to consider any change in value of the property by reason of knowledge of the proposed taking or improvement. The property may actually have increased in what it will bring or in price, but it is not proper to consider this increase, and it must be excluded from before market value.[10]

Likewise, in an after market value, there are items which actually affect price in the market which are not to be considered. One of these is a diminution in value by reason of exercise of the police power. Stated a little differently, after market value is the same as before market value altered only by the loss of the part taken, and *some* of the uses to which it is put, not by some other occurrences such as an exercise of the police power or the building located on the property burning down simultaneously with the taking. Fair market value for condemnation purposes is not in all instances the same as the price which the property will bring in the market.

Many of the cases, when discussing the measure of damages generally, fail to recognize the hypothetical nature of before and after market value. It is this very language which gives rise to the confusion concerning police regulations, change of grade, and other noncompensable items. Language from *R. R. v.*

Manufacturing Company [11] has been repeated by the North Carolina Supreme Court on many occasions, and is included in many a charge to the jury by a trial court. It is as follows:

. . . It may be safely asserted that no element should be excluded in arriving at the market value of the premises which it is customary for the business world to consider in determining such market value, or which an ordinary prudent man would take into account before forming a judgment as to the market value of the property which he is about to purchase.

Taking Doesn't Change Picture

This broad language would certainly lead one to believe that the effect of police regulations or any other injury to the value of the property could be considered, regardless of their source, once the door is opened by a taking. To further give rise to confusion, the courts are apparently consistent in holding, in those cases in which the question is presented, that injury due to police power exercised by the taking authority is not compensable. However they have beclouded the issue by permitting considerations of the effect of police power on market value, both before and after taking, when the regulation is imposed by other than the condemning authority. An example is zoning, as in the Barnes case: [12]

The weight of authority in other jurisdictions is well declared as follows: "As stated in *Beverly Hills* v. *Anger* (1932), 127 Cal. App. 223, 15 P. 2d 867, a zoning ordinance restricting the use of property is proper evidence for determining the market value of land being condemned, for the reason that in determining the market value of realty, all circumstances and conditions which become either an advantage or a detriment to the property should be considered. . . . If the land taken is not presently available for a particular use by reason of a zoning ordinance or other restriction imposed by law, but the evidence tends to show a reasonable probability of a change in the near future in the zoning ordinance or other restriction, then the effect of such probability upon the minds of purchasers generally may be taken into consideration in fixing the present market value. However if the possible change in a zoning ordinance restricting the use of the property condemned is purely speculative, such possibility is not to be considered." Anno: 173 A. L. R. 265, 266.

The principle is well stated in *Board of Education v. 13 Acres of Land* (Del. 1957), 131 A. 2d 180, in the seventh headnote: "In ascertaining market value in an eminent domain proceeding reasonable probability of a rezoning of the condemned property, to permit the highest and best use, may be considered in determining such market value."

One wonders whether median strip affects the purchaser's mind any less than zoning?

The confusion created by the broad language of the cases on measure of damages and the inconsistency of the courts, coupled with the fact that most state appellate courts have not passed on the point directly, has made it difficult for trial lawyers to convince some trial courts that these damages should not be considered, despite the fact that every state which has passed on it has held it to be noncompensable. I believe that the majority of states will hold it noncompensable since logic and precedent indicate so.

Even if this were so, we are left with some of the practical aspects. It is difficult to get many appraisers to go along with excluding noncompensable damages. Most of them are hesitant to accept the theory that market value for condemnation purposes is hypothetical and not necessarily the same as sale price. It seems to be a new concept to them, and it is difficult to apply. Sales of comparable property on the same project after the taking will reflect damages by reason of police power, and therefore require an adjustment which is difficult to make. Unfortunately many trial lawyers find that when some appraisers are instructed to disregard these damages, in many cases they merely remove the discussion of these items from the report but not the values reflected in the report. If it is difficult to sell to appraisers, it is many times more difficult to sell to a jury. You can't hide the median strip; it is there, and if it damages the property the jury will more than likely compensate the property owner regardless of their instructions. This is particularly so where appraisers have admitted that their estimates were affected by police power considerations.

Condemnation appraisal is a specialized field and its entire basis is to be found in the law. To be of any use to the condemner, or condemnee for that matter, the appraisal must be based upon the law and not upon the appraiser's personal feelings. If an appraiser is worried about the apparent inequity of not reflecting police power damages in his appraisal when they actually exist, it should be remembered that highway authorities are continuously imposing police restrictions without taking property. No appraisal is made on these parcels and the property owners affected by these recover no compensation. To pay others for the same injury because a small portion of their property is taken is hardly justice.

REFERENCE NOTES

1. *Nichols on Eminent Domain,* I (3rd Ed.), § 1.42 (2).
2. *Ibid.,* (7).
3. Pennsylvania Coal Company *v.* Mahone, 260 US 393, 412; 43 Supreme Court 158, 159; 67 Law Ed. 322, 323, 28 A. L. R. 1321 (1922).
4. Nichols, *op. cit.,* § 1.43 (3).
5. Highway Commission *v.* Black, 239 NC 198.
6. The State of Washington *v.* Fox, 53 Wash. 2d 216, 332 Pac. 2d 943.
7. The People *v.* Ricciardi, 23 Cal 2d 390, 399, 144 Pac. 2d 799, 804.
8. State *v.* Ensley, 164 N. E. 2d 342 (Ind. 1960).
9. Iowa State Highway Commission *v.* Smith, 248 Iowa 869, 82 N. W. 2d 755; Anno: 73 A. L. R. 2d 680.
10. Shoemaker *v.* U. S. 147 U. S. 282, 29 C. J. S. Em. Dom. § 136, p. 972, 973, 18 Am. Jud., Em. Dom. §§ 242, 246.
11. R. R. *v.* Manufacturing Company, 169 NC 156, 165.
12. Barnes *v.* Highway Commission, 250 NC 378.

STUDY PROJECT 8

A RETURN TO FUNDAMENTALS

This study project is intended to stimulate some reflective thinking about the economic characteristics of real estate.

Real Estate Economics: A Return to Fundamentals *

Real estate prices behave quite differently in the market place than do prices of other economic goods. Why is this so? Can the differences be explained in

* Edward E. Edwards, "Real Estate Economics: A Return to Fundamentals," *The Appraisal Journal* (April, 1949).

terms of economic principles? Will an understanding of economic principles help to explain price behavior in the past? Will such an understanding help to predict future real estate prices?

A study of the behavior of prices for single family homes leads to the conclusion that real estate prices can be explained and predicted in terms of five economic principles, which are as follows:

1. The supply of real estate is relatively fixed.
2. The demand for real estate is dependent in the first instance on income.
3. Effective demand is dependent largely on the availability and terms of financing.
4. The real estate market is a local, disorganized one.
5. The influence of government is very great.

These economic principles are well known and are not the discovery of the author. Perhaps, because they are so well known, they are frequently overlooked. This article, which deals with these five simple concepts only, may be considered a return to fundamentals in real estate economics.

Supply of Real Estate Relatively Fixed

This first principle hardly needs to be proved. Our present supply of real estate includes structures that have been built over a long period of years. The new structures added in any one year occasionally exceed in number the old structures that are torn down, but only in a building boom do they add as much as two or three per cent to the existing supply. When new construction ceases, the supply declines slowly, since neither government nor private enterprise can afford wholesale destruction of accumulated capital investment in real property.

Because the supply is relatively fixed, demand is the most important factor in determining price. When demand exceeds supply, as at the present time, real estate prices rise and continue to rise for quite some time, since there is little chance that the supply will catch up. Conversely, when demand falls below the existing supply, real estate prices fall and continue to fall or remain at low levels for a prolonged period.

The inflexibility on the supply side probably is such that there never is a time when supply and demand are equated. By the time an inadequate supply has caught up with a heavy demand, the demand has already shifted downward. On the low side, supply is never reduced to a depression-low demand, and the real estate market must wait until demand has again moved upward.

Demand for Real Estate Dependent in First Instance on Income

Real estate, as it is known in this country, is not a necessity of life, but a luxury. The amount of real estate actually needed for the bare necessity of shelter is very small. This is especially true when real estate is measured in terms of dollar value rather than in dwelling units. The demand for dollars' worth of real estate, therefore, behaves very much like the dollar demand for any other luxury good.

What are the characteristics of the demand for luxury goods, particularly real estate? First, the demand for real estate increases sharply with increased personal incomes. In this connection, it must be remembered that the increase in demand is an increase in the dollars offered for real estate. This is not necessarily an increase in the number of houses demanded; in fact, it is more likely to be an increase in the dollars that the prospective buyer will put in a single house. An increase in total demand therefore may be accompanied by a decrease in demand for certain properties.

Second, the demand for real estate decreases sharply with falling off of personal incomes.

Third, the maintenance of demand, or the increasing of demand, except in periods of rising incomes, requires aggressive selling to meet competition of other luxury goods.

By putting the first two principles together, the conclusion may be reached that the most important factors in determining the price of real estate are the level of personal incomes and the competition of other luxury goods for those incomes. If the subject of real estate economics had to be reduced to a single theorem this would be it. The idea that real estate values over the long run must equal cost of construction is of little use in explaining the real estate market. Real estate prices practically never equal cost of construction; they are either higher or lower.

Effective Demand Dependent Largely on Availability and Terms of Financing

Most buyers of real estate enter the market with some money of their own and as much or more of some financial institution's money. The amount that they are prepared to bid for real estate is therefore largely dependent on the amount that they can borrow.

While it is true that most mortgage lenders apply some standards which relate the amount of the loan to the income of the borrower, these standards change from time to time. Unfortunately, the changing standards tend to accentuate differences in personal income levels rather than to equalize them. For example, lending institutions generally have been more liberal in periods of prosperity when the level of personal incomes is high than during depressions when the level of personal incomes is low.

The amount of funds which a financial institution will place in the hands of a prospective buyer of real estate is dependent not only on the borrower's income but also on the institution's judgment as to the appraised value of the property. Here again the judgment of the lending institution frequently rises and falls with the level of personal incomes. The result is that the action of the financial institutions tends to exaggerate the effect of changes in personal incomes on real estate prices.

There are, of course, many factors other than the level of personal incomes and appraised values which affect the amount of funds available for the financing of real estate. One very important factor is the relative attractiveness of other forms of investment. Mortgagors must compete in an open-money market for their funds. The availability of funds and the interest rate that must be paid are determined at least in part by conditions and events entirely outside the real estate market.

The relative attractiveness of an investment is not solely a matter of yield. All too frequently, in the past, this country has had periods when the investor would much prefer money in the bank or in his safety deposit box to any income producing investment. This has resulted in a drying up of mortgage funds, hence a virtual elimination of the demand for real estate.

The influence of the financial institutions on demand for real estate is especially significant in view of the fact that the lending policies of so many financial institutions are regulated or influenced by federal government action. The insurance and guarantee of particular types of loans has a profound influence on the demand for real estate. The influence of the federal government on real estate prices is so important that it has been listed separately as one of the five factors necessary to explain real estate prices.

Real Estate Market a Local, Disorganized One

Real estate cannot be moved from one market to another, nor can demand be shifted from a market in tight supply to one having a surplus of properties. A vacant house in Indianapolis cannot be moved to Detroit, nor can a Detroit family solve its housing problem by moving to Indianapolis. Even within a single city separate markets exist for houses in different neighborhoods and for houses of different sizes and prices. For any given piece of property there are very few potential purchasers; for any prospective purchaser there are very few properties that will satisfy his wants.

As a result, the so-called real estate market is in reality a large number of separate markets. One market may be enjoying a real estate boom while another is in a real estate depression. Comparable properties sell at widely differing prices, and there is no national market of investors and speculators to equalize prices as there is in securities and commodities.

Even within a single real estate market the equalization of prices is difficult if not impossible because of the cumbersome, slow, costly, and risky procedures involved in real estate transfer. Compared with a well organized securities or commodity market, real estate market can only be described as highly disorganized.

Influence of Government Very Great

No other economic goods with the exception of narcotics is so greatly affected by government as is real estate. Perhaps this is inevitable in view of the fact that real estate after all is not a commodity but merely a bundle of rights created by government.

Until comparatively modern times only the state and local governments had much interest in real estate. In recent years, the federal government has moved rapidly into this field and its influence upon real estate prices is now of prime importance.

Real estate prices are affected by two more or less separate and distinct types of federal action. The federal government is now dedicated to the proposition that it must maintain a high level of personal incomes in this country. To the extent that the federal government's actions in this direction are successful, the demand for real estate is stimulated and a continuing strong demand is more or less assured.

But the federal government is not limiting its influence to the indirect effects of its full employment policies. It supervises the lending policies of many mortgage lending institutions. It guarantees and insures mortgage loans, it controls rents, it expedites the construction of new housing units, and at times it encourages public housing.

The actions of the federal government are not always consistent. The insurance of mortgage loans developed as a means of stimulating new construction during a depression, yet guaranty and insurance of mortgage loans continue during a period when there is full employment and runaway inflation is threatened. Rent control continues when there is a shortage of supply, and rationing is needed. Inconsistencies such as these are likely to continue. Perhaps politics is more important than economics, and no one should explain real estate prices except in political terms.

Summary

This discussion of real estate prices perhaps can be summarized in the form of a prediction of future real estate prices. Such a summary might read as follows:

The present real estate boom will not end because of new construction; it may end because of reduced demand. A reduced demand for real estate may come from a reduction in the national income, from a reduction in the proportion of personal incomes that people are willing to spend for housing in competition with other luxury goods, or from further tightening of real estate financing. No matter what happens, real estate prices will behave differently in each real estate market. Finally, the federal government, both directly in the field of real estate and indirectly in monetary and fiscal policy, will be a major influence.

On the assumption that the federal government will seek to maintain or increase the present level of personal incomes and to continue easy financing of home ownership, the prediction might be made that real estate prices will continue high on the national average, but that weak spots may develop in individual markets with changing local demands for real estate and widely varying increases in supply from new construction.

STUDY PROJECT 9

BROKERS TO THE WORLD *

One of the offshoots of the world economic boom is an international boom in real estate. From Rhodesia to Rochester, land shoppers are clamoring for attractive parcels of property. Only ten years ago Switzerland was the only European country in which a foreign broker could easily do business in real estate; today, firmer currencies have made the task much easier—and tremendously profitable. The firm that stands to benefit most by the boom is Manhattan's Previews, Inc., the world's only international clearinghouse for real estate, and an experienced dealer in both the exotic and the practical.

Previews considers itself a sort of stock exchange for world property, brings far-flung buyers and sellers together through twelve offices in the U.S. and abroad and 20,000 cooperating brokers in almost every country in the world. Each year it handles $75 million worth of property, in 1957 sold $28 million worth—and made $2,250,000 in fees. Last week Previews' president, white-haired John Colquhoun Tysen, 45, was off on an annual world tour to sew up new deals with pashas and parvenus, unemployed royalty and hard-headed businessmen.

Careful Eye

Tysen is convinced that some of the best buys are in the sunny resort lands of southern Europe. His Spanish subsidiary, formed only last month, is already

* *Time* (July 14, 1958). Copyright, Time, Inc., 1958.

dickering to develop a three-mile stretch of virgin coastline above Valencia into Europe's fanciest resort. "The world has gone sun crazy," says Tysen—and Previews intends to grab a place in the sun.

Previews also keeps a careful eye on depreciated slum areas that may go industrial, is gradually increasing its trade in land for industrial purposes. Tysen is negotiating with Belgian government officials about industrial development of the Inga Rapids area of the Congo River, a vast, water-rich slice of the Belgian Congo (*Time*, Nov. 25) which engineers fondly describe as "the Ruhr of the 21st century." Tysen will also shop around for three kings interested in plush homes, has hunting licenses for land for a British firm that wants to build 700-room luxury hotels in Lisbon and Vienna, a U.S. hotel chain interested in London.

Do-It-Yourself Parliament

Previews still does 90% of its business in residential land ("The appreciation can be fantastic"), specializes in finding buyers for U.S. residences such as Bing Crosby's seven-room lodge on Hayden Lake in Idaho, now for sale at $95,000. "We don't live by soufflés alone," says Executive Vice President Robert T. Furman, Jr. But Previews has made its reputation peddling white elephants and exotic properties. For $300,000 Tysen will sell a half share in an Irish distillery, for $182,000 the title to the Windward Island of Mustique, which Previews claims includes the right to appoint one's own parliament.

Whether a customer wants to sell a house in which all the rooms are round (Previews sold one in New Jersey) or turn his farm into a tourist paradise, Previews' approach is the same. Previews gets 1½% of the asking price for handling a property on a three-year contract, advertises it with attractive brochures, often distributed to as many as 5,000 other brokers. When the property is sold. Previews picks up another 2%. The local broker also gets a commission.

Just Looking

Previews was founded in 1933 by three young New Yorkers who realized that many people could not spare the time and effort to shop for just the house they wanted. They took movies of properties for sale (at a cost of $50 to the owner), showed them to prospective buyers. The firm lost money steadily for six years, largely because it could not get enough listings from unfriendly brokers. It finally switched to brochures, upped its fees—and began making money.

Trim (6 ft. 1 in., 170 lbs.) John Tysen, Paris born and British educated, got hired at Previews in 1936, when he dropped in to do an errand for a friend. Despite a dandy's flair for clothes and a Cantabrigian accent that sometimes made him almost unintelligible, Tysen proved to be a crack salesman, became sales manager in 1940, president in 1950 (at $25,000 a year, plus fat commissions and bonuses), boosted volume fourfold. Tysen holds as sacred writ that there is more money to be made in land than any other commodity, but he himself owns nothing more than a nine-room penthouse apartment in Manhattan. Says he: "There's a conflict of interest. You can't serve yourself and serve a client."

STUDY PROJECT 10

APPRAISAL REPORT *

APPRAISAL REPORT

1044 W. Dale Road
Cosmopolis, Indiana
Address of Appraised Property

Roger Sportsman
Owner's Name

1 Family - Residence
Type of Property

Riverdale Bank and Trust Company
Appraisal Made for

8-7-   8-12-
Date   Effective Date

T. Lorin Driscoll, M.A.I.
Appraiser

APPRAISAL SUMMARY

APPRAISED VALUE—LAND	$ 4,000.00
APPRAISED VALUE—LAND IMPROVEMENTS	$ 1,300.00
	$ 5,300.00
APPRAISED VALUE—IMPROVEMENTS	$18,200.00
ESTIMATED MARKET VALUE OF PROPERTY	$23,500.00

PURPOSE OF APPRAISAL

To estimate "Market Value" of the subject property, in fee simple,
free and clear of any encumbrance, as of August 12, 19 .

CONTINGENT AND LIMITING CONDITIONS

The value shown in this appraisal is market value, defined as: "The highest price estimated in terms of money that a willing and well-informed buyer would be warranted in paying and a willing and equally well-informed seller justified in accepting for a property if placed on the market for a reasonable period of time; with both parties acting free of compulsion or duress and with all rights or benefits inherent in or attributable to the property included in said value."

The value of the property is expressed in dollars on the date above specified and is subject to any changes in the value of the dollar. All existing liens and encumbrances have been disregarded and the property is appraised as though free and clear under responsible owner-ship and competent management.

The legal description furnished us is assumed to be correct. No survey was available (unless otherwise stated) and the dimensions used are from sources deemed reliable.

All information and comments concerning the location, neighborhood, trends, construction quality and costs, loss in value from what ever cause, condition, rents, or any other data of the property appraised herein represent the estimates and opinions of the appraiser, formed after an examination and study of the property.

While it is believed the information, estimates and analyses given and the opinions and conclusions drawn therefrom are correct, the appraiser does not guarantee them and assumes no liability for any errors in fact, in analysis, or in judgment. No attempt has been made to render an opinion of title or of the status of easements or of any other matter of a legal character.

Possession of this report, or a copy thereof, does not carry with it the right of publication, nor may it be used for any purpose, by any but the applicant, without the previous written consent of the appraiser, or the applicant, and in any event only with the proper qualification.

The distribution of the total valuation in this report between land and improvements apply only under the existing program of utilization. The separate valuations for land and building must not be used in conjunction with any other appraisal and are invalid if so used.

The fee for this appraisal does not provide compensation for conference or, testimony or attendance in court, with reference to the property in question.

This appraisal represents the independent opinion of the appraiser free from any commitments and free from any present or expected future interest in the property with the sole compensation for the employment being a fair professional fee.

* Appraisal report form by permission of T. Lorin Driscoll, appraiser, Indianapolis, Indiana.

LOCATION OF PROPERTY
1044 W. Dale Road
Cosmopolis, Indiana

LEGAL DESCRIPTION
Lot 104, Block 4
Tract No. 4401

TYPE OF PROPERTY
1 Family, Residence, 1 Story, No Basement, Slab Construction

TAX INFORMATION

Assessed Value—Land	$	420.00
Assessed Value—Improvements	$	5,100.00
Assessed Value—Total	$	5,520.00
Rate . . . . Year	$	7.229
Taxes Payable . . . . Year	$	399.04

NEIGHBORHOOD DATA
Section of City North East   [ ] Urban   [X] Suburban
Distances: Center of City 9 miles   Transportation At Door   Shopping ½ Mi.
                Churches   Elem. School Twp. Bus   High School Twp. Bus
Adverse Influence: [ ] Yes   [X] No   Age: Years   Built-up 85 %
Transition: [ ] Yes   [X] No   Trend: [X] Up   [ ] Down   [ ] Static
Neighborhood Developed With Comparable Homes; Except Vacant Ground
Immediately Across Dale Road, Zoned Residential.

SITE ANALYSIS
                                                 Lot Size: 105' x 190'
Zoning: Residential   Highest and Best Use: Residential 22 - $28,000
[ ] At Street Level   [X] Above   [ ] Below   [ ] Well Drained   [ ] Poor Drainage
Services: [X] City Water   [X] Gas   [X] Electricity   [ ] Sewer   [ ] Well   [X] Septic System
              [ ] Curb   [ ] Cement Walks   [ ] Alley   [X] Street Paved Asphalt Top
Yard Improvements: Drive Crushed Stone & Curb   Service Walks Brick
         Lawn Good   Trees Large Shade Trees   Shrubs Good
         Other
A good wooded lot among good, well maintained homes.

PICTURE, DRAWING, ETC.

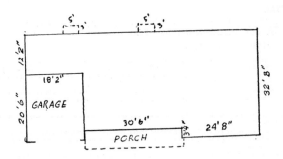

BUILDING ANALYSIS

Exterior Detail

EXTERIOR WALLS		ROOF STRUCTURE			ROOF COVER		WINDOWS	
X	Frame siding P & Gable		Flat	☐ Mansard	210#	Asphalt shingle		Double hung
	Metal siding	X	Gable	☐ Gambrel		Asbestos shingle	45	Casement Single Anderson
	Wood shingle		Hip	☐ Mixed		Wood shingle		Awning type
	Asbestos shingle		Extra Gables			Slate		Picture
	Stucco on frame		Dormers	lin. ft.		Tile		Weatherstrip
	Stucco on masonry	3'	Overhang F & R 1'3" ends			Tar and gravel	X	Screens
	Brick					Other	All	Storm sash
X	Brick veneer	Good	Condition		Good	Condition	3	Storm doors W. Comb.
	Stone		FOUNDATION			GUTTERS AND DOWNSPOUTS	1	Porch Open Front
	Concrete block	X	Poured conc. Slab		X	Galvanized	2	Stoops Rear
	Comp. siding		Concrete block			Copper		
	Other		Beams Grade			Aluminum		
			Posts or piers			None		
			Other					
Good	Condition		Condition		Good	Condition	Good	Condition

Interior Detail / Mechanical Detail

BASEMENT				1st flr.	2d flr.	Attic	ELECTRICAL			PLUMBING	
☐ Full		☐ Part					Knob and tube		1	Number bathrooms	
☐ Crawl		☒ Slab 4"					Cable ☒ Armored ☐ Non met'l		1	Number lavatories (2 fix. ea.)	
Partition							Rigid conduit			Extra fixtures	
Floor Joists							Low voltage system Mercury			W-softener	
Subfloor							HEATING AND AIR-COND.			W-heater 80 gal. G.E.	
FLOORS							Gravity warm air			Sump-pump	
Hardwood, avg.							Forced warm air				
Hardwd., fancy							Hot water ☐ Steam			MISCELLANEOUS	
Soft wood							Radiant Electric		X	Insulation:☒ Walls ☒ Ceil.	
Tile, comp.							Floor or wall furnace			Fireplaces: No. & Mirrors	
Tile, ceramic							Stove			Venetian blinds	
Linoleum				X X XX X				☐ Butane		Built-in cabinets Kit. & Laundry	
Concrete				X X X X			☐ Oil-fired	☐ Gas-fired	1	Kitchen vent. fan Air King	
							☐ Hand-fired	☐ Stoker	1	G. diposal Hot Point	
WALLS							Air-conditioned	tons		Dishwasher	
Plaster				X X X			Condition			Blt.-in range	
Dry wall							SOCIAL ROOM			Attic fan	
Wood panel Knotty P				X X X			Floor			Incinerator Yard	
Tile, plastic							Walls			Books & Cab.	
Tile, ceramic				X			Ceiling		Good	Condition	
Asbestos				X						**Garage & Accessory Bldgs.**	
CEILINGS							**Age & Condition**			GARAGE	
Plaster				X X X X XX X X X			Year built—Est. 19			☒ Attached ☐ Carport	
Dry wall							Year remodeled—Est.			☐ Detached ☐ Bsmt.	
Acoustic							% remodeled			No. cars 2	
Asbestos				X				E	G A F P	Walls asbestos 2 walls—ceil	
TRIM							Foundation			Floor Concrete	
Stock				X XX XX XX X X			Ext. walls			Roof Asph. Sh.	
Special							Ext. trim			Doors 16' O. H.	
Painted							Roof			Dimensions X	
None							Int. walls				
DOORS							Int. ceilings			ACCESSORY BLDGS.	
1⅜"				X XXX X			Floors			Description	
1¾"							Electric				
Slab				X XXX X			Heat sys.				
Panel							Plumb. sys.			Dimensions X	
CLOSETS				4 4			Avg. Tot. Cond.			Dimensions X	

(Interior floor-plan column headers: Living, Dining, Halls, Kitchen, Bedrms., Baths, Lavs., Utility rm., Activities, Bedrms., Baths, Hall)

COMMENTS:

LR 15'10 x 16'8; 11'9 x 27'7; BR 11'ELL; Kit. 11' x 11'4; Master BR 12' x 15';
BR 10'6 x 11'4; 9'2 x 11'4; Full Bath and Half Bath

Carpets are cemented to Slab. Doubtless will need to be purchased with the
house.

```
Estimated Value to Sale of Property  - Carpets    $600.00
     "        "     "    "   "    "   - Drapes      200.00

If left with property then add       - Total      $800.00
```

COST APPROACH TO ESTIMATE OF VALUE

Estimated Land Value   105' @ $40   per front foot, wooded $4,000.00
Land Imprmts: Drive $ 100   Lawn, Trees, Shrubs $ 325
  Walks $ 80   Well $ Septic $ 550 Fence $ 200 Other $ 45 $1,300.00 $5,300.00
Estimated Replacement Cost—Building:
Measurements: Perimeter Wall 205   Sq. Ft. 1,920   Cu. Ft. 30,720
Method of Cost Estimate: Wenzlick #58
  .6425 x 30,720 = $19,737.00
  Additions & Deductions   2,713.00

Total Feet 30,720 @ $ .73   per cu. Ft. (Estimated Replacement Cost) $22,450.00
Loss in Value from Various Causes:
  Physical—Incurable   Age 4 Years   6 % $ 1,350.00
  Physical—Curable $
  Functional Incurable $
  Functional Curable   Elec. Heat $ 3,000.00
  Environmental Influence $_____ $ 4,350.00
  Value of Major Improvement $ 18,100.00
Garage 372   Sq. Ft. Cost New $ 1,300   Net Value $ 1,225.00
Other Improvements   Net Value $
                                           Net Value $
Major Rehabilitation $_____ $ 1,225.00
Total Replacement Cost—Less Loss in Value $19,325.00
Market Value Indicated By Cost Approach $24,625.00

In year 19- the electric bill was: Water Heater $59.32 Gen.Serv.& Heat $441.00
  "   "   19 (8 mo.) "   "   "   "   " $36.62 "   "   " $366.04
It seems probable that the heating cost is $300 per year or 1½ times oil or gas.

INCOME APPROACH TO ESTIMATE OF VALUE

Rent—Actual or Estimated $ 200   x   110 (Gross Multiple) $ 22,000.00
Capitalization of Net Income   Not Practical $
Market Value Indicated By Income Approach $ 22,000.00

MARKET DATA APPROACH TO ESTIMATE OF VALUE

Former sale of subject property:
                        Date   Indicated price $ Adjusted $
                        Date   Indicated price $ Adjusted $
Comparable sales data:
1050 W. Dale Road   Date Asking   Indicated price $ 24,250 Adjusted $ 22,500
     Variation from subject
1101 W. Dale Road   Date   Indicated price $ 26,000 Adjusted $ 26,000
     Variation from subject
1310 W. Dale Road   Date   Indicated price $ 21,500 Adjusted $ 23,500
     Variation from subject   Less attractive, smaller, G. E. Counterflo Oil

Market Value Indicated By Market Data Approach $ 23,000.00

Market Value is without carpets.

ANALYSIS, INTERPRETATION AND CORRELLATION

Value Indicated By Cost Approach	$ 24,625.00
Value Indicated By Income Approach	$ 22,000.00
Value Indicated By Market Data Approach	$ 23,000.00

There seems only about 10% variation between the values indicated by the 3 approaches. Normally the cost approach is the upper limit. In a single family dwelling little dependence should be placed in the income approach. The Market data approach is the best indication of value.

FINAL ESTIMATE OF VALUE

It is therefor my opinion that the "MARKET VALUE" of the subject property; as of   August 12, 19
in fee simple, free and clear of encumbrance, is:

Twenty-three thousand five hundred   Dollars ($ 23,500.00)

CERTIFICATION

I, do hereby certify that to the best of my knowledge and belief the statements and opinions contained in this appraisal are correct, subject to the limiting conditions herein set forth; also that neither the employment to make the appraisal nor the compensation is contingent on the amount of the valuation reported; also that I have no interest present or prospective in the said Real Estate appraised; and that this appraisal has been made in conformity with the rules of professional ethics of the:

American Institute of Real Estate Appraisers
and
Society of Residential Appraisers

This appraisal dated this 14   day of   August   19 .
consists of 5   pages and no   exhibits.

T. Lorin Driscoll, M.A.I.

STUDY PROJECT 11

THE ROLE OF THE APPRAISER *

The appraiser performs a critical and important function in our economy. He is not an investor nor an entrepreneur; he is not an initiator nor a decision-maker. He is not an adviser in the sense of recommending a course of action. He is, however, closely associated as an expert in a great many of the important real estate decisions and the ensuing transactions which comprise real estate market activity and which result in real estate capital formation. Few major real estate developments are initiated without his participation; few advances of credit on mortgage security are made without an appraisal; and few large investments in existing properties are consummated without the benefit of a value figure estimated by the appraiser. The appraiser needs no capital to perform his function except a wealth of information concerning the behavior of the real estate market. He is not a risk-taker himself but he must understand the nature of risk-taking in the real estate market and the calculus and psychology of the risk-taker.

The social contribution which the appraiser is in a position to make is of considerable consequence. Our cities grow and are redeveloped parcel by parcel as owners and investors make investment decisions which result in growth and change. The appraiser's role in such decisions on the part of both equity and loan capital has already been suggested. As the appraiser influences the nature of these decisions, so he affects the nature of the investment and thus the rate and quality of urban growth. In the public as well as in the private investment sector, the appraiser takes a leading part. His findings, in effect, determine the cost of acquiring the billions of dollars worth of land required for highways and expressways and both the acquisition costs and sales proceeds in urban redevelopment areas which contain thousands of acres of valuable close-in land.

No one goes to a doctor or retains a lawyer or calls in an appraiser unless he has a problem; neither doctor, lawyer nor appraiser initiates his own assignments. It follows as night the day that the professional service which is requested must be directed to the problem which gave rise to the request if the client's needs are to be served. The problem, then, dictates the nature of the service to be provided. This is a truth which many appraisers ignore; armed with a standard definition of value they proceed to estimate this value figure without reference to its relevance to the problem which faces their client. The fact is that there are several value figures which are associated with any parcel of real estate and, depending on circumstances, one or several such value figures may have relevance to the client's problem and will assist him in arriving at the decision which may be required. To the extent that the appraiser views his function as simply placing a value on a piece of property, he is limiting his usefulness to his client and thus the chance of a repeat assignment.

* Richard U. Ratcliff, "A Restatement of Appraisal Theory," excerpt from *Wisconsin Commerce Reports*, Vol. VII, N. 1 (1963), p. 11.

STUDY PROJECT 12

ZONING REGULATION *

See pages 628–29.

* By permission of the City Planning Commission, Los Angeles, California.

STUDY PROJECT 13

A QUESTION OF FEDERAL CONCERN *

What is the proper role for the federal government to perform in dealing —with problems of cities and metropolitan areas? Do such apparently localized questions as urban blight or traffic congestion really demand federal action? Does the transition to a nation composed of urban dwellers mean that more of the responsibility for local conditions should be shifted to the national capital?

Observers who tend to answer these questions in the affirmative seem to base their reasoning upon two related propositions:

a) The United States is now largely urban in nature with the bulk of the nation's wealth, national income and population residing or being generated in the urban areas. All evidence seems to indicate that the pace of urbanization will be maintained or increased. The 1960 Census, for example, showed that the number of people living in the 212 Standard Metropolitan Statistical Areas increased by 26.4 per cent in the preceding decade while the rest of the nation grew by only 7.1 per cent. The facts are clear. Urbanness is extensive pervasive, and general. The next step in the argument, however, is not nearly so evident because many writers then go on to assert that the generality of the urbanness, somehow or other, automatically makes the problems of urban areas a matter of federal or national concern.

I find this reasoning somewhat difficult to understand. How does the change from a relatively rural culture and economy to a more urban one seemingly give rise to a need for an increased role and scope of federal action? It could just as well be argued that somewhat greater homogeneity in patterns of living and production might reduce the need for federal action. None of this questioning denies the premise that the federal government must have concern for the smooth functioning of the general economy with the aid of the appropriate monetary, fiscal and regulatory instruments. But, it seems to me that the real question at issue is whether or not increased urbanness gives rise to problems which are not capable of being handled by existing institutions: households, firms, markets, and state and local government agencies. This deficiency cannot be taken on faith. It needs to be demonstrated that deficiency or imperfection exists and that federal action is the appropriate way to deal with the problem.

b) The second proposition is quite similar to the first, although it does represent an attempt to point toward special problems arising out of urban areas that seem to require federal attention. The argument takes this general shape: Rising urbanization brings about greater economic interdependence between cities and regions. Individual communities have more closely-knit ties to the national economy. Some of these ties are reflected in the increased flows of

(Continued on page 630)

* From a speech by Professor J. W. Milliman, "Urban Crisis—a Question of Focus."

SUMMARY OF ZONING REGULATIONS

	ZONE	USE	HEIGHT — STORIES	HEIGHT — FEET	YARDS — FRONT	YARDS — SIDE	YARDS — REAR	AREA — PER LOT	AREA — PER DWELLING UNIT	MINIMUM LOT WIDTH	PARKING SPACE	EAGLE PRISMACOLOR PENCIL CHART
RESIDENTIAL	RE	RESIDENTIAL ESTATE — ONE-FAMILY DWELLINGS, PARKS - PLAYGROUNDS, COMMUNITY CENTERS, TRUCK GARDENING - HORSES	2 / IF SHOWN IN HEIGHT DISTRICT 3	28' / 45'	25 FT.	3' MIN. / 5'-2 STORIES / 6'-3 STORIES	25' MAX.	11,000 SQ. FEET	11,000 SQ. FEET	70 FT.	1 GARAGE PER DWELLING UNIT	950 GOLD
	RS	SUBURBAN — ONE-FAMILY DWELLINGS, PARKS - PLAYGROUNDS	2 / IF SHOWN IN HEIGHT DISTRICT 3	28' / 45'	25 FT.	3' MIN. / 5'-2 STORIES / 6'-3 STORIES	25' MAX.	7,500 SQ. FEET	7,500 SQ. FEET	60 FT.	1 GARAGE PER DWELLING UNIT	911 OLIVE GREEN
	R1	ONE FAMILY DWELLING — R S USES-INCIDENTAL COMMERCIAL FARMING ON 20,000 SQUARE FOOT LOTS	2 / IF SHOWN IN HEIGHT DISTRICT 3	28' / 45'	20 FT.	3' MIN. / 5'-2 STORIES / 6'-3 STORIES	25' MAX.	5,000 SQ. FEET	5,000 SQ. FEET	50 FT.	1 GARAGE PER DWELLING UNIT	916 CANARY YELLOW
	R2	TWO FAMILY DWELLING — R1 USES, TWO-FAMILY DWELLINGS	2 / IF SHOWN IN HEIGHT DISTRICT 3	28' / 45'	20 FT.	3' MIN. / 5'-2 STORIES / 6'-3 STORIES	25' MAX.	5,000 SQ. FEET	2,500 SQ. FEET	50 FT.	1 GARAGE PER DWELLING UNIT	917 YELLOW ORANGE
	R3	MULTIPLE DWELLING — R2 USES-BOARDING HOUSES, MULTIPLE DWELLINGS	3	45'	15 FT.	3' MIN. / 5'-2 STORIES / 6'-3 STORIES	25 FT. / 15 FEET IF NO ACCESSORY BLDG. IN YARD	5,000 SQ. FEET	800 to 1,200 SQ. FEET	50 FT.	VARIES FROM 1 FOR 1 TO 1¼ FOR 1	918 ORANGE
	R4	MULTIPLE DWELLING — R3 USES - CHURCHES, SCHOOLS - HOTELS	6 / UNLIMITED * IF IN HEIGHT DISTRICT	75' / 150'	15 FT.	3' MIN. / 5'-2 STORIES INCREASE 1 FT. THEREAFTER 16' MAX.	25 FT. / 15' TO 20' IF NO ACCESSORY BLDG. IN YARD	5,000 SQ. FEET	400 to 800 SQ. FEET	50 FT.	VARIES FROM 1 FOR 1 TO 1¼ FOR 1	943 BURNT OCHRE
	R5	MULTIPLE DWELLING — R4 USES - CLUBS - LODGES, HOSPITALS - SANITARIUMS	13 / UNLIMITED * IF IN HEIGHT DISTRICT	150'	15 FT.	3' MIN. / 5'-2 STORIES INCREASE 1 FT. THEREAFTER 16' MAX.	25 FT. / 15' TO 20' IF NO ACCESSORY BLDG. IN YARD	5,000 SQ. FEET	200 to 400 SQ. FEET	50 FT.	VARIES FROM 1 FOR 1 TO 1¼ FOR 1	946 DARK BROWN
AGRICULTURAL	RA	SUBURBAN — R1 USES-LIMITED AGRICULTURAL USES-LIBRARIES-MUSEUMS, CHURCHES-HORSES	2 / IF SHOWN IN HEIGHT DISTRICT 3	28' / 45'	25 FT.	3' MIN. / 5'-2 STORIES / 6'-3 STORIES	25 FT.	20,000 SQ. FEET	20,000 SQ. FEET	70 FT.	1 GARAGE PER DWELLING UNIT	910 TRUE GREEN
	A2	AGRICULTURAL — RA USES-EXTENSIVE AGRICULTURAL USES ON FIVE ACRE FARMS-HOSPITALS OR SANITARIUMS	2 / IF SHOWN IN HEIGHT DISTRICT 3	28' / 45'	25 FT.	3' MIN. / 25' MAX.	25 FT.	2 ACRES	1 ACRE	MINIMUM AVERAGE LOT WIDTH 150 FT.	1 SPACE PER DWELLING UNIT	912 APPLE GREEN
	A1	AGRICULTURAL — A2 USES-ALL AGRICULTURAL PURSUITS-DAIRIES ON TWENTY ACRE FARMS	2 / IF SHOWN IN HEIGHT DISTRICT 3	28' / 45'	25 FT.	3' MIN. / 25' MAX.	25 FT.	5 ACRES	2½ ACRES	MINIMUM AVERAGE LOT WIDTH 300 FT.	1 SPACE PER DWELLING UNIT	909 GRASS GREEN
PARKING	P	AUTOMOBILE PARKING — PROPERTY IN A P ZONE MAY ALSO BE IN AN A OR R ZONE. PARKING PERMITTED IN LIEU OF RESIDENTIAL OR AGRICULTURAL USES.	2	—	0-5 TO 10' DEPENDING ON ZONING IN BLOCK	5 FT. IF ABUTTING A OR R ZONE	5 FT. IF 2 STORY AND ABUTTING A OR R ZONE	AREA PER LOT AND UNIT: NONE	LOADING SPACE: —	-NONE- UNLESS ALSO IN AN A OR R-ZONE	—	967 COLD GREY LIGHT
	PB	PARKING BUILDING — P ZONE USES						NONE	—	NONE	—	936 SLATE GREY

	Use / Description	Stories	Height	Side Yard	Front / Corner Yard	Rear Yard	Yards for Dwellings	Loading Space	50 Ft. Use	Automobile Parking	No.	Color
CR	LIMITED COMMERCIAL — MOST R5 USES—OFFICE BUILDINGS BANKS—BUSINESS SCHOOLS NO MERCHANDISE DISPLAY OR SALE	6	75'	10 FT INTERIOR LOT EXCEPT ON MAJOR HIGHWAY	5' to 0'—CORNER LOT ONLY	25 FT 15' TO 20' IF NO ACCESSORY BLDG IN YARD	SAME AS R5 FOR DWELLINGS OTHERWISE NONE	WHERE LOT ABUTS ALLEY →	50 FT FOR RESIDENCE USE	1 SPACE FOR EACH 500 SQUARE FEET OF FLOOR AREA	939	FLESH
C1	LIMITED COMMERCIAL — R3 USES—LOCAL RETAIL STORES, OFFICES OR BUSINESSES	3	45'* UNLIMITED IF IN HEIGHT DISTRICT	ONLY IF PART OF BLOCK IN DWELLING ZONE	NONE UNLESS LOT ADJOINS DWELLING ZONE	25 FT 15 FEET IF NO ACCESSORY BLDG IN YARD	SAME AS R3 FOR DWELLINGS OTHERWISE NONE	MINIMUM LOADING SPACE 400 SQUARE FEET.	50 FT FOR RESIDENCE USE	1 SPACE FOR EACH 500 SQUARE FEET	929	PINK
C2	COMMERCIAL — C1 AND R5 USES—RETAIL BUSINESS WITH LIMITED MANUFACTURING	6	75'* UNLIMITED IF IN HEIGHT DISTRICT	NONE	NONE FOR COMML BLDGS RESIDENTIAL USES—SAME AS IN R4 ZONE	25 FT IF NO ACCESSORY BLDG IN YARD	SAME AS R4 FOR DWELLINGS OTHERWISE NONE	ADDITIONAL SPACE REQUIRED IN BUILDINGS CONTAINING	50 FT FOR RESIDENCE USE	OF FLOOR AREA IN BUILDINGS CONTAINING 5,000 OR MORE SQUARE FEET.	922	SCARLET RED
C3	COMMERCIAL — SAME AS C2	13	150'	NONE	ABOVE SIXTH STORY FOR COMML BLDGS RESIDENTIAL USES—SAME AS IN R4 ZONE	NONE FOR COMML BLDGS RESIDENTIAL USES—SAME AS IN R4 ZONE	SAME AS R5 FOR DWELLINGS OTHERWISE NONE	REQUIRED FOR BUILDINGS CONTAINING MORE THAN 5,000 OR MORE SQUARE FEET.	50 FT FOR RESIDENCE USE	CONTAINING	923	SCARLET LAKE
C4	COMMERCIAL — C2 USES (WITH EXCEPTIONS)	13	150'* UNLIMITED IF IN HEIGHT DISTRICT	NONE	NONE FOR COMML BLDGS RESIDENTIAL USES—SAME AS IN R4 ZONE	NONE FOR COMML BLDGS RESIDENTIAL USES—SAME AS IN R4 ZONE	SAME AS R5 FOR DWELLINGS OTHERWISE NONE	50,000 MUST BE LOCATED WITHIN	50 FT FOR RESIDENCE USE	MUST BE LOCATED WITHIN	924	CRIMSON RED
C5	COMMERCIAL — C2 USES—LIMITED FLOOR AREA FOR LIGHT MANUFACTURING	13	150'* UNLIMITED IF IN HEIGHT DISTRICT	NONE	NONE FOR COMML BLDGS RESIDENTIAL USES—SAME AS IN R4 ZONE	NONE FOR COMML BLDGS RESIDENTIAL USES—SAME AS IN R4 ZONE	SAME AS R5 FOR DWELLINGS OTHERWISE NONE	750 FEET OF BUILDING.	50 FT FOR RESIDENCE USE	750 FEET OF BUILDING.	925	CRIMSON LAKE
CM	COMM'L MANUFACTURING — C2 USES—WHOLESALE BUSINESS STORAGE BUILDINGS LIMITED MANUFACTURING	3	45'* UNLIMITED IF IN HEIGHT DISTRICT	NONE	NONE FOR INDUSTRIAL OR COMML BLDGS RESIDENTIAL USES—SAME AS IN R4 ZONE	NONE FOR COMML BLDGS RESIDENTIAL USES—SAME AS IN R4 ZONE	SAME AS R5 FOR DWELLINGS OTHERWISE NONE	WHERE LOT ABUTS ALLEY →	50 FT FOR RESIDENCE USE	1 SPACE FOR EACH 500 SQUARE FEET	905	AQUA-MARINE
M1	LIMITED INDUSTRIAL — C M USES—LIMITED INDUSTRIAL AND MANUFACTURING USES	3	45'* UNLIMITED IF IN HEIGHT DISTRICT	NONE	NONE FOR INDUSTRIAL COMML BLDGS RESIDENTIAL USES—SAME AS IN R4 ZONE	NONE FOR COMML BLDGS RESIDENTIAL USES—SAME AS IN R4 ZONE	SAME AS R4 FOR DWELLINGS OTHERWISE NONE	MINIMUM LOADING SPACE 400 SQUARE FEET	50 FT FOR RESIDENCE USE	OF FLOOR AREA IN BUILDINGS CONTAINING 5,000 OR MORE SQUARE FEET.	904	LIGHT BLUE
M2	LIGHT INDUSTRIAL — M1 USES—(EXCEPT NO "R" USES) ADDITIONAL INDUSTRIAL USES STORAGE YARDS OF ALL KINDS	13	150'* UNLIMITED IF IN HEIGHT DISTRICT	NONE	ABOVE EIGHTH STORY NONE IF IN HEIGHT DISTRICT	NONE	NOTE. R ZONE USES PROHIBITED	ADDITIONAL SPACE REQUIRED FOR BUILDINGS CONTAINING MORE THAN 50,000 SQUARE FEET.	NONE	MUST BE LOCATED WITHIN 750 FEET OF BUILDING.	902	ULTRA-MARINE
M3	HEAVY INDUSTRIAL — M2 USES ANY INDUSTRIAL USE—NUISANCE TYPE 500 FEET FROM ANY OTHER ZONE	13	150'* UNLIMITED IF IN HEIGHT DISTRICT	NONE	ABOVE EIGHTH STORY NONE IF IN HEIGHT DISTRICT	NONE	NOTE R ZONE USES PROHIBITED	MUST BE LOCATED WITHIN 750 FEET OF FLOOR AREA	NONE		931	PURPLE

Rows CR–C5 are grouped as **COMMERCIAL**; rows CM–M3 are grouped as **INDUSTRIAL**.

SUPPLEMENTAL USE DISTRICTS
(ESTABLISHED IN CONJUNCTION WITH ZONES)

[O] OIL DRILLING [S] ANIMAL SLAUGHTERING [G] ROCK AND GRAVEL

[*] HEIGHT DISTRICT

BUILDING HEIGHT UNLIMITED IN THE R4-R5-C1-C2 C4-C5-CM-M1-M2 AND M3 ZONES

No 1 FLOOR AREA OF MAIN BUILDINGS MAY NOT EXCEED THREE (3) TIMES THE BUILDABLE AREA OF THE LOT.

No 2 FLOOR AREA OF MAIN BUILDINGS MAY NOT EXCEED SIX (6) TIMES THE BUILDABLE AREA OF THE LOT.

No 3 FLOOR AREA OF MAIN BUILDINGS MAY NOT EXCEED TEN (10) TIMES THE BUILDABLE AREA OF THE LOT.

No 4 FLOOR AREA OF MAIN BUILDINGS MAY NOT EXCEED THIRTEEN (13) TIMES THE BUILDABLE AREA OF THE LOT.

NOTE: ALL INFORMATION GENERAL • FOR SPECIFIC DETAILS CHECK WITH DEPARTMENT OF BUILDING AND SAFETY

CITY PLANNING COMMISSION

goods, people, and messages between cities and regions. Such linkages are said to be proxy indicators of a developing "national system of cities." It is clear, for example, that the economic health of Detroit or Pittsburgh is directly dependent upon the national market for automobiles. Trends in national markets for labor and for capital usually have direct local impacts. The metropolis, therefore, must be seen as an integral part of the national economy and the national economy, in turn, may be affected by special regional or metropolitan forces.

If we stop the argument at this point, it is generally quite plausible and acceptable even though it should be pointed out that urbanization could conceivably reduce some kinds of interdependencies among the particular economic functions displaced and acquired in the process. Difficulties may arise, however, when an attempt is made to go beyond such generalized observations to some direct federal policy pronouncements. Do interrelationships between the metropolis and the national economy necessarily imply that "the federal government must have a deeply-rooted concern for urban areas?" I think not. Economic and social linkages, transactions, or bonds are indications of relationships but nothing more. Linkages, in themselves, do not tell us that centralized or overall coordination is required. The fact that business firms in some cities sell products to households in other cities does not make it self-evident that national urban planning is desirable. Instead, there is need to examine explicitly the workability of existing decision-making institutions.

It is important, of course, that federal policies be designed with a strong awareness that their impact may not be uniformly felt in particular regions. Moreover, we can argue quite strongly for better coordination of diverse federal programs in terms of their impact on urban areas. Not only do some federal programs work at cross purposes with each other but it is clear that some programs undercut effective metropolitan area planning:

There is no question but that the federal government plays a vital role in metropolitan areas. Its programs have had varying effects. Some have tended to accentuate the forces operating to expand metropolitan regions and reinforce characteristics of diffusion; others have been directed towards opposite ends. Some federal programs have supported and reinforced traditional operations of local governments, while others have given rise to new institutions on the local level. At times, activities or projects of one agency have been in direct conflict or at variance with projects or activities under another program.[1]

Without going into an extensive analysis and cataloging of the proper role of the federal government in the on-going urbanization process, it will be helpful to point to several lines of activity which appear to warrant greater federal participation. At the outset we must make it clear that urban policy cannot be viewed apart from the overall objectives for the conduct of the public economy. Urban policy must be consistent with and actually a part of a general federal program designed to promote such general objectives as: 1) an efficient allocation of resources; 2) provision for full employment, economic growth and price level stability; and 3) establishment of a distribution of income and wealth that has social sanction and acceptability.

Naturally, these objectives are somewhat generalized and in actual practice important policy conflicts occur when a particular program gives rise to a conflict of objectives. Nevertheless, a great deal of confusion about the intent and

[1] Robert C. Weaver, "Growing Metro Areas Make Case for Department of Urban Affairs," *Journal of Housing* (January 31, 1963).

rationale for a national urban policy results from a failure to place urban activities within an overall framework. Can we assume, for example, that federal and local interests in particular urban expenditures coincide? I think it is important that we distinguish between the local gains which result from federal expenditures in a particular community from the benefits said to accrue to the nation as a whole. The localized gains are usually quite real and obvious, particularly when the funds and resources come from the nation at large. These resource transfers necessarily involve sacrifices of alternative production possibilities elsewhere in the economy. The important and troublesome questions arise when we attempt to define the national interest in the local expenditure against a backdrop of real costs representing real alternatives sacrificed in the economy as a whole.

There are two general guidelines which seem appropriate in helping us gain perspective as to the federal responsibility and interest in the urban "crisis": 1) Would the solution of a particular urban problem lead to the achievement of the overall objectives for the public economy? 2) Do the particular methods proposed to deal with the problem promise to provide benefits in excess of the expected real costs in terms of public and private alternatives sacrificed? It seems to me that many, though not by any means all, of the urban problems said to be demanding of federal action do not meet the first test and, moreover, that a great many of the proposed solutions have not been scrutinized in light of the second rule.

STUDY PROJECT 14

WHO IS TO SAVE OUR CITIES? *

Should government take the lead and use its power and authority to revitalize our cities?

Or should business, in this area as it has in others, take the initiative, using the power of free enterprise to rebuild those areas which are the main centers of industry?

As America evolves from an overwhelmingly rural to an emphatically urban society, we are experiencing severe growing pains. Undirected or misdirected growth has created problems of all types in our cities. Today there is unanimous agreement that a severe urban crisis exists, but few are prepared to deal with it straightforwardly. There are those who think things will take care of themselves; those who feel that easy compromise solutions will do the trick; and only very few who are willing to engage in major efforts which will go to the heart of the problem. Thus, in the face of a severe and very real urban crisis, the majority of American cities either limp along in accordance with a do-nothing policy or at best get a meaningless surface cosmetic treatment.

What is the reason for this bungling approach? To put it bluntly, I believe that the responsibility for it lies largely in the lethargy of the American businessman. In an area of complex and vital self-interest, it appears that free enterprise is proving itself neither free nor enterprising, but timid, passive, and defeatist. Even in those cases where individual businessmen in a community, committee, or chamber of commerce have shown concern, their efforts are reminiscent of an anxious bather slowly entering the water: brave enough to get his toes wet but never working up enough courage to jump in and swim.

* Victor Gruen, *Harvard Business Review* (May–June, 1963).

I have had many years of experience working with federal authorities, state governments, municipalities, private developers, and citizens' organizations. On the basis of this experience and the research and studies conducted in dozens of cities in America, as well as large cities of the Western World generally, I have to conclude that—with a few exceptions so slight that they tend to confirm the rule—it is government that has taken the initiative while free enterprise has proved to be either hostile, unconcerned, or, if interested, rather ineffectual.

State of Revitalization

Government has shown concern for the fate of our cities for some time; it has developed methods of approach over the last five years, though slowly and sometimes hesitantly. The legal and administrative tools shaped for this purpose are still far from perfect, but a steady effort toward improvement and sharpening of the tools can be observed.

In the main, government action toward the revitalization of our cities proceeds in the framework of urban redevelopment legislation. In the short history of urban redevelopment and renewal, the approach has undergone significant changes.

Lack of Success. In the beginning, all attention was concentrated solely on residential buildings, and the program sailed under the flag of slum clearance. Blighted residential areas were razed by bulldozers; structures which were found to be physically unsound were demolished and replaced with new ones of sound structural qualities and up-to-date plumbing. However, urban redevelopment was a new field and, because of inexperience, the results were not always satisfactory. There was sterility in planning and design, and there were well-meant but mistaken concepts concerning density and land coverage. These resulted, more often than not, in rather inhuman, institutionalized projects.

It also soon became obvious that these efforts did not succeed in removing the slums. Economically or racially underprivileged population groups were driven out and replaced by those who could afford to pay the rent in the new projects. Those who had to leave settled nearby, causing new conditions of overcrowding and resultant blight.

Slowly, urban redevelopment procedures in residential sectors are becoming more sophisticated. The idea that only total clearance can help is being abandoned and replaced by a combination of spot clearance, rehabilitation, and conservation. Increasing attention is being paid to the aim of saving not only structures but the community itself. Thus, in many cases at least part of the original population remains but is better housed. Where considerable relocation is necessary, procedures for resettlement are being improved.

Even more significantly, redevelopment authorities now insist on the furnishing of over-all plans of either the entire community or general neighborhood in order to gain assurance that redevelopment efforts will indeed lead to genuine improvement. There is also evident a striving toward the abandonment of large, one-income-group developments, and at least the beginning of efforts to avoid these ghetto-like, single-income projects.

Widening Circle

But the greatest and most dramatic change is to be found in the broadening of the redevelopment concept from its original application (residences exclusively) to include all types of land-use functions: retailing, offices, industry, recreational and cultural facilities, civic administration, and so forth.

This change in governmental approach should effectively eliminate every excuse private enterprise can offer for its lethargy and inaction, since now the concern of redevelopment is so broad that it can deal effectively with the business and cultural life of the city.

Decline of the City. This approach is of great importance, since the most troublesome aspects of our urban crisis express themselves in the central cores of our metropolitan areas. With very few exceptions, city cores are stagnating, and statistics registering the number of visitors entering the city cores as workers, shoppers, or participants in urban activities show a steady and increasingly steep downward trend.

This trend is most easily traceable in the fate of retailing. Merchants have emigrated en masse from central business cores to suburbia where they have found havens in new, shiny, Lilliputian towns—regional shopping centers, exemplified by those giants of the species: Northland and Eastland near Detroit; Bergen Mall and Garden State Plaza in New Jersey; Old Orchard and Randhurst near Chicago; and many others. The flight of retailing has been joined by other enterprises: headquarters offices of corporations, hotels and motels, professional offices of all types, cultural and recreational facilities, and so on.

The reason for this hegira is not difficult to identify. Whenever and wherever people find it increasingly difficult and dangerous to move within a city in the advanced stages of automobile congestion, when the trip to the central core becomes a time-consuming and tiring adventure, the attraction power of the city dwindles and it becomes unprofitable to conduct any business there at all.

The mass flight of people, retailing, business, and other urban functions into the countryside has created the phenomenon of spreading, sprawling metropolis. In some highly urbanized areas, such as on the East Coast, the result has been the growing together of metropolitan influence areas into an amorphous and disorderly pattern, which has given birth to the new term "megalopolis."

Dissatisfaction with the new spread-out pattern is beginning to set in. Sprawl cannot be continued indefinitely. Communications become overextended, public improvements cannot keep pace with the tremendous costs that sprawl involves, and, most important of all, we are running out of one national resource that is irreplaceable, that can neither be manufactured nor imported; namely, land. The flight to the countryside has effectively destroyed the landscape, and many feel now that suburbia is a place which offers neither the advantages of the city nor those of the country.

Thus, during the last few years, some counterforces have arisen and a trend back to the city has become apparent. This has spurred new interest in the fate of the central core: an increasing awareness of its problems and the desire to do something about them.

Government, responding to the as yet uncrystallized popular change of mind, has broadened, as already shown, its concepts for redevelopment to the point where it has steered efforts from the so-called "gray areas" surrounding the city cores straight into the hearts of urban communities. Dozens of American cities of all sizes are now taking advantage of the widened legal possibilities and have filed applications for federal assistance in their efforts to rebuild and revitalize their languishing and suffering city centers.

. . . .

Mayor Collins of Boston in 1962 described the cooperative effort between business and city government as "without parallel in the history of the United States." This cooperative effort is directed toward the rehabilitation of the 160-acre "core area" of Boston, to be jointly undertaken by the city government and a citizens' committee known as the Committee for the Central Business District, Inc. Since it soon became apparent that retailers were not the only businessmen interested in the redevelopment of the downtown core, the CCBD, as the committee is called, includes leading figures in public utilities, banking, publishing, and the hotel, restaurant, and real estate fields. The planning effort, the Mayor announced, would not only be jointly undertaken but jointly supported monetarily as well by the citizens' committee and the Boston Redevelopment Authority.

Members of the CCBD already have raised over $200,000 to finance preliminary planning for the Central Business District and have entered into a planning contract. What is perhaps most important, they have proceeded, with the aid of the Mayor and the Boston Redevelopment Authority staff, with the preparation of a memorandum of understanding which provides for close teamwork among the CCBD, the Authority, and the city. This will be the foundation of a cooperative effort that will guarantee that the eventual plan will represent the best thinking of the city authorities and the citizens interested in the district. Total costs of the revitalization are presently estimated to be $200 million.

In Paterson, New Jersey, a group known as P.L.A.N., Inc. (Paterson Looks Ahead Now), a businessmen's organization, is cooperating with the Redevelopment Agency and the Mayor. In Fresno, California, a similar pattern of cooperation has been achieved by the "Fresno Hundred Percenters." Although in neither of these two cases has the cooperation between city and business community and their joint relationship been as clearly formulated as in Boston, satisfactory progress is being made.

Crucial Role of Timing. What persists throughout these examples is the element of timing as a crucial determinant. It is important not only that private enterprise should show interest and initiative in a given city, but that this should happen at the right time, i.e., in synchronization with governmental efforts. It is important that this interest and activity should constitute a continuing and never-abating effort until the goals are fully reached.

This vital need for simultaneity is illustrated in the case of Cincinnati, Ohio:

Here, as in Boston, free enterprise cooperation was an important factor, but the trouble in Cincinnati was that recognition of the problems and action toward their elimination came very late. Instead of leading governmental action, business followed it, in a delayed fashion. The fate of Cincinnati's revitalization effort, therefore, still hangs in the balance.

In Cincinnati, recommendations were based on the businessmen's awareness and the planner's conviction that without implementing basic improvements designed to reverse past and continuing downward trends (most clearly expressed in the diminishing number of people entering the downtown city core daily), redevelopment of individual parcels was economically unsound. It either would not take place at all or would result in attracting tenants and businesses from other downtown buildings into the new ones, resulting in new blight formation. Planners emphasized such basic trend-reversing measures as:

Better accessibility.

Increased and improved public transportation.

A distribution system for automobile traffic over loop road systems with adjoining car-storage facilities along the fringe of the core area.

Construction of a public transportation terminal located in the geometric center of the core and effectively reached by underground roads located within the core (this was a key measure).

Finally, the plan demonstrated that through the introduction of the distributing road and garage systems, and underground public transportation roads, it was possible to free all major public surfaces within the core from the dangers, disturbances, and inconveniences of surface automobile traffic. Also, by reserving special roads for service or truck traffic, a convenient solution for the servicing of all buildings could be found.

. . . .

Guiding Principles

The experiences of . . . a number of other cities across the country amply demonstrate that urban renewal is by no means a do-it-yourself project. Fortunately, the trials and tribulations encountered in bringing about the more successful instances of urban revitalization can be converted into a number of proven concepts for the businessman.

You have to take the lead. The businessman should decide that it is up to him to take the initiative, for he has the most to gain from urban renewal. Knowing his own needs and requirements intimately, he is best equipped to work with planners in formulating a program.

Your enthusiasm will be contagious. Because of the actual participation of businessmen, not only in a monetary role but in support of the planning activity, the continued interest of all parties is assured. A psychological atmosphere is created which results in the heightened enthusiasm of the business community for the development of its own city. This optimism is contagious and has resulted, in Paterson and Fresno, for example, in—

the introduction of new enterprises of all types, including department stores,

investment in the form of major building construction,

the attraction of new industries.

Your presence blocks opposition. An educational task is performed within the membership of the business community since, as a result of its active participation, a greater understanding of the problems, potentials, and goals of its city is fostered. The effect of this self-education is that the kind of opposition based on ignorance, misunderstanding, and lethargy is removed in advance of final planning or implementation.

Your dollars multiply. Financial contributions by the business community enable the planners to delve much more deeply into the individual needs and requirements of the various elements which make up the core area, with the result that a more human, more realistic, and more successful plan can be achieved.

Your interest is paramount. The responsibility for implementing master plans should not be left to outside developers alone. The outsider obviously can be motivated only by the direct profits of a redevelopment venture. He cannot possibly perform as effectively as the insider who has the advantage of intimate knowledge of local conditions and the additional motivation of protecting his own investment and the well-being of his own city. This is not to say that local free enterprise should not call for assistance from professional developers who have acquired experience in the field. But local free enterprise should assume a leadership role and participate significantly in the program.

You must realize that flowerpots are not enough. It is certainly true that thousands of members of committees, Chambers of Commerce, and other civic groups have spent millions of highly valuable man-hours in thoughtful discussions, and in attending lectures and talks on city planning. Yet the time invested in these events, though given in good faith, has rarely led to results because it was not directed toward positive action. Only too often these groups ease their collective conscience by prescribing palliatives like the decoration of downtown streets with flowerpots and flags, the holding of special downtown days, or possibly the improvement of lighting and, here and there, construction of a garage or parking lot. These beautification measures are about as effective as the treatment of cancer by aspirin, and whatever time and money is spent on them results in short-lived effects or none whatsoever.

You have to work with government. Besides those businessmen who feel that government should carry the ball, with free enterprise sitting in the bleachers, sometimes applauding but more often booing, there are others who feel just as strongly that government should get out of the city-saving business and leave the task solely to the genius of private enterprise. The fact is, of course, that neither group is right. Successful urban revitalization depends on the unstinting and full cooperation of all the groups involved. Indeed, the roles of local and federal governments and the businessmen are all inseparable and interdependent.

STUDY PROJECT 15

ECONOMIC CLIMATE FOR FUTURE URBAN DEVELOPMENT *

An important question at the present time involves the economic justification of clearing and redeveloping blighted areas in the center of cities. This involves tearing down and paring for obsolete buildings, and some sound buildings, in order not only to remove the structures but to consolidate the land holdings and to replat the scattered parcels into a single tract of sufficient size to enable a new environment to be created. There can be no doubt that the razing of a heterogeneous collection of buildings with an uneven skyline and inadequate parking followed by the building of a newly planned group of buildings with harmonious architectural design will give a more attractive appearance to the downtown area. It may bring added business to the central business merchants. It may well improve the morale of the entire urban region and be the first step in a progressive plan for gradually rebuilding all the worn out or obsolete areas in the city. If accompanied by improvement in mass transit and by rebuilding apartments in the renovated downtown sections, this central urban redevelopment may pay off financially.

However, alternatives to huge expenditures in downtown areas must also be considered. Vast new tracts of vacant land have been made accessible to the

* Homer Hoyt.

metropolitan population by the belt highways and expressways and by new jet airports. On these lands there is no cost involved in tearing down and paying for old buildings and no comparable problem in condemning and paying for numerous small plots of land because the suburban lands are usually in large, single ownership tracts. These outlying tracts are often actually closer to the homes of most residents of the metropolitan area by reason of belt highways than the downtown districts. The land is cheap enough to enable the developer to offer free surface parking. The parking areas have numerous entrances and exits and are often surrounded by highways, reducing traffic congestion. Downtown parking areas or parking garages usually have entrances and exits on congested streets, which become bottlenecks in rush hours.

Examples of the new type of development are Northland at Detroit, where apartments, restaurants, 8 and 10 story office buildings are being erected adjacent to the Northland regional shopping center, and Ward Parkway in Kansas City, Missouri, where office buildings are being completed adjacent to the regional center.

What then is the economic justification of urban redevelopment in central city areas? The economic justification of rebuilding downtown is to be found in the real function of the city center—the office headquarters of the metropolitan area or of the region, the government center, the seat of the courts and law offices, the art and cultural center, the retail center where there is the greatest depth and diversification of merchandise, the medical center where are the most specialists, the theatre and amusement center and the motor hotel, hotel and apartment places of residence for families who want to live within walking distance of all of these attractions.

In order to bring all these functions together in one integrated planned center, with access highways and parking garages, it is necessary to clear away buildings and city patterns inherited from the past pre-automobile age. The advantages which such a grouping together of these functions will have in attracting more office building headquarters, more visitors, more suburbanites back to the city center apartments, more shoppers, and in affording savings in time and travel cost for workers moving between central offices and central apartments will justify economic rents sufficient to yield a net return on the cost of new buildings and leave some surplus for the land. It is not necessary of course, to recapture all the acquisition cost of the land, because the increased real estate taxes on the new buildings will absorb the difference between acquisition cost and resale value in a few years. It is necessary, however, to receive rents high enough to cover operating costs, real estate taxes, interest and amortization on the cost of new buildings and to have something left over for the land. Otherwise an annual subsidy will be required to make up the deficit, which will be a burden on other real estate owners. Also there is no check on overbuilding, once the principle of paying an economic return is abandoned.

Every urban community does not have an economic climate for renewing its central areas. The trend of suburbanization cannot be reversed. The automobile explosion, which increased the number of private autos from 26 million in 1946 to 66 million today, burst the old city patterns apart at the seams. With 100 million private cars projected for 1980 on the basis of expected population growth by that year, it will be impossible to restore the old central retail areas to the dominant position they held in 1910. In the case of numerous smaller cities, it is possible to reach open vacant areas in a 15 to 20 minute drive from the center of the city. In cities of such size it seems questionable whether large sums should be spent in rebuilding downtown areas when vacant land nearby could be developed at far lower costs.

Urban redevelopment is thus not, or should not be considered, a panacea for all urban ills. A careful study should be made of the type of new uses that can be justified on the basis of their economic return. Tall elevator office or apartment buildings are costly to construct, but one or two-story office structures, or walkup apartments might rent for enough to yield an economic return. The right combination of uses in a central area might yield a good economic return, while the wrong combination might be a financial failure. In every proposed urban redevelopment, a careful economic study should be made prior to drawing any plans to ascertain what the community needs and to determine what new uses or expansion of existing uses or what new highways or parking facilities would strengthen and enhance the value of the uses already in the downtown areas.

STUDY PROJECT 16

A THEORY OF FLUCTUATIONS IN RESIDENTIAL CONSTRUCTION STARTS *

Housing production, which has earned the dubious distinction of ranking among the most cyclically volatile industries, is important in the economy because of its large size. Since shifts in housing starts have both an immediate impact on earnings and a delayed reaction on shelter standards, fiscal and monetary policies frequently include programs aimed directly at control of the rate of construction. This article focuses on housing fluctuations and presents a market model designed specifically to aid in their analysis.

Figure 1 illustrates the violent movements which have characterized housing starts. On an annual basis, movements of 30 to 40 per cent from peaks to troughs occurred three times between 1950 and 1962. Starts in the highest quarter exceeded those in the lowest by more than 50 per cent—a difference at annual rates of more than 600,000 dwelling units.[1]

Table 1 relates these starts for 1950–60 to the more basic market forces of demand and inventory changes. Final demand (12,478,000), which approximated 91 per cent of starts, is measured by net houshold formation plus net removals. For that period, household formations (9,645,000) equaled approximately 70 per cent of private starts; net removals (2,833,000), covering a wide variety of gains and losses to the stock that may offset or augment construction of new dwellings, equaled an additional 21 per cent.[2]

Houses not absorbed by final uses increase the inventory. Table 1 shows a rise in available vacancies and a small drop in the inventory of units under construction. Inventory increases for the decade of only 9 per cent of starts reflect

---

* Excerpted from the article by Sherman J. Maisel, *American Economic Review* (March, 1963).

[1] The starts data in this article are based on official Census estimates for the period since 1959. For 1950–58 the original data of the Bureau of Labor Statistics have been revised to agree with both the new Census concepts and the 1960 Census. The appendix contains both data and explanations of the revised series of starts, plus those for other series estimated especially for this study.

[2] For the decade of the 1920's, final demand balanced approximately 75 per cent of starts. For the 1930's it was about 110 per cent. The low demand and high vacancy factor for the 1920's was clearly important in aggravating the depression.

the well-recognized fact that, over any extended period, basic demand normally accounts for a greater percentage of the total.

Figure 1, however, presents the opposite picture. For the decade, quarterly changes in inventories account for 85 per cent of the variance in starts, while the complementary movements in basic demand were related to less than 15 per cent. In shorter periods such as a quarter or a year, the market forces are reversed. The primary correlation is that between starts and inventory shifts.

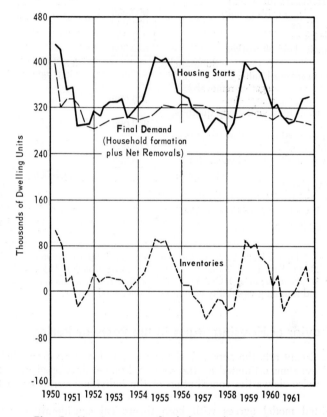

Fig. 1. Housing starts, final demand, and changes in housing inventories in the United States—quarterly totals, 1950–61.

The theory of the market developed in this article explains this sharp divergence. The short run instabilities that characterize housing starts have numerous causes deeply imbedded in the construction process. These forces primarily create fluctuations in vacancies and inventories under construction. The movements shown in Figure 1 are of a type similar to the inventory cycles experienced in manufacturing. In contrast, movements in underlying demand form a more stable equilibrium around which inventories fluctuate. While shifts in demand could cause sharp movements in starts, the forces necessary for such reactions—particularly heavy income declines—have not occurred in the postwar market.

Table 1. Disposition of Total Estimated Starts of Private Housing Units in the United States, April 1, 1950, to March 31, 1960

Net Additions to Households:			9,645,000
Net Removals:			
Losses from available stock:			
Mergers from existing units	900,000		
Demolitions	2,050,000		
Other losses	1,947,000		
Vacancies held off market	692,000		
Subtotal:		5,589,000	
Increase in seasonal units:		337,000	
Offsetting gains (negative removals):			
Public housing completions	425,000		
Trailers, institutional, group quarters, etc.	962,000		
From conversions of other structures, splits, etc.	1,700,000		
Decrease in dilapidated vacancies	6,000		
Subtotal:		−3,093,000	
Total Net Removals			2,833,000
Increase in Available Vacant Units			1,245,000
Change in Inventory under Construction			−37,000
Total Private Housing Starts:			13,686,000

SOURCE: Adapted from *U. S. Census of Housing 1960 Components of Inventory Change*, HD(4), Part 1A-1, Table C; *U. S. Census of Housing 1950*, Vol. 1, Part I; and 1960 *Advance Reports*, HC(A2)-1. Adaptation necessary because of change in definitions and sampling variability compared to decennial census.

The Behavior of Housing Starts in the Postwar Period

Figure 2 contrasts the actual deviations of housing starts from their means with the deviations estimated by the statistical model developed in this article. The figure also shows the contribution of the individual variables to the estimates.

The fitted model agrees with both theoretical considerations and other knowledge in assigning a low importance to household formation and net removals as a cause of postwar housing fluctuations. With the exception of a movement in 1950–52 related to the Korean War and reflected in starts, final demand forms a relatively stable equilibrium around which the critical disturbances take place. This theory clashes sharply with those expressed in many recent articles that attribute movements in housing starts primarily to the effect of changes in interest rates, maturities, and loan-to-value ratios on consumers' demand for space.

While starts are influenced by credit, as is evident from Figure 2, the channel of causation appears to be through inventories rather than final demand. Both analysis and policy will differ significantly, depending upon whether credit causes a temporary disequilibrium of inventories or a basic change in the number of housing units demanded by consumers.

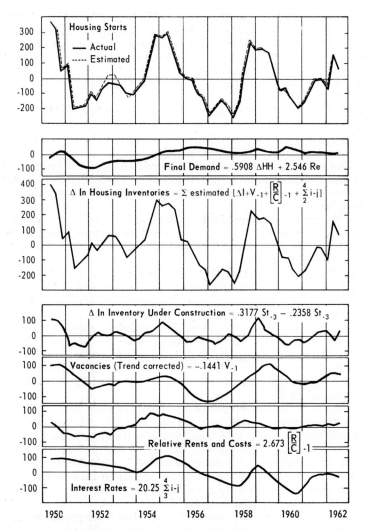

Fig. 2. Relationships between housing starts and the independent variables (thousands of starts—seasonally adjusted annual rates).

It is difficult to find any logical channel of causation between credit and household formation.[3] Few newly formed households purchase homes. In 1960 census components of change show that only 7.5 per cent of households formed in 1958–59 owned their own homes. Since these households include a large

---

[3] There is, of course, almost certainly a relationship between credit and the average expenditure of households on housing. A failure to distinguish between demand for a certain number of houses and the average value of each leads to some of the errors in analysis.

number of reconstituted ones (i.e., households formed by widowed, divorced, separated persons, etc.) whose members probably owned homes under their previous marital status, it is likely that only one or two per cent of new households purchase dwellings during their first two years of existence. Almost certainly, only a small fraction of these, and therefore an insignificant part of the total, would delay marriage or refrain from forming their own households because of credit changes.

For financing to affect the formation of non-owner households, it must first alter rents; then, higher rents must deter people from marrying or undoubling. There is no reason to expect credit to have short-run impact on rents. Furthermore, rents, averaging about 15 per cent of income, are only part of the cost of establishing a household. Given the high psychic costs of delayed marriages or merged households, it appears that reactions to changed prices or rents are likely either to be small or to influence long-run rather than cyclical changes in household formation.

Given the normal situation of a large stock of households growing at a slow rate, an acceleration could make even small percentage increases in total households important for new starts; but such movements do not seem to have occurred in recent years.

Figure 2 shows little relationship between credit and household formation (it actually is negative). This lack of any positive correlation between household change and credit or house prices has generally been found in previous studies as well.

In the three cycles since 1950, actual disequilibrium movements consisted of almost equal changes in inventories of units under construction and available vacancies. The larger actual movements in inventories under construction result from shocks transmitted through the remaining variables. The amplitudes of the endogenous movements are increased by the other forces particularly in 1954, 1958, and 1960.

The level of vacancies appears to play a role in each cycle. Below-normal vacancies gave impetus to additional building in 1950 and accounted for most of the rise in starts in 1957, 1958, and 1961. On the other hand, the expansion of starts in 1954 and 1955 caused a backlog of empty units which were an important cause of decreased building in 1956–57. A similar reaction occurred in 1959. Throughout the period, vacancies appear to have had far more influence on starts than most observers noted.

The data used to represent the ratio of rents to costs are not as sensitive an index as one would hope for because of the notorious inadequacies in the underlying data. Still the relatively low level of rents resulting from rent control seems to have had a depressing effect on starts through most of 1952, causing demand to be deferred during this period. In 1953 and 1954, rents shot up much faster than costs, thus adding to the expansion.

The high level of starts in 1954 and 1955 led to a rapid rise in costs, which in turn helped to make building or speculating on starts less profitable. Since 1956, except for a small impetus given to the boom of 1958, the influence of these variables has been slight.

The final variable consists of lagged short-term interest rates. According to the equation, credit, vacancies, and the inventory cycle account for approximately equal parts of the total variance in starts. As explained earlier, our hypothesis states that changes in the cost and availability of credit cause important disturbances in the rate of inventory accumulation. Builders and promoters increase starts because their potential profits grow as discounts fall or the amount of equity required is decreased. In addition, with more favorable terms, they may attract existing households from other parts of the market. As long as their inventories remain low, their profits grow. However final demand does not expand with starts. When the increased inventory is mainly in units under construction, builders feel only slight pressure to change their action. Eventually, however, as the number of empty completed units grows, pressure mounts to cut back starts. Timing depends on both the period of production and the lags between starts and particular types of vacancies.

Finally, Figure 2 shows significant longer-run movements. In 1950 there was still a backlog of final demand. Builders were more likely to receive premiums than to pay discounts for their financing; vacancies were below a desirable level; households were still doubled up; rent control was in the process of being dismantled; the high demand allowed only minimum removals. Between 1950 and 1956, most of these aftereffects of the war worked themselves out of the system. Since 1957, the number of starts has averaged about 1,366,000 units per year, with a high quarter rate of 1,604,000 and a low of 1,162,000. With this production, available vacancies have accumulated at the rate of about 60,000 per year, slightly below the assumed equilibrium.

There is no obvious reason for the average level of starts to vary much in the near future. Only if sudden economic changes or governmental policy should drastically alter the present levels of basic demand or if vacancies begin to change rapidly, would the number of units constructed over the next five years vary sharply from the previous five.

The probabilities of continued instability also appear to remain unaltered. Basic factors of lags, acceleration, and poor information have not changed, and the system continues to be plagued by unstable forces. The possibility of serious outside shocks remains strong. Only a major increase in knowledge, combined with government policies specifically designed to compensate for, rather than accentuate, normal market instability would appear to offer much hope for improvement.

STUDY PROJECT 17

INPUT-OUTPUT ANALYSIS FOR MISSISSIPPI *

Introduction

Input-Output analysis is associated with the work of Professor Wassily Leontief and, simply stated, is concerned with the quantitative analysis of the interdependence of producing and consuming units in an economy. The genesis of input-output analysis can be traced to the Tableau Economique of Quesnay published in 1758. Leontief was the first to formulate (1936) an empirical input-output analysis based upon the interdependence of producing and consuming units. Since 1936 a considerable amount of work has been done in this area. Over twenty countries have published some type of input-output table including the massive 1947 table published for the United States by the Bureau of Labor Statistics. . . . With the considerable amount of interest in this type of analysis, Leontief and others have made a significant amount of variations

* John G. D. Carden, *Bureau of Business & Economic Research,* Vol. XX, No. 4 (February, 1960), University of Mississippi.

and improvements upon his original formulation. One of the more significant developments, perhaps, is the use of linear and non-linear programming methods. However, the ordinary input-output techniques as opposed to various adaptations employing linear programming still have a greater practical value because of the severe data requirements imposed by the more demanding system of linear programming. Because meaningful statistical information concerning the Mississippi economy is limited, the "economy features" of the ordinary input-output analysis model are better suited for our problems.

The Basic Theory of Input-Output Analysis

The description which follows will present three tables or matrices. Each matrix, culminating with the third matrix, represents a distinct step in the development of the final input-output matrix. Once the final matrix is developed, specific questions about the economy can be answered.

The analysis begins with the assumption that in order to produce outputs (for example, canned poultry) inputs are necessary (feed, manpower, fuel, to mention a few). To analyze an economy all the inputs required to produce a commodity or service are assembled and this process, in turn, is repeated for all goods and services produced by the economy. Table 1 shows this relation.

Table 1. X Matrix in Dollars—Total Dollar Amount of All Goods and Services Purchased and Produced in a Hypothetical Economy in a Given Year

| Producing Sectors–Outputs | Purchasing Sectors–Inputs | | | |
	Manu-facturing	Agri-culture	Final Demand	Total
Manufacturing	10	30	60	100
Agriculture	30	20	50	100
Land, Labor Capita	60	50		
Total	100	100		200

Table 1 (the X matrix) shows the total dollar amount, in a given year, which each sector has purchased and produced in our hypothetical economy. For purposes of illustration our economy has been aggregated into a 3×3 matrix containing three purchasing sectors–inputs (manufacturing, agriculture, and land, labor and capital). It should be recognized that an actual matrix for Mississippi would be subdivided into considerably more sectors.

We can see by reading down any column how much that industry purchased from all other industries in the economy including itself. Manufacturing, for example, in order to produce its total output or final bill of goods ($100), purchased $10 of inputs from itself (manufacturing), $30 of inputs from agriculture and $60 of inputs from land, labor and capital. Similarly, by reading across the rows, the allocation of the total output of a specific industry can be determined. For example, manufacturing sold $10 of its output to itself, $30 to agriculture and $60 to final demand. The analytical system by definition is balanced, i.e., total inputs must equal total outputs for each industrial sector and therefore for the entire economy.

For the sake of presentation, the assumption has been made that our hypothetical economy neither imports nor exports goods or services. Because

Mississippi is not a self-contained economy, the problem of incorporating exports and imports into the system will be treated in a later portion of this article.

The Sectors

It is important that the significance of the sectors be explained. The first two columns and the first two rows (manufacturing and agriculture) represent the processing sectors in our hypothetical economy. The third column (final demand) and the third row (land, labor and capital) represent the final demand sectors of our economy. The column labeled final demand consists of construction, maintenance, government purchases, consumption by households and savings. The row entry labeled land, labor and capital is the counterpart of the final demand sectors. It represents the output of the final demand sectors. For example, households purchase manufactured and agricultural goods and produce labor (farmers and machinists) as the payment for these goods.

The values in the final demand sector must be stated before answering any problems concerning the processing sectors. Moreover, the analysis is based on the assumption that the combined consumption requirements of the final demand sector determines the production levels of the processing sectors (manufacturing and agriculture). The relation between the final demand sectors and the processing sectors are similar to the concepts of induced and autonomous demand.

To make the model more operationally effective, it must have incorporated into it, as non-autonomous factors, segments of the final demand sector such as savings and exports by assuming that these previously autonomous elements are in some way determined by the level of production. The discussion of imports and exports later in the article will give an example of this problem.

The usefulness of Table 1 (the X matrix) is limited to examining the underlying economic interrelationships which bind together the various segments of our hypothetical economy. The economic interrelationships can be stated in terms of a series of input coefficients which are expressed as direct purchases per dollar of output. Table 2 (the A matrix) introduces the concept of input coefficients.

Table 2. A Matrix—Input Coefficients Indicating Direct Purchases per Dollar of Output

Producing (Output)	Purchasing (Input)	
	Manufacturing	Agriculture
Manufacturing	.10	.30
Agriculture	.30	.20

Table 2 (the A matrix) is derived from Table 1 (the X matrix) by dividing each individual input of the processing sectors by the total amount of inputs for that processing sector. The final demand sectors have been eliminated from Table 2 because of the earlier statement that this sector will be considered outside the system. The table indicates the direct amount of inputs required per dollar of output. Thus an increase of $1.00 in the output of manufactured goods will require an increase of $.30 of agricultural goods.

The figures in Table 2 are input or production coefficients representing direct purchases per dollar of output. The concept of input coefficients is central to the theory: for input-output analysis is based on the premise that all productive activities in the economy can be divided into sectors whose interdependence can be stated in terms of input coefficients. The concept of input coefficients is derived from three basic assumptions.

1) Each commodity is supplied by a single producing sector. From this assumption, two subsidiary assumptions are made. (a) Only one production method is used for producing each group of goods. (b) Each sector has only a single primary output. Referring to Table 2, manufactured goods are supplied by only the manufacturing sector, not by the agricultural sector. Moreover, only one scarce factor (or fixed relative prices of factors) and no joint produc-sector is manufactured goods, not agricultural goods.

2) Each sector's purchase of inputs is a direct linear function of that sector's level of outputs. This is a further refinement of the earlier statement that each producing sector's level of total output is a function of final demand. By assuming a direct linear relation, the system precludes both the effects of price changes of inputs and substitution of inputs.

3) The possibility of external economies and diseconomies is ruled out of the system by the assumption that the total effect of carrying on several types of productions is the sum of the separate effects.

The stability of the input-coefficients is the main criticism of input-output analysis. The argument is that the input coefficients are not stable over any meaningful period of time and the system, therefore, loses its effectiveness.

The degree of stability of the input coefficients depends partially upon how the sectors of the matrix are selected and partially upon the underlying properties of the productive system.

Changes in the productive process can arise from (1) technological alternatives, (2) composition of demand and (3) relative prices of the inputs. Over the long run, technological changes do take place which can affect technological alternatives and the composition of demand. However, the changes occur in a gradual process whose direction and rate of change are predictable. Adjustments to the coefficients can then be made. Concerning the relative prices of inputs, Samuelson and others have shown that in a competitive system having only one scarce factor (or fixed relative prices of factors) and no joint production, relative commodity prices will be fixed.

The input-output system described so far only portrays the structural inter-relationships of our hypothetical economy. The system is incomplete as a tool for measuring the total multiplicative impact of a change in final demand. By introducing Table 3 (the inverse matrix) the total multiplicative impact of any change in final demand can be directly measured.

Table 3. Inverse of the (I-A) Matrix—Direct and Indirect Purchases per Dollar of Final Demand

	Manufacturing	Agriculture
Manufacturing	1.269	.476
Agriculture	.476	1.428

The inverse matrix can be derived by either determinants or the process of iteration. Table 3 was derived through iteration. The process of iteration used to obtain the inverse matrix represented the following summation for each cell: $I + A + A^2 + A^3 + A^4 + \ldots$, where I equalled the indentity matrix

1	0
0	1

and A is the matrix of coefficients shown in Table 2. While Table 2 showed the direct purchases per dollar of output, Table 3 shows both the direct and indirect purchases per dollar of final demand. By inverting the 1-A matrix we are able to express in single coefficients the direct and indirect requirements from each industry associated with a given final demand after all requirements have had a chance to diffuse themselves throughout the economy. By telescoping the total repercussive effects of a given change in final demand input-output analysis assumes its real significance. The logic of the inverse matrix is analogous to Keynes' simultaneous multiplier which shows the total effect on income after all transactions have been completed through the economy.

To illustrate the value of the inverse matrix, assume that the final demand sector should increase its demand for manufactured goods by $100. By referring to Table 3 the total requirements placed upon the economy to fulfill the increased demand will be $126.90 of goods from manufacturing and $47.60 of goods from the agricultural sector. This is the total direct and indirect impact upon the economy. The A matrix, on the other hand, would show only the first round effects of an increase in final demand and considerable calculations would have to be performed in order to know the total multiplicative impact upon the economy.

The article to this point has attempted to show how input-output analysis, by providing a conceptual framework, can allow considerable statistical material to be assembled so that the structural interrelationship can be examined in terms of input coefficients which can be used to project the total multiplicative impact upon the economy of any change in final demand for any specific commodity.

Specific Application to Mississippi

The Mississippi Industrial and Technological Research Commission is in the process of applying input-output analysis to Mississippi as a tool for the state's economic development program.

The analysis is the responsibility of Mr. F. Brown Whittington and the author. The data for the matrix will come from *The Census of Manufactures* statistics, United States Department of Agriculture figures and data from individual accounting records within the state. It is intended that approximately a 35 × 35 to 45 × 45 matrix will be completed . . . . Further modifications of the Mississippi matrix would be the development of individual matrices for such sectors as agriculture, food and kindred products and lumber and wood products.

Several results are expected from the analysis of Mississippi:

1. By establishing a series of "production multipliers," those economic opportunities which will have the greatest multiplicative impact upon the economy per dollar of total output, can be indicated. With this information, a perennial question of economic development personnel can be partially answered: "What type of industry should we seek for our state?"

2. The Mississippi matrix will indicate the ratio of imports and exports to total output for each economic sector. The import information will indicate where and to what extent the state is losing significant manufacturing opportunities. Development personnel can then analyze this information, and possibly correct the reasons for these lost opportunities.

The export information will indicate quantitatively where the economy is most dependent upon trade outside of the state. This information can then be analyzed in terms of (1) the impact upon the Mississippi economy resulting from shifts in national demand; and (2) where Mississippi is losing manufacturing opportunities by shipping goods out of the state for further processing.

3. The matrix, by showing the interrelationship of all economic activity in the state, will assist the analyst in determining the combination of economic activities which will balance the desire for an accelerated growth of per capita income with the desire for growth which minimizes cyclical fluctuations.

4. The Mississippi matrix will provide a valuable tool for projection. With the help of input-output analysis, the Research Commission plans to project future labor requirements for specific industrial sectors. This information should be invaluable to the state educational system in planning technical and industrial training programs to meet the future labor requirements of Mississippi industry.

Another application for governmental purposes would be the projection of state tax revenues. Given certain estimates of final demand, the gross revenue of various economic sectors can be projected.

Input-output analysis has immediate application for the individual industrialist. Given certain estimates of final demand, industry by industry projections can be made of total output. These projections, for example, can be equated in terms of power needs or transportation needs.

As long as the information which the industrialist might require is a function of the total output of an industry or a group of industries, input-output analysis is a valuable tool for projection.

5. As an inevitable by-product, input-output analysis is highly effective in organizing previously existing statistical information. The fact that each output of each industry has to be balanced with its inputs, demands an accuracy and preciseness which can only be equalled in national income accounting. It is quite natural to expect that a considerable amount of new information and insights will evolve for the analysis. New areas for research will surely be indicated. The statistical by-products, in themselves, are a strong argument for the study.

In conclusion, it should be emphasized that input-output analysis is only a tool, not a panacea, for the state's economic development problems. The analysis surpasses other systems in providing a framework for understanding the structure of the Mississippi economy. However, for the analysis to be truly effective, it must be coupled with other techniques and good judgment.

STUDY PROJECT 18

ECONOMIC BASE ANALYSIS
BEL AIRE

Bel Aire is located in an agricultural and mining area of a state having no large cities. Bel Aire is several hundred miles from a major industrial center. Employment opportunities have diminished and there has been a reluctance on the part of the residents to move on; hence, there is a surplus of labor in Bel Aire.

In the past half century the rate of population growth in the town of Bel Aire has not kept pace with that of the rest of the nation. Except for the decade of the thirties the population has decreased in every decade since 1910. By the way of contrast, the nation as a whole has had significant population increases in the same period (see Table 1).

Table 1. Population Changes: Bel Aire and the United States

Year	Bel Aire	Per Cent Change	United States	Per Cent Increase
1960	12,000	−4	180,676,000	19.1
1950	12,500	−3.84	151,689,000	14.8
1940	13,000	+23.8	132,122,000	7.2
1930	10,500	−8.69	123,188,000	15.7

In Bel Aire at the last census the male population was 48.9 per cent of the total. This ratio is slightly under the national average of 49.7 per cent. There is a significant difference in age groups of the population of Bel Aire as compared with the rest of the nation. The percentage of preschool (under 5) and school age (5 to 19) population is under the national average, whereas the percentage of the older age groups (60 and over) is higher than the national average.

Approximately 95 per cent of the Bel Aire population are native-born caucasians. The median number of school years completed is 8.5 years, which is slightly under the national average.

Three-fourths of the labor force of Bel Aire is male.

The major sources of employment by type of industry are agriculture, retail trade, mining, and manufacturing (see Table 2). The firms are small in size, the largest firm employing less than 200 persons and only three firms employing more than 100 persons.

Bel Aire has an adequate urban plant.

Table 2. Employment in Bel Aire

	1958	Per Cent
Total employed	4,000	100
Agriculture	900	22.5
Mining	600	15
Construction	250	6.25
Manufacturing	450	11.25
Transportation	200	5
Utilities	100	2.5
Wholesale trade	50	1.25
Retail trade	850	21.25
Medical, educational, and professional services	300	7.5
Public administration	300	7.5

STUDY PROJECT 19

HAWAII *

Hawaii, Our New Pacific State

Statehood for Hawaii means that the Pacific States will not be three but five —Washington, Oregon, California, Alaska and Hawaii. Thus, America fills out its Far West, reaching from the crest of the Rockies to the far Aleutians and now to the sunny beaches of Hawaii.

Hawaii is a major market for products of the Pacific Northwest and accounts also for an important share of waterfront activity in Puget Sound and the Columbia River.

The list of goods that move from our ports to the Islands reads like the roll call of Pacific Northwest industry. At the top of the list are lumber, plywood, shingles, piling and paper products—output of our evergreen forests destined for the homes and industry of tropical islands.

Next largest group of products shipped to Hawaii are flour and feed—the products of the wheat and grain farms of our interior. Then come the products of our fields and orchards—canned and frozen fruits, berries and vegetables and canned milk. Machinery made in Oregon and Washington also goes to Hawaii, plus a wide variety of consumer products.

Hawaii, in turn, ships a number of products for use in this region. The big items are sugar and canned pineapple. Other items include by-products of the sugar industry—molasses and also an insulation board made from bagasse which competes here with insulation boards made from Northwest trees. But the volume of goods brought to Oregon and Washington from Hawaii is only about one-third as large as the volume we ship out.

Attraction to Investors

Growth in Hawaii, particularly in Honolulu, brings other direct ties with the Pacific Northwest. Recent years have seen important examples where private capital, built up in earlier days of lumbering, salmon packing and shipping, has made important hotel and airline investments in Hawaii. Capital is attracted to Hawaii for a number of reasons. For one thing, westerners naturally look westward for expansion—to Alaska, the Orient and Hawaii. In addition, investment in Hawaii offers diversification and an opportunity to participate in the growth of a coming section of the West.

This looking westward to our newest state is seen in other industries too. Most insurance companies with home offices in Oregon and Washington are licensed to do business in Hawaii. This is true both of those writing life insurance and annuities and those offering fire and casualty insurance. For these companies Hawaii offers opportunity for new growth.

Weyerhaeuser Timber Company last year opened a plant to make container board for Hawaiian industry. Crown Zellerbach Corporation, in co-operation with the Hawaiian Sugar Planters Association, is operating a pilot plant at

* By permission of the Pacific 1st Federal Savings & Loan Association, Tacoma, Washington.

Crown's research center, Camas, Washington, that uses sugar cane residue as raw material for paper.

Lure For Tourists

In many ways the most glamorous aspect of Hawaii is the tourist trade. One sign of this is the increasing number who board a plane to spend anywhere from a week end to a month on the Islands. Another sign is the frequency with which manufacturers and retailers, in launching promotions for consumer products, offer a fully paid vacation in Honolulu as the top prize. Few promotions, they find, have the appeal of one that beckons, "the Islands are calling you to the land of year-round sunshine."

Not all the passengers who fly from the Pacific Northwest to Honolulu live here. A good number come from the Midwest, some on individual trips, others on tours. The lure of Hawaii brings these people through our area and offers an opportunity to promote a side visit and local sightseeing. Airlines, for example, currently are promoting stopovers in Portland to visit the Oregon Centennial this summer. Fishing and mountain scenery are other attractions offered to encourage stopovers.

Thus Hawaii, like Alaska, becomes another magnet to draw America ever westward. In that movement, the West itself is helped to reach its aspirations in growth and maturity.

STUDY PROJECT 20

CITIES DO NOT ALWAYS GROW *

The record of most American cities, with the exception of mining and lumber towns, during the entire period of our national history, has been one of almost continuous growth. There is no universal law that guarantees the growth of cities without any setback. However, as a result, usually of capture or bombing, some cities in both ancient and modern times have been almost blotted out but then have come back again from total destruction to new heights. Some examples are as follows:

City	Population at Peak Before Decline	Population at Bottom	Latest Population
Rome	1,100,000 (A.D. 200)	1,000 (A.D. 475)	2,160,000 (1963)
Athens	110,000 (460 B.C.)	2,000 (1822)	1,852,000 (1963)
Constantinople-Istanbul	700,000 (A.D. 400)	2,000 (1453)	1,924,000 (1963)
Tokyo city	7,800,000 (1942)	1,607,000 (1944)	8,800,000 (1964)
Warsaw	1,179,000 (1930)	–	1,232,000 (1964)
Cologne	757,000 (1930)	450,000 (1940)	1,300,000 (1963)
Alexandria, Egypt	700,000 (100 B.C.)	20,000 (1800)	1,348,000 (1963)
Cuzco, Peru	200,000 (A.D. 1500)	0 (1536)	65,000 (1963)
Baghdad	750,000 (A.D. 800–900)	15,000 (1650)	1,000,000 (1963)
Moscow city	1,506,000 (1910)	1,028,000 (1920)	6,388,000 (1964)
Leningrad city	1,911,000 (1919)	706,000 (1920)	3,607,000 (1964)

No modern city of any substantial size has been wiped out and abandoned. Yet there are a number of the greatest ancient cities, once teeming with thousands of people, that are now either desolate wastes or unpopulated ruins. Thebes and Memphis in Egypt have left only stone monuments. Babylon, once the greatest city on earth, with a population of at least 350,000 at its peak,

* Homer Hoyt, April 26, 1965.

after being destroyed four times and rebuilt, at last came to the end of its existence after a life of 1,374 years. Other great cities near its site, Selucia and Ctesiphon, lasted for 476 and 957 years respectively. Nineveh, capital of Assyria, was blotted out after a short life of 93 years, from 705 B.C. to 612 B.C. Knossus, in Crete, with a population of probably 40,000, lived from 1700 B.C. to 1400 B.C. Pataliputra, which with 500,000 inhabitants, was the world's largest city of the time (300 B.C.) has completely disappeared. Angkor, in Cambodia, which in the year 1000, with 1,500,000 inhabitants, was the largest city on earth, is now deserted and has left only the vast temple Angkor Vat. Long gone, of course, are man's earliest cities, Ur and Uruk in Babylonia, dating back to the third and fourth millennia B.C., as is also Mahenjo-Daro in India, a highly civilized city of 4,500 years ago, whose ruins were only discovered in 1925.[1]

> The lion and lizard keep the courts where Jamshyd
> gloried and drank deep.
>
> *Omar Khayyam*

Instead of a prospective decline, it is now predicted that existing metropolitan areas will, barring an atomic war, knit together into a series of megalopolitan urban agglomerations. Not only will Washington, D.C., and Baltimore merge into one city, but the entire area from Norfolk, Virginia, to Boston will become virtually a prolongated urban mass, extending for a distance of over 500 miles. Vacant gaps are now being filled in with such projects as the 16,000-acre Columbia City and 1,600-acre Crofton, between Washington and Baltimore. Everywhere there is a rush from rural areas to the metropolis, even if the newcomers have to live in the huts and favellas of Rio de Janeiro, the ranchitos of Caracas or the barrios of Lima. The author has estimated that the world urban population of 3.4 billion in the year 2000 would exceed the entire population of the earth in 1965.[2]

All of the 6,000 years of recorded human history, beginning with the first cities to the present, is but a few seconds in geological time. It seems, however, a long time to real estate men of today who calculate in terms of 1 to not over 25 years into the future. The six millennia of land transactions in thousands of cities seems to have little application to current real estate problems of today. However, there are some records of density of population in ancient cities that afford a basis of measurement with urban densities today.

Ancient cities were practically all enclosed by walls, except Knossus, with very narrow streets of 6 to 8 feet in width, excepting the ceremonial avenues, as in Dubrovnik today, a 1,000-year-old city on the Dalmatian Coast of Yugoslavia.

The density of population per square mile of ancient cities was very great, as is shown in the next table.

Great as these densities are, they were equalled or exceeded on the Lower East Side in Manhattan, New York City, in 1910, when 500,000 people lived in six-story tenements on 1,000 acres, which is a density of 320,000 to the square mile. The population density of ancient cities is also equalled or exceeded by present densities in some areas in Hong Kong, Calcutta, and Bombay.

On the other hand, as a result of the automobile and concrete highways, which increases commuting distances to work, cities in the United States today

[1] Wolf Schneider, *Babylon Is Everywhere* (1960) (English trans.; New York: McGraw-Hill Book Co., 1963), p. 55.

[2] Homer Hoyt, *World Urbanization,* Urban Land Institute, *Technical Bulletin #43* (April, 1962), Table 17, p. 50.

POPULATION DENSITIES OF ANCIENT CITIES

City	Population	Area in Square Miles	Population per Square Mile
Rome, A.D. 100	1,100,000	5.2	211,500
Rome (within Servilian walls)	600,000	1.55	389,000
Alexandria, Egypt, A.D. 100	700,000	3.6	195,000
Pataliputra, India, 300 B.C.	500,000	10.8	46,000
Carthage, 200 B.C.	300,000	7.7	39,000
Nineveh, 650 B.C.	120,000	2.6	46,000
Uruk, 3000 B.C.	100,000	1.7	59,000
Syracuse, Sicily, 300 B.C.	400,000	5.4	74,000
Total	3,220,000		
Average all ancient cities above		3.70	87,000

SOURCE: Wolf Schneider, *Babylon Is Everywhere* (1960) (English trans.; New York: McGraw-Hill Book Co., 1963), p. 138.

have far less densities than the ancient cities enclosed by walls. In our 213 urbanized areas, the average density of population in central cities is only 5,349 persons to the square mile and 2,575 persons per square mile in our urban fringe areas. While the seven walled cities of ancient times, with a total population of 3,220,000, were concentrated within walled areas totaling 37 square miles, the United States urbanized population of 213 areas of 95,848,487 in 1960, was spread out over 25,544.3 square miles of land.[3] The population density of our central areas has declined from 7,786 per square mile in 1950 to 5,349 in 1960,[4] as a result of the movement to the suburbs.

The land area from the center of the city increases with the square of the radius and the automobile and the new highways have made it possible to use the entire periphery of American cities rather than only the narrow bands along suburban railroads. The lower values for the raw land opened up by the automobile and expressways, permit the construction of single-family homes on wide lots instead of the dense apartments on narrow streets. In ancient Rome some of the tenements were 115 feet high, or up to 11 stories, with but one room for each apartment. As many as 500 people lived under one roof. Rents were so much higher in Rome than in the suburbs that even the free bread barely made living costs in Rome equal to those in areas beyond the walls.

Thus the effect of density on high rents and land values was apparent 1,800 years ago.[5]

The highest population densities today are in central apartment areas like Manhattan, New York City, 77,200 to the square mile, and New York City as a whole, 24,697 to the square mile; Chicago, a mixture of large and small buildings and single-family houses, where the density is 15,836 to the square mile; or row house cities like Philadelphia, Washington, D.C., and Baltimore, with population densities respectively of 15,743, 12,442, and 11,886 to the square mile.

[3] 1960 Census of Population, Table 22.
[4] In 1950 there were only 157 urbanized areas compared to 213 in 1960.
[5] Schneider, *op. cit.*, p. 139.

STUDY PROJECTS

The Largest Cities of Antiquity

Population

1. Rome   1,100,000–2d century A.D.
2. Alexandria   700,000–1st century B.C.
3. Seleucia   600,000–3d century B.C.
4. Pataliputra   500,000–4th century B.C.
5. Syracuse   400,000–4th century B.C.
6. Babylon   350,000–6th century B.C.
7. Antioch   350,000–3d century B.C.
8. Carthage   300,000–3d century B.C.
9. Cuttack (India)   300,000–2d century B.C.
10. Agrigento   200,000–400 B.C.
11. Ephesus   200,000–3d century B.C.
12. Caesarea   200,000–2d century B.C.

Cities That Were the World's Largest in Their Time

				Population
4th millennium B.C.	Ur	Babylonia	Iraq	30,000
3rd millennium B.C.	Uruk	Babylonia	Iraq	100,000
1700–700 B.C.	Babylon	Babylonia	Iraq	150,000
6th century B.C.	Nineveh	Assyria	Iraq	120,000
600–400 B.C.	Babylon	Babylonia	Iraq	350,000
400–300 B.C.	Pataliputra	Magadha	India	500,000
300–150 B.C.	Seleucia	Seleucid Empire	Iraq	600,000
150 B.C.–A.D. 350	Rome	Roman Empire	Italy	1,100,000
350 B.C.–A.D. 800	Byzantium	East Roman Empire	Turkey	700,000
A.D. 800–900	Baghdad	Empire of the Caliphs	Iraq	750,000
900–1100	Angkor	Khmer Empire	Cambodia	1,500,000
1100–1300	Hangchow	China	China	2,000,000
1300–1850	Peking	China	China	2,550,000
1850–1920	London	England	England	8,000,000
1920–1957	New York	U.S.A.	U.S.A.	14,100,000
Since 1957	Tokyo	Japan	Japan	20,000,000

SOURCE: Wolf Schneider, *Babylon Is Everywhere* (1960) (English trans.; New York: McGraw-Hill Book Co., 1963).

These central cities had their main growth before the automobile came into general use.

On the other hand, in Los Angeles, which has grown chiefly during the automobile age, the average population density, even in the central city, is only 5,451 persons per square mile.

STUDY PROJECT 21

MARKET SURVEY OF CHESTNUT GROVE, MAY, 1965

Estimated Rents at Chestnut Grove

As Table 2 shows, rents on minimum guarantees at Chestnut Grove are estimated at $190,100 for 1966 when the center is in full operation. This is an average of $2.06 for the 92,520 square feet in all the stores. The minimum rents estimated for stores not leased are given in Table 2. In Table 2 rents on percentage leases are estimated at $258,600 which should be realized by 1968.

Estimated Cost of Constructing Chestnut Grove

Chestnut Grove should be constructed at a cost of $1,110,000 for the 92,520 square feet of buildings, or $12.00 a square foot which would include paving of parking areas, air conditioning in all stores, architect's fees, builder's profit, and interest during construction.

Table 1. Estimated Sales of Stores at Chestnut Grove, 1966

Type of Store	Building	Sales	Area in Square Feet	Sales per Square Foot
Supermarket	A	$3,000,000	18,000	$167
Furniture	A	500,000	18,000	28
Women's lingerie	B	150,000	3,000	50
Family shoe store	B	150,000	2,500	60
Household appliances, TV	B	300,000	6,500	46
Beauty shop	B	100,000	1,500	67
Barber shop	B	60,000	860	70
Cafeteria	B	250,000	4,040	62
Bakery	B	90,000	1,500	60
Optician	B	60,000	1,000	60
Book store, stationery	B	100,000	1,500	67
Drug store	C	1,000,000	15,360	65
Cleaning establishment	C	300,000	7,500	40
Restaurant	C	500,000	7,860	64
Candy	D	70,000	700	100
Florist	D	30,000	750	40
Greeting cards	D	40,000	550	73
Bank	E	–	1,400	–
Total: all buildings		$6,700,000	92,520	$ 73.53
Ground area occupied by stores			59,160	
Balance of area for mall and parking or 3.12 times leasable area			289,320	
Total area			348,480	

Interest and Amortization Charges

The cost of the buildings should be entirely financed by a mortgage loan of $1,100,000 at an 8 per cent constant rate of which 5¾ per cent or less would be interest and the balance amortization, which would also represent depreciation.

Operating Expenses

Operating expenses should not exceed 55 cents a square foot of gross leasable area. This includes real estate taxes, insurance, exterior maintenance,

Table 2.   Estimated Rents of Chestnut Grove, 1966–1968

Type of Store	Gross Leasable Area in Square Feet	Minimum Guarantee per Square Foot	Per Cent of Sales	Estimated Sales	Rents Received	
					On Minimum Guarantee 1966	On Percentages 1968
Building A						
Supermarket	18,000	$2.05	1.5	$3,000,000	$ 36,500	$ 45,000
Furniture store	18,000	1.25	5	500,000	22,500	25,000
Total Building A	36,000	1.64	2	3,500,000	59,000	70,000
Building B						
Women's lingerie, sportswear	3,000	3.00	6	150,000	9,000	9,000
Family shoe store	2,500	2.50	5	150,000	6,250	7,500
Household appliances, TV	6,500	1.50	5	300,000	9,750	15,000
Beauty shop	1,500	4.00	10	100,000	6,000	10,000
Barber shop	860	4.00	10	60,000	3,440	6,000
Cafeteria	4,040	2.50	6	250,000	10,100	15,000
Bakery	1,500	2.00	5	90,000	3,000	4,500
Optician	1,000	3.00	10	60,000	3,000	6,000
Book store	1,500	3.00	10	100,000	4,500	10,000
Total Building B	22,400	2.46	6.6	1,260,000	55,040	83,000
Building C						
Drug store	15,360	2.20	4	1,000,000	33,790	40,000
Cleaners, etc.	7,500	2.00	6	300,000	15,000	18,000
Restaurant	7,860	2.00	6	500,000	15,720	30,000
Total Building C	30,720	2.10	4.9	1,800,000	64,510	88,000
Building D						
Candy	700	4.00	8	70,000	2,800	5,600
Florist	750	2.00	8	30,000	1,500	2,400
Greeting cards	550	3.00	10	40,000	1,650	4,000
Total Building D	2,000	2.98	8.6	140,000	5,950	12,000
Bank	1,400	4.00	–	–	5,600	5,600
Total All Stores	92,520	2.06	3.8	$6,700,000	$190,100	$258,600

management, advertising, and general administration. This is the average for neighborhood shopping centers in the northeastern states.[1]

Vacancy Allowance

No vacancy allowance is necessary for national chain stores with triple A credit but a vacancy allowance of 10 per cent is made for local stores without a national rating.

Estimated Net Return on Investment in Chestnut Grove

After making the deductions from the minimum guaranteed rentals of $190,100 there remains $44,814 as the annual net return on the land. Capitalized at 6 per cent this would produce a land value for the 8 acres of $747,000 or $93,375 an acre, or $2.14 a square foot, when the center is in full operation. The combined land and building value then would be $1,847,000. (Table 3.)

Table 3. Estimated Net Income of Chestnut Grove Shopping Center, 1966, Based on Minimum Guaranteed Rents *

Rents on minimum guaranteed rents	$190,100
Vacancy allowance 10% on local tenants with minimum guarantees of $56,000	5,600
Rents received	$184,500
Operating expenses	
55¢ per square foot on gross leasable area of 92,520 square feet (average for northeast area for neighborhood shopping centers)	50,886
Balance available for mortgage charges	$133,614
8% constant (5¾% interest balance amortization or depreciation) on building cost of $1,110,000 at $12 per square foot for 92,520 square feet buildings	88,800
Annual net return on land	$ 44,814
Land value capitalized at 6%	$747,000
Or	$ 93,375 per acre
	For 8 acres
Or	$2.14 per square foot

* With all leases signed but before center is in operation.

When and if percentage rents are realized by 1968, as Table 4 shows, the annual net return would be $110,000 as a result of the increase of rents from $190,100 to $258,600. The land value then would be $1,833,000 or $229,000 an acre or $5.25 a square foot. Nearly all of the increase in rents would accrue to net income and the $68,500 increase in rents would produce a $65,000 increase in net income. The land value would increase two and one-half times. The value of Chestnut Grove in 1968 for land and building would then be $2,933,000.

[1] Urban Land Institute, *The Dollars and Cents of Shopping Centers* (Washington, D.C.: The Institute, 1963), Table 6, p. 26.

Table 4. Estimated Net Income on Percentage Leases at Chestnut Grove, 1968 *

Rents on percentage leases		$ 258,600
Vacancy allowance 10% on local tenants with percentage rents of $88,000		8,800
Rents received		$ 249,800
Operating expenses 55¢ per square foot		50,886
Available for mortgage charges		$ 198,891
Interest and amortization at 8% constant on loan of $1,110,000 to cover building costs		88,800
Annual net income on land		$ 110,091
	Say	$ 110,000
Land value capitalized at 6%		$1,833,000
	Or	$ 229,000 per acre
	Or	$5.25 per square foot

* After all leases are signed and center is in operation with sales volumes actually realized.

STUDY PROJECT 22

BUILDING BOOM AND PRICE DECLINES *

The building boom that reshaped the face of America's cities in the postwar period is bearing bitter fruit for many real estate investors: A serious weakening of prices for older buildings.

Acute shortages of rental space until recently keep most pre-war buildings fully occupied despite mushrooming new construction. But shortages are ending, and new buildings are luring tenants away from older and less attractive apartments, factories, and offices. Vacancies mean falling income for these older properties and declining investment values.

A fall in rental income forces the seller of a commercial building to lower his selling price, because buyers often calculate what they'll pay on the basis of yield or return on their investment. Even after price concessions now being made, property shoppers view yields on many old buildings as too low. Current prices are still just below post-war highs and far above the original cost of these pre-war buildings.

The increasing number of vacancies, of course, is good news for many tenants. Over 7.5% of the nation's rentable office space and apartment units are now empty, roughly double the rate of a decade ago. Owners of some older buildings are cutting rents and many are launching extensive fix-up programs to keep tenants happy. But in some cases these measures only eat into profits of such properties.

Price Troubles Watched

Price troubles of investors owning older buildings will be watched closely. Pre-war buildings represent over half of the total value of the nation's income-

* *The Wall Street Journal*, Vol. XLIV, No. 85 (Wednesday, February 12, 1964), by Laurence G. O'Donnell, Staff Reporter.

producing properties. No precise figures are available on their value, but observers figure such structures are worth at least $100 billion and probably much more.

Already, softening prices have curtailed sales of older buildings in many areas as buyers and sellers haggle over prices. And they are plaguing some major property traders who buy buildings for quick resale, counting upon fast price appreciation for profits.

Webb & Knapp, Inc., one of the biggest traders, has been forced into a sweeping voluntary liquidation program, partly because it bought a number of properties in 1962 for quick resale. It found, "owing to the softness of the real estate market," that it couldn't turn them over as fast as it had expected.

The Real Estate Board of New York reported a few days ago that fewer properties changed hands on Manhattan last year than in any year since 1937. Only 1,812 buildings, chiefly walk-up apartment houses, were sold in 1963, down 14% from the previous year and 41% under the total five years earlier.

There's considerable controversy over the long-term significance of recent price weakness in older buildings. Says Warren P. Hunnicut, a St. Petersburg, Fla., real estate counselor, "Real estate prices (here) are at least 20% under those prevailing in 1956 to 1958. While property sales and asking prices are generally off their peaks, most of them were not worth their peak prices. Today's values are more realistic, but indications are they will not remain on the present plateau. Values are expected to rise as the slack is taken up."

Past Is No Guide

Others are less certain about price recovery. "You no longer can count on being rescued from investment mistakes by general price inflation," Jules Backman, professor of economics at New York University, warned in a recent speech to real estate investors. "Significant changes in market conditions mean that the earlier post-war experience is not a guide to the future," he said.

A Wall Street Journal survey of about 50 real estate brokers, counselors, investors and appraisers active in 32 cities from Birmingham, Ala., to Spokane, Wash., shows the extent of sagging prices on older buildings.

In Chicago, Detroit and 18 other cities, some or most types of old structures, including walk-up apartments, office and motels, now are changing hands at prices lower than levels reached a few years ago when such buildings hit their post-war price highs.

In some instances prices have dropped as much as 25% and a few buildings are being offered at what experts say is only slightly more than the value of land under them. The relentless pace of new building is blamed by most experts for downward pressure on prices of older buildings. "The minute you get over-building you reduce prices," declares one Boston real estate veteran.

Builders Unconcerned

The general easing of property prices doesn't worry builders—or so they say. They argue that new buildings have a competitive edge in attracting tenants because they're equipped with the air conditioning, automatic elevators and bright lighting which many older buildings lack.

Any overbuilding is temporary anyway, builders assert. And they note that the general economy is booming, a situation entirely different from that prevailing after the 1929 crash when a building glut accompanied the nation's plunge into depression.

Liberal financing available on new construction is also contributing to the woes in the marketing of older properties. Lenders often will provide up to 90% of the cost of a new building in a first mortgage loan. By contrast, lenders generally limit first mortgage loans to about two-thirds of the value of old buildings.

In Springfield, Ill., broker James P. McClernon says prices of older apartment houses there have tumbled 20% to 25% because large mortgage loans are harder to obtain on older buildings than on new ones.

The collapse of real estate syndication—a method of raising real estate investment funds through the sale of securities—is another reason for the drop in transfers in many areas. Syndication has been placed under a cloud in the past year and a half because of charges of fraud against certain promoters and the financial difficulties of many syndicates and companies. The trouble stemmed in some cases from vacancies in older buildings they owned.

It was the earlier buying programs of the syndicates that helped bid up prices of many older buildings in the first place. "I think we are letting some of the water out of prices in some buildings, particularly in metropolitan areas where big-time syndicates operate," says one real estate trust manager who has been seeking investments.

Interest in older buildings also is waning because of the exodus of people and jobs from some areas. "Cleveland's industrial (real estate) market is weak and deals are being made at rock bottom prices," says a broker with Cragin-Land-Free & Co., a Cleveland real estate firm. "Companies have consolidated and others have moved South," he adds, noting that one sizable industrial plant recently sold for $500,000, although the owners originally asked $1.5 million.

Apartment Price Drop

The tug-of-war over prices across the nation is most pronounced in the apartment house field. In Houston, appraiser V. P. Ringer reports medium-sized garden apartment projects that sold two or three years ago for 6 to 7½ times their gross income now bring only 5 to 7 times total revenues.

Louie Reese, a Birmingham, Ala., broker, says a garden apartment project there which was bought with a $30,000 cash investment four years ago was sold recently for only $10,000 cash, with the buyer assuming the existing mortgage. The former owner thus lost $20,000 plus whatever amount he had invested in mortgage payments.

Brokers report that buying interest is drying up for "strips" of retail stores in Detroit, Chicago and many other cities. Such groups of adjoining stores usually don't have enough parking space to compete with large shopping centers. Industrial and loft buildings, too, have fallen from favor with investors.

In Galveston, Tex., according to a real estate advisor there, "bargains are available and going begging." A Pittsburgh broker, Joseph J. Gumberg, says he handled a recent sale of an old warehouse in which the $90,000 final price was $35,000 under the owner's asking price.

The Cold Shoulder

Motels, too, are getting the cold shoulder from investors in most areas. Motel prices broke in 1963 after a seven-year boom, according to Stephen W.

Brenner, vice president of Helmsley-Spear. Inc., a New York brokerage firm and a consultant to many motel owners. The number of motels sold also has fallen off sharply.

"Many buyers are steering clear of motels today," says Mr. Brenner. "Statements of motel concerns for 1962 and business last year indicate a decline in gross income, mainly because of new motels and hotels." He says motels that cost $6,500 a room to build four years ago were fetching up to $10,000 a room a year ago. But now they're settling "at cost or below—even 30% below in some cases."

Even "bargain" prices for many older commercial buildings pegged below prevailing market levels sometimes fail to whet investor interest. Says one real estate man in a small Southwestern city, "One two-story office building here has been on the market for some time with no takers. This is an old building which was completely remodeled about two years ago. Although it is still well occupied, the tenancy is insecure and it cannot be sold for its cost."

STUDY PROJECT 23

SOME ASPECTS OF LAND PLANNING: THE LONGVIEW VALLEY CASE *

Growth of Longview Valley to 1956

Longview Valley, for the purposes of this study, is defined as all the area within the political limits of the city of Metropolis located north of the State Mountains, with the exception of the cities of Baxter and St. Regis. As such, it is a large basin containing 212 square miles extending to the base of the mountains on three sides—the north, south, and west and to the city of Baxter on the east. The mountains serve to isolate the Valley from the central city and roads and transportation routes connecting it with the central area are limited to the passes created by the breaks in the mountain formation.

The climate of the Valley is characterized by hot, dry summers and cool winters. Rainfall is usually concentrated in the months between November and April and falls in such volume that areas in the Valley have had to be reserved for drainage channels. Rainfall in the rest of the year, however, is so light that much agriculture can be conducted only with the aid of irrigation. Indeed, it was the completion of the aqueduct assuring a continuous and adequate water supply for farming that provided impetus for the annexation of a large portion of the Valley to the city in 1915.

In the early development of the Valley, wheat growing and stock raising were the predominant activities, although the very fertile soils in the west central area of the region were devoted to more intensive agricultural uses. With the advent of water, more and more of the land was utilized for fruit growing.

The street and highway pattern in Longview Valley conforms generally to the United States government land surveys, so streets are primarily oriented north and south or east and west. However, in the north and east section of

* Adapted from a study by Fred E. Case and James Gillies, "Some Aspects of Land Planning: The San Fernando Valley Case," first reported in *The Appraisal Journal* (January, 1955).

the Valley, the St. Regis Road and the city of St. Regis (which were established prior to the survey) influence the pattern of roads. In the central eastern section the topography of the area has made necessary certain deviations from the basic survey pattern. However, with these exceptions, major and secondary highways are located on section and quarter-section survey lines.

By 1930 some subdividing had taken place and small scattered communities were being formed. The impetus for such activity lay in the generally flat character of the area which made it possible to develop the land for suburban uses with minimum development costs. The Valley gradually became recognized as an attractive peripheral area in which to live and during the thirties and forties, the Valley population increased at a rapid rate. However, between 1950 and 1960, the Valley changed so completely that it became not only physically and politically, but also economically and socially an integral part of the central city.

Although the population of Longview Valley in 1950 was only 112,712 or less than 8% of the population of the city of Metropolis, the rate of population growth in the Valley between 1940 and 1950 was far greater than the rate of growth in either the city or the standard metropolitan area. The population increase in the Valley was generally concentrated around the new established centers, some of which grew as much as 150% in that period.

The rapid increase in population during the forties accelerated the demand for residential dwelling units. In 1940 there were about 15,000 units in the Valley and by 1950 the number had increased to approximately 36,200. Consequently, during the decade when population increased 123%, there was an increase of 130% in the number of housing units.

Industrial activity was practically nonexistent in Longview Valley in 1950. Although almost no official data of any kind were collected about industry in the area prior to 1950, some idea of the amount and kind of industrial operations which did exist may be obtained by a study of the industrial directories of Metropolis. These data indicate that the industry in Longview Valley during the period from 1940 to 1949 was chiefly light and of a service nature. The majority of the firms were small in terms of number of persons employed and the total number of these firms never averaged more than 80 per year during the entire decade of the thirties. Manufacturing and quasi-industrial activities within the group were food processing, furniture making, publishing (newspaper and printing), wholesale baking, ceramics, motion picture production, and wholesale dry cleaning and laundering.

Data on employment in Longview Valley in 1950 may be estimated by reference to the population and employment ratios for Metropolitan County and the city of Metropolis. On the basis of such estimates there were between 41,000 and 43,000 employed persons living in Longview Valley in 1950. This figure, however, does not indicate the number of persons employed by firms located in Longview Valley, since a substantial number of Valley residents were employed elsewhere.

Longview Valley in 1950, therefore, did not differ markedly from the Longview Valley of earlier years. The bulk of the area was used for agriculture and the urbanization which was occurring was largely associated with residential growth in established urban centers. Therefore, little conflict among land uses existed simply because the vast amounts of land available in the Valley provided adequate space for concurrent development by a variety of users. Land uses were controlled by means of the Residential District Ordinance of 1931 which was originally intended to be only an interim measure and although the Valley was largely used for agricultural purposes, the zoning regulations made no provision for agricultural uses within the city limits. The lack of reports of a large number of requests for changes in the control of land uses is probably the best indicator of a lack of land use conflicts.

Valley Growth, 1956–1960

Indexes of bank debits, retail trade, industrial activity, income, building, and real estate all showed favorable increases in the period from 1956 to 1960. Analysis of the 1959 Census of Manufacturers indicated that manufacturing was well diversified and was well balanced between heavy and light manufacturing and between durable and nondurable goods. Manufacturing played an increasing role in the area to such an extent that by the end of 1961 factory payrolls were higher than at any time. The aircraft industry became the most important source of industrial employment.

This general prosperity in the Metropolis district was reflected in Longview Valley. By 1960 the population of the Valley exceeded 310,000—an increase of 175% over 1950. This tremendous increase in population caused a continually increasing demand for residential dwelling units.

In 1960 there were 101,746 residential dwelling units in the Valley compared with 56,970 in 1956—an increase of 78.5% in five years. An important aspect of this new construction in the Valley was the part played by subdividers. Tract houses were constructed as builders integrated the entire real estate process—buying land and constructing and selling units, all within one enterprise. Such an operation, known as tract building, is essentially the application of some mass production methods to house construction. However, mass building is only possible when land is available and a large volume of sales can be made rapidly. Both these conditions were present in Longview Valley in this period as there was a large amount of level land suitable for building and there was a very active demand for housing.

An analysis of tracts recorded during the period of 1955–1962 shows that about 66% of all subdivisions recorded in the city were located in the Valley area. These subdivisions occupy 13,995 acres and consist of 51,020 lots. Units constructed on individual lots accounted for only a fraction of new residential construction in the Valley.

Growth in Valley, 1960–1965

Competition between industrial and residential developers for attractive building sites was extremely marked by 1960, and the continued urbanization of the Valley between 1960 and 1965 did not improve this situation. However, the 1956 plan for land use was sufficiently flexible that the Planning Commission was able to meet the needs of all parties by rezoning agricultural land for residential or industrial purposes, without apparently doing too great injustice to either residents or industries.

In the period between 1960 and 1965 the population of the Valley increased by 50.2% and housing by 42.8%. These increases were reflected in the sustained level of building permits and the increase in industry which amounted to an additional 50 firms. Employed persons increased to 220,000 and employed persons in manufacturing rose to 57,600. In response to these increases the amount of land zoned for urban uses was equal to almost 40% of the total area zoned and the amount of industrially zoned land was increased by 27.8%

Changes in land uses were typically accomplished only after the Planning Commission had made a thorough study of the physical problems involved and had estimated the amount of change required. In addition, conferences were held with those persons most interested in or likely to be affected by the proposed changes. For instance, on December 24, 1963 the City Council approved the changing of 1,380 acres zoned for RA, A1, A2 and C2 to M1 and M2 after the Planning Commission had conferred with the West Valley Property Owners Association and interested real estate firms.

Changes in land zoning resulting from actions of this nature were tacit recognition of the changing character of the Longview Valley and the inappropriateness of the original planning approach. The original plan had been based upon four premises—two of which involved prediction of the future course of Valley development. By 1960 these two predictions had not been realized—agriculture had not maintained its expected importance and the series of small, self-contained communities had not developed. The changes in zoning which were permitted between 1960 and 1965 were rejections of the validity of these premises.

The rapid urbanization of the Valley during the past ten years has led to a conflict of opinions over the appropriateness of the manner in which land uses have been permitted to develop. Some persons believe that more industry should be located in the area in order to maintain the present population and provide for further growth. Other persons believe that industrialization would be detrimental to further residential growth and should not be encouraged. However, even though these conflicts have not been completely resolved, the Valley continues to grow into a large and continuous urban area.

The amount of industrialization to be permitted in the Valley remains a matter for debate. The absence of large vacant industrially zoned areas under single ownership means that further industrial expansion has to be accomplished by rezoning of additional land. Even this often fails to solve the problem of providing sufficient industrial land because present zoning regulations permit residential uses to occupy industrial land. Up to the present time the demand for residential land has been greater than the demand for industrial land with the result that the percentage of industrially zoned land occupied by other uses has remained constant even though the amount of industrial zoning has increased.

The changes in zoning which have taken place since 1956 indicate that the Planning Commission has rejected some of the original premises of the comprehensive zoning plan. The Valley is developing as a continuous urban area and the approach which the Commission uses to solve each new request for additional industrial zoning further suggests that it is seeking a formula for the proper and harmonious development of both industrial and residential land uses for the entire Valley as a unit. The problems to be solved currently are completely new and ones not considered in the original planning of 1956; namely, How much and what kinds of industrial development are to be en couraged in the Longview Valley?

STUDY PROJECT 24

THE IMPACT OF OUTLYING SHOPPING CENTERS ON CENTRAL BUSINESS DISTRICTS *

Cities basically are trading centers. Buying and selling is one of their oldest and most universal functions. Therefore, there may be greater novelty and significance in the current tendency of retail merchandising to shift from the central to the peripheral, or hinterland, areas of the city than in the comparable moves of population and industry.

Emergence of the Regional Shopping Center

There has always been a certain amount of decentralized trading activity. The village and the crossroads stores have been with us from time immemorial. The hit-or-miss retailing enterprises strung out along well-traveled highways have been an accompaniment of the automobile age. But the postwar period has brought something new and different—the regional shopping center.

In a fertile burst of creativity, the merchandising world has produced this phenomenon that is changing the shopping habits and attitudes of America and is also spreading to foreign countries. The three prewar developments that made possible the postwar regional shopping center are the chain store, the branch department store, and the supermarket.[1]

Chain stores are very ancient, but it is only within recent decades that they have become one of the leading components of American merchandising. The food supermarket received its great impetus during the thirties as the A & P fought against chain store taxes by closing smaller outlets and concentrating on large self-service units. The branch store movement was originally apparently merely a reaching out of the parent store for the suburban trade. Later it became definitely tied in with shopping center developments. At the moment there appears to be in it a strong element of the edging against declining profits in the central city.

The chain store-supermarket-department store branch sequence led rapidly in the postwar era to the emergence of an even more gigantic and revolutionary merchandising development—the regional shopping center. Far-reaching economic and sociological developments made possible the development of the shopping center in this merchandising sequence. The regional center represents the merchants' adaptation to the revolutionary changes in population and transportation patterns that have become of such extraordinary significance in recent years.

Nature of Regional Shopping Center

The modern shopping center has been defined as a "group of commercial establishments planned, developed, and managed as a *unit*," with parking facili-

---

* By Mabel Walker, *Executive Director, Tax Institute, Incorporated*. Reprinted from *Public Management*, XXXIX (August, 1957), through the courtesy of the International City Managers' Association.

[1] "Modern Merchandising and Municipal Finance," *Tax Policy*, April–May, 1955, p. 3.

ties and with integration to the trade area.[2] These centers fall into three main categories: neighborhood centers, community centers, and regional centers.

The regional center is the type that represents the fullest flowering of the shopping center idea and is the one that offers the greatest potential threat to the central business district of a city.

Conclusion

The regional shopping center movement is of very recent origin. The movement may have passed its peak with respect to construction, but the peak of the shopping center retail volume is still in the future. Even if there should be a moratorium on the construction of new centers, which seems unlikely, we shall have to wait a few years to appraise the sales effect of those already constructed, or being constructed.

The sales volume of the shopping centers will be conditioned partly by the growth of the suburbs, partly by the ability of the centers to satisfy shopper needs, and partly by the income level of the consumers.

There seems no reason to doubt that they are already having an impact on the central business districts of the city, nor that that impact will increase.

Does this mean bankruptcy and stagnation for the central business district? Not necessarily. Although downtown can anticipate a continued decrease in its share of total retail sales, it will still have the resident population of the central city, which probably will continue to do the bulk of its buying there. Moreover, specialty shops catering to rare and unusual tastes will probably continue to be found mainly in the central cities.

It is also being widely said that downtown will continue to be pre-eminent in the sale of luxury items. Perhaps, but even here we can anticipate substantial inroads. The large department store branches in some of the giant centers are definitely catering to the carriage trade. For example, Livingston's (San Francisco) will take its entire fur stock twice yearly to its branch stores in two regional shopping centers. It seems likely that this practice will be copied by other stores.

Downtown merchants are becoming increasingly interested in urban redevelopment as a means of protecting their market. They are concerned about traffic congestion and feverishly urge that the city provide facilities to enable motorists to use their cars in downtown shopping. In the smaller cities much can probably be done along these lines, but in the larger cities this seems a futile endeavor.

A little pencil and paper work should soon demonstrate the physical impossibility of providing driving and parking space for the shoppers necessary to maintain, let alone increase, the sales volume in the large downtown stores in New York, Chicago, Philadelphia, Detroit, Boston, and many others. The city can never compete with the open periphery in appealing to the motorist. Its appeal must be rather for the pedestrian and the transit rider. There is some evidence here and there that the pedestrian may become increasingly important in the urban scheme of things.

It is claimed that one of the reasons why Manhattan office buildings are

[2] J. Ross McKeever, *Shopping Centers: Principles and Policies*, Technical Bulletin No. 20, Washington: Urban Land Institute, 1953, p. 6.

being erected in clusters is so the companies can be within walking distance of their business contacts in order to avoid the midtown traffic jams.[3]

Some dynamic planners dream of redesigning the old congested central areas so that buildings would be grouped in functional clusters, within which traffic would be on foot and which would be surrounded by transportation loops for public transportation.[4]

It seems unlikely that urban redevelopment will attract many suburbanites back into the city, or that it will completely stop the outward push of the population. What it can do is to make the city a healthy, prosperous place for those who wish to remain in it, and an appealing focal point for such activities as attract the peripheral population to visit the city from time to time.

[3] Jane Jacobs, "New York's Office Boom," *Architectural Forum,* March, 1957.
[4] "Downtown Needs A Lesson," *Business Week,* October 22, 1955. Article outlining views of Victor Gruen.

STUDY PROJECT 25

SUBDIVISION AND LAND DEVELOPMENT

Sans Souci Estates Subdivision

The purpose of this study project is to illustrate the nature of subdividing and subdividing decisions.

The Flamingo Development Company, subdividers and builders since 1953 purchased 40 acres in the Eastwood section of a West Coast metropolitan area. The Eastwood section had its greatest development in the post-World War II years when land formerly used for growing citrus fruits was developed with low- to medium-priced homes financed by VA-guaranteed and FHA-insured mortgages. Though the heyday of Eastwood has passed, the Flamingo Development Company believes that there is a strong market in Eastwood for medium-priced conventionally-financed homes.

The Flamingo Development Company decided to call the 40-acre subdivision Sans Souci Estates. The land to the north, south, and east is almost fully developed. The houses built in the immediate post-World War II period are in a general price range of $11,000 to $13,000. The homes most recently built are larger and sell in the general price range of $14,000 to $16,000. Sans Souci Estates is about three miles from Eastwood Shopping Center, a class II regional center.

The Flamingo Development Company considered three alternative land patterns:

1. A gridiron pattern with lot sizes ranging from 50 x 110 feet to 55 x 125 feet. This plan would provide for 160 lots. Total costs as follows:

(a)	surveying	$ 8,100
(b)	grading	12,000
(c)	sewers	25,000
(d)	roads and curbs	45,000
(e)	water mains	14,800
(f)	street lights and corner signs	3,100
	Total Cost	$108,000

2. A gridiron pattern with lot sizes ranging from 70 x 110 feet to 75 x 125 feet. This plan would provide for 120 lots with costs as follows:

(a)	surveying	$ 7,600
(b)	grading	12,000
(c)	sewers	22,000
(d)	roads and curbs	41,400
(e)	water mains	13,000
(f)	fire hydrants	3,000
	Total Cost	$99,000

3. A curvilinear street pattern with cul-de-sacs. Lot sizes would range from 70 x 110 feet to 75 x 125 feet except some irregularly shaped lots of at least 7,500 square feet. This plan would provide for 120 lots.

(a)	surveying	$ 7,800
(b)	grading	12,000
(c)	sewers	23,000
(d)	roads and curbs	43,000
(e)	water mains	13,200
(f)	fire hydrants	3,000
	Total Cost	$102,000

Eastwood has a comprehensive zoning plan. The restrictions applicable to the Sans Souci Estates and the neighboring area provide, among other things, that:

1. No buildings or land shall be used except for the following purposes:
   (a) single-family dwellings
   (b) parks and playgrounds owned and operated by a governmental agency
2. No buildings shall be erected having a height in excess of two and one-half stories or 35 feet.
3. No main building shall be erected unless the following yards and lot area are maintained:
   (a) a front yard of not less than 20 feet or 20 per cent of the depth of the lot, whichever is the lesser of the two
   (b) side yards of not less than 5 feet or 10 per cent of the width of the lot, whichever is the lesser of the two
   (c) rear yard of not less than 25 feet or 25 per cent of the depth of the lot, whichever is the lesser of the two
   (d) a lot area of not less than 5,000 square feet, and the lot frontage shall not be less than 50 feet in width

The Flamingo Development Company plans to provide the following restrictive covenants:

1. All the lots herein described are declared to be residential in character, and no dwelling or structure, except a private dwelling house, designed to accommodate one family only, and garage and outbuildings appurtenant thereto, shall at any time be erected or maintained on any building lot.
2. No building or fence of any character shall be constructed upon any lot in this tract without the approval as to location, height, and design first having been obtained from Grantors or their nominee. No dwelling or

structure erected on the property shall be erected closer to the front boundary line of the property than the setback shown upon the map of the tract on file with and accepted by the city of Eastwood.

3. No person shall reside in any dwelling or structure until and unless the construction has been completed.

4. No boundary or fence exceeding 7 feet in height above the ground shall be constructed upon said property.

5. No store, shop, or factory shall be erected or placed on any lot, nor any business or trade conducted or maintained thereon.

6. No fowl or animals other than reasonable and usual number of household pets, such as domesticated dogs, birds, and felines, shall be permitted.

7. No lot shall be subdivided or portion thereof sold, transferred, or conveyed, excepted that a portion thereof may be transferred or conveyed for the purpose of forming a part of an adjoining lot, but no lot shall be left with a principal frontage of less than 50 feet or an area less than 5,000 feet square.

8. No noxious or offensive activity shall be allowed in the tract, nor shall anything be done which may be or become an annoyance or nuisance to the neighborhood.

9. All covenants and restrictions are to run with the land and shall be binding on all parties and all persons claiming thereunder until July 1, 1978, at which time said covenants and restrictions shall automatically extend for successive periods of ten years, unless by a vote of the majority of the then owners of the lots it is agreed to change said covenants and restrictions in whole or in part.

10. If the parties hereto or any of them or their heirs or assigns shall violate or attempt to violate any of the covenants or restrictions herein, it shall be lawful for any person or persons owning any other lots in the development or subdivision to prosecute any proceeding at law or in equity against the person or persons violating or attempting to violate any such covenant or restriction, and either to prevent him from so doing or to recover damages or other dues for such violations.

The Flamingo Development Company purchased the property with a down payment of $40,000, and executed a purchase-money blanket mortgage for the balance of $160,000. The mortgage calls for payment of $40,000 or more annually plus 6 per cent interest. There is no prepayment penalty. The mortgage has a release clause providing that 10 acres will be released for each $40,000 payment on the mortgage. There is no subordination clause. The Flamingo Development Company is considering the alternative of developing the land in 4 units of 10 acres each, 2 units of 20 acres each, or 1 of 40 acres.

The Flamingo Development Company has, in addition to their capital equipment and the $40,000 equity in the land, the sum of $100,000 in cash available for the development of Sans Souci Estates. Flamingo Development Company also has contact with a number of investors who would be willing to participate in the development on a joint-venture basis. The investors would be willing to furnish the capital and participate in 50 per cent of the profit.

STUDY PROJECT 26

THE NEW ARCHITECTURE *

1. Drama in Baltimore

The centerpiece of Baltimore's Charles Center will be a new 1,500-seat
legitimate theater by Architect John M. Johansen. Raised on a platform above
street-level shops, the theater will be approached across wide terraces. The
rugged exterior expresses the rough fan shape of the seating: sections crop out
between piers. Four stair towers, a pair flanking the entrance, are to be exits to
the terrace. Owner: Morris Mechanic.

1

° *Architectural Forum* (May, 1964).

2

671

2. Science in Florida

As part of a $93 million golden anniversary program, the University of Miami in Coral Gables assigned priority (and about a third of the money) to the science center above and a medical center. The first science unit, by Caudill, Rowlett & Scott, will house the departments of zoology and chemistry, together with service facilities for the center. Services feed vertically through columns grouped in fours and horizontally through paired cross beams.

3. Research at M.I.T.

Helped by grants from several sources, M.I.T. is expanding its Alfred P. Sloan School of Management with this new building for research in the social sciences and in management. Named for Grover M. Hermann, chairman of the board of the Martin Marietta Corp. and a benefactor of M.I.T., the new building will be four stories high, built of reinforced concrete. The nearly solid second floor will be a poured-in-place girder transmitting the upper floors' weight to the sturdy tapered columns below. Architects: Eduardo F. Catalano, associated with Robert C. Brannen and Paul S. Shimamoto.

3

4. Music in Colorado

An inexpensive hall to replace the Aspen music tent is the goal set by the Music Associates of Aspen. They commissioned Herbert Bayer to develop the design, which will hold 1,300 people during festival concerts and cost in the neighborhood of $300,000. The unusual shape, with its two-way flare, was determined by acoustical considerations. The structural frame will be a steel column and exposed truss system. Associate architects: Leon Brin, Frederick R. Bates.

4

5

5. Apartments in Houston

Houston House, an $8 million apartment building, will be one of Houston's tallest structures, stretching up to 33 stories. The blocky base is an eight-level garage atop ground-floor stores, a lobby, and a sheltered promenade. Inside the patterned tower will be 403 apartments, those immediately above the garage to be duplexes with walled roof gardens. The Texas sun will be kept at bay by closely spaced steel fins striping the garage and precast concrete louvers fixed at angles on the tower. Architects: Charles M. Goodman Associates and Irving R. Klein & Associates. Owner: The Lumbermens Co.

6. Illinois Hall

The manipulation of space which marked Paul Rudolph's Art and Architecture Building at Yale also distinguishes this much smaller building for the Christian Science Organization at the University of Illinois in Urbana. Ostensibly it has two floors, a pale description of the many levels within. Behind the blank wall of fluted block and directly off the entrance is the tallest space, a meeting room lit by skylights.

6

7. Los Angeles Restaurant

Peaked witches' hats roof the restaurant planned for the new Los Angeles Zoo. Not only do they provide a lighthearted touch, but they also serve the very practical purpose of being readily seen from every corner of the zoo. The two spires above the restaurant are to be 104 feet tall; the smaller roofs shelter exhibits. Architects: Charles Luckman Associates.

8. Cleveland Apartments

A tree-studded site in Cleveland, once an estate overlooking a city park, will keep much of its natural quality despite two high-rise apartment buildings on a corner plot. Architect Don M. Hisaka's plan places most apartments within view of the park and a valley (top left). Also on the site will be split-level

7

8

garages (foreground), a small motel, and two groups of townhouses. The apartment buildings, 16 stories high, will be strongly modeled of poured-in-place concrete and will contain 150 apartments. Developer: A. J. Bruscino.

9. California Church

This small, elegant chapel by Callister and Payne of Tiburon is the First Church of Christ Scientist in Mill Valley, Calif. It was designed as "an oasis for religious contemplation with much of the shingle-church-in-the-redwoods tradition." The auditorium will be lighted by clerestories beneath the spire, slit windows, and a chandelier.

9

10. Sacramento Shops

Within a stone's throw of Capitol Mall, Sacramento's downtown redevelopment area, shoppers will be able to park, shop, and sample gourmet specialties, all in the same block. Leo A. Daly & Associates designed the Convenience Motor Shopping Center for Northern California Developers, Inc., parking 800 cars on three levels above an international restaurant and a supermarket.

11. New York School

The Wiltwyck School, which is both a school and a treatment center for emotionally disturbed children, is planning a new campus in Yorktown, N.Y., one of the dormitories shown above. Architect Richard G. Stein specified the same simple materials throughout—brick and concrete with precast roofs—yet achieved variety in each group.

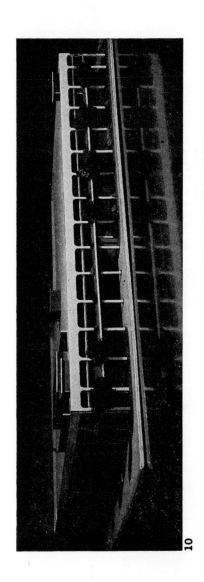

10

11

12

13

12. Capital Offices

Instead of hiding "the largest privately owned office building in Washington" behind a classical temple, Morris Lapidus Associates' design gains a monumental character from a rhythmic façade of reinforced concrete. There are to be 12 floors of 54,550 square feet each and four more underground. Cost: $28 million, including land. Owner: Northwestern Development Co. of Washington.

13. Denver Needle

A tower proposed for the outskirts of Denver would dwarf the Empire State Building, topping it by 230 feet, and provide spectacular views from lofty observation platforms and a restaurant. Structural Engineer Lultcho Boduroff plans to build the tower from elongated cones joined by a narrow neck of concrete strung with cables through the center shaft. Inside the bottom cone would be offices, a hotel and convention center. Developer: Towerland Leasing Corp. of Denver.

STUDY PROJECT 27

HOUSING PROFESSIONALS PAY OFF BEST WHEN THEY WORK TOGETHER AS A TEAM *

Builder Matt M. Jetton, who makes the above statement, can back it up with a remarkable sales record in one of the sickest U.S. Housing Markets, Tampa.

Jetton, president of Sunstate Builders Inc. (75-houses-a-year), used a distinguished team of professionals on his most recent promotion house. The payoff: The house won a top design award for the architect, a top merchandising award for the builder; it helped sell 34 houses averaging $29,000 while it was being promoted and immediately afterwards; it produced a wealth of local publicity for the subdivision where it was built; and, as important as anything else, it sold the first week it was offered for sale—right after the promotion.

Jetton's use of talented professionals on the promotion house was not a one-shot effort. His Carrollwood subdivision, which won a top land-planning award in 1962, is a full-blown product of professional teamwork: It was planned by a professional land planner and involved the work of a score of architects, landscape architects, and interior designers. Jetton has his own realty firm which handles all his new sales and resales. Like many builders, he works closely with his mortgage lender—First Federal S&L of Tampa. Says First Federal's executive vice president, Joseph W. Dalton: "We're so convinced that Jetton's concepts are sound that we've invested more than $7 million in mortgages at Carrollwood. It can't lose."

Jetton and his professional team exemplify a powerful trend in housing. More and more builders are using more and more professionals. Examples abound.

Last year big Builder William J. Levitt, who had handled most design and planning problems within his own organization, retained noted Architects George Nemeny, George Nelson, Donald Lethbridge, and Carl Koch as consult-

* *House and Home* (January, 1964).

ants for his ever-widening operation, which now includes Long Island, New Jersey, Maryland, Florida, Puerto Rico, and Paris, France.

Rochester, New York, Builders Caldwell & Cook, eager to retain design leadership in their market, have just retained prizewinning architect John Anderson—a move urged by their marketing consultant, Stanley Edge.

Builder Ross Cortese, developer of Rossmoor and Leisure World, California's most successful retirement community, has engaged Collins & Kronstadt, architects, engineers, and planners, to plan a new community in the Washington, D.C., area and design a variety of houses for it.

The most attractive and successful urban renewal efforts in the U.S.— Washington's River Park and San Francisco's Diamond Heights and Western Addition—are prime examples of teamwork by professionals and farseeing entrepreneurs who retained them.

Developers of satellite cities, now abuilding from California to Florida, from Michigan to Texas, are using the best professionals they can retain: Howard Ahmanson of Los Angeles' Home Federal S&L hired Land Planner and Architect William Pereira to plan three tracts totaling 10,000 acres in California; Baltimore Mortgage Banker James W. Rouse hired away William E. Finley, director of the National Capital Commission, to plan a satellite city for 100,000 residents between Washington and Baltimore; T. Jack Foster & Sons retained Land Planners Ruth and Krushkhov and Landscape Architects Royston, Hanomoto, Mayes & Beck for $500 million Foster City, California.

The list is almost endless, and Publisher Paul Hornsleth of *House & Garden* phrases the trend aptly when he says, "America is on a design jag."

Says Builder Jetton: "My whole future in building is based on the increasing use of professionals. Only with them can I compete." He recently provided office space in his own headquarters building for Architect Eugene R. Smith and Interior Designer Edwina Black because "I need professionals closer to my customers."

Jetton offers this advice on coordinating the work of professionals and making the most of their talents:

"The building entrepreneur—the man who holds the check book—must lead the team." How does Jetton lead? He follows three hard-and-fast rules:

1. He makes sure all his professionals realize they are working in a competitive market: "They must be taught to design and plan within a price range and at a profit to the builder. An architect with no previous experience in merchant building takes about six months to learn how to design a house that can be built at a profit. Too often his initial detailing, for example, costs twice as much as standard detailing. So in the beginning he must lean on the builder to be sure his designs are both workable and economical. But eventually he designs a better, more salable house."

2. He spells out his objectives for each professional: Does he want a mass-built house or an individually designed one? Does he want to be right with the market or a little ahead of it? Does he need a house to sell quickly or a promotion house to draw traffic?

3. He gets all his professionals together at the outset and stresses the importance of working as a team: "An interior designer can do little about furnishing a room with badly-placed windows unless he can make his point to the architect at the start. A landscape architect can't provide a better planting scheme or suggest modifications to help marry a house to its land unless he gets in at the beginning. No one professional has all the answers, but he can give better answers when he hears other professional opinions."

Sums up Jetton: "Professionals, working together for a builder, produce far more than a better end product. They save his time—the most valuable time in his organization. And they even help him tap new markets. Every professional has a following that will come out to see what he has done. I'm convinced that professionals don't cost—they pay."

STUDY PROJECT 28

SIX GREAT MOTIVATORS *

Competition for savings is by far the greatest now that it has been since World War II. Our public relations effort must be intensified, expanded and made even more effective if we are to keep our place in the sun and if we are to continue approximately the same rate of growth that we have enjoyed recently.

To a very great degree, the success of these efforts will depend upon the measure of understanding we have of the basic emotions and impulses—motivational forces—that govern people. I think it can be argued that this understanding of people is the paramount consideration involved in developing our various public relations and promotional programs.

Some years ago, the advertising people gave the fancy-sounding title of "motivation research" to the job of understanding people. It is this understanding of people and why they act as they do that might be called the golden key to public relations success.

The first important motivational force that has direct influence on public relations activities is that people like to feel that they are needed. This basic desire to be needed suggests a variety of approaches as far as public relations programs are concerned.

One such approach is that people's savings are needed to build a safe future for the family. Another is that their savings are needed now so that the saver can enjoy new and wonderful products of the future. Still another approach is that savings are needed to provide the fuel of capital for the expansion and growth of our economy. And a fourth approach is that savings are needed for patriotic reasons—currently this patriotic reason is the fighting of inflation.

The second great basic motivational force which can influence our public relations programs is that people like to be successful. An obvious major public relations approach here is that people who save are successful people because they have mastered the problem of putting away part of what they earn. Similarly, people like to feel that they are part of a successful, progressive enterprise, which accounts, incidentally, for the sense of proprietorship that many families display in the growth of the savings association in their community.

The third great force that should affect public relations planning is that people like a sense of physical well-being.

There are at least three considerations here that apply to public relations programs—office quarters, personnel and the dress of personnel. With respect to office quarters, the building of new buildings, the remodeling or modernization of old quarters has played a vital part in developing new business. With respect to personnel, people like warm, friendly employees to handle their affairs. As to the dress of personnel, studies have shown that people are greatly

---

* An article by William B. O'Connell in *Saving and Loan News,* as reprinted in *Director's Digest* (March, 1959), pp. 21–24.

impressed by the appearance of other people; this suggests that employees be suitably and conservatively attired.

The fourth great moving force affecting public relations programs of associations is that people like to feel secure.

The search for security has brought remarkable changes in American life. It has developed a tremendous life insurance industry; it has inspired passage of unemployment compensation and social security laws; it brought the Blue Cross and Blue Shield health insurance into being; it caused the establishment of literally thousands of private retirement and pension plans.

. . . .

There is still another element involved in the search for security, and that is the seeking of assurance that savings placed with a savings association are safe In the past 10 years I have given a great deal of thought and study to this matter and long ago reached the conclusion that public confidence in the safety of our institutions is more vital to our prestige than anything else.

This suggests immediately the necessity of placing repeated emphasis on such factors of safety as sound and careful management, including auditing, the federal-agency insurance of savings accounts and the assistance available through the Federal Home Loan Bank System.

The fifth great motivational "mover" is that people like to be appreciated. Look for opportunities to say "thank you" in many different ways, not only to persons when they open new accounts but on the anniversary dates of the day on which the accounts were opened. You can say "thank you," too, to persons who have shown consistency and regularity in adding to their accounts.

The sixth great mover is that people like to be informed.

This is more true today than it ever was. Our educational levels have advanced generation by generation, and today a higher percentage of youngsters go through college than went through high school 50 years ago. As a result, the hunger for knowledge and information is more active than ever before.

❊   ❊   ❊

STUDY PROJECT 29

OMNIBUS REALTY COMPANY, PROPERTY MANAGEMENT POLICIES

The following is an abstract of the minutes of a meeting of Omnibus Realty Company.

Mr. Omnibus: Gentlemen, today we will consider some alternative policies for the property management department which we are planning to add to our operation. First, we will consider the question of flexibility of rents.

Mr. Maxim: If we are to maximize the income for our property owners, it will be necessary to adjust rents frequently in accordance with changes in market conditions. Also, this means changing rents for occupied apartments, not just changing rents as space becomes available.

Mr. Axim: We should not be so concerned with maximizing scheduled gross income. If we raise rents frequently we may find large vacancy and collection losses and high expenses. That is, we may expect that tenancy turnover will be quite high and maintenance expenses would rise. I, therefore, believe the policy should be only to raise rents when space becomes available or under conditions where our rents fall substantially below the prevailing market rental levels. Not only will this maximize long-run net returns but I think it leads to better tenant relations. I don't anticipate any problems because of rent differentials due to different dates of beginning occupancy.

Mr. Novis: Wouldn't the requirements for long term leases solve this problem for us?

Mr. Omnibus: Some interesting questions have been raised. We will consider these and come back to them later. Let's now turn to the question of selection of tenants.

Mr. Maxim: Since we are trying to maximize income I see no reason to ever let an apartment stay vacant as long as there is someone willing to pay the rent. Therefore, as long as a prospective tenant seems able to pay and is of apparently good character, I think that we owe it to the property owners to immediately rent the space and thereby minimize vacancy losses.

Mr. Axim: While it is true that we do not wish to have vacancy losses, I think that if we carefully select our tenants we will have a lower turnover and thus less vacancies. This should also minimize losses since we may then select a good caliber tenant, not to mention the possibilities of minimizing repair expenses and other maintenance charges. I don't think that we need to check back to see if the ancestors of prospective tenants came over on the Mayflower, but I would at least like to see a policy of requiring an application and a deposit giving us sufficient time to check credit references and background.

Mr. Novis: Checking out the tenants seems to be a good idea, but I think that most prospective tenants would be offended if we questioned their character. Therefore, why don't we just adopt a policy of accepting tenants if they make a nice appearance?

Mr. Omnibus: Well, this brings us to the question as to whether we should require leases which will spell out the terms of our agreement.

Mr. Maxim: Since I think we should have flexible rent and therefore short term leases or no leases at all, the question comes down to how we should spell out the terms of the agreement. We may from time to time desire to change the rules by which we operate; therefore, I would rather not commit ourselves as to terms of tenancy. The alternative of setting up general rules posted in the building and in our office letting all tenants know what we expect and what we will do would be sufficient. In this way we have the flexibility of changing our rules and yet the tenants can know what is expected of them by merely looking at our rules from time to time.

Mr. Axim: When we lease a space for a period, whether it is short or long, I think the terms of the tenancy should be specifically spelled out and should be held for the period. Therefore, I believe that all the essential elements of the agreement should be contained in a lease and if changes are necessary they would be made at time of renewal. In this way, the tenants having signed the lease will certainly know what is expected of them and what they may expect of us.

Mr. Novis: There are certain conditions of the lease which we will want to have written in order to be enforceable. And therefore I think that we ought to adopt a policy of requiring written leases. As for operational rules, we may desire to vary these from property to property so why not just inform the tenant whenever an issue arises? In this way, we can always adjust to the situation.

Mr. Omnibus: This brings us to the general area of tenant relations. I would like you gentlemen to render opinions on collection of rents and policies for providing maintenance and repairs.

Mr. Maxim: I think the less contact we have with the tenants the less difficulties will arise. Therefore, I would be in favor of a policy of having the tenants mail their checks to the office. With regard to repairs, when the building needs repairs, the tenants will certainly let us know. So I would not be in favor of going out and looking for things to do.

Mr. Axim: Good tenant relations in the long run can mean more income for our property owners. I think we should have considerable personal contact with our tenants. Therefore, I recommend that a representative of the office call for the rent on the due date and at that time inquire as to any needs, complaints or recommendations on the part of the tenants. Also, preventive maintenance is important for prolonging the economic life of the property and hence the earnings of the property so I recommend periodic inspection of the property to see that it is being kept up. Deferred maintenance in the long run can be costly. While such a policy may mean a lower net income for some period, in the long run we will benefit the property as well as the tenants.

Mr. Novis: In regards to rent, I don't think people like to be reminded, so I would be in favor of having them mail their checks. As for maintenance, if we go ahead with our plans to provide our own maintenance crews we might as well keep them busy by having them going to each of the properties and doing whatever they see necessary rather than waiting for someone to complain.

STUDY PROJECT 30

A CLOSER LOOK AT THE RENTAL OF SINGLE FAMILY UNITS *

When we talk with our colleagues in the management profession, invariably the subject of single dwellings management arises. You, as well as I, have had the experience of hearing someone say that the management of single dwellings is a non-profitable nuisance, one which many managers will not touch.

* Reba E. Claytor, C.P.M., *Journal of Property Management*, XXIX, No. 6 (July–August, 1964), pp. 309–13.

Someone will say there are too many problems, and not enough profits. Lets examine single family dwellings critically, and see if the profits really need to be so small, and the problems so large.

How would an alert manager approach the management of single dwellings? Why do owners rent single family dwellings?

1. Absentee owner transferred out of town—for some reason he doesn't want to sell just now. Maybe depressed market—if he sells now—can't get investment back. Maybe he hopes transfer is temporary, and if he comes back, he certainly wants his own home back. Maybe he has no reason—but we know he has sentimental attachment to it. He can't give it up—not yet, anyway.

2. Estates—owner gone, heirs have no need for the house—executor can let the house set vacant during probate, or rent it, and add the income to the estate.

3. Builder of tract homes—sales are slower than anticipated. Inventory of unsold homes—with payments—hurts. So he offers them for rent, to help him make those payments. This trend is growing—in fact it was noticed and commented on in the September *House and Home* magazine. "Hint of New Trend in the Housing Market—One Family Homes for Rent."

The biggest surprise was spotted by real estate analyst Roy Wenzlick of St. Louis: 2.8 per cent of new homes built in 1963 are being rented instead of sold. A year ago the percentage was negligible. Why are builders renting their homes? The trend is so new that answers from owners provide no clear reason. Most of them are renting homes that have remained unsold for a long while simply to keep them from standing idle. A new census look at house building shows merchant builders are taking 6–7 months to sell a home after completion now.

A new NAHB forecast for housing the rest of the decade indicates the trend to one-family homes for rent may continue. Says NAHB, 9.1 million single family homes will be built this decade, including those already built, but only 7.1 million will be sold. The remaining 2 million will be either rented or vacant. NAHB predicts demand for rental and sale quarters will be about equal. And the new sampling of market prospects among renters shows the rental of a house might be an important sales tool. A survey of 19,000 renters in all 50 states by Panelboard Mfg. Company of Newark shows many renters are fearful about taking on the chores of home-ownership and would like trial runs as renters. Some want builders to rent homes on trial before buying. Others want builders to take homes back if families decide to move.

From the sound of that article, management of single dwellings is going to boom in the next decade. I know a builder in Castro Valley, with a tract called Sleepy Hollow. He built 400 homes, and upon selling 300, found he was paying out far more of his profit in income tax than he was keeping. He thought about this, and upon the advice of his tax consultant, stopped selling homes. He rented the last 100, and sells a few each year. He has a lifetime retirement, for each year his homes increase in value, and he carries back mortgages or deeds of trust on part of the payment. His homes now, just 4 years after selling the first one, sell for $3000–$4000 more per home than the original sales price.

A Need and a Challenge

I have mentioned a few of the reasons why homes come on the rental market, and you can think of many more. The important point is that—if homes are being rented, management is needed. And where there is a need for management there is both a challenge and an opportunity for the CPM.

What problems are there in managing single dwellings? I don't think they are much different from a multiple unit building. The techniques and methods differ. We must always ask what we should charge for rent. What is the fair rental value of this property? As in multiple dwellings, the rental agent must know his market, and set a realistic evaluation. Keep in mind though, that with one single dwelling, you never have a 5 per cent or 10 per cent vacancy factor. It is 0 or 100 per cent. If that house would rent immediately at $150, but might take 3 months to rent at $175, if it would rent at all at that price—the owner who held out for $175 per month would have collected $225 less in the first year than the owner who rented immediately for $150.

It is difficult for owners to realize this concept when we talk of rental value. A friend and fellow manager—dramatizes this well with a $5 bill. He shows the bill to the owner—and asks what the reaction might be if he tore the bill into tiny pieces and threw it away. Most owners respond that they'd think he needed to have his head examined. He turns the tables on them and explains they are doing about the same thing every day their $150 per month is idle and unrented. Convince the owner that he has only time to sell, and that a day's rent lost due to vacancy is gone—it can't be recovered. Convince him to be realistic about the rental value.

He must not expect to make a profit on renting a single dwelling. In fact, in my area, he's lucky to break even. His motivation for renting single dwellings must be something other than profit. His motivation may be simply to preserve his asset—until he can later decide what to do with it.

. . . .

Some Specific Problems

If you properly merchandise your single dwelling, you'll find a tenant, then you will have the problems of management to meet. Some problems exist here that are absent in multiple units. One might be the gardening. With a large apartment building, you hire a gardener. Often an owner has left valuable plants and shrubs that must be maintained. Most tenants will water, some will cut lawns, but few will weed, spray, and fertilize. If the grounds are extensive, and with valuable plants and large lawns, the owner must retain a professional gardener. Rarely can he regain this cost in additional rents.

If the grounds are modest and without extensive plantings, owners expect the tenant to keep and maintain them. Expecting and getting are often far different. We help to boost the tenant's good intentions with a clause in our lease, stating that if he doesn't do the work, we'll hire a gardener to do the work, and add the cost to the rent. This device has worked for us more than once, when a tenant has been derelict in his duty, and we've called to say unless the lawn was shaped up, we'd have a professional gardener start working the first of the month. We have never yet had to hire a gardener, under those circumstances.

In a single dwelling lease, we usually require a substantial security deposit. This should be at least equal to one month's rent, but definitely not applicable as the last month's rent. For this reason, we never make the amount exactly equal to a month's rent, always a little more or less.

I make it clear that this deposit may never be used as the last month's rent. This security deposit is worth nothing if it is gone before the tenant moves out. It is refunded after the tenant has moved, returned the key, and the house checked and found to be in good condition. In the case of a furnished house, the deposit should be higher, particularly if the owner has left his own furnishings which are usually of higher quality than found in normal rental units. Only with an adequate security deposit can one insure the owner against loss.

Once the house has been rented, the management problems become routine. There is little difference in management of homes as compared to managing multiple units. After all, if you have 58 single dwellings, you have the same number of tenants as you'd have in a 58-unit multiple—only a little more spread out. There is, of course, more travel time caring for maintenance, repairs, showing, inspections. For this reason, if you will manage single dwellings you must build a volume. If you have 6 houses in a 6 block area, it takes little more time to inspect 6 than 1.

Accounting is especially important when you manage single dwellings. Certainly it must be simple—streamlined. When you have an account where the income is only slightly greater than the expenses going out, ask the owner to provide you with a "kitty" to handle unexpected expenses such as maintenance and repairs.

Many of you may be thinking—it sounds good—but how can we do all this work for the small fee involved, and still make a profit?" My answer—you can— if you:

1.   Establish realistic fees.
2.   Build volume
3.   Take full advantage of the by-products of management
Lets elaborate—

1. Forego the idea of per cent of gross for your fee. Charge a minimum fee that will cover your cost and return a profit, even though it be a nominal profit. The fee must be based particularly on your individual costs of handling. So, you must make a cost analysis of your management department, so you are sure that every home pays its own way. Our firm includes 6 per cent monthly management fee based on monthly rent, but with minimum fee of $10 per dwelling. Also 10 per cent supervision on all maintenance and repair items. Quick arithmetic shows a $200 per month house yields fees of $24 per month or $288 per year, without any extra fees for supervision or maintenance, and without any other benefits from management.

2. If you build a volume, of say 200 accounts, you can see you will be approaching a gross revenue of about $60,000 per year. This begins to add up to something worthwhile. Also with volume, per unit costs of handling go down, and thus profits go up. The same bookkeeper needed to handle $30,000 per year gross could, with proper accounting procedures, handle the $60,000 gross. One rental agent can show 2 or 3 homes in one area in little more time than it takes to show one house only.

3. Fringe benefits—or side benefits from management. The most obvious is management into sales. Previously the absentee owner was mentioned. He still has sentimental attachment, and elects to rent rather than sell. Time proves that after several years of renting, that sentiment weakens, the roots he had in the neighborhood begin to wither, his hopes for returning home dim, maybe if he still hopes to return, his family size may have changed, making the home no

longer fit his needs. One year, when the lease is coming up for renewal, you will receive a letter asking your opinion on selling at this time. This will be a good listing as you will be asked for your opinion of price. Motivation is strong —as expenses go on while income may be nil if he didn't renew a lease. One management firm counts on their management department to yield 12 to 14 good listings per year from absentee owners, and from management of single dwellings.

Another side benefit may be insurance on the property. You will be asked for advice on the amount and kind of coverage desirable. You are in a prime spot—the insurance account can be yours, along with its extra income to you.

Maybe the owner will need to refinance. If so, you can provide this service for him, for a fee.

None of these are necessarily large commissions, but they are bread and butter, and can be regular. Occasionally, you will find that what you thought was bread is really cake. Some years ago, I agreed to manage a house for an absentee owner. It was a nice house, but at $10 per month commission. I managed it for several years, until the owner returned to occupy the home again. He had been pleased with the service, and later, upon coming into an inheritance, he decided to invest in income property, and come to me. Over the years we've helped him to buy and sell over a million dollars worth of property—and we manage his holdings. He presently owns about one-half million in property, which we manage. This came to us because we pleased one owner with our management of his single dwelling.

No one can deny that there are problems in handling another person's single dwelling. But—do not forget—one man's problems become another's opportunities. And where there are opportunities, there are potential profits.

STUDY PROJECT 31

FLYNN *ET AL. V.* KENRICK *ET AL.**
285 Mass. 446, 189 N.E. 207 (1934)

This was an action by Nellie T. Flynn and others (plaintiffs) against William A. Kenrick and others (defendants). Judgment for plaintiffs and defendants appealed. Judgment affirmed.

Property was sold under an agreement of purchase and sale, containing the following recital: "Said premises are to be conveyed on or before September 1, 1930, by good and sufficient warranty deed of the party of the first part, conveying a good and clear title to the same, free from all incumbrances except a first mortgage of $5,000 . . . and for such deed and conveyance the party of the second part is to pay the sum of $6,500 of which $100 has been paid this day, balance above mortgage, are to be paid in cash upon delivery of said deed." According to the contract the property was deeded to the purchasers. The mortgage debt was not paid, and on foreclosure the property was sold for $4,500 and a deficiency decree was entered against the mortgagor, which he has paid. Suit is brought against the purchaser by the mortgagor to recover the amount paid on the ground that the purchaser agreed to pay the mortgage debt. The deed was drawn subject to the mortgage.

---

* Harold F. Lusk, *Business Law: Principles and Cases* (4th ed.; Homewood, Ill.: Richard D. Irwin, Inc., 1946), p. 306.

CROSBY, J.—It has long been held in this commonwealth that where land is conveyed subject to a mortgage the grantee does not become bound by mere acceptance of a deed to pay the mortgage debt. In the absence of other evidence, the deed shows that the grantee merely purchased the equity of redemption. If a deed contains a stipulation that the land is subject to a mortgage which the grantee assumes or agrees to pay, by his acceptance of the deed the law implies a promise to perform his promise. The contention of the defendants that they purchased merely the plaintiff's equity of redemption and did not assume and agree to pay the mortgage cannot be sustained in view of the agreement, the deed, and the agreed facts. The agreement recites that the defendants for such conveyance are to pay "the sum of Sixty-five hundred dollars of which One Hundred dollars have been paid this day, balance above mortgage, are to be paid in cash upon delivery of said deed." It thus appears that for the deed and conveyance the defendants agreed to pay the sum of $6,500; that $100 was paid on the date of the agreement, and on delivery of the deed $1,400 was to be paid. The words "balance above mortgage" properly construed mean that the defendants having paid $100 obligated themselves to assume and pay the mortgage, and that the balance above the mortgage of $1,400 is to be paid upon the delivery of the deed.

The words of the deed "for consideration paid" interpreted in the light of the agreement mean that the defendants under the terms of the agreement are to pay $6,500 as the entire consideration. This seems to have been the construction put upon the agreement and the deed by the parties, as it is agreed that after the defendants entered into possession of the property they paid the interest installments on the mortgage until July 7, 1932. The agreement of the defendants to pay $6,500 for the property is equivalent to a stipulation that they assumed or agreed to pay the mortgage.

STUDY PROJECT 32

THE CHANGING ROLE OF GOVERNMENT *

During the decade of the '50s, the federal government exerted its influence on the savings and loan business largely by *not* changing the basic legislation that had been enacted in the '30s. Continued attention by the Congress to housing and home finance presented rather constant and at times serious legislative problems for the business. In retrospect, however, the government's housing programs probably did more to stimulate association growth than to lessen the importance of associations in the housing and mortgage markets, although this result does not appear to have been either planned or anticipated. Much the same kind of result seems to have occurred in the area of taxation, with the new tax law early in the decade failing almost completely to bring in revenue but serving most effectively to stimulate growth.

Before the decade was over, and perhaps as a result of savings and loan's rapid growth, thoughtful persons both inside and outside of government began to look at the business more carefully, and to ponder and discuss the proper role of financial institutions and their regulatory agencies. Although the Congress failed to provide for a major inquiry into our financial system, as had been

* U.S. Savings and Loan League, A *Second Look at the Decade of the Sixties* (Chicago: The League, 1963).

recommended by President Eisenhower near the end of his first term, this kind of investigation was undertaken by an independent Commission on Money and Credit, sponsored by the Committee for Economic Development. Following publication of the Commission's report in 1961, President Kennedy appointed a high-level Committee on Financial Institutions (popularly known as the Heller Committee) to review this report and to recommend what action should be taken by the government to change the character and operation of the range of America's financial institutions.

Meanwhile, several other apparently unrelated developments were serving to make the government's role during the decade of the '60s one of direct rather than indirect influence on the savings and loan business. *First, the long fight and eventual showdown on the tax question brought to the attention of both legislative and executive branches of government the facts of savings and loan growth.*

Second, determination of appropriate government policy with respect to commercial banking has been coming to the forefront as banking's major problem. Discussions both within banking circles and in government quickly turn to competition, especially with savings and loan associations, which in so many cities now have passed the leading commercial bank as the largest financial institution.

Third, housing has lost much of its political appeal, and there is relatively less interest in government housing programs than there was in the previous decade.

Fourth, occasional criticism of the Federal Home Loan Bank System and the supervisory policy and procedure of the Board *has brought the entire regulatory framework under study.*

Fifth, the introduction and rapid spread of the holding company idea into savings and loan has brought the business to the attention of investment bankers, brokers and other agencies in the securities markets, and also their regulatory agencies in government.

Finally, the mutual savings banks and their national trade association have begun an aggressive campaign to get Congress to provide for *federal chartering of mutual savings banks and for the conversion of savings and loan associations into mutual savings banks.*

We can conclude therefore that during the decade of the '60s, the *federal government will be taking a close look at the savings and loan business, and very likely will be considering and re-shaping government policy with respect to it.* The present decade could easily be one in which major changes in basic legislation could be as significant as they were back in the '30s when the ground work was laid for savings and loan to become such an important part of our economic system. Whether these changes will be conducive to further growth or serve to impede it undoubtedly will depend on how well the business understands and portrays its proper role in a growing economy.

Housing

Four years ago it seemed that "without a major domestic or international crisis during the '60s, little in the way of radical change will take place in federal housing policy." Thus far in the decade, this forecast has been quite accurate. In fact, housing has lost much of its political appeal, largely because housing needs are being satisfied without further federal intervention.

As predicted, the more liberal terms available under conventional mortgages have led to a marked reduction in the volume of mortgage loans insured by FHA. The VA guarantee program has been continued but not extended to veterans of the cold war. Public housing, slum clearance, urban renewal, housing for minority groups and other controversial programs continue to receive some federal support, but in total they do not constitute a major portion of residential construction volume.

What has happened thus far in the decade may represent only a temporary period for something approaching a "hands-off" policy. *By 1965 or soon thereafter a rapidly increasing number of households could again make housing a favorite topic in the political arena.* Also, before 1970 it is quite possible that the civil rights question will be centered more on housing than on schools and public facilities as at present. Thus there may well be some doubts as to the soundness of the conclusion four years ago that "it is questionable whether many real changes in housing policy will occur during the decade."

Taxation

Before the decade ends, taxation may again become an issue of government policy. This most certainly will be true if the new tax law for the savings and loan business fails in this decade, as the 1951 act did in the past decade, to produce the anticipated revenue. *But even with associations paying taxes in the amounts anticipated, a reconsideration of the tax law may be in order. The special tax arrangements for the business now depend on associations' meeting a rather strict definition as to what kind of business Congress had in mind to benefit from these arrangements.* If the nature of the business changes, or needs to be changed in order to serve its objectives, this part of the tax controversy may be expected to be reviewed.

Time will tell what effect taxation will have on the business, but *there seems to be no reason now to believe that taxes will interfere with association progress in the long run, although they are bound to have some adverse effect on the business both in the short and long run.* Owing to efficiencies of scale, continued growth brings continuous reduction in operating costs other than cost of money. If high dividend rates have resulted more from competition within the business than from the necessity to compete with other types of savings institutions, as very likely is the fact, some diversion of income from savers to the Treasury should be possible without damaging results to the business.

Taxation of course is having its indirect effects, some of which may impede progress, but most of which will eventually strengthen the business. Improved accounting and financial practices at the management level and more rational consideration of reserve and capital requirements at the supervisory level should be expected as a result of taxation. Leadership in the business can now direct its energies into more constructive programs than a tax fight that was destined to be lost eventually. Also, now that the charge of unfairly escaping taxes can no longer be made, the business cannot help but gain in prestige, and its people cannot help but gain strength and confidence for whatever stand they wish to take on any public issue, including, for example, *a program to improve the tax position of savings accounts in individuals' thrift and investment efforts.*

Changes in the tax status of home owners as compared with renters undoubtedly will continue to be proposed, and before the end of the decade the Congress might be more disposed toward considering them. The present ratio of home owners to renters does not make these proposals attractive politically except in highly populated metropolitan areas, but that's where the increase in population is taking place. Quite obviously any loss by home owners of their present tax advantages could affect the single family home market and hence the savings and loan business.

Liquidity and Capital Requirements

Among the recommendations of the Heller Committee were two that strike right at the very heart of the savings and loan business. After favoring a cash reserve requirement similar to that imposed on banks, the Committee concluded that "federal agencies that supervise financial institutions should be endowed with sufficient authority to assure that the institutions maintain adequate liquidity over and above cash reserve requirements." *To the Committee, liquidity meant liquid assets and not unused credit lines from the Federal Home Loan Bank, hence the conclusion must be interpreted as a recommendation that the associations carry much more of their own liquidity, reducing the proportion of mortgages and increasing the proportion of low yielding, highly liquid assets in their portfolios.*

While a conclusion of a committee, even a high level one like the Heller Committee, may never result in any legislation or regulatory change, the possibilities of that occurring before the decade is over certainly add to the problems of estimating savings and loan growth.

The Committee also concluded that "supervisory and insuring authorities should have adequate powers to assure that all institutions subject to their respective jurisdictions maintain at all times ample capital in accordance with guidelines established by those agencies." Although no one really can quarrel with this basically "sound" proposition, the danger to the savings and loan business lies in the possibility *that associations will be subjected to the same high capital requirements that have kept commercial banks from competing effectively in the savings and home mortgage markets.*

From a public policy standpoint, adequate liquidity for the savings and loan business as a whole *can be provided best and at lowest cost by maintaining a strong and liquid Federal Home Loan Bank System. Protection against loss to the public is provided in the final analysis by a strong Federal Savings and Loan Insurance Corporation.* Meeting the basic problems of liquidity and safety in this way does not prevent individual associations from insuring their own continued existence through wise and careful management of their own liquidity and reserve positions. In fact, this approach permits and encourages associations to develop and use their own judgment and experience. It also requires that supervisory agencies manage the Insurance Corporation and the Bank System effectively, which from the standpoint of growth and development of the savings and loan business *would be a more important contribution than trying to manage every individual association through exercise of supervisory powers.*

Lending and Investment Powers

Without much question savings and loan associations will be given somewhat broader lending and investment powers. Liberalization already has begun, both at the Congressional and Board levels. How far this trend will go, and in which direction, could profoundly affect savings and loan growth.

To illustrate, rather than to forecast, one direction that liberalization might take would be to relax or eliminate altogether the geographical limitations on home mortgages. The results of this government action would be quite different than if geographical limitations were retained, and restrictions on types of properties and types of loans were relaxed or eliminated.

The broadening of lending and investment powers into new types of loans and investments, such as municipal bonds and personal and automobile loans, could easily have a different result than might first appear. *Permitting associations to look more like banks in their loans and investments might lead to requirements that would make associations more like banks in terms of liquidity and capital. Far from stimulating growth, the net effect could be quite the opposite.*

Federal Charters for Mutual Savings Banks

The efforts to obtain legislation for federal chartering of mutual savings banks are not unrelated to the broadening of lending and investment powers.

One way for associations to get such powers would be to convert to a federally chartered mutual savings bank. Currently, one way to weaken the savings bank campaign would be to broaden associations' powers until conversion no longer seems attractive.

As of now, the possibility of federal charters within this decade seems far less than the likelihood of broader lending and investment powers for associations. *By the end of the decade, therefore, associations may have about the same powers as mutual savings banks whether or not they convert.*

Branching

Savings and loan associations generally are subject to the same powers and limitations on branching as those authorized for commercial banks. If this general rule continues to be followed, the whole structure of the savings and loan business could change if and when major changes take place in branching arrangements for banks. While such changes may not occur in this decade in view of the strong political pressures for retaining the status quo, there never has been a time when opportunities were any better for legislation favorable to branching.

Regulation by Rules or Objectives

The rapid growth of the savings and loan business has made it difficult for the regulatory agencies to keep pace. *Too many rules and regulations now in effect seem to be inheritances from the time most associations were small and perhaps needed to be told "how to do it."* Too few regulations state in terms of basic principles the objective to be sought, leaving associations freedom to reach it in their own way.

If the savings and loan business is to continue to grow and to serve more effectively the objectives for which it exists, *strong and well-managed associations need freedom to manage, to innovate and to take new risks.* Greater freedom to develop new and different types of savings and investment contracts could result in a larger net inflow of funds at a lower average cost. Similarly, greater freedom to tailor home mortgages to the individual needs and debt paying abilities of the borrowers could make associations more competitive on the lending side. The combination of lower cost funds and greater freedom on the lending side could make an association a far more influential force in community service and development.

Greater freedom involves risk and greater competition between associations, which both association managements and supervisory authorities should be willing to assume and see develop in view of the possible gains. How soon and to what extent associations will be given more freedom will affect the future growth, but cannot be predicted very well. One obstacle will be the difficulty of measuring association performance in terms of how well broad objectives are being met, rather than in terms of what rules or regulations were violated. Still another will be the reluctance of many savings and loan managers and at least some members of the Congress to moving in this direction.

STUDY PROJECT 33

OUR STRONGER FHLB SYSTEM *

The FHLB System grows stronger, and noticeably so compared with its own size and financial condition a few years back. Because of this improvement, the danger exists that we will be satisfied with the banks' performance and not ask ourselves how much more improvement is necessary or desirable. For example, *when we observe that the assets of the bank system have grown more rapidly than the assets of member associations, we may forget that the ratio of bank assets to association assets was pitifully small not too long ago, hence may still be.*

One way to correct for this possible error in our thinking would be to take a look at the assets of the Federal Reserve Banks and of their members. Here we find that the Reserve banks are approximately ten times as large as the FHL Banks, but the assets of Federal Reserve members are only twice those of FHLB members. In other words, the FHL Banks would need to be about five times their present size to be comparable to the Reserve banks on this measure. Looked at somewhat differently, *Reserve Banks hold approximately 20 per cent of the combined assets of the banking system, whereas FHL Banks hold only around 5 per cent of the combined assets of the FHL Banks and their members.*

Granted that this comparison proves little if anything, the whole point we are trying to make is that recent rates of growth prove very little either. The important question is how big should the bank system be.

As most of you know, *we would like to see the FHL Bank System much, much bigger, and much, much more liquid.* The FHL Bank of San Francisco is no longer a peanut stand, as Eddie Edwards once described it, but we aren't sure it and the eleven others are big enough to meet all possible demands on them. They could be, and at no great cost. The small difference in rate the banks would have to pay on their own obligations and the rate they would receive on Treasury bills makes warehousing of liquid assets a cheap form of insurance.

---

* *Economics for Savings and Loan Executives,* Graduate School of Savings and Loan, Bloomington, Indiana.

Chairman McMurray, in whose administration the banks have grown substantially, cites 1963 performance as evidence the banks can meet any anticipated demand. While it is true the banks made record advances in 1963 without any sign of financial difficulty, *the making of advances for loan expansion is quite a different matter than making emergency advances to meet withdrawals.* Members can anticipate their needs for funds on the lending side, and they can schedule their disbursement. Such may not be the case in the event of any withdrawal emergency.

How big should the bank system be? We may know when the first real need arises, but let's hope we don't learn it should have been bigger than it was.

STUDY PROJECT 34

A MORTGAGE LOAN APPLICATION BY JOHN J. SMITH

Assume you are a mortgage loan officer of a Savings and Loan Association and an application is made for a $12,000 loan secured by a first mortgage on a property to be purchased by the applicant at a price of $20,000. The purpose of this loan is to finance part of the purchase price of the property.

The applicant, John J. Smith, 45, married, has 4 children, ages 12, 9, 6, and 4. Mr. Smith has been president of the A & B Manufacturing Company for the past fifteen years. The A & B Manufacturing Company manufactures specialty goods distributed on a regional basis.

Mr. Smith receives an annual salary of $15,000. He has no other source of income except the several hundred dollars in interest per year that the savings account earns. Mrs. Smith is not employed. Mr. Smith carries a checking account which ordinarily has a balance of about a thousand dollars. He has insurance policies to the amount of $30,000; his wife is named as beneficiary.

Mr. Smith stated on his loan application that he owns no real estate and owes no personal debts. He provided no credit references and explained that he always pays cash.

A local retail credit company was engaged for a credit investigation. The investigation report stated that the federal bankruptcy records were checked and no record was found of the applicant. The credit company further reported that to their knowledge he had no present or recent credit account with any of the local stores. The credit company estimated his net worth to be approximately $20,000.

The property which the applicant offers as security for the loan is located at 130 West 46th Street. The property is in a residential neighborhood that is completely built up and located within the city limits. The neighborhood is well kept and may be said to have an upward trend. Though the older buildings in the area were constructed in the pre-World War II era, most of the development took place in the immediate postwar period.

The property is four blocks from an elementary school and one mile from a high school. There is a church across the street. One block from the property is a main thoroughfare with bus transportation. Three blocks north on the thoroughfare is a small retail shopping center.

The street is paved and is in good condition. There are concrete sidewalks and curbs. The neighborhood is served with city water, the city sewage system, natural gas, electric power, and telephone lines. There is adequate police and fire protection. The neighborhood is without any kind of zoning ordinance,

Form LD 100—Rev.

RAILROADMEN'S FEDERAL SAVINGS AND LOAN ASSOCIATION OF INDIANAPOLIS
MORTGAGE LOAN APPLICATION

New Loan ☒
Renewal Loan ☐
Renewal with Additional ☐
F. H. A. Title II ☐   VI ☐
G. I. Loan ☐

All Facts set out in black face type must be answered. Otherwise this Application is not complete.	

Present Holder..
Loan Number...
Date of Loan-Contract..................................
Original Amount..
Balance for ....19........ $........
Delinquent $.....................Ahead $..........
Orig. Appr. $......................Date...............

To Railroadmen's Federal Savings and Loan Association:

I/we hereby apply for membership in Railroadmen's Federal Savings and Loan Association and desire to borrow from said Association **the sum of $.12,000**...................for the purpose of securing said credit and in order to assist the Association in acting upon my/our **request for such credit, I/we furnish the following as a true and correct statement, with reservations, of my/our financial condition.**

Name of Applicant ....John J. Smith...Joint Title.. **Yes**......Age.. **45**......
Wife or Husband......Mary Smith..Age..............
Mailing Address......1466 Shannon Ave,..................................Zone........Telephone. Fl 6 - 3040
Property Location......130 W. 46th St,..

Occupant's Name........Jones............................ Owner ☒ Tenant ☐ Contract ☐ Lot Size...50'.. x...160'.
No. of Rooms......7........M ☒ SM ☐ NM ☐ Water Supply...City............ Acreage.....................
Amount of Loan Desired $.12,000............Int. Rate............% To extend..........20.........years. Standard ☒ Reg. ☐
Purpose of Loan...
.........................PURCHASE FOR HOME...
....
....

Repairs Planned......No.......................Underway.................... **Fully Completed**.............................
Contractor..Estimate ....$.................
Date of Purchase..Proposed.......Price Paid $..20,000...........Home ☒ Investment ☐ Down Payment ..$500.........
Present Owner's Name or Agent...Improvements Added $...........
Inspection Time......Any.........Key..

PERSONAL STATEMENT
Employer..A. & B. Mfg. Co,............... Position......President.............No. of years.....15.....
Previous Employer...Position....................No. of years..............
Dependents—Number....4....Age..12....Age....9....Age..6....Age....4....Age............Age............
Net Amount of Life Insurance $.30,000.........Beneficiary...

CASH ASSETS		INCOME	
Bank Account	$..1,200......	Base Pay . .	$..15,000......
Savings Accounts	$..12,000......	Ave. Overtime .	$..................
Savings Accounts	$..................	Net after Deductions	$..11,000......
Other Assets	$..13,000......	Net income from business or profit . .	$..................
Net Worth in Mortgagor's Business .	$..................	Dividends	$..................
Other Real Estate Owned:		Net Rents	$..................
Location..................................		Pensions (Type....................)	$..................
Mortgage $..........@..........mo. Eq.	$....None......	Income from other sources:	
Location..................................		....	$..................
Mortgage $..........@..........mo. Eq.	$..................	....	$..................
Location..................................		Total Net Income	$..11,000......
Mortgage $..........@..........mo. Eq.	$..................	Credit References:	
Total Value of All Property . .	$..26,200......	Bank..................................	
AMOUNTS OWED		Misc.......Pays cash...............	
For..........@..........mo. $..........		....	
For..........@..........mo. $..........		....	
For..........@..........mo. $..........		....	
Total Amount of Personal Debts .	$......None......	....	
NET WORTH	$..................		

REMARKS
....
....
....

A ☒   B ☐   C ☐   D ☐   E ☐

Signed............John J. Smith.................
                Applicant — Owner — Agent

Application prepared by......J. B.... **Date**..2/2/......

Mortgage loan application.

Form LD102

APPRAISAL REPORT
RAILROADMEN'S FEDERAL SAVINGS AND LOAN ASSOCIATION OF INDIANAPOLIS

1. Location of Property....130 W. 46th St...Owner Occupied.......**X**.....Rented.................
   Name of Occupant...Sold on Contract...
2. New Construction ☐, Old Construction ☒ est.
3. Plot Area.......50'......frontage x.......160'......depth, Acres No................., Lot Level......**X**......., Rough............., High.........
   Low..................., Regular......**X**......., Irregular....................
4. Community: Residential ☒, Business ☐, Semi-business ☐, Suburban ☐. Transition if any to.....No.............................
5. Trend: Up ☒, Down ☐, Static ☐, ...100.....% Built Up. Outside City Limits—Yes ☐, No ☒.
6. Distance to Schools...........4........., Churches..across st.., Transportation.........1........., Shopping Center......3.......
7. Streets: Paved ☒, Graded ☐, Blacktop ☐, Sidewalks ☒, Curb ☒, Sewer ☒, City Water ☒, Well Water ☐, Gas ☒, Power ☒, Septic Tank ☐,
   Electric Pump ☐, Hand Pump ☐.
8. Age of Property: Less than 1 year ☐; 1-5 ☐; 6-10 ☐; 11-20 ☒; Over.....................Years.
9. Design of Residence: Best☐, Good ☒, Fair ☐, Poor ☐. Room Arrangement: Good☒, Fair ☐, Bad ☐.
   Is House Above ☐, Equal ☒, Below ☐ value of typical near-by homes?
10. Number of Stories...1 3/4...... No. of Rooms: Base....Full......., First Floor.....5......., Second Floor......4......., Attic...............
    Finish: Down....Pine...., Enamel....Paint.... Baths: Up....Yes......, Down....Yes...., Shower..Basement also toilet
    Up: Enamel..............., Extra Plumbing................, Bath Room Location: Good ☒, Fair ☐, Bad ☐.
    Bathroom Finish: Walls....Glass......, Floor....Tile......... Equipment: Good☒, Fair ☐, Bad ☐.
    Kitchen: Floors...Lin....., Built-in Cabinets.....Yes...., Cabinet Sink................, Drainboards...Lin...., Breakfast Nook...Yes.....
    Modernized: Yes☒, No ☐.
    Wall Finish: Canvas ☐, Paper ☒, Paint ☒. Condition: Good ☒, Fair ☐, Bad ☐.
    Plumbing: Good ☒, Fair ☐, Bad ☐. Electric Fixtures: Good ☒, Fair ☐, Bad ☐.
    Floors: ......Hardwood.................................. Sub. Floor....Yes....; Condition: Good ☒, Fair ☐, Bad ☐.
    Heat: Stoker ☐, Oil ☒, or Gas Burner ☐, Hot Air ☒, Radiant ☐, A. C. ☒, Blower ☒, Steam ☐, Hot Water ☐, Coal Stove ☐, Fireplace ☒.
    Porches: Wood ☐, Concrete ☒, Brick ☒, Open Terrace ☐, ...Screened........ In ☒, Storm Windows ☒; Screens: Good ☐, Bad ☐.
    Drive: ...Front.............Entrance ☒, Ribbon ☐, Cinder ☐, Stone ☐, Cement ☒, Gravel ☐.
11. Construction: Frame ☒, Brick Veneer ☒, Stone Veneer ☐, Block ☐, Stucco ☐, Prefabricated ☐.
    Asbestos Siding ☐, Imitation Brick ☐, Aluminum ☐; Insulation: Full ☐, Part ☒, Weather Strips ☐.
    Foundation: Concrete ☐, Concrete Block ☒, Tile ☐, Brick ☐; House Settling: Yes ☐, No ☒
    Basement: ...Concrete Floor ☒, Plastered ☐, Wall Boarded ☐, Painted ☐, Fire Safe ☒, Social Room ☒, Damp ☐, Dry ☒, Light ☐, Dark ☐,
    ....Inside.......... Entrance.
    Roof: Asphalt Shingle ☒, Strip Roll ☐, Plain Roll Comp. ☐, Asbestos ☐, Tile ☐, Slate ☐; Condition: Good ☒, Fair ☐, Bad ☐; Gutter: Galvanized ☒,
    Copper ☐, Box ☐; Condition: Good ☒, Fair ☐, Bad ☐.
    Condition of Exterior: Good ☒, Fair ☐, Bad ☐; Termites......No..................., Dry Rot ☐.
12. Garage.....2.....Cars; Wood ☒, Cement Block ☐, Brick Veneer ☐, Stucco ☐; Roof same as house ☒, Overhead Doors ☒, Sealed ☐.
    Other Buildings......No.......
13. Condition of House and Premises: Neat ☒, Fair ☐, Dirty ☐; Rental $..Owner.......Est. Rental $.100.00......; Lot Landscaped: Yes ☒, No ☐
    Condition: ......Good.......
14. Time of Loan: (Based on age of property and trend of community) 5 - 10 - 12 - 15 - 19 years.
15. Is This Property Readily Saleable ☒, Slow ☐, Difficult ☐.
16. Remarks: ..This is a quality built 1 3/4 story brick veneer with frame gable dwelling...
    Has 5 rooms and bath first floor, 4 rooms & bath second floor. This house is arranged.
    into a duplex having separate entrances. Hardwood floors. Fireplace in first floor.
    living room. Both kitchens have modern type built in cabinets and breakfast space.
    Glass wall baths and tile floor. Large screened in rear porch. Full basement. Oil.
    fired hot air a.c. furnace. Sealed social room in basement with fireplace. Automatic.
    water heater. Extra shower & toilet in basement. Front concrete drive to a 2 car frame
                                                OVER *—

Appraisal:			Date:	
Land Value . . $ 2,500	Good	☐ Collateral	Cubic Value per foot . .	
Improvements . $ 17,500	Fair	☒ "	Total Cubage . . .	
Outbuildings . . $	Fair Only ☐	"	Garage	
Total Value . . $ 20,000	Poor	☐ "	Total Replacement .	

Report submitted by

_____   _____
Appraiser   Appraiser

Appraisal report.

and the deed to the property contains no restrictive covenants. The property is approximately equal in value to the other properties in the area.

The main building is a typically-constructed, conventionally-styled, 1¾-story of brick veneer over wood frame. The gabled roof is of asphalt shingle and is in good condition. The first floor has five rooms and a bath. The second floor has four rooms and a bath. The house is arranged into a duplex with separate entrances. The property has hardwood floors, a fireplace in the first-floor living room, modern built-in cabinets in the kitchen, and glass enclosed tubs and tile floors in the baths. There is a large screened-in rear porch and a full basement. The basement has an oil-fire, hot-air, a.c. furnace, automatic water heater, and bath. There is a sealed social room in the basement with a fireplace. There is a two-car garage with access over a concrete driveway. The appraiser from the savings and loan association appraised the property at $20,000.

STUDY PROJECT 35

THE FUTURE OF MORTGAGE CREDIT: CHANGING CHARACTER OF THE REAL ESTATE MORTGAGE MARKETS *

Since 1945, non-farm mortgage debt has risen from $30 billion to approximately $260 billion. Today's mortgage debt now exceeds, but not by much, the publicly held Federal debt. In 1945 it was a mere 12 per cent of the Federal debt. Today's mortgage debt is more than double the demand deposits of our commercial banks. Then it was less than one-half. Today's mortgage debt is also more than double the policy reserves of life insurance companies. Then it was substantially less. Today's mortgage debt is four times as large as the total assets of all Federal Reserve Banks, approximately four times the outstanding consumer debt, three times the state and local government debt, and 60 per cent greater than long-term corporate debt.

From what study of the mortgage markets I have been able to make, I have reached a few conclusions that seem worthy of discussion. Among these are the following:

1. After many years of relative decline, as compared with home mortgages, mortgages on income properties are now gaining rapidly.

2. Savings and loan associations, by continuing to grow more rapidly than other mortgage lenders, have not only become the dominant force in the home mortgage markets but are beginning to move in this direction in the income property field.

3. Geographical restrictions on mortgage lending, especially in the case of savings and loan associations, continue to fragment the mortgage markets, and are now beginning to interfere with and distort the sound growth of our savings institutions.

4. The second mortgage and other means of secondary financing have again returned to the home mortgage markets.

* Edward E. Edwards. Reprinted by permission, *The Journal of Finance*, XIX, No. 2, Part 1 (May, 1964), 313–20.

5. The federally insured or guaranteed mortgage has declined as compared with the conventional mortgages, the terms of which have continued to be liberalized.

6. Foreclosures have again become a normal feature of mortgage lending.

7. The annual increase in mortgage debt, as compared with construction expenditures or other measures of increased real estate values, suggests that mortgage credit is being used extensively to get money out of real estate. This in turn suggests that mortgagee interests in real estate are both increasing and becoming more permanent.

8. Further growth in the supply of mortgage funds is now being threatened by a variety of proposed changes in laws and regulations governing our financial institutions, especially savings and loan associations. However, further growth might well be more seriously threatened by failure of supervisory authorities to deal with unsafe and unsound practices if in fact these do exist.

Rather than add to this list, I wish now to explore and develop these points. Let's look first at the changing distribution of our mortgages as between homes and income properties. During the past five years, when the total non-farm mortgage debt increased by $96 billion, mortgage debt on income properties increased by $30 billion, almost one-third of the total. During the preceding five years (1954–58), debt on income properties increased by only $15 billion, which was less than one-fourth of the total increase. Stated somewhat differently, lending on income properties has doubled while home mortgage lending was growing by less than 30 per cent. More significantly, mortgage lending on income properties as a percentage of their total non-farm mortgage lending increased from 29 to 50 per cent for life insurance companies, from 32 to 50 per cent for commercial banks, from 19 to 30 per cent for mutual savings banks, and from 5 to 14 per cent for savings and loan associations. While I do not necessarily agree with those who believe this is a sign of deterioration in credit standards, I do believe it is a significant development, and especially so in view of the structural rigidities in our mortgage markets.

Without offering reasons why this might occur, let's assume a continued rise in mortgage debt on income properties. Who will hold it? Will life insurance companies and commercial banks remove themselves still further from the home mortgage field? Even if they do, will they have adequate funds to meet the mortgage demand for income properties? My guess, and that's about all it is, would be that at least some insurance companies and some banks would stay in the home mortgage field, and that mutual savings banks and savings and loan associations would continue to push into income property lending. But for savings and loan associations that will require changes in laws, regulations, examination procedures, and attitudes at the supervisory level, and new methods of doing business at the association level.

Present restrictions on associations in making loans on multi-family and commercial properties do not really encourage this type of business, and in fact do not give a well-managed association sufficient underwriting freedom to acquire the highest quality loans or to incorporate the safest and best terms. What lending powers associations possess in this area have come about primarily as exceptions to the basic idea that these are home financing institutions. The exceptions do permit some lending to be done, but they do not give associations anything like the broad powers the life insurance companies have.

The extent to which associations move into this field will depend largely on what the Congress and the FHLB Board do to broaden lending powers. If geographical limitations on home mortgage lending are extended or removed, there may be less need for relaxing present restrictions on income property lending. I would much prefer to see the geographical limitations removed first, but that is not a prediction of what will happen. I am afraid most savings and loan managers would prefer to keep their present position of oligopoly or near monopoly in a limited geographical market, and I am afraid also that their wishes are likely to prevail in any changes to laws and regulations.

If savings and loan associations become more significant lenders on income properties, the market will take on a much different aspect. When life insurance companies tended to dominate this area of the market, decisions were made in part at least on the basis of national experience. Decisions by commercial banks presumably were made in part if not largely on the basis of experienced judgment as to business risk and potential. On what basis will local savings and loan associations make their decision? Will we have a "good" market for mortgage loans for unsound promotions that more experienced lenders might turn down? Will "sound" projects have more difficulty getting financed because of inexperienced analysis?

Questions of this type might be asked also if associations stayed in the home mortgage field but extended the geographical area of their markets. Many students of mortgage lending experience in the early thirties concluded that it was the distant loan that caused trouble, either because it was not properly underwritten in the first instance or could not receive adequate supervision or servicing. Transportation and communication have greatly shrunk distances since then, however, and associations have grown in size sufficiently that distant lending need not be scattered or isolated lending.

The fragmentation of the home mortgage market shows up most clearly in the case of rapidly growing areas such as California, where substantially higher mortgage interest rates continue to prevail. While associations in other parts of the nation can now buy participations in California loans, they cannot make conventional loans or buy them outright. California associations thus can and do pay higher dividend rates, but this has not as yet moved sufficient funds to equalize either mortgage interest rates or dividend rates across the nation. Proposals for secondary markets for conventional mortgages or privately insured mortgages have not made much headway, nor has the FHLB System done very much in moving substantial sums from capital-surplus to capital-short areas.

✿　✿　✿

STUDY PROJECT 36

QUALITY OF CREDIT *

Lee Kendall, in a speech to the Investment Analysts Society of Chicago on the subject of quality of credit, suggested that while he was obviously worried about the possibility that the quality of mortgage credit had deteriorated, *he*

* *Economics for Savings and Loan Executives*, Graduate School of Savings and Loan, Bloomington, Indiana, 1964.

pointed out that liberalization of terms and deterioration in quality were not necessarily the same thing.

He questioned—and rightly so—the idea that "the quality of credit is the composite of the characteristics of the property, the borrower, and the loan." Under such a concept, presumably, the best loan would be (1) on a soundly constructed, well designed property, in a good neighborhood; (2) to a stable and responsible borrower with a high income relative to monthly payment; and (3) for an amount representing a low debt-to-value ratio. The poorest loan would have the opposite of these characteristics, and all other loans would fall somewhere in between.

Omitted from these criteria, he said, is an all important element, "the condition of the local real estate economy." Also omitted, it seems to us, is the most important factor of all—time. Mortgage loans stay around for many years. Good loans become bad, bad ones good. *The idea that quality is fixed for all time by the characteristics present when the loan is made just will not hold up.*

But even if it were true that these characteristics determined quality, we still are faced with an almost impossible job of measurement. The trouble is that loans for a high percentage of value are made on new houses; loans with a low loan-to-value ratio are likely to be on properties in a poor neighborhood or poorly maintained; what's a well designed house—and even a well constructed one—is a matter of opinion, as to a considerable extent also is the quality of a neighborhood, and so on. How do we put these contradictory elements into a formula? Or if we develop a formula, how do we know whether it is any good?

Individual associations probably should have a method of classifying their own loans, in order that management will know the changing characteristics of the loan portfolio. Very likely it would be a good idea for associations to measure loan performance separately by broad categories of loans in the portfolio. This might permit adjustment in policy to get a different portfolio mix as time brings actual experience. But this is quite different than rating loans on the basis of their initial characteristics and assuming this measures quality.

Getting back to Kendall, he believes that home mortgage lending is experiencing a "rolling" adjustment, at a time when the economy can withstand it. He looks forward, as we do, to the latter half of this decade, when another housing and mortgage lending boom should reappear. It would be a shame to lose this opportunity by "going broke" now through careless lending. But an even worse catastrophe would be the collapse of the real estate market because mortgage lenders quit making loans except on what they thought were the very best properties, or what they thought were the highest credit risks, and for only a small percentage of "value."

STUDY PROJECT 37

WHAT POPULATION TRENDS AND MIX MEAN *

Total population growth during the '60s will be relatively high, although it is apt to be under the growth rate of the '50s. The crude birth rate (births per 1,000 total population) and the fertility rate (births per 1,000 women 15–

---

* Philip M. Hauser. *Director's Digest* (April, 1964) condensation from *The Mortgage Banker* (January, 1964).

44 years) have turned downward. Other evidence indicates our postwar boom birth rate may decline perceptibly.

The absolute increase in population, however, will not decline as much as the birth rate, because the number of women of reproductive age will increase rapidly as our postwar baby crop matures.

The number of births annually is likely to remain about 4 million, even while the rate drops. Had the birth rate remained at its postwar level, the U. S. population would number 214 million by 1970. However, now the population is likely to be below 210 million—about 30 million for the decade—still a substantial increase in total market.

Predictions of a boom economy in the "soaring '60s," based in part on the continuation of the postwar baby boom, have thus far failed to materialize.

The postwar upsurge in population growth undoubtedly provided a stimulus to economic growth, but population changes during the '60s contain bearish as well as bullish implications. Two of the bearish aspects are the flooding of the labor market and the disproportionate increase in younger and older households compared with intermediate-aged households. Arising largely from our changing age structure, these factors will greatly alter the character of consumer demand.

Babies born after demobilization in 1946 are reaching labor force age in the '60s. New workers under age 25 entering the labor force now average 600,000 a year, three times as many as between 1955 and 1960. The bulge in new entrant workers—at a time when we have a high level of chronic unemployment and increasing automation—may constitute the gravest peacetime challenge our economy has ever faced.

If the unemployment volume rises as postwar offspring begin to reach age 18 in 1964, we may anticipate mounting unemployment compensation and relief costs and that the government will be obliged to experiment with various types of programs to cut unemployment.

Under such circumstances, it also may be anticipated that consumer demand will slough off in many areas—the teenage market, the marriage market, and other markets oriented to it—and that general consumer demand may decline, as the public interprets rising unemployment as indicating an uncertain economic outlook.

Between 1960 and 1970, households may increase by about 11 million (or 20%) from the total of 52.6 million in 1960. Households with heads under 25, however, will increase by over 90% and those with older heads—55 and over—by about 30%. In contrast, households with heads of intermediate age—25 to 54 years—will increase by only 10%.

Less than one-third of the increase in households will have heads of intermediate age. These constitute the bulk of the home buying market. Consequently the demand for housing during the '60s is likely to be stronger for apartment units than owned homes.

A drop in the rate of young households formed in the '60s would diminish the demand for apartments but would not adversely affect demand for homes; however, it probably would lessen the demand for owned homes in the '70s.

The changing age structure, all other things being equal, will adversely affect savings volume. Of the increase expected in persons 20 years of age and over in the '60s, 12.4 million (or three-fourths) will be under 25 or over 55. Only 4 million (or one-fourth) will be of intermediate age, 25 to 54 years.

Since the younger and older persons tend to save less than those of inter- mediate age, savings volume during the '60s will not rise as rapidly as if the population increases were more concentrated in the intermediate age groups.

STUDY PROJECT 38

CONSUMER ASPIRATIONS AND HOUSING DEMAND IN THE 1960's *

Locational Preferences

One of the dynamic factors in the construction market throughout the 1950's was the shift of population to the suburbs and the consequent growth of shopping centers and outlying community facilities. Some experts believe that this outward movement may be reaching a limit now for two reasons: (1) the scarcity of land in reasonably convenient suburban locations and (2) the time and cost involved in commuting longer distances to work. However, studies of consumer preferences and commuting patterns strongly indicate a further outward movement in the future.

Replies to the question, "If you could do as you please, would you like to live closer to the center of (. . . METRO AREA . . .) or farther from the center or just where you are?" indicated that about 70 per cent of people ex- press satisfaction with their present location; among the remaining 30 per cent, the answer "farther out" is three times as frequent as the answer "we would like to live closer in." Similar results were obtained in earlier Survey Research Center surveys in 1961 and 1963. Thus the finding that many people prefer to move farther out is confirmed by a large number of measurements.

The contrary wish—to live closer to the downtown area—is most frequent among older people, families with incomes under $3,000, and people who do not engage in outdoor activities at all (a characteristic associated with ad- vancing age and low income). The desire to live farther out is particularly pronounced among married couples with children; one-fourth of this group would like to live farther out. Significantly, the desire to live farther out does not diminish at all with the distance which people already live from the center of the metropolitan city.

Of particular interest is the proportion of the mobile population who would like to move farther out. Among those families who said they would move or might move within the metropolitan area during the *next five years*, about 40 per cent reported that they planned to move farther out. This very high pro- portion corresponds to recent experience. Among the group who moved within the metropolitan area during the *past five years*, as many as 42 per cent re- ported that they moved farther out.

❋   ❋   ❋

* Eva Mueller, *The Outlook on Consumer Behavior* (Ann Arbor, Mich.: The Foundation for Research on Human Behavior, 1964), pp. 52–57.

STUDY PROJECT 39

SOME FACTS AND FIGURES ON THE
OFFICE BUILDING MARKET *

Manhattan Island valued initially by the appraisers, shrewd then as now, at twenty-four dollars has grown in valuation and occupancy far beyond the expectation or imagination of the Indians and the Dutch. For tax purposes, its present valuation is $11,094,658,435. You could buy a lot of wampum at Tiffany's or Cartier's today for that kind of money!

A great deal of the history and development of our City has its origins in the background of our early beginnings. No one will deny that the port facilities of New York contributed to its settlement and growth. Today, this influence is still felt in our transportation, commercial and travel industries, and our favorable geographical location may link our further expansion to the growing European Economic Community.

.   .   .   .

At the beginning of the 19th Century, according to the Census Bureau, New York's built-up area extended to Eighth Street. By 1822, it ran to Thirty-first Street and thirty years later to Forty-second Street. But we must remember for all of this period, Telephone and Telstar were not part of the daily business life; and personal contact, business luncheons, and personal messengers were the communication channels. So, of necessity expansion in area did not occur; rather, concentration was desired. In 1848, when James Bogardus introduced the cast-iron structure which could rise vertically to ten or fifteen stories, the growth trend upward began. In the 1870's, came the efficient elevator, and floor stacking became practical. The nine story New York Tribune building was erected in 1875, and is still standing—one of the oldest office buildings in New York City. Compared with the 102 story Empire State of 1931, we can say that we have at least made a great deal of upward progress in fifty years.

At the turn of the Century, midtown Manhattan, our present location, presented a different aspect to the visitor. Saint Patrick's Cathedral was called "Hughes' Folly" when its site was selected; its location was way up in the country. The shops were in lower Manhattan. This area, Grand Central was a residential one with Hotels scattered about to accommodate the travelers and businessmen who thronged here. The great names of New York lounged, dined, and partied in this area. Sherry's, the Ritz-Carlton, Diamond Jim Brady's Residence, the Vanderbilt Mansion, the Gould Home, the Murray Hill Hotel— all were adjacent to this Hotel and have been replaced with office buildings.

The twenties brought a perceptible change to the area, Grand Central in particular. The tower-type building was the favorite then—the Chrysler, the Chanin, and the Lincoln rose to mock the staid converted Hotel-office buildings surrounding them everywhere. A change was felt and an upswing of interest in office building construction was evident. The Depression halted the activity, building ceased, and it was not until Rockefeller Center was conceived and initiated that any new construction was added to the inventory of New York's office buildings. It was in the 'Twenties too, that the steam locomotive was

* Dr. Gordon D. MacDonald, Vice President, The Real Estate Board of New York, Inc., Wednesday, November 13, 1963.

banished from sight on Park Avenue. With its withdrawal from view, apartments proliferated and the elegant residential aspect of the midtown section was established. The poor people, that is, those with no mansion on Fifth Avenue, lived in the brownstones of the fifties or in the spacious apartments of Park Avenue.

World War II brought controls and no building, and now in the post World War II era, we have building because of controls. The rent controlled apartments, homes and brownstones are yielding to commercial ventures and the office building, owned by private entrepreneur, or a syndicate, is replacing them rapidly. Every possible plot of land, regardless of configuration, is considered, purchased and utilized by builders. Every design is used, zigs, zags, and straight up and down. Side streets which once were peopled by dog-walkers, party-goers, visitors, and residents suffer from six o'clock shadow. After dark, no one is here to walk the streets, seriously that is,—all are on trains, riding to suburbia to rest, so they can return to the glass and steel canyons at nine A.M.

The Real Estate Board of New York has records which state that there were 74 office buildings in Manhattan in 1900. But, year after year in the early 1900's, and more especially in the 1920's, New York's architects and builders etched in the City's famous skyline. In the first ten years of the Century, 76 new office buildings were constructed in Manhattan, more than as many as had existed in 1900; 99 went up in the years 1911–1924, and another 138 between 1925–1933, making a total of 387 by 1933. The progress of office building in the New York Region, like everything else, slowed down and came to an almost complete stop during the Depression of the 1930's. The optimism that had prevailed in the twenties began to wane. As the vacancy rate in the City's office buildings soared to almost 25 per cent in 1934, it was commonly believed that the demand for office space had declined to a permanently lower level, and that the great days of office building would never come back. New York, it was widely believed, had passed its zenith. The wave of the future lay in decentralization, suburbanization—anywhere—but away from the City.

After World War II, the office building was distinterred as it were, and the death notice which had been tentatively posted, was rescinded. During the sixteen years after 1946, Manhattan added approximately 55 million square feet of office space through the construction of tall buildings. This was more office space than existed in any other city. It represented more office construction than took place in that period in all the rest of the country put together. Exploding or expanding, call it what you will, the metropolis began to take on a new look. The old look is fast disappearing: the small delicatessen shop, the vegetable store, and the convivial pub located for the most part in the old and sub-standard structures which previously existed in many of the business areas have already gone or are fast disappearing. Such neighborhood services cannot afford space in the gleaming splendor of the new structures, and their clientele has disappeared—the residents replaced by workers who cannot dally after work—their recreation has a time table to govern it.

It is a difficult task to attempt to compress a report on the facts and figures of Manhattan Real Estate Activity into ten minutes; actually, it is impossible. But, we would like you to have some feeling for the pageant of New York City, and to be able to feel some competency in judging it, and relating its activity to the situations you encounter in your own communities. Undoubtedly, as you saunter about, along Fifth and Park Avenues, you must of necessity suffer from "Busman's holiday" syndrome: inspect, appraise, and speculate on the new construction which you see about you. Park Avenue from Forty-fifth to Fifty-ninth Streets will give you some of the best examples we have of old, new, and transitional areas in Manhattan. The Pan American Building dominates the scene; the islands planted with chrysanthemums provide a sample of Community beautifying action, and the new offices, and the ones in process, show the new activity in the area. The Racquet and Tennis Club, and Saint Bartholomew's Church are monuments to past living; how long can they survive in the competitive office market area? Any of the apartments left on Park Avenue are almost totally cooperative, representing a new thought and new trend in real estate in a changing world. New thoughts in Real Estate trends are well represented by this Avenue. Just imagine, how extensive this trend is when you consider all the other Avenues which are witnessing the same type of growth and reuse.

*   *   *

STUDY PROJECT 40

SHOPPING CENTERS: NEW SHAPE *

The suburban shopping center, a building standing in a serried sea of cars, is architecture's most unique and successful response to the automobile age. It is about to acquire a new shape.

The design is the work of Skidmore, Owings & Merrill, who were asked by Macy's to design a new store on a cramped site in Elmhurst, L.I., a crowded New York suburb. Since there wasn't enough room for the conventional parking lot, SOM architects simply wrapped the parking space around the store.

The result is a circular building flanked by two spiral ramps. Customers drive up a ramp, peel off at the level they choose. There are two parking levels for each selling floor, and the customer parks diagonally on the outside or inner rim. Eliminated is the long walk from the distant parking lot.

Theoretically at least, no customer need walk more than 75 ft. from car to counter. Says Project Manager Albert Kennerly: "For the first time in modern times the auto is brought to the curb of the store. It will be just like parking on Main Street in front of your favorite shop."

* *Time* Magazine (April 10, 1964), p. 54.

STUDY PROJECT 41

IN THE REALTY BUSINESS IN SPITE OF THEMSELVES *

Companies that assure transferred employees they won't lose on sale of their homes are finding they have taken on more real estate dealing than they like.

Company housing today means something quite different from the dreary row upon row of frame houses that made up the traditional mill town.

Some U.S. corporations find themselves almost as actively in the residential real estate business as the 19th Century mill and mine owners. But these days their holdings are likely to consist of commodious homes in fashionable suburbs.

* *Business Week* (August 10, 1963).

The reason, of course, is the increase in executive mobility, especially since World War II. When General Motors, or International Business Machines, or General Electric transfers a management man, it may cushion the shock for him by taking responsibility for disposing of his old house—and absorbing any loss he might suffer. As a result, companies are handling homes in this manner at a rate put by one estimate at $100-million a year.

Landlord Troubles

Getting into the realty business adds up to a whole series of new problems for corporate management.

One Pittsburgh-based executive insisted that his rock garden be shipped with him to his new location out west. Over company protests of "Can you imagine the tonnage!" his rock garden went west with him.

In another case, an executive refused to give up any of his 15 cats of assorted sizes and colors in order to make renting a home easier. After weeks of trying to get someone to rent him a house, the executive, happily in possession of his cat kingdom, was forced to buy a home at his new location.

A vice-president moving to the New York area told company representatives that any new house had to be checked by his wife—because she had a fear of the color green. Even the slightest trace of green caused her to reject the home whatever its other merits.

And then there's the executive who got his company to ship and curry his string of polo ponies—and even build new stables for them. And the executive's wife who insisted that the company find her husband a suitable house, at their new location, within walking distance of the Methodist church with the best paid choir.

Add to these the more common problems of dogs, parakeets, children with special educational needs, and wives who want "just the right kind of house."

Dealing in Houses

Relocation programs may range in other respects between the extremes of silver-platter treatment and almost nothing. But nearly all companies try to smooth transfers by guaranteeing the employee against loss on the sale of his home. This is where a manufacturer soon discovers he is wading knee-deep in the real estate business.

The company may absorb brokers' commissions, pay closing fees and appraisal costs, and even take care of mortgage prepayment penalties. For a relatively inexpensive $20,000 house, these costs can easily amount to $2,000 or $2,500.

Finally, Ownership

Some companies go so far as to buy the houses of transferred employees at fair market value.

General Motors, for one, will offer to buy the private homes of employees at the average price of three independent appraisals. Through Argonaut Realty, a separate division that handles the company's real estate problems, GM arranges for the purchase and holds the house for resale.

While the house sits in GM's inventory, waiting for a buyer, the company has to pay for maintenance, taxes, and costs of keeping the house in show condition (grass cutting, painting). The longer the house stays on the market, the more expensive it becomes to the company.

Top Secret

Companies label these costs "top secret," but it is not unusual for larger companies to have more than $1-million worth of single-family houses in inventory.

Under normal circumstances, most companies feel that costs are justified—more or less—if they help speed the transfer of employees. But as costs soar, and the real estate market softens, companies are going through an agonizing reappraisal of policies.

Some companies, for instance, now sanction executive moves only when "absolutely necessary." Others have adopted a tougher policy on home appraisals in order to escape some of their bigger losses.

One company lost $7,000 when a home, appraised at a high value on a weekday, turned out to be worth far less on weekends when bumper-to-bumper traffic passed by the front door. And a 20-room mansion has been on the hands of another company for four years because it was over-appraised.

"Actually," a company spokesman says, "nobody wants a white elephant quite that large."

Pain Killer

To ease the pain, at least two brand-new nationwide companies just this year have gone into the business of handling employee transfers. Relocation Finance Corp., based in St. Louis, has signed trial contracts with two large companies. Homequity, Inc., with main offices in New York, Houston, and Los Angeles, is presently helping 10 major companies with their realty problems, and has firm contracts with two others.

Both Homequity and RFC will take over all of a company's realty problems —from house purchase to resale—for a fee, which they claim is less than what companies are now spending. Homequity plans sometime soon to set up an IBM sorter to match corporate buyers and sellers of private homes on a nationwide basis. With the added efficiency of the sorter, Homequity expects to knock 2% off the current average broker's fee—dropping the fee from 6% to 4%.

Self-Help

Though most companies don't broadcast their unhappiness over finding themselves in the real estate business, it is evident that management is searching for answers.

Interest in a recent American Management Assn. seminar on corporate housing problems was so strong that three additional seminars had to be scheduled to handle the overflow. And more major companies—so says a recent survey by the National Industrial Conference Board—are beginning to ask their employees to handle their own realty problems.

STUDY PROJECT 42

AN ADAPTIVE PROGRAM FOR AGRICULTURE *

Three Possible Approaches to the Problem of Agriculture

The problem of agriculture is not unique. It is the leading case in a large class of problems. Other problems in this class include the industry in which workers are being rapidly displaced by technological changes; the industry experiencing increased competition from imports; and the area depressed by the exhaustion of some natural resource.

The common characteristic shared by these problems is that, as a result of changes in the economy, the labor and capital employed in the industry cannot all continue to earn, by producing goods for sale in a free market, as much income as they formerly earned, or as much as they could earn if employed in some other use; that is—*the industry is using too many resources.*

MEMORANDUM OF COMMENT, RESERVATION OR DISSENT

By Fred C. Foy: "I agree with all of this paragraph except the italicized statement. It is true that in some industries or areas of the economy labor and capital cannot earn as much income as they could if employed in some other use but who is CED to say that in this situation "too many resources" are being used. In a free economy the owner of the labor or capital must be free to decide how he wishes to use them. It will always be true that some capital will earn less than others in the market place, but their earning less does not necessarily mean that they are being wasted or should be withdrawn."

Agriculture is the largest problem in this class, as measured by the number of people involved. It is also the case in which we have the longest experience with a variety of attempts to find a solution. This experience, if properly interpreted, holds valuable lessons for dealing with other similar problems.

There are three general kinds of policy possible in the kind of situation we have described.

The laissez-faire approach

If nothing is done to prevent it, the incomes of labor or capital or, usually, both in the affected industry or area will decline, at least relatively to incomes earned by similar resources elsewhere, and often absolutely. This will deter the flow of new labor and capital into the industry or area. Some of the resources engaged there will not be replaced when they are retired. Other resources engaged will move to other uses. The resources that move will raise their incomes, and the incomes of those that remain will be improved by the reduction of the resources still in the industry. This is the process upon which we normally rely for adjustment to economic change, and normally it works well. It works best—that is with the smallest and shortest decline in the incomes of resources in affected industries—when: (1) opportunities for employing labor and capital in the rest of the economy are numerous, (2) the shift of resources needed to restore incomes in the affected industry or area is relatively small, and (3) there is no serious obstacle to the movement of the

* Excerpted from the policy statement by the Committee for Economic Development, *An Adaptive Program for Agriculture* (New York: The Committee, 1962).

resources involved. Where there is a substantial departure from these conditions it is necessary to consider other approaches.

The protectionist approach

This approach to the problems of an industry using too many resources attempts to sustain the incomes of persons attached to the affected industry, or area, even though the incomes they could earn by selling their product in a free market have declined. This approach usually requires government action. In some cases it can be followed by concerted action of the workers or businesses involved, although this in turn often depends upon government support or sanction. A variety of measures can be employed. For example, the government may purchase the product of the industry at prices above the free market. The government may limit the industry's production or sales in order to keep prices up. The government may, as in the marketing orders and agreements used for perishable farm products, try to support prices, and income of producers, by regulations aimed to secure "orderly marketing" of output. The government may attempt to sustain prices and income by limiting imports. The businesses and workers concerned may adopt rules limiting the introduction of new technology or holding hours of work artificially low. In particular areas the government may subsidize the continuation or introduction of industries that would be unprofitable without the subsidy. Whether such measures in fact help to sustain incomes depends upon circumstances that vary from case to case. But even where successful this approach sacrifices the basic national interest in efficiency and growth; it must be regarded as inferior to approaches that would reconcile this interest with the interests of the particular industries or areas affected. At its worst it can grossly distort the use of the nation's resources.

The adaptive approach

The adaptive approach utilizes positive government action to facilitate and promote the movement of labor and capital where they will be most productive and will earn the most income. Essentially this approach seeks to achieve what the laissez-faire approach would ordinarily expect to achieve but to do it more quickly and with less deep and protracted loss of income to the persons involved than might result if no assistance were given. The adaptive approach requires improved knowledge of available employment opportunities, and measures to finance movement and retrain workers; that is, a generally improved labor market. It works best when there is a high rate of economic activity and employment.

The adaptive approach seeks to achieve adjustment to economic reality without imposing hardships, by means of programs that promote adjustment but cushion the effects upon people and property. Although the adaptive ap-

---

MEMORANDUM OF COMMENT, RESERVATION OR DISSENT

By Allan Sproul, in which Messrs. Emilio G. Collado, Fred C. Foy and Thomas B. McCabe have asked to be associated: "What we are seeking is a return to economic reality without imposing *unnecessary* hardships upon particular people or property. Adjustments to the economic realities of a free market do impose hardships on some people some of the time. Attempts to protect everyone from hardship all of the time eventually throttle free markets."

---

proach, like the protectionist approach, requires government action, the objectives of the government action are entirely different. The adaptive approach calls for action by government working with the free market, not against it. It seeks to achieve the results of the free market more quickly and easily, rather than to keep those results from occurring. The adaptive approach works by permitting full production, rather than by limiting production. And, government adaptive programs applied to particular industries can ordinarily be temporary, whereas protectionist government actions generate the need for their own indefinite continuance.

Consequences of the Policies Followed Since 1947 Are Summarized Briefly Here

1. Farm policy may have moderated the decline in farm incomes, per person engaged in agriculture, that would have occurred if there had been no farm program after 1947, but it has not prevented a growing gap between farm and nonfarm earnings. In addition, it has left many farmers in a situation where withdrawal of government programs would cause a sharp drop in their incomes.

2. The program has not helped most the farmers who were most in need of help. Since the attempt to support farm income has been made by way of supporting the prices of key farm goods, farmers who market the most get the most out of the support program. Smaller farmers, who market less, do not receive large amounts from the price-income support programs.

3. The support of prices has deterred the movement of resources out of agriculture. It has given farmers erroneous expectations of the earnings their labor might yield in agriculture in the future. The high support prices, plus the technological change increasing the amount of land a farmer could efficiently work, have raised land prices and misled the farmer about the income he was actually earning. These same factors, plus the financial capacity created by the higher land values, have encouraged the investment of capital in agriculture.

4. Other aspects of farm policy have done too little to bring about the withdrawal of resources from agriculture. Little of the considerable withdrawal of resources that has occurred was the result of policy.

5. Controls have diverted some land from its most economic use to less economic uses, tending to reduce efficiency in agriculture.

6. Taxpayers have borne a heavy burden which, given the character of the Federal tax system, has impeded the growth of the economy generally. In recent years Federal outlays simply for carrying accumulations of surpluses have come to about $1 billion annually.

7. The negotiating position of the United States in bargaining for freer access for American agricultural products to European markets has been impaired by the fact that the United States was subsidizing its own exports and imposing quotas to protect high domestic prices.

8. Underdeveloped countries have received more assistance from the United States in the form of more agricultural commodities than they would otherwise have received. But without these programs, and the burdens they imposed on the American taxpayer, they might have received other assistance more valuable to them and less costly to us.

9. Some segments of agriculture have been subjected to controls on their freedom of action.

STUDY PROJECT 43

REALTORS TAKING BUSINESS ABROAD *

WASHINGTON, March 28 (UPI)—Voulez-vous acheter un supermarket à Chicago?

This is the kind of question six U.S. real estate men are going to be asking in Brussels one day this spring.

Or if you don't want to buy a supermarket, how about an office building, hotel, high-rise apartment, industrial plant, industrial site or shopping center?

They'll be peddling this kind of property in half a dozen European countries.

For the realtors it's a chance to make a buck. For the government it's a chance to cut the U.S. balance of payments deficit by bringing more dollars into this country from abroad.

Both want to take advantage of the new tendency for real estate money to go international. A British firm has taken a 50 per cent interest in New York's new 59-story Pan American building.

An Italian group is building a $60-million apartment complex near the Lincoln Memorial in Washington. Another British outfit is behind Boston's first big speculative office building.

The Commerce Department has been helping American manufacturers get abroad to sell their products. So why not American real estate men, commerce asked. The Society of Industrial Realtors liked the idea and picked six of its most prominent members to go.

They're Harold Hess of Philadelphia, C. Pat Lumpkin of Houston, J. J. Harrington Jr. of Chicago, James Brett of San Francisco, J. D. Sawyer of Middletown, O., and A. Kyle Bettilyon of Salt Lake City.

The mission will talk to leading investors, bankers, mortgage lenders and industrialists in Sweden, the Netherlands, Belgium, West Germany, Switzerland and Italy.

Their sales pitch will run something like this:

Land costs much less in the United States. Land that brings $300 a foot in downtown Paris, London or Rome can be bought for $50 a foot in Washington, $85 a foot in Philadelphia and comparable prices elsewhere.

The United States is growing. Property bought cheaply now will be worth a lot more later on.

Foreigners often don't have to pay any capital gains tax when they sell property in the United States.

The United States is a stable country. Investors here don't have to worry about a revolution.

You only need about 40 per cent cash to throw up a building in this country. In Europe, a builder often has to pay 60 per cent of his costs in cash.

The call has gone out to realtors and others to offer property. The society has sent special notices to the firms on Fortune Magazine's 500 list. So far, more than $200 million worth of property has been offered.

The Society is being choosey about what it accepts. "The Europeans are very sophisticated and very sharp," says one official. "We're only going to take over first-class offerings."

* *The Indianapolis Times* (Sunday, March 29, 1964).

To be eligible for the mission, a property will have to list at $200,000 or more.

And it can't be some old dud that no one's been able to unload at home. Only new listings or ones recently on the market will qualify.

—John Pierson

STUDY PROJECT 44

THE DISTRIBUTION OF NATIONAL INCOME AMONG LABOR, LAND, AND CAPITAL *

The significance of the distinction between reproducible assets and land as shown in the table is obvious—broadly speaking, the quantity of reproducible assets can be changed by saving and investment, while the quantity of land is given.[1] International assets are placed in the former category because their value can be changed by domestic saving even though they may take any physical form or represent financial claims.[2]

Nonfarm residences are grouped here with other reproducible capital, but except where the focus of discussion is the relationship between saving and investment, I shall nearly always treat them separately from business capital in further analysis. The fact that decisions to purchase a house for the owner's own use are not based closely on a hypothetical comparison of their "earnings" with those of alternative investments and that the realized rate of return (exclusive of capital gains) apparently is, in fact, much below that on other capital, when combined with the great importance of houses in the capital stock and current investment, makes this distinction necessary. Decisions to buy a house are in large part consumer decisions.[3] Their peculiar status requires that they be given separate treatment. Formerly, they may be thought of as a kind of input separate from business capital.

The estimates of the distribution of national income serve two key purposes in our investigation:

1. They make it possible to estimate the amount by which the national income could be increased by increasing the quantity of any one of the factors of production by a small percentage.

The returns to the various factors of production—labor, land, and the various types of capital goods that I have distinguished—exhaust the value of the

---

* Excerpted from Edward F. Denison, *The Sources of Economic Growth in the U.S.*, Committee for Economic Development Supplementary Paper No. 13 (New York: The Committee, 1962), pp. 29–32.

[1] This is not, of course, literally true; see Chapter 10 [of the paper].

[2] The reader should be aware that the distribution provided in Table 4 [1, 2, and 3 not shown] is a distribution of the national income as measured by the Department of Commerce. This means that no return is included on government or (with minor exceptions) institutionally-owned property or consumer durable goods (except houses); that undistributed profits of foreign subsidiaries of U. S. corporations are excluded; and that profits and rents are computed on the basis of depreciation procedures (largely use of accounting charges) followed by the Department of Commerce and are gross of depletion of natural resources.

[3] At one time, the purchase of a house by the prospective occupant was handled in the national income statistics like a consumer purchase and no return was imputed to its owner. Despite my comments here, I believe the decision to switch to the imputed-rent treatment was a correct one.

Table 4. Percentage Distribution of National Income Among Factors of
Production, 1909–1958

Period	National Income	Labor	Land	Total	Non-farm Residential Structures	Other Structures and Equipment	Inventories	U.S. Holdings of Private Assets Abroad	Less: Foreign Holdings of U.S. Private Assets
						Reproducible Capital Goods			
1909–13	100.0	69.5	8.9	21.6	3.3	13.9	4.6	.4	.6
1914–18	100.0	67.0	8.8	24.2	3.5	15.3	5.3	.4	.3
1919–23	100.0	69.5	7.0	23.5	3.4	14.8	4.7	.8	.2
1924–28	100.0	69.7	6.4	23.9	4.3	14.6	4.3	.9	.2
1929–33[1]	100.0	69.2	6.2	24.6	4.5	15.3	4.2	1.0	.4
1934–38[1]	100.0	70.4	5.6	24.0	3.6	15.6	4.3	.8	.3
1939–43[1]	100.0	72.1	4.9	23.0	2.8	15.5	4.3	.6	.2
1944–48[1]	100.0	74.9	4.0	21.1	2.2	14.6	3.9	.5	.1
1949–53	100.0	74.5	3.4	22.1	2.5	15.4	3.8	.5	.1
1954–58	100.0	77.3	3.0	19.7	3.0	13.1	3.0	.7	.1
1909–58[1]	100.0	71.4	5.8	22.8	3.3	14.9	4.2	.6	.2
1909–29	100.0	68.9	7.7	23.4	3.7	14.6	4.8	.6	.3
1929–58[1]	100.0	73.0	4.5	22.5	3.1	15.0	3.9	.7	.2

[1] For 1930 through 1940 and 1942 through 1946 these represent interpolated distributions, not the actual distribution for those dates. See text [of the paper].

national income. Under competitive conditions, in equilibrium, each unit of any factor of production of uniform quality will receive the same income. According to the marginal productivity theory, the amount of this income will equal the value of the marginal contribution to production of one unit of the factor—that is, the amount by which the national income or product would be changed by adding or subtracting one unit. Hence, the average income per unit and the marginal income per unit will be the same, and both will equal the value of the marginal product of a unit of the factor. The basic assumption of my approach is that the economy of the United States is not so different from this description as to invalidate the use of the average return per unit of each factor as a measure of its marginal value product. For the broad categories with which this paper deals—labor, and a few broad classes of labor classified by education or by age and sex; land; nonfarm residences; and other reproducible capital—this is a reasonable assumption. The chief requirement for its validity is that firms tend to employ each factor up to the point where its marginal value product equals the price of its services (however that price may be established) and that departures from this practice tend to be offsetting.

As a first approximation we can assume that, with the productive technique and other conditions actually prevailing in any year, if we had (and used) an additional 1 per cent of *all* the factors of production the national income would also be 1 per cent larger. This implies that the economy operates under constant returns to scale. Later, I shall examine and modify this assumption but it will suffice for the present.[4]

The question I now ask is, if only one of the factors of production were increased, while the others were unchanged, how much would the national income increase? Table 4 [1, 2, and 3 not shown] shows that during the latest period (1954–58) labor earned 77.3 per cent of the national income. The marginal value product per unit of a small addition to the supply of any one factor would be about the same as the actual marginal value product per unit. It follows that if the quantity of labor employed had been 1 per cent larger than it actually was during this period, the national income would have been 0.773 per cent larger. Similarly, it can be read directly from Table 4 that if the quantity of land had been 1 per cent larger, the national income would have been 0.030 per cent larger. If the quantity of reproducible assets of each type had been 1 per cent larger, the national income would have been 0.197 per cent larger. Each of these statements presumes the quantity of other productive resources to be unchanged. These estimates do not mean that labor is in any sense more productive than capital (or capital than land) but only that a 1 per cent increase in labor involves a bigger quantity of resources than a 1 per cent increase in capital. In other words, 650,000 workers are much more resources than $10 billion of capital; they produce more and earn more.

For substantial changes in the quantity of any one factor, consideration must be given to the principle of diminishing returns. This tells us that, as the quantity of any one factor of production is increased without increasing the others, the addition to output provided by the same addition to the varying factor will progressively decline. Hence, if only one of the factors were increased substantially, the percentage increase in national income would have been a smaller fraction of the percentage increase in that factor than is indicated in Table 4, although it is not possible to say how much smaller.

All these statements assume that, if an additional supply of any factor had been available, the changes in the structure of the economy required to use it efficiently could have been made and also that demand would have sufficed to put it to use. For our purpose, which is to judge the contribution that an increase in the supply of each factor has contributed or can contribute to *long-term* growth of our productive *capacity*, these particular qualifications do not loom large.

The proportions shown in Table 4 are suggestive in themselves of the prospects for affecting the growth rate via changes in the supply of each of the productive resources. I shall consider this subject in following chapters. Before developing that theme, however, it will be convenient in each case to examine our past experience.

2. It is possible to develop time series that measure changes in the quantity of each category of productive resource. The percentages shown for successive periods in Table 4 provide appropriate weights by which these series can be combined to secure a measure of the total resources used in production. This in turn will permit us to distinguish that part of the growth in national income which is due to the increase in the supply of productive resources, including in the case of labor the improvement of its quality, from the part which is due to technological advance, economies of scale, and the many other influences affecting the rate of growth. In this context, as I shall repeatedly have occasion to note, the fact that the growth of the society's stock of knowledge permits

[4] The modification is described on page 47 and in Chapter 16 [of the paper].

each factor of production to produce more (including the fact that it permits capital goods to be better designed) is not considered as an increase in factor input but, rather, of output per unit of input.

STUDY PROJECT 45

SOME LIMITATIONS OF LONG-RANGE PLANNING *

Many businessmen, and some economists, view with pride the increased use of long-range planning by business firms, believing, apparently, that the longer look will be helpful in dampening down wide fluctuations in business spending for new plant and equipment. Hence in total business activity this optimistic view has never appealed to me, primarily because of my own personal experience in the big depression of the early thirties.

When I graduated from college in 1928, I started to work for AT&T, then the greatest exponent of long-range planning. After several months of training at Western Electric, I was assigned to the business methods organization, and my first project was to revise the standard practice instruction on capital budgeting and the control of capital expenditures, which brought me in close contact with AT&T's celebrated long-range planning. But what sticks in my memory is a speech made by a highly placed company official to a group of 25–30,000 employees in the back yard at Hawthorne Works a few days before the company's first—and I think America's first—two-week uniform vacation period in July, 1929.

We were told to enjoy ourselves, to drive safely, to watch for the "Hello Charlie" stickers on other cars, and not to worry about our jobs. Because of AT&T's long-range planning for continued improvement of telephone service, Western Electric had orders on the books to keep all of its factories running at capacity until 1934, even if they never received another order. And this was true.

Unfortunately, by 1930 AT&T began revising its long-range plans, and this quickly resulted in the cancellation of many of Western's unfilled orders. By 1931 about the only organizations at Western with any activity were the order cancellation and the employment termination departments.

For a long time I thought AT&T's performance resulted from a lack of courage, a failure to follow through on long-range plans when the time came to stand up and be counted. To some extent this was true, for AT&T's top management was caught in the same disillusioning experience as everyone else. We were supposed to be in a new era, where depressions were impossible. Statistical studies had proved that demand for telephone service could be maintained at any desired level merely by raising or lowering advertising expenditures. And $300 a share for AT&T stock merely confirmed the rosy future that lay ahead. Thus when the market crashed, the demand for telephone service dropped, and business firms and financial institutions of every kind were failing, AT&T could hardly be expected to hold out as the one big optimist for the future.

But I have since changed my mind about AT&T's lack of courage, and concluded instead that long-range planning guarantees this type of performance rather than preventing it. And that's one of the things I wish to talk about.

* A lecture by Professor Edward E. Edwards at the Indiana Executive Development Program, June 15, 1964.

Another, an important corollary of the first, is that depressions must be avoided, not planned for.

Before going further into an analysis of long-range planning, it might be helpful to draw a line between long-range and short-range. This presents quite a few difficulties, even for an individual firm. In terms of years, long-range might be thought of as anything beyond five years, perhaps beyond one or two years, although I would consider that a bit too close to the present. Perhaps I can illustrate this better by going back to AT&T. Its plans in 1929 for telephone exchanges, lines, and other services to be built in 1934 were long-range, and they were long-range primarily because they could be cancelled before they were executed. If something is a plan today, and still a plan next month or next quarter, rather than a project underway, let's call it a long-range plan.

Now we can begin to see at least one of the dangers in long-range planning. Long-range plans by definition are plans that can be changed or cancelled before anything is done about them. This, of course, is a plus factor, too, but we should see that long-range plans can easily result in an atmosphere of unjustified optimism or wishful thinking about an uncertain future.

But the danger here does not arise from the possibility that top-management will run scared and fail to follow through on the plans. The danger lies in the fact that the planning process practically guarantees that plans will be changed or dropped should depression occur.

Let's think for a moment of the year immediately preceding a depression. Such might very well be a year much like 1964, although this is no forecast of what next year will be. By that I mean that businessmen would be optimistic, would be pushing hard their short-range plans for increasing profits, and most likely would be raising their sights for the longer run, too. If they weren't, the depression very likely would have started already, and we should be considering the previous year.

Now let's look at just one piece of a long-range plan, and let's say that this is an accepted proposal to increase capacity another 10 per cent by 1967, with new machinery and other facilities to be put under order or contract by the fall of 1965, but nothing more than further refinement of plans to be done during the next year. Assume also that this proposal was accepted on the basis recommended by capital budgeting theorists, namely, that the present value of the expected inflows exceeds the present value of the outflow. Our question is: will this project become a reality a year from now? The answer: probably not.

When the present value of the net inflow from our proposed project was computed, the estimated returns for each year very likely were discounted at a high rate, reflecting the company's estimated cost of capital plus some allowance for risk and uncertainty. This process results in giving a large weight to cash flows—earnings plus depreciation—during the early years, and a small weight to cash flows in later years. With estimates for the early years being optimistic, under our assumption, it is easy to see that a revised look at the proposal next year, when there is still time to change plans, and after optimism has changed to pessimism, may easily show the proposal as being undesirable.

To remind ourselves of the importance of the short-run in the discounting process, let's take a look at a simple case, a proposal to add machinery for increased capacity. Let's assume the machine costs $30,000 installed, has an estimated economic life of five years, will increase profits by $4,000 each year, after depreciation of $6,000, and will thus produce a total cash inflow of $10,000 annually. If our capitalization rate is 15 per cent, we find the present value of the estimated inflow to be $33,600, giving us a positive net present value of $3,600 for the project, and an index of desirability of 1.12. Thus we proceed with the project.

Now let's consider the same proposition in the first year of a depression, when our forecasts suggest the added machine will not begin to contribute to profits until year 3, rather than year 1. Even if we now give the machine an estimated life of seven years—two years with no profit, then five of $4,000—and even if we take credit for the early depreciation for tax purposes, which generally assumes we will still be making a profit elsewhere in the firm, we will have a difficult time justifying the project. For example, if we still hold to the 15 per cent capitalization rate, the present value of the inflows, even though the inflows themselves have not changed in amount, but only in timing, drop to $27,860, and we have a negative net present value and an index of desirability of less than 1. So we postpone the project.

From a practical, rather than long-range planning, approach, we would cancel the project anyway, because our judgment would tell us we would be better off to wait. Converting liquid assets into plant and machinery at the start of a depression is a luxury few companies can afford. Even if we could afford it, why take a chance on starting the next period of prosperity with unused but obsolete machinery and equipment?

Notice that we have been talking about depression, not recession. The downturns we have had since World War II have been so small in volume, and their duration so short in time, that there has been little need to modify or postpone long-range plans. In fact, firms would have done very well during most of the years to step up their capital spending in recession, and to work overtime rather than try to increase capacity in prosperity.

. . . .

People have a right, I believe, to expect better public performance by American businessmen in the economic sphere. And I think businessmen are beginning to do better. My own observations lead me to believe that most businessmen are not the poor economists their printed and spoken words suggest, which makes me wonder if most of the trouble doesn't arise out of the delegation of these matters to public relations men. Thus I am optimistic that as more businessmen sense the need to keep our economy moving, their record as leaders of economic thought will improve.

How will this affect long-range planning? It might just possibly overcome the limitations I have mentioned. If individual firms make their own long-range plans on the assumption that the future will be the best of all possible worlds, with maximum growth—and freedom from depression—and if individual businessmen in honesty and with dedication seek to bring about that kind of world, perhaps all these good things will come true. But until that time comes—and even after it apparently has arrived—businessmen would be well advised to remember that

> Making long-range plans on the assumption there will be another depression is unworthy of our abilities
>
> No long-range planning by individual firms can prevent depression, but perhaps appropriate economic policy can

This to me is a wonderful and tremendous challenge for business leadership —to make our economy a steadily and rapidly growing one, free of depression, and one in which long-range plans can appropriately be made on an optimistic basis. We don't have that kind of economy yet, but it is within our reach.

STUDY PROJECT 46

LIPPMANN EYES OUR WORLD IN 1964 *

✣　　✣　　✣

There is nothing unusual about having to relearn and rethink. It has been going on furiously throughout this century, this century of great changes, during which the United States has been transformed from a provincial and rural society into the leading industrial and military power in the world.

Indeed, though sometimes the evolution of ideas is rapid, and sometimes it is slower, we may say that the need and the ability to rethink and to relearn is the hallmark of a free society.

It is most surely the inner principle of our own American society. The question to which the Founding Fathers of the Republic sought an answer was, as Alexander Hamilton put it, whether "societies of men are really capable of establishing good government from reflection and choice." The commitment to establish such a government is the essence of the revolutionary turn in human affairs which created the United States. But for that, we could go on thinking what we always thought, with never a worry that we might be wrong.

From time immemorial, men have been governed by custom and heredity, by accident and force. The newly liberated Americans attempted to do what on the scale of a nation had never been done before. They had to invent, contrive and learn how to operate a new kind of government—a government established and operated by reflection and choice.

This was a daring and revolutionary enterprise, and so it was held to be throughout the world.

To attempt it, the Founding Fathers had to make certain assumptions about the nature of man and about the world he lives in. They had to assume that at least a sufficient number of Americans would be capable of reflecting correctly and then of choosing wisely. For the Founding Fathers had no illusions about the capacities of unregenerate and uneducated men. They did not assume that the capacity to reflect soundly would instinctively appear in every man when he became eligible to vote. On the contrary, they realized that the incentives and restraints of well-designed political institutions were necessary to produce sound reflection.

They had to assume something more. They had to assume that those who emerged and became the legislators and executives of the Republic would be capable of something more than reflection—that they would be inspired also with the grace to choose rightly—and that they would have the gift of preferring the good when they saw it.

These are the fundamental assumptions of the American ideology, and insofar as they are lost in our schools and in our public life, popular government, as we intend to have it, becomes extremely difficult to make work. At the root of all these assumptions is a commitment to a continuing process of self-education and self-discipline. It is a vast and complicated process of re-examining,

* Walter Lippmann. Reprinted with permission of Los Angeles Times Syndicate. Copyright 1964, the Washington Post Company.

reappraising, rethinking and relearning what goes into the making of public policy.

. . . .

What I wish to say today is that now we have come to a different time. You will—quite rightly—take what I am saying with a grain of salt and keep your fingers crossed. But it is true, I believe, that the threat of war—the threat of great nuclear war which could devastate the whole Northern Hemisphere—has become decidedly less than it was a few years ago, while you were still in school and college.

It is hard to believe that this is true. Indeed, all of us have a kind of superstitious fear that we may be tempting fate if we dare to say that the danger, the greatest danger in the history of mankind, has receded. But I think you may believe that it has receded enough so that we can begin again to plan our lives and our public affairs on the assumption that our civilization is going to survive. This is an assumption which no one has dared to make for decades. You can make it. You can look once more beyond mere survival to the improvement of our own affairs.

I am, I must warn you, venturing onto dangerous and slippery ground. Many men who have played an honorable and leading part in the wars of this century will say that if the people are allowed to think of peace they will lose the will to prepare for war. They will cease to make the effort, they will refuse to accept the sacrifices which are required if we are to play our part in the world.

The older generation are haunted by the memory of how, after the first and again after the second world war, the country demobilized its military power as soon as an armistice was reached and long before peace was secured. I know I shall be warned that even if the cold war has in fact been, as I believe it has been, defused of its malignant nuclear sanction, it is a mistake to talk about preparing for peace.

And indeed, it could be a catastrophic mistake. If the generation who are now taking over are incapable of continuing to prepare for war while they prepare for peace, then there is grave trouble ahead. I do not doubt that for some the mere talk of peace is a sedative and a sleeping pill.

But I refuse to believe that we are doomed inevitably to make again every mistake we have made before. I am that much of an optimist. I do not believe that men are incapable of learning anything from experience. They can learn something. To be sure they do not learn enough. But they do learn something.

And so, while I admit that the talk of preparing for peace may provide the selfish and the lazy with a reason for closing their eyes and folding their hands, I believe that we must speak of preparing for peace and that you especially must think of it.

        ❉   ❉   ❉

APPENDIXES

APPENDIXES

A

Glossary [*]

abstract of title. A historical summary of the conveyances, transfers, and other facts relied on as evidence of title; a summary of the documents having a bearing on the history of the title to a property.

accessibility. Ease or difficulty of approach to real property via public land or private land maintained for public use.

acre. A unit of land measure containing 43,560 square feet.

ad valorem. According to value.

administration of real estate resources. The efficient utilization of real estate resources in the achievement of desired results, usually in combination with other resources.

adverse possession. The open and notorious possession of real property as a claim to title. Thus, a method of acquiring title.

advertising real estate. The act of informing the public with the intent to induce some desired impression, feeling, or action relative to real estate. Public announcements and messages, the purposes of which are to aid directly or indirectly in the sale of real properties or property services.

institutional advertising. Advertising that pertains to real estate in general and has for its purpose the creation of favorable public attitudes toward real estate, investments in real estate, or the people engaged in the real estate business.

name advertising. Advertising that has for its main purpose the popularizing of the name, activities, and reputation of a specific real estate firm.

specific advertising. Advertising that pertains to individual properties and property services. Its purpose is to aid in the selling or renting of a specific property.

agent. One who acts for and has the authority to represent another who is known as a principal.

air rights. Rights in real property to use the space above the surface of the real estate without precluding the use of its surface area for some other purpose.

[*]Prepared by Maurice Seldin; revised by D. Jeanne Patterson, Bureau of Business Research, Indiana University.

allodial tenure. A system of ownership of real property where ownership may be complete except for rights held by government. Allodial tenure is in contrast to feudal tenure.

amenities, amenity return. Pleasant satisfactions that are received through using rights in real property but that are not received in the form of money.

American Bankers Association. A trade association of commercial bankers.

American Institute of Real Estate Appraisers. A trade association of real estate appraisers. *See* **appraiser, MAI (*Member Appraisal Institute*).**

amortization. The process of payment of a debt or obligation by a series of payments over time. Generally the payments are in equal amounts that include principal and interest; and generally the payments are made at uniform intervals of time.

amortized mortgage. A mortgage in which repayment is made in accordance with a definite plan that requires the repayment of certain amounts at definite times so that all the debt is released by the end of the term. *See* **amortization.**

appraisal, valuation. An estimate of value. In real estate, an estimate of value of specific rights in a specific parcel of real estate as of a specific date for a specific purpose.

appraisal report. A report, usually written, of the appraised value, together with the pertinent information regarding the property appraised and the evidence and analysis leading to the reported value estimate.

appraiser. One who is in the business of making appraisals on the basis of a fee or salary or in conjunction with some other compensated service.

  MAI (Member Appraisal Institute). A professional designation of an appraiser who is a member of the American Institute of Real Estate Appraisers, an association affiliated with the National Association of Real Estate Boards.

appurtenance. Property that is an accessory to or incidental to other property to which it is annexed.

assessment. The valuation of a property for the purpose of levying a tax. The tax so levied.

  special assessment. An assessment levied for specific purposes such as providing streets, sewers, sidewalks, and the like. An assessment related to benefit derived by the taxed.

assumption of a mortgage. Agreement by the grantee of real property that is encumbered by a mortgage that he, the grantee, will pay such a mortgage; the assumption of a personal liability under an existing mortgage.

axial growth. City growth that takes the form of prongs or finger-like extensions moving out along main transportation routes.

base line. *See* **legal description, land description.**

basic employment, urban growth employment. Employment in establishments that receive their income from outside the community. Basic employment is in contrast to nonbasic employment.

basic income. Income commanded from outside the community.

blanket mortgage. A mortgage that has two or more properties pledged or conveyed as security for a debt, usually for subdividing and improvement purposes.

blight. Decay; withering away, as of a neighborhood.

broker. An agent who negotiates for the sale, leasing, management, or financing of a property or of property rights on a commission basis that is contingent on success.

builder. One who undertakes the improvement of land by erecting structures; one who undertakes the production of real estate resources by improving land through the erection of structures.

custom builder. A builder who builds for a specific owner.

operative builder, speculative builder. A builder who builds for sale to the public rather than for a specific owner.

building codes. Government regulations that specify minimum construction standards for the purpose of maintaining public health and safety.

building permit. Authorization or permission by local government for the erection, alteration, or remodeling of improvements within its jurisdiction.

bundle of rights. The assortment of rights in real property. *See* **estate; property.**

buyer's market. *See* **market,** *buyer's market.*

CPM (Certified Property Manager). *See under* **Institute of Real Estate Management.**

capital market. *See* **market,** *capital market.*

capitalization. The process of reflecting future income in present value; the discounting of the future income stream to arrive at a present value.

capitalization rate. The rate at which future income is discounted.

split rates. Use of different capitalization rates for land and buildings in the income approach to value.

central city. Sometimes used to refer to the "downtown" center; also a city that is the center of a larger geographic trade area for which it performs certain market and service functions.

chattels. Personal property; personalty.

closing statement. A listing of the debits and credits of the buyer and seller to a real estate transaction for the financial settlement of the transaction.

cloudy title. *See* **title,** *cloudy title.*

commercial properties. Properties intended for use by all types of retail and wholesale stores, office buildings, hotels, and service establishments.

commitment. For a mortgage, a promise or statement by the lender of the terms and conditions under which he will lend.

common law. Rules based on usage; judge-made law in contrast to legislative or constitutional law.

common property. *See* **property,** *common property.*

community property. In certain states, the property jointly owned by husband and wife.

condemnation. The process of forcing a sale under eminent domain.

condominium. A form of property ownership providing for individual ownership of a specific apartment or other space not necessarily on ground level together with an undivided interest in the land or other parts of the structure in common with other owners.

conformity. In real estate, the blending of an improvement with the surroundings or the essentially similar use of land in relation to its surroundings; the appearance and use of real estate that is harmonious with the surrounding real estate.

construction loan. A loan to finance the improvement of real estate.

contract. An agreement between two or more persons that is legally enforceable; a written evidence of such an agreement.

contract for deed. *See* **land contract, contract for deed.**

contractor, general contractor. One who supervises the improvement of land by erection of structures or other improvements; one who has the responsibility for such improvement but does not necessarily initiate the process as is done by a builder.

conversion. A change in the use of real estate without destruction of the improvements; a change in the use of real estate by altering improvements.

conveyance. Transfer of an interest in real property from one person to another person.

cooperative ownership. A form of apartment ownership. Occupant acquires ownership by purchasing shares in a corporation but typically must consult the corporation for such actions as sale or improvement.

corner influence table. A statistical table, sometimes used in real estate appraisal, that attempts to reflect the added value of a lot located on a corner.

corporeal rights. Possessory rights in real property.

cost. That which is, was, or would be given up to obtain property (or other things).

> *replacement cost.* The cost of replacing real estate improvements with an alternative of like utility but that is not necessarily an exact replica.

> *reproduction cost.* The cost of replacing real estate improvements with an exact replica.

cost approach to value, summation approach. Valuation approached by estimating the cost of providing a substitute for that which is being valued.

covenant, restrictive covenant. A contract between private persons usually to regulate land use or relating to land use.

cul-de-sac. A dead-end street that widens at the end to form a circular area sufficient to enable an auto to make a U turn.

curtesy. The life estate of the husband in the real estate owned by his wife.

custom builder. *See* **builder,** *custom builder.*

cycle. *See* **cyclical fluctuation.**

cyclical fluctuation. Variations around a trend in activity that recur from time to time; fluctuations remaining after removal of trend and seasonal factors.

data plant. A file of information on real properties maintained usually by an appraiser, mortgage lender, and the like.

dealer-builder. A builder who erects structures from prefabricated components, usually as a local representative of a prefabricated house manufacturer.

deed. An instrument conveying title to real property.

> *deed of trust. See* **trust deed.**

> *grant deed.* A deed in which the seller warrants that he has not previously passed title.

> *quitclaim deed.* An instrument transfering only such title as the seller may possess.

> *warranty deed.* A deed in which the seller warrants that title is "good and merchantable."

deed restrictions. Limitations placed upon the use of real property in the writing of a deed.

defective title. *See* **title,** *defective title.*

deficiency judgment. A judgment for that part of a debt secured that was not liquidated by the proceeds from the sale of foreclosed real property.

demographic. Pertaining to the structure of population, e.g., size, density, statistical characteristics.

depletion. *See* **depreciation,** *depletion.*

deposit, earnest money. A sum of money or other consideration tendered in conjunction with an offer to purchase rights in real property.

depreciation. Loss in property value due to any cause.

>*contingent depreciation.* Loss in property value because of expectations of a decline in property services.

>*depletion.* The exhaustion of a resource such as the removal of a mineral deposit.

>*economic obsolescence.* Loss in property value from events outside the property that unfavorably affect income or income potentials.

>*functional depreciation, functional obsolescence.* Loss in property value because of a loss in ability of the physical property to provide services as compared with alternatives.

>*physical depreciation.* Loss in property value due to wearing away or deterioration.

depth table. A technique for real estate appraisal using statistical tables based on the theory that added depth increases the value of land.

developer. One who undertakes the preparation of land for income production, the construction of buildings and other improvements, and the making available of completed properties.

district. A city area that has a land use different from adjacent land uses, e.g., commercial, industrial, and residential. *See* **neighborhood.**

double, duplex. Two dwelling units under one roof. A double usually means dwelling units side by side; a duplex, one dwelling unit above the other.

double taxation. *See* **taxation,** *double taxation.*

doubling up. The occupation of one dwelling unit by two or more families.

dower. The life estate of a wife in the real estate owned by her husband.

drainage. The running off of water from the surface of land.

earnest money. *See* **deposit.**

easement. The right to make limited use of real property owned by another; a right to use property without taking possession.

economic base. The major economic support of a community; economic activities that enable it to compete effectively with others.

economic base analysis. A technique for analyzing the major economic supports of a community; analysis as a means of predicting population, income, or other variables having an effect on real estate value or land utilization.

economic goods. Goods that have scarcity and utility; goods that provide desired services but that are not in sufficient abundance to be free.

economics. The branch of organized study dealing with the social organization for the utilization of resources in the attainment of objectives that the society or community sets for itself.

economy. Getting as much as possible of what one wants by the use of the means available.

effective age. A statement regarding the amount of depreciation that has occurred on a property. The amount is stated in terms of the number of years that would ordinarily be associated with the degree of depreciation.

eminent domain. The right of government to take private property for public use with just compensation.

encroachment. An improvement on a parcel of land that intrudes on or invades a contiguous parcel of land.

encumbrance. A claim against a property such as a debt secured by a mortgage.

equity. In finance, the value of the interest of an owner of property exclusive of the encumbrances on that property; also, justice.

equity of redemption. *See* **redemption,** *equity of redemption.*

erosion. The wearing of a ground surface.

escheat. The reversion of private property to the state.

escrow. An instrument in the hands of a third party that is held for delivery until certain acts are performed or conditions fulfilled; the arrangement for the handling of such instruments.

estate. The degree, quantity, nature, and extent of an interest in real property.

estates in expectancy. A classification of estates by time of enjoyment when possession will be at some future time. *See* **remainder; reversion.**

estates in possession. A classification of estates by time of enjoyment when possession is present. *See* **corporeal rights.**

estates in severalty. Ownership in a single individual; a classification of estates by number of owners where the number is one.

freehold estate. A nonleasehold estate such as a fee simple estate, fee tail estate, and life estate.

fee simple estate. The most complete form of estate ownership; the "totality of rights" in real property.

fee tail estate. An estate or a limited estate in which transfer of the property is restricted in that the property must pass to the descendants of the owner. Originally used to insure the passing of land in a direct ancestral line.

life estate. An estate that has a duration of the life of an individual. *See* **curtesy; dower.**

joint estates. A classification of estates by number of owners where the number is two or more. *See* **tenancy,** *joint tenancy, tenancy in common.*

nonfreehold estate, leasehold estate. The rights of tenants as distinguished from those of a freeholder. Includes estate for years, estate at will, and estate at sufferance.

estate at sufferance. Rights of a tenant in real property after the expiration of a lease if the tenant holds over without special permission.

estate at will. Rights of a tenant in real property that may be terminated by either landlord or tenant.

estate for years. Rights of a tenant in real property for a definite period of time.

estate taxation. *See* **taxation,** *estate taxation.*

eviction. The taking possession of real property from one in possession.

exclusive agency listing. *See* **listing,** *exclusive agency listing.*

exclusive right-to-sell listing. *See* **listing,** *exclusive right-to-sell listing.*

featherbedding rules. Rules that preserve outmoded and inefficient work methods.

Federal Deposit Insurance Corporation. Agency of the federal government that insures deposits at commercial banks and savings banks.

Federal Home Loan Bank. A District bank of the Federal Home Loan Bank System that lends only to member financial institutions such as savings and loan associations.

Federal Home Loan Bank Board. The administrative agency that charters federal savings and loan associations and exercises regulatory authority over members of the Federal Home Loan Bank System.

Federal Home Loan Bank System. The network of Federal Home Loan Banks and member financial institutions.

Federal Housing Administration (FHA). An agency of the federal government that insures mortgage loans.

Federal National Mortgage Association. An agency of the federal government that buys and sells FHA insured and VA guaranteed mortgage loans.

federal savings and loan association. A savings and loan association with a federal charter issued by the Federal Home Loan Bank Board. A federally chartered savings and loan association is in contrast to a state-chartered savings and loan association.

Federal Savings and Loan Insurance Corporation. An agency of the federal government that insures savers' accounts at savings and loan associations.

fee simple estate. *See* estate, *fee simple estate.*

fee tail estate. *See* estate, *fee tail estate.*

feudal tenure. A system of ownership of real property where ownership rests with a sovereign but where lesser interests are granted in return for loyalty or service. Contrast to allodial tenure.

feuds. Grants of land.

fidelity bond. A bond posted as security for the discharge of an obligation of personal services.

filtering down. In housing, the process of passing the use of real estate to successively lower income groups as the real estate produces less income.

financial institutions. Organizations that deal in money or claims to money and serve the function of channeling money from those who wish to lend to those who wish to borrow. Such organizations include commercial banks, savings and loan associations, savings banks, and insurance companies.

fixity of location. The characteristic of real estate that subjects it to the influence of its surroundings and prohibits it from escaping from such influence.

flow of funds. An accounting method (used primarily by the Federal Reserve) to describe the sources and uses of the nation's funds in a given period of time.

foreclosure. The legal steps required by law to be taken by the mortgagee after the default of a debt before the property can be proceeded against for payment of the debt.

    foreclosure by sale. Foreclosure either under court action resulting in a decree of sale or under power of sale contained in a mortgage or trust deed.

    strict foreclosure. Action by a court that, after determination that sufficient time has elapsed for a mortgagor to pay a mortgage past due, terminates all rights and interest of the mortgagor in the real property.

freehold estate. *See* estate, *freehold estate.*

functional plan. The special arrangement of real estate improvements as it relates to property services.

grant. A transfer of real property by written instrument as in a deed.

    private grant. The transfer of real property from one person to another.

    public grant. A government grant of real property to a private party; a transfer of real property from government to a person.

grantee. One who receives a transfer of real property by deed.

grantor. One who transfers real property by deed.

gridiron pattern, gridiron plan. A layout of streets that resembles a gridiron;

a system of subdivision with blocks of uniform length and width and streets that intersect at right angles.

gross income multiplier. A technique for estimating real estate value based on some factor (multiplier) times the gross income derived from the property in the past.

gross national product (GNP). The total value of all goods and services produced in the economy in any given period; also, the accounting method used to list the major income and expenditure (product) accounts of the nation.

guaranteed mortgage. A mortgage in which a party other than the borrower assures payment in the event of default by a mortgagor, e.g., Veterans' Administration guaranteed mortgages.

highest and best use. The utilization of real property to its greatest economic advantage; the use that provides the highest land value; the use of land that provides a net income stream to the land that when capitalized provides the highest land value.

home associations. *See* **property owners' association.**

Home Owners Loan Corporation. An agency of the federal government that refinanced mortgages in default in the early 1930's.

homestead (right of), homestead exemption. The interest of the head of a family in his owned residence that is exempt from the claims of creditors.

improved value. The difference between the income-producing ability of a property and the amount required to pay a return on the investment in the property.

improvement. That which is erected or constructed upon land to release the income-earning potential of the land; buildings or appurtenances on land.
    overimprovement. An improvement of real estate in excess of that justifiable to release the earning power of land.
    underimprovement. An improvement insufficient to release the earning power of land.

incorporeal rights. Nonpossessory rights in real estate.

inheritance taxation. *See* **taxation,** *inheritance taxation.*

input-output analysis. A technique for analysis of an economy through description of the production and purchases of specific sectors of the economy.

Institute of Real Estate Management. A professional organization of property managers.
    CPM (Certified Property Manager). Official designation for members.

insured mortgage. A mortgage in which a party other than the borrower, in return for the payment of a premium, assures payment in the event of default by a mortgagor, e.g., FHA insured mortgages.

interurbia. A contiguous urban development larger than a city or metropolitan area.

intestate. Legal designation of a person who has died without leaving a valid will.

joint estates. *See* **estate,** *joint estates.*

joint tenancy. A joint estate with the right of survivorship.

judgment. The acknowledgment or award of a claim through a court of law; an obligation or debt under a court decree; also, the decree.

junior mortgage. A mortgage having claim ranking below that of another mortgage.

jurisdictional disputes. As between two labor unions or trade unions, a disagreement as to which union's members shall perform certain services.

land. In a physical sense, the earth's surface; may include the minerals below the surface and the air above the surface.

land contract, contract for deed. A written agreement by which real property is sold to a buyer who agrees to pay in installments the established price, with interest, over a specified period of years, with title remaining with the seller until the purchase price or some portion of the purchase price is paid.

land description. *See* **legal description.**

land economics. The branch of general economics that deals with the social organization for the utilization of land resources in the attainment of the objectives that the society or community sets for itself.

land planning. The designing of land area uses, road networks, and layout for utilities to achieve efficient utilization of real estate resources.

law. A generalization from experience that applies almost universally. A demonstrated relationship between cause and effect. Also, in a legal sense, an established rule or standard of conduct or action that is enforceable by government.

> *license law.* A law that regulates the practices of real estate brokers and salesmen.

lease. A transfer of possession and the right to use property to a tenant for a stipulated period, during which the tenant pays rent to the owner; the contract containing the terms and conditions of such an agreement.

> *graded or step-up lease.* A lease with a rental payment that increases to specified amounts at specified periods of time.
>
> *ground lease.* A lease for vacant land upon which the tenant may erect improvements.
>
> *index lease.* A lease in which the rental payment varies in accordance with variation of an agreed-upon index of prices or costs.
>
> *lease with option to purchase.* A lease in which the lessee has the right to purchase the real property for a stipulated price at or within a stipulated time.
>
> *leasehold, leasehold estate.* An estate held under a lease.
>
> *net lease.* A lease in which the tenant pays certain agreed-upon property expenses such as taxes or maintenance.
>
> *percentage lease.* A lease in which the rental is based on a percentage of the lessee's sales income.
>
> *reappraisal lease.* A lease in which an arrangement is made for determination of the amount of rent at some future period by independent appraisers.
>
> *tax participation clause (in a lease).* An agreement in a lease where the lessee agrees to pay all or a stated portion of any increase in real estate taxes.

leasehold estate. *See* **estate, nonfreehold estate.**

legal description, land description. A means of identifying the exact boundaries of land by metes and bounds, by a plat, or by township and range survey system.

metes and bounds. "Metes" refers to measures; "bounds," to direction. Metes and bounds descriptions are means of describing land by measurement and direction from a known point or marker on land.

plat. A recorded map of land that identifies a parcel by a number or other designation in a subdivision.

township and range survey system. A system of legal description of land with a township as the basic unit of measurement.

    base line. A parallel that serves as a reference for other parallels.

    meridians. North-south lines of survey 6 miles apart.

    parallel. East-west lines of survey 6 miles apart.

    principal meridian. A meridian that serves as a reference for other meridians.

    range. A north-south row of townships; the 6-mile strip of land between meridians.

    section. A 1-mile square in a township.

    tier. An east-west row of townships; the 6-mile strip of land between parallels.

    township. A 6-mile square of land bounded by parallels and meridians, and composed of 36 sections.

lessee. The tenant under a lease; one who receives possession and use of real estate for a period of time in return for the payment of rent.

lessor. The landlord under a lease; one who grants permission and use of real estate for a specified period for a specified rent.

license law. Law that regulates the practices of real estate brokers and salesmen.

lien. The right to have the property of another sold to satisfy a debt.

lien theory of mortgage. The mortgage arrangement whereby title to mortgaged property vests in the borrower, with the lender having a lien against the property.

life estate. *See* estate, *life estate.*

listing. An agreement or contract between a principal and an agent providing that the agent will receive a commission for finding a buyer who is ready, willing, and able to purchase a particular property under terms specified by the agreement.

    exclusive agency listing. A listing contract providing that the agent shall receive a commission if the property is sold as a result of the efforts of that agent or any other agent, but not as a result of the efforts of the principal; the contract further provides that the agent will receive a commission if he secures a buyer under the terms of the contract.

    exclusive right-to-sell listing. A listing contract providing that the agent shall receive a commission if the property is sold irrespective of whether as a result of the efforts of that agent or another agent or the principal; the contract also provides that the agent shall receive a commission if he produces a buyer under the terms of the contract.

    multiple listing. A listing that in addition to employing the agent, provides for the services of other agents who have agreed among themselves that they will cooperate in finding a purchaser for the property.

    open listing. A listing contract providing that the agent shall receive a commission if the property is sold as a result of the efforts of that agent or if the agent produces a buyer under the terms of the contract before the property is sold.

localization of income. Income production at fixed locations; i.e., from real estate, which has a fixed and unique location.

location. Position of land and improvements in relation to other land and improvements and to local or general economic activity.

location quotient. An analytic technique using proportionality comparisons as, for example, the comparison of the percentage of an activity in a city with the percentage of the same activity in the nation.

lot. A specific plot of land.

MAI (Member Appraisal Institute). *See under* **appraiser.**

map. A representation of some feature on the earth's surface such as physical features or boundary lines and the like. *See* **plat, plat map; Sanborn insurance maps; time interval maps; topographical map.**

market. A set of arrangements for bringing buyers and sellers together through the price mechanism.

    buyer's market. A market in which buyers can fulfill their desires at lower prices and on more advantageous terms than those prevailing earlier; a market characterized by many properties available and few potential users demanding them at prevailing prices.

    capital market. The activities of all lenders and borrowers of equity and long-term debt funds.

    market analysis. A study of the supply, demand, and price forces at work in a particular market; also the process of studying supply, demand, and prices in a particular market, e.g., the real estate market.

    money market. A market for borrowed funds, generally short-term.

    seller's market. A market in which potential sellers can sell at prices higher than those prevailing in an immediately preceding period; a market characterized by very few properties available and a large number of users and potential users demanding them at prevailing prices.

meridian. *See* **legal description,** *township and range survey system.*

metes and bounds. A system of land description; "metes" refers to measures; "bounds," to direction. *See* **legal description,** *metes and bounds.*

model house. A house used for exhibition in order to sell other houses.

modular planning. The designing of structures using a designated size minimum dimension of length and width such as 4 feet.

money market. *See* **market,** *money market.*

mortgage. The pledge of real property to secure a debt; the conveyance of real property as security for a debt; the instrument that is evidence of the pledge or conveyance.

mortgage bonds. Evidences of debt secured by a mortgage in favor of individual parties as a group, usually with the mortgage held by a third party in trust for the mortgage bond creditors.

mortgage broker. An agent who, for a commission, brings a mortgagor and mortgagee together.

mortgage company. A firm that, for a fee, brings mortgagor and mortgagee together or that acquires mortgages for the purpose of resale.

mortgagee. The creditor or lender under a mortgage.

mortgagor. The debtor or borrower under a mortgage.

motivation research. Analysis of consumers in an attempt to determine why prospective buyers react as they do to products or services or to advertisements used in attempting to sell them.

multifamily structure. A dwelling for (usually) five or more household units.

multiple listing. *See* listing, *multiple listing.*

National Association of Real Estate Boards. A national real estate trade association. Includes such trade associations as American Institute of Real Estate Appraisers, Institute of Farm Brokers, Institute of Real Estate Management, and others.

national income accounting. Statistical technique used in developing gross national product calculations; *see* **gross national product (GNP).**

national wealth statistics. Accounting technique for measuring the size and composition of wealth of the economic system and the changes in them.

neighborhood. A small area within a city that may be differentiated from adjacent areas, e.g., an area with homes of the same price range or people of the same income bracket. *See* **district.**

nonbasic employment, secondary employment, urban service employment. Usually refers to employment in establishments that receive their income from within the community. Contrast to basic employment.

nonbasic income. Usually refers to income that comes from within the community.

nonfreehold estate. *See* estate, *nonfreehold estate.*

obsolescence. Loss in property value because of the existence of a less costly alternative that provides comparable or more desirable property services.

open house. A house that is available for inspection by potential purchasers without appointments.

open listing. *See* listing, *open listing.*

open-end mortgage. A mortgage with provisions for future advances to the borrower without the necessity of writing a new mortgage.

operative builder. *See* builder, *operative builder.*

opinion of title. *See* title, *opinion of title.*

option (to purchase real estate). The right to purchase property at a stipulated price and under stipulated terms within a period of time; the instrument that is evidence of such a right.

ordinance. A public regulation such as a law (usually local laws).

orientation. The position of a structure on a site and its general relationship to its surroundings.

overbuilding. The building of structures of a particular type more than can be absorbed by the market at prevailing prices.

overimprovement. *See* improvement, *overimprovement.*

ownership of real property. The holding of rights or interests in real estate. *See* estate, *fee simple estate.*

package mortgage. A mortgage in which the collateral is not limited to real property but includes personal property in the nature of household equipment.

parallel. *See* legal description, *township and range survey system.*

parcel of real estate. A particular piece of land and its improvements.

parking lot. A parcel of real estate used for the storage of automobiles. Usually about 300 square feet per auto is required for parking space and aisles.

partially amortized mortgage. A combination of an amortized mortgage and a term mortgage (straight-term mortgage).

perpetuity. Without limitation as to time, perpetual; as in capitalization in perpetuity.

personal property. The exclusive right to exercise control over personalty; all property objects other than real estate.

personalty. All property other than realty; chattels.

plat, plat map. A map that shows boundary lines of parcels of real estate, usually of an area that has been subdivided into a number of lots. *See* **legal description,** *plat.*

plat book. A book containing a series of plat maps.

plottage. The extent to which value is increased when two or more lots are combined in a single ownership or use.

police power. The authority for governmental regulations necessary to safeguard the public health, morals, and safety and to promote the general welfare.

prefabrication. The process of manufacturing component parts of a structure in a factory for later assembly on-site.

present value. *See* **capitalization.**

price. That amount of money at which property is offered for sale or is exchanged for at a sale; value in terms of money.

principal. One who has another act for him; one who is represented by an agent. Also, the amount of a debt.

private property. *See* **property,** *private property.*

probate. The proof or act of proving at a court that a last will and testament is actually the last will and testament of a deceased person.

property. The exclusive right to exercise control over economic good. *See* **real property; personal property.**

    common property. Ownership of a parcel of land by a number of people who hold their interests by virtue of ownership of adjoining parcels.

    private property. Property held by individuals or by groups of individuals except when such a group constitutes a public organization.

    public property. Property held by government.

property brief. A folder that presents pertinent information about a property.

property management. The operation of real property including the leasing of space, collection of rents, selection of tenants, and the repair and renovation of the buildings and grounds.

property owners' association, property owners' maintenance association. Organizations with the purpose of administering private regulations affecting residential land uses.

property services. The benefits accruing from the use of property.

property taxation. *See* **taxation,** *property taxation.*

public housing. Housing owned by a governmental body.

public property. See **property,** *public property.*

purchase money mortgage. A mortgage that is given in part payment of the purchase price in contrast to a mortgage that is given as security for repayment of funds.

purchase on contract. The purchase of property on installments with title remaining with seller. *See* **land contract.**

range. *See* **legal description,** *township and range survey system.*

real estate. In a physical sense, land with or without buildings or improvements; in a legal sense, the rights in such physical objects.

real estate administration. *See* **administration of real estate resources.**

real estate appraisal. *See* **appraisal.**

real estate broker. An agent who negotiates the sale of real property or real property services for a commission that is contingent on success.

real estate business. The business that deals in rights to income or income potentials at fixed locations. It is concerned with production, marketing, and financing of these rights.

real estate developing. The process of preparing land for use, constructing buildings and other improvements, and making the completed properties available.

real estate financing. The channeling of savings into the production and use of real estate; facilitating the production and use of real estate through borrowed or equity funds. Also, the area of study dealing with the foregoing.

real estate investment corporation. A corporation that sells its securities to the public and has a special interest in real estate or is a builder or developer of real estate.

real estate investment trusts. A trust established in a form similar to that of an investment or mutual fund for the purpose of allowing investors to channel funds into the real estate market.

real estate marketing. The process of putting real properties and their services into the hands of consumers. Brokerage and property management are the two main subdivisions of real estate marketing.

real estate operator. An individual engaged in the real estate business acting for himself rather than as an agent.

real estate syndicate. A partnership organized for participation in a real estate venture. Partners may be limited or unlimited in their liability.

real property. The exclusive right to exercise control over real estate; a parcel of real estate.

real property taxation. *See* **taxation,** *real property taxation.*

realtor. A broker who is a member of a local real estate board that is affiliated with the National Association of Real Estate Boards.

realty. The property objects of land and all things permanently attached to it.

recording acts, registry laws. Laws providing for the recording of instruments affecting title as a matter of public record and that preserve such evidence and give notice of their existence and content; laws providing that the recording of an instrument informs all who deal in real property of the transaction and that unless the instrument is recorded, a prospective purchaser without actual notice of its existence is protected against it.

redemption. The regaining of title to real property after a foreclosure sale.

> *equity of redemption.* The interest of the mortgagor in real property prior to foreclosure.
>
> *statutory right of redemption.* The right under law of the mortgagor to redeem title to real property after a foreclosure sale.

redevelopment. Typically the processes of clearance and reconstruction of blighted areas.

regional analysis. When applied to real estate, pertaining mainly to local economies and the surrounding area; for other purposes, the area of a "region" may be defined more broadly.

registrar of deeds, recorder. Officer in charge of a land records office.

registry laws. *See* **recording acts.**

rehabilitation. The removal of blight by repair and renovation rather than by destruction of improvements.

remainder. The right of a person to interests that mature at the end of another estate; a classification of estates by time of enjoyment.

    contingent remainder. An interest that will become a remainder only if some condition is fulfilled.

renewal. The process of redevelopment or rehabilitation in cities; often used in relation to rebuilding or restoration of blighted areas.

rent controls. The legal provision for a maximum rental payment for the use of real property.

rent multiplier. A factor or number used to estimate value by multiplying the rent. A rent multiplier may be either a gross rent multiplier or a net rent multiplier.

restrictive covenant. *See* **covenant.**

reversion. The residue of an estate left with the grantor that entitles him to possession after the end of another estate; a classification of estates by time of enjoyment.

rod. A unit of linear measure representing a length of 5½ yards.

sale-leaseback. An arrangement that provides for a simultaneous transfer of ownership and execution of lease—the grantor becomes the lessee and the grantee the lessor.

sales kit. A file of information about the properties a broker has for sale.

Sanborn insurance maps. Maps showing locations of individual structures in many cities. Developed for underwriting insurance.

search of title. *See* **title,** *search of title.*

seasonal fluctuations. Variations in economic activity that recur at about the same time each year.

seasoned mortgage. A mortgage in which the principal has been reduced through amortization.

secondary employment. *See* **nonbasic employment.**

secondary income. *See* **nonbasic income.**

section. *See* **legal description,** *township and range survey system.*

sector theory. A theory of city growth that considers the city as a circle with wedge-shaped sectors pointing to the center.

secular trend. *See* **trend.**

seller's market. *See* **market,** *seller's market.*

senior mortgage. A mortgage having a claim ranking above that of another mortgage.

single-family home. A dwelling intended for occupancy by one household only.

site. A parcel of real estate that is improved or suitable for improvement.

situs. Location.

slum clearance. The removal of blighted improvements by destruction of the improvements. *See* **redevelopment; rehabilitation; renewal.**

Society of Real Estate Appraisers. A trade association of residential real estate appraisers.

special assessment. *See* **assessment,** *special assessment.*

specific performance, specifically enforceable. The requirement that a party must perform as agreed under a contract in contrast to compensation or damages in lieu of performance; the arrangement whereby courts may force either party to a real estate contract to carry out an agreement exactly.

Statute of Frauds. Legislation providing that all agreements affecting title to real estate must be in writing to be enforceable.

statutory right of redemption. *See* **redemption,** *statutory right of redemption.*

straight-term mortgage. A mortgage in which repayment of principal is in one lump sum at maturity.

subcontractor. A contractor who contracts from another, usually a general contractor. A subcontractor usually is concerned only with one particular part of the improvement of real estate such as plumbing, masonry, carpentry, and the like.

subdivision. An area of land divided into parcels or lots generally of a size suitable for residential use.

suburb. A development of real estate in areas peripheral to the central area of a city.

survey. A measurement of land to determine boundaries or points of location on land; the process of determining, or the map that shows, the exact dimension and location of a site and possibly such things as levels of the land by contour lines, boundaries and their relationship to natural formations, and the location of streets, sewers, water, and gas and electric lines.

tax lien. A claim against property arising out of nonpayment of taxes; the claim may be sold by the taxing authority.

tax participation clause. *See* **lease.**

tax title. *See* **title,** *tax title.*

taxation. The right of government to payment for the support of activities in which it engages.

> *double taxation.* In real estate, the taxation of the property as an asset and the taxation of the property income the owner receives.
>
> *estate taxation.* Taxation imposed by government on property passed by will or descent.
>
> *inheritance taxation.* Taxation imposed on property received through inheritance.
>
> *property taxation.* Taxation imposed upon owners of property.
>
> *real property taxation.* Taxation imposed upon the owners of real property.

taxing district. The geographical area over which a taxing authority levies taxes.

tenancy. An interest in real property; the right to possession and use of real property.

> *joint tenancy.* A joint estate that provides for the right of survivorship; a joint estate in which the interest of joint tenants passes to the surviving joint tenant or tenants.
>
> *periodic tenancy.* The rights to use and occupancy under a lease that is renewed from period to period.
>
> *tenancy by entirety.* An estate held by husband and wife where both are viewed as one person under common law, which thus provides for the right of survivorship.
>
> *tenancy in common.* A joint estate in which each tenant in common (co-owner) may dispose of his interest by devise or descent.

term mortgage. *See* **straight-term mortgage.**

tier. *See* **legal description,** *township and range survey system.*

time interval maps. A series of maps that show land use or some other feature as of different dates.

title. Proof or evidence of ownership or ownership rights.

abstract of title, abstract. A historical summary of the conveyances, transfers, and other facts relied on as evidence of title; a summary of the documents having a bearing on the history of the title to a property.

cloudy title. A title that would be impaired if an outstanding claim proved to be valid.

defective title. A title that would be impaired if an outstanding claim proved to be valid and where such a claim could be shown to be valid.

opinion of title. The statement, usually of an attorney, as to whether he believes a title to be clear or defective.

search of title. A study of the history of the title to a property.

tax title. The title to real property acquired through a forced sale for taxes; an interest in real property that will become ownership if the defaulting taxpayer does not redeem the property.

title by descent. Title acquired by the laws of succession; title acquired by an heir in the absence of a will.

title by devise. Title received through a will.

title insurance. Insurance that a title is clear or clear except for defects noted; a policy of insurance that indemnifies the insured for loss occasioned by unknown defects of title.

title theory of mortgage. The mortgage arrangement whereby title to mortgaged real property vests in the lender.

topographical map. A map that shows the slope and contour of land; a map of the physical features of a parcel of real estate or an area of land.

topography. Contour and slope of land and such things as gullies, streams, knolls, and ravines.

Torrens system. A system of land title registration in which the state guarantees title.

township. *See* **legal description,** *township and range survey system.*

trade area. That geographical area from which purchasers of particular goods and services will ordinarily be drawn.

trade association. A voluntary organization of individuals or firms in a common area of economic activity; the organization has for its purpose the promotion of certain aspects of the common area of activity.

trend. A prevailing tendency of behavior of some observable phenomenon such as economic activity over time; a tendency that is exhibited over a long period of time despite intermittent fluctuations.

trust deed. An instrument that is evidence of the pledge of real property as security for a debt where the title to the real property is held by a third party in trust while the debtor repays the debt to the lender; the debtor is known as the *trustor;* the lender is known as the *beneficiary,* the third party is known as the *trustee.*

United States Savings and Loan League. A trade association of savings and loan associations.

urban growth employment. *See* **basic employment.**

urban plant. The community facilities that enable the community to function as a unit; e.g., the system of streets, sewers, water mains, parks, playgrounds, and the like.

urban renewal. *See* **renewal.**

urban service employment. *See* **nonbasic employment.**

valuation. *See* **appraisal.**

value of property. The usefulness of the property relative to its scarcity.

Veterans' Administration (VA). An agency of the federal government that, among other activities, guarantees loans made to veterans.

zoning. Government regulation of land use; regulation by local government under police power of such matters as height, bulk, and use of buildings and use of land.

B

Real Estate License Laws *

Alabama. Alabama Real Estate Commission (January 1, 1929).[1]
Alaska. Alaska Real Estate Commission (1964).
Arizona. State of Arizona Real Estate Department (1939).
Arkansas. Arkansas Real Estate Commission (1929).
California. California Real Estate Commission (1919).
Colorado. Real Estate Brokers Board (April 20, 1925).
Connecticut. Insurance Department (October 1, 1953).
Delaware. Delaware Real Estate Commission (July 1, 1927).
District of Columbia. Real Estate Commission of District of Columbia (August 25, 1937).
Florida. Florida Real Estate Commission (1927).
Georgia. Georgia Real Estate Commission (January 1, 1926).
Hawaii. Real Estate License Commission (May 2, 1933).
Idaho. Idaho Real Estate Brokers Board (not available).
Illinois. The Department of Registration and Education (June 29, 1929).
Indiana. Indiana Real Estate Commission (March, 1949).
Iowa. Iowa Real Estate Commission (1930).
Kansas. Kansas Real Estate Commission (July 1, 1947).
Kentucky. Kentucky Real Estate Commission (1938).
Louisiana. Louisiana Real Estate Board (1920).
Maine. Maine Real Estate Commission (1937).
Maryland. Maryland Real Estate Commission (1939).
Massachusetts. Board of Registration of Real Estate Brokers and Salesmen (1957).
Michigan. Michigan Corporation and Security Commission (January 1, 1920).
Minnesota. Securities Division (1955).
Mississippi. Mississippi Real Estate Commission (May 6, 1954).
Missouri. Missouri Real Estate Commission (January 1, 1942).
Montana. Montana Real Estate Commission (1921).

* Compiled by George F. Bloom, Indiana University.
[1] In each case, effective date or date of approval of state's license law.

Nebraska. Nebraska Real Estate Commission (1936).

Nevada. Real Estate Division (July, 1963).

New Hampshire. Insurance Commission (July 1, 1960).

New Jersey. Division of New Jersey Real Estate Commission in the Department of Banking and Insurance (1921).

New Mexico. New Mexico Real Estate Commission (June 9, 1951).

New York. Department of State, Division of Licenses (1922).

North Carolina. North Carolina Real Estate Licensing Board (July 1, 1957).

North Dakota. North Dakota Real Estate Commission (1957).

Ohio. Ohio Real Estate Commission (1927).

Oklahoma. Oklahoma Real Estate Commission (January, 1950).

Oregon. Real Estate Division of Department of Commerce (May 29, 1919).

Pennsylvania. State Real Estate Commission (January 1, 1930).

Rhode Island. Rhode Island Real Estate Commission (July 1, 1959).

South Carolina. South Carolina Real Estate Commission (July 1, 1956).

South Dakota. Real Estate Commission (July 1, 1955).

Tennessee. Tennessee Real Estate Commission (July 1, 1951).

Texas. Texas Real Estate Commission (1939).

Utah. State Securities Commission (1921).

Vermont. Vermont Real Estate Commission (June 28, 1957).

Virginia. Virginia Real Estate Commission (1924).

Washington. Department of Licenses, Real Estate Division (1953).

West Virginia. West Virginia Real Estate Commission (1937).

Wisconsin. Wisconsin Real Estate Brokers Board (1919).

Wyoming. Wyoming Real Estate Board (1929).

C

Capitalization Tables

Table 1. Present Value of One.

Years		5	5¼	5½	5¾	6	6¼	6½	6¾	7	7½	8	8½	9	9½	10
						Per Cent										
1........		0.952	0.950	0.948	0.946	0.943	0.941	0.939	0.937	0.935	0.930	0.926	0.922	0.917	0.913	0.909
2........		.907	.903	.898	.894	.890	.886	.882	.878	.873	.865	.857	.849	.842	.834	.826
3........		.864	.858	.852	.846	.840	.834	.828	.822	.816	.805	.794	.783	.772	.762	.751
4........		.823	.815	.807	.800	.792	.785	.777	.770	.763	.749	.735	.722	.708	.696	.683
5........		.784	.774	.765	.756	.747	.739	.730	.721	.713	.697	.681	.665	.650	.635	.621
6........		.746	.736	.725	.715	.705	.695	.685	.676	.666	.648	.630	.613	.596	.580	.564
7........		.711	.699	.687	.676	.665	.654	.644	.633	.623	.603	.583	.565	.547	.530	.513
8........		.677	.664	.652	.639	.627	.616	.604	.593	.582	.561	.540	.521	.502	.484	.467
9........		.645	.631	.618	.605	.592	.579	.567	.556	.544	.522	.500	.480	.460	.442	.424
10........		.614	.599	.585	.572	.558	.545	.533	.520	.508	.485	.463	.442	.422	.404	.386

Table 2. Present Value of Declining Annuities.

Years	Per Cent														
	5	5¼	5½	5¾	6	6¼	6½	6¾	7	7½	8	8½	9	9½	10
15	7.29	7.20	7.10	7.01	6.92	6.83	6.75	6.66	6.58	6.42	6.27	6.12	5.98	5.84	5.71
16	7.70	7.60	7.49	7.39	7.29	7.20	7.10	7.01	6.91	6.74	6.57	6.40	6.25	6.10	5.95
17	8.11	7.99	7.88	7.76	7.65	7.55	7.44	7.34	7.24	7.04	6.86	6.68	6.51	6.34	6.19
18	8.51	8.38	8.25	8.13	8.01	7.89	7.77	7.66	7.55	7.34	7.14	6.94	6.76	6.58	6.41
19	8.90	8.75	8.61	8.48	8.35	8.22	8.09	7.97	7.85	7.62	7.40	7.20	7.00	6.81	6.62
20	9.28	9.12	8.97	8.82	8.68	8.54	8.41	8.27	8.15	7.90	7.66	7.44	7.22	7.02	6.83
21	9.65	9.48	9.32	9.16	9.01	8.86	8.71	8.57	8.43	8.16	7.91	7.67	7.44	7.22	7.02
22	10.01	9.83	9.66	9.49	9.32	9.16	9.00	8.85	8.70	8.42	8.15	7.89	7.65	7.42	7.20
23	10.37	10.17	9.99	9.80	9.63	9.45	9.29	9.12	8.96	8.66	8.37	8.10	7.85	7.60	7.37
24	10.72	10.51	10.31	10.11	9.92	9.74	9.56	9.39	9.22	8.90	8.59	8.31	8.03	7.78	7.53
25	11.05	10.83	10.62	10.41	10.21	10.01	9.82	9.64	9.46	9.12	8.80	8.50	8.21	7.94	7.69
26	11.38	11.15	10.92	10.70	10.49	10.28	10.08	9.88	9.70	9.34	9.00	8.68	8.38	8.10	7.84
27	11.70	11.45	11.21	10.98	10.75	10.54	10.32	10.12	9.92	9.55	9.19	8.86	8.55	8.25	7.97
28	12.02	11.75	11.50	11.25	11.01	10.78	10.56	10.35	10.14	9.74	9.37	9.03	8.70	8.39	8.10
29	12.32	12.04	11.77	11.51	11.26	11.02	10.79	10.56	10.35	9.93	9.55	9.18	8.84	8.53	8.23
30	12.61	12.32	12.04	11.77	11.50	11.25	11.01	10.77	10.54	10.11	9.71	9.33	8.98	8.65	8.34
31	12.90	12.59	12.30	12.01	11.74	11.47	11.22	10.97	10.74	10.29	9.87	9.48	9.11	8.77	8.45
32	13.18	12.85	12.54	12.25	11.96	11.69	11.42	11.16	10.92	10.45	10.02	9.61	9.24	8.88	8.55
33	13.45	13.11	12.79	12.47	12.18	11.89	11.61	11.35	11.09	10.61	10.16	9.74	9.35	8.99	8.65
34	13.71	13.35	13.02	12.69	12.38	12.09	11.80	11.52	11.26	10.76	10.29	9.86	9.46	9.09	8.74
35	13.96	13.59	13.24	12.91	12.58	12.27	11.98	11.69	11.42	10.90	10.42	9.98	9.57	9.18	8.83
36	14.20	13.82	13.46	13.11	12.77	12.45	12.15	11.85	11.57	11.04	10.54	10.09	9.67	9.27	8.91
37	14.44	14.04	13.66	13.30	12.96	12.63	12.31	12.01	11.71	11.17	10.66	10.19	9.76	9.36	8.98
38	14.66	14.25	13.86	13.49	13.13	12.79	12.47	12.15	11.85	11.29	10.77	10.29	9.84	9.43	9.05
39	14.88	14.46	14.06	13.67	13.30	12.95	12.62	12.29	11.98	11.41	10.87	10.38	9.93	9.51	9.12
40	15.09	14.66	14.24	13.84	13.47	13.10	12.76	12.43	12.11	11.52	10.97	10.47	10.00	9.58	9.18
41	15.30	14.85	14.42	14.01	13.62	13.25	12.89	12.55	12.23	11.62	11.06	10.55	10.08	9.64	9.24
42	15.49	15.03	14.59	14.17	13.77	13.39	13.02	12.67	12.34	11.72	11.15	10.63	10.15	9.70	9.29
43	15.68	15.21	14.75	14.32	13.91	13.52	13.15	12.79	12.45	11.81	11.23	10.70	10.21	9.76	9.34
44	15.87	15.38	14.91	14.47	14.05	13.65	13.26	12.90	12.55	11.90	11.31	10.77	10.27	9.81	9.39
45	16.04	15.54	15.06	14.61	14.18	13.77	13.38	13.00	12.65	11.99	11.38	10.83	10.33	9.86	9.43

Table 2. Present Value of Declining Annuities—Continued

Years	Per Cent														
	5	5¼	5½	5¾	6	6¼	6½	6¾	7	7½	8	8½	9	9½	10
46	16.21	15.70	15.21	14.74	14.30	13.88	13.48	13.10	12.74	12.07	11.45	10.89	10.38	9.91	9.47
47	16.37	15.85	15.35	14.87	14.42	13.99	13.58	13.20	12.83	12.14	11.52	10.95	10.43	9.95	9.51
48	16.53	15.99	15.48	14.99	14.53	14.10	13.68	13.29	12.91	12.21	11.58	11.00	10.47	9.99	9.55
49	16.68	16.13	15.61	15.11	14.64	14.20	13.77	13.37	12.99	12.28	11.64	11.05	10.52	10.03	9.58
50	16.83	16.26	15.73	15.22	14.74	14.29	13.86	13.45	13.06	12.35	11.69	11.10	10.56	10.06	9.61

Table 3. Present Value of Level Annuities

PER CENT

Years	3½	3¾	4	4¼	4½	4¾	5	5¼	5½	5¾	6	6¼	6½	6¾	7	7½	8	8½	9	9½	10
1	0.97	0.96	0.96	0.96	0.96	0.95	0.95	0.95	0.95	0.95	0.94	0.94	0.94	0.94	0.93	0.93	0.93	0.92	0.92	0.91	0.91
2	1.90	1.89	1.89	1.88	1.87	1.87	1.86	1.85	1.85	1.84	1.83	1.83	1.82	1.81	1.81	1.80	1.78	1.77	1.76	1.75	1.74
3	2.80	2.79	2.78	2.76	2.75	2.74	2.72	2.71	2.70	2.69	2.67	2.66	2.65	2.64	2.62	2.60	2.58	2.55	2.53	2.51	2.49
4	3.67	3.65	3.63	3.61	3.59	3.57	3.55	3.53	3.51	3.49	3.47	3.45	3.43	3.41	3.39	3.35	3.31	3.28	3.24	3.20	3.17
5	4.52	4.48	4.45	4.42	4.39	4.36	4.33	4.30	4.27	4.24	4.21	4.18	4.16	4.13	4.10	4.05	3.99	3.94	3.89	3.84	3.79
6	5.33	5.29	5.24	5.20	5.16	5.12	5.08	5.04	5.00	4.96	4.92	4.88	4.84	4.80	4.77	4.69	4.62	4.55	4.49	4.42	4.36
7	6.11	6.06	6.00	5.95	5.89	5.84	5.79	5.73	5.68	5.63	5.58	5.53	5.48	5.44	5.39	5.30	5.21	5.12	5.03	4.95	4.87
8	6.87	6.80	6.73	6.66	6.60	6.53	6.46	6.40	6.33	6.27	6.21	6.15	6.09	6.03	5.97	5.86	5.75	5.64	5.53	5.43	5.33
9	7.61	7.52	7.44	7.35	7.27	7.19	7.11	7.03	6.95	6.88	6.80	6.73	6.66	6.59	6.52	6.38	6.25	6.12	6.00	5.88	5.76
10	8.32	8.21	8.11	8.01	7.91	7.82	7.72	7.63	7.54	7.45	7.36	7.27	7.19	7.11	7.02	6.86	6.71	6.56	6.42	6.28	6.14
11	9.00	8.88	8.76	8.64	8.53	8.42	8.31	8.20	8.09	7.99	7.89	7.79	7.69	7.59	7.50	7.32	7.14	6.97	6.81	6.65	6.50
12	9.66	9.52	9.39	9.25	9.12	8.99	8.86	8.74	8.62	8.50	8.38	8.27	8.16	8.05	7.94	7.74	7.54	7.34	7.16	6.98	6.81
13	10.30	10.14	9.99	9.83	9.68	9.54	9.39	9.25	9.12	8.98	8.85	8.72	8.60	8.48	8.36	8.13	7.90	7.69	7.49	7.29	7.10
14	10.92	10.74	10.56	10.39	10.22	10.06	9.90	9.74	9.59	9.44	9.29	9.15	9.01	8.88	8.75	8.49	8.24	8.01	7.79	7.57	7.37
15	11.52	11.32	11.12	10.93	10.74	10.56	10.38	10.21	10.04	9.87	9.71	9.56	9.40	9.25	9.11	8.83	8.56	8.30	8.06	7.83	7.61
16	12.09	11.87	11.65	11.44	11.23	11.03	10.84	10.65	10.46	10.28	10.11	9.93	9.77	9.61	9.45	9.14	8.85	8.58	8.31	8.06	7.82
17	12.65	12.40	12.17	11.93	11.71	11.49	11.27	11.07	10.86	10.67	10.48	10.29	10.11	9.93	9.76	9.43	9.12	8.83	8.54	8.28	8.02
18	13.19	12.92	12.66	12.41	12.16	11.92	11.69	11.46	11.25	11.03	10.83	10.63	10.43	10.24	10.06	9.71	9.37	9.06	8.76	8.47	8.20
19	13.71	13.42	13.13	12.86	12.59	12.34	12.09	11.84	11.61	11.38	11.16	10.94	10.73	10.53	10.34	9.96	9.60	9.27	8.95	8.65	8.36
20	14.21	13.90	13.59	13.29	13.01	12.73	12.46	12.20	11.95	11.71	11.47	11.24	11.02	10.80	10.59	10.19	9.82	9.46	9.13	8.81	8.51
21	14.70	14.36	14.03	13.71	13.40	13.11	12.82	12.54	12.28	12.02	11.76	11.52	11.28	11.06	10.84	10.41	10.02	9.64	9.29	8.96	8.65
22	15.17	14.80	14.45	14.11	13.78	13.47	13.16	12.87	12.58	12.31	12.04	11.78	11.54	11.29	11.06	10.62	10.20	9.81	9.44	9.10	8.77
23	15.62	15.23	14.86	14.50	14.15	13.81	13.49	13.18	12.88	12.58	12.30	12.03	11.77	11.52	11.27	10.81	10.37	9.96	9.58	9.22	8.88
24	16.06	15.64	15.25	14.86	14.50	14.14	13.80	13.47	13.15	12.85	12.55	12.27	11.99	11.73	11.47	10.98	10.53	10.10	9.71	9.33	8.98
25	16.48	16.04	15.62	15.22	14.83	14.45	14.09	13.75	13.41	13.09	12.78	12.49	12.20	11.92	11.65	11.15	10.67	10.23	9.82	9.44	9.08

Name Index

Subject Index